WHOLE GOSPEL WHOLE WORLD

WILLIAM R. ESTEP

WHOLE GOSPEL WHOLE WORLD

*The Foreign Mission Board of the
Southern Baptist Convention
1845-1995*

BROADMAN
& HOLMAN
PUBLISHERS

Nashville, Tennessee

4210-41
0-8054-1041-4

Dewey Decimal Classification: 266.023
Subject Heading: MISSIONS, FOREIGN / FOREIGN MISSION BOARD— HISTORY
Library of Congress Card Catalog Number: 94-8237

Library of Congress Cataloging-in-Publication Data
Estep, William Roscoe, 1920-
    Whole gospel—whole world: the Foreign Mission Board of the Southern
Baptist Convention: 1845-1995 / William R. Estep.
        p.   cm.
    Includes bibliographical references and index.
    ISBN 0-8054-1041-4
    1. Southern Baptist Convention. Foreign Mission Board— History
2. Southern Baptist Convention— Mission— History. 3. Baptist— Mission—
History. I. Title
    BV2520.A5S684 1994
    266'.6132— dc20
                                                        94-8237
                                                        CIP

his history of the Foreign Mission Board of the Southern Baptist Convention is unusual on several accounts. First, it presents the story of an organization called into being and supported by voluntary cooperation of what is now 38,741 churches. This in and of itself indicates that more is at work here than the efforts of human beings alone. Second, the story deals with an organization that currently has 3,911 missionary men and women living around the world. These missionaries have a primary purpose of sharing the gospel message of Jesus Christ in a personal way with men and women and boys and girls who, otherwise, may never meet a follower of Jesus Christ. Finally, this history came into being through the cooperative efforts of two diverse institutions. The idea was conceived and shepherded through writing and editing by personnel of the Foreign Mission Board. The Broadman & Holman Division of the Baptist Sunday School Board then produced the book. As the Publisher of record, I would like to say a word of personal thanks to Robert E. Shoemake and William R. Estep who, along with others, brought this book into being. Oversight of the sesquicentennial manuscript was assigned to the Policy Subcommittee of the Foreign Mission Board. After careful review and dialogue with the author, the subcommittee approved the manuscript.

As you read through this history, I trust that you will see God's hand at work, and that you will be encouraged at the prospects for the future of this institution committed to taking the gospel message of Jesus Christ to the very corners of the world.

Sincerely,

Charles A. Wilson Publisher, Broadman & Holman

Whole Gospel–Whole World

*T*able of Contents

PART I: PROLOGUE

From Kettering to Augusta, 1792-1845

CHAPTER 1

Beginning Again and Again:
From Carey to Judson, 1792-1812

CHAPTER 2

"The Hand of God", 1812-1846

The FMB Seal

The Foreign Mission Board of the Southern Baptist Convention 1845-1995

CHAPTER 3

PART II: BEGINNINGS

The Era of Beginnings
The Southern Baptist Foreign Mission Board, 1846-1888

CHAPTER 4

CHAPTER 5

CHAPTER 6
Two Crucial Decades, 1872-1893 135

PART III: HORIZONS

Expanding Horizons
and Diminishing Resources, 1893-1932

CHAPTER 7
Enlarging the Vision, 1893-1914 159

CHAPTER 8
Rising Expectations—Diminishing Returns, 1915-1932

PART IV: ADVANCE
Renewal and Advance, 1933-1976

CHAPTER 9
A New Spirit, 1933-1944

CHAPTER 10
An End and a Beginning, 1945-1953 251

CHAPTER 11
A Shared Vision, 1954-1979

PART V: ADVANCE
Bold Mission Thrust, 1976-1992

CHAPTER 12

PART VI: EPILOGUE
Promise of a New Day

*The
trustees of the
Foreign Mission Board
wish to dedicate this sesquicentennial volume to*

Acknowledgments

The task of research and writing this history of the Foreign Mission Board was made possible by the cooperation and collaboration of many knowledgeable persons. The bare listing of the names of those who have helped in various ways can never adequately express my gratitude nor indicate the numerous authors, editors, and historians to whom I am also indebted. Their works have helped to make possible this narrative history of the board's efforts to facilitate the missionary mandate of the Southern Baptist Convention through 150 years. I have grouped the names of those upon whom I have been most dependent in categories in which their major contributions have been made.

The following persons permitted me to interview them concerning various aspects of the board's history: Ben Bruner, Norman N. Burnes, Eloise Glass Cauthen, Louis R. Cobbs, Edna Frances Dawkins, Minette Drumwright, Helen Falls, Jesse Fletcher, H. Cornell Goerner, Samuel H. James, Don Kammerdiener, Rebekah Naylor, Frank Means, Lewis I. Myers, William R. O'Brien, R. Keith Parks, Jerry Rankin, Bob Shoemake, Ebbie Smith, Elmer West, Gene Newton West (interviewed by Elmer West).

The following have read the manuscript critically and have made several suggestions for its improvement, many of which I have incorporated in the final draft: Karen Bullock, Edna McDowell Estep, Edie Jeter, Don Kammerdiener, Johnni Johnson Scofield, and Chester Young.

Without archives and libraries, such a work as this would not be possible. Four libraries and their archival holdings have been particularly useful and their personnel extremely helpful. They are: L. Howard Jenkins Research Library, the Archives of the Foreign Mission Board, A. Webb Roberts Library of Southwestern Baptist Theological Seminary, Dargan Carver Library and Archives of the Historical Commission of the Southern Baptist Convention, James P. Boyce Centennial Library of the Southern Baptist Theological Seminary, and Hunt Library of the Woman's Missionary Union.

I wish to express my sincere appreciation to a special group of colaborers in the preparation of the manuscript. The help of Edith Jeter, archivist of the Foreign Mission Board Archives has been indispensable in my research. Johnni Johnson Scofield, editor, has done much more than read the manuscript, she raised many questions and made incisive comments which led to its improvement. She also has helped in numerous other ways, including the selection of graphics and the compiling of the Appendixes. Victoria Bleick has painstakingly aided in the selection of the photographs, maps, and charts that have illuminated the text throughout the book. Jennifer Schuch has typed the manuscript, transcribed the interviews, and transferred the manuscript from one software to another. Dan Schuch, her husband, has served as a consultant in the complicated process. My wife, Edna McDowell Estep, has also made her own unique contribution from aiding in the basic research to proofreading. My indebtedness to her is incalculable.

To Southwestern Baptist Theological Seminary and to President Russell H. Dilday and Dean Bruce Corley, are due a special word of appreciation for providing me with a well-equipped office and secretarial help, without which the manuscript could not have been completed in the three years of its preparation.

I will always be grateful for the gracious manner in which Bob Shoemake, assistant to the president of the Foreign Mission Board, has expedited the entire project. He has served as liaison between the board and the author. His attention to detail in providing for my needs in the process of research has made my many trips to Richmond an enjoyable experience.

Robert A. Baker, my esteemed mentor and friend, died just after I had completed the first draft of the fourth chapter. Before his death, I read at his bedside the chapters I had completed in order to receive the benefit of his counsel. Even though blind, he was still alert and his memory good. His encouragement meant much to me in the initial stages of this formidable undertaking.

Preface

This is the most important book I have ever written. When the Foreign Mission Board asked me to consider the possibility of writing its sesquicentennial history, I was hesitant to agree to do so. Friends advised me not to attempt it, with good reason.

Yet, even though the task was a formidable one, the impression grew that God had uniquely prepared me for this very opportunity. My conversion and call into the ministry were the beginning. In retrospect, my call to the ministry was in reality a call to foreign missions. It was accompanied by a vision of the lost multitudes of many races and nations passing in review without hope to a Christless grave. Before the week was over, I had conveyed my sense of call to my pastor, Dr. Paul Bagby, and to the members of the First Baptist Church of Williamsburg, Kentucky.

After finishing high school, four years of college followed and seven years of seminary—three at The Southern Baptist Theological Seminary, and four at Southwestern Baptist Theological Seminary. During those years I was privileged to study missions with Dr. H. Cornell Goerner at Southern and with Dr. Frank K. Means at Southwestern. After graduating from Southern, my wife and I applied to the Foreign Mission Board for missionary appointment but were told by J.W. (Bill) Marshall, personnel secretary, that the board would never send us because of a health problem.

After graduating from Southwestern I became pastor of a church in Houston,

Texas, which sponsored two Hispanic missions. During the three years we lived in Houston, I joined Dr. Goerner on two mission tours, first to Cuba, and later to Central America and Mexico. One reason I accepted the invitation to join the faculty at Southwestern was the opportunity it would give me to share my own missionary vision with the students. During those early years, I delivered a series of lectures at the International Baptist Seminary in Cali, Colombia. This experience led me to accept the invitation of the seminary faculty there to teach on my first sabbatical leave, provided I would teach in Spanish. Since I didn't know Spanish, I took a crash course in San José, Costa Rica the summer of 1959. The year in Colombia was followed by sabbatical years in Switzerland, England, Spain, and numerous lecture tours in a half dozen Latin American countries as well as extensive travels in Europe and Asia. These experiences not only enriched my life but enhanced my understanding of missionary service by permitting me to be involved in many facets of the work.

Although most of my articles and books have been devoted to some aspect of the history of the Reformation of the sixteenth century or to Baptist history, I am not a stranger to the history of missions since it is a major division within the history of Christianity. I did write a mission study book for 1968, *Colombia, Land of Conflict and Promise,* and most recently, a chapter on Lottie Moon for the book titled *More than Conquerors.* The three years I have devoted to this manuscript have challenged me to use many of the skills developed through more than forty years of teaching and writing church history. Added to the difficulties of reading handwritten minutes, diaries, and correspondence, has been the difficulty of maintaining a degree of objectivity. I recognize that complete freedom from bias is unattainable for one who is as much a part of the history recorded in the following pages as I am. Again, the developments within the denomination since 1979 have so divided Southern Baptists that regardless of the sympathies of the reader, he or she is likely to detect bias where none was intended. I do not claim to be devoid of an opinion, but I have attempted to be honest and fair in handling the materials available to me.

I consider myself exceedingly fortunate to have been privileged to live vicariously through two hundred years of Baptist missionary history in the process of writing this book. I speak of two hundred years for the story of a century and a half of the Foreign Mission Board's life could not be adequately told without some understanding of the English and American Baptist missionary experience that preceded it. In the process of perusing the historical records, biographies, and minutes (seemingly without end), I have learned much—and more than that, I have been impressed again and again with the evident blessing of God upon the people called Southern Baptists. May those who read be as blessed and challenged by this account of the Foreign Mission Board's attempt to take the whole gospel to the whole world as I have been.

W. R. Estep
Fort Worth, Texas

PART I

Prologue
*From
Kettering
to Augusta
1792-1815*

PROLOGUE: 1732-1845

From Kettering to Augusta

WORLD HISTORY EVENTS

1789: Constitution of the United States ratified by the original thirteen colonies.

We the People

insure domestic Tranquility provide for the common and our Posterity, do ordain and establish this Consti

1731: Moravians begin foreign mission work with support of Denmark.

1776: American Declaration of Independence and Revolutionary War

1768: Captain James Cook's voyage to the Pacific

| 1730 | 1740 | 1750 | 1760 | 1770 | 1780 |

BAPTIST MISSIONARY MOVEMENT

1783: William Carey's baptism

1785: William Carey becomes pastor at Moult

1761: William Carey's birth

1785: Andrew Fuller publishes *The Gospel Worthy of All Acceptance* and breaks the grip of Jo Gill's hyper-Calvinism or English Baptists.

1803: The Napoleonic Wars

9: The French Revolution

1845: Rising tension over the slavery issue divides the churches in America.

1815: Waterloo

1841: Anglo-Catholic "Oxford Movement"

1830-1874: The rise of "Modern German Theology"

1812: The British-American War

00   **1800**   **1810**   **1820**   **1830**   **1840**   **1850**

1812: The great fire at Serampore

1837: John L. and Henrietta Hall Shuck begin missionary witness in Macao.

AN
ENQUIRY
INTO THE
OBLIGATIONS OF CHRISTIANS,
TO USE MEANS FOR THE
CONVERSION
OF THE
HEATHENS.

IN WHICH THE
RELIGIOUS STATE OF THE DIFFERENT NATIONS
OF THE WORLD, THE SUCCESS OF FORMER
UNDERTAKINGS, AND THE PRACTICABILITY OF
FURTHER UNDERTAKINGS, ARE CONSIDERED,

BY WILLIAM CAREY.

LEICESTER:

MDCCXCII.

1812: First Congregationalist missionaries sent out by the American Board of Commissions.

92: Carey publishes *An Enquiry* *the Obligations of Christians to Means for the Conversion of Heathen,* "The Charter of dern Missions." Preaches the eathless Sermon" on "Expect at Things. Attempt Great ngs" at association meeting at ttingham. The Particular otist Society for Propagating Gospel Among the Heathen anized.

1814: Adoniram and Ann Judson baptized in Calcutta.

8 May, 1845: Baptists meet in Augusta, Georgia, to organize the Southern Baptist Convention.

1814-1835: Luther Rice, agent of the Triennial Convention

3

Beginning Again and Again:
From Carey to Judson, 1792-1812

Perilous travel

The heartbeat of the Southern Baptist Convention is missions. It has been so from its beginning in 1845. On 8 May when the 293 messengers convened in Augusta, Georgia, for the consultative convention that launched the Southern Baptist Convention, they envisioned no break with the cause of missions.

Although these Southern Baptists felt compelled to sever ties with the Triennial Convention on the basis of principle, the messengers had no intention of forsaking its missionary vision. This was made explicit in the convention's Address to the Public.

The Constitution we adopt is precisely that of the original union; that in connection with which, through his missionary life, Adoniram Judson has lived, and under which Ann Judson and Boardman have died. We recede from it no single step. We have constructed for our basis no new creed; acting in this matter upon a Baptist aversion for all creeds but the Bible. We use the very terms, as we uphold the true spirit and great object of the late "General Convention of the Baptist Denomination of the United States." It is they who wrong us that have receded. We have receded neither from the Constitution nor from any part of the original ground on which we met them in this work.[1]

If the "peculiar institution," which no responsible Southern Baptist would defend today, was the negative catalyst which galvanized Southern Baptists into action, the cause of missions was the positive. The missionary vision alone made possible the survival of the con-

William Carey

vention even after the collapse of the Confederacy. Obedience to the imperative of the Great Commission enabled the convention to transcend its provincialism and to establish its own distinctive identity. Southernness, although an integral aspect of the emerging body, in itself could never have created what has become the Southern Baptist Convention.

The missionary vision of William Carey (1761-1834) that challenged the English-speaking world of the eighteenth century was the vision that has shaped, to a considerable extent, the life of the convention for much of its history.

In Kettering, England on 2 October 1792, the modern missionary movement was born— the fruit of a new understanding of Calvinism, a "Concert of Prayer," and Carey's vision. There can be little question that Carey was a catalyst. His proposal to form a missionary society was preposterous if you leave God out of the picture, and indescribably difficult if you don't. Because William Carey "expected great things from God and attempted great things for God" the Baptists and the missionary movement were both permanently altered.

5

In between the modern mission movement and the formation of the Foreign Mission Board of the Southern Baptist Convention were Adoniram Judson and the Triennial Convention. Southern Baptists were in a sense beginning again that which had begun in 1792 among English Baptists. The Moravians have frequently been cited as the progenitors of the modern mission movement when in reality they were its eighteenth century antecedents. Their missionary exploits were used by

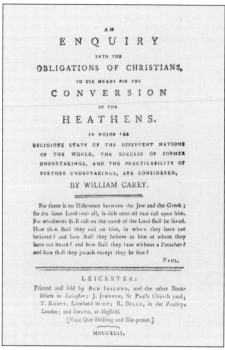

Carey's Enquiry, *1792*

Carey to prod his Baptist brethren into action. It is with Carey, however, that the modern missionary movement is generally dated.

From Enquiry to Action

Carey argued the call to foreign missions was no less binding on Christians than the command to baptize. In his *An Enquiry into the Obligations of Christians*, he set forth this premise in the first of his arguments that Christians, not just the apostles, were obligated to use means in proclaiming Christ to the heathen:

> *First, If the command of Christ to teach all nations be restricted to the apostles, or those under the immediate inspiration of the Holy Ghost, then that of baptizing should be so too; and every denomination of Christians, except the Quakers, do wrong in*

baptizing with water at all.[2]

In this remarkable little book, Carey called his reluctant Baptist brethren to action. After demolishing one by one all the current arguments against attempting foreign missions, he proceeded to remind his readers that the call to missions was not a recent innovation but the essence of the Christian faith.

After briefly reviewing Paul's missionary journeys, he gave his readers a glimpse of the history of missions, including a passing reference to what the Moravians and others, such as David Brainerd, had attempted with meager resources. Next, he spread the world out before their eyes by using the most recent population estimates of the various continents, indicating their major religions, and by underlining the spiritual destitution his statistics revealed. The last two chapters comprise the "how to" section of the *Enquiry*. Here Carey anticipated many of the problems that missionaries in every age have faced and suggested ways in which they could be solved. In the last few pages he gave attention to the purpose of the book—to call for the formation of a foreign mission society that would sponsor a fresh missionary beginning among English Baptists. In this call he laid bare his heart:

> *If there is any reason for me to hope that I*

shall have any influence upon any of my brethren, and fellow Christians, probably it may be more especially amongst them of my own denomination. I would therefore propose that such a society and committee should be formed amongst the particular baptist denomination.[3]

What Carey proposed was in the eyes of many of his peers an "impossible dream." When he first dared to ask at a ministers' meeting (1789), for the sake of discussion, "Whether the command given the apostles to teach all nations was not obligatory on all

Carey's world

ministers to the end of the world," he was unceremoniously put down. Dr. John Ryland Sr., the respected Baptist minister of Northampton and host pastor, is reported to have said: "Sit down, young man. You are

a miserable enthusiast to ask such a question. When God wants to convert the world, He can do it without your help; and at least nothing can be done until a second Pentecost shall bring a return of miraculous gifts."[4] Various historians have given slightly different versions

Fuller memorial window, Kettering Baptist Church

of Ryland's response; however, there is no question in the meaning of the exchange. The response was characteristic of both the man and the hyper-Calvinism predominant among the Particular Baptists at the time. But all of this was destined to change.

If the hyper-Calvinism of Dr. John Gill, the one celebrated Baptist theologian of the day, and his followers had continued unabated among the Particular Baptists, Carey's vision would have perished with him, and possibly the denomination as well. At least such was the opinion of Andrew Fuller. "Had matters gone on but a few years," observed Fuller, "the Baptists would have become a perfect dunghill in society."[5] It was Fuller, pastor of the Kettering Baptist Church (Gill's home church), who became the most articulate critic of this barren theology. Fuller wrote in his *The Gospel Worthy of All Acceptation*:

I believe it is the duty of every minister of Christ plainly and faithfully to preach the Gospel to all who will hear it;. . . I therefore believe free and solemn addresses, invitations, calls, and warnings to them to be not only consistent, but directly adapted, as means, in the hand of the Spirit of God, to bring them to Christ.[6]

Some time before, the works of Jonathan Edwards became widely read in England. The younger John Ryland discovered in Edwards's *Inquiry into the Freedom of the Will* how one could reconcile evangelism with Calvinism. He soon shared his new found insights with his fellow ministers and the

Fuller's The Gospel Worthy of All Acceptance, *1732*

walls of the impregnable fortress of hyper-Calvinism began to crumble. A few years before Abraham Booth, a Particular Baptist preacher, formerly a General Baptist, published in 1768 an assault on Gill's teachings in *The Reign of Grace*, in which he declared:

> *Complete provision is made for the certain salvation of every sinner, however unworthy, who feels his want, and applies to Christ. The gospel is not preached to sinners, nor are they encouraged to believe in Jesus, under the formal notion of their not being elected. No: these tidings of heavenly mercy are addressed to sinners, considered as ready to perish.*[7]

By the time Carey had published his *Enquiry*, a number of young preachers in the Northamptonshire Association had been engaged for eight years in what was termed a "Concert of Prayer," led by John Sutcliff. In addition to praying for spiritual renewal, Sutcliff had challenged them by asking that the "spread of the Gospel to the most distant parts of the habitable globe be the object of your most fervent requests."[8] *The Journal of Captain Cook's Last Voyages* had just been published and its impact was per-

vasive. The book that was a curiosity for most Englishmen became for Carey a window on the world—a world of teeming millions without Christ—and a missionary vision was born. For him, Cook had removed the greatest obstacle to missionary advance by demonstrating that the "habitable globe" was, indeed, accessible, but not without risks.

When Carey preached his "deathless sermon" at the Nottingham meeting of the Northampton Association, all the pieces in the providential pattern were in place. Yet after pouring out the deepest convictions of his soul, it appeared as if Andrew Fuller, who was presiding, was determined to go on with business as usual. To Carey, this was simply unacceptable. For years they had prayed for the conversion of the "heathens." Now neither theology nor geography presented an insurmountable barrier for missions. Carey had given himself to intensive study of the world's spiritual needs,

Carey's house and cobbler shop, Moulton

preached on missions, and finally put the fruits of his studies into print. The time had come to act! Impulsively he grabbed Fuller by the arm and impatiently asked: "Is noth-

The Wallis House

Plaque: IN THIS HOUSE OCTOBER 2nd 1792
A meeting was held to form a society for propagating the Gospel among the heathen, and 13 pounds, 2 shillings, 6 pence was contributed for the purpose. Andrew Fuller was elected Secretary and Reynold Hogg, Treasurer. William Carey, to whose sermon at Nottingham in May of the same year, the movement was due embarked for India on June 13th 1793. This meeting marks the founding of the Baptist Missionary Society and the inauguration of modern foreign missions.

ing going to be done again?" The year before in the meeting of the association at Clipstone, before his *Enquiry* was published, Carey had pleaded for action, but to no avail. Both Sutcliff and Fuller, the preachers upon that occasion, advised delay. This time Andrew Fuller responded. Before noon on 1 June 1792, Fuller proposed "that a plan be prepared against the next Ministers' Meeting at Kettering, for forming a Baptist Society for propagating the Gospel among the Heathens."[9]

Kettering, 2 October 1792

The year 1792 marks the birth of the modern mission movement, a movement whose time had come. The proposal was preposterous if you leave God out of the picture, and difficult even if you don't. Carey reminded the readers of the *Enquiry* that Christianity was a missionary religion. The journal of David Brainerd and the work of the Moravians were matters of common knowledge, but for Baptists, and only a handful at that, to propose to form a foreign missionary society was unthinkable. It is not remarkable that Carey's fellow ministers were hesitant. To the contrary, it would

have been surprising if they had not been. Baptists bore the label of "dissenters" with the stigma and discrimination that the term implied. Their pastors were generally dirt poor and self-educated. And, as if all of that were not deterrent enough, Dr. John Gill was dead set against "offering the gospel to the unconverted." Yet, the twelve young pastors, a layman, and a ministerial student forged ahead to organize a society for foreign missions and the world has never been quite the same since.

The resolution on that eventful October evening like "the shot heard around the world" meant little, if anything, to anyone outside the room, for no one, or almost no one, realized the significance of the occasion. The resolution finally agreed upon read:

Humbly desirous of making an effort for the propagation of the Gospel among the

Heathen, according to the recommendations of Carey's Enquiry, we unanimously resolve to act in Society together for this purpose; and, as in the divided state of Christendom each denomination, by exerting itself separately, seems likeliest to accomplish the great end, we name this the Particular Baptist Society for the Propagation of the Gospel among the Heathen.[10]

A committee was then formed to carry on the work of the Society. Fuller was named secretary, and Reynold Hogg, the most financially secure of the group, became the treasurer. Carey, John Ryland, and John Sutcliff completed the committee. At the next meeting, Samuel Pearce, a pastor in Birmingham, was added. The next order of business was to secure pledges to undergird the work. A total of 13.2.6 (13 pounds, 2 shillings, and 6 pence) was subscribed, including 6/10 (6 shillings and 10 pence) pledged by a visiting ministerial student by the name of William Staughton from Bristol. Proceeds from the sale of Carey's *Enquiry* were added. The next move was to determine where to begin the work and find a missionary or missionaries committed to the task.

An Unequal Yoke

Unknown to the committee at the time the society was organized, a young physician who had served as a surgeon on the *Earl of Oxford* (an English ship which sailed between India and England) was seeking support from the Baptists of London to finance his return to India as a missionary. In his previous trips, he had learned Bengali and had begun to translate the New Testament into the language, but due to financial difficulties had been forced to suspend his work. Someone told him of Carey, whom he promptly wrote. Carey turned the letter over to Fuller and together they sought to learn as much as possible of this new missionary candidate. Convinced that John Thomas was a man sent from God, they determined to recommend him for the Society's first missionary. However, Thomas had no intention of going back to India alone. Would Carey go with him? The answer was evident before the question was asked, for Carey's vision not only involved the sending of others, but it also included his own personal commitment, regardless of the cost.

Carey was no longer the "poor cobbler" that John Ryland baptized in the River Nen; he had become one of the most respected and beloved pastors in the association. The Leicester Church, which had been beset by internal dissention for years, had under his preaching and pastoral care begun to enjoy a new found harmony. The waters of baptism were disturbed frequently by those converted through his evangelistic efforts and his family life was as happy as it had ever been. His wife had at last learned to read and their marriage was blessed by three bright little boys. The church was reluctant to release its pastor but finally consented. But his wife, Dorothy, was a different matter. At the time, she was pregnant and dead set against going to India. She had never been out of her home county and had never shared the vision of her husband. Yet, once Carey had put his hand to the plough, there was no turning back.

Resolved to go without his family to India, Carey decided to take his eight-year-old son, Felix, with him. But when the ship upon which he and Dr. John Thomas had booked passage refused to take them for want of a license from the East India Company, this development gave them a reprieve. Thomas took advantage of the opportunity to lay upon Dorothy Carey's conscience her duty to join her husband. Since baby Jabez had arrived, she finally agreed, provided she could take her unmarried sister, Kitty, with her. Soon a Danish ship was found on which Carey booked passage for the whole party but now they lacked even enough funds to pay for the passage of the two missionaries, since a full refund was not forthcoming from the *Earl of Oxford*. The situation appeared hopeless. A two hundred pound gift from John Fawcett of Yorkshire, who had heard Carey preach, changed the picture from impossible to barely possible. Carey renegotiated the fare downward from 700 to 315 pounds. On 13 June 1793, a year after Carey had preached on the theme, "Expect Great Things from God and Attempt Great Things for God," the entire party of eight set sail for India on the Danish *Kron Princessa Maria*.

Five long tiresome months later, the ship arrived in Calcutta. The voyage had not been without its perils. French privateers had wreaked havoc on the shipping lanes, but the *Kron Princessa Maria* arrived safely. Carey

Eighteenth century sailing vessel

could not refrain from drawing a parallel between the trials of the journey and the Christian life when he wrote in his journal on 9 November 1793:

For near a month we have been within two hundred miles of Bengal, but the violence of the currents set us back when we have been at the very door. I hope I have learned the necessity of bearing up in the things of God against wind and tide, when there is occasion, as we have done in our voyage. We have had our port in view all along, and there has been every attention paid to ascertain our situation by solar and lunar observation: no opportunity occurred that was neglected. . . . Now, though this is tiresome work, and (especially if a current sets against us) we scarcely make any way; nay, sometimes, in spite of all that we can do, we go backwards instead of forwards; yet it is absolutely necessary to keep working up, if we ever mean to arrive at our port. So in the Christian life, we often have to work against wind and currents; but we must do it if we expect ever to make port.[11]

At last, the missionaries arrived in India but with scarcely enough money to sustain them for a month. Dr. Thomas had assured the committee of the Society that once the missionaries were in India they could support themselves through secular employment while carrying on their missionary work. Thomas immediately went about setting up his practice of medicine, but Carey spent weeks trying to find employment without success. In the meantime, Thomas managed to use all the mission's funds in his own interests, leaving Carey and his large family destitute. Through it all Carey continued the study of Bengali that he had begun on shipboard with Thomas.

Out of desperation to feed his family,

Carey began to clear forty acres of land in what he called a "jungle forest," three days journey from Calcutta. Because the house was already occupied into which he had hoped to move, Carey and his family were compelled to accept the hospitality of an Englishman until he could build his own bamboo dwelling. Fortunately, Ram Ram Basu, a well-educated high-caste Brahmin who had been won to Christ by Dr. Thomas years before but had not been baptized, became Carey's "pundit" or *munshi* to assist him in studying the languages of Bengal, its people, and their culture. Even in all the setbacks that Carey had thus far experienced, he doggedly forged ahead in his determination to translate the whole Bible into the language of the people.

Before the first harvest was gathered or his house completed, Carey and his family were on the move again. Dr. Thomas's renewed contact with a former friend had opened a new door of opportunity for both Carey and Thomas. They were invited to supervise the cultivation and processing of indigo. A house would be provided with a 250 pound salary a year for each. The factories were located sixteen miles apart, but close enough to enable Thomas and Carey to preach and witness together. To Carey the new opportunity was an answer to prayer. The secular work in which he was to be engaged was seasonal, leaving most of the year free for his missionary work which soon involved, in addition to preaching and teaching, horticulture and education.

Carey's spirit soon revived in Mudnabatty. It was thirty-two miles north of Malda in northern Bengal. Both Thomas and Carey enlarged their ministries by using their skills to meet human needs—Thomas with his medicine and Carey with his horticulture. Carey's first letter to England did not arrive until 29 July 1794, and he received no letter from the Society for two long years. He was beginning to feel that he had been abandoned but he kept writing. Since he now had an income sufficient for his needs, he asked Fuller not to send any more money but to use it to send out another missionary. He also asked for a "few instruments of husbandry" and "a yearly assortment of all garden and flowering seeds, and seeds of fruit-trees, that you can possibly procure . . . as it will be a lasting advantage to this country; and I shall have it in my power to do this for what I now call my own country. . . ." [12]

Even in all the setbacks that Carey... experienced, he doggedly forged ahead in his determination to translate the whole Bible into the language of the people.

Carey and Thomas also began a school for boys that included in its curriculum mathematics, science, Sanskrit, Persian, and the Bible. But that which brought the greatest joy was the opportunity to preach again. S. Pearce Carey wrote: "Every Sunday, with the factory closed, and during two or three evenings a week—except in the rains—Carey would be out in some of his two hundred villages." [13] Reflecting upon the experience Carey wrote: "Preaching the gospel is the very element of my soul. Over twenty miles square I published Christ's name."[14] Upon another occasion, he expressed his feelings. "Preached on Christmas day, and twice on the Lord's day, the 28th; and I think I may say with truth, that the whole of this time was a time of real refreshing to my soul, which had long been in a languid state."[15]

From his correspondence and his journal, it is evident that Carey was settling in at Mudnabatty. His house provided sufficient room for his growing family and his study. The indigo factory provided contacts that made possible a hearing for the gospel that would have been difficult to secure otherwise. Audiences frequently numbered as many as five hundred on a Sunday. Carey remarked that they were eager "hearers of the gospel but so slow to understand." A part of the problem, he admitted, was his inability to express himself clearly in the Bengali idiom of the region. Some complained that he gave them "mental trouble." Such responses continually challenged him to improve his use of the language. When it appeared that Carey's vision of a bivocational missionary was at last finding fulfillment in India, his five-year-old son, Peter, took sick and, in spite of all that Dr. Thomas and his medicine could do, he died.

Peter, the Careys' third son, was already fluent in Bengali. His cheerful nature was a delight to his father, who in spite of the long hours devoted to his missionary labors and the demands of the indigo factory, loved his children dearly. Little Peter's death hit hard. The sorrow was compounded by the difficulty of finding anyone willing to help with the burial. The caste system, which Carey had come to despise with a passion, prohibited any Hindu from volunteering for the task. Finally four Muslims were persuaded to help. After the funeral Carey was faced with a distraught wife whose mental condition began to deteriorate rapidly. Carey now faced the realities he had not faced before—the death of Peter, the shackles of the caste system, Dorothy's insanity, and the suspicions of some members of the Society that he was becoming too absorbed in his secular work to the detriment of his missionary task. Little did his critics back home understand the situation or the caliber of their missionary. Besides, there was no way the meager allocations of the Baptist Missionary Society could have sustained him and Thomas and their families.

Carey was hurt by the unwarranted criticism but hastened to explain the way in which he attempted to utilize his time and opportunities.

Our labours will speak for us. I may declare that, after a bare allowance for my family, my whole income, and some months much more, goes for the purposes of the gospel, in supporting pundits and school-teachers and the like. The love of money has not prompted me to this indigo-business. I am indeed poor, and always shall be, till the Bible is published in Bengali and Hindustani, and the people need no further instruction.[16]

By 1796, he reported to the Society that the magistrates in India were ordered to return all Europeans who were not employed by the East India Company or the British government. Since he was employed in the manufacturing of indigo dye and licensed through the influence of an official of the East India Company, it was now evident that he had been saved from deportation. His responsibility at the factory demanded his personal attention only three months of the year. During the remaining months, he was free to devote virtually all of his time to missionary responsibilities.

It became apparent to Carey that, if he were going to master Bengali, he would have to learn Sanskrit. With his usual determination, he set about to do exactly that. First, he translated a Sanskrit grammar and dictionary into English and then he compiled his own Sanskrit-Bengali-English dictionary. In view of the demands of his preaching, translation work, and language study, it is surprising that he found time for gardening, but this, too, he viewed as an essential element of his witness. As he gathered plants and seeds and developed his skills in Indian agriculture, he also collected and collated information on the birds, beasts, fish, and reptiles of India.[17]

Even though a church of four members, including Carey and Thomas and two other Englishmen, had been formed by 1798, work among the indigenous people was making no discernable progress. In fact the mission was in disarray. A new missionary by the name of John Fountain was so shocked at the exploitation of the people by the East India Company and the British government alike that Carey, who had no love for the monarchy nor for the East India Company, feared Fountain's unbridled tongue would get them all deported. Dr. Thomas, pursued by his creditors, forsook his indigo factory and his missionary work for a medical practice in Calcutta by which he hoped to make enough money to pay off his debts. Because of Dorothy's condition, Carey found himself forced to spend more time with his domestic responsibilities. In 1798, he had to give up keeping a journal for lack of time. It was a despondent missionary who wrote Andrew Fuller on 9 January 1798: "Mr. Thomas is gone far away and my domestic troubles are sometimes almost too heavy for me. I am distressed, yet supported, and I trust not totally dead in the things of God."[18] Carey had been unequally yoked, first with Dorothy, who had never shared his missionary vision, and then with the erratic but gifted Dr. Thomas. Although Carey was apparently unconscious of the impact he was making on his fellow Englishmen, "His purpose in India had become known also to the European community and, such was the respect in which he was already held, that no one sought to prevent him from furthering it."[19]

Serampore

In spite of the hardships and the handicaps of Carey's years in India, Christ had been lifted up in word and deed. Although no public confessions were made and consequently no baptisms were recorded among the Hindus or Muslims, a number of Englishmen in Malda had been won to Christ. Too, the translation of the entire Bible into Bengali was almost complete. A printing press had been set up in Carey's house. But everything came to a standstill when a flood destroyed the indigo crop and the factory. Since his license did not run out for three more years, Carey made plans to move to Kidderpore, a village twelve miles from Mudnabatty, which was on higher ground. His plans included a missionary compound which would accommodate the four families who were on their way to join him in the work.

The new missionaries with their children had arrived on an American ship at Serampore, fourteen miles north of Calcutta. Since they had no licenses which would allow them to work in India, British authorities ordered them to return immediately, but Colonel Bea, governor of the Danish colony of Serampore, offered them asylum and promised to protect them from the British. William Ward, who was formerly the printer and editor of the *Hull Advertiser*, and whom Carey had challenged years before to use his skills in printing the Scriptures, was sent to Mudnabatty to confer with Carey and Fountain.

Once again, Carey was faced with a major decision. He had not anticipated this turn of events. Besides, he had invested much in the property at Kidderpore. He wrote Fuller: "It was all so affecting to my mind that I scarcely remember having felt more on any occasion soever. No one could gauge the conflict of this trial but myself."[20] The next morning, nevertheless, Ward recorded: "Monday, December 2,—Carey has made up his mind to leave all, and follow our Saviour to Serampore. Indeed, whilst He has opened a door there to us, He has shut all others."[21]

It was not easy, in spite of the lack of conversions among the Hindus and Muslims, to leave his school and the hundreds who continued to give the gospel a hearing week by week. It was particularly difficult to part with English friends who had committed their lives to Christ, but he

was reassured that they would not let the work die. On 1 January 1800, the boats were loaded with Carey's family, the printing press, his precious manuscripts, assorted plants, and household belongings. They docked at Serampore ten days later. Going down the river took only a third of the time the trip upstream had taken almost seven years earlier.

Serampore became not only a "city of refuge" from the hostility of the East India

India

Company and British authorities, as well, but also a beachhead for the gospel in all of Asia. For Baptists, it was to become the symbol of their commitment to global missions that challenged and quickened Baptist life on both sides of the Atlantic. John Richter expressed it well: "The Jews might as well forget Jerusalem as the Baptists Serampore."[22]

The promise of Serampore was not self-evident. A Moravian mission station had ceased operation after fifteen fruitless years that saw only one questionable convert. Carey suffered no illusions regarding the difficulty of the task, but he relished the new possibilities for proclaiming the gospel that Serampore offered. It seemed to be at the crossroads of the world as the ships of many nations plied its waters daily. Yet on the threshold of this new beginning, death claimed three young missionaries: Grant, Brunson, and Fountain. The three families that survived, Carey, Marshman, and Ward were, under Carey's leadership, to write a new chapter in missionary history.

Once property was purchased, buildings were erected to accommodate the families, the church, a printing press, schools, and a workshop. Almost immediately Carey planted a garden without which in the early years the mission would have been hard pressed for food. Even while at Mudnabatty, Carey had planned to organize the mission on Moravian lines under which all the missionaries would live, eat, and share the work together. He made one important change, however, in the Moravian pattern. He designated no one person as the mission's "housefather" whose major function in the Moravian missions was to settle disputes that naturally arise. At Serampore all missionaries were to be equal, sharing alike in the work and witness of the mission. No one was to work for personal gain. All were to pool their income in order to support and expand the work. Each was to receive a frugal allowance sufficient for individual and personal needs. And amazingly enough it not only worked, but the mission thrived.

Carey discovered that his colleagues were as committed to the cause as he was,

and that they also brought abilities and talents that supplemented his own. William Ward soon had the press set up and began to print the first edition of Carey's Bengali Bible. The Marshmans established two schools, one for boys and another for girls.

Hannah Marshman threw herself into the work as completely as did her husband. In addition to the major responsibility for the girl's school she brought Carey's sons a mother's touch with firm discipline that they much needed. The all important translation work did not consume all of Carey's time for he was frequently out in the "byways and hedges" preaching in Bengali. Services weekly in English attracted others from as many as a half a dozen different nationalities, representing a mixture of religions.

Before the first year was up in Serampore, Marshman and Ward had begun to preach in Bengali. In spite of the taunts and sneers of the Europeans and the sticks and stones of the Hindus, they persisted. Finally, a Bengali made his profession of faith and expressed a desire for baptism but

At Serampore all missionaries were to be equal, sharing alike in the work and witness of the mission... All were to pool their income in order to support and expand the work.

soon afterwards disappeared and was never seen again. The missionaries' joy quickly turned to sorrow and then again, the unexpected happened.

First, Dr. Thomas reappeared just at the God-appointed hour. He was eating with the missionaries when word came that a guru "at his morning bath and homage, [had] slipped and fell on the ghat" and dislocated his shoulder. He was in such great pain that he sent to the mission for the "doctor-padre." Thomas left his uneaten meal on the table and rushed with Marshman and Carey to the stricken man's side. After replacing the shoulder, they left him to think through the meaning of "A father chastises a child whom he loves." Years before, it turned out that Krishna Pal had heard the gospel from one Johannes Grassman for whom he had done some carpentry work. Now, it was that same gospel that Thomas, Ward, and Felix Carey, who had only recently confessed his faith in Christ, shared with him day after day as he came to the mission for therapy. On Monday, 22 December 1800, Thomas asked Krishna if he understood what he had been learning. To which he replied that "the Lord Jesus Christ had given His very life for the salvation of sinners, and that he and his friend Gokul did unfeignedly believe this." "Then you are our brothers," declared Thomas. "Come, and in love let us eat together."[23]

Krishna Pal was the mission's first Hindu convert, and Dr. Thomas was the "means." The invitation to eat together was by design. This meant that Krishna Pal was breaking caste and that he realized his action would have dreadful consequences

for him and his family. His public baptism followed on 28 December 1800. Ward recorded the moving event:

Krishna Pal

After our English Service, at which I preached on baptism, we went to the riverside, immediately opposite our gate when the Governor, a number of Europeans and Portuguese, and many Hindus and Mohammedans attended. We sang in Bengali, "Jesus, and shall it ever be?" Carey then spoke in Bengali, particularly declaring that we did not think the water sacred, but water only, and that the one from amongst them about to be baptized professed by this act to put off all sins and all debtahs, and to put on Christ. After prayer, he went down the bank into the water, taking Felix in his right hand, and baptized him. Then Krishna went down and was baptized, the words in Bengali. All was silence. The Governor [who was present] could not restrain his tears, and almost every one seemed struck with the solemnity of this new ordinance. I never saw in the most orderly congregation in England anything more impressive. . . . When Krishna came from dressing—a quick thing here—a Danish lady took him by the hand, and thanked him from her heart. . . . In the afternoon we kept the Lord's Supper in Bengali for the first time. "How amiable are Thy tabernacles, O Lord of hosts!" Krishna said he was full of praise. Felix and I accompanied him to his home. We talked with unusual feeling to the women. About nine o'clock Krishna came joyfully to the Mission to tell us that they again wished for baptism. Blessed day![24]

The Impact

After Krishna Pal had confessed faith in Christ and accepted Dr. Thomas's invitation to eat with him, the persecution which the missionaries had known was now turned against the new converts with renewed fury. A mob of Krishna Pal's neighbors carried him before the magistrate and charged him with having become a European. His oldest daughter was kidnapped and mobs gathered around his house to chant *"Feringhi."* In the midst of the tumult, "Carey met Rasamayi, Krishna Pal's sister-in-law, in the road weeping and wept with her, which," as S. Pearce Carey wrote, "she never forgot."[25] Braving the unbridled wrath of Hindu neighbors, Krishna Pal's wife, Jaymani was baptized and by February, her sister Rasaymayi followed suit. These were the first fruits of the gospel in India. The missionaries thanked God and rejoiced.

On 5 March 1801, a bound copy of the Bengali New Testament was laid on the communion table in the chapel of the mission. It had taken seven months to print on the mission's press under Ward's supervision and represented seven and a half years of Carey's diligent effort. Marshman composed a hymn commemorating that high hour, the first stanza of which reads:

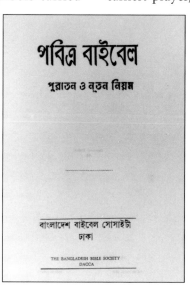

Bengali Bible title page

Hail, precious Book divine!
Illumined by thy rays,
We rise from death and sin,
And tune a Saviour's praise:
The shades of error, dark as night,
Vanish before thy radiant light![26]

A byproduct of Carey's expertise in Bengali was an invitation to become a professor of Bengali in the newly established Fort William College in Calcutta. After earnest prayer, the missionaries agreed that such an opportunity must be of God for purposes beyond their understanding. Carey accepted the invitation but, because he was a Baptist, and not an Anglican, he was given the title of tutor, not professor. He soon discovered his new position not only gave him much needed income for the expansion of the mission's printing enterprise but also gave him an opportunity to sharpen his language skills with the most knowledgeable pundits available. It also laid to rest fears that the missionaries could be returned to England at the insistence of the East India Company, although the mission was located in a Danish colony. In fact, shortly after Carey began to teach at the college, the British took over Serampore. The British Commissioner, however, assured the missionaries of their freedom to continue their missionary work as before. The next year, with peace restored in Europe, the colony was returned to Denmark.

The missionaries saw the hand of God

in much that had transpired. The Old Testament was in the process of being printed in Bengali. Also, the New Testament in Sanskrit was published in 1808. Carey's new position gave him an opportunity to witness to many a bright young Englishmen in the service of the East India Company, and some were won to Christ. His own knowledge of Bengali and Sanskrit continued to grow. The mission was soon publishing two papers, one in English and the other in Bengali, in which Carey attacked relentlessly the age-old practice of *sati* (the burning of widows alive along with the bodies of their deceased husbands). Carey's own investigation uncovered the fact that in a nearby section of Bengal 438 widows, some of them child brides, had been burned in one year alone. To his campaign against *sati* was added a vigorous attack upon infanticide and human sacrifices to Hindu gods.

But always the central concern in the mission's work was evangelism. By 1821, 1,400 converts had been baptized. Others were to follow but so would opposition. Many a new convert was put to death by Hindu fanatics and others simply disappeared never to be heard from again. In spite of repeated threats on their lives, Krishna Pal and his friend, Gokul, remained, despite relapses, faithful unto death. Gokul was the first of the two to go, and in his death India witnessed that which only the gospel could do: provide a graphic repudiation of the caste system.

Krishna Pal and Gokul, although longtime friends and brothers in Christ, had their differences that were allowed to fester into bitter confrontations. But, during the two months before his death, Gokul sought reconciliation and forgiveness. When he died, it was Krishna Pal who constructed the casket at his own expense. The coffin was carried on the shoulders of Marshman, Krishna Pal, two of Carey's sons, Felix and William, a Christian Brahmin and the first Muslim convert. To a rigid caste society, this was a witness more powerful than words.

The impact of the mission upon Hindu society did not go unnoticed by those who opposed its efforts, among either the English or the Indian population. The work of the missionaries was blamed for the mutiny at Vellore and its bloody aftermath. With the change of English governors in Calcutta, all missionary work in Bengal by the missionaries or the Indian preachers was strictly prohibited, and the new British governor ordered the Serampore printing press moved to Calcutta. Even the services in the Lall Bazar Chapel, in Calcutta, were forbidden. Both in England and India, the missionaries were slandered and maligned. As if this were not enough, death visited the mission again and again and on 12 March 1812, fire broke out in the storage room where the paper for the printing of the Bible was stored. In spite of the almost superhuman efforts of Marshman and Ward and the employees of the press, all appeared lost.

I saw the ground strewn with half-consumed paper, on which the Words of Life would soon have been printed. The metal under our feet amidst the ruins was melted into misshapen lumps—the sad remains of types consecrated to the service of the sanctuary. A few hours ago all was full of promise—now all is rubbish and smoke.[27]

Precious manuscripts representing ten years of labor were consumed in the flames. Carey estimated it would take a year before the printing of the Bible could be resumed. But God used the fire to publicize and advance the cause of missions as nothing else could have done.

As soon as word reached Fuller in September, the news of the disastrous fire spread throughout England. S. Pearce Carey wrote of the reaction:

> Some event thus dramatic seemed needed to reveal the work to British Christendom, which learned with astonishment that the mission could lose, and in one building, from 9,000 to 10,000 pounds, and still more that the translations were so polyglot. Till then they had heard without hearing. This catastrophe unstopped their ears. In the blaze of this fire they saw the grandeur of the enterprise; the facts were flashed out.[28]

Upon the Baptist Missionary Society's twentieth anniversary, Fuller wrote: "When your late disastrous intelligence reached us, a strong sensation was felt throughout the kingdom, not only in our own denomination but amongst Christians of every name, each vying with the rest to repair your loss."[29] Later Fuller could report that the entire monetary amount of the loss incurred had been raised within only two months, but that which was of greater importance, the cause of missions, now captivated England and Scotland as never before.

The British Indian Administration seemed completely oblivious to the rising tide of support for the Serampore mission. To the contrary, this arm of the government aggressively pursued an anti-missionary policy more vigorously than ever. The first missionary of the London Missionary Society to India was immediately ejected. Others, including newly appointed missionaries

from America, were also ordered deported. Serampore came under even greater censure when it became known that the Judsons and Rice had become Baptists, even though this decision had been reached only after their own careful and independent study of the Scriptures. In spite of the War of 1812, Baptists in America were becoming increasingly aware of the difficulties that the missionaries faced. But the situation in India was to change sooner than anyone had anticipated.

On 12 March 1813, the House of Commons began a debate on the renewal of the East India Company's charter. Wilberforce, who had contributed personally to the Baptist Missionary Society, seized the opportunity to strike a blow for freedom in India.

"Now that the slave trade is abolished," he argued, "the exclusion of missionaries from India is by far the greatest of our national sins."[30] Since the fire at Serampore, public opinion, in spite of the calumnies against and denigration of the missionaries, was dead set against the anti-missionary policies of the East India Company. This was clear from the 837 petitions, representing more than 500,000 signatures, presented to the House of Commons on behalf of the missionaries. Andrew Fuller and the Baptists spearheaded the campaign among the people and Wilberforce led the pro-missionary forces in the Commons and Lord Wellesley in the House of Lords. The opposition's major arguments against the Baptists, who were called "Anabaptists" and "tub-preachers," consisted of prejudicial remarks designed to denigrate the missionaries. Charles Marsh, a leader of the opposition scornfully referred to the missionaries as "apostates from the loom and anvil, these renegades from the lowest handicraft employments."[31] At last the pro-missionary forces carried the day. When the resolution which changed the charter of the East India Company was passed, Wilberforce wrote: "It was late when I got up. I thank God I was enabled to speak for two hours and with

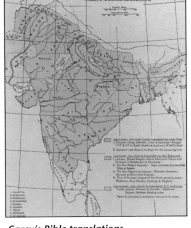

Carey's Bible translations

great acceptance, and we carried it by 89 to 36."[32] The charter was changed and the first missionary to receive a license from the Company was Carey's nephew, Eustice Carey.

The newly won freedom did not solve all the vexing problems that plagued the Serampore trio and their co-laborers. In fact, it added others of which the appointment of an Anglican bishop was not the least. In spite of this development, which Carey opposed, he still maintained an ecumenical attitude toward other Christians. The Baptist Missionary Society, itself, also contributed to the mission's problems by insisting upon the immediate transfer of the Serampore property that had been purchased and maintained by the missionaries themselves at great personal sacrifice. Since the death of Fuller in 1815, John Ryland had served as secretary and nineteen new members had been added to the committee charged with supervising the work. This "change of the guard" created problems for the committee and the Serampore mission-

aries. The new missionaries, including Eustice Carey, sided with the committee. Thus, for some time the missionaries in India presented a divided front before reconciliation was achieved.

In spite of the problems of the mission, the fire, and floods which inundated the property and wiped out Carey's beloved garden, the measurable results of the work were remarkable. By 1817, the Baptist missionaries had opened 103 schools with an average attendance of 6,703 students. By 1837, the Serampore missionaries under Carey's leadership had also accomplished the phenomenal task of translating the Scriptures into some forty languages and dialects. Carey, himself, translated the entire Bible into "Bengali, Oriya, Marathi, Hinki, Assamese, and Sanskrit, as well as portions of it into 29 other tongues."[33]

Not only did the missionaries translate the Bible, the mission also printed on its own presses the Scriptures in these languages. This was a chapter in missionary history possibly never equaled and surely never surpassed. It was all a part of the design for doing missions that Carey had brought to India with him. Carey had been greatly influenced by the missionary work of the Moravians. His mission strategy followed a pattern which they had pioneered. The Baptist Missionary Society, however, lacked the financial support of a government and, of course, was not an "established church" in any nation. The Baptists, the most denigrated of all dissenters in England, were on their own with meager financial resources. This is why Carey felt the necessity of self-support in order to maintain the missionary enterprise. Employment at the indigo factory and later at Fort William College, however, were always only a means for sustaining the work, not an end in itself. The heart of the work for Carey was the translating and printing of the Scriptures into the language of the various people which he sought to reach for Christ. Joshua Marshman called the first two thousand copies of the New Testament in Bengali two thousand missionaries, for the New Testament could penetrate areas where missionaries had never been able to go.

A Calcutta neighborhood today

For Carey, evangelism and education went hand in hand, one was incomplete without the other. He was the most miserable during the early months in India when he could not preach to the Bengalis. Before leaving Mudnabatty, he had organized two small churches of Europeans, but he and Thomas also established a school for Bengali boys. As soon as Joshua and Hannah Marshman were able, they organized schools at Serampore. By 1818, Serampore College was founded as a Christian College open to students of all denominations, religions, colors, races, and nationalities.[34] Its

teachers were required to be Christians. Nineteen of the thirty-seven students in the first class were also Christians. In addition to the church at Serampore, Carey had begun in 1803 to preach in both English and Bengali at a chapel in the Lall Bazar of Calcutta, a section of the city abounding in bars and prostitutes frequented by the sailors of many nationalities. This ministry was designed to reach the international community as well as Bengalis. Notable conversions reinforced the work of the missionaries and made possible the expansion of the work. Several of the converts won here also became missionaries.

The Social Implications

From the beginning of the work in India, Carey and Thomas recognized the need of meeting the physical needs of its people. At Mudnabatty, Thomas treated the ailments of those who came daily to his house. After Thomas left, Carey carried on the medical work as best he could with the knowledge and medicines he had acquired from Thomas. Carey was a skilled gardener. Upon reaching India, he saw immediately the need for applying his skills for the good of the native population. Hence for Carey, his hobby and scientific pursuit became also a ministry. At Serampore by necessity he cultivated a large garden to help provide

Serampore College, Administration Building, 1821

food for the mission; but at the same time, he developed an extensive knowledge of the plants of India and the East Indies to which he ascribed Latin names. But the garden at Serampore was more than a laboratory, it became for Carey a sanctuary—a garden of prayer. Here he sought and found communion with God and strength for his tasks.

The mission published two monthly magazines, one in English and the other in Bengali, and a weekly newspaper in Bengali. These became the media through which Carey and his colleagues carried on their running battle against the social evils that plagued Hindu society. On a trip from Mudnabatty to Calcutta, Carey witnessed *sati* for the first time. He wrote Fuller a graphic account of the burning of the widow with her husband's corpse and his unwelcomed protests. As the bamboo poles held the woman down amidst the flames, Carey wrote: "We could not bear to see more, and left them, exclaiming loudly against the murder, and filled with horror at what we had seen."[35] From that time, Carey and the missionaries carried on a relentless campaign against the practice and other traditional murders of infanticide, the sacrifice

of children to various gods, and *ghat*. (*Ghat* was the abandonment of the aged and infirm to die alone on the banks of the rivers from starvation or the ravages of nature.)

The caste system for the Baptists was completely unacceptable. For these ardent abolitionists, it was simply another form of slavery but more diabolical because it was sanctioned by religion and hallowed by tradition. The Moravians accepted it as an unmovable rock. From the beginning of their work, Carey and Thomas determined to do otherwise. Thus, for them the gospel was both personal and social. By the same token a privatization of the Christian faith that shut its eyes to social and moral evil was both unthinkable and unacceptable.

Southeast from Serampore

The Serampore mission of the Baptist Missionary Society not only became a beachhead for the gospel in Bengal but also a staging area and model for Southeast Asia. Ernest Payne has shown in his book, *South-East from Serampore*, that this effort remains a little known chapter of the heroic struggle of Baptist missionary efforts to proclaim the gospel in the East Indies in spite of insurmountable obstacles.

After the death of his first wife and considerable friction in working with other missionaries, William Robinson agreed to go to Java. He and his second wife, Margaret Gordon, the daughter of a deacon of the Calcutta Church, sailed on 6 March 1813. The Robinsons took with them a boy by the name of Charles Leonard. He was thirteen years of age. His father was from Ireland and a deacon in the Calcutta church. The missionaries thought that it would be helpful for the Robinsons to have a boy in the company of the missionaries who could become the first student in a school that Robinson hoped to start in Java. The Robinsons carried with them a letter of instructions from the Serampore Mission. After reminding the missionary (women were not considered under appointment) of the ethnic and language diversity he would doubtless encounter, the Serampore missionaries wrote:

> We wish you to consider yourself, however, as a Javanese missionary. You must, depending on the Divine blessing, secure their language so as to preach to them, and to give them the Holy Scriptures in their own tongue. You will find a necessity for the Dutch and Malay languages; but if you should not be able, by calls of immediate duty to learn accurately the three languages, let the Javanese at any rate be first secured. . . .
>
> If you should have a clear opening to begin an English school, we would have you embrace it, that you may meet as much as possible the extremely low state of the Society's funds. We recommend to you the most rigid economy, remembering that poverty in a missionary never lowers his character in the sight of his neighbors. . . .[36]

On 3 May 1813, William and Margaret Robinson with young Charles Leonard arrived in Batavia and, as Payne wrote: "The Baptist Mission to the East Indies had commenced."[37]

That which began with such high expectations soon met with disappointment and frustration, largely due to the Dutch colonial authorities. As the British began to relinquish control of island after island, the Baptist missionaries found themselves confronted by hostile governments that resented Baptist missionary efforts above all others. Jabez Carey, who had gone to Amboyna was one of the first to have his work curtailed by the Dutch. Then, William Robinson whose activities were censured by the Dutch colonial government, felt compelled to leave Batavia after eight years of rather fruitless effort. He transferred to Sumatra which was still under British rule.

By the death of Carey in 1834, there were fourteen missionary societies in England and many others in Europe and the United States.

A number of missionaries from the Baptist Missionary Society arrived in Sumatra in response to the open door provided by Sir Stamford Raffles, the governor. The center of activities was Bencoolen. The response to the gospel was once again disappointing. Nathaniel Ward (a nephew of William Ward) and Richard Burton, a newly appointed missionary from Olney, did make a dangerous trip, however, into the interior for the purpose of making contact with the Battas, a primitive tribe of cannibals. When the British in 1824 turned Sumatra over to the Dutch, the English missionaries departed for other fields of service. The pioneering efforts of the Baptists, however, were not as fruitless as they might appear. Initial translation of the Scriptures had been made in Javanese and Malay. Some few notable conversions had taken place and seed was sown that the Netherlands' Missionary Society and Dutch Mennonites would cultivate.

West from Serampore

The influence of Carey and his Serampore colleagues began to kindle anew the fires of missionary enthusiasm the church had seldom known. Latourette later wrote: "It [the Baptist Missionary Society] inaugurated a new era in the geographic spread of the faith outside the Occident, an era in which Evangelicals of the British Isles and America were to take the lead. . . ."[38] The truth of this observation first became evident when in the summer of 1794 John Ryland shared one of Carey's letters with David Bogue, a Congregational minister. Bogue and his friends were so moved that they met at Baker's Coffee House in London to pray and to plan for their own missionary society. In 1795 they formed the London Missionary Society. The Anglicans soon followed with a society of their own. Led by Charles Simeon, an Evangelical pastor at Cambridge with the support of Wilberforce, John Newton, and Thomas Scott, the Church Missionary Society was formed in 1799. By the death of Carey in 1834, there were fourteen missionary societies in England and many others in Europe and the United States.[39]

In spite of the fact that at the turn of the century, intercontinental communication was a slow and uncertain matter, news did travel. Baptists in the United States were still involved in the birth of a new nation in which they had taken an active part, when in England the "deathless sermon" was preached and the Baptist Missionary Society was born. The time and energies of American Baptists had been involved for more than a quarter of a century in the struggle for religious liberty. Yet they were aware of the epoch-making events of 1792-1801. Correspondence between Serampore and leading ministers in Boston kept them informed. Too, often missionaries bound for India were forced to sail first to America and then take passage on American ships to their destination since English ships would not carry them to India without a license from the East India Company. Hence, it is not surprising to learn that the first mission society formed in the States was the Massachusetts Missionary Society of Boston.

Acknowledging the stimulating influence of the new day of awareness of missionary responsibility on "both sides of the Atlantic," Samuel Stillman, pastor of the First Baptist Church of Boston, and Thomas Baldwin, pastor of Boston's Second Baptist Church wrote: "We propose the forming of a Missionary Society, for the purposes hereafter mentioned." In Article IV, the purpose of the society was stated:

The object of this Society shall be, to furnish occasional preaching, and to promote the knowledge of evangelic truth in the new settlements within these United States; or farther, if circumstances should render it proper.[40]

Even though the primary purpose of the society was to launch a home missionary effort in a rapidly expanding nation, 26 May 1802, marks the beginning of a number of local missionary societies organized in the United States before 1814. The

Massachusetts Missionary Society almost immediately contacted Carey. In a letter of 1 December 1804, he expressed his willingness to write for the society's magazine in order "to contribute to its promotion. . . ."[41]

That the influence of Carey was making itself felt in the new nation is unquestionable. Yet no Baptists were answering the call to missionary service outside the United States. This situation was destined to change quite suddenly when the Judsons and Luther Rice embraced Baptist views upon reaching India in 1812.

ENDNOTES

1. Proceedings, Southern Baptist Convention, 1845, 14. Hereafter referred to as Proceedings, SBC. See also Robert A. Baker, *The Southern Baptist Convention and Its People, 1607-1972* (Nashville: Broadman Press, 1974), 169-71.

2. William Carey, *An Enquiry into the Obligations of Christians, to Use Means for the Conversion of the Heathens. In Which the Religious State of the Different Nations of the World, the Success of Former Undertakings, and the Practicability of Further Undertakings, Are Considered* (Leicester: Ann Ireland, MDCCXCII), 8-9.

3. Ibid., 84.

4. William Owen Carver, *The Course of Christian Missions*, rev. ed., (New York: Fleming A. Revell Company, 1939), 139.

5. John Ryland, *Life and Death of the Rev. Andrew Fuller* (Philadelphia: American Baptist Publication Society, 1818), 106; quoted in A. C. Underwood, *A History of the English Baptists* (London: Carey Kingsgate Press, 1947), 164. Gill's *Body of Doctrinal Divinity* continued to find publishers until 1815.

6. Ibid., 163-64. See H. Leon McBeth, *The Baptist Heritage* (Nashville: Broadman Press, 1978), 178-83 for a fuller discussion of the introduction of hyper-Calvinism into English Baptist life and the rise of "Fullerism."

7. Cited in McBeth, *Baptist Heritage*, 179.

8. Cited by Timothy George, *Faithful Witness: The Life and Mission of William Carey* (Birmingham, Alabama: New Hope, 1991), 48. This is one of the more recent biographies of William Carey. It gives special attention to the theological background of the Particular Baptists of England in the eighteenth century.

9. Mary Drewery, *William Carey: A Biography* (Grand Rapids: Zondervan Publishing House, 1979), 40.

10. Cited in S. Pearce Carey, *William Carey, D. D., Fellow of Linnaean Society* (London: Hodder and Stoughton, 1923), 91. The biographer gives in minute detail an account of the meeting, including the names of those who made pledges and how much each pledged.

11. Cited in Drewery, *William Carey*, 60.

12. Ibid., 84.

13. Carey, *William Carey*, 165.

14. Ibid.

15. Ibid., 85, 86.

16. Ibid., 164.

17. Drewery, *William Carey*, 99.

18. Ibid., 101.

19. Ibid., 107.

20. Quoted in Carey, *William Carey*, 179.

21. Ibid.

22. Cited in Ibid., 183.

23. Ibid., 195.

24. Cited in Carey, *William Carey*, 197.

25. Ibid., 196.

26. Ibid., 199.

27. Quoted from a letter of Chaplain Thomason in ibid., 289.

28. Ibid., 292.

29. Ibid., 291.

30. Drewery, *William Carey*, 163.

31. *Ibid., 308.*

32. *Ibid., 309.*

33. *George, Faithful Witness, 140-41.*

34. The original charter of the college read: "No caste, color, or country shall bar any man from admission into Serampore College." Ibid., 148.

35. Carey, *William Carey*, 177. See also Drewery, *William Carey*, 104, 105.

36. Ernest A. Payne, *South-East from Serampore* (London: The Carey Press, 1945), 14.

37. Ibid.

38. Kenneth Scott Latourette, *Christianity in a Revolutionary Age*, vol. II, *The Nineteenth Century in Europe* (New York: Harper & Brothers, 1959), 328.

39. George, *Faithful Witness*, 136.

40. William H. Brackney, ed., *Baptist Life and Thought: 1600-1980* (Valley Forge: Judson Press, 1983), 158.

41. Ibid.

"The Hand of God," 1812-1846

Adoniram Judson

In the one trip that Adoniram Judson made back to his native land after leaving thirty-three years earlier, he managed to visit Richmond, Virginia. Upon that occasion (8 February 1846) a mass meeting, sponsored by the Foreign Mission Board of the newly formed Southern Baptist Convention, was held in his honor. J. B. Jeter, president of the board and pastor of the First Baptist Church, said in referring to Judson's career and specifically to his becoming a Baptist, *"The hand of God was in it."*[1] "The change," Jeter continued, "was the means of arousing among the Baptists of the United States the missionary spirit, and forming the Baptist Triennial Convention, under whose patronage you have so long labored."[2] Virtually all Baptists also were convinced that they had seen the hand of God in Judson's baptism and in his subsequent remarkable missionary career.

Judson was the living link between the American Board of Commissioners for Foreign Missions (1812) under whose auspices he first sailed to the East, the Triennial Convention (1814) whose formation his baptism had inspired, and the Foreign Mission Board of the Southern Baptist Convention. The Judson saga, no less than that of William Carey, constitutes an indispensable chapter in the history of missions and particularly that of the Baptist missionary movement in America of which the Southern Baptist Convention became a part. Without the labors of Luther Rice, however, it would have been a far different story. He, too, in the providence of God, became the catalyst who put feet to his dreams, challenging Baptists in the United States by an unfailing vision and tireless efforts to form their first national denominational organization. But it all began with a revival and a prayer meeting in a small college in Massachusetts.

Of Revival, Prayer, and a Book

On a steamy August afternoon in 1806 a group of five students from Williams College in Massachusetts, led by Samuel J. Mills, Jr., was walking toward a grove in Sloan's Meadow for a prayer meeting when they were intercepted by

Burmese Bible title page

When an American Congregationalist, Adoniram Judson, en route to India became convinced that the Baptist were right in regard to baptism, a new chapter in the foreign mission movement was written. It was an American chapter to which Baptists in the South also contributed. Without the Judson legacy and the labors of Luther Rice, there possibly never would have been a Triennial Convention, Baptists' first national organization in the United States.

a sudden thunderstorm and forced to take refuge under a haystack. What began as a routine prayer meeting turned into a decision service. Earlier in the same year, a revival swept through the student body, increasing the students' awareness of the spiritual needs of a pagan world. Upon this occasion that awareness became particularly acute. Before the storm subsided, four of the five had dedicated themselves to foreign mission service.

The impact of William Carey and the Serampore Mission was clearly making itself felt among all Christians, not just Baptists. Before Carey, the work of the Moravians, particularly that of Bartholomeus Ziegenbalg and Christian Frederick Schwartz had stirred not a few to think of carrying the gospel to the ends of the earth. But the Moravians were German-speaking and sponsored by the Danish government. With Carey and the English Baptist Missionary Society, the possibility of forming similar societies and sending forth missionaries had become a reality. Letters from the Serampore missionaries, sermons, and books spread the news of their work throughout the English-speaking world. Among these, a published sermon titled *The Star in the East* by Claudius Buchanan, who had served as a chaplain of the East India Company, came to the attention of Adoniram Judson shortly after his conversion. It fell as seed on fertile ground. Although later he realized that it was a romanticized account; nevertheless, Judson confessed that God used it to call him to foreign mission service in the East.[3]

Andover 1808-1810

Andover Theological Seminary was founded in 1808 by Congregationalists as an alternative to Harvard, which had come increasingly under Unitarian influence. It would have been natural for Judson to have gone to Harvard since he was skeptical and inclined toward deism. In fact during his years at Brown, where he graduated first in his class, he had become a deist. After graduation, he taught school for about a year, only to give it up in order to try his luck on the stage in New York. Instead of fame and fortune, his life as a vagabond actor soon turned sour.

> *The impact of William Carey and the Serampore Mission was clearly making itself felt among all Christians, not just Baptists.*

He returned to Massachusetts in order to continue his wanderlust, until one night in a country inn in western Massachusetts, his life was turned around.

After a long and tiresome day, he sought lodging in an inn and was told that there was only one room left and that it was next door to a sick man who was possibly dying. Judson assured the innkeeper that that would not bother him in the least. He was mistaken. The sounds coming from the room kept him from sleep. Then when all grew silent, thoughts of death—that of the man next door and of his own—flooded his mind. The next morning upon enquiring, he learned that the man had, indeed, died and that his name was Jacob Eames, Judson's best friend and lighthearted skeptic of his college days. "Stunned," his son

Edward wrote years later, "he resolved to abandon his scheme of travelling, and at once turned his horse's head toward Plymouth."[4] Arriving home on 22 September 1808, a few days later he entered Andover, not as a candidate for the ministry, but as a special student, although not even a professing Christian. Before the end of the year, however, he had come out of the shadows into the light of a new day and a new life. He dedicated himself unreservedly to God. On 28 May of the following year he made his profession public and joined the Third Congregational Church of Plymouth where his father was pastor. He was twenty-one years old.[5]

Even before making his public confession of faith, Judson was convinced that God was calling him to become a missionary. It was then that Burma first came to mind. In scouring the library at Andover for books on missions, he came across one by Michael Symes, a British army officer who had served as an ambassador to Burma from India, titled *An Account of an Embassy to the Kingdom of Ava*. The time of decision had come; of it he wrote in his journal:

> It was during a solitary walk in the woods behind the college, while meditating and praying on the subject, and feeling half inclined to give it up, that the command of Christ, "go unto all the world and preach the Gospel to every creature," was presented to my mind with such clearness and power, that I came to a full decision, and though great difficulties appeared in my way, resolved to obey the command at all events.[6]

So far as Judson knew, he was the only student at Andover considering the call to foreign missions. Unknown to him there were others and by 1810 still others from Williams College, including Luther Rice.

Finally, there were six who were willing to sign a petition to the General Association of [Evangelical] Congregational Churches of Massachusetts meeting at Bradford in 1810 asking to be sent as foreign missionaries. Judson was chosen by the group to formulate the petition. It closed with a fittingly humble plea.

> The undersigned, feeling their youth and inexperience, look up to their fathers in the Church, and respectfully solicit their advice, direction, and prayers.
> (Signed)
> Adoniram Judson, Jr.
> Samuel Nott, Jr.
> Samuel J. Mills.
> Samuel Newell.[7]

The names of Luther Rice and James Richards, which were initially included with the others, were left off for fear of alarming the association due to the apparent impossibility of supporting so many missionaries and their spouses.

The Congregationalists also heard the personal testimonies of the petitioners and were visibly moved by the earnest enthusiasm of the youthful missionary candidates. As a result the association proceeded to organize the American Board of Commissioners for Foreign Missions. At first, doubting their own ability to support such a formidable enterprise, the American Board, as it became known, sent Judson to confer with the London Missionary Society about a possible joint relationship. After an eventful trip that saw his ship interrupted by a French Man of War and subsequent imprisonment in France, Judson reached England four months after leaving Boston. He was graciously received but was informed by the London Society that a joint venture was hardly feasible although the Society was willing to send the American candidates out under its auspices. In the light of Judson's report the American Board of Commissioners determined to proceed alone.[8]

Missionaries under Appointment

After Judson's return in September 1811, matters moved rapidly. The American Board appointed Judson and his colleagues to establish missions in Asia, specifically naming the Burman Empire, Surat, Prince of Wales Island, "or elsewhere as, . . . Providence shall open the most favorable door . . . ."[9] On February 5, Adoniram was married to Ann Hasseltine, whom he first met on the day of the General

Ann Hasseltine Judson

Association meeting at Bradford. Three days later, Adoniram Judson, Samuel Newell, Samuel Nott, Gordon Hall, and Luther Rice were examined and later that evening ordained in the Tabernacle Church of Salem. As the missionaries knelt for the laying on of hands, Ann slipped out of her pew, according to an unknown observer, to kneel near those being ordained. It was a never-to-be-forgotten service. Through their tears, the congregation caught a fleeting glimpse of the world as the courageous young candidates had come to see it.

The Newells and Judsons, after much delay, sailed on the *Caravan* from Salem on the morning of 19 February. Five days later

Luther Rice, the Notts, and the Halls departed from Newcastle on board the *Harmony*. They joined a missionary party already on board sent out by the English Baptist Missionary Society. On 13 June, the *Caravan* arrived in Calcutta, India.

Immediately upon arriving, Judson and Newell sought permission to remain in India but without success. Enquiries about Burma brought discouraging information. The missionaries were told it was a "living hell" controlled by a capricious and arrogant despot who delighted in torturing his enemies and insulting foreigners. In the light of such news, the Newells decided to take passage on a ship preparing to sail to Mauritius (the Isle of France). Because the captain would carry only two passengers, the Judsons were left behind.

Since the plight of the Americans was common knowledge in the international community in Calcutta, an English Baptist family invited the Judsons to stay with them until they could arrange to join the Newells. Their hosts, the Rolts, possessed a fine library of theological works that gave Adoniram an opportunity to continue his study of baptism in the New Testament that he had begun on shipboard, much to the consternation of his wife Ann, whom he called Nancy. In a letter she wrote to a friend on 7 September 1812, Ann candidly reported:

I felt afraid he would become a Baptist, and frequently urged the unhappy consequences if he should. But he said his duty compelled him to satisfy his own mind and embrace those sentiments which appeared most concordant with Scripture. I always took the Pedobaptist side in reasoning with him, even after I was as doubtful of the truth of their system as he.[10]

In a letter to her parents on 14 February 1813, Ann described in some detail the remarkable development in their thinking that led them both to become Baptists:

I will now, my dear parents and sisters, give you some account of our change of sentiment, relative to the subject of baptism. Mr. Judson's doubts commenced on our passage from America. While translating the New Testament, in which he was engaged, he used frequently to say that the Baptists were right in their mode of administering the ordinance. Knowing he should meet the Baptists at Serampore, he felt it important to attend to it more closely, to be able to defend his sentiments. After our arrival in Serampore, his mind for two or three weeks was so much taken up with missionary inquiries and our difficulties with government, as to prevent his attending to the subject of baptism. But as we were waiting the arrival of our brethren, and having nothing in particular to attend to, he again took up the subject. I tried to have him give it up, and rest satisfied in his old sentiments, and frequently told him, if he became a Baptist, I would not. He, however, said he felt it his duty to examine closely a subject on which he had so many doubts. After we removed to Calcutta, he found in the library in our chamber many books on both sides, which he determined to read candidly and prayerfully, and to hold fast, or embrace the truth, however mortifying, however great the sacrifice. I now commenced reading on the subject, with all my prejudices on the Pedobaptist side…. But after closely examining the subject for several weeks, we were

constrained to acknowledge that the truth appeared to lie on the Baptists' side. It was extremely trying to reflect on the consequences of our becoming Baptists. We knew it would wound and grieve our dear Christian friends in America—that we should lose their approbation and esteem. We thought it probable the commissioners would refuse to support us; and, what was more distressing than any thing, we knew we must be separated from our missionary associates,…. These things were very trying to us, and caused our hearts to bleed for anguish. We felt we had no home in this world, and no friend but each other. Our friends at Serampore were extremely surprised when we wrote them a letter requesting baptism, as they had known nothing of our having had any doubts on the subject. We were baptized on the 6th of September, in the Baptist chapel in Calcutta.[11]

A copy of the letter to the Serampore missionaries to which Mrs. Judson referred in her letter to her parents was sent to Samuel Baldwin by Adoniram with permission for Dr. Baldwin to use as he thought best. It gave in a few words the conclusion of months of intensive and careful study. Dated 27 August 1812 and addressed to the Reverend Messrs. Carey, Marshman and Ward, Judson wrote:

As you have been ignorant of the late exercises of my mind on the subject of Baptism, the communication which I am about to make, may occasion you some surprise.

It is now about four months, since I took the subject into serious and prayerful consideration. My inquiries commenced during my passage from America, and after much laborious research and painful trial, which I shall not now detail, have issued in entire conviction, that the immersion of a professing believer is the only Christian Baptism.

In these exercises I have not been alone. Mrs. Judson has been engaged in a similar examination, and has come to the same conclusion. Feeling, therefore, that we are in an unbaptized state, we wish to profess our faith in Christ by being baptized in obedience to his sacred commands.[12]

Next, Judson also sent a copy of the letter to the corresponding secretary of the American Board of Commissioners for Foreign Missions and a personal letter in which he said:

The Board will, undoubtedly, feel as unwilling to support a Baptist Missionary, as I feel to comply with their instructions, which particularly direct us to baptize "credible believers with their households."

The dissolution of my connexion [sic] with the Board of Commissioners, and a separation from my dear Missionary brethren, I consider most distressing consequences of my late change of sentiments, and indeed, the most distressing events which have ever befallen me.[13]

Judson went on to express what was undoubtedly his fervent hope:

Should there be formed, in accordance with the ideas suggested therein, a Baptist Society, for the support of a mission in these parts, I shall be ready to consider myself their Missionary; and remain, dear Sir,

Your obliged friend and servant,

Adoniram Judson, jun.[14]

To Lucius Bolles, a Baptist minister of Salem, Judson wrote on 1 September, even before his baptism, of his change of convictions and of his hopes that the Baptists in America would form a foreign mission society.

I recollect that, during a short interview I had with you in Salem, I suggested the formation of a society among the Baptists in America for the support of foreign missions, in imitation of the exertions of your English

Carey Baptist Church, Lall Bazar, Calcutta

brethren. Little did I then expect to be personally concerned in such an attempt. . . . Under these circumstances [a reference to his forthcoming baptism], I look to you. Alone, in this foreign, heathen land, I make my appeal to those whom, with their permission, I will call my Baptist brethren in the United States.[15]

On the same day which Judson wrote the letter to Lucius Bolles, Joshua Marshman wrote a long letter to Samuel Baldwin in which he recounts the events that led the Judsons to submit to believers' baptism by immersion. He then closed his letter with an impassioned plea for the Baptists of the United States to assume the responsibility of supporting them.

I would wish then that you should share in the glorious work, by supporting him. . . . After God has thus given you a Missionary of your own nation, faith, and order, without the help or knowledge of man, let me entreat you, and Dr. Messer, and brethren Bolles and Moriarty humbly to accept the gift.[16]

After the Judsons were baptized and it appeared that Luther Rice would also follow their lead, Carey added the weight of his influence to that of Judson and Marshman in urging American Baptists to form their own missionary society. In his letter of 20 October to Dr. William Rogers, a highly regarded Baptist minister of Philadelphia, he wrote that he had written to William Staughton "a detailed account of the change of sentiment which has induced brother and sister Judson, American Missionaries, to be baptized publickly at Calcutta, and of the probability that brother Rice will follow their steps." He concluded the letter with a strong recommendation that "our Baptist brethren in America" form a mission society since "the change of sentiment in brethren Judson and Rice . . . lays the church in America under obligations different from any under which they lay before."[17]

Three days later, Luther Rice wrote Dr. Thomas Baldwin of his change of convictions. He does not give, however, a detailed account of his own pilgrimage but leaves no doubt as to his sincerity and the firmness of his new convictions. "I am now satisfactorily convinced," he wrote,

> that those only who give credible evidence of piety, are proper subjects, and that immersion is the proper mode of baptism. This being the case, we think it expedient and proper that I should unite with brother Judson in a mission, rather than with the other brethren.[18]

Rice's change of convictions had not come without a struggle. He had sailed to India on the *Harmony,* with several English Baptist missionaries. Whenever the subject of baptism came up, Rice was the most vehement of the Congregational missionaries in arguing for infant baptism. Upon his arrival in Calcutta, he was shocked to learn of the Judsons' decision to become Baptists. His reaction was sharply negative. Adoniram reported that after Luther moved

over to Calcutta that "he was disposed to give me fierce battle." Adoniram and Ann refused to argue with him but suggested that he search out the questions on his own in prayer. For two months, he searched the Scriptures. On 12 October, he wrote his brother Asaph indicating that he was almost persuaded; and that if he did become a Baptist, he would join the Judsons in establishing a mission in Java, since the East India Company would not allow them to live and work in the territory governed by the British. On 1 November, he was baptized by William Ward in the Lall Bazar Chapel (Carey's church in the Lall Bazar, Calcutta).[19]

Luther Rice, Advocate of Missions

Rice and Judson first met at Andover where Rice had led in organizing a secret society dedicated to the study and promotion of foreign missions. He, like several others at Andover, was a graduate of Williams College. It was there that he first became an enthusiastic advocate of missions. He almost missed, however, being appointed for a number of reasons. Once the possibility of going became a live option, he raised the necessary funds in six days and was ordained along with the others who had been previously appointed. Thus, Rice early demonstrated both his ability to enlist others in the cause of missions and to tap funds for their support: two activities that were to consume his time and energy for the remainder of his life.

Nothing could have been further from his mind when he and the Judsons, forced out of India, sailed for Mauritius. He had left the United States in order to serve as a missionary, and with the Judsons, he deter-

William Staughton

mined to cast his lot in establishing a mission station wherever the Lord led. Plans changed, however, once they finally reached the Isle of France. Luther suffered another attack of his liver ailment. After a period of prayer and thoughtful consultation, it was decided that he should return to the States in order to sever connections properly with the American Board of Commissioners and to secure recognition and support from the Baptists. They also hoped the sea voyage would prove beneficial to his health. Therefore on 13 March 1813, Rice departed for the United States. The route was a circuitous one through a South American port. En route from South America, he found himself on board a ship carrying passengers and prisoners bound for New York. Opportunities for proclaiming the gospel enabled him, he estimated, to have a part in leading possibly as many as twenty to Christ. At least two became Baptists and one of these, a Baptist minister.

First Baptist Church, Philadelphia

The Triennial Convention, 1814

Unknown to the new Baptist missionaries, by the time Rice arrived in New York City there were four or five Baptist foreign mission societies organized and functioning in New England. The first had been formed at Salem shortly after the five missionaries and the four wives had set out for India. Baptists in New England had already contributed to the American Board of Commissioners which had widely circulated its non sectarian character, for which Rice now took the commissioners to task because of their curt dismissal of him and the Judsons upon their becoming Baptists.[20] The first society organized upon learning of the Judsons' decision to become Baptists was the one initiated by Thomas Baldwin in Boston. In the home of Baldwin, Boston Baptists organized the Baptist Society for the Propagation of the Gospel in India and other Foreign Parts.

After visiting the Boston brethren, Rice left the city on 29 September 1813 and after a brief visit with his family in North-borough, he arrived in Philadelphia during the annual meeting of the Philadelphia Baptist Association. He addressed the association, giving an account of the work of English Baptists in Serampore and something of his own pilgrimage of faith and that of the Judsons. The effect was electrifying. The association voted to form a foreign mission society after the pattern of the Salem and Boston societies to be known as "The Philadelphia Baptist Society for Foreign Missions." A committee of the most prominent leaders of the association, including Henry Holcombe, pastor of the First Baptist Church of Philadelphia, and two former pas-

Richmond, Virginia, 1862

tors, William Staughton and William Rogers, was appointed to "devise a plan of such a society, to submit said plan to the churches and the public for signatures, and to give it full effect."[21]

From Philadelphia, Rice began the first of his many trips south. First, he stopped at Baltimore, then came Washington, and Richmond, where the Virginia Baptist Foreign Mission Society had just been organized. From Richmond, he continued his travels into North Carolina, South Carolina, and Georgia. Increasingly, as he slowly made his way by stagecoach from city to city and state to state, the need for a national society to coordinate Baptist missionary efforts of the scattered societies became clear. In a letter to Judson, Rice described the plan as it first occurred to him.

While passing from Richmond to Petersburg in the stage, an enlarged view of the business opened upon my contemplations. The plan which suggested itself to my mind, that of forming one principal society in each state, bearing the name of the state, and others in the same state, auxiliary to that; and by these large, or state societies, delegates be appointed, to form one general soci-

ety. The society in Richmond, in the outset, took the name of the state, as did one afterwards, in North Carolina; but in no case, have auxiliaries been formed to these state societies.[22]

Lucius Bolles proposed that Philadelphia be chosen for the first national gathering of Baptists. Rice concurred. The Philadelphia Society began to make preparations for this historic occasion. The date was set for 18 May 1814. Dr. Richard Furman, pastor of the First Baptist Church of Charleston, South Carolina, presided. After several days of deliberation and prayer, the decision was made by the thirty-three delegates present

Richard Furman

to form "The General Convention of the Baptist Denomination in the United States for Foreign Missions." And by 24 May, a constitution was drawn up and officers elected. Shortly afterwards the General Convention became known as the Triennial Convention, since it met only once every three years.[23]

Luther Rice

A board of twenty-one commissioners which soon became known as The Baptist Board of Foreign Missions was formed of which Thomas Baldwin of Boston was elected president. The two vice presidents, Henry Holcombe and William Rogers, were from Philadelphia, and William Staughton, who was present at the

Kettering meeting when a handful of English Baptists formed their foreign mission society, was named corresponding secretary. Luther Rice now officially became the agent of the convention. Before he had acted largely upon his own initiative as an ambassador but without portfolio.

The second meeting of the board convened in New York City on 19 June 1816. It was a time of rejoicing since the cause of missions had received such widespread support among Baptists throughout the entire country despite some early vocal opposition. Another cause for optimism was the response of laymen who began to support the work with money and services. One such was Edward Thompson, of Philadelphia, merchant and owner of two new copperclad sailing ships. He offered to provide passage free of charge to a missionary appointee printer by the name of George Hough, his wife, two children, and a Mrs. White to India. The board reported that the Hough party, with printing press and necessary equipment, "had put out to sea" about 20 December on the *Benjamin Rush* and should have reached Calcutta by the time of its meeting. In gratitude for his services, the board invited Thompson to become an honorary member of the board, which offer he accepted.

The board also registered its gratitude for the herculean efforts of Luther Rice on behalf of missions and his determination not to be turned aside from his calling by the "offered emoluments and honours of the presidency of a respectable University in Kentucky."[24] After commending Rice for turning down the offer of Transylvania University, the board appointed a committee to confer with him about his work in the

coming year. Their expectations were high, in fact in the light of road conditions, travel by horseback, and the limitations of human energies—impossible. An excerpt is enlightening. The committee recommended

that as soon as the Report is published, he proceed to Virginia, supply the associations with the Report, and attend the General Meeting of Correspondence in North Carolina, the 1st of August, where he will enjoy facilities in supplying the associations in the latter State, and accomplishing those objects of importance which circumstances may encourage. Let him attend as many associations in the south and west as may be in his power, visiting, if possible, St. Louis and its vicinity; and spend the winter forming mission societies, collecting monies, and effecting arrangements for keeping up a regular intercourse between the Board, and all the associations and mission societies in the United States.[25]

Two other actions of note were taken at this meeting of the board. A committee was appointed to look into the feasibility of establishing a "Western mission, on a large scale, embracing the country beyond the Mississippi, . . . that men shall 'fear the name of the Lord from the West,' as well as 'his glory from the rising of the sun.'"[26] The second matter was in reference to the American Board of Commissioners. Recognizing a certain indebtedness to both the Congregationalists and the Serampore missionaries, the corresponding secretary was

requested to address a letter to the American Board of Commissioners for Foreign Missions, and also to the Baptist Missionary Society in England, inviting them respectively to a friendly and steady reciprocation of reports, publications, missionary information, and mutual good offices in aid of our united efforts for the glory of God, and the everlasting welfare of immortal souls.[27]

Whether they realized it or not, Baptists in America had not only organized for missions, they had become a denomination, for the Triennial Convention was something other than a mission society. When the Triennial Convention met in 1817 in its second meeting, the denominational character of its organization was affirmed by a change in its constitution that made possible the appointment of John Mason Peck and James E. Welch for a "Western mission." It was understood that they would proceed as soon as possible to Saint Louis and thus begin their missionary efforts in the Missouri Territory.[28] The Convention also launched an educational enterprise that was largely initiated by Luther Rice with the staunch support of William Staughton, who had been training young men for the ministry in his own home. In his travels, Rice had come to see the need of a college that would seek to raise the educational level of the Baptist ministry and that would be accessible to ministerial candidates, North and South. Washington,

> *An element in the antimission sentiment among Baptists was based on the fears of an all encompassing organization that would threaten the autonomy of the local church.*

District of Columbia, appeared the ideal location for such an institution. With the fervent backing of Richard Furman, elected president at this meeting, the convention adopted this proposal also. Columbian College, therefore was chartered in 1821. The incorporation of home missions and education, however, under the umbrella of the General Convention was short lived. It seems that there were some misgivings on the part of Francis Wayland and others almost from the beginning, regarding the changing nature of the Triennial Convention, which gained momentum from this time until 1826 when Columbian College was separated from the Convention.

The Focus on Foreign Missions

Robert A. Baker points out that two thirds of the delegates attending the meeting of the Triennial Convention in 1826 were from New York and Massachusetts.[29] Since Wayland led the Convention to withdraw its support from Columbian College, it appears that not only the precarious financial status of the college was involved but that also sectionalism and the concern for Brown University may have been factors in the reversal of policies implemented in 1821. Also, perhaps it was too early for Baptists who had such a strong local church ecclesiology to think in terms of an all encompassing denominational body. At least societies, whose membership consisted only of those interested in the cause for which the society existed, posed no threat to any local church or association. An element in the antimission sentiment among Baptists was based on the fears of an all encompassing organization that would threaten the autonomy of the local church.

At least this was the perception in the eyes of some like John Taylor, pioneer Kentucky Baptist preacher.[30] As if to emphasize this withdrawal from its educational enterprise, the board removed its center of operations from Washington to Boston. From this point on the Triennial Convention would concentrate its energies on foreign missions. Eventually, other societies would form to support a variety of causes.

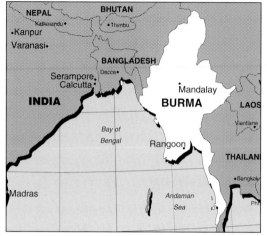

Burma (Myanmar)

As late as 1818, Judson thought it possible that Luther would return to labor with him in Burma. Even Ann wrote, imploring him to rejoin them in Rangoon where they had begun to live and work after parting on Mauritius. Those early years had been fraught with difficulties. The Judsons found mission work on Mauritius virtually impossible. They next sailed to Madras, but the East India Company hounded them even there, threatening to send them to England. The inescapable choice, against which their friends continued to warn them, was Burma. It seemed the only option left, unless they returned to the states. This was unthinkable. At the first opportunity on 22 June, they went on board the *Georgiana,* a Portuguese ship, to which Adoniram referred as a "crazy old vessel." It was on board the *Georgiana* that Ann gave birth to a stillborn baby.

Three weeks later on 13 July, Ann and

Adoniram arrived at one of the mouths of the Rangoon River. The next day before the ship docked, they caught sight of the fabled golden Shwe Dagon pagoda towering over every other building in sight, an ominous sign of the entrenched superstitious worship of the great Buddha, the Gautama. Adoniram could not resist going on shore that evening. He returned to the ship quite despondent. Later he wrote Rice:

I went on shore, just at night, to take a view of the place, and the Mission-house, but so dark, and cheerless, and unpromising did all things appear, that the evening of that day, after my return to the ship, we have marked as the most gloomy and distressing that we ever passed.[31]

In spite of his foreboding, the indescribable filth of Rangoon, the hostility of both a despotic monarch and the Buddhist priests, Adoniram and Ann applied themselves to the study of Burmese (Pali). Ever so slowly they began to gain a proficiency in the language and a greater knowledge of Burma, its religion and culture. After six years in attempting to establish a Christian witness in the strange land, the first convert, Maung Nau, was baptized. It was a Sunday, 27 June 1819. This was but the beginning of a great harvest that none present would ever live to see.

Although the cost of discipleship had

been high—little Roger Williams Judson born in Rangoon suddenly sickened and died—it would be higher still. When war broke out between Burma and England, Adoniram was accused of being a British spy. Even before his arrest, he had described Burma as "a most filthy and wretched place." With his imprisonment, he was to find himself a part of that filth and wretchedness. For twenty-one months, he was prisoner of the Burmese. Irons and fetters bound him hand and foot, the scars of which he bore the remainder of his life. By her own ingenuity, Ann saved both Adoniram's life, with food she brought him daily, and his Burmese Bible, upon which he had been working for ten years.

With the end of the war, sealed by the treaty of 24 February 1826, he was released. He had been conscripted as an interpreter for the Burmese government in the treaty negotiations. His services received the acclaim of the British, who now attempted to employ him with the promised amenities of a high salary, prestige of government service, and security for his family. But Adoniram would not be turned aside. "This one thing I do," he replied, "preach Christ! I have no time to make money," he added.[32]

He and Ann returned to Rangoon to find the town devastated and the mission destroyed. Only four converts could be found. He determined to leave Rangoon, the scene of so much joy and sorrow. It was in Rangoon that Adoniram had erected his first *zayat* (a bamboo enclosure on stilts) for teaching the faith to the curious "drop-ins" and Ann had begun the first Christian school for girls and translated a catechism for their instruction. Here the first fruits of

the gospel had been baptized in a pond behind the mission and gathered into a church. It was also near the pond where the first converts had been baptized that little Roger Williams was buried. But now there seemed little else to do but abandon the city. Conditions were chaotic. Rangoon was rapidly returning to the jungle. Tigers were roaming the streets at will. Once the decision was made, the move began. They would leave Rangoon but not the work. The converts, a number of girls from Ann's school, and the faithful servants joined them in the move to the new British colony of Amherst. On 2 July 1826, the party arrived in the new town.

The British again sought Adoniram's services in the treaty negotiations with the promise of imposing religious liberty upon the Burmese government. This promise, as did Amherst itself, proved illusory. It was Moulmein and not Amherst that became the headquarters of the British protectorate in Burma. In Adoniram's absence, Ann supervised the building of both a schoolhouse and their new home. She had scarcely settled into the new house when the dysentery from which she had suffered periodically since arriving in Burma, struck with a vengeance. On 24 October 1826, just when everything, except little Maria's health, looked so promising, Ann died. She was thirty-seven. It had been just fourteen years since she knelt in the Tabernacle Church at Salem while hands were laid on the head of her husband. Since Adoniram was in Ava at the time, he did not receive the news until a month after his beloved Nancy was buried. Six months later, while he was still reeling from the blow, little

Maria, who was born while he was in prison, also died. It proved almost too much.

Death had stalked Judson's missionary career from the beginning. Of the tiny group that left Salem fourteen years before, Henrietta Newell was the first to die, even before a mission station had been established. Of the missionaries sent out by the Triennial Convention, both Wheelock and Colman were dead, and Dr. Price had lost his wife. With the death of his gifted and faithful wife and Maria's death six months later, something in Adoniram died.[33] On 4 December 1827, he wrote Ann's sisters: "Death mocks at us and tramples our dearest hopes and our lives in the dust."[34]

He further isolated himself to engage in a most intensive self examination. An irrepressible sense of guilt welled up within him. He now faced and rejected every vestige of ambition and pride. In 1828, he even asked Brown University through the *American Baptist Magazine* and the *Columbian Star* to withdraw the doctorate bestowed upon him five years before. He withdrew more and more from all earthly friends, including his missionary associates. It appeared his usefulness as a missionary was coming to an end smothered in despair until he reached the conclusion that his self-imposed exile and ceaseless mourning were leading nowhere.[35]

Shortly after Ann's death, Judson moved the mission from Amherst to Moulmein. Three *zayats* were built and two schools, one for boys and another for girls. George and Sarah Boardman took over the school work. Jonathan Wade began teaching in one of the *zayats* and his wife, Deborah Wade,

worked with Sarah Boardman in teaching the girls. Maung Ing, the faithful convert from Rangoon, read the Scriptures daily in one *zayat* and Adoniram taught in another. And, at last, Adoniram finished his Burmese New Testament. He also made significant progress in completing his translation of the

Title page, Burmese Bible

Old. New tracts began to come from his pen and converts multiplied. At last, after eighteen years and indescribable hardships, the harvest had begun.

Before this change became evident to the missionaries, a breakthrough came with the Karens. The Karens constituted in the eyes of the Burmese a wild and uncivilized mountain tribe. They had few contacts with the Buddhist society. There was a legend circulating among them that a white teacher would come some day from across the water bringing with him the book of gold and silver which Y'wa [God] had made long ago. The missionaries had little contact with these strange, mountainous, nomadic people until the conversion of one of their own by the name of Ko Tha Byu. His first contact with Christianity came as an employee in the print shop of George Hough. Through a series of misadventures, he was turned over to Judson as a laborer. Although the man was a known robber and murderer, the missionary began to make a lasting impression on him. As he read the Burmese New Testament, his uncontrollable temper was tamed and his life was changed.

When the Boardmans left Moulmein to establish a mission among the Karens at Tavoy, they took Ko Tha Byu with them. This seemed the Lord's doing in their eyes for Ko Tha Byu, once baptized, focused all his talents and energies in making Christ known among his own people. As Anderson writes, "He became the virtual father of Karen Christianity."[36] It was also among the Karens that the Wades labored. To them George Boardman gave the last ounce of his strength and died. From Prome, Adoniram ventured to preach to Karens through an interpreter and directly to the Burmese in a rebuilt *zayat*. By the end of 1829, he had begun to come out of the depression that had persisted in spite of his rigorous self denial and forty days of ceaseless meditation. Once again, it was sharing the good news with those who had never heard that "God so loved the world that he gave his only begotten Son" that brought the most joy to his heart. Yet he forced himself to limit his preaching in order to do what no other could do—complete the translation of the Old Testament—which he had begun years before.

By 31 January 1834, Judson completed this translation. Two years later it was print-ed.[37] Although the entire Bible was now in the Burmese (Pali) language, this was not the end of Judson's linguistic efforts, the last of which was an English-Burmese dictio-nary. In addition to this six hundred page section, which he completed on 24 January 1849, he planned a Burmese-English section, that he never lived to complete.[38]

Nevertheless, what he had done would prove an invaluable tool for learning and using the language for generations to come. Before his death, Adoniram's numerous tracts were being circulated in the thousands in Burmese. Other missionaries, as they acquired the necessary linguistic tools, trans-lated portions of the scriptures and Adoniram's tracts into Siamese, Taling, and Karen.

Under Cephas Bennett's supervision, two printing presses were set up. They enabled the printshop to turn out five hun-dred thousand pages of tracts and portions of the Scriptures in one year, 1832. This included three thousand copies of the New Testament, and thirty-three thousand tracts and catechisms. Therefore, through the printed page, as Carey had learned, the gospel was able to penetrate areas where the missionaries could not go.[39]

In 1834, after completing his translation of the Old Testament, Adoniram and Sarah Boardman, who had remained in Burma fol-lowing the death of her husband three years before, were married. It had been eight years since Ann had died. Finally, Adoniram became whole again. But Sarah was ill. It appeared at times that she would not have survived but for the tender care of her husband who nursed her back to health. As dedicated to the work as Ann had been, Sarah, too, began the study of another lan-guage in order to translate Adoniram's cate-chism and tracts. This time it was Taling for there were many Peguans living in Moulmein whose language none of the mis-sionaries knew. After his marriage to Sarah the new home which Adoniram built for his family was no longer an isolated hut but in the middle of the mission compound—symbolic of the new lease on life that he now began to share with Sarah—and the work prospered.

Luther Rice and the South

In spite of his dreams of returning to the Far East and once again joining the Judsons in Burma, it became apparent that Rice was virtually indispensable in raising the awareness of the missionary cause in the United States. His ability to form missionary societies and to raise funds for the Triennial Convention's work soon became evident. His zeal and dedication endeared him to Baptists everywhere but particularly to those in the South. J. B. Taylor, the first corresponding secretary of the Foreign Mission Board, called Richmond, Virginia, Rice's second home.

In fact, before the General Convention was organized, Rice had already begun his southern itinerary. In the fall of 1813, he preached in the Richmond Baptist Church, Richmond, Virginia. In recalling the occasion, a member wrote: "The church was stirred to its depths."[40] As a result, the Foreign Missionary Society of Virginia was organized and became a participating member of the Triennial Convention at its organizational meeting in Philadelphia in 1814. Rice visited Richmond frequently during the remainder of his life. Upon one of these occasions, the treasurer of the Richmond Female Missionary Society presented him with one hundred and fifty dollars, its annual contribution for foreign missions, and a "love gift" of forty dollars for Luther, himself.[41] Such gifts were recorded and reported by the agent to the General Convention.

Although Luther became increasingly preoccupied with the affairs of Columbian College, which he founded at the nation's capital, missions were never out of mind. A letter from Judson to Rice dated 9 May 1835, in which Adoniram expressed his appreciation for a file of the *Religious Herald* that Rice sent him by the Wades, confirms this concern. The last letter Rice ever wrote to Judson gives the same impression. Columbian College and the mission enterprise were inseparable in Rice's thought. He expressed the wish on 15 June 1836 that he might not die "till from that institution some laborers shall have gone forth into some part of the heathen world, to preach among the gentiles the unsearchable riches of Christ."[42]

After returning to America, Rice had thrown himself with all the energies of his fervent soul into enlarging the base of support for the missionary enterprise. In the process, he was largely responsible for including in the vision home missionary expansion and Columbian College, primarily for the education of ministers, particularly in the South. New England had two Baptist colleges, but there was none in the South. With the founding of the college in 1821, Rice became its agent.

For eight years Rice had given himself unreservedly to the work of the Triennial Convention but from 1822 until his death, he was obsessed with his dream of a Baptist university in the nation's capital. However, his dream began to tarnish with his inability to raise enough cash to save the college from an impending financial disaster, for which many Baptists held him responsible. He was, therefore, relieved of administrative duties but was asked to continue as agent of the college. His apparently inept administration was possibly due to a vision too large for the small Baptist constituency to sustain and his own incurable optimism.[43] There is also little doubt that Rice's emphasis upon an educated ministry contributed to the birth of at least half a dozen academies and colleges in the South that in turn diverted funds which would otherwise have gone to Columbian College.[44] Inevitably, money that might have been available to save Columbian College were now funneled to these more visible local institutions. Even though the college eventually failed, for Baptists, missions and education would henceforth be inevitably linked. For this alliance present-day Baptists have Luther Rice largely to thank.

William C. Crane

It was Rice who helped Baptists in the South become full partners in the work of the Triennial Convention. His sacrificial labors, first on its behalf and then as the agent of Columbian College, won their undying esteem. Their confidence in him was never shaken, for they knew him as few in the North did and they believed in his integrity. They well knew that no one in the entire country had preached in as many churches and associations, or had organized as many missionary societies at such personal sacrifice as had Luther Rice.[45]

In spite of his super human efforts in raising funds for the causes to which he had given his life, Rice was never physically strong. By 1835, it was evident that he had literally worn himself out. He was unable to preach for six months. Finally, when Luther realized that death was imminent, he calmly gave instructions that his horse, sulky, and other belongings be given to Columbian College. He died in his fifty-third year on 24 September 1837 at Edgefield, South Carolina. The news of his death was accompanied by widespread sorrow. A memorial service was held at the First Baptist Church of Richmond at which J. B. Jeter preached from Matthew 19:29.

In One Lifetime

At the time of Rice's death, the thirty-five years since the first contingent of missionaries left New England for India had seen changes that no one could have anticipated in 1814. The Triennial Convention, which had begun as a super foreign mission society to coordinate the work of numerous local mission societies, for a time became a denominational body. Due largely to Francis Wayland, however, and also perhaps to the fear that many Baptists entertained of any organization beyond the local church, it soon reverted to a foreign mission society. Its work was expanded to include new stations not only in Burma but also in Siam, Africa, France, Germany, Denmark, Greece, China, South India, and Assam. Of these new fields, Africa was the one with which the First Baptist Church of Richmond, Virginia was the most closely associated.

In 1815, the Richmond African Baptist Missionary Society, Auxiliary to the Baptist General Convention of the United States, was organized. The society grew out of a school for Blacks that William Crane, a merchant, had initiated. Three years before, Crane and his wife had moved from New Jersey. Shortly after joining the Richmond Baptist Church, he was ordained a deacon. Rice visited the church in 1813. As a result of this visit, the Foreign Missionary Society of Virginia came into being. Two years later the Richmond African Baptist Missionary Society was organized largely due to the enthusiasm for missions that characterized the church in the wake of Rice's visit and to Crane's interest in the education of the blacks of the church and community.

Lott Cary

Crane's school met in the church building three nights a week with twenty students enrolled. In addition to the basic subjects, reading, writing, and arithmetic, Crane and two other teachers taught the Bible and shared with the students news of the mission work of the General Convention. As a result, the missionary vision that captured the imagination of the students, just at the time that the American Colonization Society was promoting Liberia, led to the formation of the new society.[46] Three years later, two of its members, Lott Carey and Collin Teague, expressed a desire to serve as missionaries in Liberia. Crane wrote a letter on their behalf to the American Baptist Board of Foreign Missions in which he gave a biographical sketch of the two missionary candidates.[47]

Lott Carey and Collin Teague were appointed missionaries to Liberia by the Triennial Convention but were financed by the Richmond African Missionary Society. They sailed for Africa with their families in January 1821. Shortly before leaving, the newly appointed missionaries and five other members of the Richmond Baptist Church met in the home of William Crane and constituted themselves into a Baptist church of which Lott Carey was chosen pastor. This church became the Providence Baptist Church of Monrovia. The American Colonization Society provided the usual stipend for each emigrant to Liberia.[48]

The State of Missions, 1845

By 1845, although much work remained to be done and internal tensions once again threatened its unity, the General Convention could view with a degree of satisfaction its accomplishments over the past thirty-one years. Baker summarizes its report.

> *In a recapitulation of this significant work, the 1845 report named 17 distinct missions, 130 stations and outstations, 109 missionaries and assistant missionaries of whom 42 were preachers, 123 native preachers and assistants, 79 churches, 2,593 baptisms, more than 5,000 church members, and 1,350 students in 56 schools.*[49]

It is evident that Baptists were making significant advances in establishing beachheads for Christ in difficult and remote parts of the world. It had not been, however, without its failures and its high cost in human sacrifice. The earliest American missionaries had patterned their work in so far as possible after that of Carey. But it was largely "learning on the job" that taught them valuable lessons from which subsequent generations could benefit, if they would. When Howard Malcom, pastor of the Federal Street Baptist Church of Boston, visited Burma in order to observe for the Triennial Convention the work of the missionaries, he was struck by the differences in church life that Judson had adapted as a matter of course. From his earliest attempts to reach the Burmese with the gospel, he had adapted the *zayat,* the common teaching center of Buddhist priests, as the most promising format for his own work. Courtney Anderson describes Malcom's impressions:

> On his very first Sunday in Moulmein, Malcom was struck with differences that Adoniram never even noticed. At morning worship with the Burmese congregation in the zayat, for instance, everyone sat— Adoniram on a chair, the audience on mats on the floor. Long horizontal bamboos about a foot and a half above the floor served as back rests. In prayer, the Americans knelt; but the Burmese merely leaned forward from their sitting position and, resting their elbows on the floor, placed their palms together. Sermon, prayer and all, were in Burmese except for one word which surprised Malcom when he heard it. As Adoniram concluded his prayer, every person in the congregation spoke the "Amen!" aloud.[50]

Baptists were beginning to realize that conducting mission work involved much more than learning the language and proclaiming the gospel. Through the voluminous correspondence of the Judsons and their colleagues, the principles by which the missionaries were learning to become effective witnesses were becoming clearer. Among these were the following: 1. A missionary must first seek to learn the language or appropriate languages, but also seek to understand the culture and religions of the region. 2. It is paramount that the Scriptures be translated as soon as possible into the languages or dialects of the people of a given region. 3. Also, missionaries should give their undivided attention to the work and never engage in secular work unless it advances the gospel. 4. The missionary must commit himself, or herself, to a lifetime of service. 5. Missionaries should be free of debilitating disease at the time of appointment. (Colman and Wheelock were both tubercular.) 6. The primary purpose is to make disciples, therefore, no person should be baptized without evidence of a genuine conversion. 7. Schools break down barriers and open minds for the reception of the gospel. 8. Missionaries should receive their support from the sending body, therefore any money earned on the field should go into a common treasury. 9. As soon as possible, churches must be formed that are truly Christian and truly indigenous. 10. Missionaries are limited, therefore, gifted nationals will of necessity bear a heavy responsibility of winning their own people to Christ. (The example of Ko Tha Buy was not lost on Judson and his colleagues.)

Although the science of missiology was not yet born, the principles by which mission work would henceforth be carried on by the Triennial Convention and after 1845 by the Foreign Mission Board of the Southern Baptist Convention, were the same. It is fortunate that the lessons were also learned by those who helped to shape the nature of the Southern Baptist Convention. With Augusta, came an opportunity not only to implement the policies formulated in the light of thirty-one years' experience within the national body, but also to improve upon them as Southern Baptists sought to return to a denominational structure that the General Convention had abandoned.

ENDNOTES

1. Robert T. Middleditch, *Records of the Life, Character, and Achievements of Adoniram Judson* (New York: Edward H. Fletcher, 1854), 380.

2. Ibid.

3. T. B. Ray, *Southern Baptists in the Great Adventure* (Nashville: The Sunday School Board, 1934), 88. Many biographies also refer to Judson's remarks concerning the impact of Buchanan's sermon upon him.

4. Edward Judson, *The Life of Adoniram Judson* (Philadelphia: American Baptist Publication Society, 1883), 13.

5. Ibid.

6. Cited by Courtney Anderson, *To the Golden Shore: The Life of Adoniram Judson* (New York: Doubleday & Company, Inc., 1956), 68.

7. Cited by Robert T. Middleditch, *Burmah's Great Missionary* (New York: Edward H. Fletcher, 1854), 230.

8. The details of these events are given in a number of biographies, including the following: Anderson, *Golden Shore;* Judson, *Life of Adoniram Judson;* Middleditch, *Records of the Life, Character, and Achievements of Adoniram Judson;* and Francis Wayland, *Memoir of the Life and Labors of the Rev. Adoniram Judson, D.D.,* Vol. I (Boston: Phillips, Sampson, and Company, 1853).

9. Judson, *Life of Adoniram Judson,* 32.

10. Wayland, *Life and Labors of the Rev. Adoniram Judson,* 103.

11. Ibid., 106-7.

12. *Massachusetts Baptist Missionary Magazine* 3, no. 9 (March 1813): 266-67.

13. Ibid., 267.

14. Ibid.

15. Ibid., 268.

16. Ibid., 270.

17. *The Massachusetts Baptist Missionary Magazine* 3, no. 10 (May, 1813): 289-90.

18. Ibid., 293.

19. Evelyn Wingo Thompson, *Luther Rice: Believer in Tomorrow* (Nashville: Broadman Press, 1967), 77.

20. James B. Taylor, *Memoir of Rev. Luther Rice: One of the First American Missionaries to the East* (Baltimore: Armstrong and Berry, 1840), 134-36. Rice was informed upon enquiry that the American Board of Commissioners considered his relationship to the board "dissolved from the date of my letter from Calcutta, announcing the fact of my change of sentiment." His attempt to seek a formal letter of dismissal was ignored. However, the treasurer of the board was instructed to ask for repayment of that which the board had spent on his behalf. Whereupon, he replied if they would communicate with him, he would certainly attend to the matter. Reflecting upon the acrimonious feelings the American Board of Commissioners had exhibited toward him, he wrote:

I rather wished for a fair and fit opportunity to remind them of their *non sectarian professions;* of the fact that so handsome a portion had been drawn from the *Baptists;* of the light in which I had viewed the relations between myself and their body, consistently too, with their own professions; and of the fact, that my own outfit in particular, had been provided for *specially,* and very much by my own personal exertions. (136)

21. *The Massachusetts Baptist Missionary Magazine* 3, no. 12 (December, 1813): 353.

22. Taylor, *Luther Rice,* 142.

23. William Williams Keen, *The Bi-Centennial Celebration of the Founding of the First Baptist Church of the City of Philadelphia, 1898* (Philadelphia: American Baptist Publication Society, 1899), 81, 82. Keen gives a list of the thirty-three delegates present at the organization of the Triennial Convention. Among those present from the South were: Robert B. Semple, Virginia; Richard Furman, South Carolina; and W. B. Johnson, Georgia.

24. *The Massachusetts Baptist Missionary Magazine* 4, no. 11 (Sept., 1816): 340.

25. Ibid., 343.

26. Ibid., 341.

27. Ibid., 342.

28. Robert A. Baker, *A Baptist Source Book* (Nashville: Broadman Press, 1966), 67.

29. Robert A. Baker, *The Southern Baptist Convention and its People* (Nashville: Broadman Press, 1974), 111.

30. In 1820, John Taylor wrote a pamphlet titled *Thoughts on Missions,* which expressed this fear.

31. Taylor, *Luther Rice,* 154.

32. Later Judson was persuaded for a short time to help the British in the final negotiations with the emperor upon Ann's insistence. Following his own recommendation, "he later turned over to the Board some 2000 rupees realized from presents made him at

Ava and 2500 rupees paid him by the East India Company." Anderson, *Golden Shore,* 356.

33. An unusually gifted woman, Ann felt her calling every bit as much as Adoniram. Once in Burma, she gave herself to learning the language with all the dedication of her fervent soul. She wrote that she was more fluent than Adoniram in conversing in Burmese, although she added that he knew more about the structure of the language than she. Ann also translated Job into Burmese as well as Adoniram's first tract, and a catechism for use in her girls' school. She also began to acquire a knowledge of Siamese and to translate these works into that language. In addition to orienting new missionary wives into the art of managing a Burman household, she learned to use native vegetables and herbs to prepare some special New England dishes. Her efforts to make prison life more bearable during the twenty-one months Adoniram was in the "Death Prison" were truly as heroic as they were ingenious. Remarkable in any era, none excelled her in her own.

34. Middleditch, *Burmah's Great Missionary,* 230.

35. One suspects that the fact that Adoniram was pressed into service by the British against his better judgment, which also forced him to be absent during Ann's last sickness and death, was the basis of his great sense of guilt.

36. Anderson, *Golden Shore,* 374.

37. Wayland, *Life and Labors of the Rev. Adoniram Judson,* 75.

38. Anderson, *Golden Shore,* 478.

39. Ibid., 396.

40. Blanche Sydnor White, *The First Baptist Church, Richmond, 1780-1955* (Richmond, Va.: Whittet and Shepperson, 1955), 28.

41. Ibid.

42. Taylor, *Luther Rice,* 319.

43. J. B. Taylor wrote regarding Rice's role in the financial failure of Columbian College:

He was willing to assume too much responsibility in the erection of the buildings, and thus incurring heavy expenses, without an immediate prospect of funds to meet them. . . . In all this, the error he committed was an error of judgment. While there was allowed a degree of heedlessness in the accumulation of debt, he was, nevertheless, governed by motives of a high and noble character. The good of the denomination, and the prosperity of the Redeemer's kingdom, were the great objects he sought to accomplish; and, if he merited censure for injudiciously contracting these liabilities, he was not alone in the imprudence. Taylor, *Luther Rice,* 201-2.

44. These institutions included Furman Academy and Theological Institution (1827), Georgetown College (1829), Mercer Institute (1833), and Wake Forest College (1834). Richmond College did not begin classes until 1843 but the Virginia Baptist Seminary which preceded it, was founded in 1832. See the *Encyclopedia of Southern Baptists,* vols. 1 and 2.

45. Excerpts from Rice's letters and journal give a glimpse into his remarkable career. The following are taken from J. B. Taylor's *Memoir of Luther Rice* from the pages indicated. That Luther Rice was as much a missionary at home as Judson was abroad is indicated from a letter written on 29 October 1816:

The 25th of July, I left Philadelphia, and arrived in Warrenton, N. C. on the evening of Friday 2d August, at least 370 miles. After attending the North Carolina general meeting of correspondence, near that place, I took stage the night of Monday, about midnight, having been occupied after meeting, till that hour, in writing, without going to bed, and about 2 o'clock, on Wednesday morning, arrived again in Richmond, Va. more than 100 miles from Warrenton. In the evening of the same day, preached in Richmond, wrote twenty-one letters on Thursday, besides doing some other necessary business, and at 3 o'clock, on Friday morning, left that city, and preached in the evening of the same day, in Goochland county, forty miles from Richmond. At a yearly meeting, same place, preached again on Saturday at 12 o'clock, and on the Sabbath, that is, the next day, was with the Appomattox Association; preaching in Prince Edward county, about sixty miles from where I was in Goochland county. (164-65)

He then continues in much the same vein to report that he was in the Mountain Association in Burke county, North Carolina, and then the following Saturday with the Shiloh Association in Culpeper county, Virginia, after riding more than 400 miles in less than six days. Then back to Virginia and to Kentucky, he traveled 290 miles through the rain, "excessively bad roads, mountains, rivers, creeks, and mud—my health began to be impaired." (166) In Kentucky he was with the Franklin Association near Frankfurt and then continued later to Lexington and to the Union Association in Knox County, and his journeys carried him to Warren County, Tennessee on the sabbath, all by horseback. He attended the Flint River Association, in Bedford County, Tennessee. The next sabbath he was with the Tennessee Association, in Blount County, Tennessee, and the Broad River Association, in Rutherford County, North Carolina. In all of his wanderings, he said he was forced to ride at night, and Friday night he got lost in North Carolina.

The roads in this part of our country, are none of them fenced, and are mostly through woods; I had to go that night in by roads, but little travelled—missed the way, got out of roads, at length, into mere paths, and ultimately, lost the path—found myself alone in a dreary wilderness, unable to discover the point of compass; totally ignorant which way to direct my course, to find any road or habitation of men. I stopped, and besought the Lord to lead me out—rose from my supplications and attempted to advance. In less perhaps, than two minutes, certainly, in less than five, fell into the road which conducted me to the place that I calculated to reach that night, at which, I arrived about 1 o'clock. (166-67)

The Triennial meeting of the Convention was held in Philadelphia in May 1817. Just before the meeting, Rice observed his thirty-third birthday. He wrote:

By my journal, it appears that I have travelled, since entering upon my thirty-third year, which closes this day, seven thousand eight hundred miles, and, since leaving Philadelphia the 25th of last July, have received from various sources, and on various accounts, $3,629.44 ¼. As this amount has been mostly contributed for missionary purposes, the fact, and the amount, furnish gratifying proof of the progressive state of missionary views, impressions, and zeal among the Baptists in the United States. (168-69)

In giving his report for 1817, Luther Rice indicated since 19 June 1816 he had traveled 6000 miles and raised over $4,000 for the cause of missions. Acting on a suggestion of Rice, a quarterly publication was begun titled *Latter Day Luminary*. After indicating that he would be forced to spend more time in Boston than previously, due to his responsibilities for the missionary publication, he shared his travel plans. "My route onward will take me into North Carolina, then back again north-westwardly to Pittsburg, through Ohio, Kentucky, Tennessee, and into Georgia, and then back again to Philadelphia." (178)

46. White, *First Baptist Church, Richmond,* 28, 29.

47. William Crane wrote:

Ever since the missionary cause began to be agitated, these two men have wished they could do something to aid their unhappy kindred in Africa. Now, stirred up by the letters published from Sierra Leone in *The Latter Day Luminary,* they have determined to go themselves. Brother Lott has a wife and several little children. He owns a little place below Richmond which cost him $1,500. Brother Collin has a wife, a son fourteen years of age, and a daughter of eleven, for whom he paid $1,300. Both wives are Baptists, the children are docile, and have been schooled considerably. Collin is a saddle-and-harness-maker. He can read, though not a good reader. He has good judgment. Lott was brought up on a farm; and for a number of years has been chief manager among the laborers in the largest tobacco warehouse in Richmond. He has charge of receiving, marking and shipping tobacco, and receives $700 a year wages. They have been trying to preach for ten to twelve years, and are about forty years of age. Cited in ibid., 29.

48. Ibid., 30.

49. Baker, *Southern Baptist Convention,* 113.

By 1845 the reports of the General Missionary Convention revealed an impressive achievement in foreign mission work. Curiously enough, until 1865 work among Indians in North America was included in the foreign mission program. By 1845 the convention had work among the Ojibwas, Ottawas, Tonamondas, Tuscaroras, Shawanos, Cherokees, Creeks, and Choctaws. In the European field, which included France, Germany, Denmark, and Greece, the report in 1844 showed 3 missions, 21 stations and 34 outstations, 4 preachers and 5 female assistants, 28 native preachers and assistants, 28 churches with 900 members and 123 baptized the previous year, and 1 school with 50 pupils. In the African field, the report showed 1 missionary, 2 stations and 1 outstation, 2 preachers with 1 assistant and 2 female assistants, 2 native assistants, 1 church with 24 members, and 2 schools. In the Asiatic field, which included Burma, Siam, China, Assam, and India, the report showed 7 missions with 51 stations and outstations, 66 missionaries and assistants and 84 native assistants, 34 churches reporting 2,360 baptisms in 1844 along with 2,257 members, and 42 schools with about 1,000 students. Ibid.

50. Anderson, *Golden Shore,* 407.

"Imperatively Demanded," 1845

First Church, Augusta

On 24 April 1844, the Triennial Convention,[1] convened in the city and the church where it began thirty years before. Some feared it would be its last. Unfortunately, this was no baseless fear. The first national Baptist body founded on a shared missionary vision now faced dissolution over the slavery issue.

The rise of the immediate emancipation movement brought the issue to the forefront even within the Triennial Convention. This development brought with it serious implications for Baptists from the South. Although southern Baptists had never been as fully represented in the convention as had those in the North, due to a number of factors, they had held prominent places of leadership within the organization from the beginning.[2]

The presence of southerners in the infrastructure of the convention, however, was more apparent than real. In 1841 when W. B. Johnson was elected president, Daniel Sharp of Boston was

From the Preamble of the Southern Baptist Convention, May 8, 1845.

Purpose: "A plan for eliciting, combining and directing the energies of the whole denomination in one sacred effort, for the propagation of the Gospel."

appointed president of the Board of Managers. The two corresponding secretaries of the convention were from Massachusetts, as was the treasurer, Heman Lincoln. There were forty managers, thirty-two of whom were from the North.[3] In spite of this imbalance, the southern delegates and the societies that they represented, had supported the missionary efforts of the Triennial Convention from its inception. The mutual respect of brethren united in a common enterprise and sharing the same missionary vision had appeared to be a foretaste of days to come until the slavery issue was interjected into the organization's deliberations. At this point (1839) tensions mounted, and southerners who had always been minor partners in the work of both the Triennial Convention and the Home Mission Society felt themselves increasingly under suspicion and attack.

In spite of heroic efforts on the part of leaders, both North and South, to maintain the conven-

By 1844, it became evident to all that division was inevitable. The Emancipation movement had succeeded in dividing the Baptists as it had other Protestant denominations. Without its missionary vision, however, it is doubtful if the loosely related Baptist churches in the South would ever have formed the Southern Baptist Convention. Missions became its primary reason for being. A difference over the slavery issue had divided— missions united.

tion's neutrality on the issue, the cords that bound Baptists together in the work of missions were finally severed in 1845. By that time the slavery issue had become extremely complicated, economically and politically, involving questions of morality and sectionalism. Even antislavery forces were divided between those who called for immediate emancipation and the advocates of gradual emancipation.[4]

The Slavery Issue

The Spanish, Portuguese, Dutch, and English had inundated the Western Hemisphere with slaves imported from Africa. From time to time Indians were also enslaved, against which both Roger Williams (1637), among the English, and Bartolomé de Las Casas (1510), among the Spanish, protested.[5] The first public group protest against Negro slavery in the English colonies was lodged in 1688 with the Quaker Monthly Meeting at Dublin, Pennsylvania. A century was to pass before Baptists would publicly question the practice, although they had begun to preach the gospel to the slaves much earlier.

The Revolutionary War turned the colonials' attention from the festering problem of slavery to independence from England. Most Baptists supported the war with the hope that once independence was achieved and a new nation founded, religious liberty would become a reality. In the meantime, slaves had become an integral part of the colonial social structure. Generally, Baptists were not of the slaveholding class and for them slavery had not become the burning issue that, in time, it would become. Several prominent Baptists of Virginia who did own slaves freed them soon after 1782, when it

became legal to do so.[6] The Ketocton Association in Virginia resolved in 1787 "that hereditary slavery was a breach of the divine law." And two years later the General Committee, meeting on August 8, 1789, passed a strong resolution offered by John Leland against slavery. It ended with a plea "that our honorable legislature may have it in their power to claim the great jubilee, consistent with principles of good policy."[7]

The advent of the nineteenth century witnessed the rise of antislavery sentiment in the South and the proliferation of antislavery societies.

The advent of the nineteenth century witnessed the rise of antislavery sentiment in the South and the proliferation of antislavery societies. By 1807, the antislavery movement was so strong in Kentucky that an association of antislavery Baptist churches was formed which took the name "Friends of Humanity Association." These "Emancipation Baptists," however, disbanded their associations some ten years or so later.[8]

The humanitarian phase of the antislavery movement, the roots of which were largely in the South, began to fade with the call for immediate emancipation. With the publication of the *Liberator* in Boston on 1 January 1831 by William Lloyd Garrison, the antislavery campaign shifted gears. Gradual emancipation and the colonization movement were forsaken for "freedom now," and the center of agitation moved north.[9] By this time slavery had become a socially accepted institution widely thought necessary for the economic survival of the South. Climate, geography, and King Cotton dictated the concentration of slaves below the Mason-Dixon line. The mountain sections of the South were relatively free of slavery but the large plantations of the eastern seaboard and other southern states apparently could not prosper without slave labor.

The Rise of the Abolition Movement

Although antislavery had become divisive among some Baptist churches and associations before 1830 in a few states, such was not the case with most Baptist churches when the General Convention was organized in 1814. Since the northern states had freed their slaves, slavery was largely a dead issue among American Baptists until 1834. English Baptists had led in the campaign to emancipate the slaves in Jamaica. Flushed with victory, a group of London ministers wrote the Board of Managers asking the Triennial Convention to take the lead in pressing for the end of slavery in the United States. Upon receiving the letter, Daniel Sharp and Lucius Bolles of the Boston Board answered that the General Convention was a missionary society and slavery was not one of the issues to which the convention and its board could give their attention.[10]

In another letter Bolles indicated that slavery was an extremely complicated issue in the United States due to the nature of the union of sovereign states. He also informed the English that many of these states had already outlawed slavery and he felt in time that the southern states would follow, but that instant emancipation was out of the question. "We are confident that a great portion of our brethren at the south would rejoice to see any practicable scheme devised for relieving the country from slavery."[11] He then closed the letter very much as he and Sharp had written previously, "It is not the duty of the Baptist General Convention, or the Board of Missions, to interfere with the subject of slavery."[12]

As the abolition movement gathered momentum, several prominent Baptist ministers began to make their views known to Baptists both in England and the South. For example, Baron Stow, recording secretary of the board, in a letter of 11 January 1839, to the London Union, identified himself as an abolitionist and assured the brethren: "God is on our side and the cause will prevail."[13] Elon Galusha, a pastor in New York and a member of the Board of Managers, was a strong abolitionist who did not hesitate to express his views to any and every audience. But what precipitated the anxiety that marked the meeting of the Triennial Convention in 1841 was the formation of the American Baptist Anti-Slavery Convention in April 1840 and the aggressive tactics it adopted to pressure Baptists in the South to join the crusade.[14] The Board of Managers, experiencing pressure now from both sides of the issue, attempted a compromise statement on 2 November 1840, declaring that members of the board as individuals had every right to act as they wished, but as officers of the Triennial Convention, they had no right to say anything regarding slavery.[15] Such a statement

Richmond slave auction, 1861

slavery, and the timidity of the Free Baptist Foreign Missionary Society organized in 1840, the more militant abolitionists in 1843 formed the American and Foreign Baptist Missionary Society to begin the appointment of home and foreign missionaries at once.[16]

For many Baptists, the meeting of the Triennial Convention of 1844 held frightening possibilities. Although the Southern delegates were outnumbered more than five to one (of the 460 present only 80 were from southern states), some still hoped a schism could be avoided. But the high attendance was ominous. The 1844 meeting saw the largest number ever to attend a triennial meeting of the General Convention. An additional number of visitors raised the total attendance to an estimated six or seven hundred. It was clear that abolitionists were there in force and that they had captured the minds and hearts of the majority of those present. A last ditch effort, however, was made to preserve the integrity of the national body. A pre-convention prayer meeting became a strategy meeting. W. B. Johnson, who had been elected president in the previous meeting of the convention in Baltimore, asked not to be considered for another term for reasons of poor health and the fact that southerners had served as presidents for twenty-one out of the thirty years of the convention's life.[17] Doubtless,

satisfied neither the abolitionists nor the southerners.

As the 28 April meeting of the Triennial Convention in Baltimore in 1841 drew near, tensions mounted, but so did efforts to avoid a breakup of the convention. A secret caucus was held by leaders from both North and South to explore means by which the convention could avoid its impending demise. Fervent prayers were offered that the union might be preserved. Northern leaders who wished to preserve the Triennial Convention and confine its activities to missions, along with southern leaders, drew up a compromise statement disclaiming any participation in the abolition movement. The statement was signed by seventy-four delegates. Thus the neutrality of the Triennial Convention was preserved but this action was viewed as an evasive tactic by those caught up in the new abolition movement. Disappointed by the failure of the General Convention to take a stand against

although not expressed, Johnson believed that a division was inevitable, and he did not want to be soundly defeated (and thereby repudiated by a majority of the delegates) or to preside over the convention's dissolution.

J.B. Jeter

On Thursday evening, 25 April, Richard Fuller, a prominent pastor from Charleston, South Carolina, presented a resolution asking the convention to restrict itself only to the missionary enterprise. Nathaniel Colver, pastor of Boston's West Cambridge Baptist Church, argued that this simply evaded the slavery issue. After continued debate the resolution was withdrawn. George B. Ide, pastor of the First Baptist Church of Philadelphia, where the convention was meeting, offered an alternate motion:

> *Therefore Resolved, That, in cooperating together as members of this Convention in the work of Foreign Missions, we disclaim all sanction, either expressed or implied, whether of slavery or of anti-slavery; but, as individuals, we are perfectly free both to express and to promote, elsewhere, our own views on these subjects in a Christian manner and spirit.[18]*

However ardently some wished to preserve the unity of the convention, this appeared, short of a miracle, impossible. And no miracles were forthcoming. Instead, very human emotions took over. Northern abolitionists were determined to press for an unequivocal stand while southern delegates felt censured and repudiated by their brethren. Concentration on the missionary task of the Triennial Convention and the Home Mission Society became extremely difficult.

Failure of Attempts at Reconciliation

In spite of the efforts of W. B. Johnson and the diplomacy of the irenic Francis Wayland, who was elected president of the General Convention in 1844, the dissolution of both the convention and the Home Mission Society appeared imminent. Even though the Home Mission Society had issued in 1841 a circular declaring its neutrality on slavery, by 1844 by a vote of 123 to 61, the society declared "our cooperation in this [society] does not imply sympathy with slavery or anti-slavery, as to which subjects societies and individuals are left as free and uncommitted as if there were no such cooperation."[19] From this action, it was clear that the sentiment of the society was overwhelmingly abolitionist.

Flyleaf inscription, J.B. Jeter's Bible

As the debate continued, Nathaniel Colver reported that William Lloyd Garrison was making a strong appeal to the churches in the North. Richard Fuller and J. B. Jeter did not attempt to defend slavery, but they explained that it was an institution that had been inherited and, like some diseases of the physical body, it could only be cured by purifying the blood rather than by radical surgery. They further observed this was already in process and gradually the South would do away with the institution.[20] Besides, they argued, the constitution of the General Convention only provided for an organization to appoint missionaries and support them in the field, therefore, slavery was not a germane subject under the present constitution. The abolitionists countered that the Home Mission Society had a right to examine the qualifications of individuals who offered themselves for missionary service. Finally, faced with the reality of the situation, a committee of eleven was appointed to consider "the amicable dissolution of the society and to make its report at the board meeting the following year."[21]

As the General Convention and the Home Mission Society adjourned their meetings, there was an uneasy feeling that the schism was already an undeniable fact. Scarcely had the delegates arrived in their home states when a series of events began that left no doubt regarding the outcome.

Rumors were circulated that the Home Mission Society was attempting to pressure the resignation of a popular missionary to the Indians, Jesse Bushyhead, because he was a known slave owner. Baptist papers North and South editorialized on the problems facing both the Triennial Convention and the Home Mission Society. The language became abusive and advocates of both the abolitionists and defenders of the "peculiar institution" became more strident. Since it now became evident to all parties that missionaries who were also slave holders would not be appointed by either the

While… the slavery issue had shattered the fellowship of the nation's Baptists before 1845, it was the missionary imperative that precipitated the call for a consultative convention in Augusta.

Home Mission Society or the Triennial Convention, a test case was offered by the Georgia Baptist Executive Committee in 1844. The committee nominated James E. Reeve for appointment under the Home Mission Society. It also informed the society that Reeve was a slave holder. This action was a blatant violation of the neutrality agreement of 1841. The society sought to evade the issue by refusing to consider the application. This action did not sit well with Georgia Baptists nor apparently with many other Baptists in the South.

A similar attempt by the Alabama Convention to clarify the issue followed in November 1844. Upon this occasion a resolution was addressed to the General Convention asking for a statement affirming that slave holders were eligible for appointment as missionaries on the same basis as non-slave holders. The acting board replied that if such a missionary should offer himself and insist upon retaining slaves as his property "we could not appoint him. One thing is certain we can never be a party to any arrangement which would imply approbation of slavery."[22] This turn of events prompted the call of the Virginia Baptist Foreign Mission Society to Baptists of the South to convene a convention for the purpose of discussing the feasibility of forming a separate missionary convention.

The Missionary Imperative

While it is apparent that the slavery issue had shattered the fellowship of the nation's Baptists before 1845,[23] it was the missionary imperative that precipitated the call for a consultative convention in Augusta, Georgia. The southerners were convinced that the Home Mission Society and the Boston Board had shut them out of the missionary enterprise.[24] Since the majority of Baptists in the South were not of the slave-owning class and were hardly prepared to form a separate convention simply in the defense of slavery, *without a more compelling motive,* it seems unlikely that enough support for the formation of a separate Baptist "missionary" convention would have been forthcoming. In making its report, the Committee on the Preamble and Resolution in 1845 explained to the assembled delegates, "That this convention was imperatively demanded, must be apparent to all."[25]

Augusta, 1845

The Virginia Baptist Foreign Mission Society issued a call for a consultative convention that was addressed "to the Baptist churches of Virginia and the Baptist denomination of the United States generally." It was signed by James B. Taylor, president of the society. The call disavowed any interest in forming a "sectional convention." The reason given for the call was the Boston

Board's adoption of "an unconstitutional and unscriptural principle to govern their future course." Even though Taylor had no desire to defend slavery, he did not accept the implications of the Boston Board's action that in effect said "that holding slaves is under all circumstances, incompatible with the office of the Christian ministry...." The call emphasized that the consultative convention "would consider the formation of a new foreign mission society and possibly a separate Bible society, publication society, and a 'Southern' theological institution." The date was set for the

First Baptist Church, Augusta

convening of the convention on "Thursday before the 2d Lord's day in May next, in Augusta, Georgia."[26]

The leading exponents of a southern convention came from the states of Virginia, South Carolina, Georgia, and Alabama, which were also the major slave states where as many as a third of the Baptists owned slaves. Even though there had been calls for a separate western convention from Kentucky, this time, W. C. Buck, editor of the *Western Recorder,* and others from Kentucky, Tennessee, and Mississippi advised delay. The hesitant brethren explained they did not have time to elect delegates for the consultative convention, and they believed that there was the possibility that both the Home Mission Society and the General Convention would reverse the actions of their boards. The slavery issue was not such a divisive issue to these "western brethren," for they knew that there were persistent pockets of antislavery sentiment in the South, particularly in Appalachia. However, once the assembled delegates had formulated their plans in Augusta, Baptists in these states liked what they saw and supported the new missionary organization. Possibly they caught in the proposed convention a glimpse of the vision of a more encompassing denominational organization that was the shared plan of Richard Furman and Luther Rice that for a brief period had found expression in the Triennial Convention. However, there was no question that the major purpose of the new convention was to promote missions.

William Bullein Johnson

A few weeks after the Virginia Foreign Missionary Society's call for a consultative convention, the South Carolina State Convention met in a called meeting to discuss the nature of the proposed organization. At that time W. B. Johnson, president of the South Carolina Convention, addressed that body outlining the options that lay before concerned Baptists. First, he suggested the possibility of forming "separate and independent bodies for the prosecution of each object (benevolence)," or one convention with "separate and distinct boards for each object of benevolent enterprise...."[27]

When the 293 delegates from nine states met in Augusta on 8 May 1845, many insisted that they had met just to form a foreign mission society. Among these was Richard Fuller, who preferred the term "society" since, he believed, it would not divide "the Baptist church."[28] By Saturday, 10 May, however, the denominational plan which Johnson favored was adopted. Article 2 set forth what was conceived to be the nature of the new convention. "It shall be the design of this Convention to promote Foreign and Domestic Missions, . . ."[29] Many Baptists throughout the country continued to think of the new convention as a missionary society. Barnes points out that for the next half century Baptist papers, North and South, frequently referred to the "southern missionary convention." Although the convention's organization also provided for other benevolences, it was the cause of missions that had captured the imagination of the delegates and dictated the nature of the new convention.

W. B. Johnson was asked by the convention to prepare a statement explaining why Baptists of the South felt it necessary to form a separate convention. Some memorable phrases from that address capture the spirit of the hour and the reasons underlying the "painful division." First, Johnson sought to minimize the extent of the disunity. "At the present time it involves only the Foreign and Domestic Missions of the denomination. Northern and Southern Baptists are still brethren. They differ in no article of the faith. They are guided by the same principles of gospel order."[30] Then, he proceeded to lay the onus of schism at the feet of a "few ultra Northern brethren." The remainder of the "Address" was divided into three sections, the first of which allowed Johnson to give a brief historical sketch of the Triennial Convention with which he had been so closely related. In the second section, he reiterated a theme that recurs repeatedly.

> *The constitution we adopt is precisely that of the original union; that in connection with which throughout his missionary life, Adoniram Judson has lived, and under which Ann Judson and Boardman have died. We recede from it no single step. We have constructed for our basis no new creed; acting in this matter upon a Baptist aversion for all creeds but the Bible. We use the very terms, as we uphold the true spirit and great object of the late "General Convention of the Baptist denomination in the United States." It is they who wrong us that have receded. We have receded neither from the Constitution nor from any part of the original ground on which we met them in this work. . . .*[31]

In the third section, Johnson again emphasized the objects for which the Southern Baptist Convention was organized. "Our objects, then, are the extension of the Messiah's kingdom, and the glory of our God." After explaining the nature of the structure of the new convention, Johnson returned to the compelling missionary vision "the Macedonian cry from every part

of the heathen world, . . ." As much as he lauded the purpose of the new convention he could not help but betray the anguish experienced in the attempt to work within the Triennial Convention: "We have shaken ourselves from the night mare of a six years' 'strife about words to *no* profit,' for the profit of these poor, perishing and precious souls."[32]

Although logic was on the side of Johnson, the break had not come without emotional trauma. Strong ties of personal friendship with William Staughton, Lucius Bolles, and Francis Wayland had grown through the years. Each of these, in spite of personal sympathy with the abolitionists' cause, attempted to maintain neutrality on the slavery issue within both the Triennial Convention and the Home Mission Society but without success. Although logic may have been on the side of neutrality, as Johnson so effectively delineated, abolitionists had made their cause the hallmark of Christianity. For them there could be no compromise, even for the sake of missions. The abolition movement had captivated large segments of the population of the North and endued them with the spirit of a holy crusade, and Baptists had joined their forces. In the consultative convention at Augusta, those who for various reasons had not joined the abolitionist crusade, sought to form a new missionary convention without distraction.

The officers elected by the convention paralleled those of the General Convention and the Home Mission Society. Even the requirements for missionaries were identical. Article X specifically stated: "Missionaries appointed by any of the Boards of this Convention, must, previous to their

> *"Missionaries … must, previous to their appointment, furnish evidence of genuine piety, fervent zeal in their Master's cause, and talents which fit them for the service for which they offer themselves."*

appointment, furnish evidence of genuine piety, fervent zeal in their Master's cause, and talents which fit them for the service for which they offer themselves."[33]

It was proposed that the Southern Baptist Convention would hold its meetings "triennially, but provisions were made for extra meetings, if called by the President with the approval of any of the Boards of Managers."[34]

On Monday morning, a number of "resolutions"[35] were passed that meant, in spite of some misgivings on the part of Johnson that the convention may have been acting without the expressed approval of the Baptist constituencies of the states involved, the convention in the minds of the delegates was a functioning organization. Convinced that they were in the will of God, the delegates proceeded as if they had the unqualified support of Baptists who were neither present nor represented in Augusta. One resolution asked that funds for foreign or domestic missions be forwarded to the treasurers of the respective boards "as promptly as convenient." Another resolution expressed its concern and interest in Indian missions. It was followed by a resolution instructing the Board of Domestic Missions "to take all prudent measures for the religious instruction of our colored population." Two resolutions sought to seek an equitable settlement with the Triennial Convention regarding "any claim we may have upon the convention, or any claim which that body may have, or think they have, upon us, . . ." The convention authorized the Foreign Mission Board to enter into any prudent arrangement "with the acting Board of the Baptist General Convention, to take a portion of its Missions under the patronage of this Convention." Further, the Board of Domestic Missions was instructed to establish a missionary thrust in the city of New Orleans.[36]

While it is undeniable that the primary cause of division between the northern and southern Baptists was the slavery issue, it is also evident that the missionary spirit was the new convention's breath of life.

William Bullein Johnson (1782-1862)

There is no question that William Bullein Johnson was the most commanding figure among notables at Augusta. At the time, he was pastor of the Edgefield Village Baptist Church of Edgefield, South Carolina, and rector of the Edgefield Female Academy. He traced his ancestry on both sides of the family back to the First Baptist Church of Charleston. For twenty-eight years he served as President of the South Carolina Baptist Convention, and one term as President of the Triennial Convention

"...the missionary spirit was the new convention's breath of life."

(1841-1844). Both his mother and father were well educated by the standards of the day. His mother taught him to read when he was four years of age and he began the study of Latin two weeks before he was six. Apparently he later attended an academy taught by a Mr. Waldo, where he added French to his study of Latin and English classical literature. He was awarded a Masters of Arts degree from Brown University in 1814 and a D. D. degree in 1833.

The missionary movement came to his attention even before his conversion and baptism, for he was only ten years old when he met William Staughton, with whom he later was associated in the organization of the Triennial Convention. In his boyhood years he was greatly impressed by Richard Furman, and recalled that both Richard Furman and Oliver Hart wore robes in the pulpit. Indeed, Henry Holcombe, pastor of the First Baptist Church in Philadelphia at the time the General Missionary Convention held its organizational meeting, was Johnson's pastor in Beaufort, South Carolina, before going to Philadelphia, and Johnson was a guest in his home during the convention.

Johnson was practicing law but was not a Christian when he first met Holcombe. The Second Great Awakening was sweeping through the South when the young lawyer's attention was drawn to Holcombe. Beaufort was not exactly a stronghold of Baptists, Johnson wrote in his autobiography, that

the new birth was held in contempt, & a violent prejudice prevailed against the Baptists. Here the Doctor raised the standard of the cross, & though attempts were made by the ungodly to turn his ministerial exercises into ridicule, he maintained his ground unmoved.[37]

Neither Holcombe nor Joseph B. Bullein Cook, however, had the decisive influence upon his life as that of Miss Lydia Turner from London, England. She impressed upon Johnson the necessity of a personal commitment to Jesus Christ. As Johnson reflected upon her insistence, the conviction grew that he needed to do exactly that. Consequently, he made his confession public and was baptized in October 1804. Three months later, he preached his first sermon. His wife, the former Henrietta Hornby, had been reared an Episcopalian, but shortly after marriage she became a Baptist. Johnson wrote that he preached his first sermon in the pulpit of the Euhaw Baptist Church, which was in the Beaufort district. Shortly thereafter the pastor died, and Johnson was called to the pastorate of the church, which responsibility he assumed in January 1806.

Most of his years as a pastor were spent in South Carolina, but at a significant period in his life (1811-1815) he served a Baptist church in Savannah, Georgia. While in Savannah he led in the formation of a missionary society. As a delegate from that society he attended the meeting of the Triennial Convention in 1814 and served on the committee that drew up its constitution.

Also while pastor of the Savannah church he visited Boston when Lucius Bolles and his wife united with the church to which Bolles had been called as pastor. Johnson liked the method of receiving members into the church there. Later when he attempted to inaugurate the same practice of requiring personal testimonies from those who came with letters in hand before receiving them into the membership of the church, he met with some vocal opposition. This led to his resignation. A few weeks later, much to his surprise, fifteen members also asked for their letters from the Savannah church and proceeded to form a new church which then called him as pastor. However, Johnson soon left Savannah in answer to the call of the Edgefield Village Baptist Church, which he served as pastor twenty-two years.

As President of the Triennial Convention (1841-1844), Johnson found himself attacked by both the abolitionists and the southern advocates of separation. Viewing the situation he wrote the *Edgefield Advertiser:*

> With these evidences from our Northern brethren that they were not Abolitionists, the question with the South, as it appeared to their Delegation, was: Can we remain in the convention with the few Abolitionists there, though their treatment of us has not been of the kindest sort? Can we, for the sake of the noble cause in which we are embarked, and which has received such blessing from God, bear with Christian fortitude such unkindness from these good but mistaken brethren? Can we remain with them in Convention to carry, without division, the GRAND MISSIONARY ENTERPRISE? The answer is plain. We can.[38]

Perhaps no one worked harder to hold the factions together than did Johnson.

The Foreign Mission Board, it was decided, would be located in Richmond, Virginia, and the Board of Domestic Missions, in Marion, Alabama.

It is surprising that he found himself the subject of suspicion and innuendo among his own South Carolina compatriots. He was using Francis Wayland's *Moral Science* in the academy at Edgefield when he came under attack in November 1842 because of its alleged antislavery teachings. Upon the occasion of his absence from Edgefield, a group of parents whose children attended the academy condemned the book. One who signed himself "A Parent" said that any teacher who still would use the book

> ought to be held up to public view, to enable those parents who wish their children brought up in the Southern faith, to know them, so that they may guard against the evils of having their children taught whilst young, doctrines which they themselves know to be obnoxious and unsafe towards our free institutions.[39]

Johnson later wrote in answer to these charges:

> It is true that the Professor teaches that slavery is wrong, and he is thus an anti-slavery man, but not an abolitionist. Nowhere does he denounce the slaveholder as a thief. . . . Immediate abolition would result in the greatest possible injury to slaves who are not competent of self government.[40]

Johnson held that it was just as wrong for southerners to wish to exclude abolitionists from the work of the General Convention as for abolitionists to desire southerners to withdraw from the convention. His legal mind saw the controversy as a constitutional matter, but his southern culture conditioned him to tolerate slavery.[41] "Southernness" was an essential ingredient in this development. For him slavery was not always an unmitigated evil, because it was an inherited condition with which the South was peculiarly afflicted. But immediate emancipation was not the answer either. Johnson's efforts to reconcile the opposing factions were frustrated. Although he was not the first to call for a convention to determine the future course for southern Baptists, he became the chief architect of the Southern Baptist Convention and, at sixty-two years of age, its most effective leader.

The Foreign Mission Board Organized

Missions had long been an obsession with W. B. Johnson. In 1813 in the name of the Savannah Society for Foreign Missions he wrote to the people of Georgia and South Carolina about the prospects of a national missionary organization:

> These societies have for their object the establishment and support of foreign missions; and it is contemplated that delegates from them all will convene in some central situation of the United States for the purpose of organizing an efficient and practicable plan, on which the energies of the whole Baptist denomination, throughout America, may be elicited, combined and directed, in one sacred effort for sending the word of life to idolatrous lands. . . .[42]

Daniel Sharp described this address "the most able appeal in behalf of Baptist missions which was written by anyone in that period."[43] The terms "elicit, combine, direct," as Hortense Woodson points out, are also found in the constitution of the Triennial Convention. They have appeared frequently in mission literature through the years.

Article II of the constitution adopted in Augusta called for two boards "to promote Foreign and Domestic Missions, and other important objects connected with the redeemer's kingdom, . . ."[44] The Boards of Managers for Foreign and Domestic Missions were elected. Jeremiah Bell Jeter was elected president of the Foreign Mission Board, and Basil Manly president of the Domestic Mission Board. There were fourteen vice presidents of the Foreign Mission Board, and in addition to the president and vice presidents, there were a corresponding secretary, a recording secretary, a treasurer, an auditor, and fifteen managers. A parallel slate of officers and managers was named for the Domestic Mission Board.[45]

The first task of the Foreign Mission Board, once the managers convened in Richmond, was to seek a corresponding secretary who would, in effect, be the executive officer of the board. The search began almost immediately after the convention adjourned, and for months it appeared that the board was engaged in a fruitless effort. In the meantime, J. B. Jeter, president of the board, acted in the capacity of the corresponding secretary.

The First Year, 1845-1846

Delegates attending the consultative convention had very little time for rest. Sessions were held morning, afternoon, and evening. It appears when the convention was not in session, committees met, agreements were reached, and a sense of direction was achieved that enabled the delegates in Augusta to transact a considerable amount of business. On Saturday afternoon several far-reaching motions were passed, apparently without spoken opposition. The first of which determined that the next meeting of the convention (the first of the proposed triennial meetings) would convene on "Wednesday after the first Lord's Day in June, 1846, in Richmond, Virginia: . . ." The second related to the location of the two boards. The Foreign Mission Board, it was decided, would be located in Richmond, Virginia, and the Board of Domestic Missions, in Marion, Alabama. In the evening session, which convened at eight o'clock, a motion was offered that underlined the major concern of the assembled delegates, "*Resolved*, That a collection be taken up at the close of the service, in the Baptist meeting-house tomorrow morning, for Foreign Missions, and in the evening for Domestic Missions."[46]

The cause of missions, which had been so prominent during the proceedings of the Augusta meeting, now became the special responsibility of the Board of Managers for Foreign Missions. Most managers of the board lived in Richmond or its proximity. This had been the pattern of the Acting Board of the Triennial Convention. Since transportation was difficult, this was a necessary expedient. During the first year, meetings of the Board of Managers were held virtually every month, and at times twice a month.

In the first action that the board took before leaving Augusta, it asked William B. Johnson to "make a tour among the churches on behalf of the foreign mission enterprise and that his traveling expenses be paid by the Board."[47] Since C. D. Mallory of Georgia had been elected corresponding secretary in Augusta, the board proceeded to set his salary at $1,200 a year. The next month, however, when the board met on 30 June, the managers received word that Mallory had declined to serve. Undaunted, the board immediately turned to William B. Johnson, inviting him to become its corresponding secretary. The members of the board well knew Johnson's commitment to missions and his experience with the work of the General Missionary Convention. But he, too, informed the board that he could not see his way clear to become the corresponding secretary.

In the meantime, under J. B. Jeter's leadership, the board did not hesitate to take whatever steps were necessary in order to carry on its work. One of the most significant decisions of the board in that first year was the choice of China as the first field in which Southern Baptists would attempt to establish work. In its meeting on 7 July 1845, the board voted "that, with as little delay as possible, we will proceed to establish missions in the seaports of China, or such of them as may be selected for the purpose."[48]

While the board corresponded with I. J. Roberts, a missionary who had been serving under the Triennial Convention in Canton, China,[49] a young man by the name of S. C. Clopton wrote the board, offering himself for missionary appointment to China. In the 1 September meeting, Clopton appeared for examination in view of appointment by the board. After the interview he was approved unanimously. It was a high day, indeed, for a board that was having such a difficult time finding a qualified person to accept the position as corresponding secretary. Hence, less than six months from the time the Foreign Mission Board had been organized, its first missionary was appointed. The next day the board was informed that a young man by the name of George Pearcy had offered himself as a career missionary. A letter was received from J. I. Dagg of Georgia recommending still another candidate.

It soon became apparent that the board would have no difficulty in fielding missionaries, if the money could be raised for their support. The first step, therefore, was taken to finance the work by the appointment of the first of a number of agents who would spend varying amounts of time in designated areas, promoting foreign missions and soliciting funds for the work. The first such agent officially elected was "an Elder A. Williams of Georgia."[50] Several such agents were appointed in the following years. In addition to officially elected agents, others volunteered their services, such as Robert Herndon who declined appointment but was willing to "accept a voluntary agency," responsible for Alabama and Mississippi. In these years before the Cooperative Program was even a dream, the financing of foreign missions was a touch and go affair, largely dependent upon agents for both publicizing the work of the board and raising the financial support necessary for sustaining its work. As a result, the board was at the mercy of an uncertain income that trickled in only when and where agents lived and worked. Yet with an undimmed vision and unbridled hope the managers made plans for the future expansion of the work.

The board took a number of actions relative to its decision to give China the priority of its sustained missionary thrust. J. B. Jeter was asked to visit the China Missionary Society in Kentucky. Upon his return he reported that this society agreed to turn its funds over to the Foreign Mission Board and to cooperate with the board in its work. The board also decided to correspond with Baptist missionaries in China and to invite them to come under "the patronage of this Board."[51] In the hopes of receiving both property and funds from the Triennial Convention, possibly in China, the board met with little encouragement. A letter from Albert Day, chairman of the Boston Board, rejected any claim that Southern Baptists naturally felt they had on the property or other assets of the Triennial Convention. The letter flatly stated:

"… that, with as little delay as possible, we will proceed to establish missions in the seaports of China, or south of them as may be selected for the purpose."

> that it is inexpedient either for the General Convention, for those who may have retired from it, to make any claims, the one upon the other respecting the property of said General Convention on the one hand or the payment of its present debts on the other.[52]

However, another letter from Francis Wayland, who chaired a committee charged with answering the enquiry, softened the blow somewhat by stating that "in the spirit of fraternal regard" if any missionary wished to transfer from the Triennial Convention to the new Southern Board, "he would be allowed every facility for doing so."[53] George Pearcy was interviewed at the same meeting of the board and after "deliberate consultation" was unanimously accepted.

Since the board already had approved two missionaries to serve in China and was consulting with two others at work there who desired to transfer to the "Southern Board," the question of rules or regulations governing the conduct of missionaries on the field arose. This situation led to the initial step in drawing up a set of policies that eventually would provide guidelines for those who desired to serve under the auspices of the Foreign Mission Board.

One real problem facing new missionaries was the matter of the lack of medical facilities or of adequate medical care in missionary service. In response to this practical need, the board requested all those who were under appointment, if at all possible, to attend a lecture given by a medical doctor by the name of Albert Snead. The board also asked Snead to provide each appointee with a medicine chest supplied with the basic medicines that he anticipated new

James B. Taylor

missionaries would need in the country of their destination.

The early months of attempting to raise necessary funds and to find a competent pastor to serve as corresponding secretary of the board met with much frustration. The popular and eloquent R. B. C. Howell of Nashville, Tennessee, was only the most recent in a series of able Southern Baptist ministers who declined to accept the position of corresponding secretary of the board.[54] Finally, the board voted "by ballot" to ask James B. Taylor of the Grace Street Baptist Church in Richmond to serve. Taylor had been an assistant secretary of the Triennial Convention before becoming secretary in 1844. He was also the president of the Virginia Baptist Foreign Mission Society and one of the major leaders in the formation of the convention. He declined appointment but at the same time told the board

If no competent individual can be found who will be likely to give satisfaction to the whole south and who may be certainly expected to accept this office I am willing until the first of June, to devote two entire days in each week, to the duties of the secretaryship and if it be necessary I am willing to take a journey to the south.[55]

While such a hesitant and tentative offer might have discouraged a less determined group of men, after having been turned down by so many able churchmen from other states the board was in no mood to delay longer.[56] Jeter informed Taylor by letter that he would have been asked in Augusta

> *but for the influence of the Virginia delega-tion, who were anxious to obtain an officer from a State south of this, you would have been appointed Corresponding Secretary. No appointment could be made which would be so generally acceptable to the denomination, and which would inspire so much confidence of success, as that which has been made. . . .[57]*

The managers promptly accepted the offer and in doing so they acted more wisely than they knew, for J. B. Taylor, was among the most able and knowledgeable pastors in the convention. He would shortly give himself to the work without reservations but the decision did not come easily. As A. M. Poindexter wrote: "A sense of duty led him to accept the office of Secretary, and its duties were thenceforth the work of his life."[58]

The meeting of the board on 22 February 1846, continued on the high note on which the last meeting of 1845 concluded. One of the first actions was to consider establishing a mission on the coast of Africa. The corresponding secretary was instructed to "make inquiries concerning suitable persons for missionaries for the African mission."[59] The board also voted to outfit each missionary at a cost not to exceed $500 each. In further action the board asked the pastors of the Baptist churches in Richmond to form a committee to make arrangements for Judson's visit.

J. Lewis Shuck

Before the close of the February meeting of the board, it was reported that Issachar J. Roberts, a native of South Carolina, who first went to China under the China Mission Society of Kentucky, had asked to become a missionary of the Foreign Mission Board to labor in Canton. Jehu Lewis Shuck, a native son of Virginia and a ten year veteran of missionary service in China under the General Missionary Convention, was present at this meeting and addressed the board regarding the needs of China. He asked the board to adopt Canton and Shanghai as mission stations. Both I. J. Roberts and J. L. Shuck were consequently appointed missionaries to serve in Canton. Clopton and Pearcy were requested to postpone their planned departure for China in order to do deputation work among Southern Baptists in the interim. The Young Men's Missionary Society of the Second Baptist Church of Richmond sent word that the society hoped to raise enough funds to support two native missionaries in Canton.[60]

On the eve of the first triennial meeting of the newly organized Southern Baptist Convention, the Foreign Mission Board adopted a series of *Regulations* governing the relationship of the board to the missionaries on the field, their conduct, and the monetary responsibilities of the board to the missionaries and their families. The first regulation stipulated that the missionaries were not to engage in "any secular business for the purpose of personal gain." Second, missionaries were not to labor for monetary reward for themselves. It is evident that the influence of William Carey and the self-sacrificing Serampore missionaries and the struggle of Adoniram Judson with the problems his service on behalf of the British government had not been without its influence upon Taylor, Jeter, and the managers of the board. Article four spelled out the salary scale and stipulated that salaries were not to begin until one had arrived on the field. The salary of a single man serving as missionary was set at $500 a year and $50 additional in the first year of service. A husband and wife were granted $750 per year and an additional $100 during the first year of service.[61] A single woman missionary was to receive "$400 per annum, if she keeps her own table, or $300 a year if she boards in a mission family." Eighty dollars a year was designated for each child until seven years of age. From seven to thirteen the allocation for boys was set at $100, and girls would be given the same amount until fifteen. A ceiling of $1200 was placed on the total any one family could receive in a given year. Other regulations stipulated amounts to be received by returning missionaries up to five years and all children "orphaned or otherwise either remaining in heathen lands or in this country shall be provided for as above." With these regulations in place the Foreign Mission Board was prepared to make its first report to the Southern Baptist Convention.

First Baptist Church, Richmond

The 1846 Convention Meeting in Richmond

The 1846 meeting of the convention was called to order "in the meeting house" of the First Baptist Church of Richmond, at 11 o'clock on 10 June by W. B. Johnson, president. Shortly after convening the afternoon session, a motion was made and passed that

> *Rev. J. L. Shuck, of Canton, China, missionary of the Board of Foreign Missions, and Yong Seen Sang, a native preacher of the above Board, both now present, be introduced by the President to the body, to-morrow morning at 11 o'clock, or as soon thereafter as may be convenient, and the President of the Convention be requested to receive them with a fraternal address, and tender to them the hand of recognition.*[62]

The next day, after greetings from Shuck, a brief address by a national Chinese worker, Yong Seen Sang (Yeung Hing), followed. Sang closed his remarks with one request *"that all disciples in their prayers, morning and evening, would remember China."*[63] The presentation of the missionaries moved the convention to an interlude of spontaneous prayer and praise, after which "Brother Shuck" was "requested to address the Convention" on any one of several topics relative to the new door of opportunity that had been opened in China.[64]

In addition to hearing the first annual report of the Board of Foreign Missions, the convention also received a number of committee reports that stirred the imagination and sparked the enthusiasm of those who realized the challenge of the task to which they had put their hands. The first of these was given by Richard Fuller, Chairman of the Committee on the China Mission, a central paragraph of which read:

Yong Seen Sang

Your committee regard China as the province where our forces ought chiefly to be concentrated. They will be pardoned for expressing the hope, that your body will confine its attention to a very few fields, and not divide, and thus weaken your energies. They recommend the most prompt and vigorous measures for prosecuting your enterprise in this land of promise; respectfully advising your body to send out as large a band of missionaries as possible, and with them, men qualified to become theological instructors to the Chinese candidates for the ministry; that, thus, your power may be increased, and your efficiency, as well as economy, may be consulted, by large accessions of native talent and piety to the work of the mission.[65]

Fuller closed his remarks with an appeal for funds for the erection of a chapel in Canton under the direction of J. Lewis Shuck.

Brother T. Hume, chairman of the Committee on Agencies, acknowledged that there were many different ideas abroad regarding the best way of raising money for the missionary cause. Those who opposed the "system of agency," he asserted, "have failed to suggest a course which may be safely pursued by us. . . ." Hence the committee determined "that a judicious system of agency is a chief mode which should be relied on." Financing the foreign mission enterprise of Southern Baptists was to become increasingly burdensome for the new convention, with no satisfactory answers in sight.

B. M. Sanders, chairman of the Committee on the Instruction of the Colored Population, struck a note of concern for the spiritual and physical welfare of the African-American population. After explaining that in many churches "the pastors devote one sermon on the Sabbath for the particular benefit of this class," the committee encouraged the formation of "Sabbath Schools" for the instruction of children who generally were not present in worship services. Sanders pointed out that there was much lacking in the religious instruction of the "colored persons" and reminded the masters that it was part of their duty to see that their servants received such instruction for they (masters) were

the moral guardians of their servants as of their children. If they receive their services it is reasonable that they should provide for their spiritual, as for their physical wants.

If all pastors of churches should feel the claims of this part of their charge upon them, as is now felt by many, very much more might yet be affected for them, by their special labors.[66]

Sanders closed his remarks with the suggestion that in cooperation with the masters, domestic missionaries might find ways of achieving the goal of religious instruction of children as well as adults in their service.[67]

The first annual report of the Board of Foreign Missions carried a rather full account of the activities of the board during its first year of operation. In addition to giving an account of its meetings and decisions, the board announced that a journal entitled the *Southern Baptist Missionary Journal* had been published, the first issue of which was ready for distribution. While the *Religious Herald* of Virginia had carried several articles on the work of the convention and its Foreign Mission Board, the board emphasized that the new journal would by design carry much more missionary information than a state Baptist paper could be expected to do.[68]

The Southern Baptist Missionary Journal, 1846

Finances received considerable attention. The first treasurer's report informed the 113 delegates present that $11,735.22 had been paid into the treasury, with a balance in hand of $9,504.13.[69] Next it was pointed out that the board "will soon be absorbed by the demands of the missionaries now appointed by the Board." It was emphasized that "some plan which would reach all our churches and bring forth the free-will offerings of our brethren, may be considered as a desideratum among us."[70] The report ended with a challenge. "The chief enquiry of interest is, how shall the means be obtained? The whole subject is respectfully submitted to the Convention."[71]

In the section of the report devoted to fields of labor, it explained that China was opening up to the western nations.

Regular steamers from Great Britain and America will soon enter all her ports, and an opportunity will soon be furnished of sounding in the ears of her teeming millions, the gospel's joyful sound. This field, "white already to harvest," the Board have determined to occupy with all the force they can command.[72]

If China were the field to which Southern Baptists would send their first contingent of missionaries, the second was Africa.

Another important position which the Board consider themselves especially invited to occupy, is Africa. . . . Various considerations combined to urge upon our sympathies, her spiritual interest. Many of her sons are among us, and from them we may hope, in the process of time, to select those who become immanently qualified to preach to their countrymen "the unsearchable riches of Christ."[73]

The report continued in a most positive tone to relate that recent communications had indicated "the most encouraging prospects of success" that call for the "immediate occupancy of the field." Apparently the board assumed that the financial outlay of sending missionaries to Africa would be minimized since they would be African-American and bi-vocational missionaries, who would go to Liberia, where

English could be spoken and the necessity of acquiring another language would be unnecessary. Lott Carey and Collin Teague had operated largely in this fashion.

A most interesting feature of the entire convention was a historical sketch introducing to the convention the newly appointed missionaries, Samuel C. Clopton and George Pearcy, as well as I. J. Roberts and J. Lewis Shuck. Shuck had transferred from the Triennial Convention, under whose auspices he had served in China for some time. The presence of Shuck was a poignant reminder of the investment that Virginia Baptists had already made in China. Shuck's father-in-law, Addison Hall, had proposed the name of the new convention adopted in Augusta.[74] Also, two of those present in 1845, Robert Ryland and James B. Taylor, had served on Shuck's ordination council.[75]

Henrietta Hall Shuck

J. Lewis and Henrietta Hall Shuck

The appointment of J. Lewis Shuck (1812-1863) was particularly gratifying to the assembled delegates. A native of Alexandria, Virginia, and educated in the Virginia Baptist Seminary, he was appointed by the General Convention for China in 1835. Shuck baptized his first Chinese convert two years later, and by 1843 he had founded in Hong Kong the first Baptist church in China. The death of his wife, Henrietta, forced his return to the States in February 1845 to place three of the five children with his wife's relatives. However, little Henrie (named for his mother) died at sea. Added to his already heavy load was the news that the Boston Board refused to pay for his passage home or any allowance for his children.[76] He was accompanied upon his return to the United States with a Chinese convert and co-laborer by the name of Yong Seen Sang.

Henrietta was also well known in Richmond. It was under the earnest preaching of Taylor that she made her public profession of faith in Christ at thirteen years of age. A short time later she was baptized by her pastor, J. B. Jeter. When Lewis proposed to her, it was with the understanding that she would go to China as his wife. She agreed to both proposals and two days after their marriage on 8 September 1835, Lewis and his seventeen year old bride were set apart, along with Robert D. and Frances Davenport, for missionary service in the Far East. Few among those attending the meeting of the 1846 convention would fail to remember that emotionally charged occasion that helped Baptists in the South to feel so much a part of the foreign missionary movement.

It was in that very building that the Youth's Missionary Society of First Church chose J. Lewis Shuck to represent the society at the 1835 meeting of the Triennial Convention. When the offering plate was passed, he dropped in a piece of paper upon which he had scribbled: "I give myself."[77] Shuck was a member of the Third (Grace Street) Baptist Church of Richmond and in his senior year as a student in the Virginia Baptist Seminary (later Richmond College) when he met Henrietta Hall.

Converted just before her fourteenth birthday, Henrietta had often dreamed of becoming a missionary. In March 1834, she wrote: "Reading the memoirs of Mrs. Judson caused me first to think of the subject. A deep and abiding yearning for their souls and a conviction that God pointed me thither caused me to decide."[78]

Twelve days after the farewell services at the First Church, Richmond, and a long arduous trip by steamboat and train, the Shucks set sail on the *Louvre* the morning of 22 September 1835 with twenty other missionaries. The voyage was particularly difficult for

China 1860

Henrietta. She called it "dreadful" for she was seasick most of the time. However, between bouts of nausea, she did find time to write letters and make entries in her journal. En route from Calcutta to Singapore Lewis and Henrietta spent a few days in Burma. While there they visited the grave of Ann Hasseltine Judson, whose life held such profound meaning for Henrietta. During their five-month stay in Singapore the Shucks acquired a fluency in the Malay tongue comparatively easy. But Henrietta was informed that American women could not learn Chinese. However, when she heard that a woman in Singapore spoke

Chinese fluently she said, "What woman has done, woman can do,"[79] and she did.

A year after leaving Boston, the Shucks landed in Macao some ninety-five miles from Canton. At last they had reached their destination and now there were three of them, since little Lewis Hall Shuck was born in Singapore. Shortly after arriving, they took into their home two orphaned Chinese boys and not long afterwards their Chinese servant, Ah Loo, professed his faith and was baptized by Shuck—the "first Chinese convert that was ever baptized within the confines of this vast and idolatrous Empire."[80]

It was not long, however, before there arose a serious difficulty with the Boston Board. A sea captain reported that the Shucks were living in luxury and extravagance. The Shucks were crushed by the news and the harsh letters they began to receive from Heman Lincoln, the treasurer. A part of the problem lay in the lack of a clear understanding regarding financial arrangements. The board had not informed the Shucks regarding salary, living expenses, or allowances for language study. Besides, in caring for orphans, destitute people, and a fellow missionary, I. J. Roberts, who paid them only $50.00 during the five months he lived with them, all added to the financial burden. Finally, in an attempt to alleviate board criticism, the Shucks broke up housekeeping for three months, during which time they all slept in one room, before moving into a smaller house. Deprived of the basic comforts, if not the necessities of life, and laboring under suspicions of the Boston Board took its toll in emotional stress and physical well-being before the situation changed for the better.

A letter finally reached them on 1 January 1841, saying that the board did not hold Lewis responsible for the overdrafts before he was told what his salary would be.[81] The change in the board's attitude apparently was the result of a visit by Robert Dean, a Baptist missionary in Bangkok and one in whom the board had confidence. After living with the Shucks for some time, he wrote the board a glowing account of the Shucks and their work.[82] It took a while but by 24 March 1843, the tension between the Shucks and the board had been replaced by expressions of appreciation accompanied by a new harmonious relationship. Henrietta never shared these problems in her letters to her family. Through it all Virginia Baptists kept supporting their beloved missionaries

by designating their offerings for their support through the Triennial Convention.[83]

In 1842, the Shucks moved to Hong Kong, some forty miles East of Macao. Shortly after arriving in this British enclave, they received the startling news that the firm through which they and the other missionaries received their funds had failed. In this dark hour an offer to co-edit an English language newspaper was accepted and provided the needed support for the missionary labors to continue. On 5 May 1842, Shuck led in constituting the Queen's Road Baptist Church with five members, which was the first Protestant church established in China. In addition, three chapels were begun and buildings erected, and a mission house built, largely from privately donated funds, including those contributed by the Shucks themselves.

Henrietta, as was her custom, opened a school, and through the generosity of a friend a building was soon erected. By May 1844, some fifty girls and boys were enrolled. The school prospered and a larger building was soon required to replace the first one.

As always the Shuck household often included a variety of other residents, some for a short stay, others for longer. The mission house must have resembled the proverbial Grand Central Station if Thomas Dunaway's account is reasonably accurate.

The year 1843 brought Henrietta increased domestic burdens and anxieties. Mr. Dean and his family having moved to Hong Kong, took up their residence with the Shucks and greatly added to Henrietta's household duties. A young Chinese lad, who had embraced Christianity and had been baptized in Baltimore, Maryland, arrived in

Hong Kong, and as he had no means of support, the Shucks took him in and shared with him their pittance. On March 14, Dr. McGowan arrived, and he, too, made his home with the Shucks. He bore kind letters from the Board, formally acknowledging for the first time that the American Baptists had a regularly organized mission on the soil of China. Dr. McGowan made his home with the Shucks until he went to Ningpo, to be in charge of a station there.[84]

In addition to the cares of the household, Henrietta continued a schedule of teaching in the girls' division of the school. Lewis preached regularly in English at Queen's Road and three times a week in Chinese at the Bazaar Chapel. All together services were held thirty-three times a week. In the midst of the exhilarating work, Henrietta's heart was heavy because one of her most intelligent and promising students was taken from school by her parents who bound her feet and betrothed her to "an opium-smoking derelict." This prompted Henrietta to write a friend about the heartaches of missionaries. "They toil and labor and are often discouraged. . . . We need great faith, *we* indeed are compelled to walk by faith alone."[85]

By the time other missionaries arrived to help carry the load, Shuck was conducting some twenty Chinese services a week. Converts were made, instructed, and baptized. Among those confessing Christ as Lord were a cook, a Buddhist priest, and Yong Seen Sang, for six years Shuck's teacher and a Confucian scholar. After such close association with the missionaries and the Shucks, Yong became a true disciple of Christ and a faithful co-laborer until his death.

In Hong Kong, the work was firmly established and prospered not just because of the preaching and teaching of the preachers, but to no little degree because of Henrietta. Her gracious hospitality and genuine dedication were evident in everything she did, from tract distribution among British soldiers, and openness toward the international community to her special care for the Chinese students. Then abruptly it all came to an end. Shortly after her twenty-seventh birthday Henrietta took seriously ill. Never strong, the rigors of life in the Orient were too much for her. She sickened and on 27 November 1844, she died and all Hong Kong wept.

Back in Richmond when Shuck stood before the gathered delegates and visitors attending the Southern Baptist Convention that June 1846, visions of Henrietta and a life so young laid on the altar of sacrifice could not fail but come to mind. It was a high hour and the delegates came to a fresh realization of why they had met. The missionary vision that had called the convention into being now demanded the best Southern Baptists had to offer. Plans were already made for Shuck and Yong Seen Sang to return to China in the fall.[86] Upon the

> *... the first Foreign Mission Board report to the Convention... upbeat and loaded with encouraging news... closed on a somber note.*

Foreign Mission Board's insistence, they delayed their return in order to tour the South in the interest of the missionary cause and to raise sufficient funds for the proposed chapel in Canton. The tour was highly successful. Thousands heard of the needs in China and responded with their hearts and offerings.[87]

First Report on Missions

While the first Foreign Mission Board report to the Convention was upbeat and loaded with encouraging news and the promise of greater things to come, it closed on a somber note. Under the subhead "Difficulties to be Overcome" the committee called the delegates to frankly face the problems of the small Baptist constituency in the South and the lack of missionary vision that was characteristic of some churches, particularly where extreme forms of Calvinism prevailed. The lack of funds to undergird missionary stations already established, and most of all the widespread spiritual lethargy among Southern Baptist churches, were of special concern. To this latter condition the report addressed itself:

> *If the church, the body of Christ, be sickly and feeble, how can her energies be efficiently exerted. Shall we expect a vigorous aggression to be made upon the powers of darkness, while loyalty to heaven's king is so doubtfully evinced. Although these obstacles present themselves, the Board have not yielded to discouragement.*[88]

And, indeed it had not. It was all quite evident as the convention turned its attention to matters relating to the Board of Domestic Missions and later participated in the "designation service" (commissioning service) for the newly appointed missionaries.[89]

William C. Crane, chairman of the Committee on the African Mission, gave a brief sketch of attempts on the part of the Moravians and the English Baptists to establish missions in Africa. He reminded delegates that twenty-five years earlier "two colored Baptist missionaries were sent from this city, by the Board of the Triennial Convention to disseminate the word of life in the same region, supported mainly by the African Missionary Society of this city." After mentioning those who had already given their lives in missionary service in Africa, Crane recounted the formation of the First Baptist Church of Monrovia, Liberia.

[... the Committee on New Fields of Labor for Foreign Missions] ...

envisioned... the future would open up to Southern Baptists other fields besides China and Africa, the first of which should be Mexico and all Latin America.

> *Twenty-five years ago, a little church of only seven members, with Lott Carey as pastor was organized in an upper room of a private dwelling in this city. That church is now First Baptist church in Monrovia. It has been the mother of some seven to ten other churches, and also of the Providence Baptist Association in Liberia.*[90]

Although Crane, a deacon, never indicated that it was in his home that the church had been formed or mentioned his part in the organization of the African Missionary Society, this was common knowledge.[91] The heart of the man is seen in his appeal to his brethren:

> *And whether we view this great subject in the light of simply sending the gospel to the heathen, or in the light of repairing the wrongs of oppressed Africa, or in the light of employing and benefiting the piety and zeal of probably one hundred and fifty thousand cold-hearted Baptists in our own country, your committee cannot but earnestly urge that our enquiries, our prayers, and our efforts, may be energetically employed in this behalf.[92]*

The committee, while not disparaging the work in Liberia of missionaries of African extraction, emphasized the need for better prepared pastors from among Southern Baptists.

> *But your committee deem it peculiarly important that at least two well educated, well qualified missionaries, fitted for the work, should be employed there as leaders in an African Mission; and they would affectionately inquire, whether some of our good southern pastors cannot feel that God had called them to this important service.[93]*

Crane closed his remarks with a challenge "We feel that a solemn obligation rests not only upon this Convention, but upon all christians, to furnish them with the gospel, and a suitable christian ministry."

On Friday evening at 8:00 the delegates, joined by a large congregation of local Baptists, gathered in the Second Baptist Church to hear a message by J. Lewis Shuck on China. In this first worship service during the convention, devoted to the foreign missionary work of Southern Baptists, Yong

Seen Sang gave a short address which was followed by Brother Thomas Simons, a missionary to Burma, who described some of his experiences in Burma.

On Saturday morning the convention reconvened to consider the report of the Committee on Bible and Publication. The two mission boards were charged with the responsibility of distributing the Bible. The delegates also heard a recommendation that the board should cultivate the most friendly relationships with the American and Foreign Bible Society and its work of translation and distribution "in all lands."

J. B. Taylor, Chairman of the Committee on Selecting Missionaries, recommended that in addition to appointing more missionaries for China and Africa as soon as possible, that the board be instructed to secure a missionary to devote himself to "theological training of such native converts in China, as may be employed in the Christian ministry." The third recommendation emphasized the importance of sending as soon as possible a Christian physician "who shall also be engaged in imparting the knowledge of divine truth."[94]

After the report was approved, motions were passed that at the next meeting of the convention the second night would be devoted to the promotion of domestic missions and that the convention sermon "be appropriated to the promotion of foreign missions."[95] C. D. Mallory, chairman of the Committee on New Fields of Labor for Foreign Missions, presented what must have appeared to the assembled delegates an impossible dream. Yet it was a far-reaching missionary vision that had captivated the imagination of this man who was the first choice of the Augusta Convention for the corresponding secretary's position. He envisioned the possibilities that the future would open up to Southern Baptists other fields besides China and Africa, the first of which should be Mexico and all of Latin America. He also predicted that Jews would continue to return to Palestine, where they should also be included in the missionary vision of Southern Baptists. Although, as the committee suggested, Mallory agreed that it would be unwise to divert the board's energies from the present work in China and the contemplated mission in Africa, nevertheless, he insisted, preliminary preparations should be made to enter "especially Mexico, South America, and Palestine, with a view to the future establishment of missions in those regions. . . ."

In this historic meeting of the convention, the delegates could not fail to be reminded in the "Preamble" that the "law of Christ requires not only of his ministers, but of all his disciples, to bear a part in the great work of evangelizing the world, . . ."[96] In the light of this truth the convention called upon "intelligent merchants and mechanics" to join the missionary force while practicing their respective trades. In this recommendation were echoes of the Serampore mission

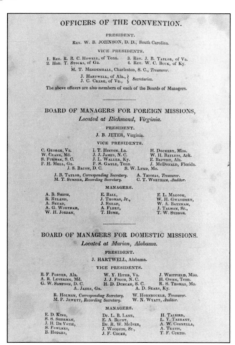

Board of Managers for the Foreign Mission Board, 1846

and an anticipation of missionary strategies yet to come.

Heritage and Promise

Robert A. Baker correctly observed that: "For many decades the convention was looked upon simply as a missionary body, not a structure for implementing all of the varied benevolences of Baptist people in the South as the constitution originally envisioned."[97] One thing is certain, Southern Baptists were in the missions business. However, it remained to be seen if the convention would meet expectations or even survive. In the proceedings of this, the first of the triennial meetings of the Southern Baptist Convention, there was more promise than substance. Only one missionary was on the field, and he was to prove, at times, more of a problem than an asset. The new missionary appointees were full of enthusiasm, with visions of worlds to conquer for Christ, but finances were virtually non-existent and with no system other than free will offerings and bequests, quite uncertain. In spite of the lack of financial assets, one thing was clear: Southern Baptists had taken a step in faith and even though it had been a painful step of separation from brethren with whom they had worked for more than thirty years, they still considered themselves a part of the Baptist missionary movement. Although institutional alignment was no longer the same, the heritage of the Judsons, Luther Rice, and the Boardmans they claimed as their own, and above all, the Great Commission they accepted as their mandate.[98] Little did Southern Baptists know, or could possibly foresee, that by severing the cords that bound them with their brethren of the North, they were contributing to the inevitable conflict that would further divide the nation in bloody strife. That the Southern Baptist Convention survived that conflict was little short of miraculous.

ENDNOTES

1. The official name was the "General Missionary Convention of the Baptist Denomination in the United States of America for Foreign Missions." It became more widely known as the Triennial Convention since it met every three years.

2. Another reason white Baptists in southern states were not as well represented as those in the North was due to the fact that white Baptists were often in a distinct minority. Winthrop Hudson gives some examples of this imbalance.

In Richmond, Virginia, for example, there were 387 white members of the First Baptist Church in 1841 and 1,708 black members. In 1846 the First Baptist Church of Charleston, South Carolina had 261 white members and 1,382 black members; at Georgetown, South Carolina, there were 33 and 798; at Natchez, Mississippi, there were 62 white and 380 black. *Religion in America,* 4th ed. (New York: Macmillan Publishing Company, 1987), 211.

Even though some of these were freed slaves, they were lacking in funds to belong to societies that required a membership fee. Therefore, while membership figures for Baptist churches in the South seemed much larger than those in the North, those able to bear the expense of attendance at the national meetings of the Triennial Convention were considerably fewer.

3. *Baptist Missionary Magazine,* 121, no.6 (June 1841): 7.

4. As regrettable as those actions appear 150 years later, the task of the historian is not to sit in judgment upon one side or the other but to understand.

5. William Warren Sweet suggests that the first pronouncement against the slave trade in the English colonies may have been made by Roger Williams: "In 1637 he protested against the enslavement of the Pequot Indians and, although he did not mention the Africans, a statute of 1652 granted ultimate freedom to the negroes of Providence Plantation." William Warren Sweet, *Religion on the American Frontier: The Baptists, 1783-1830, A Collection of Source Material* (New York: Henry Holt and Company, 1931), 77. Unfortunately, Las Casas supported the use of African slaves in the place of Indians whose protector he became. See William Warren Sweet, *A History of Latin America* (New York: The Abingdon Press, 1919), 111.

6. Three of these were Dr. Thomas Chisman of Grafton, Robert Carter III of Nomini, and David Barrow of Mill Swamp. Carter was said to have owned six to eight hundred slaves. Sweet, *Religion on the American Frontier,* 79, and Robert Baylor Semple, *History of the Baptists in Virginia,* first published in 1810, revised and extended by G. W. Beale (Lafayette, Tenn.: Church History Research and Archives, 1976), 178.

7. Cited by Semple, *History of the Baptists of Virginia,* 105.

8. For more information on this early antislavery movement and the Emancipation Baptists, see Sweet, *Religion on the American Frontier,* 77-101. W. W. Barnes points out that Elihu Embree published in Jonesborough, Tennessee in 1820 the first antislavery paper in the United States under the title of *The Emancipator.* See William Wright Barnes, *The Southern Baptist Convention, 1845-1953* (Nashville: Broadman Press, 1954), 18-20, for further information regarding the antislavery movement in the South. In Illinois the Emancipation Baptists took the name "Friends to Humanity."

9. Sweet, *Religion on the American Frontier,* 101. Sweet explains the demise of the "Friends to Humanity" in Illinois:

Finally, the trend taken by the anti-slavery movement after 1830 served to alienate the Friends to Humanity. Earlier, the interest had been in gradual emancipation and in schemes of colonization. William Lloyd Garrison first published the *Liberator,* January 1, 1831 in Boston, and soon afterward started founding anti-slavery societies. In December, 1833 the American Anti-slavery Society was organized in Philadelphia to stimulate the agitation. The new movement called for immediate abolition and violently and indiscriminately denounced southern slave holders. The leaders were northerners such as Phillips, Lowell, Palfrey, Follen, Burleigh, Parker, and Lovejoy. The Illinois Friends to Humanity were mostly of southern ancestry, and were out of sympathy with the radical abolitionists.

10. Barnes, *Southern Baptist Convention,* 20.

11. Ibid., 20, 21.

12. Ibid., 21.

13. *Christian Index* (February 12, 1841): 105. Cited in Barnes, *The Southern Baptist Convention,* 24.

14. See Baker, *Southern Baptist Convention and its People,* 157, for more details regarding the significance of this antislavery organization.

15. Robert G. Torbet, *A History of the Baptists* (Valley Forge: Judson Press, 1963), 288.

16. Barnes, *Southern Baptist Convention,* 22.

17. *Baptist Missionary Magazine* XXIV, no. 7 (July 1844): 155.

18. Ibid., 158.

19. Barnes, *Southern Baptist Convention,* 24.

20. Jeter wrote: "I grew up with a determination never to own a slave." Jeremiah Bell Jeter, *Recollections of a Long Life* (Richmond: The Religious Herald Co., 1891), 67. In fact neither J. B. Taylor, elected secretary of the Triennial Convention in its 1844 meeting, and pastor of the Grace Baptist Church in Richmond, nor J. B. Jeter, pastor of the First Baptist Church, Richmond, were advocates of slavery. Taylor never owned slaves in his entire life, and Jeter only became involved with the management of slaves when he became responsible for those which his wife had inherited.

21. Robert A. Baker, *Relations Between Northern and Southern Baptists* (Fort Worth: Baker, 1948), 73.

22. Cited by Baker, *Southern Baptist Convention and Its People,* 159.

23. Two foreign mission societies were organized by the abolitionists before 1845, the first in 1840 and the second in 1843.

24. Johnson in the "Address" delivered on 12 May 1845 in Augusta declared: "Were we asked to characterize the conduct of our Northern brethren in one short phrase, we should adopt that of the Apostle. It was 'FORBIDDING US *to speak* UNTO THE GENTILES.'" *Proceedings,* Southern Baptist Convention, 1845, 18. Hereafter referred to as *Proceedings,* SBC.

25. Ibid., 12.

26. The complete text of the call is found in the following: Baker, *A Baptist Source Book,* 109-12; Barnes, *Southern Baptist Convention,* 26-27; William H. Brackney, ed., *Baptist Life and Thought: 1600-1980* (Valley Forge: Judson Press, 1983), 231-33; H. Leon McBeth, *A Sourcebook for Baptist Heritage* (Nashville: Broadman Press, 1990), 262-64.

27. Cited by Barnes, *Southern Baptist Convention,* 27.

28. At this time Baptists often referred to all Baptists represented in the General Convention as "the Baptist Church." Fuller apparently felt that another society of which there were many among Baptists would not be as schismatic as an all encompassing denominational organization. He also apparently had hopes of an eventual reconciliation.

29. *Proceedings,* SBC, 1845, 3.

30. Ibid., 17.

31. Ibid., 19. Robert A. Baker also reproduces the "Address" in *A Baptist Source Book,* 120. Baker gives the "Address" the title of "Address to the Public." The *Proceedings,* SBC, 1845, 17, carry a longer title: "To the Brethren in the United States; to the congregations connected with the respective Churches; and to all candid men."

32. *Proceedings,* SBC, 1845, 19. In the phrase, "perishing and precious souls," Johnson included "the Macedonian cry from every part of the heathen world, . . . the four million of half stifled Red Men, our neighbors; with the sons of Ethiopia among us. . . ."

33. Ibid., 4.

34. Ibid.

35. The term "resolution" did not mean in the societies and conventions what it means now. Rather, in most cases it can best be understood as a motion.

36. See *Proceedings,* SBC, 1845, 14-15, for resolutions.

37. Cited in Hortense Woodson, *Giant in the Land* (Nashville: Broadman Press, 1950), 8.

38. Ibid., 100-101.

39. Ibid., 104.

40. Ibid., 104-5.

41. Johnson was a slave owner.

42. Woodson, *Giant in the Land,* 35.

43. Ibid. See also Baker, *Southern Baptist Convention and Its People,* 161-77 for a detailed discussion of the formation of the SBC and Johnson's role in this development.

44. *Proceedings,* SBC, 1845, 3.

45. The Domestic Mission Board listed only thirteen vice presidents. Ibid., 6.

46. Ibid., 15.

47. Minutes, Board of Managers for Foreign Missions, 12 May 1845, 8. Hereafter referred to as Minutes, FMB.

48. Ibid., 12.

49. Roberts initially had gone to China under the auspices of the China Missionary Society, located in Louisville, Kentucky.

50. Ibid., 17.

51. Minutes, FMB, 3 November 1845, 21.

52. Ibid.

53. Ibid.

54. Minutes, FMB, 1 December 1845, 23.

55. Minutes, FMB, 29 December 1845, 24.

56. Ibid.

57. Cited in George B. Taylor, *The Life and Times of James B. Taylor* (Philadelphia: The Bible and Publication Society, 1872), 158.

58. Cited in ibid., 177.

59. Minutes, FMB, 22 February 1846, 27.

60. Ibid., 25.

61. This salary scale had been recommended by Shuck who had suffered embarrassment and a tarnished reputation due to the Boston Board's unclear policies. Shuck in a letter to James B. Taylor of 9 May 1846 wrote:

Let it be distinctly understood that your missionaries must have separate and *definitely settled* salaries whatever the sum may be, and that they never could consent to draw their supplies according to their necessities from a *common fund*. . . . A missionary under any circumstances has enough to do to meet the demands of his *own* conscience, without being called upon to submit his food & raimant [sic] to the square & compass of *other* consciences.

Cited in Thelma Wolfe Hall, *I Give Myself: The Story of J. Lewis Shuck and His Mission to the Chinese* (Richmond: Thelma Wolfe Hall, 1983), 70.

62. *Proceedings,* SBC, 1846, 5.

63. Ibid., 6.

64. Treaties were signed between China and western nations, including the United States in 1844, opening port cities to their citizens.

65. *Proceedings,* SBC, 1846, 31.

66. Ibid., 16.

67. The report was received and ordered printed.

68. The first issue of the *Southern Baptist Missionary Journal* carried considerable information on China, its culture, language, and ethnic diversity. J. L. Shuck wrote an article emphasizing the importance of building the chapel in Canton.

69. There were 136 delegates listed in the *Proceedings,* SBC, 1846, 8-9, but this list included 23 absentees. The reason for this peculiar listing is that the 23 absentees had paid their "subscriptions" (membership dues). This was also the practice of the Triennial Convention. The new convention was still functioning like a society based on interested individuals who had paid a stated amount in order to be seated as a delegate.

70. Ibid., 24.

71. Ibid.

72. Ibid.

73. Ibid.

74. Hall, *I Give Myself,* 67.

75. Ibid.

76. Ibid., 69.

77. White, *First Baptist Church, Richmond,* 82.

78. Thomas S. Dunaway, *Pioneering for Jesus: The Story of Henrietta Hall Shuck* (Nashville: Sunday School Board, 1930), 28.

79. Ibid., 53.

80. Ibid., 60.

81. Ibid., 107.

82. Ibid., 106.

83. Ibid., 109. The Shucks were scrupulously honest in the use of missionary funds, often supporting Chinese students at their own expense.

84. Ibid., 126.

85. Ibid., 129.

86. *Proceedings,* SBC, 1846, 25.

87. Hall, *I Give Myself,* 74-80.

88. *Proceedings,* SBC, 1846, 28.

89. I. J. Roberts was not present for this service even though he had been appointed after writing that he was ready to transfer from the Boston Board.

90. Ibid., 11.

91. Crane took the lead in establishing a school at First Baptist Church, Richmond, for the African Americans. He, like many others, was an antislavery advocate who supported the colonization movement. It was in his home that the First Baptist Church of Monrovia, Liberia, was organized.

92. Ibid., 11.

93. Ibid.

94. Ibid., 15.

95. Ibid.

96. Ibid., 13.

97. Baker, *Southern Baptist Convention and Its People,* 176.

98. William B. Johnson, "Address to the Public," in *Proceedings,* SBC, 1845, 20.

PART II

The Era of Beginnings

The Southern Baptist Foreign Mission Board 1846-1888

1846-1888

The Era of Beginnings

WORLD HISTORY EVENTS

1845: Texas becomes a state.

1859: Charles Darwin, *The Origin of the Species*

1854: Admiral Perry opens trade with Japan.

1853: Taiping Rebellion

1858: Second British-Chinese War

China

1860: Treaty with China opens ports.

1861-1864: Rising tens brings War between the States.

1840   **1850**   **1860**

BAPTIST MISSIONARY MOVEMENT

1846: J.B. Taylor (1846-1871) elected first secretary of the Foreign Mission Board.

Nigeria

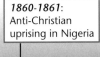

1860-1861: Anti-Christian uprising in Nigeria

1854: Nigeria entered from base in Liberia.

1845: China becomes the first foreign mission field entered by Southern Baptists.

1861: Foreign Mission Board's missionary effor almost come to a standstill.
Missionaries in Africa and China forced to fin secular means of suppo The board buys and sel cotton in England to finance work. At end of Civil War, the board is impoverished.

1859: J.R. Graves confronts the Foreign Mission Board in Richmond.

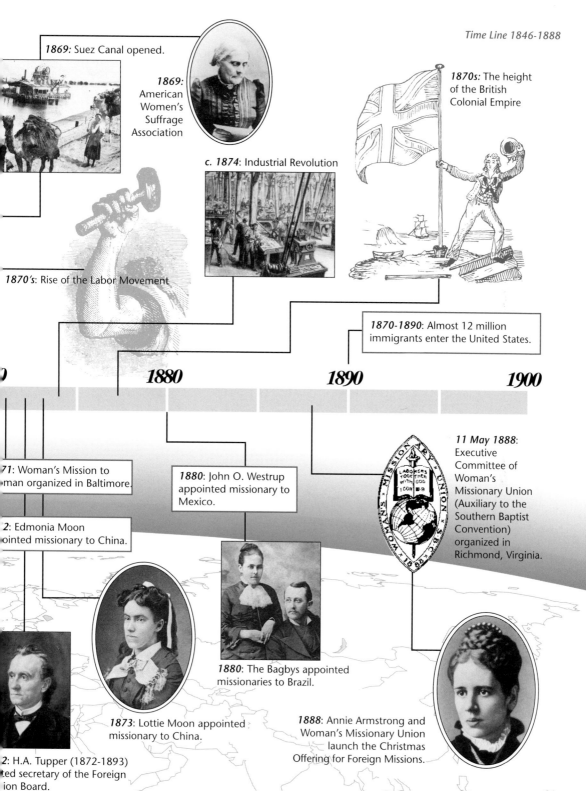

1869: Suez Canal opened.

1869: American Women's Suffrage Association

1870s: The height of the British Colonial Empire

c. 1874: Industrial Revolution

1870's: Rise of the Labor Movement

1870-1890: Almost 12 million immigrants enter the United States.

1880

1890

1900

71: Woman's Mission to man organized in Baltimore.

1880: John O. Westrup appointed missionary to Mexico.

11 May 1888: Executive Committee of Woman's Missionary Union (Auxiliary to the Southern Baptist Convention) organized in Richmond, Virginia.

2: Edmonia Moon ointed missionary to China.

1880: The Bagbys appointed missionaries to Brazil.

1873: Lottie Moon appointed missionary to China.

1888: Annie Armstrong and Woman's Missionary Union launch the Christmas Offering for Foreign Missions.

2: H.A. Tupper (1872-1893) ted secretary of the Foreign ion Board.

81

Survival Through the Storm

J.B. Taylor

Little did the founding fathers of the Southern Baptist Convention realize that the failure of the Triennial Convention to reconcile the factions that finally pulled it apart foreshadowed the division that threatened the very life of the nation itself. Few if any could have foreseen that the twenty-five years through which James Barnett Taylor would guide the fortunes of the Foreign Mission Board, the board would be threatened by dissolution not only by the War between the States but also by dissension within the denomination.

Perhaps, it was due, in part, to the preoccupation with the threat of the Landmark movement that more attention was not given to the changing political climate in the South. Before the convention faced the possibility of its own demise from civil strife, its mission boards became the object of strident criticism by a faction within the denomination that even questioned the new convention's right

"Upon reaching the suburbs, as the train slowly approached, we saw the blue uniform of the soldiers . . . I hastened home . . . But deep was my grief to find my beautiful city in flames . . ."

J.B. Taylor, April 2, 1865

to exist. In addition to these major crises, the board was continually struggling to enlarge its financial base without which it was frequently less than a year from insolvency.

That the convention and the Foreign Mission Board survived is a testimony to the dedication, faith, and ability of those who guided it through the storm. Like a ship at sea with sails torn and masts broken but still afloat, the convention and its Foreign Mission Board emerged in the post-civil war years (1866-1871) still viable institutions. Symbolic of the convention's tenacity in refusing to forsake its missionary vision was the Foreign Mission Board's first corresponding secretary.

James Barnett Taylor, 1804-1871

On the evening of 15 June 1846, the day the convention adjourned, the first "designation" (commissioning) service was held at the Second Baptist Church, Richmond. C. D. Clopton and

Almost as soon as the fledgling convention was organized, its organization came under fierce attack by J. R. Graves and his followers. Thus the very life of the convention was threatened even before the Civil War engulfed the whole nation in a fratricidal conflict. That the Foreign Mission Board survived was due to the dedication of its first corresponding secretary and the determination of laymen and missionaries. Above all missionary vision enabled the convention to survive.

George Pearcy had been recently appointed to China. The newly elected corresponding secretary, J. B. Taylor, only six months in office, delivered the charge. His was hardly the voice of a novice, for in addition to his pastoral experience at the Second and Third (Grace Street) Churches in Richmond, he had been deeply involved in the missionary efforts of the Triennial Convention. Too, prior to his first pastorate, Taylor served briefly as a missionary of the Baptist General Association of Virginia.

The primary task of the missionary, [Taylor] emphasized, is the preaching of the gospel: "This is your appropriate work. For this you are distinctly sent forth..."

A few excerpts from his address upon that occasion give insights into Taylor's own personality and inner strength which gave him "staying power" through the years of turbulence and uncertainty which were to follow.[1] "We are your friends, your brethren in Christ. . . . It will be important that the Board hear from you frequently." He emphasized that the information from missionary correspondence would be used to inspire sacrificial giving by Southern Baptists. He also reminded the young missionary appointees that they were but human and subject to "saying or doing that which may tempt to alienation of heart. Beware of strife among yourselves. . . . Love

as brethren, pray for each other regularly, bear each other's burdens, and provoke each other only to love and good works." He warned them, once they were on the field, that they would be tempted to move in elite circles with Europeans and other Americans who were accustomed to an expensive lifestyle. "You will be everywhere regarded as specimens of self-denial—as those who in an eminent measure walk even as Christ walked. Let this peculiar glory of the Christian missionary be yours. In your dress and style of living study simplicity." Taylor also admonished the young men to give themselves to language study by seeking to understand the culture and mentality of those to whom they would minister, then "they will be ready to listen to the word because they respect and love you." The primary task of the missionary, he emphasized, is to preach the gospel: "This is your appropriate work. For this you are distinctly sent forth; you go from this land not to engage in scientific research or pecuniary speculation, not to represent the best form of government or to exhibit the various stores of human knowledge, but to preach the gospel."[2] As a young man Taylor was subject to periods of depression. He spoke, therefore, out of his own experience when he cautioned them "against the spirit of despondency."

Taylor then described for the audience the circumstances missionaries would likely face, as though he had been there himself. "Under such circumstances," he said,

you will be in danger of yielding to discouragement. But you need not despond. By whose command do you go forth? Is it not the glorified Redeemer's? On whose promise do you rely for support? Is it not that of the immutable God? He who sends you to preach the gospel has said, "Lo, I am with you always, even to the end of the world."[3]

A few days after this service, Taylor accompanied Pearcy and Clopton to New York where he arranged for their voyage to China on board the *Cahota* which he described in a letter on 24 June 1846.

> *The* Cahota *is a fine vessel, and the accommodations are ample. She has a cow on board giving milk, several sheep and pigs for the use of the table, about one thousand fowls, with all the luxuries of the season for present use, and an abundant supply of everything necessary for the comfort of the passengers.*[4]

Afterwards he went to Boston where he made arrangements with a financial house for the transmission of funds to China. He also met once again with Baptist brethren, Baron Stow and Daniel Sharp, of the Boston Board. Similar trips were to follow with the missionaries in tow to the seaport cities on the Atlantic seaboard.

Thus, the gentle and devout pastor, with a gift for writing, began his new responsibilities as the first executive officer of the Foreign Mission Board. The man who loved his family and his pastoral ministry above everything else, had been persuaded after much hesitation, to give himself without reservation to the missionary effort of Southern Baptists when any sane observer would have said, and many probably did, "This foolhardy venture could only fail."

Who was this man that took such a calculated risk? James B. Taylor was born in Lincolnshire, England, on 19 March 1804. A year later his family moved to the United States and settled in New York City. One Sunday while walking by the First Baptist Church with his parents, he was drawn by the sound of music and persuaded them to enter. His father and mother were later converted and baptized. At the age of thirteen he became convicted of his sins and sought counsel from a devout deacon, J. J. Graves, who apparently advised James and his friends to visit the pastor, William Parkinson. Soon afterwards, conviction and confession were followed by baptism.

A short time later his family moved to a farm near Christiansville, Virginia, where his father followed the trade of cabinetmaker. James and his parents promptly united with the Blue Stone (now Bethel) Baptist Church. At sixteen years of age he responded to the call to preach. Preaching, he was convinced, was to be his life's work. Although a formal university education escaped him, he received the rudiments of an education from Bartholomew Egan, principal of the academy in Christiansville who gave him instruction weekday nights and on Saturdays. His natural love of books and a desire to learn did the rest. When only twenty-two years of age and not yet ordained, he was appointed a missionary of the General Association "to occupy the lower section of Meherrin District for six

> *[Taylor], the gentle and devout pastor, with a gift for writing, began his new responsibilities as the first executive officer of the Foreign Mission Board.*

months, making a tour once a month, and to render a particular account of his labors."[5]

It was during his six months service as a missionary of the association that he met Jeremiah Bell Jeter. James had not yet been ordained but Jeremiah had. He wrote his father how pleased he was to meet Jeter, whom he admired greatly. Since Jeremiah had been preaching two or three years longer and was ordained, young Taylor looked up to him as an elder brother. "I find I am but a babe to him, however, in preaching talents. He speaks plainly and forcibly, and is sometimes quite eloquent."[6] The friendship that developed between Jeter and Taylor was of lifelong duration. Jeter later said "Our intimacy and friendship commenced from the moment of our introduction, and was never interrupted from that time to the day of his death."[7] Early in his ministry Taylor took particular interest in the evangelization of the slaves and in the Colonization Society, which was largely a southern expression of antislavery sentiment.

Shortly after his ordination on 2 May 1826, young Taylor preached a series of sermons in Richmond. William Carey Crane, a deacon in the Second Baptist Church, saw in the twenty-two year old preacher the qualities of the pastor he was convinced the church needed. Finally, after much hesitation Taylor was persuaded to become pastor of the small congregation which at that time had only thirty-seven members, eighteen white and nineteen black. Within six months, sixty converts were added to the church. The salary was inadequate, but at the time he was unmarried with few expenses other than his books. Two years later his status changed with his marriage on 30

October 1828 to Mary Williams of Beverly, Massachusetts, whose father was also a Baptist minister.[8] Mary was a devout Christian, sharing her husband's poverty without complaint, if a letter to his father about the time of his marriage truly reflected her attitude. "We have both determined to pursue a course of the most rigid economy, and to buy nothing which we can dispense with, and especially to avoid involving ourselves in debt."[9]

Among these [principles], Taylor resolved in his human relationships: "As much as I can to alleviate the sufferings of the poor and afflicted."

During the thirteen years in which he was pastor of Second Church, 664 new members came into the church, which also became the mother congregation of three churches: Third Baptist (now Grace Street Church), a church in Baltimore, and the Walnut Grove Church, located a few miles from Richmond. It was early in this pastorate that Taylor penned a memorandum of principles meant for his eyes alone—a code by which he intended to live. Among these, he resolved in his human relationships: "As much as I can to alleviate the sufferings of the poor and afflicted."[10] In relationship to the world at large, he determined to "Make increased endeavors to promote the spread of the gospel throughout the earth." In these two resolutions we catch a glimpse of an earnest young minister with a world vision and a heart of compassion.

During the last year (1839) of his pastorate at Second Church, Taylor took a leave of absence in order to serve a term as chaplain of the University of Virginia. He felt this responsibility would not only give him a great opportunity to minister to bright young students, but also the privilege of auditing classes in subjects which would supplement knowledge gleaned largely by his own efforts.

At the close of his pastorate at Second Church, he confided in his diary: "Among the poor I have delighted to go, to do them good in body and soul." The poorest of the poor in Richmond were both slaves and freedmen. As he continued to reflect upon his thirteen-year pastorate, he expressed his satisfaction in that only five or six members of Second Church had forsaken the Baptists to follow Alexander Campbell. Other Baptist churches had lost considerably more.

Corresponding Secretary of the Foreign Mission Board

Apparently Taylor's health was always somewhat delicate, and upon occasion he was seriously ill from various ailments. It also seemed he was constantly engaged in a balancing act in dividing his time between his pastoral responsibilities, the board, and his family. At the first meeting of the board in January 1846, shortly after becoming corresponding secretary, Taylor was requested, in addition to the two days a week devoted to the board, to take a public relations tour of the South on behalf of foreign missions. This was an indication that the work of the board demanded more time than he was able to give it. He attempted to solve the problem of time management by dividing

each day between the demands of his pastorate, and the duties of the corresponding secretary. Within a few months, however, he made the decision to resign his beloved church and give himself without reservation to the work of the corresponding secretary.

When 8 February 1846 arrived and a mass meeting was held at the Second Church in honor of Adoniram Judson, Taylor was unable to attend. According to his diary he was ill on Sunday, 1 February 1846, and unable to preach in the afternoon. The next day he spent four hours in a meeting of the Foreign Mission Board and later visited a dying woman. The day before he had counseled and prayed with a man who was apparently on his death bed. On 3 February he met Judson and the next day talked with the veteran missionary at length. Later in the week he made a trip to Petersburg in the interest of the board. It is not surprising that on 5 February he returned home quite ill and was compelled to call for the doctor.[11] On the eighth, the day of the mass meeting, he felt somewhat restored but not well enough to leave the house. The following day Judson came to his home and they remained together in earnest conversation an hour or so. Taylor recorded in his diary:

> *It was a heavenly interview. Here was before me the very man who had given the whole Bible in their own tongue to millions of dark pagans, and yet so modest, so humble was his bearing that one would scarcely know that he was aware of it. An unaffected simplicity of manner is a striking characteristic of the man. May I be improved by the privilege of seeing him! Before he left our family he led in prayer.[12]*

On 11 February he was off again, this time on an extended trip to the South on behalf of foreign missions, as requested by the board.

In the fall of 1850 Taylor was very ill for several months. It was feared that he would not recover. During this time while convalescing he wrote to his dear friend W. C. Crane, who had moved to Baltimore with a contingent of members from the Second Church in order to form a new congregation,

Remember me to Drs. Fuller, Wilson, Adams, and all friends, especially of the cause of missions, and to sister C. Adieu. My soul is bound to you as David's was to Jonathan's.

When does the Liberia packet sail? Poor Africa! But she will see the salvation of the Lord. I wish to work for her good.[13]

From Mecklenburg on 20 January 1851, he informed his wife, "My hand is yet swollen and useless. I find it quite a task to write, and sometimes fear it will not be in my power to confine myself to the writing-table as I have done."[14] Little did the corresponding secretary know that his writing-table was to become, conceivably, the most important pulpit of any minister in the Southern Baptist Convention for the next twenty years. There was much more, however, than correspondence involved in the work of the board's corresponding secretary.

In order to relieve the burden for the financial support of the work on the agents, Taylor took upon himself more responsibility for fundraising. Critics charged that the "agency system" was a poor way to raise money for missions since the money collected, according to them, did not justify the expenditure. An excerpt from a letter to his son George in 1858 opens a window on this aspect of his work:

I have been absent from home about a fortnight, and during that time have secured about $510, of which $335 is in cash, for the Board. It will be three weeks or a month before my return home, and I must, if possible, secure $1000 in cash. But it is hard work. If I go where they have done anything, this is plead as an excuse; if nothing has been done, a painful disposition is apparent. Still, I like to work on, nothing dispirited. If I can only keep my own heart right, all will be well.[15]

There were some bright spots in the drudgery of fundraising as he indicated in a 23 March 1858, letter to his wife.

[I] am spending a little time with our excellent brother, H. A. Tupper, a wealthy minister, who gives seven hundred dollars for the support of Mr. and Mrs. Reid. His wife is a sister of Brother Boyce. They have six little children, five of them boys. I am resting a little. Having preached ten times, counting one address, in eight days, repose is necessary.[16]

In between his itinerant fundraising trips and growing correspondence, Taylor accompanied the newly appointed missionaries, who were sailing for the Orient or Africa, to the cities of embarkation.

The corresponding secretary also put on another hat, that of the personnel secretary. Among those students cultivated, encouraged, and at last interviewed for appointment were Matthew T. Yates of Wake Forest College and Roswell H. Graves. Yates was appointed in 1846 and Graves in 1856. Under the leadership of Taylor, the "Designation Services" became an unforgettable experience for the appointees and others who witnessed or participated in them. This was particularly true of the designation service at the First Baptist Church on the night of 18 December 1846.[17] The plans were that the Yateses, the Tobeys, the Shucks, Yong Seen Sang (Yeung Hing), and Francis Johnson, who was expected to inaugurate theological education for China in Canton, would take part in this service. Although Johnson was ill at the time, all the others participated in a memorable service that lasted for hours.

Under... Taylor, the "Designation Services" became an unforgettable experience for the appointees and others who witnessed or participated in them.

The next day Taylor left with his band of missionaries for Philadelphia, where they were received with warm Christian greetings in two churches, and later in New York where they were to board a ship for China. Mrs. Yates, however, became suddenly ill, which compelled the Yateses to delay their departure. A Baptist family took them in not so much as guests, it was reported, but more as their own children. The cordial relationship that James B. Taylor continued to enjoy with Northern Baptists was evident with every contact he made. Frequently, in New York and Philadelphia or Boston, the newly appointed Southern Baptist missionaries met Baptist brothers and sisters who encouraged and blessed them just before their departure for their overseas assignments.

Roswell H. Graves told his father of Taylor's personal attention as he accompanied him to the ship. Later Graves's father wrote a son of Taylor:

Upon my son's departure for China, April, 1856, your father accompanied him to New York, and attended him with fatherly care and advice up to the moment of his sailing, and expressed more than usual official pleasure and personal interest in sending forth the grandson of Deacon Graves to proclaim the gospel of Christ to the idolatrous heathen of the "land of Sinim". . . .[18]

On such occasions, Taylor often had a brief farewell service with the new missionaries and others who cared to join in prayer and worship on the deck of the ship just before departure. He well knew, due to the nature and uncertainty of life, and the perils of the voyage, that the possibility of ever seeing the young missionaries again was by no means certain.

In a letter of 31 October 1858, to his wife Mary, Taylor gives a glimpse of the flurry of activities in which he was engaged in the last minute preparations for the J. B. Hartwells' departure for China.

The next morning I found Brother Hartwell and lady. We at once began our work, selecting and purchasing all needful articles, and by Friday night had nearly completed the outfit. Saturday morning, until the last half hour, I was busy in settling accounts. I then bade Brother and Sister H. farewell, rapidly passed to the hotel, paid my bill, jumped into an omnibus, and reached the ferry two minutes before the boat left. Was not able to leave Philadelphia until eleven o'clock, and consequently did not reach Baltimore till this morning about day. I went to a hotel and slept a little. On com-

ing to Brother Crane's to breakfast, I
learned that I had been relied on to supply
Dr. Fuller's pulpit. I preached for him at
eleven o'clock. The house was quite full.
This evening we had a crowded congregation, to pray for the missionaries previous to
their embarkation. Addresses were delivered
by Brethren Berg, Stone, and myself; prayer
offered by Brother Sharp and Brother Van
Meter of the Burman mission. It was a
pleasant meeting.[19]

After three more days of purchasing
needed supplies, he wrote in his diary:

This morning went down with them to the
Mary Caroline Stephens, lying in the stream
some three miles distant. Twelve or more
other missionaries of different persuasions
were also passengers. Had religious services, and then bade them a long farewell.
Returned to the city, transacted some business, and at five P.M. left for home, expecting to travel all night.[20]

Though there was "sweet sorrow" in
such partings, sorrow was compounded in
Charleston (1849) with the news of sudden
death among the missionaries. The Foreign
Mission Board reported to the convention
that

The young, ardent, and devoted Clopton, is
no more. He had just begun to speak in the
language of the Chinese, and by his amiable disposition and courteous manner, had
secured the regard of the natives residing
immediately near him, when he was suddenly arrested by the hand of death.[21]

The same report carried news of the
death of two missionaries in Africa.

The African mission has also suffered
painful bereavements. Beside the death of
Brother A. S. Jones, at Cape Palmas, which
occurred in 1846, about the time he was
expected to enter our service, the Board are

compelled to record the sudden removal of
F. S. James, of New Virginia. He was a
good man. In the language of one of his co-
adjutors in the work, he was pious, amiable,
laborious, self-denying, beloved by his people and all who knew him.[22]

The Case of I. J. Roberts

As painful to Southern Baptists as the
loss of the missionaries was, they could
accept it within the will of God. It was not
the same with the troublesome case of I. J.
Roberts. Roberts had first gone to China
sponsored by the Chinese Missionary
Society of Kentucky and later transferred to
the Boston Board of the Triennial
Convention. Shortly after the formation of
the Southern Baptist Convention, he indicated a desire to serve as a missionary of the
Foreign Mission Board. At the time, J. Lewis
Shuck warned the board that Roberts could
not always be trusted. Despite the warnings,
Roberts was appointed without appearing in
person before the board. At the time, he
was serving alone in Canton. Clopton and
Pearcy were sent out to reinforce the mission. Shortly after his appointment, the
Foreign Mission Board became aware that
Roberts was attempting to raise money
through the Kentucky-based China
Missionary Society and learned that he was,
at the same time, receiving support from a
Canton Missionary Society. Upon their
arrival in Canton, the R. B. W. Whildens
learned that Roberts was also in conflict
with some missionaries in the Canton
Mission. During a trip back to the States to
defend himself against a variety of charges,
additional problems arose in his treatment
of a Chinese valet who had accompanied
him. After an admission of sin and an
expression of repentance, the board reluc-

tantly agreed to send him back to China. This proved to be a poor decision.

Once back in Canton, Roberts, it was reported, was guilty of indefensible conduct in relation to the suicide of a missionary of another denomination in whose home he and Mrs. Roberts and Harriet Baker, a recently appointed single Southern Baptist missionary, were living. This was the last straw as far as the board was concerned. After Roberts was recalled, he continued to agitate the issue, accusing the board of grave injustice, which was given wide publicity in Kentucky and Tennessee Baptist papers. Finally, the board brought the unsavory matter to rest by the publication of the "Case of Reverend I. J. Roberts" in the 1855 *Proceedings* of the Southern Baptist Convention.[23] The article had been prepared originally for publication in the *Western Recorder* and hand delivered by J. B. Taylor to the senior editor. Up to this time the *Western Recorder* had been very critical of the Foreign Mission Board for dismissing Roberts. Even though the article was reported lost, the editor did sign a statement exonerating the Foreign Mission Board for any alleged wrongs done in the Roberts affair. Nevertheless, the board thought that it was important in defense of its own integrity to publish a rather full account of its dealings with Roberts.

The Landmark Crisis

The I. J. Roberts affair taxed the patience of J. B. Taylor and the Foreign Mission Board as few events had. As personally aggravating as the Roberts affair had been, it was not nearly as threatening to the life of the convention as would be the Landmark movement under the leadership of J. R. Graves.

Graves and his followers attacked the structure of the Southern Baptist Convention upon the basis of ecclesiology, which Graves claimed to have derived from his understanding of the New Testament. He went to the convention determined to be heard—and he was. If it had not been for the integrity and patience of the corresponding secretary and his associate Abram Maer Poindexter (1809-1872), the outcome would have been far different. Graves was editor of *The Tennessee Baptist,* perhaps the most influential Baptist paper in the Southwest. He was also pastor of a church in Nashville, Tennessee. He had taken a group of followers out of the First Baptist Church, Nashville, which consisted of only a minority of its membership but claimed to be the true First Church. This maneuver led to an acrimonious relationship with R. B. C. Howell upon his return to the pastorate of the original First Baptist Church.

When the convention of 1859 convened in Richmond, Virginia, Graves was determined to challenge the reelection of Howell to the presidency of the convention and to confront the Foreign Mission Board regarding the scriptural basis of its existence. A total of 574 delegates attended this session of the convention, 241 of which were from Virginia and 97 from North and South Carolina.[24] Howell was elected president on the first ballot, but declined to serve out of fear of dividing the convention. Richard Fuller was then elected president.

The convention gave Graves ample opportunity in which to present his objections to the boards. These were already well known since he had published them in the 4 September 1858, issue of *The Tennessee Baptist.*

The scriptural plan is clearly exemplified in the New Testament, and it is simple and effectual, and the sooner we return to it as a denomination, the better for us and for the world. . . .

We do not believe that the Foreign Board has any right to call upon the missionaries that the churches send to China or Africa, to take a journey to Richmond to be examined touching their experience, call to the ministry, and soundness in the faith. It is a high-handed act, and degrades both the judgment and authority of the church and presbytery that ordained him, thus practically declaring itself above both.[25]

Since the idea of local churches acting as missionary organizations, collecting funds, sending, and supervising missionaries was obviously impractical, Graves suggested that local churches could unite informally in order to send missionaries to a foreign field and could use a commercial house for transferring funds. This plan Graves attempted to promote in Richmond. The convention did give Graves a full day in which he presented his objections to the organization of boards, particularly the Foreign Mission Board, and in which he introduced an alternate plan.

A committee was appointed to bring a recommendation the following day regarding the disposition of Graves' objections and suggested solution. Since Graves was not satisfied with the reception he had received on the floor of the convention, J. B. Taylor and his associate, A. M. Poindexter, continued the discussion in the foreign mission rooms at the First Baptist Church, which lasted throughout the night. Taylor's youngest son, Charles, who was with his father at the time, fell asleep but was awakened, he later wrote, "The east was glowing

and the roosters crowing when, at last, the brethren shook hands and parted. . . ." He recalled: "There was plain talking, but many a time since I have thought of that occasion as proving that Christian men can differ widely, express themselves freely, and even charge each other with having said and done wrong things, and yet not lose their tempers."[26]

The next day "The committee of inquiry as to the improvement of the system of missions and missionary operations," previously appointed, brought a report that satisfied Graves's objections and saved the Foreign Mission Board. It contained two significant recommendations:

1. Resolved, That in the judgment of this Convention, it is inexpedient to make any change in the existing plans of missionary operation.

2. Resolved, That in case any churches, associations, or other bodies entitled to representation in this Convention, should prefer to appoint their own missionaries, and to assume the responsibility of defraying their salaries and entire expenses, that the respective Boards are authorized, under our present organization and fundamental rules, to become the disbursing agents of the bodies so appointing missionaries and appropriating funds, whether such contributions be intended for the civilization or the evangelization of the heathen; provided that such expenses of forwarding the money, as have to be specially incurred, be borne by the contributors.

All which is fraternally submitted,

W. P. CHILTON, Chairman.[27]

The report was received and adopted. Two weeks later, after the close of the convention, Graves wrote an editorial in his paper that supported the report of the committee. His appeal to the churches was forthright. "Here are two plans of operation submitted to the brethren. Let them make their election. Let them remember that they have no good excuse for doing nothing. The missionary spirit enters essentially into a church organized according to the gospel."[28]

By the close of the convention, healing had begun to take place and a motion was made by G. W. Samson of Washington, D. C., which read "*Resolved,* That, as members of this Convention, we express our earnest conviction that personal controversies among pastors, editors, and brethren, should, f r o m this time forth, be more than ever studiously avoided." This was followed by a motion by I. T. Tichenor of Alabama: "That the Editors of our religious papers be requested to publish the above resolution."[29]

Sooner, perhaps, than anyone expected the personal animosities that had emerged in the 1859 convention and the issues raised by the Landmarkers were soon drowned out by a call to arms.

Missions During the War, 1861-1865

Scarcely had the attacks on the Foreign Mission Board by the Landmark faction sub-

> *Taylor was primarily concerned about the disastrous consequences that the impending war would have upon the missionaries far from their homeland.*

sided when the thunder of the shore battery firing on Fort Sumter turned the nation's attention from more beneficial pursuits to war. For some time South Carolina had determined that the only "honorable course of action" was to secede from the Union, if Lincoln were elected president. The state's more vocal agitators had attempted to get other Southern states to secede first but without success. For at least ten years before South Carolina dissolved its ties with the Union, talk of war had escalated, fueled by politicians and their debates. The appeal to "Southern Rights" (a euphemism for slavery), coupled with the fear of slave rebellion, made secession an emotional issue designed to rally Southerners to the cause of independence. Reasonableness and attempts at negotiation became the first casualties. As emotionalism spawned fanatics both North and South, both sides miscalculated the severity and length of the impending conflict.

With Lincoln's election, South Carolina promptly seceded, followed by five other states of the lower South. Together their delegates organized the Southern Confederacy at Montgomery, Alabama, on 4 February 1861. While many Southerners could not conceive of defending slavery at the risk of war, most eventually rallied around the crossed bars in defense of hearth and kin. This was particularly true of states in the lower South where feelings ran high. Still significant minorities, even in the lower South, held out for negotiations rather than war. "Union men" were particularly active in Virginia and Tennessee. Even after the mortar attack launched by the Charleston harbor defenses against Fort Sumter on 12 April, the Virginia Convention hesitated to act.

Those states of the upper South that finally joined the Confederacy did so against sizable opposition and only after Lincoln issued a call for troops. Virginia is a case in point. Of course, Kentucky and Maryland never left the Union, although an estimated 35,000 Kentuckians joined the Confederate forces, there were some 75,000 who marched under the stars and stripes.[30]

A Virginia Convention had been called to meet on February 13 to consider the matter of secession and had been in session almost two months without reaching a decision. The secessionists with the aid of influential editors of the Richmond newspapers pulled out all the emotional stops to persuade a state, which was at best lukewarm to the idea, to secede from the Union. Advocates of the Confederacy were given free rein on the floor of the convention to do what they could to fan the flames of patriotism against the "submissionists." Finally a former governor, Henry A. Wise, called a Peoples' Convention on 16 April. The Confederate flag was raised during the night over the capitol and an expedition was sent to seize the arsenal at Harper's Ferry. Under the mounting pressure the convention finally voted on 17 April, 88 to 55, to join the Confederacy.[31] On 29 May, the capital of the Confederacy was moved from Montgomery, Alabama, to Richmond. Jefferson Davis, who had been provisional president was elected president on 6 November 1861 and formally inaugurated on 22 February. Thus, Richmond, a city of thirty-five thousand with 2,500 freed blacks, found itself the headquarters of the Confederacy.

Upon the eve of the outbreak of the war (4 January 1864), Taylor wrote in his diary, "We are living in perilous times, the whole fabric of our confederated Union being likely to be broken to pieces. South Carolina has seceded, and other states are soon to follow. God alone can preserve us from ruin."[32] Taylor was primarily concerned about the disastrous consequences that the impending war would have upon the missionaries far from their homeland. The board was already beginning to feel the financial strain. Hence, Taylor recorded in his diary the following after a hard day on Friday as he left at night by train for Alexandria:

> *It becomes necessary to go out visiting as many churches as possible, that in this sad condition of the country, when all the avenues of trade are obstructed and money for our Board is coming in slowly, means may be secured for the support of our beloved missionaries. We must not allow them to suffer.*[33]

Finances of the Board, 1861-1865

At the outbreak of the war, there were thirty-eight missionaries serving overseas; fourteen in China and twenty-four in Africa. Among these was T. J. Bowen, who had led in opening the work in Yoruba (Nigeria) and was attempting in 1861 to establish a mission in Brazil.[34] The work in China was carried on through three missions located in Canton (South China), Shanghai (Central China)[35], and Shantung (North China). The work in Africa, which was initiated by the Richmond African Missionary Society (organized in 1815), counted missions in Liberia, Sierra Leone, and Yoruba (Nigeria).[36]

Although income from various sources

began to decline sharply by October, the balance at the end of the year was $10,869.41. Disbursement of funds to the missions became more and more difficult. Meetings of the board became less frequent with only two meetings held in 1862. On 2 December, the board decided to set up a provisional committee in Baltimore "to act on behalf of the Board in securing and transmitting funds for the use of missionaries. . . ."[37] The committee was also authorized to fill "any vacancies which may occur" and borrow funds up to $10,000.00, if necessary.[38]

In order to relieve the board of responsibility for his salary, A. M. Poindexter, Taylor's able associate, retired to his farm and Taylor, himself, took a part-time position as a colporteur and chaplain with the Sunday School and Publication Board of the General Association of Virginia, concentrating on military hospitals. Since cotton was the source of much of the income of Baptists in the lower South, it was important that the board find ways of getting its cotton through the Union blockade. The cotton then would be sold in England, and the proceeds sent to the missionaries overseas. There were shipping firms willing to take the risk of running the blockade for high profits. Taylor made the arrangements in Charleston. Conse-

quently, in 1863 and 1864, the board's disbursements included $845.00 for cotton.[39] However, England stocked up on cotton before the war and India and Egypt began to raise cotton, thus forcing the price down on the international market. Hence, the missionaries never received the anticipated income that the board had hoped the sale of cotton would bring.

Matthew T. Yates was enjoying unusual success in winning Chinese to Christ when the news of the impending conflict finally reached him. He wrote on 20 March 1861:

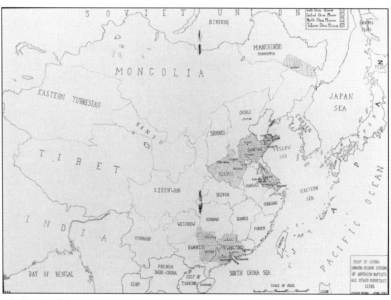

Missions in China

"That the Board should have to resolve to send out no more missionaries under existing circumstances, confounds me beyond measure."[40] After receiving a letter from Taylor dated 25 December and the news that five states had seceded, the distraught missionary exclaimed, "May the God of nations save our country from a fratricidal

IN MEMORY OF

REV⁰ MATTHEW TYSON YATES,D.D.,

FOR 40 YEARS A MISSIONARY TO CHINA OF THE
SOUTHERN BAPTIST CONVENTION.U.S.A.AND FOR
33 YEARS PASTOR OF THIS CHURCH.

BORN IN NORTH CAROLINA JAN.8.1819.
DIED AT SHANGHAI.MCH.17.1888.

*Blessed are the dead which die in The LORD; —
that they may rest from their labors and their
works do follow them.*

Yates Memorial, North Gate Baptist Church, Shanghai

letter dated 9 May 1861 sounded a far different note, "We pray God that He Himself will step in as a mediator between the contending parties. I do assure you that the disturbance there adds nothing to our peace here."[44] At the outbreak of hostilities there was heightened anxiety concerning the effects of the war upon both the income of the board and its ability to sustain the missionaries overseas. Soon fears became realities and both the board in Richmond and the missionaries in China and Africa were faced with a dwindling income from a people now preoccupied with a war that would not go away. The incalculable cost of the

Roswell H. Graves

war in terms of human suffering and the human spirit sapped the strength of the churches. Spiritual vitality eroded and with it the cause of missions in many churches vanished. Graves wrote from Canton about his concern for the effect of the war upon Southern Baptists and their churches.

war! Viewing the whole matter from this distant point of observation our people, North and South, seem to be mad."[41]

Roswell Hobart Graves wrote from Canton that he saw no end of the war until the North recognized the independence of the Confederacy.[42] But T. P. Crawford, who for eleven years labored alongside Yates, wrote in a far different vein on 3 October 1861, "The South has the better cause. The argument is exhausted; the time for secession has come, and let her stand by her rights. My sympathies are fully with her, and I am prepared to share her troubles and her fate."[43] Joseph Harden, an African-American missionary serving in Liberia, in a

And I believe the churches at home need something to keep their souls from being swallowed up in this war. If they had some enterprise before them to call forth their energies, absorb their thoughts, and examine their hearts, it would do their souls good.[45]

Graves's concern was not financial but spiritual, for he was hardly in a position to know how desperate the board was for finances by the end of the war. He had apparently received a rather steady income through the Baltimore committee. This does not seem to have been true of other missionaries in China or Africa.

When the board became unable to continue to pay his salary Yates's fluency in spoken Chinese enabled him to make a living as an interpreter in the Chinese courts and as vice coun-

Yates' family home in Shanghai

sul for the United States Embassy. There were other sources as well. Almost by accident, he received title to what he thought was a worthless piece of property from a grateful Chinese who had asked Yates to see that he and his wife received a decent burial. From this gift that he considered providential, Yates went on to make a number of investments that gave him more than an adequate income during and even after the war. On 19 April 1869 Yates wrote: "The board has not been able for the last sixteen months to send me more than half the amount required for our salaries and to keep up the Mission property."[46] In spite of the necessity of working a few hours each week in order to sustain himself, his wife, and the mission in Shanghai, Yates never forgot the purpose which brought him to China or lost his love for the Chinese. The missionary was never subsumed in the businessman.

Perhaps of all the missionaries those in Africa were most impoverished during the war. Joseph Harden supported himself by making bricks but died in May 1864. Other missionaries, including Beverly P. Yates, supported themselves in various ways as best

they could and yet the work went on and Africa proved the most fruitful field of Southern Baptists' mission endeavor. T. A. Reid was stranded due to a civil war raging in Nigeria; his fellow missionaries lost contact with him and he with the board. Finally the long years of silence were broken in 1864. For three years he did not hear from the board. He declared that no missionary in Africa had suffered such privations and "been so alone as I have."

Back home the board was faced with rampant inflation and a war that collected its wages in human lives, suffering, and bitterness. In fact, J. B. Taylor did not attend the convention of 1863, which was finally held in Augusta, Georgia, 8-12 May. Plans were first made to meet in Columbus, and the location was changed because of military action, to Montgomery, Alabama. This city proved unsafe as well. Taylor had planned to leave for Augusta on 5 May, but after the Battle of Chancellorsville on Sunday, 3 May, Taylor wrote in his diary, "I did not esteem it my duty to be absent. Hundreds of wounded men are coming in, and our hospitals are filling up. I am constantly employed in visiting the wounded and the dying."[47]

It is difficult to imagine what it must have been like, for Chancellorsville represented the greatest victory of Lee's army against a Union army. The casualties of the Union were 17,000 killed, wounded, and captured. Lee's losses numbered 10,281 killed and wounded.[48] Taylor ministered to the wounded and dying of both armies who were frequently placed together in the same wards in the improvised hospitals. The convention, however, met and heard the report of the Foreign Mission Board, even in the absence of its corresponding secretary.

The report began with an expression of gratitude for the "divine goodness" of God who had wonderfully preserved the South. In an allusion to the war, (the onus of which was placed on the Union) the report declared that the South had been invaded by "powerful and fierce armies" and "yet remains before the world, a spectacle of indomitable courage, a monument of Jehovah's care and kindness."[49] The report continued, "again we meet, amid the carnage and desolations of war, to confer on interests relating to a kingdom not of this world, to kindle afresh on the missionary altar, the fires of devotion, and to encourage each other to higher, holier consecration to the Redeemer's glory."[50]

It is not surprising that Southern Baptists registered their disapproval of "the invading armies of the North" but that which was truly notable was their concentration on the missionary task. The reports from the missions were mixed. From China the Canton mission reported that "Brother Gaillard's" splendid work was brought to a halt by a typhoon that claimed the lives of an estimated 10,000 people, including that of the promising missionary. Mrs. Gaillard remained in China as a single missionary. She later married Roswell H. Graves. Regarding Graves, the report read

He had performed much labor in the practice of medicine, having in the course of a year vaccinated 415 children, and prescribed otherwise to 2,620 patients. He regarded these attentions to the sick as valuable auxiliaries to the work of teaching the people the way of salvation.[51]

Since the convention met after the Battle of Chancellorsville, there was no hint in the convention's proceedings that anyone expected other than a Confederate victory at the end of a long and distasteful war. This was the attitude generally reflected by most Southern political leaders, especially by Jefferson Davis. But after the decisive Battle of Gettysburg, it became evident that the fortunes of war had turned against the Confederacy.

In fact, after 1863 the signs were ominous. The Confederacy's financial condition worsened. The government had printed so much paper money—in fact three times as much as the "greenbacks" issued in the North—that inflation became uncontrollable.[52] Also, large amounts of counterfeit Confederate bills were printed in the North in a deliberate attempt to debase southern currency. The glut of Confederate dollars became so great that the Confederate congress passed a law on 17 February 1864, requiring an exchange of paper bills for long term bonds at 4 percent interest.[53] Consequently, the Foreign Mission Board invested around $45,000 in Confederate bonds of one kind or another for varying rates of interest, which, of course, proved worthless.[54] At the close of the war the board reported a balance of $1.78.[55]

As the war drew to a close many a Southerner, like Jefferson Davis, refused to recognize the obvious. On Sunday, 2 April 1865, Davis was sitting in his pew at St. Paul's Episcopal Church in Richmond when an usher brought him a note from General Robert E. Lee that the city must be evacuated. Seven days later Lee and his half starved army surrendered to General Ulysses S. Grant at the Appomattox Courthouse, near Lynchburg. Lee refused to continue the war on the basis of guerilla warfare, knowing in the end it meant the senseless sacrifice of many a young man. Davis, however, continued attempts to rally the troops, but failed. He was captured on 10 May at Irwinville, Georgia, and imprisoned at Fort Monroe, Virginia.

The war had lasted longer than anyone had thought possible, and its cost to the South and the nation was beyond computation. On Sunday, 2 April, J. B. Taylor preached at Ashland where he heard that Petersburg had fallen and that Richmond would likely be evacuated. The next day the rumors were confirmed. He wrote in his diary:

> About nine o'clock I took the cars for Richmond. Long before reaching the city, the dark, rolling clouds of smoke and the sound of bursting shells too fearfully told of the destruction which was going on. Upon reaching the suburbs, as the train slowly approached, we saw the blue uniform of the soldiers already posted in the fields, showing that the city had fallen. Having assisted some ladies out of the cars, I hastened home, and was happy to find all safe. But deep was my grief to find my beautiful city in flames. . . .[56]

Before the Confederate troops retreated from the city, they had torched the tobacco warehouses to keep them from falling into the hands of the federal troops. But the wind shifted, and a fourth of the city was soon engulfed in the inferno.

Reconciliation and Hope

Although Richmond had fallen and the Confederacy with it, the missionary spirit that had sustained the Foreign Mission Board and the convention throughout the war was still alive. The board was in debt approximately $10,000, and there was nothing left in the treasury with which to meet the obligations. Nevertheless, in its meeting on 7 August 1865, plans were made for raising $12,000 during the remainder of the year with the hope that this could be increased to $20,000. A Committee on Future Operations recommended that the corresponding secretary give special attention to Maryland, Kentucky, and Missouri, where federal currency had been used throughout the war.

With renewed vigor and enthusiasm,

The missionary spirit that had sustained the Foreign Mission Board and the convention throughout the war was still alive.

Taylor visited these states and attended the 1866 meeting of the Southern Baptist Convention in Russelville, Kentucky, the first held after the end of the war. Taylor also reopened correspondence with Baron Stowe of Boston. Stowe asked Taylor not to misjudge "the disposition of your Northern brethren by taking the noisy utterances of extremists as indicative of the prevailing spirit." He asked Taylor to "use your whole influence to persuade your Southern brethren not to misjudge us, as I fear many of them do. Let us '*study* the things that *make* for peace, and things whereby one may edify another.'" Stowe closed the letter: "The nearer we get to Christ, the nearer shall we come to all who resemble him."[57]

Doubtless there were many in the South, including Baptists, who harbored deep resentment against the North and allowed their bitterness to be engraved upon their hearts. Evidently this was not so of J. B. Taylor and W. C. Crane, or of R. H. Graves and Matthew T. Yates. Graves wrote Taylor: "God has granted the South to be overcome in their struggle for

[1861], a committee of Southern Baptist Convention ... declared: "Resolved, That we will pray for our enemies in the spirit of the Divine Master, who 'when He reviled, reviled not again' ..."

independence. Whatever our feelings may be, I think it is the duty of Christians to forgive their enemies."[58] Even at the outset of the war (1861), a special committee of the Southern Baptist Convention on the state of the country declared: "*Resolved*, That we will pray for our enemies in the spirit of that Divine Master, who, 'when He was reviled, reviled not again'. . . ."[59] Now Southern Baptists were called upon to do exactly that—to forgive and seek forgiveness.

The "delegates" in Russelville had a lot of catching up to do. Only then did they begin to realize how death had invaded their ranks. First, they heard from China that the A. L. Bonds, who had sailed on 3 August 1860, on the *Edwin Forest*, were never heard from again. They were also shocked to learn that J. L. Holmes, and an Episcopal missionary, stationed at Chefoo, in the Shantung Province, were murdered by Chinese rebels during the Taiping Rebellion.[60] Also, that John and Sarah Rohrer, who were appointed to serve in Japan, were lost on the same ship as the Bonds. From Africa the word came that Joseph M. Harden had died on 15 May 1864. Although he had been supporting himself, the Baltimore Committee had sent his widow some financial assistance.

For about three years Reid continued his missionary labors in Awyaw separated from his colleagues. Before going to England in hopes of recovering his health, he worked for a short period in Abeokuta. News came that B. J. Drayton, who had served as a missionary in Liberia, had drowned. During the war, James Bulluck, of Millsburg, and S. W. Britten of New Georgia had also died. The report observed that all the missionaries in

Liberia were "colored men, with more or less of qualifications for their work."[61] Unfortunately, Lott Carey, the most able man among the African-American missionaries, met an untimely death a few years after having immigrated to Liberia. The once flourishing mission in the country was reported by missionary Beverly P. Yates to be in disarray. The death of so many had taken its toll in mission operations. A civil war in Nigeria brought the missionary work to a standstill.

[R.H. Graves] felt the medical work opened doors that would otherwise have been closed to him.

In the spite of such a dismal report, there was still reason for hope, exemplified by R. H. Graves. After the death of C. W. Gaillard, Graves married Eva Gaillard. She became ill and had to be taken to Hong Kong in the hope of regaining her health. On 12 December 1864, in spite of all he and other physicians could do, she died. Graves wrote upon this occasion: "I miss her much, but would not recall her. Our season of companionship was pleasant, though short. I now look forward to the time when she will welcome me in Heaven."[62] Kate Schilling also died and the Canton mission went into mourning again. She left two children, a girl of three, and a little boy of eighteen months. J. G. Schilling was forced to leave the field in order to take his children back to the United States.

Once again Graves found himself the only Southern Baptist missionary in Canton. But the indomitable missionary reported that in 1863 and 1864 eight were baptized in Canton and seven at Shiu Hing. By 1865, he reported that twelve more were baptized in Canton and that the two churches had a total of ninety-one members. He further related a new and important development: "I have given two hours a day to the instruction of the native preachers. . . . At Shiu Hing my time has been specially given to the instruction of the native brethren."[63] In reference to his medical work he wrote, "The number of patients prescribed for during the year [1864] has been 2,160, a slight increase over last year. About one hundred children have been vaccinated; some [cysts] have been extracted, and other minor operations performed."[64]

From Graves's report it is apparent that his interest was far more in preaching and teaching than in practicing medicine. Yet he felt that the medical work opened doors that would otherwise have been closed to him. He reported having visited Uu Chau, a city in the Province of Kwang Si. "I hope, by God's help, we may soon be able to establish a station there."[65]

This was the word of hope that the convention needed to hear. In spite of wars in America, China, and Africa, and in spite of the loss of so many missionaries, the work had survived. Although the response to the gospel had been slower in China than in Africa, the missions there had fared better during the war. This was undoubtedly due to the "staying power" of three able missionaries: Matthew T. Yates, Shanghai; T. P. Crawford, Shantung; and Roswell H. Graves, Canton. Too, they concentrated their efforts on winning the Chinese, and thus saved themselves from an overwhelming preoccupation with the war back in their homeland. At Russelville, the survival of the work in China and Africa was cause for rejoicing and Southern Baptists gave God thanks.

With new hope and the financial support of Baptists in Kentucky, Maryland, and Missouri, the convention received the necessary finances without which the work possibly could not have continued. From this point the board was able to make a fresh start. By 1868 the *Home and Foreign Journal,* after being suspended during the war, resumed publication and by 1869 subscriptions numbered 4,000. Finances improved, and a new chapel was built in Canton, but the work in Africa still lagged behind. T. A. Reid could not return to Nigeria and the board was not immediately able to raise the funds for the resumption of its work in Liberia. But by 1871 all debts were paid and the board reported receiving $25,700 for the year 1870-71. Even a balance of $3,000 remained in the treasury.[66] The news brought renewed hope to the missionaries who had relied largely upon their own resources for sustaining the work in China. Chief among these was Matthew T. Yates.

Matthew T. Yates

Matthew Tyson Yates (1819-1888)

The year 1866 found Yates at mid-career in his work in Shanghai. He was easily the most prominent foreigner in the city. His mastery of the Chinese language and his work with the American Consul during the Civil War had catapulted him into a place of unique prominence.

Yates was converted at eighteen years of age during a summer revival meeting held by the Mount Pisgah Baptist Church near Raleigh, North Carolina. For some time he had been stopping daily unseen by anyone at an oak tree to pray. The burden of his prayer was that God might have mercy upon him, a sinner. After an intensely personal struggle, he committed his life to Christ and shortly after his baptism experienced a call to preach. As a farm boy his educational opportunities had been limited. Upon entering Wake Forest College he felt outclassed by his peers. What he lacked in preparation, however, he soon made up with hard work. His funds were meager but since he was a candidate for the ministry, the North Carolina Convention gave some financial assistance. He also taught singing schools to help with incidental expenses.

In the process of his studies Yates became convinced that the Lord was calling him to foreign missions. J. B. Taylor was alerted to Yates's intention to serve as a missionary and made a special trip to Wake Forest to meet him. After several interviews, Taylor wrote that he was much impressed with the college student. His call to missions also became a call to China. He wrote the corresponding secretary:

I am now resolved, and I hope that I have

been guided by the Holy Spirit—that, let others say what they may about rushing into danger, I will go wheresoever God, in His providence, may direct me. Since coming to this irrevocable conclusion my feelings and affections seem to have winged their way to China. This enterprise has swallowed up every other.[67]

Once the commitment was made, Matthew shared his vision with Eliza E. Moring, his childhood sweetheart. They were married on 27 September 1846. The Yateses arrived in Shanghai harbor on 12 September 1847, but no one was there to meet them. Since they had their own bedding, an Episcopal missionary offered to let them sleep on the floor of his living room until they could find a house to rent. Thus began their forty-two year ministry to the Chinese in the name of Christ.

Like everything he did, Yates tackled the language with tenacity and persever-

Eliza Moring Yates

ance. He studied such long hours that his eyes began to fail. Instead of despairing, he saw this development as providential, for it drove him to use his keen musical ear in acquiring a fluency in the difficult tone language. As a result, he became so fluent in Chinese that a Methodist missionary observed, "A Chinaman, if his eyes were shut, could not distinguish between Yates' talk in Chinese and that of a native." Yates had so identified with the Chinese and mastered their language with an understanding of the culture that the Chinese were accustomed to say, "Yates is no foreigner; he is a

Chinaman with his queue cut off."[68]

It would have been impossible for Yates to pretend to be Chinese, for when sixty-six years of age he still stood six feet two inches tall and weighed 244 pounds. His was a commanding presence. His own experience in learning Chinese had been so difficult since he had only a Chinese-English dictionary to work with, that he felt compelled to write a beginner's grammar, *First Lessons in Chinese,* to aid subsequent missionaries in acquiring the language.[69] For twenty-three years, the Yateses labored in Shanghai alone. Other missionaries had come and gone but they were two who had come and stayed—through the Taiping Rebellion, the Civil War in America, typhoons, the cholera epidemics, and his own recurring illnesses. When his voice failed a second time, he could not make an audible sound for forty days. A return to the States and a trip to Europe brought rest and healing. His voice was back to normal by the end of 1875.

Through the war years and for some time afterwards he had taken advantage of an opportunity to serve as an interpreter in the Chinese courts and worked with the American consul. He then invested his money in real estate without once forgetting his calling. He explained his work as an interpreter took little time and helped to provide the means by which he could sustain not only himself and his wife, but also the mission in the absence of an income

Matthew T. and Eliza Yates with daughter, Annie

from the Foreign Mission Board.

Yates used every means at his command to advance the cause of Christ, e.g., tract distribution, Bible translation, instruction of national assistants, and above all—preaching. He held to a firm conviction that the gospel alone was the power of God unto salvation. As early as 1855 he baptized "the first female member from among the multitudes of this city."[70] This was indeed a breakthrough. Women in China were segregated, and most were out of the sight and sound of men.

Yates, like most missionaries before and since, did not always agree with the policies of the Foreign Mission Board, but unlike some, he declared himself ever ready to abide by whatever policies the Richmond board determined to establish for the operation of its missions overseas. A case in point was a disagreement that arose among the missionaries in Shanghai in 1856. Some agitated for freedom "to do their own thing" without regard to the concerted action of others. Apparently these unhappy missionaries persuaded the board to consider this *laissez faire* approach as the best option for conducting missionary work in China. Yates was somewhat exasperated by this turn of events and said so. "What I desire is for the Board to adopt a policy and maintain it firmly. It will be seen that I have no selfish ends to attain by these remarks. The Board may adopt a policy which may be as much against my views as those of other people. May you have wisdom from above!"[71]

The last twenty years of Yates's ministry in China were the most fruitful and the most satisfying. Yates claimed that some other denominations were receiving members simply upon the basis of their willingness to reject idols, without giving any evidence of a personal confession of faith in Christ or of an understanding of the demands of Christian discipleship. He was convinced that such "evangelism" would produce only "rice Christians." On 24 April 1869, he wrote with evident satisfaction:

After more than twenty-one years of labor, I have reached the Chinese heart. Oh, there is joy in my little church.

My church of believers only, is attracting more and more attention. There seems to be something in the simple act of immersion that impresses the Chinese favorably. It carries with it the idea of truthfulness and stability.[72]

Yates insisted upon a membership which understood the requirements of discipleship. He set forth his convictions in four principles, the second and third of which read:

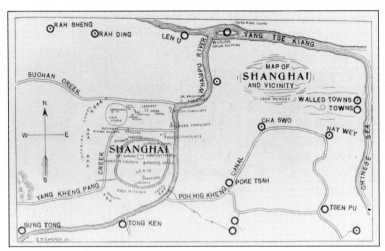

Matthew T. Yates' Shanghai

They [membership] should be taught that, when they embrace Christianity, they become the disciples of Jesus Christ, and not the disciples of the missionary. . . . As they have become the disciples of Jesus, they should become thoroughly acquainted with his teachings in the language in which they think and speak. They should be encouraged to commit to memory precious and practical portions of the New Testament in the spoken language of their particular locality.[73]

After twenty-three years in Shanghai, Yates found his audiences more receptive to the gospel than ever before, and his preaching attended by anxious "enquirers." Mystified, he asked one of the native preachers, Wong, how to explain the apparent change in the congregation. He replied: "Your preaching goes to the heart now: formerly it only went in at one ear and out at the other. You preach much better than in former years."[74]

Upon a return visit to the States, his brother invited him to make his home Matthew's home as well. He answered,

"Thank you for your kind invitation to make your house my home. I shall not stay long at any place. *My home is in China.*"[75] Indeed, it was in Shanghai in his own home that Matthew T. Yates died after suffering a second paralytic stroke—but not before he had completed translating the New Testament into Chinese. Mrs. Yates wrote on 8 April 1888: "He had to give up preaching almost altogether; but two objects occupied his mind constantly, the completion of the translation of the New Testament and a house for Mr. Bryan (a fellow missionary). Both of these he lived to see accomplished."[76] Mrs. Yates lived six years longer than her husband.

Sung Way Dong Baptist Church, Shanghai

Without the efforts of J. B. Taylor, the work of the Yateses would have been impossible. Although forced to rely upon his own efforts for financial support, Yates knew there were always back home those who cared and prayed.

Postwar Developments

Upon the death of J. B. Taylor, the President of the Foreign Mission Board, J. L. M. Curry said, "Humanly speaking, he was the soul of the work—its moving, energizing representative." The entire twenty-five years in which J. B. Taylor served as Corresponding Secretary of the Foreign Mission Board tend to bear this out and particularly the last five years. These years were marked by certain events affecting the board's life, the first of which was a change of presidents.

J. B. Jeter, who had served as President of the Foreign Mission Board from its very beginning in 1845, was succeeded by J. L. Burrows. Taylor and Jeter had worked as yokefellows in the missionary task, now he apparently felt it was time to step down.

Shift in the Board's Financial Support

Before and during the war, the board had been dependent largely upon the financial support of states of the lower South. But with the loss of income from this section of the country, Kentucky, Maryland, and Missouri became the board's major sources of income. Beginning with the meeting of the convention at Russelville in 1866, the board began to make a comeback. This first became evident in its financial status. On 1 April 1865, the board reported a balance of $20,677.73. Two days later, the treasurer reported that there were no available funds. The balance reported on 1 April was in Confederate bonds which, of course, were worthless. To reduce the debt from eight to ten thousand dollars,[77] the board looked to Kentucky, Maryland, and Missouri for help, and the churches responded. The Baptist General Association of Kentucky gave two thousand dollars in cash and pledges. Later when J. B. Taylor made more visits to the state, renewed interest in foreign missions was manifest wherever he went and additional funds were raised.

From all sources, the board reported since 3 April, that $6,630.56 had been given. The committee in Baltimore reported having sent directly to the missionaries and for other expenditures a sum of $2,794.06, making a total of funds raised from Kentucky and Missouri, and Maryland in addition to gifts from other sources a total in excess of $10,000. To be exact, $10,026.48 had been received and disbursed during the last fiscal year.

A policy of the board established in its first year of operations prohibiting missionaries from any secular employment for remuneration was suspended during the war. This was essential and flexibility became the mark of wisdom. Therefore, Matthew T. Yates and T. P. Crawford had managed to support themselves and contribute considerable amounts to the work by the income derived from their investments.[78] The same was true, to a lesser extent, of the missionaries of the board still working in Africa.

The Convention Acts

From the 1867 meeting of the Southern Baptist Convention in Memphis, Tennessee, two significant actions by the convention were to have a positive effect upon foreign missions. The convention held its first mass meeting for foreign missions, at which an offering of $4,000 was received[79] and revised its constitution again to provide for annual, rather than biennial, meetings. From 1849 to 1866 the convention voted to meet every two years, but this became impossible due to the war. After the war the convention began to meet annually and the change was made official in 1867. This meant that the

Foreign and Domestic Mission boards could keep the cause of missions before the Southern Baptist people not only at the mass meetings held during the convention but also through the reports of the Baptist state papers and the *Home and Foreign Journal.* The information conceivably would stimulate both more interest in missions and consequently more financing for missionary projects. This certainly seemed to be the case, for subscriptions to the *Journal* rose from 4,000 in 1869 to 10,000 in 1870.[80]

The possible reunion of Southern Baptists with Baptists of the North was in the minds of some. The board raised the question in order to secure feedback from its constituency. The question was addressed by the Sunday School Board in 1870, which declared that cooperation with Northern Baptists was desirable but reunion was not. The report concluded "that while fraternization with Northern Baptists is desirable, and will be sought, separate action in general denominational enterprises is a policy of true peace and surest progress."[81]

Missionaries Appointed for China, Africa, and Italy

The last years of Taylor's life were marked by frequent illnesses and sometimes prolonged periods of convalescence. In spite of these involuntary periods of rest, the pace that the corresponding secretary set for himself would have felled a man of lesser vision or determination. In those last years there were only two agents to "collect" funds for the board. Taylor, therefore, did the work of a "super agent" of the board, traveling constantly by day and sometimes at night when his health permitted. It was

Graves of Matthew T. and Eliza M. Yates

particularly gratifying to him to bring in 1871 the most encouraging report to the convention since the war.

> *Since the last annual meeting the Board have appointed the following brethren to labor as missionaries: Robert S. Prichard, to be employed temporarily at Shanghai, with the view of commencing a new mission in the interior. E. Z. Simmons and wife, assigned to the Canton Mission. M. J. Herndon, with authority to employ an associate with reference to a school, both to operate among the Bassas, in Africa.*[82]

The report continued by indicating that four, including W. M. Cote, M. D., had been appointed as Baptist missionaries in Rome. Further, under the caption of European Mission, W. M. Cote was quoted:

> *One fact is certain, Rome is now open to the Gospel. The power of the Anti-Christ has come to an end, and his spiritual power is fast decreasing. A bountiful harvest in Rome and the Provinces awaits the diligent sowers of the truth. Let the Baptists be up and doing. Let them reclaim from error and perdition the fallen descendants of the primitive Roman Church, whose faith and sufferings for the cause of Christ had earned the commendation of the Christian churches throughout the world.*[83]

107

The event to which Cote referred was the triumph of Victor Emmanuel in reuniting Italy and reducing the Papal States to 108 acres in Vatican City. Previously the Papal States had included about three million people who lived in the heart of Italy dividing the North from the South. Although the victory had not been confirmed as yet by parliament, it was a forgone conclusion. Pius IX already regarded himself a prisoner in the Vatican. Vatican Council I had been brought to a premature close, but not before approving the concept of papal infallibility in which the council declared:

> We teach and define that it is a dogma divinely revealed: that the Roman pontiff, when he speaks ex cathedra, that is, when, in discharge of the office of pastor and teacher of all Christians, by virtue of his supreme Apostolic authority, he defines a doctrine regarding faith or morals to be held by the universal Church, is, by the divine assistance promised to him in Blessed Peter, possessed of that infallibility with which the divine Redeemer willed that His Church should be endowed in defining doctrine regarding faith or morals; and that, therefore, such definitions of the Roman pontiff are of themselves, and not from the consent of the Church, irreformable.[84]

For Baptists, as for most of the Protestant world, this change in the fortunes of the Roman Catholic Church appeared providential. By the time of the Foreign Mission Board's report there was already a Baptist church organized in Rome with eighteen members. This development was particularly gratifying to the aging secretary. During the postwar years the Taylorsville church, which Taylor had served after resigning the Grace Street Church asked him

to return to the pastorate. But he declined, indicating that his work as corresponding secretary demanded all of his time. It was his custom to spend Sundays in various churches preaching and calling upon the brethren to share the gospel with a heathen world.

Found Faithful

On 30 April, a Sunday, Taylor recorded in his diary: "Preached at First Colored Church, Alexandria, from Galatians iii.22. Delivered addresses at two colored churches in the afternoon. At night preached at Second African Church, from Luke xxiv.36, 37. Quite unwell all day."[85] When C. H. Rowland, pastor of the white Baptist church in Alexandria, questioned Taylor's spending an entire day in black churches, he replied "that his visit was special—that a crisis had been reached in the African mission, and he desired to enlist the colored churches in the work."[86]

There was always manifest in Taylor's ministry a love for the African-Americans. His son George said of him and his interest in work among the Blacks, "He had, when entering the ministry, decided to remain in the South—partly, as he declared, that he might labor for the benefit of that race—and during all his pastorate[s] he had paid special attention to the colored people, while as Secretary his heart had been peculiarly enlisted in the African missions. . . ."[87]

Failing health caused Taylor to think some were critical of his continuing in the office of corresponding secretary, so he offered his resignation. But the board would not hear to it. Instead, it offered to find an assistant. Because of the board's insistence, he wrote in his diary on 24 July, "I have this day written my purpose to withdraw my letter of resignation as Corresponding Secretary of the Foreign Mission Board."[88] Although he felt his strength ebbing away, he still refused voluntarily to cease his efforts on behalf of the board and the missionaries whom it supported.

On 2 November, he wrote in his diary: "Left for Norfolk for the purpose of seeing the emigrants for Liberia, and of sending letters, etc. by the vessel for the missionaries."[89] The next day he added: "Spent the day in writing and in visiting the emigrants. It has been a busy time, and I am to-night very weary." On 15 November, he referred to the Chicago fire which caused the failure of insurance companies and banks, producing a financial crisis throughout the nation. "Our Board is feeling the pressure sorely. This necessitates more vigorous endeavors and more numerous appeals, so that I have prepared and sent off, with the assistance of my wife, more than five hundred letters."[90]

In spite of the fact that A. D. Phillips, a missionary to Africa, had been enlisted to assist him in his work, he felt it absolutely necessary to resign, and he did so on 11 December. This time the board did not ask him to reconsider, recognizing that he had given his all and that there was nothing more to give. The last eleven days he still continued to dictate answers to letters and worked on an editorial for the *Home and Foreign Journal* until Thursday, 14 December 1871. On 22 December, with his family gathered around him; he died at six o'clock in the evening.

Perhaps no better summation of the life and work of J. B. Taylor has been given than that which the President of the Foreign Mission Board, J. L. M. Curry, gave at his funeral.

Whatever of history belongs to the foreign mission-work of the Southern Baptist Convention is closely, inseparably interwoven with Brother Taylor. Humanly speaking, he was the soul of the work—its moving, energizing representative. His labors were abundant. Consummate caution and wisdom marked his counsels and actions. Body, soul, and spirit, he identified himself with the cause and the missionary. To those laboring abroad he was a brother and a father. He put his heart in closest sympathy, in loving union, with their hearts. He shared in their toils, labors, sacrifices. His prayers went up with theirs. His tears mingled with theirs. All their comforts and joys were shared equally by him. He had so allied and identified himself with labors in foreign fields that he was himself almost a foreign missionary, and certainly caught the character and spirit of Brainerd and Martyn and Boardman and Judson.[91]

Perhaps the greatest contribution that J. B. Taylor made to the cause of Christ and the work of the board was that he, with the help of J. B. Jeter, W. C. Crane, and A. M. Poindexter, held the board together and never allowed the war or denominational strife eclipse its missionary vision.

ENDNOTES

1. Taylor, *Life and Times of James B. Taylor*, 1779-81.
2. Ibid., 180.
3. Ibid., 181.
4. Ibid., 183.
5. Ibid., 34.
6. Ibid., 37.
7. Ibid., 39.
8. Ibid., 70.
9. Ibid., 72.
10. Ibid., 126.
11. Ibid., 160-61.
12. Ibid., 161.

13. Ibid., 222.

14. Ibid., 222-23.

15. Ibid., 247.

16. Ibid., 248.

17. F. Catharine Bryan, *At the Gates: Life Story of Matthew Tyson and Eliza Moring Yates of China* (Nashville: Broadman Press, 1949), 65.

18. Ibid., 21. This "Deacon Graves" was Dr. J. J. Graves who had advised the thirteen-year-old James when he and his friends were seeking to become Christians in New York City.

19. Ibid., 248.

20. Ibid., 249.

21. *Proceedings,* SBC, 1849, 44.

22. Ibid., 44-45.

23. *Proceedings,* SBC, 1855, 75-89.

24. Baker, *History of the Southern Baptist Convention and Its People,* 217.

25. Cited by ibid., 216-17.

26. Charles E. Taylor, "My Most Memorable Convention," *Religious Herald,* 8 May 1902, 2. Cited by Barnes, *Southern Baptist Convention,* 111.

27. *Proceedings,* SBC, 1859, 95-96.

28. Baker, *Southern Baptist Convention and its People,* 218, 219.

29. Ibid., 29.

30. Clement Eaton, *A History of the Southern Confederacy* (New York: The Macmillan Company, 1954), 35. While Eaton's figures may be accurate as far as Kentuckians serving in the Union army are concerned, figures for those serving with the armies of the Confederacy are probably less so. J. G. Randall, in *The Civil War and Reconstruction* (Boston: D. C. Heath and Company, 1937), 322, indicates that 75,000 Union enlistments were a matter of official record, but that in February, 1862 only 7,950 soldiers from Kentucky were serving with the Confederacy and Confederate recruiting efforts in Kentucky declined after this.

31. Eaton, *A History of the Southern Confederacy,* 31.

32. Taylor, *Life and Times of James B. Taylor,* 260.

33. Ibid.

34. T. J. Bowen had written the first grammar of the Yoruba language which was published by the Smithsonian Institute.

35. Winston Crawley in his *Partners Across the Pacific* (Nashville: Broadman Press, 1986), 44, prefers the term "East China" to "Central China" and explains why:

The second area of Southern Baptist mission work in China was based In the city of Shanghai. That area came to be known as the Central China field (and it is so named in all Foreign Mission Board reports). At the time the work began, only coastal areas were open to missionaries, and Shanghai is located in the central part of the China coast. However, the area is actually more properly understood as East China.

36. The eighteen missionaries in Liberia were African-Americans as was J. M. Harden who transferred from Liberia to Lagos.

37. Minutes, FMB, 2 December 1862. Cited by Jesse Fletcher in "A History of the Foreign Mission Board of the Southern Baptist Convention During the Civil War," *Baptist History and Heritage* X, no. 4 (October 1975): 209.

38. Ibid.

39. See ibid., 214, for a fuller account of the financial crisis of the latter years of the war.

40. Charles E. Taylor, *The Story of Yates the Missionary* (Nashville: Sunday School Board of the Southern Baptist Convention, 1898), 144.

41. Ibid., 145. The letter from which this quotation is taken was written on the next day, 21 March 1861.

42. Cited by Fletcher, "A History of the Foreign Mission Board," 206.

43. Ibid.

44. Ibid., 207.

45. Graves's Letters, Letter to Franklin Wilson, 10 May 1865, cited in ibid., 218.

46. Taylor, *Story of Yates the Missionary,* 161.

47. Taylor, *Life and Times of James B. Taylor,* 265. The Battle of Chancellorsville took place from 1 May to 5 May. See Randall, *The Civil War and Reconstruction,* 513, 514.

48. Eaton, *A History of the Southern Confederacy,* 197.

49. *Proceedings,* SBC, 1863, 22.

50. Ibid.

51. Ibid., 25.

52. Eaton, *A History of the Southern Confederacy,* 238.

53. Ibid.

54. See Fletcher, "A History of the Foreign Mission Board," for details of the disbursement of funds in the years 1863 and 1864, 214-15.

55. Minutes, FMB, 27 December 1865.

56. Taylor, *Life and Times of James B. Taylor,* 269.

57. Ibid., 274-75.

58. Graves's Letters, letter to J. B. Taylor, 10 May 1865, cited by Fletcher in "A History of the Foreign Mission Board," 218.

59. *Proceedings,* SBC, 1861, 63.

60. *Proceedings,* SBC, 1863, 26-27.

61. *Proceedings,* SBC, 1866, 65.

62. Ibid., 59.

63. Ibid., 60.

64. Ibid.

65. Ibid.

66. *Proceedings,* SBC, 1871, 37.

67. Taylor, *Story of Yates the Missionary,* 34-35.

68. Ibid., 55.

69. Ibid., 53.

70. Ibid., 108.

71. This is from a letter dated 30 July 1857, cited in ibid., 116.

72. Cited by ibid., 162.

73. Ibid., 160.

74. Ibid., 162.

75. From a letter written from Syracuse, New York, on 1 August 1870, cited in ibid., 170.

76. From a letter of Mrs. Yates given in full in ibid., 294.

77. Both figures are given. The board reported in 1866 that the indebtedness amounted to "about $8,000." *Proceedings,* SBC, 1866, 57. In 1868 the indebtedness was reported to amount to "about $10,000," of which $2,000 had already been paid.

78. Yates not only contributed generously to the work in China but also donated sizeable sums to Wake Forest College, Richmond College, and Southern Seminary.

79. *Proceedings,* SBC, 1867, 20.

80. *Proceedings,* SBC, 1870, 2.

81. Ibid., 35-36.

82. *Proceedings,* SBC, 1871, 40.

83. Ibid., 48-49.

84. Anne Fremantle, *The Papal Encyclicals in their Historical Context* (New York: Mentor-Omega Books, 1963), 27.

85. Taylor, *Life and Times of James B. Taylor,* 291.

86. Ibid.

87. Ibid.

88. Ibid., 294.

89. Ibid., 295.

90. Ibid.

91. Ibid., 302.

The Dawn of a New Era, 1872-1893

H. A. Tupper

Lottie Moon

The contrast in backgrounds between the Foreign Mission Board's first and second corresponding secretaries, J. B. Taylor and H. A. Tupper, could hardly have been greater. Taylor's formal education was meager as were his finances. In contrast, Tupper was both well educated and a man of means. It was he who tactfully sought the support of women in the board's work and made possible their services as single missionaries. He paved the way and encouraged the formation of Woman's Missionary Union.

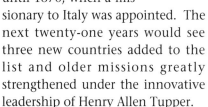

For twenty-five years, James B. Taylor had guided the fortunes of the Foreign Mission Board from its feeble beginnings through the painful years of the Civil War into a new day of promise and renewed hope. Due to the Civil War, no new countries were entered until 1870, when a missionary to Italy was appointed. The next twenty-one years would see three new countries added to the list and older missions greatly strengthened under the innovative leadership of Henry Allen Tupper.

The new corresponding secretary brought with him, in addition to superb preparation for such a demanding task, a long-standing commitment to missions, home and foreign. He took a fresh look at the board's organization and its always precarious financial condition. New approaches were attempted and committees for mission support were established in each state. His bold yet tactful support of the involvement of women in missions led to a giant step in Southern Baptist missionary support.

In addition to the marked achievements of this period, the board was faced with an increasing number of problems. The failure of missionaries to measure up to the demands of their calling coupled with theological deviation proved among the most vexing. The Taiping Rebellion in China and civil war in Nigeria interrupted the work in both countries. The indebtedness of the Foreign Mission Board took its own toll in frustration and anxiety on the missionaries as well as on Tupper and his colleagues on the board.

The personal conflicts in which Tupper and the board found themselves with I. T. Tichenor of the Home Mission Board and Annie Armstrong of the Woman's Missionary Union involved principles regarding a division of missionary work and its support that he would not abandon for the sake of a truce or "peace at any price."

Even though Tupper desired a closer working relationship with the American Baptist Missionary Union, he was not prepared for reunion with Northern Baptists. During this period, however, the board's ties with other denominations were quietly strengthened.

The problem of T. P. Crawford and the Gospel Mission movement in China proved as exasperating as his friendship with Charlotte Diggs Moon was satisfying. With both Crawford and Moon, Tupper exemplified both patience and understanding. Through it all, the relationship of Tupper with Lottie Moon and with Armstrong proved a manifold blessing to the cause of Christ in China and around the world.

Issac T. Tichenor

Henry Allen Tupper, 1828-1902

The contrast between James B. Taylor and H. A. Tupper as far as personal backgrounds are concerned could hardly have been greater. Taylor was the son of an artisan, a cabinetmaker, Tupper, the son of a wealthy businessman. Taylor, born to poverty, was largely self-taught with no formal education beyond elementary school, while Tupper had the advantages that wealth affords, including the finest theological education available in the United States. Yet both were uniquely fitted for the challenges that demanded their best.

H. A. Tupper's family was one of the most prominent in Charleston, South Carolina, and his parents were long-time members of the historic First Baptist Church. Although reared by devout parents, prominent in the life of the congregation, Henry, who first came under conviction at age nine, at eighteen resisted the gospel and every attempt to win him to Christ. Hence during his years as a student in Charleston College, he was known for his skepticism and love of pleasure, not piety. Through the efforts of Richard Fuller, who was conducting a six weeks' evangelistic crusade, the teenager's stubborn resistance was broken down and with the help of *The Anxious Inquirer,* a book which Fuller had loaned him, he was soundly converted.

The night Tupper was baptized (17 April 1846), Fuller announced, "This young man wants to go to Africa, but we need him at home."[1] The truth of the matter was that the new convert was besieged by doubts prompted, so he thought, by his refusal to enter the ministry, to which he had been called. Once the decision was made, he was off with his friend, James P. Boyce, to Hamilton, New York, to enter the theological department of Madison University (Colgate).

Shortly after his graduation from the university with his Bachelor and Master of Arts degrees, he married Nannie Johnstone Boyce, the sister of his friend James P. Boyce. Nannie and Henry had known each other since childhood. Her father, Ker Boyce, was reported to have been the wealthiest man in South Carolina, but he was not a professing Christian. It was with the Boyce family that the young couple made their home, which enabled Henry to serve in his first pastorate in Graniteville, South Carolina, without remuneration.

In 1853, Tupper was called to the First Baptist Church of Washington, Georgia, which he continued to serve until elected corresponding secretary of the Foreign Mission Board in February 1872. While in Washington, he won the respect and appreciation of the entire city. Of this idyllic situation, he wrote: "Between the denominations the utmost cordiality prevailed. . . . The whole community became a spiritual family. . . . No man could be more perfectly identified with a place than I was with 'dear old Washington.'"[2] In fact he was so loved by his congregation that when he attempted to resign in order to accept a chaplain's commission in the Confederate Army, the church refused to accept his resignation.

Annie Armstrong

As satisfying as was his pastorate in Washington, he felt there was still something lacking. Tupper longed to be a missionary and in a certain sense, he was. In fact he wrote James B. Taylor, "You know that I am now a missionary as well as a pastor. Preaching regularly . . . to the negroes on the surrounding plantations."[3] "Before the War," he reported, "I preached every Sunday and Tuesday night to the colored people and had appointments on the plantations in the vicinity. This was service in which my heart rejoiced. . . . I had a large colored membership and many of them devoted Christians."[4]

Tupper also led his church to give more generously to missions than did any other Baptist church in Georgia. He admitted that the amount of the church's financial involvement appeared greater than it actually was because he gave personally an amount sufficient for the support of two missionaries, one to the Indians and the other for a missionary couple in Africa. Yet, he said, "The monthly Concert of Prayer for the salvation of the world was regularly kept up. . . . The church was thoroughly indoctrinated on the subject of missions, as their large contributions indicated."[5]

It was Tupper who led the Georgia Baptist Association to establish an Executive Committee on Missions of which he became chairman. Even this involvement with the missionary efforts of the denomination did not satisfy his desire to serve as a foreign missionary. At last he came up with a proposal to establish "a sustaining colony" in Japan. He made two visits to Richmond to discuss his plan with Taylor and even corresponded with the State Department. He proposed endowing the colony with $250,000, but the Civil War derailed this grandiose scheme.[6]

Like so many of his peers, Tupper identified with his native South Carolina when the break with the Union came and immediately volunteered his services as a chaplain. Although his involvement in the Confederate cause earned him the nickname "The Fighting Parson," he never carried a weapon. He received his commission to serve without remuneration as a chaplain with the Ninth Georgia Regiment Volunteers. When he heard that the Morris Street Baptist Church, Charleston, had been converted into a silver factory, he was horrified and promptly bought it "for my

Master." He turned the former church building into a "Soldiers' Chapel" and proceeded to minister to the spiritual needs of the war-weary troops. Of this experience he wrote: "[I] had the happiness of preaching to my old regiment, the 9th Georgia stationed at James Island. The meeting with those war-worn men was delightful. Their religious condition is most gratifying. Fifty have been converted. Some [are] waiting now for baptism."[7]

Tupper's ministry was undergirded by an unshakable faith.

Although Tupper's military service lasted only a few months, from June 1861 to January 1862, his concern for Confederate soldiers continued throughout the conflict. He bought the Goodlett Hotel in Greenville, South Carolina, to be used as a refuge for the soldiers. After the war it was given to The Southern Baptist Theological Seminary.[8] What Tupper and other ardent patriots of the Confederacy never dreamed would happen, did. With dramatic finality, the reality of the defeat was engraved upon Tupper's memory when Jefferson Davis and his entourage arrived in Washington, Georgia, on 3 May 1865. The next day Davis and his cabinet met for the last time in the local bank. At 10:00 A. M., Davis spoke to Tupper in the town square and repeated the words of Job, "Though He slay me, yet will I trust Him."[9] He then mounted his horse and rode away.

Tupper, like Davis, had never expected the fall of the Confederacy, but unlike Davis, there was a cause far greater than the political fortunes of the South to which he had pledged his supreme allegiance long before. To this cause he would give most of his waking hours during the next twenty-one years.

The church that had refused to release its pastor twice before, now reluctantly did so, recognizing his election to the office of corresponding secretary was in Tupper's mind a missionary call he could not resist. For Tupper, it was what God had been preparing him for all his life, and for the Foreign Mission Board, he was, indeed, God's choice. J. L. Burrows, president of the board, presented three names to the committee without indicating a preference. H. A. Tupper was elected corresponding secretary on the first ballot by a unanimous vote.[10] His salary was set at $2,000 a year.

Before Tupper had a chance to respond, the *Religious Herald* of 25 January 1872 published a profile of the successor of James B. Taylor, as envisioned by the "search" committee. No more succinct description of Tupper's qualifications could have been devised:

> Its incumbent should be pious, an earnest friend of foreign missions, of popular, at least respectable speaking talents, discreet, industrious, of business habits, of financiering skill, acquainted with the world, of enlarged views, free from objections in all sections and among all parties; in short fitted to be a wise counsellor of the Board, and to make a favorable impression everywhere in behalf of foreign missions.[11]

Three days later, Tupper accepted the call to the Foreign Mission Board as from the Lord and informed the church of his decision on 1 February. On his last Sunday as pastor of First Church, the other churches of the city canceled their services in order to hear his last sermon. All met together again in the evening at the Methodist church for a farewell service in his honor.

A few days later the new secretary arrived in Richmond. In his first meeting with the board, Tupper responded to the president's greetings: "I have come because you called me, and I shall do all I can for the cause of missions."[12] On Sunday evening 25 February at the "designation" service held in the Second Baptist Church, Jeremiah Jeter announced: "We have called you to think for us."[13] It was evident to those present that Tupper had already given considerable thought to his new assignment. This would become increasingly evident within the following months.

Among the assets Tupper brought with him to Richmond were two of immeasurable value—his wife and his faith. Nannie Boyce Tupper was a remarkable woman. Even before her marriage she had distinguished herself by a selfless spirit in serving others. From the beginning of her married life, Nannie Tupper was completely supportive of her husband's ministry. She also was the mother of twelve children, two of whom died in infancy. Upon the family's arrival in the city, she became involved in the life of the First Baptist Church, serving as president of the Female Missionary Society, chair of the Mite Box Committee (a cause dear to the heart of her husband), and vice president of the Woman's Missionary Society of Richmond. In spite of such demanding roles, she found time to create a gracious home in which her husband and children

delighted. Upon the death of his wife in 1888, Tupper wrote: "How changed all of life! October 12th, at 2 A. M., the noblest woman of earth went into sleep. . . ."[14]

Tupper's ministry was undergirded by an unshakable faith. Characteristic of the First Church, Charleston, it was a blend of Calvinism and Baptist ecclesiology motivated by a thorough-going missionary vision. This much was evident in an article he wrote for the *Alabama Baptist* titled "Be Not Deceived." In the article, designed to raise the consciousness of Baptists regarding the board's financial obligations, he listed five points in which his readers should not be deceived. By the fifth point, he admonished:

> *Be not deceived in supposing that, though God works within his people to will and to do of his own good pleasure, their salvation or the salvation of the world can not be accomplished without his people working it out with fear and trembling, and with no little self-denial.*[15]

Getting Organized

Tupper was an organized person. This was evident in his personal affairs, his studies, and the life of the Foreign Mission Board during his administration. Shortly after arriving in Richmond, he found a house that appeared suitable for his large family and bought it. About the same time he purchased for his family what he called a "long home" (a lot in Hollywood Cemetery).[16] By this gesture, he was making a statement about tenure. He had come to stay. Upon the arrival of his family in June, his wife and children joined him in uniting with the First Baptist Church. Almost immediately he began to teach (lecture) in the church's

Sunday School, which he did regularly except for interruptions due to his travels and his nemesis--hay fever.

A. D. Phillips, a missionary home from Africa, had been called to assist Taylor during his last illness. Therefore, from Taylor's death to Tupper's arrival, Phillips served as the interim corresponding secretary. Tupper was indeed fortunate to have his services and the counsel of Jeremiah Bell Jeter, pastor of First Church (1836-1849) and president of the Foreign Mission Board, during those first few months. In May, Phillips became an agent of the board, leaving Tupper the board's only full-time staff member. Discussion of moving the mission rooms from First Church began during Tupper's first meeting with the board, apparently at his initiative. On 6 June 1872 the board voted to rent meeting rooms over the store of J. T. Ellyson, a Baptist layman, for $300 a month.

In June the managers (trustees) of the board were organized into committees on China, Africa, Europe, New Fields, Agencies, and Publications. By the following year the committee on New Fields became the Committee on New Missions and Missionaries, reflecting enlarged responsibilities. A Committee on Finances also was added to the roster of committees. This structure allowed the board to expand its committees and change assignment as new developments demanded.

In the *Home and Foreign Journal*, Tupper took a broader look in attempting to formulate a plan for the support of foreign missions that would enlist Baptists in every church and every state convention. He called for each state association or convention to establish a missions committee in cooperation with the Foreign Mission Board. The article went on to make specific suggestions regarding ways in which state committees could assist local churches in promoting missions, for example, by: "1. Circulating the *Home and Foreign Journal.* 2. Establishing and fostering the monthly concert of prayer for missions." Of the three other suggestions, the most significant was the fifth.

> Encouraging "Woman's Mission to Woman," and distributing "Mite Boxes," with the plan of using them, throughout the churches and Sabbath-schools, collecting funds, and advancing the interest of the work by such other agencies and instrumentalities as may be deemed expedient, in consultation with the Richmond Board.[17]

It was evident that Tupper was already beginning to emphasize elements of his plan for a more effective involvement of the whole convention and its churches in foreign missions. Information, adequate financing, and the involvement of women in every aspect of the work were indispensable in his mind for the future of the Southern Baptist foreign mission effort. All would be coordinated by the Foreign Mission Board in cooperation with the Central Committee of each state. Tupper's "cherished plan," however, would not be fully implemented until another fifteen years when the Woman's Missionary Union was organized.[18]

The Role of Women in Missions

When the Foreign Mission Board appointed Harriet Baker to China on 5 March 1849, it took a bold step. A missionary career for a single unmarried woman was unadvisable in the eyes of many. Women in American society were generally, like children, to be seen but not heard. Consigned to domestic life, they may have had a voice but certainly no vote. The woman's suffrage movement had existed only in the minds of some free spirits like that of Abigail Adams.

Lottie Moon

The first national meeting "to discuss the social, civil, and religious rights of women" was held in Seneca Falls, New York, the year before Harriet sailed for China. This meeting marked the beginning of the woman's suffrage movement. But there was no national organization until 1869, when the American Woman's Suffrage Association broke with the Equal Rights Association. It would be another sixty-one years before women would win the right to vote in the United States.[19]

In the light of the national climate and particularly of that within the Southern Baptist Convention, with its strong Landmark element, it is not surprising that the board decided not to appoint single women as missionaries. Harriet Baker's brief career only served to confirm the board's opinion that single women were not suited for foreign missionary service.

If Tupper had not determined to change the board's policy before becoming the corresponding secretary, it soon became evident that this was his intention. Lula Whilden offered herself for missionary service to China. Her sister and brother-in-law, Nicholas B. and Jumille Williams were also candidates for China. This meant that if the board appointed all three few could object to Lula's appointment since she would have the support and protection of her brother-in-law.

Edmonia Moon, a younger sister to the more famous, Charlotte (Lottie), also determined to apply for appointment to China. She, like all the Moon sisters, broke the mold of a demure Southern belle of the Old South. Intelligent and gifted, she received her formal education at the Richmond Female Institute. She was appointed on 9 April 1872 without appearing before the board. Since the board's funds were depleted at the time, she proposed supporting herself. This situation provided Tupper the perfect opportunity to challenge the Baptist women of Richmond to raise Edmonia's salary. The able Mrs. Jeremiah Bell Jeter led the women of several societies to form the Richmond Missionary Society for the purpose of supporting Edmonia with their prayers and offerings.

The following year Charlotte Diggs Moon, inspired by Edmonia's letters and the preaching of her pastor in Cartersville, Georgia, offered herself for missionary service. Almost immediately the women of the Cartersville Baptist Church and the First Baptist Church of Washington, with prompting from Tupper, undertook Lottie's support. The pattern was beginning to take shape: woman's missionary societies in South Carolina, Georgia, and Virginia were bonded with single missionaries. Women were soon on the field as they felt called of God, supported by equally dedicated women in the States. The work was coordinated by the Foreign Mission Board.

Even before 1872, the Baptist women of Baltimore, Maryland under the leadership of Ann Jane Graves, the mother of Roswell H. Graves, missionary in Canton, China, formed a society under the name of Woman's Mission to Woman in 1871. The name was chosen on the basis that no one could object to women missionaries who were appointed to work with heathen women. In China the women were segregated to the extent that they were forbidden to have any social contacts with men outside their own families. The pioneer missionaries in China welcomed women to work with women and conduct girls' schools. Besides, Sallie Little Holmes, the widow of the martyred missionary, James Landrum Holmes, had stayed on in China since his death in 1858 to labor among the Chinese with remarkable effec-

... the corresponding secretary... realized... that the women were providing the leadership and the finances for an ever expanding missionary movement.

tiveness. This was exactly the kind of missionary that the Woman's Mission to Woman was designed to support. Its stated purpose was "to give light to the women that sit in darkness because of Bible destitution, by taking the gospel of Christ in their homes, through the agency of native Bible women, aided and superintended by their Christian sisters from Bible lands."[20]

The work in Baltimore was just the spark the woman's missionary society movement among Southern Baptists needed. A few women from Society Hill, South Carolina visited Baltimore where they witnessed a designation service in which missionaries had been set apart. They promptly organized a Woman's Mission to Woman Society of which Ellen Edwards, J. B. Hartwell's sister, became president. The Foreign Mission Board asked Tupper to do all he could to multiply such societies and to inform the "Woman's Missionary Society of Baltimore" that the Board heartily approved of its objects.[21]

The causes which the Woman's Missionary Societies supported began to broaden from missionaries to buildings for schools and chapels; in so doing the movement gained momentum and added support. No one could have been more encouraging than the corresponding secretary, for he realized, perhaps more than any one else, that the women were providing the leadership and the finances for an ever expanding missionary movement. Tupper commended the women publicly and wrote numerous personal letters expressing his sincere appreciation for and encouragement in their work.

Tupper well knew that he had a selling

job on his hands if the Southern Baptist Convention were going to support the more aggressive role of women in missions. In making his first annual report to the convention in 1872, he addressed "for the first time in the Convention's history the role of women."[22] After reporting on the missionaries who were then on the high seas, including Lula Whilden, and the appointment of Edmonia Moon, under the caption of "Bible-Women," Tupper told the convention:

> The necessity of Christian women to carry the word of God as men cannot do it, to the women of heathen lands, is increasingly felt. Women societies are organizing to support Bible-women at our Missionary stations. God helping them, our sisters, on the way, will do good work. The sisterhood of our Southern Zion should be aroused to the grand mission of redeeming their sister-woman from the degrading and destroying thraldom of Paganism.[23]

With the Foreign Mission Board's financial backing and Tupper's personal involvement, the 1878 meeting of the Southern Baptist Convention approved a report of a Committee on Woman's Work that recommended the boards organize Central Committees of women in every state. The purpose of the Central Committees, as projected by the committee, was to foster the organization of "Missionary Societies, and by the circulation of periodicals and other means to cultivate the missionary spirit." The committee went on to clarify the relation of the Central Committees with the State Conventions and the Southern Baptist Convention. "These Societies should be auxiliary to the State Conventions, or to the Southern Baptist Convention."[24]

After ten more years of vigorous growth

in the number of societies and corresponding missionary enthusiasm, it became apparent that the women were moving toward a convention-wide organization of some kind. Before this could happen, they attempted to allay fears on the part of some within the convention that the women were attempting to set up their own mission program in competition with that of the Southern Baptist Convention. Apprehension mounted after the 1883 meeting of the convention

Broad Street Methodist Church, Richmond, Virginia

in Waco, Texas, where the women met separately in the largest gathering of Southern Baptist women to date. In their second annual meeting, the women passed a series of resolutions. They were presented to the 1885 meeting of the convention by N. A. Bailey of Florida. The second resolution read: "*Resolved 2.* That we desire to prosecute our work directly through the churches, and to have representation in the S. B. C., through our respective State Conventions, as heretofore."[25]

Apparently successful in clarifying their objectives with most men, though not all, plans were made at Louisville in 1887 during the women's annual meeting for representatives of each state Central Committee to meet the following year in Richmond for forming a national executive committee with appropriate officers. A minor problem emerged. Since Virginia had never formed a Central Committee and was to be the host state, how could this rather embarrassing situation be handled? As Robert Alton James observed, Tupper personally intervened: "Tupper again affected the first meeting by persuading Mrs. Theodore Whitfield, wife of the pastor of Fulton Church, Richmond, to serve as hostess for the sessions."[26]

While the Southern Baptist Convention was meeting in the First Baptist Church of Richmond, the women met in the Broad Street Methodist Church. Present were duly elected delegates from twelve Central Committees and representatives from three other states. On 11 May 1888, the Executive Committee of the Woman's Missionary Union (Auxiliary to the Southern Baptist Convention) was formally organized. Annie Armstrong, who had emerged as the most forceful leader of the Southern Baptist woman's missionary movement, was elected corresponding secretary and Martha McIntosh of South Carolina, president. The women once again made their intentions clear. They did not intend to administer funds, only raise them, nor appoint missionaries, only inform the churches about them and pray for them. In short, they envisioned their role as solely educational and supportive.[27]

A part of the purpose of the new national organization stated: "To secure the earnest systematic co-operation of women and children in collecting and raising money for missions."[28] This aspect of the missionary society movement had been

Lottie Moon with fellow missionaries Ella Jeter, left, and Jessie Pettigrew

foremost in Lottie Moon's mind for some time. She and her sister Edmonia knew by experience the importance of the financial support of the societies of Richmond, as well as Cartersville and Washington, Georgia. In September 1887, Lottie wrote Tupper that the women needed a better organization and suggested that an offering for missions should be taken during the Christmas season. (Methodist women were already doing this very thing.) Another letter from the lonely missionary of P'ingtu, dated 24 May 1888, spelled out the urgent need for more women missionaries. Tupper sent the letter on to Armstrong with the suggestion that "your Executive Committee might give special attention to this matter, until it should be accomplished. What do you think?"[29]

Armstrong liked the idea and so did the

Executive Committee. Lottie had requested two additional women missionaries and prayer. The appeal was made and sent out in time for a Christmas offering to be taken in the churches. A total of $3,315.26 was raised at the cost of $72.82 to the Foreign Mission Board. This was the beginning of what was to become the Lottie Moon Offering for Foreign Missions and a token of greater things to come.

With the organization of the Woman's Missionary Union, Southern Baptist women had found a way in which their energies and talents could be used to advance the cause of missions among Southern Baptists. The denomination would be immeasurably strengthened thereby. If Tupper had done nothing other than to foster the growth and development of the Woman's Missionary Union, it would be enough to mark his administration as the dawn of a new era in the Southern Baptist missionary expansion. For evidence of this fact one needs to look no further than the financial record.[30]

New Fields and Missions

No new field had captured the imagination of Southern Baptists as did Italy. With the unification of Italy under Victor Emmanuel and the reduction of the Papal States to 108 acres in Rome, Protestants around the world rejoiced. Within the same year (1870) Southern Baptists learned that an independent Baptist missionary, working in Rome, desired appointment under the Foreign Mission Board. Without careful investigation, which would have proved time-consuming, William N. Cote was accepted and placed on salary. Almost immediately the euphoria Baptists felt with

these developments was cut short by internal problems within the Italian mission. It became evident that if the mission were going to be saved from dissolution and a golden opportunity lost, a capable missionary must be sent to Rome. In the absence of a volunteer, the board appointed W. H. Whitsitt, who had recently been elected to the faculty of the Southern Baptist Theological Seminary, but he declined appointment.

While the board was pondering its next step, it asked J. B. Jeter, who was in England in an attempt to raise funds for the Italian mission, to make a fact-finding trip to Rome. In response to Jeter's recommendation, J. B. Gioja, an Italian evangelist in the employment of the board, was dismissed. Further the board registered its opinion.

It is the conviction of the Board that for Dr. Cote's sake, as well as for the future peace and best interest of our Italian mission, bro. Cote should be counselled to withdraw from the mission and service of the Board as the simplest solution of the perplexed and endangered state of our church in Rome.[31]

When Whitsitt declined his appointment, the board proceeded to elect George B. Taylor, a son of James B. Taylor, who accepted the appointment and requested the immediate return of Jeter for a briefing on the Italian situation. Whereupon Tupper wired Jeter the request (the first time the minutes record the use of wireless communication). Upon arriving on the field, Taylor asked the board to restore Cote to his former missionary status but when the board declined to do so, Taylor employed him as an evangelist of the mission. It seems to have worked out well for both Cote and the mission for in spite of an inhospitable climate and the difficulty of finding suitable places for worship, a strong church developed. Taylor wrote the board that a house had finally been purchased and renovated. Dedication services were held on 2-3 November 1878 with all evangelical missionaries and evangelists, working in Italy, in attendance.

Due to the shortfall in anticipated offerings from Northern Baptists as well as the estimated income from Southern Baptists for the chapel in Rome, the board asked Taylor to return home to conduct a fundraising campaign on behalf of the project. He complied but soon returned to the field, where he served faithfully until the death of his wife, Susan Spottswood Taylor, in 1884. After another short stay in the States, Taylor returned to Italy where he continued his missionary labors until 1907.

Mexico

The first new country Southern Baptists entered during Tupper's tenure was Mexico. A number of new fields came under consideration. Some recommendations came from young missionary volunteers eager to be a part of the action. Prussia, Brazil, Argentina, Cuba, and Mexico were among the candidates. Mexico was chosen, in part because the financial support was pledged by Texas Baptist Convention and in part because a courageous Baptist missionary was already on the field. Tupper kept a sharp eye on the financial status of the board. He was a trained accountant. For two years he had served in this capacity in his father's business enterprises. He well knew how soon the board could lose credibility, if its obliga-

tions outran its income. Therefore, regardless of the urgency of the call, he was resolved no country would be entered unless the board had the means to open and sustain the work.

Although Southern Baptists had been asked to initiate work in Mexico as early as 1875 the board did not think it feasible at the time. Besides, the American Baptist Home Mission Society was still supporting missionaries and a few small churches, but withdrew in 1876. Finally, in cooperation with Texas Baptists, the board agreed to appoint John O. Westrup, a missionary who had been laboring in Mexico for ten years. He was appointed on 5 April 1880. Two months later near Progreso, Mexico, Westrup and his traveling companion, Basilio Flores, were assassinated by unknown assailants said to have been Indians from New Mexico.[32]

The death of Westrup was a tragic blow but not a fatal one for the Baptist witness in Mexico. A few struggling, little churches survived with national pastors. Thomas M. Westrup, an older brother of the martyred missionary, was appointed to take his brother's place but a few months later transferred to the American Baptist Home Mission Society, which had decided to re-enter Mexico.

Shortly after the death of his brother, Thomas Westrup baptized William M. Flournoy, from Alabama, who was living in Laredo at the time. Shortly afterwards, he was married and ordained to the gospel ministry. Westrup had so laid the burden of Mexico on his heart, that Flournoy and his bride moved to Progreso, near the very site of John Westrup's murder, in order to begin their missionary careers. Texas Baptists undertook their support. Within the year (1881) the Flournoys were appointed by the Foreign Mission Board to serve in Mexico. Thus they became the first Southern Baptist Missionaries to Mexico from the United States and provided a living link between the Westrup brothers and Southern Baptists.[33]

Although the Flournoys returned to Laredo, giving up the work after approximately six years, W. D. Powell, a recent graduate of The Southern Baptist Theological Seminary and a man of culture and unusual ability, took up his mantle. Powell had served over four years as the "general field man" of the Sunday School and Colportage Convention of Texas. After a reconnaissance trip to Mexico on behalf of the Texas Baptist Convention, he felt an irresistible call to Mexico. His work in Texas had been marked by boundless enthusiasm and remarkable results. He organized hundreds of Sunday Schools and traveled thousands of miles, preaching as he went. He and his wife, Mary Florence Mayberry Powell were appointed by the board in July 1882. The State of Coahuila was unusually receptive to the gospel as presented by the Powells. Within three months, the two earnest young missionaries had

organized a church in Saltillo, established a school, formed an association of churches, and launched a Baptist paper. Subsequently, Saltillo was to become the site of the Madero Institute and the center of Baptist work in the state. John Westrup, who had first sown the seed in the State of Coahuila, had not labored, nor had he died, in vain.[34]

Brazil

Thomas J. Bowen, missionary to Nigeria, attempted to establish a church in Brazil as early as 1859-1861 but without success. After the Civil War some disillusioned Southerners who had emigrated to Brazil called upon Southern Baptists to adopt work

Brazil

already established as a mission of the Foreign Mission Board. It was then that the decision was made to enter Brazil.

Disheartened citizens of a variety of denominations who refused to be reconciled to the postwar state of affairs in the South began to arrive in Brazil in 1866. Although Brazil, originally a colony of Portugal and nominally Roman Catholic, opened its doors to Protestant immigrants from the United States, Emperor Dom Juan VI had previously welcomed English and German immigrants promising them religious toleration. Dom Pedro II, emperor at the time the southerners arrived in Brazil, followed the same policy. As a result, several colonies of North Americans were established, but that of Santa Barbara, in the state of Sao Paulo, proved the most prosperous. It was here that the first Baptist church organized in Brazil was constituted on 10 September 1871. In October of the following year, the congregation asked the Foreign Mission Board to accept the church as a mission of the board with no financial obligations. Subsequently, a member of the church by the name of E. H. Quillen was appointed a missionary in 1879.

The major promoter of the southern colonization movement was a former Confederate general by the name of A. T. Hawthorne. He visited Brazil in the interest

William Buck and Anne Luther Bagby

of locating the best sites for future colonies. He returned to the United States in hopes of recruiting others to join those already in Brazil but was interrupted by the death of his only daughter. In his grief, he turned to God for the first time in his life and under the influence of the able Texas lawyer-turned-evangelist, William Penn, Hawthorne experienced a profound conversion. Shortly afterwards, the former Confederate general was ordained to the ministry. Although he longed to return to Brazil as a missionary, he reluctantly gave up the idea since he was fifty years old. Instead, he determined to lay the cause of Brazil upon the consciences of Southern Baptists.

Texas became the center of Hawthorne's activities. As a result of his efforts, the W. B. Bagbys and the Z. C. Taylors heeded the call to Brazil. Altogether, some fifteen missionaries to Brazil were enlisted by this self-appointed "personnel secretary" of the Foreign Mission Board. Hawthorne's impassioned pleas before the churches and conventions led to his appointment as chairman of the Committee on South American Missions, which gave its report at the 1880 meeting of the Southern Baptist Convention in Lexington, Kentucky.

The committee report naturally reflected Hawthorne's convictions when it recommended that Southern Baptists expand its missionary force in Brazil. Speaking for the committee, he argued that the government was "stable" and "wisely administered" amply affording "security to life, liberty, and property." In addition Hawthorne emphasized that the people were favorably inclined toward North Americans and he believed that they would be receptive to the gospel. As a further inducement, he gave a "chamber of commerce" report on the beauty of the country and its healthy climate. Above all, he pleaded, that "God, by His overruling Providence, has specially prepared that country and those generous people for the evangelizing armies of our denomination, and especially for the Baptists of the South."[35]

The convention adopted the report and proceeded to appoint William Buck Bagby and Anne Luther Bagby to Brazil. The Bagbys were first led to consider Brazil as a mission field in which they could invest their lives before they were married. Upon making their desires known, Tupper wrote the couple, invit-

Mission, Sao Paulo, Brazil, 1892

ing them to appear before the board for examination "as to qualifications for the field may be had." Tupper went on to assure them of the nature of the "examination." "You will find yourself surrounded by loving brethren who regard you as a beloved one in the Lord."[36] The board was

obviously attempting to tighten up the appointment process, which had up to this time been somewhat lax.

The board was favorably impressed by the two recent graduates of Baylor University. Consequently, they were appointed in 1880 and sailed for Brazil a month later. Upon arriving in Brazil they found a letter awaiting them, offering the young couple a place to live in Santa Barbara. While learning the language, the Bagbys lived in Santa Barbara and worked with the English-speaking churches, as did the Zachary Clay Taylors after their appointment in 1882.

On 8 March 1882, Bagby wrote the board that the Presbyterians had Santa Barbara "well fortified" and suggested that it might be "prudent" if the Committee on Brazil agreed "to make our headquarters for missionary operations in some other and equally accessible and promising province." The committee agreed. In October, the Bagbys and the Taylors moved a thousand miles to the north and opened a mission in Bahia, the Roman Catholic center of the country. On 15 October 1882, the two couples and one convert organized the first Portuguese-speaking Baptist church in Brazil.

Within a few months, the Bagbys moved to Rio de Janeiro where in less than two years they established a church on 24 July 1884. But it was not without difficulty. First they rented a hall but nobody came. They took their folding organ into the street and began to play and sing. Soon they had an audience. The next night a curious crowd gathered on the street and filed into the hall. C. E. Maddry later related that when the news reached the local Catholic priest, it was not long until he sent some fanatical followers to run the missionaries out of town and close down the work. But when the leaders of the mob descended on the Bagbys, they discovered to their disappointment that they did not run, and that, which was even more disconcerting, the missionaries were supported by a group of those who liked what they heard. The mob rushed into the building, and destroyed furniture and lights, and resorted to throwing stones, one of which hit Bagby in the head. For a few minutes he lay unconscious on the floor but then arose and continued his preaching.[37]

News of the attack spread and even the newspapers took up the cry of the mob, claiming that there was no room in Rio de Janeiro for such people. The news brought others out of curiosity to the chapel, even some young men from the more affluent level of Rio's society. Among these were three whose hearts were touched by the gospel, which they had heard for the first time in their lives. Subsequently all three, F. F. Soren, Theodore Teixeira, and Thomas de Costa, became gifted leaders of Brazilian Baptists. With the work of the Bagbys in Rio and the Taylors in Bahia, the seed was sown that in time would produce an abundant harvest. Among those who would reap the

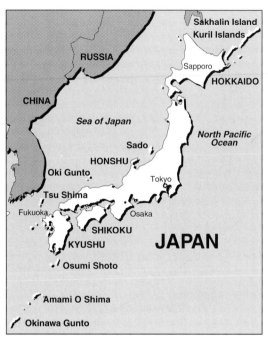

Japan 1860

harvest and sow seed on their own would be six of the nine Bagby children who became missionaries to Brazil.

Japan

Southern Baptists' first attempt to establish a mission (1860) in Japan ended in tragedy. The ship on which missionaries John and Sarah Rohrer, and Alfred and Helena Bond (missionary appointees for China) were sailing was lost at sea. With the advent of the Civil War it became impossible to send out new missionaries. After the war other needs proved more pressing but Japan was not forgotten. Before the war, Tupper had even entertained thoughts of going to Japan himself and establishing a Christian beachhead by endowing a Christian colony with $250,000.

Japan Mission, around 1915

From China, the veteran missionary Matthew T. Yates continued to beseech the board to enter Japan. He even offered to underwrite the salary of a missionary. Those like Yates, who were familiar with the Japanese people, were well aware of the potential of such an intelligent and gifted people, but the Japanese had thus far resisted every attempt to establish a lasting Christian witness in Japan. With the death of Yates in 1888, the board once again took up the possibility of establishing a mission in the island nation. Further delay was inconceivable.

While the conviction was growing among the managers (trustees) of the board that a mission to Japan should be undertaken, two able students at Southern Seminary, John A. Brunson and J. W. McCollum, offered themselves for the task. The board reported to the 1889 convention that contact had been made with the American Baptist Missionary Union, which had encouraged them to send Southern Baptist missionaries to Japan. The board also reported, "Two admirably qualified young men . . .

have been appointed as our pioneers in this most hopeful enterprise."[38]

Northern Baptists had maintained a missionary presence in Japan almost continuously from 1860 and, like three or four other denominations, initially had enjoyed an unusually favorable response until a reaction against the missionaries and Christianity set in just at the time that the Brunsons and the McCollums arrived in Yokohama on 5 November 1889. In consultation with the Northern Baptist missionaries, the two missionary couples began their language study in Kobe and Osaka. At the end of two years, it was decided that the Southern Baptist mission should be established on Kyushu, the island furthest south of the Japanese archipelago. McCullom had made good use of his opportunity to study the language and the Japanese culture. Upon moving to the city of Kokura, he immediately began to establish a number of preaching points. Brunson, who had studiously applied himself to the written language, found himself unable to communicate. He came to the conviction that he was unsuitable for missionary service and returned to the States in September 1892, leaving the McCollums alone to represent Southern Baptists in Japan.

Not long after the departure of the Brunsons, the E. N. Walnes arrived in Japan and moved to Kokura. For six months the two missionary families lived in the same compound. They reinforced one another as

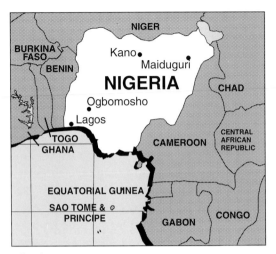

Nigeria

they shared the same problems of discrimination and rejection. They discovered to their dismay that they had no legal status since they did not live in one of the port cities protected by treaty guarantees. When the Northern Baptist missionaries became aware of their plight, they sent a Japanese Christian, Kawakatsu Sensei , to their rescue. Kawakatsu remained with the Southern Baptist mission in which he served effectively eighteen years. In spite of open resentment by the people and the inability of the mission to rent suitable houses for worship, the work began to make headway. In 1892 and 1893, twenty-five converts were baptized. Since no church yet had been formed in Kyushu, the new converts were nominally members of a church in Shimonoseki sponsored by the American Baptist Missionary Union.

By October 1893, the missionaries had succeeded in organizing the Moji Baptist Church with thirty members. Subsequently this church became the mother church of all the Baptist missions and churches in

Kyushu. At last Southern Baptists had established the long sought beachhead for Christ in Japan.[39]

The African Missions

Even before the Southern Baptist Convention came into existence many Baptists in the South carried in their hearts a deep concern for Africa and African-Americans. Deacon William Carey Crane and Corresponding Secretary James B. Taylor were among those who constantly reminded Southern Baptists of the needs of the "dark continent" and their struggling missionaries. H. A. Tupper shared their vision and in his more affluent days supported the T. A. Reids, missionaries to Africa. In spite of the interest and financial investment in Africa by the various Baptist missionary bodies, after an initial gratifying response, the work had not prospered.

Missionary doctor George Green (assisted by wife, Lydia, and pharmacist John Dare), performs surgery, Ogbomosho, 1910.

Disease and death stalked the white missionaries and tribal warfare frequently disrupted the work. The mission in Liberia was abandoned and the board shifted its attention to Nigeria which appeared to give greater access to the interior of the continent.

Nigeria was under British rule and was much larger than Sierra Leone and Liberia together. C. E. Smith, a missionary to Nigeria, wrote, that "Our work in the Yoruba country really began with the settlement of Brethren Bowen and co-laborers at Ijaiye in 1854."[40] Shortly afterwards eight men and five women were serving in several stations, but six of these were soon dead.

T. J. Bowen transferred to Brazil in 1859. Mrs. Mary Canfield Reid died in Ogbomosho the year before, and Joseph M.

Green baptizes near Ogbomosho.

Harden, who had transferred from Liberia, died at Lagos in 1864. A civil war in 1860-1861 and a fierce anti-Christian uprising destroyed virtually all mission property and brought the work to a standstill. Southern Baptists were devoid of a missionary presence in Africa until W. J. David and W. W. Colley reestablished the mission.

William Joshua David was appointed to Africa in 1874, and reached Nigeria the fol-lowing year. During the next three years, he and W. W. Colley, sent out by the Colored Baptist Convention of Virginia, worked together to close out the work in Liberia and reopen the mission in Nigeria. They discovered in Lagos that a young carpenter by the name of M. L. Stone, a national convert, had been preaching, as time permitted, to the converts that remained. David employed him full time and soon a large self-supporting church was developed. David also visited Abeokuta and Ogbomosho. Although anti-Christian feelings were running high, a few converts were found at each place, more at Ogbomosho, where a church was gathered underneath a tree. In time Ogbomosho would become the most important Baptist center in Nigeria.

David suffered frequent bouts of illness that forced him to return to the United States for treatment, but he refused to give up his work, remaining a missionary under appointment until 1894. Upon his return to Richmond on 15 October 1878, the board made arrangements with the Colored Baptist Convention of Virginia for Solomon Cosby "to locate temporarily in Lagos and use our chapel there" (Stone had already gone to Ogbomosho) and "our missionary Rev. W. W. Colley," the Minutes read, "will go to Abeokuta, and occupy Brother David's station—Thus each of our three stations will have a missionary, and the work will go on much as before but apart from Bro. David."[41]

Up to this time (1878) David had served as a single missionary. It had been a lonely and difficult life. While on furlough he met a devout young woman by the name of Nannie Bland willing to serve the Lord in Africa with him. Together they left New York on board the *Cordenas* on 8 December 1879. Upon this occasion, David wrote Tupper:

> *Off at last—to him be the glory who hath removed all our obstacles, and granted us the long felt desire of our hearts. Joyfully Mrs. David and I turned our faces toward the 'dark continent,' believing that he who hath lived and cared for us in the past, will order our future in that way, that will bring most honor to his name. Our desire is to glorify Christ whether in life or death. Mrs. David says I must put 'Amen' to the above for her.*[42]

Little did they realize that Africa would claim their first born, a girl, their only son, and finally the courageous young missionary mother herself. A British doctor in the colony of Lagos prescribed a trip to Madeira as the only hope for Nannie's life. David wrote the board: "On May 20 (1885) while we were lying at anchor off Cape Coast Castle, she fell asleep without a struggle. Among her last utterances were, 'Never give up Africa.'"[43]

Although Southern Baptists never gave up Africa, at times they were sorely tempted to do so. By 1893, the work was nearing the half-century mark. "A total of forty-two white and six colored missionaries had been appointed to the work. Thirteen of these had died in Africa, or on the voyage home . . ."[44] Africa had taken its toll in human life and suffering. For ten years the board appears to

have reached an impasse. Only one couple was appointed from 1891 to 1901, that stayed only a few months. In 1893, there were four "male" missionaries and three missionary families remaining on the continent. But as Nannie David prayed, Southern Baptists refused to "give up Africa." By the turn of the century the board reported (1900) six churches and six outstations with 385 baptized members, fifty-six of whom had been baptized in the year 1899-1900.[45]

The words of S. G. Pinnock proved prophetic.

> *The few who have been won are but a handful of the glorious harvest which the Master wishes from the whitening fields. Never were the nations better prepared to receive the Gospel. Never were the facilities for reaching them so good. Never were there so many praying and giving for the advancement of the Master's kingdom. Never was the power of the cross to save greater than to-day.*[46]

The Christian hope expressed in these words was also an echo of the spirit that still characterized Tupper who, although no longer the corresponding secretary, left his imprint upon the board. In spite of the controversies in which he inevitably found himself by virtue of his office, his robust faith provided the support and balanced perspective that hard pressed missionaries on the field continued to receive.

ENDNOTES

1. Cited in George Braxton Taylor, *Virginia Baptist Ministers*, Fifth Series, 1902-1914 (Lynchburg, Va.: J. P. Bell Company, Inc., 1915), 22.

2. Ibid., 25.

3. Cited in Robert Alton James, "A Study of the Life and Contributions of Henry Allen Tupper" (Th.D. diss., New Orleans Baptist Theological Seminary, 1980), 39.

4. Taylor, *Virginia Baptist Ministers*, 25.

5. Ibid.

6. Ibid., 26.

7. Ibid., 28. Slight changes were made to smooth out the rather cryptic report.

8. James, "Henry Allen Tupper," 48, 49.

9. Ibid., 51.

10. The other two names presented along with that of H. A. Tupper of Georgia were William E. Hatcher of Virginia, and I. T. Tichenor of Tennessee.

11. *Religious Herald*, 15 January 1872, 2.

12. Quoted in Taylor, *Virginia Baptist Ministers*, 30.

13. Ibid.

14. Quoted in ibid., 35.

15. *Alabama Baptist*, 28 April 1887, 2.

16. Hollywood Cemetery was so named from the ancient holly bushes that cover a large wooded area overlooking the James River and downtown Richmond. The lot that Tupper purchased was adjacent to that of President James Monroe.

17. H. A. Tupper, "Plan For Promoting Foreign Missions," *Home and Foreign Journal* 6 (July 1873): 2.

18. Fannie E. S. Heck referred to the organization of Central Committees as Tupper's "cherished plan." Cited by James, "Henry Allen Tupper," 169.

19. For more information on the status of women in the United States from the Revolution to the present see Anne F. Scott and Andrew M. Scott, eds., *One Half the People: The Fight for Woman Suffrage* (Philadelphia: J. B. Lippincott Company, 1975).

20. Cited in Catherine Allen, *A Century to Celebrate: History of Woman's Missionary Union* (Birmingham: Woman's Missionary Union, 1987), 25.

21. Ibid., 27.

22. James, "Henry Allen Tupper," 157.

23. Proceedings, SBC, 1872, 42.

24. Proceedings, SBC, 1878, 32.

25. Proceedings, SBC, 1885, 34.

26. James, "Henry Allen Tupper," 181.

27. There are numerous sources that support this statement, both primary and secondary. See Alice Armstrong, "Woman's Missionary Union," *Baptist Standard*, 10 May 1894, 2. Also see Allen, *A Century to Celebrate*, 48ff.

28. See Juliette Mather, "Woman's Missionary Union" in *Encyclopedia of Southern Baptists*.

29. Cited in James, "Henry Allen Tupper," 183.

30. In the first full year of Tupper's administration, the board's income almost doubled, totaling $51,023.62. In 1888, before the Woman's Missionary Union was organized, the figure was $86,340.66. During the centennial celebration of the beginning of the modern mission movement, with the help of the Woman's Missionary Union, the income of the board was $154,686.28.

31. Minutes, FMB, 28 March 1873, 269.

32. Alejandro Treviño, converted under the ministry of John O. Westrup and the head of a shoe factory in Monterrey believed that fanatical Roman Catholics were responsible for the murders. See Justo Anderson, *Historia de los Bautistas* Tomo III (El Paso: Casa Bautista Publicaciones, 1990), 28.

33. Ibid., 29.

34. Ibid., 30-32. See also J. M. Carroll, *A History of Texas Baptists* (Dallas: Baptist Standard Publishing Co., 1923), 561, 562, for an account of W. D. Powell's work in Texas.

35. Proceedings, SBC, 1880, 25.

36. Cited by James, "Henry Allen Tupper," 144.

37. Charles E. Maddry, *Christ's Expendables* (Nashville: Broadman Press, 1949), 24-25.

38. Proceedings, SBC, 1889, XXXIV.

39. See E. N. Walne, "The Japan Mission," in *Southern Baptist Foreign Missions*, ed. T. B. Ray (Nashville: Sunday School Board, 1910), 217-27.

40. C. E. Smith, "The African Mission," in *Southern Baptist Foreign Missions*, ed. Ray, 133.

41. Minutes, FMB, 4 November 1878, 381.

42. Minutes, FMB, 5 January 1880, 400.

43. Maddry, *Christ's Expendables*, 68.

44. Charles E. Maddry, *Day Dawn in Yoruba Land* (Nashville: Broadman Press, 1939), 77.

45. Proceedings, SBC, 1900, 120.

46. Ibid., 117.

Two Crucial Decades, 1872-1893

H.A. Tupper

In spite of a debilitating case of hay fever, the severity of which forced Tupper to leave Richmond every year for at least a month, he still managed to maintain an optimistic spirit. This same attitude generally characterized his entire tenure as corresponding secretary. In spite of the controversies in which he found himself involved, Tupper never appears to have lost sight of the goal toward which he attempted to lead the Southern Baptist missionary enterprise. He possessed an irenic disposition that enabled him to take other viewpoints seriously. Doubtless his ability to lose himself in his scholarly pursuits and his own healthy devotional life helped him to keep the competing demands upon the board in their proper balance. He does not appear to have harbored personal grudges nor to have taken adversities in the work as personal attacks. As close as he ever came to losing his objectivity was in the conflict with I. T. Tichenor over the Home Mission Board's appropriation of Cuba as its mission field.

"We must go out and live among the people, manifesting the gentle, loving spirit of our Lord. . . . We need to make friends before we can hope to make converts."

Lottie Moon, 1890

The Cuba Issue

A request for Southern Baptists to establish a mission in Cuba first reached the Foreign Mission Board in 1881. The committee appointed to study the matter reported to the convention meeting in Columbus, Mississippi that "the time has not yet come when the Island can be occupied by our Foreign Mission Board."[1] Four years later the board reconsidered the possibility of entering Cuba and decided it was time to act. By this time, however, the Home Mission Board, under the aggressive leadership of I. T. Tichenor had also decided to take the work in Cuba, which Florida Baptists had been supporting, under its direction. For Tichenor it was the opportune time for such a move. It was the third year of his administration and he was determined that the Home Mission Board would assume its rightful place in the life of the convention. There is little doubt that Tichenor was the rising star among the convention's leaders. Therefore, when he perceived

Personality conflicts and theological controversies are inevitable. This was certainly true during the last decade of Tupper's tenure as secretary. First it was the issue of Cuba and then it was the problem of theological deviation. Later the Gospel Mission Movement led to the loss of several missionaries and churches in North China. The late developing controversy with Annie Armstrong was not serious but taxing. All of these conflicts, personalities aside, can be interpreted as the board's attempt to define its limits and the nature of its responsibilities.

that Cuba offered an opportunity to expand the influence of the Home Mission Board, he seized it. In consultation with Florida Baptists, Tichenor pointed out that since the Foreign Mission Board had failed to respond to the invitation of Cuban Baptists for assistance that the work should be undertaken by the Home Mission Board. Tupper disagreed.

When the convention convened in 1886, a committee made up of several of the more influential leaders among Southern Baptists strongly recommended that the Home Mission Board be given the responsibility for the work in Cuba. An attempt was made to rescind this action, but was defeated by a vote of 126 to 76.[2] It is evident that Tichenor had the backing of the convention for the Home Mission Board's move to acquire Cuba as its territory.

The action of the Convention did not change Tupper's mind. He wrote Tichenor that the Home Mission Board had taken over the work of the Foreign Mission Board and thereby erased a necessary distinction between the boards' proper fields of labor. The Cuban question led to a none too flattering exchange of public letters between the two corresponding secretaries that can only be understood in the light of the situation in the convention.

I. T. Tichenor was a man with a mission. That mission was to protect the Home Mission Board against the "encroachments" of the American Baptist Home Mission Society in the South. The board was experiencing difficulties in eliciting the support of Baptists, especially in the border states, for its programs. Tichenor doubtless viewed Tupper's more irenical approach to the American Baptist Missionary Union and the

Home Mission Society as undermining his efforts to establish the hegemony of his own board and that of the Southern Baptist Convention against the claims of the Home Mission Society and the American Baptist Publication Society.[3] Even though displeased with Tichenor, Tupper did not "nurse his wrath." When the Home Mission Board asked to be included in the fund-raising drive initiated by Tupper as a part of the observance of the Missionary Centennial, Tupper graciously agreed.

Annie Armstrong's Chapel Project

Annie Walker Armstrong, like Tichenor, was a strong personality. To Armstrong goes much of the credit for leading the Woman's Missionary Union into a place of prominence and effectiveness in the life of the convention. She and Tupper had worked together effectively but not without an occasional disagreement. In such cases she found T. P. Bell, Tupper's assistant, easier to approach than Tupper. The most notorious conflict was a result of Armstrong's attempt to dictate to the board how to use the money raised by the women. At least this is the way Tupper viewed the matter.

The need for a chapel in Rio de Janeiro had been widely publicized in the *Foreign Mission Journal*. The Central Committee of the Missouri Convention desired to raise money in the state for this purpose. Annie thought it would be a great project for the entire Woman's Missionary Union and, therefore, proceeded to receive the endorsement of the Executive Committee of the Woman's Missionary Union for the plan. She wrote Tupper for his opinion. He answered: "The best thing, in the matter of foreign missions, the men and women of the country can do in my judgment is to raise money for the Board and let the Board appropriate it."[4] Annie was not so easily turned aside from that which had such appeal. She persisted and thought that she had received Tupper's personal approval of the matter and that it would be only a matter of time until the project received the board's endorsement. When no response was forthcoming from a follow-up letter, she made a trip to Richmond to confer with Tupper and learned that the board had never approved of a chapel in Rio. She promptly wrote a forthright letter to H. H. Harris, president of the board, explaining exactly how she felt. As the result of her persistence, the Rio chapel project was approved by the board in December 1890.

T.P. Bell

Although Annie Armstrong had previously enjoyed a most cordial and productive relationship with Tupper, it seems that this "run-in" with the corresponding secretary soured their relationship. From this time on, she limited her contacts with the board to T. P. Bell and John Pollard, who served as chairman of the board's Committee on Women's Work. "Fortunately," James observed, "the personality differences did not stop the great work of the Foreign Mission Board or the Woman's Missionary Union. Contributions to foreign missions continued to climb and the Woman's Missionary Union received much of the credit for the increase."[5]

The Problem of Theological Deviation

Perhaps the severest test of Tupper's diplomatic skill arose with the appointment of John Stout and T. P. Bell as missionaries to China. The Minutes of the board on 20 April 1881 reported that "the usual formal examination was dispensed with, and the brethren each proceeded to make a statement of their views and feelings on the subject."[6] Stout was appointed to serve in Shanghai and Bell in Tengchow. The appointment of such promising young pastors for missionary service was highly publicized. For some time the board had been highlighting the need for pastors. Women had responded in unusual numbers but there was a paucity of men. The board, therefore, was dismayed to hear from Tupper's brother-in-law, J. P. Boyce, that the two men were not sound in the faith.[7] Stout, himself, had begun to wonder if he could serve under the board since he had learned during a recent meeting of the convention that some members of the board held to a theory of verbal plenary inspiration and expected missionaries to affirm the same.

In the board meeting of 6 June, letters were read from Stout and Bell that set forth their views of inspiration. A committee of five was charged with the responsibility of recommending a course of action to be taken and to report at a called meeting of the board on 17 June. The committee dealt with the issue raised by Stout regarding the freedom to teach his views on the mission field. After receiving the committee's report, the board decided that,

> *Whereas Rev. John Stout has candidly and courteously presented to the Board of Foreign Missions his views on Inspiration; and whereas his views do not seem to the Board to be in accord with the views commonly held by the constituency of the Southern Baptist Convention; and whereas Bro. Stout reduces the question between himself and the Board to the simple point whether the Board will give their consent to teach or print, if thought advisable by him, these views as a missionary of our Board; therefore,*
>
> *Resolved, That, while the Board distinctly and emphatically disclaim the least right over the conscience or Christian liberty of any man, they have no right to consent to any missionary teaching or printing anything regarded by them as contrary to the commonly received doctrinal views of the constituency of the Southern Baptist Convention.*
>
> *2. Resolved, that while the discovery of this difference in views fills the Board with unfeigned regrets, they rejoice at the fraternal spirit manifested by Bro. Stout in the assurance that whatever be the issue of this difference, he shall ever be a fellow helper with the Board in giving the gospel to the heathen world.*
>
> *3. Resolved, that the Board having answered the inquiry of Bro. Stout in the same candor and Christian love that it was propounded by him, they refer the matter back to him for his decision which they await with the deepest interest.*[8]

The board next asked T. P. Bell to return to the board and present his views in person. Bell declined to accede to the board's request but indicated his substantial agreement with Stout. Stout seems to have been the more adamant of the two. It is not surprising, therefore, that he asked for the reasons for the board's decision. The board felt it inadvisable to comply. The board then left the decision with him to decline his appointment. Stout, however, insisted that it was incumbent upon the board to withdraw the appointment, which it proceeded to do, including Bell in the process. Stout then asked if the board wished him to resign as chairman of the Central Committee for South Carolina. The board assured him of its will that he continue to serve, and he did.

Throughout the whole embarrassing episode Bell maintained a cordial relationship with Tupper and continued in complete support of the board. In 1886, he was elected assistant corresponding secretary and editor of the *Foreign Mission Journal*. In March 1893, Bell was elected corresponding secretary of the Sunday School Board.

It appears that Tupper was able to maintain a most amicable relationship with both Stout and Bell while leading the board to withdraw their appointments. A clue to his ability in maintaining a degree of objectivity is found in his novel *Truth in Romance*. In discussing the controversy in the novel, Tupper speaking for the board said: "The young men made the issue, and the Board did exactly what they required, viz., to dismiss them, if their views did not accord with those of the denomination."[9]

Apparently, Tupper was more in accord with the position of these young men than with that of his brother-in-law, J. P. Boyce, chairman of the faculty at The Southern Baptist Seminary. Boyce had studied with Charles Hodge at Princeton and had incorporated much of Hodge's Calvinistic theology into his own. Hodge was an adamant opponent of higher criticism. When Crawford H. Toy began to champion this approach to the Bible, he was opposed by Boyce.[10] Stout and Bell had been students of Toy at Southern, and Stout admitted that it was Toy's position that he was espousing. If Stout had not raised the issue of inspiration of the Scriptures, neither Tupper nor the board would have done so. It is significant that both would-be missionaries continued to serve the denomination that refused to send them as missionaries.

T.P. Crawford

T. P. Crawford and the Gospel Mission Movement

As frustrating and painful as the Stout and Bell problem was to the board, it did not rival in severity or length of the controversy initiated by Tarleton Perry Crawford. Eventually Crawford's views comprised a philosophy of missions known as "Gospel Missionism." It closely resembled the Landmarkism of J. R. Graves and has often been viewed as a variant expression of that movement.[11] If this were the case, this aspect of Crawford's philosophy of missions was not evident for a number of years.

Crawford's conversion and call to the ministry came almost simultaneously. At sixteen years of age, he was mimicking some local preachers to the merriment of a few friends when he was reprimanded by his brother. The rebuke sobered him and sent him home. Here he was led to Christ by his mother, and, he almost immediately announced "I will spend my life in telling of His great mercy."[12] In 1851 he graduated first in his class from Union University. Even before his graduation, the Big Hatchie Association in Tennessee agreed to provide his support as a missionary in China. He was in Richmond discussing the prospects of missionary service with J. B. Taylor when the corresponding secretary showed him a letter he had received from a pastor in Alabama concerning a young woman who had also felt called to missions. Crawford was so impressed that he determined to meet her face to face. It was February and the rivers were swollen but after a difficult trip by horseback he finally arrived in Clinton, Alabama, where Martha Foster was teaching.

Martha was the daughter of a Baptist deacon. Even though her father was a devout man and of good reputation, he opposed his daughter's decision to become a missionary. Martha was just as determined in her calling. Her decision had not come easily and she was not about to give it up. In fact she had decided to go as a single woman to the field, if the board would send her. The sudden appearance of a young man with a similar calling was a surprising development of which she had had no advance knowledge. Their first meeting resulted in no love at first sight. To the contrary, Crawford frankly said, "The short of it is, we do not love each other, and ought not to marry."[13] In spite of the lack of a spark of romance, the couple decided to give love a chance. They were engaged two weeks later and were married in the bride's home by Basil Manley, Sr. on 12 March 1851. Martha was twenty-one and Tarleton, twenty-nine.

Martha Foster Crawford

The young couple was set apart for China at a designation service during the convention meeting in Nashville on 11 May 1851. Before the end of the year, the Crawfords sailed for China on 17 November 1851 aboard the *Horatio*. They arrived in Hong Kong 102 days later, a record for a sailing ship at the time. By 30 March, they were in Shanghai. In Shanghai they experienced some of the terrors and many of the joys of new missionaries. While learning the language, they lived with the Yateses. When the Red Turbans (a band of rebels who took over the city of Shanghai) launched their reign of terror, the Crawfords suffered from the same fears and hardships as did their fellow missionaries. They also witnessed the power of the gospel to change despair into joy and hate into love. They were privileged to see the baptism of the first Chinese woman convert in Shanghai. During their eleven years in the city, the Crawfords appear to have been productive missionaries—Martha in her girls' school and Tarleton in his evangelistic work. There is evidence, however, that Crawford

longed to be out from under the shadow of Yates and free to follow his own inclinations in missionary service. In 1863 the Crawfords transferred to Tengchow in the Shantung Province.

Not long after arriving in Tengchow, Crawford found himself in conflict with J. B. Hartwell. Hartwell, his wife and Sallie J. Holmes had been working in the area for six years. The feud between Crawford and Hartwell festered until Hartwell brought charges against Crawford before the Foreign Mission Board. The Board refused to hear the charges until the provisions of Rule 20 were met, which required that the accused first be allowed to respond to the charges before the board would hear them. The rule read:

> *If any member of a mission persists in violating any of the above regulations, it shall be the indispensable duty of the mission to give with his knowledge full information to the Board, but no information or charges affecting the Christian character of a missionary shall be made the basis of action by the Board, until they shall have communicated the said information or charges with the names of the authors to the accused, and given him ample opportunity for explanation and defense.[14]*

Forced to support himself during the War between the States, Crawford's business dealings continued after the war and involved him in embarrassing quarrels with Chinese Christians. Apparently the income that made it possible for him to buy his own home, which he later sold to the board, gave him financial independence that also fostered the idea that missionaries could support themselves on their fields of labor and should do so.

From his first visit to Hong Kong, Crawford had developed a negative view toward national Chinese colporters and preachers. He heard that two hundred Chinese workers employed by a German missionary to distribute the Bible in the interior of China had entered into a conspiracy to lead the missionary to believe that they were distributing large quantities of Bibles while they were actually selling them to a printer who resold them to the missionary.[15] This deception was appalling to the new missionary, and he was never able to free himself from his negative evaluation of native Chinese employees of the missions. Too, he became convinced that mission schools conditioned the Chinese converts to depend upon the missionaries for a livelihood whether or not they were spiritually and intellectually qualified. Hence he waged a campaign to eliminate all schools operated by the mission. Thus, a combination of factors led Crawford to champion immediate self-support as the only biblical method in missionary work.

Although by 1871 Crawford had determined not to employ Chinese workers with foreign money, he was not adverse to making demands upon the board for money to build his new chapel in Chefoo. He frankly told the board what he was doing. "I am contracting for a lot on which to build a chapel. I need three thousand dollars for the work. I cannot afford to stop labor for want of a chapel, and I shall confidently

expect the Board to furnish the means." He went on to indicate the basis of his demand. "Twenty years of constant labor in China entitles me to a chapel in which to train the congregation which, from nothing, I have gradually built to its present number."[16] Crawford advanced the money for the building of the chapel, expecting the board to compensate him for the expenditure.

In May 1877, both Martha and Tarleton read papers at a general conference of missionaries of Protestant denominations working in China. Tarleton's paper dealt with "The Employment of Native Assistants with Foreign Money," but it met with a mixed response. Martha's paper on "Woman's Work" was well

T.P. Crawford's phonetic system for the Shanghai dialect

received. By this time the matter of self-support was rapidly becoming an obsession with Crawford. While on furlough in 1878-1879, he presented his views to the board and to the 1879 meeting of the Southern Baptist Convention in Atlanta. In June, following the convention, Richmond College conferred upon him the Doctor of Divinity degree. He took advantage of his new-found notoriety to promote with all his energies a national conference on self-support with the foreign mission boards in the United States, but without success.

While Crawford was pursuing his dream

Tengchow Mission, 1910; seated, left to right: Lottie Moon, Anna Hartwell, Ida T. Pruitt, Mary W. Newton; standing, left to right: William Carey Newton, J.B. Hartwell, and C.W. Pruitt

with single-minded tenacity in the States, back in China his wife, Martha, was faithfully fulfilling her missionary responsibilities. She was conducting a day school, a boarding school, and a class for Sunday School

Tengchow Baptist Church

teachers. In the afternoons in spring and autumn she joined Sallie Holmes and Lottie Moon in making evangelistic visits to nearby villages. She was also generally in charge of the inquirers at the church, since there were no native assistants to do this work. The Crawfords' two adopted children also required much of her time. Not long after

T. P. Crawford's return to Tengchow, he and his colleagues disbanded their schools in favor of direct evangelism under the impression that the schools were more of a detriment than a help in developing an indigenous Christianity.

In October 1885, the Foreign Mission Board sent a copy of C. H. Carpenter's *Self-Support in Bassein* to all its missionaries. Crawford took this as an indication that the board had changed its position on subsidies. Without authorization or notification he returned to the states at his own expense and soon discovered that the board, which had been extremely patient with him, did not agree with his position any more in 1885 than it had earlier. The board's policy was clearly stated. While agreeing with Crawford that the ultimate purpose of all missionary work was to establish self-supporting churches, the board refused to make it an absolute demand and an inflexible rule. Instead, the board offered an alternative:

> *These are our convictions of the rightfulness and necessity of self-support as an end to be kept in view; and we do not doubt that they are shared by all the missionaries under our appointment.*
>
> *An entirely different question is presented when we consider whether we will incorporate this principle into a rule which would, in the future, forbid all appropriations for work done by native Christians, at least in the fields of missionaries that may be appointed hereafter. Should self-support assume the shape of inflexible law? We are constrained to think not.[17]*

Then the board adopted two significant resolutions regarding self-support. The committee offered two resolutions:

Resolved I, That while the principle of self-support in our mission work is essential to healthy progress and ultimate success, we believe its practice is to be established not by formal rule, but as the result of growth and development.

Resolved 2, That we urge upon our missionaries the duty of holding constantly in view self-support as an object to be attained, and of training their converts and churches in this direction with all possible diligence.[18]

Since Crawford had not given a date for his return to China, and since he was disturbing the churches in much of the South in promoting his own position against the stated policy of the board, the board asked him to return to China at the earliest possible moment, and not to "continue further discussion before our Southern churches of plans for the conduct of mission and further

C.W. Pruitt

that it would be gratifying to the Board if he should be able to return at some early date to his work in China." Apparently miffed at the rebuff of the board, Crawford offered his resignation as treasurer of the Tengchow mission. His resignation was accepted and C. W. Pruitt was elected treasurer in his place.

Four years later Crawford resigned as a missionary of the North China Mission, stating that at sixty-nine years of age "For many reasons of a physical, mental and spiritual character, I now wish to retire at my own charges from all future responsibility. . . ."[19]

He also stated that he was speaking for himself alone and not for his wife, who will "continue to labor in this field while it shall be her pleasure to do. . . ."[20] The rejection of Crawford's version of self-support was apparently a major factor in his resignation, for Pruitt replied:

I think you are mistaken in saying your position has been odious. To all real lovers of the Lord I am sure it has not been so. Even Mr. _____ has a most profound respect for the truth that lies on the other side, but remember that success is on the side opposed to your views.[21]

Anna Stewart Pruitt

Although Crawford resigned from the North China Mission with feelings of rejection, the mission was kind to him. Since Lottie Moon and Pruitt were so burdened with additional responsibilities, a number of new missionaries were turned over to the Crawfords for orientation. This seemed to have restored his self esteem and given new life to his principle of self-support. Virtually all of the new missionaries were convinced by the apparent biblical support of Crawford's position and stood in awe of the veteran missionary.

Convinced more than ever of the rightness of his theories, Crawford published a booklet entitled *Churches, to the Front,* which revealed not only a plea for self-support as the only scriptural method of mission work but which also decried the work of mission boards and conventions "as presently organized." It concluded, "But these Conventions should collect no funds, employ no men, hold no property and exercise no authority over the government or the work of the Churches."[22] The Landmark tenets were undeniable. Crawford's name was now stricken from the board's roll of foreign missionaries. But the Crawfords did not leave Tengchow until J. B. Hartwell was reappointed and assigned to China. In August 1893, the Hartwells arrived in Chefoo.

The twelve missionaries serving with the Gospel Mission organization made a courageous attempt at establishing stations in the interior, eventually all twelve settled in Taian. At its height in 1895, the Gospel Mission had twenty-one missionaries serving under its banner.[23] In six years, against almost insurmount-

T.C. Crawford's **Churches to the Front!**, *published in China, 1892*

able odds the Gospel Mission succeeded in establishing one church before the Boxer Rebellion, which was violently anti-Christian, erupted and compelled the missionaries to leave. The Crawfords returned to the States in 1901. On 8 April 1902, T. P. Crawford died. In October, Martha Crawford at seventy-two years of age returned to Taian Fu to take up the work once again at the foot of the sacred mountain, where she remained until her death

seven years later.

Upon Mrs. Crawford's decision to leave the service of the board in 1892, its members accepted her resignation "with sincere regrets that this noble worker should be separated from the board with whom she has so long and faithfully labored and with prayerful hopes that her days of usefulness may be many among the people for whose highest good she has consecrated her life."[24] Martha Foster Crawford lived seventeen years after resigning from the board, dying among the people she loved. "Thus, with her death, the last binding link holding the Gospel Mission together was broken."[25]

Lottie Moon

The relationship of Tupper with Charlotte Diggs Moon was as delightful as the T. P. Crawford affair was exasperating. It is even more remarkable that Lottie in the midst of such a hostile atmosphere was able to maintain a most cordial relationship with all parties involved in the acrimonious quarrel. Doubtless Lottie's ability to rise above the melee was due in part to Mrs. Crawford and Sallie Holmes. Her own spiritual vitality and the support she received from both the Foreign Mission Board and the Woman's Missionary Union and its antecedents go far to explain how she was able to transcend the limitations of her culture and her sex to become Southern Baptists' most beloved missionary.

Born on 12 December 1840 at Viewmont in Albemarle County, Virginia, it would be difficult to conceive of a more unpromising missionary candidate. The fourth of seven children she enjoyed all the advantages of the landed gentry of antebellum Virginia. Tutors in French, English literature, and music were brought to the home for the instruction of the children. At fourteen, Lottie left home for a boarding school, the Virginia Female Seminary.

Although Lottie's Uncle James Barclay was a medical missionary to Palestine of the relatively new Disciples denomination and her parents were staunch Baptists, Lottie was a skeptic. Apparently, the Moon children were an independently minded lot who rarely attended any church. Lottie's church attendance during her two years at Hollins Institute (new name for the seminary) greatly improved but not her attitude toward religion. Attendance at chapel was compulsory and the Enon Baptist Church, located just across the road from Hollins, made attendance the normal activity on Sundays for the hundred girls enrolled in the school. The two years Miss Moon spent at Hollins saw her excel in classical studies but she didn't do quite as well in mathematics and science. She stubbornly resisted, however, the religious influences so pervasive at the Baptist school.

On 22 December 1858, Lottie made a profession of faith in Christ as her personal Savior. Although there was a great deal of agitation for women's rights throughout the country, in Baptist circles the only time a woman could address a mixed audience of men and women was when she gave an account of her conversion. Upon this occasion, Lottie reported that during a revival

Crawford H. Toy

meeting conducted by Dr. John W. Broadus at the Charlottesville Baptist Church she went to her room to sleep, but, due to the barking of a dog, she could not. During a sleepless night she determined to examine Christianity honestly. The result was her conversion. She, as so many before her, went to scoff, but as she wrote her cousin, "I returned to my room to pray all night."[26]

The change in the gifted but frivolous student was transparent. Her friends wrote of the change that God had brought about in her life. At the time, Lottie was in the second year of her studies in the newly founded Albemarle Female Institute, an institute designed as the academic equivalent to the University of Virginia, which only admitted men. Here Lottie became known quite as much for her academic accomplishments as for her "devil may care attitude." Her influence was great and she soon became the object of earnest prayer by concerned Christian friends, students and faculty. Shortly after her baptism, the object of their prayers had assumed the leadership of the Christian students in the institute.

Four years after entering Albemarle, Charlotte Diggs Moon was awarded the Master of Arts degree. In the process, she had become a superb linguist. In addition to French, Latin, Italian, and Spanish, she had gained proficiency in Greek and Hebrew. Perhaps her desire to study the biblical languages was due to her interest in the

Going village to village, Lottie Moon often used the shentze.

brilliant, young professor Crawford H. Toy, who taught these languages and whose sister Julia was her close friend. Lottie's interest in foreign mission service also may have been stimulated by Toy, who sought appointment as a missionary to Japan. Lottie's own call to foreign mission service, however, did not come until some ten years later. In the meantime, Lottie taught school in Danville, Kentucky, and Cartersville, Georgia. It was during her second year in Cartersville that Lottie heard the call to foreign missions "as clear as a bell."

Lottie had discussed the possibility of a missionary career with her younger sister Edmonia as early as 1870. In fact, she and Edmonia were already making generous gifts to foreign missions in China and Italy. Finally, Edmonia's dream of becoming a missionary to China turned to reality when she was appointed by the Foreign Mission Board in 1872. Although Edmonia was emotionally unstable and unsuited for missionary service, her efforts were not fruitless. For one thing, devout women in five churches in Richmond, Virginia undertook

her support by organizing "Mite Societies." Edmonia reported that there was much work to be done in China for the Lord that, due to the segregated society, only women could do. This information struck a resounding chord in Lottie's heart. She was seeking to discover just where the Lord could make the greatest use of her life.

Once the decision was made, there was no turning back. On 7 July 1873, Charlotte Diggs Moon was appointed a missionary to China, and the Baptist women of Georgia were asked to provide her support. She was assigned Tengchow, where her sister Edmonia had already begun to serve. Tengchow was one of the cities opened to foreign trade and missionaries by treaties some thirteen years before. Even though Confucius, revered Chinese sage and philosopher, was born there, Christianity had managed to gain a precarious foothold in the ancient city, especially among the poor. Although the Chinese government was bound by treaty to protect all Americans, the consulate in Chefoo (the port city) could not shield them from the scorn and ridicule of the people who considered them unwanted foreign devils and said so. The six Baptist missionaries, including the newly arrived Lottie, and a few more missionaries of the Northern Presbyterian Mission constituted a tiny minority in the city of 80,000. Lottie was delighted to learn that the Baptists and Presbyterians worked together in the seemingly impossible task of establishing an effective witness for Christ in the midst of such barriers of prejudice and hatred.

To complicate matters, the Moon sisters were forced to live in the Crawford mission compound. Edmonia mastered the difficult Chinese language with remarkable speed. But the primitive conditions of Shantung Province, the constant barrage of "devil woman" that always accompanied her in the streets of the city, the curiosity of children, the denigration of women, and the wanton disregard of human life, were all too much for her. Her dream of becoming a missionary to China turned into a never-end-

With foreigners ordered out of China, Lottie Moon teaches English in Fukuoka, Japan.

ing nightmare. Culture shock coupled with poor health compelled the mission to ask Lottie to take her sister home. Edmonia never returned to China, but Lottie did. And because she did, her name has been a household term synonymous with missions in thousands of homes for more than a century.

Upon her return to China in 1877, Lottie began to develop her own mission strategy. The work that appealed to her most was the educational approach, the most commonly accepted mission methodology at the time. She opened a school for girls in Tengchow in which geography, arithmetic, and Bible were taught. The Bible and a catechism that Martha Crawford had

developed for her school comprised the heart of the curriculum. Soon Lottie reported that some of her students could quote from memory the entire Gospel of Mark or Matthew. This was a small victory. She had less success convincing parents that they should unbind the feet of their daughters but she persisted and eventually could report progress in this effort as well. What continually frustrated her best efforts was famine which kept recurring with devastating frequency. To the board and to the *Religious Herald*, she wrote of the terrible plight of the starving Chinese. Money for famine relief began to trickle in but there was never enough. She fed the hungry at her doorstep, frequently at her own expense, until funds were virtually exhausted. For years she provided for as many as fifteen destitute women at a time in her own home.

Although Lottie continually longed to win the upper classes to Christ, she loved all the Chinese, poor as they were. Her personal concern for the destitute masses as well as the influence of T. P. Crawford caused her educational work to take a back seat to direct personal evangelism. Sallie Holmes, who had served in Tengchow along with her husband until his death at the hands of bandits, led the way. She had stayed in China doing evangelistic work in the villages of

Shantung Province with a zeal that few could match. It was with this remarkable woman that Lottie had her first taste of person to person—in this case, woman to woman—evangelism, and she gradually came to realize this was the work she most loved. In the midst of China's war with Japan in 1895, Miss Moon, accompanied by a younger missionary, made evangelistic excursions into 118 villages within three months. It is little wonder that back in Tengchow it was increasingly reported that "Miss Lottie Moon is out preaching in the country."

Even before China's war with Japan, Lottie's "country" had expanded. Since arriving in North China she had never been farther into the interior than fifty miles from Tengchow until she determined to establish work in P'ingtu, 120 miles from Tengchow. At P'ingtu her mission strategy changed. Instead of going into the streets with her message of salvation, she decided to become first a friend and a neighbor and work quietly within her own neighborhood. With the help of two converts from P'ingtu, she began to make many friends in whose homes she became a welcome guest. She first won the friendship of the local children with the delicious cookies she baked from an old Virginia recipe. That first unbearably cold winter in P'ingtu forced her to adopt for the first time the padded robe worn by Chinese women.

Pastor Li baptizes in P'ingtu.

She was amazed at the difference the Chinese apparel made. No more did women ask if she were a man or a woman and no longer was she met on the streets with the epithet "devil woman." Her new strategy was working, she explained to a colleague. "Demonstrate a Chinese-style Christian life," which means, "We must go out and live among them, manifesting the gentle, loving spirit of our Lord." "We need to make friends before we can hope to make converts," she added. And this she did.

With the help of a Chinese Christian couple by the name of Chao, Lottie became something of a celebrity. As the only foreigner living in P'ingtu City, curiosity gradually gave way to friendship and friendship led to the resumption of her itinerant ministry in innumerable villages throughout the P'ingtu countryside. A Mr. Dan Ho-bang of Sha-ling, a small village about ten miles from P'ingtu City, heard of the woman who preached Jesus and who lived on the west side of the city. He sent three men to bring her to Sha-ling. Here she discovered a number of people, members of a devout vegetarian group known as the Venerable Heaven Sect, the members of which were earnestly seeking God. She sent for Martha Crawford and the two of them reaped a harvest for Christ. An elderly man who heard Miss Moon teach at Sha-ling longed to know more about the one who could forgive sins and change lives. Lottie gave him a New Testament which, since he could not read, he asked a young cousin of his, Li Show-ting, a learned Confucian scholar, to read to him. At first Li scoffed, but as he read and discussed the new religion with Miss Moon, his attitude changed. Under her careful guidance and that of two other missionaries who had come to help, Li

Miss Moon's residence in Tengchow, the "Little Crossroads"

was converted. In 1890, he was baptized and later ordained. Subsequently, he became the most effective evangelist in North China, baptizing more than ten thousand converts.

The growing response to the gospel in P'ingtu was accompanied by persecution. It came with a vengeance during the Chinese New Year celebrations in 1890. Miss Moon refused to call upon the American Consul in Chefoo for protection but encouraged the new converts to remain faithful. At the height of the persecution she thrust herself physically, all four feet three inches, between the persecutors and the young Christians. Defying the anti-Christian mob,

she declared, "If you attempt to destroy this church, you will have to kill me first. Jesus gave himself for us Christians. Now I am ready to die for him."[27] When one of the antagonists took his sword thinking to do exactly that, she confidently assured the terrified Chinese, "Only believe, don't fear. Our Master, Jesus, always watches over us, and no matter what the persecution, Jesus will surely overcome it."[28] At this pronouncement, the hand of the persecutor fell to his side. The P'ingtu Christians remained faithful but some were tortured and others were murdered.

Although Lottie returned to Tengchow and reestablished her school, she continued to keep in touch with the P'ingtu Christians. They, from this time on, had a special place in her heart and she in theirs. Upon one occasion when she did not return as expected, two men from Shaling walked 120 miles to seek her out. After her death, the P'ingtu church wrote: "How she loved us." In fact the hardships Lottie had endured and her great love for the P'ingtu Christians brought about her last illness and death. The Boxer Rebellion had subsided somewhat when the most severe famine of a series hit Shantung Province. Starvation stalked the land. Lottie fed hundreds at her doorstep but when she heard that the famine had reached P'ingtu, she refused to eat. Financial conditions made it impossible for the Foreign Mission Board to help. To Lottie the situation appeared hopeless.

The mission recognized that Lottie's resources, physical and financial, were exhausted. Her fellow missionaries believed her only hope for sanity and survival was a return to the United States. She began the journey home only to die on Christmas eve, 1912, on board a ship in the harbor of Kobe, Japan. Cynthia Miller, the missionary nurse caring for Lottie, observed her last hours, according to Una Roberts Lawrence.

Charlotte Diggs Moon and Henry Allen Tupper were of one mind and heart... They shared a common missionary vision and complete dedication to the cause of Christ.

> *For a long while that morning she had lain very quietly, unconscious, the watcher thought. Then she stirred, and seemed to be looking for someone. Her lips moved, and as the nurse bent to catch her whisper she heard a Chinese name. The frail, thin hands were clasped together in the Chinese fashion of greeting, and gently unclasped. Over and over there came that look, and the greeting to Chinese friends long since gone on before her—her Chinese women of Tengchow and Pingtu, of the villages round about, whom she had told of the heavenly home. The watcher did not venture to break that holy hour. She felt as if the heavenly visitors had come within the stateroom to greet and bear her spirit away.*
>
> *And it was thus, with the Chinese handclasp, a smile of greeting and the whisper of a friend's name that Lottie Moon went home.*[29]

Charlotte Diggs Moon and Henry Allen Tupper were of one mind and heart. Their cultural backgrounds were similar and both were well educated and endowed with unusual linguistic ability. They shared a common missionary vision and complete dedication to the cause of Christ. With mutual respect and appreciation they modeled the ideal working relationship of the Foreign Mission Board with its missionaries. Their correspondence was extensive and continued even after Tupper retired from the board. Whatever success the now legendary missionary may have enjoyed was due in part to the support she received from Tupper and the board.

The Missionary Centennial, 1892

As the centennial of the modern missionary movement drew near, the board began to think of how the celebration could be most effectively used for the promotion of missions. In its 1888 meeting, the convention appointed a Centennial Committee. Tupper suggested that a most fitting commemoration of the centennial would include the appointment of one hundred new missionaries and the building of one hundred "simple" chapels.[30] The next year plans were expanded and Tupper's suggestions were adopted as goals. Centennial Committees were set up in each state. A goal of $250,000 was projected for a permanent fund to be divided equally between the Foreign and Home Mission boards. The convention also invited Northern and Canadian Baptists to join in the celebration.

Although the financial and personnel goals were not reached, the missionary efforts of Southern Baptists were blessed with forty new missionaries appointed in the three year period ending in March 1893. The treasurer of the board reported that $154,686.28 had been received.[31] Intangible results may have been even more important than those that could be tabulated. Not only were Baptists prompted to rethink their own missionary responsibility, but other Protestant denominations did the same.

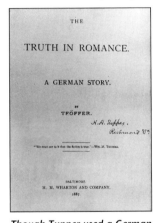

THE

TRUTH IN ROMANCE.

A GERMAN STORY.

BY
TFÖFFER.

BALTIMORE
H. M. WHARTON AND COMPANY.
1887.

Though Tupper used a German pen name for his novel, **The Truth in Romance,** *a surviving copy bears his signature*

The twenty-one years of Tupper's administration had seen a remarkable expansion of the work and a corresponding increase in receipts. The Foreign Mission Board's annual report in 1894 praised Tupper for "his consecrated devotion to the work. . . ."[32]

Sufficient funds, however, for the day to day operation of the board were never assured. His two years' experience as a bookkeeper in his father's business enterprises made him acutely conscious of the board's precarious financial condition. His personal wealth and line of credit made it possible for him to borrow money on his own signature to meet the board's pressing bills. In addition, Tupper frequently gave large sums himself to balance the books. Toward the end of his life, he estimated that he had given half of his income to missions. Even with these assets, raising the necessary finances for the board's needs was a continual struggle. To help out, he even asked the board to reduce his salary from $2,500 to $2,000 annually, which it was when he took office, but the board turned down the request. The centennial year brought the board the largest income it had ever received.

Tupper Retires

With the close of the Missionary Centennial Celebration, Tupper decided it was time to retire. Therefore, when the board met on 4 May 1893, "Dr. Tupper stated that the Convention had left the election of the Cor. Secretary with the Board, and he earnestly requested that the Board would not consider his name in connection with the office. . . ."[33] The members of the board promptly disregarded Tupper's request and unanimously elected him corresponding secretary by a standing vote. Upon learning of the action of the board, Tupper wrote: "I must beg you fervently that I may be allowed to decline the great honor that you have conferred upon me. With sentiments of the highest consideration I am dear Brethren, yours very sincerely, (signed) H. A. Tupper."[34]

H. A. Tupper was sixty-five and now without the help of his wife, who had died five years before, he doubtless felt he could not carry the burden of his office any longer. Besides, T. P. Bell who had been his able assistant the past seven years had resigned to become the corresponding secretary of the Sunday School Board. Tupper now had the full responsibility of the office alone. He had given the board and Southern Baptists his best years in attempting to make foreign missions a priority in the life of the convention. Perhaps he had grown weary with the long controversy over Gospel Missionism, as Robert Alton James has suggested. He also probably wanted some time to teach and write, while he was still able—something he had enjoyed doing on a limited basis for some time.

In spite of the controversies in which Tupper inevitably found himself by virtue of his office, his was an irenic spirit. He had demonstrated upon numerous occasions that while he was a Baptist of deep convictions with an historical understanding of the faith, he cultivated fraternal relationships with other denominations. He led the board to join the Foreign Mission Conference of North America. During the centennial year (1892), he took part in a missionary conference sponsored by twenty-two mission boards and societies.

Tupper possessed a profound respect for history and the printed page. When the convention in a fit of short-sightedness, due to a deficit of $1,200, suspended publication of the *Foreign Mission Journal* with the June issue, 1875, Tupper was understandably upset. The next year under his diplomatic prodding the convention reversed itself and allowed the board to resume publication, which it did in April 1877.[35] He also added his own contribution to the history of

H.A. Tupper's grave, Hollywood Cemetery in Richmond

Southern Baptist foreign mission efforts with two major books: *Foreign Missions of the Southern Baptist Convention* (1880) and *A Decade of Foreign Missions, 1880-1890.*[36]

Tupper was the epitome of the scholar-activist. He devised his own Hebrew grammar to aid in his study of the Hebrew text. Three years after his retirement he entered the classroom at Richmond College to teach Bible, continuing until his death on 27 March 1902. In addition to his books and articles, correspondence and published sermons, Tupper's personal legacy was great. Six of his children were actively involved in the on-going work of the Foreign Mission Board either through the Woman's Missionary Union or through their churches. Above all, he modeled for subsequent generations an utterly sincere dedication to missions. He never allowed the shadows cast on the work by controversy or the unfaithfulness of others to obscure the sunlight of God's love or eclipse his own missionary vision. While he may not have been the most eloquent or the most dynamic corresponding secretary, none felt the importance of the task to which he had put his hand more than did H. A. Tupper. As much as he supported the home mission effort, he was convinced that the Great Commission made foreign missions a divine imperative.

> *Much is to be done at home. But the power of the gospel cannot be localized. The son of Manoah was not born to be bound to a treadmill, but to bear away the brazen gates of Gaza, and to scatter singlehanded the compacted forces of Philistia. Luther said that the doctrine of Justification by Faith, was for the standing or falling of the church. But faith is manifested by works. However true to the ordinances and the doctrines, our people must come down from their position and power if they fail in this great essential duty of Christianity.[37]*

For Tupper, the life blood of Southern Baptists was missions. That conviction increasingly became the driving motivation of the Southern Baptist Convention and its reason for being.

ENDNOTES

1. *Proceedings*, SBC, 1881, 19.
2. See *Proceedings*, SBC, 1886, 21-22, 27, 28.
3. See Baker, *Southern Baptist Convention and its People*, 261-65, for a more complete discussion of Tichenor's problems in establishing a place for the Home Mission Board in the Southern Baptist Zion.
4. Cited by Bobbie Sorrill, *Annie Armstrong: Dreamer in Action* (Nashville: Broadman Press, 1984), 94.
5. James, "Henry Allen Tupper," 189. For more information on Annie Armstrong's difficulties in relationships, see Sorrill, *Annie Armstrong: Dreamer in Action*.
6. Minutes, FMB, 20 April 1881, 433.
7. Correspondence of H. A. Tupper with James P. Boyce, 1881, Jenkins Memorial Library and Archives, Foreign Mission Board, Richmond, Virginia. Hereafter referred to as JMLA.
8. Minutes, FMB, 17 June 1881, 434-35.
9. Cited by James, "Henry Allen Tupper," 107.
10. Crawford Howell Toy (1836-1919) taught before the Civil War at Albemarle Female Institute from which Lottie Moon graduated. He also was appointed a missionary by the Foreign Mission Board to Japan but the war intervened and his plans changed. At one time he seriously considered marrying Lottie Moon, whom he apparently admired. After serving as a private in the Confederate Army and then as a chaplain, he studied in Germany and came back to the United States to espouse an early form of higher criticism that he encountered in Germany at the time. He also embraced the theory of evolution. His tenure as professor of Old Testament at Southern Seminary was terminated when he refused to pledge not to teach the offensive views. During his ten years (1869-1879) he was as influential as controversial. A year after he left Southern, Toy became a professor of Hebrew and Oriental Languages at Harvard University and won international recognition for his scholarship.

11. Baker, *Southern Baptist Convention and its People*, 278-81. Adrian Lamkin, Jr., concluded in his Ph.D. dissertation, "The Gospel Mission Movement within the Southern Baptist Convention" (Southern Baptist Theological Seminary, 1980), 207-10, that T. P. Crawford developed his philosophy of missions independently of J. R. Graves and the Landmark movement. He also believed that the Landmarkers appropriated Gospel Missionism as their own. The anti-board policy of Crawford was certainly very similar to that of Graves as expressed in the 1859 meeting of the SBC in Richmond, Virginia. Crawford did attend that meeting of the convention and may have been influenced by Graves to think along those lines.
12. L. S. Foster, *Fifty Years in China: An Eventful Memoir of Tarleton Perry Crawford, D. D.* (Nashville: Bayless-Pullen Company, 1909), 25.
13. Ibid., 42.
14. Minutes, FMB, 5 March 1877, 354.
15. Foster, *Fifty Years in China*, 214.
16. Cited in ibid., 171-72.
17. *Proceedings*, SBC, 1886, XXIV.
18. Ibid.
19. Foster, *Fifty Years in China*, 222.
20. Ibid., 223.
21. Cited, ibid., 225.
22. T. P. Crawford, *Churches, to the Front* (China: T. P. Crawford, 1892), 14.
23. Lamkin, "Gospel Mission Movement," 166.
24. Foster, *Fifty Years in China*, 345-46.
25. Lamkin, "Gospel Mission Movement," 181-82.
26. Maddry, *Christ's Expendables*, 30.
27. Cited by Catherine B. Allen, *The New Lottie Moon Story* (Nashville: Broadman Press, 1980), 184.
28. Ibid. This record of Lottie's defiance was recorded by Pastor Li.
29. Maddry, *Christ's Expendables*, 37. I am indebted to Catherine B. Allen for her splendid biography of Lottie, *The New Lottie Moon Story*, for much of the material in this section.
30. *Proceedings*, SBC, 1890, xlii-xliii.

31. Ibid., vii, ix. Of the amount received by the Foreign Mission Board $21,345.90 was designated for "Permanent Fund," and $28,438.91 for "Centennial."

32. *Proceedings,* SBC, 1894, I.

33. Minutes, FMB, May 4, 1893, 388-89.

34. Ibid., 392.

35. *Proceedings,* SBC, 1876, 34.

36. Tupper also wrote the bicentennial history of the First Baptist Church of Charleston, South Carolina, and edited the centennial history of the First Baptist Church of Richmond, Virginia. His *Truth in Romance* was a novel based on the Stout and Bell episode. He also wrote *The Carpenter's Son* that set forth his philosophy of history. After Tupper retired from the Foreign Mission Board, he wrote *American Baptist Missions in Africa,* which was published in 1895.

37. H. A. Tupper, *The Foreign Missions of the Southern Baptist Convention* (Philadelphia: American Baptist Publication Society, 1880), 263-64.

PART III

Expanding Horizons and Diminishing Resources

1893-1932

1893-1932

Expanding Horizons and Diminishing Resources

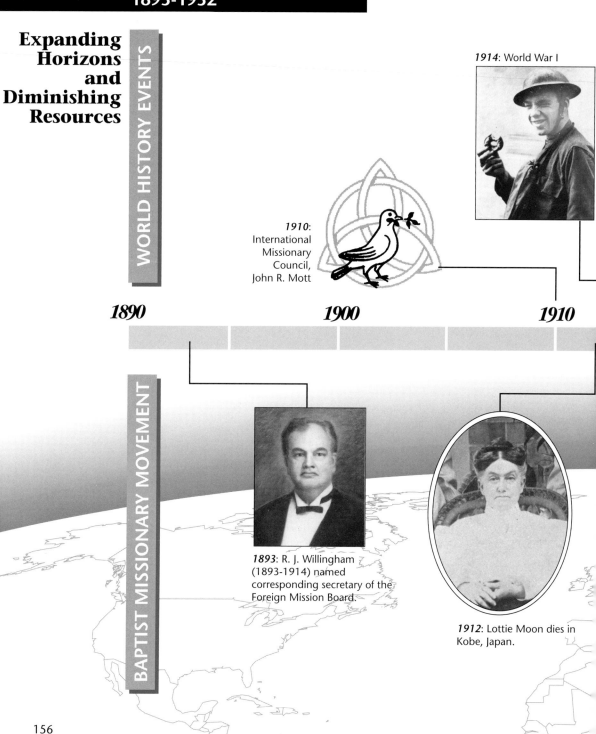

WORLD HISTORY EVENTS

1914: World War I

1910: International Missionary Council, John R. Mott

1890   **1900**   **1910**

BAPTIST MISSIONARY MOVEMENT

1893: R. J. Willingham (1893-1914) named corresponding secretary of the Foreign Mission Board.

1912: Lottie Moon dies in Kobe, Japan.

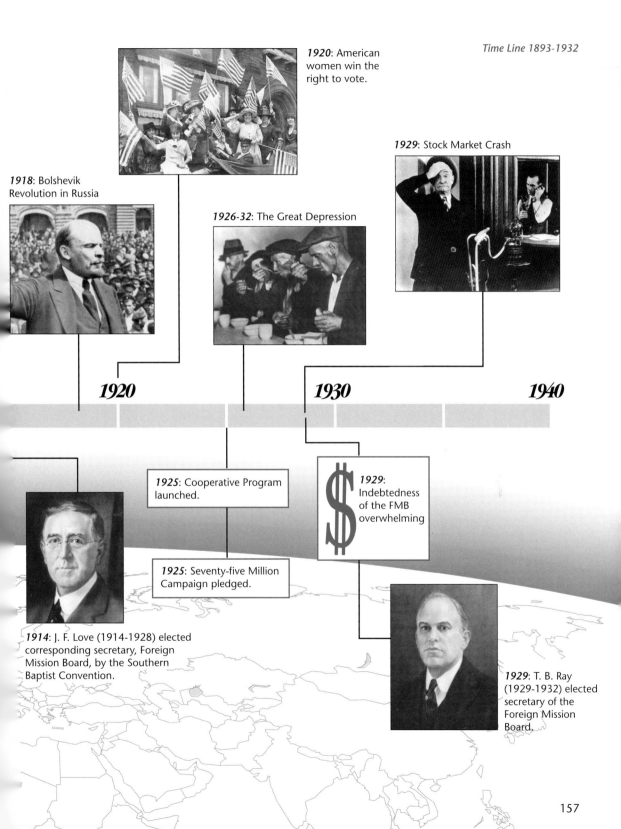

1920: American women win the right to vote.

1929: Stock Market Crash

1918: Bolshevik Revolution in Russia

1926-32: The Great Depression

1920

1930

1940

1925: Cooperative Program launched.

1929: Indebtedness of the FMB overwhelming

1925: Seventy-five Million Campaign pledged.

1914: J. F. Love (1914-1928) elected corresponding secretary, Foreign Mission Board, by the Southern Baptist Convention.

1929: T. B. Ray (1929-1932) elected secretary of the Foreign Mission Board.

157

Enlarging the Vision

During the latter years of Tupper's tenure, the Home Mission Board had moved into the forefront of Southern Baptist concerns due to the forceful and effective leadership of its corresponding secretary, I. T. Tichenor. Gradually, T. P. Bell, the assistant corresponding secretary, had emerged as the spokesman for the Foreign Mission Board. Both of these developments probably confirmed Tupper in his decision to resign. Forty-one at the time of Tupper's resignation, Bell was committed to foreign missions. He appeared to be Tupper's heir apparent. There was only one problem—he had recently been elected to the office of corresponding secretary of the Sunday School Board and had assumed his new responsibilities one month before Tupper's resignation. The managers of the Foreign Mission Board determined to elect him anyway, which they did. But he decided to remain with the Sunday School Board.

H. H. Harris, professor of Greek at Richmond College and president of the board, wrote the vice presi-

R.J. Willingham

dents of the board for their recommendations. Less than two months later, Robert Josiah Willingham, pastor of the First Baptist Church of Memphis, Tennessee, was surprised to receive a letter from Harris informing him that on 23 July 1893 he had been unanimously elected corresponding secretary of the Foreign Mission Board. Before giving the board an answer, Willingham sought advice from trusted friends and decided to meet with the managers of the board. The decision was not an easy one. He had been pastor of the church less than two years, and God's blessing upon his ministry in Memphis was evident.

Willingham met with the board on 6 August. His visit was confirming. His salary was set at $2,500 a year which was $500 less than his salary in Memphis. The board's indebtedness stood at $7,075 and by the time he took office on 1 September, it had reached $13,279.06. There were no better prospects of paying it off than had existed previously. Willingham also discovered that

R.J. Willingham assumed his new responsibility as secretary of the Foreign Mission Board at a reduction in salary. He was the first of the corresponding secretaries to travel extensively, enhancing his missionary vision. Thus, for a people who thrived on preaching, Willingham was a man sent from God. In the years before the Cooperative Program and the Lottie Moon Christmas Offering, he preached the board out of debt and missions into the hearts of Southern Baptists.

the office did not even own a typewriter, but Harris, the interim corresponding secretary, had been authorized at the 23 July meeting to purchase one.[1] In spite of its financial straits, the board voted to pay Willingham's expenses to Richmond for the meeting on 6 August. Apparently, Willingham did not believe it was the board's responsibility since the trip to Richmond was taken at his initiative, for scribbled in pencil in the Minute Book is this note: "But he declined to receive same," and initialed RJW.[2]

Among those from whom Willingham sought advice was his father's pastor, E. W. Warren of Macon, Georgia. Warren wrote him on 29 July 1893.

> You are called to a very important position—the direction and support of one hundred missionaries, and to the wise and Godly direction of all our great work abroad. Accept it; lay yourself upon this altar of active and Christly service unreservedly. I want to say a few things:
>
> 1. You will have two millions of masters, but you will be under obligation to please but One.
>
> 2. You will find ignorant pastors and uncooperative brethren by the thousands; but God always has enough willing givers to keep his work going and to make it successful.
>
> 3. You will find dissatisfaction and disaffection among the missionaries, but a wise and conservative Board will come to your aid.[3]

Willingham took Warren's advice and accepted the call of the Foreign Mission Board. He moved to Richmond the last of August, assuming the responsibilities of his office on 1 September 1893. H. H. Harris introduced the new corresponding secretary to the readers of the *Foreign Mission Journal*. "For five years," he wrote, "Dr. Willingham has been the very efficient Vice-President of our Board for Tennessee. He brings to his duties as Secretary some acquaintance with missions, a vigorous body thirty-nine years old, great capacity for work, fine talents both for public speaking and for influencing men privately. . . ."[4] As later events would reveal, this description of the new corresponding secretary, while accurate, hardly captured the spirit of the man. Perhaps, as few others could have, Willingham was destined to enlarge the missionary vision of Southern Baptists and to enlist their support for foreign missions.

The Man and his Mission

The twenty-one year and four month tenure of Robert Josiah Willingham, 1893-1914, was almost exactly the same length as that of his predecessor. There were other interesting parallels. Both Tupper and Willingham were native sons of South Carolina and both later moved to Georgia. Both were pastors with a deep commitment to foreign missions before coming to the board. Although their personalities were quite different, their contributions to the cause to which they gave themselves were both distinctive and creative. If Tupper's work was, as that of James B. Taylor, foundational, it remained for Willingham to forge a consensus among Southern Baptists as they entered the twentieth century. Because foreign missions was his own "magnificent obsession," he possessed the ability to translate his vision into language that Southern Baptists could understand and embrace.

Willingham entered the University of

Georgia at fourteen years of age without any goal in mind except to earn a degree. Two years later, he suspended his collegiate education to work for his father, mainly as a bookkeeper. Within a year he was back in school and living in the home of a university professor. Young Willingham's own consistent Christian lifestyle impressed the professor, who observed that the student never missed family prayers and he never studied on Sundays. He applied himself to his studies in spite of the temptation to do otherwise. He wrote to his sister, "[I] never visit the girls and thus am not disturbed mentally."[5] Yet the tranquility he sought was not to be. His little sister, Matchie, whom he loved dearly, died, as did his brother George, during his senior year at the university. In spite of this double sorrow, he graduated in 1873 with an M.A. degree and a gold medal in mathematics.

After graduation, Robert first taught school, becoming principal of the high school in Macon, Georgia. In his leisure hours he discovered that he enjoyed studying Latin and Greek more than mathematics. In the meantime, he found he had time

[Willingham] wrote his son Calder,… "That year [1879] with three children I got $450 and had to pay $100 rent and keep a horse and buggy to go to my churches."

for the girls, at least for one girl, Corneille Bacon, who was a Sunday School teacher in a mission where he was also teaching. They were soon engaged and shortly afterwards, married.

While working with his father in the mercantile business, he studied law at night with the intention of becoming a lawyer, but the overwhelming conviction that God was calling him into the ministry changed the course of his life. He had been converted at thirteen during a revival meeting and subsequently had given some thought to the possibility of preaching but was determined not to preach without a definite call. The call did come in his twenty-third year. He was licensed to preach by the First Baptist Church of Macon, Georgia, on 19 December 1877. Ten days later he left his wife and children with his father-in-law to enter The Southern Baptist Theological Seminary, in Louisville, Kentucky.[6]

The following fall term found him back in the seminary but this time with his wife and children. His seminary education was cut short when he accepted the call of a Baptist church in Talbottom, Georgia, to which he moved in January 1879. That first year in the pastorate was not easy. Years later he wrote his son Calder, who was a missionary, "That year with three children I got $450 and had to pay $100 rent and keep a horse and buggy to go to my churches."[7] That which concerned him more than his financial condition was the lack of conversions. During his first eighteen months as a pastor, he baptized only one convert and she confessed that she was converted as a result of the ministry of another preacher. In twenty-eight months he baptized only three converts, but he persisted. In the next few months, the confirmation which he sought finally came with the baptism of thirty-four new converts.[8]

After serving churches in Georgia, Willingham became the pastor of the First Baptist Church of Chattanooga, Tennessee in 1887. Four years later, he was elected vice president of the Foreign Mission Board for Tennessee and a member of the state's Centennial Committee, whose goal was to raise $250,000 during the centennial celebration of the beginning of the modern mission movement. Shortly thereafter in 1891, he accepted the call of the First Baptist Church of Memphis, but here his commitment to missions was to be sorely tested.

Nothing less than a missionary world vision could have moved Willingham from the pastorate to… the Foreign Mission Board.

One of the members of the Memphis church was J. R. Graves, the grand old man of the Landmark movement and the champion of some of the principles that the Gospel Mission movement had embraced to the detriment of the work in the North China Mission. Graves apparently constituted no personal problem to the new pastor but the same could not be said of the leading contributor of the church. Willingham was warned by one of the deacons that he should not preach so much on missions because, he said, "the man who gives more for your salary than anybody else doesn't believe in it."[9] The young pastor responded: "I will not preach a mutilated gospel." He was true to his word. As a result, the former opponent to missions became one of its strongest supporters. Willingham attributed the ingathering of two hundred new members to reaching out "as we had never done before for lost souls."[10]

Nothing less than a missionary world vision could have moved Willingham from the pastorate to an administrative position with the Foreign Mission Board. It certainly was not money. As the president of the board indicated, Willingham accepted the call of the board at a salary of $2,500 and no perquisites at a time when a missionary on the field with a wife and nine children would have received an allowance of $2,750.[11] His annual salary in Memphis was $3,000, excluding honoraria that pastors ordinarily received from a variety of sources. Such would not likely be forthcoming in Richmond. The corresponding secretary elect also said when discussing the salary differential that he could not call on others to go and to give unless he were willing to make sacrifices for the cause. He tendered his resignation to take effect on 1 September 1893, the very day the board had asked him to assume his new position.

The Financial Burden

One of the first problems Willingham faced upon arriving in Richmond was the suffocating debt of the Foreign Mission Board. This was common knowledge throughout the convention. The president of the board, in announcing in the *Foreign*

Mission Journal Willingham's acceptance of the position, wrote:

We do not imagine that he or any other one man possesses all the qualifications considered desirable for the position, but only that by the grace of God, the help of the brethren, and a deal of hard work, he will come nearer to filling it than any other we could get. He takes charge at a most unpropitious time. Our treasury is not only empty, but burdened with a heavy debt.[12]

It was, indeed, an "unpropitious" time. The entire country was in the throes of a financial depression. To further complicate matters, the year before the convention had accepted the report of a Committee on Methods, which had recommended dispensing with assistant secretaryships, but had left the matter with the boards.

Upon the resignation of Tupper, H. H. Harris, president of the board and professor of Greek at Richmond College, became the interim corresponding secretary. He was assisted by R. T. Bryan, missionary to China, who had delayed his return to the field in order to assist the board during the period of transition. Under the circumstances, the board decided not to employ an assistant secretary. Thus at the outset, Willingham shouldered the burden of the board's indebtedness pretty much alone. His experience as an accountant made him acutely conscious of the problem. He determined to take the matter to the convention in its annual meetings.

From the very beginning of his work with the Foreign Mission Board, it was evident that Willingham was perfectly suited for the job. His conviction that the gospel was the "power of God unto salvation," coupled with his commitment to missions and his transparent sincerity, enabled him to captivate his audiences and enlist their enthusiastic response. L. W. Beler referred to Willingham as a "master of assemblies":

I cannot begin to number the times I have heard him speak, yet not once did he fail to grip his audience with a magnetic power. . . . If the convention was excited over a spirited debate, it grew calm when he began to speak; if it was listless, he would rouse it to keen attention before a dozen sentences had fallen from his lips.[13]

In spite of his best efforts, however, the indebtedness worsened before the situation began to improve. By 14 April 1896, the liabilities of the board had risen to $49,292.89. During Tupper's administration, the corresponding secretary had often alleviated the financial crunch by a generous donation. Willingham, apparently, had no comparable personal income upon which to draw. But some missionaries were sufficiently well off to make small loans to the board upon occasion. In 1896, both Lottie Moon and R. T. Bryan loaned the board more than $2,000 each.[14] That year appears to have been the turning point in the fortunes of the board.

The impression that the board's indebtedness must be retired in order to free the board for its work was spreading. Indicative of this spirit was an editorial in the *Religious Herald* by R. H. Pitt in the 9 April 1896 issue:

The situation of the Foreign Mission Board is still distressing. Money has come in very slowly. The officers and members of the Board are sorely troubled. . . . For the Board to go to Chattanooga with a heavy debt, would be deplorable indeed. If brethren throughout the South could see our big-hearted secretary as we see him day after day–praying, struggling, working incessant-

ly, hoping that God will enlarge the hearts of his people and unloose their purse-strings, so that they may send in the needed money–they would understand the situation far more clearly than we can present it.[15]

When the convention convened in Chattanooga on 8 May 1896, a Committee on Finances of the Foreign Mission Board brought its report. The report addressed frankly the possibility of recalling missionaries from the field, if the finances were not forthcoming to sustain the work. A part of the problem, the committee charged, was due to the failure of churches and state conventions to make their contributions throughout the fiscal year, forcing the board to borrow the money to meet its monthly obligations, thus incurring charges of $2,000 in interest, "which amount ought to have gone directly to missions." The committee identified the source of the problem. "Our brethren are very sensitive as to the slightest approach to waste, or excessive expense, by our Boards. Would that they could realize their own reckless waste of so much money *for interest, for which they themselves are alone responsible!*"[16]

The committee made two significant

Willingham's burden had become the burden of the entire convention with the result that Southern Baptists became committed to foreign missions as never before.

recommendations in light of the board's financial problems. First, the committee recommended that the board encourage individuals and churches to give as much of their annual contributions as possible during the first quarter of a convention year instead of waiting until the last month, as most had been doing. Second, "We recommend that an effort be made here and now to pay off the debt of the Board."[17]

After F. H. Kerfoot, of Kentucky, spoke to the report, Willingham gave his usual moving appeal. Then an offering of $9,835.37 was taken. The challenges of the committee and R. J. Willingham did not go unheeded. From this point on, leading pastors of the convention showed a new determination to rid the board of its encumbering debt. This was particularly evident when Georgia Baptists met in their annual state convention the following year.

In April, Willingham was interrupted while addressing the Georgia Baptist Convention by J. L. Gross, who arose to offer a resolution that Georgia Baptists raise $5,000 for each of the Home and Foreign boards before the next meeting of the Southern Baptist Convention. The resolution was enthusiastically adopted. The news of what Georgia Baptists had done was reported in every Baptist state paper in the South. Just before the convention convened in Wilmington, North Carolina, for its 1897 session, the Georgia messengers learned that the board still owed $13,500. They decided to raise an additional $1,300, $300 of which was designated for flood relief in Louisiana and to alleviate suffering in Florida brought on by a freeze that devastated the citrus crop. Other states took similar action. Enough pledges were received to indicate that the board would soon be out of debt. The next year it happened. The *Foreign Mission Journal* announced in its issue of June 1898: "All debts Paid."[18] This accomplishment was even more surprising in light of the Whitsitt controversy, sparked by a resurgence of the Landmark movement, which was convulsing the convention at the time. (The next year William Heth Whitsitt was forced to resign the presidency of Southern Seminary.)

Willingham's burden had become the burden of the entire convention with the result that Southern Baptists became committed to foreign missions as never before. A jubilant corresponding secretary for the first time saw an unencumbered board able to expand and strengthen its work. The report of the Foreign Mission Board to the convention reflected the newfound enthusiasm. "At the very beginning of the year," Willingham declared, "we received from the Convention, in clear, ringing tones, the order to ADVANCE. To this order the Board gave immediate consideration, and steps were at once taken to enlarge our work."[19] Then, Willingham reported that twenty-one new missionaries had been appointed during the convention year, and that, in spite of the Boxer Rebellion in China, there were one thousand and nine baptisms on the foreign fields during the past year.

Another reason for rejoicing was the improved financial condition of the board.

Let it be noted that this is the fourth year in succession that our Board has been able to report all indebtedness paid, and the number of our missionaries has been constantly increasing, until now we have one hundred and two missionaries and one hundred and seventy-one native assistants; a force altogether of two hundred and seventy-three workers.[20]

As yet, no new countries had been entered during Willingham's tenure, but the existing work had been strengthened. With the expansion into new fields, indebtedness would return but not until 1909. Regardless, the board was now determined

Sidney M. Sowell family, Argentina

to enlarge its operations.

Enlarging the Vision

It was ten years into Willingham's tenure before the board entered a new country. The underlying reason for the delay was the lack of adequate financing to make such a venture feasible. Apparently, Willingham's strategy was to strengthen existing work when possible, since Southern Baptists were already involved in two of the largest mission fields in the world, China and Africa. With all debts paid, the convention insisted on enlarging the vision.

Only Brazil and Mexico were numbered among the board's work south of the border. A group of students at Southern Seminary, where missionary enthusiasm permeated the student body, became particularly burdened for Argentina. Under the leadership of two students, Sydney Sowell and Joseph Hart, students of the seminary raised a thousand dollars in order to prod the board into launching work in Argentina.

[In Argentina] Baptists work with a continuing existence that began with the ministry of Pablo Besson.

At seventeen years of age, Sydney McFarland Sowell (1871-1954) dedicated his life to God as a missionary to Argentina. He put his decision in writing and hid it in a hollow stump on his father's farm. His interest in Argentina had first been aroused when, as a teenager, he read a book about the country. With his call to missions came the conviction that he must prepare himself for his life's work. Graduating from the University of Richmond with an M.A. degree, he entered Southern Seminary, from which he received his Th.D. Upon graduation, he and Joseph L. Hart offered themselves to the Foreign Mission Board for missionary service in Argentina but were told by Willingham that the board was not prepared to begin work in that country. Instead, the secretary suggested that the

young men consider Palestine as their field of service. But they insisted that God had called them to Argentina, not Palestine. With the thousand dollars to back up their commitment, the board relented and in 1903 appointed both missionaries to Argentina.

Sowell left for Argentina in September, arriving in Buenos Aires in December. Enroute to his field of service the young bachelor was the guest of the Bagbys in Rio de Janeiro. While there he not only received an orientation to Latin America but met his bride-to-be, Ermine Bagby (1881-1939), whom he married in 1906. Upon arriving in Argentina, he was surprised to learn that there were already functioning Baptist churches in the country. Willingham had written a letter of introduction to a Methodist pastor in Buenos Aires since he, too, was unaware of the presence of Baptists in the city. The pastor immediately put the new missionary in contact with Pablo Besson, the pioneer Baptist preacher in Argentina.

Besson invited the new American missionary to live in his home. Thus, while learning the language, Sydney Sowell received an incomparable orientation to Argentina and the indigenous Baptist work. In the process, ties of friendship and cooperation were established with the leaders of the older Baptist work which helped to foster a spirit of unity from the earliest days of Southern Baptist missionary presence in the country.

Sowell soon learned that as early as 1818, a Scottish Baptist layman by the name of James Thomson came distributing Bibles for the British and Foreign Bible Society and

River Plate countries: Argentina, Chile, Uruguay, Paraguay

Evangelicals. English Baptists succeeded in forming a church in Malvinas by 1872 but in time it, too, disappeared without a discernable trace. Baptist work with a continuing existence began with the ministry of Pablo Besson.

Besson arrived in Buenos Aires as an immigrant in 1881. He was born and educated in Switzerland and was ordained as a pastor of a Reformed church in 1870. Difficulties with the church compelled him to examine the question of infant baptism in the light of the Greek New Testament. Once he had determined that Baptists were right in this matter, he examined their doctrines of faith and became a convinced Baptist. For six years he was a Baptist missionary in France until one of his former friends, who had emigrated from Europe to Argentina, pled with him to send a Baptist to that country to serve as pastor of a small band of believers at Santa Fe. Even though he found no mission society willing to sponsor his work in Argentina, he decided to go it alone. In the city of Sante Fe, as he began to witness and win immigrants to Christ, he encountered for the first time the fierce opposition of the Roman Catholic Church.

An incident early in his ministry there became a catalyst that changed the course of his life. A little daughter of one of the immigrant families had died and when the

establishing Lancastrian schools in Argentina and other countries of South America. Although he established no churches, Thomson sowed the seed which later others would cultivate. Robert Williams of Wales appears to have been the first Baptist pastor who attempted to form a church among Welsh immigrants around 1866. Other Welsh Baptists were to succeed in establishing schools and churches which eventually were absorbed by other

167

family attempted to have her buried in the public cemetery, the local parish priest effectively blocked it. This bit of intolerance turned Besson into a champion of religious liberty.[21] His articles on the subject were published in the leading newspapers of Argentina. His was arguably the most effective voice that led to the establishment of religious liberty in that country.[22]

Following the recommendation of Besson and Robert Hosford, Sowell and Joseph Hart began the work in Rosario. By 1905, the two missionaries had succeeded in constituting a Baptist church in the city. Sowell then returned to Buenos Aires, married, and with his bride, founded the Iglesia del Once on 30 November 1906.

From Argentina, within a decade, missionaries and nationals carried the gospel into Uruguay, Paraguay and Chile.

In 1908, Joseph Hart, pastor of the First Baptist Church, Rosario, Argentina, issued the invitation on behalf of the Argentine Baptist Mission that led to the formation of a national convention. A few years later the Central Church of Buenos Aires, founded and led by Pablo Besson, affiliated with the convention. Other churches which had been apparently reluctant initially to become a part of the new convention, for fear of losing their freedom, also joined.

Thus Baptists of a number of different nationalities overcame their differences in laying a solid foundation for the denomination in this nation of immigrants.

Sowell and Hart worked closely together in developing the infrastructure of the denomination. The River Plate Seminary, of which Sowell became president, was founded in 1918. He also held numerous positions in the fledgling denomination, and wrote a number of commentaries and Sunday School lessons. He became the first editor of the Argentine Baptist paper, *El Expositor Bautista*. Sowell and Besson provided a literary foundation for the Baptists of Argentina. Sowell died on 5 May 1954 in Buenos after fifty-one years of fruitful missionary service, leaving behind a rich legacy and four children, one of whom became a missionary.

From Argentina, within a decade, missionaries and nationals carried the gospel into Uruguay, Paraguay, and Chile. The vigorous growth of the Baptist movement in Argentina and its neighboring countries was phenomenal. Doubtless many factors contributed to this development. Some are more evident than others. The Bible was widely distributed. An example of its impact upon the lives of those into whose hands it had fallen for the first time is seen in the life of Pabla de Broda. She bought a Bible in the Chapel of San Antonio de Lattin in 1911 and was converted in the process of reading it. She immediately began to share her faith with her family. As a result they, too, became Christians. Through a Baptist layman they met Joseph Hart, who baptized the entire family. Two of Mrs. Broda's sons, Natalio and Pablo, became Hart's assistants and together with Hart and Julio Ostermann, founded five churches. Subsequently, other members of the Broda family became widely influential in Argentine Baptist life and beyond.[23]

In the experience of the Broda family is seen a combination of factors that aided the rapid growth of the Baptist work in Argentina. The seed had been sown years before by Thomson, Besson, and others. With the arrival of the first Southern Baptist missionaries, Baptists almost immediately became more aggressive in their evangelism. Funds became available with which Bibles could be more widely distributed and chapels rented. As the work expanded, hungry hearts responded to the gospel so earnestly preached by missionaries and the newly won converts alike. Since the population was largely made up of immigrants from a number of different European nations, the people were not adverse to hearing the gospel from North Americans. It was apparent that Southern Baptists had entered Argentina at the opportune moment.

Uruguay, often referred to as "the Switzerland of South America," sandwiched

In 1948, a National Convention was organized and the Uruguayan Baptist Mission was separated from the Argentine Mission in 1954.

between two powerful neighbors–Argentina and Brazil–early in the nineteenth century had experienced some of the same gospel currents as Argentina. In 1806 when English troops occupied both Buenos Aires and Uruguay, David Hill Creighton, a missionary of the London Missionary Society, arrived in Montevideo with six hundred copies of the New Testament and additional tracts in Spanish in order to lay the ground work for future Protestant missionary efforts. When the English withdrew the following year, he returned home, leaving his Bibles and tracts behind. In this first decade of the nineteenth century there seems to have been an avid interest in buying Bibles, especially on the part of Catholic priests.

When the Scotsman James Thomson arrived he was cordially received by an influential priest, Damaso Antonio Larranaga. He aided Thomson in distributing his Bibles and in organizing the Lancasterian School in Montevideo in 1821. Although a Baptist, Thomson apparently baptized no converts nor did he attempt to organize a church. Apparently, he felt that his primary task was that of a colporter and educator. Therefore, he concentrated his efforts on establishing schools in which the Bible was the principle textbook. It was not long, however, before all traces of his work had vanished.

Pablo Besson, the pioneer Baptist preacher from Argentina, for a number of years took his vacations in Montevideo during the summers. Upon these occasions, he made friends among the elite, some of whom he won to Christ and baptized. Besson did not attempt to organize a church. By the time the first Southern Baptist missionary arrived, only one of those who had been baptized by Besson, Juan Llorach, could be found to become a member of the first formally constituted Baptist Church in Uruguay.[24]

Two brothers, James and Lemuel Quarles, who had been serving as Southern Baptist missionaries in Rosario, Argentina, while Joseph Hart and his family were on furlough in the States, decided to transfer to Uruguay. They left Rosario by river boat on New Year's Day, 1911, and a few days later arrived in Colonia, Uruguay, where a colony of Waldenses from Italy had settled. After spending three months with the Waldenses, James and his family moved to Montevideo and Lemuel and his family returned to Argentina. Three months after arriving in Montevideo, James organized the First Baptist Church of Montevideo in his home on 13 August 1911 with only six members, all of whom had been members of the First Church of Rosario.[25]

Uruguay appeared as promising as Argentina had been fruitful but such was not the case. Although, like Argentina, it was a nation of immigrants, 95 percent of whom had come from Spain and Italy, it was no Argentina. With the highest literary rate of any country in South America, Uruguay was also the most indifferent to the gospel. For years, the Baptists carried on a token existence. In spite of the fact that Lemuel transferred to Uruguay from Argentina in order to labor alongside his brother James, after nine years there was still only one Baptist Church and it counted less than forty members.[26] As Justice Anderson pointed out, Baptists failed in the early years to develop able national pastors but were dependent upon "imported" preachers.[27]

The situation began to change for the better with the arrival of the B. W. Orricks in Montevideo on 1 November 1921. Less than two years later with the help of Enrique Cabral, who had been a police chief in Argentina, the Radio Norte Church was organized on 25 March 1923 with nine members. Thus the Orricks began a fruitful ministry of thirty-seven years. In 1948, a National Convention was organized and the Uruguayan Baptist Mission was separated from the Argentine Mission in 1954.

Macao, the scene of the early missionary labors of the J. L. Shucks before they transferred to Hong Kong, became the third field entered by Southern Baptists during Willingham's administration. The circumstances were unusual and reflected the board's willingness to accommodate some variation of commonly accepted Baptist positions in the interest of missions.

Sometime after the Shucks left Macao, the Bible Missionary Society, an independent Baptist organization, began a mission in the colony. After the death of the founder of the mission, the eight remaining missionaries expressed a desire to become a part of the South China Mission. Some beliefs and practices of the Bible Missionary Society's missionaries were at a variance with those of Southern Baptists, the most controversial of which was the practice of "faith healing." The initial response of the board to the request was favorable, with certain reservations.

Subsequently on 9 September 1909 articles of union were agreed upon which "spelled out" how far the board was willing to go in accepting the mission and its missionaries. While it asked that the missionaries of the Bible Missionary Society practice closed communion, the board insisted that "divine healing" should not be allowed to become a test of fellowship "on either side." Further, the board insisted that those missionaries who held different opinions from the majority on disputed points should agree not to make an issue of their views. If a missionary could not conscientiously abide by these articles, the board advised retirement from the employment of

Hwangsein Baptist Church dedication, 1907; R.J. Willingham, left, with C.W. Pruitt and J.B. Hartwell

the board. The board went on to assure the would-be Southern Baptist missionaries that they would be treated "as other missionaries of the board, and they are to be subject to all rules and regulations which may be made by the Board and the mission for their future conduct."[28]

The implications of the articles for merger were that the board was willing for the missionaries to hold to "divine healing" as long as this teaching did not become disruptive in the work. The statement on the role of women, which was also a matter of concern for some members of the board, was equivocal. The board was willing to recognize the fact that conditions on the mission field varied and that the board could not always define precisely the role of women in every situation. The missionaries of the Bible Missionary Society apparently accepted the provisions of the merger,

because the Minutes of the board on 16 December 1909 carried the announcement that the Bible Missionary Society of Macao would become a part of Southern Baptist work on 1 January 1910.[29]

The Sights and Sounds of Human Need

After fourteen years as corresponding secretary of the Foreign Mission Board, Willingham was given the opportunity of visiting the far-flung mission fields of Southern Baptists. The board recommended that he take time off from the office to see for himself the work of the missionaries within the cultural and geographical context of their labors. Friends raised the money for the trip and a personal friend underwrote Mrs. Willingham's expenses. Apart from four trips to Mexico on business for the board, and a prior trip to Palestine and Egypt, Willingham had never been out of the country.

After fifteen days at sea, the Willinghams arrived in Yokohama, Japan. While there, they were the guests of a Northern Baptist missionary family. The sights and sounds of gongs and the clapping hands of idol worshippers, in contrast with the joyous hymns of the redeemed, within the warm fellowship of small Baptist churches, moved the corresponding secretary to the depths of his being. Of this experience, he wrote: "Where on earth can a man make his life count for more than in this great land!"[30] Later his son, Calder, became a missionary to Japan.

The first Sunday in China, the Willinghams visited P'ingtu where Lottie Moon had labored so effectively. J. B. Hartwell was their host during their visit to the stations of the North China Mission. While here, Willingham took part in a dedication of a chapel at Hwanghsein. All along the way from mission station to mission station and from schools to hospitals, he could not refrain from preaching as the missionaries took turns interpreting his sermons. One of his most memorable experiences came in Shanghai, when he stood in the pulpit of Matthew T. Yates, one of the few that "fit him to a T" for Yates was also six feet, two inches tall. He made it a point to visit the hospitals, a work particularly dear to his heart.

His travels brought home to him, apparently for the first time, the harsh realities of missionary service in foreign lands. The very real sacrifices that many missionaries were making far from home and families often with inadequate housing in harsh climates was an inescapable fact not lost on the sensitive soul of the big man with a ten-

der heart. Neither was he indifferent to the condition of those who knew not Christ. Symbolic of this world of darkness to which the Willinghams were being introduced was the sight of women and girls with bound feet hobbling along as best they could. Mrs. Willingham wrote home of their "loveless life."

On the way back to the United States via Burma, the Willinghams visited Rangoon, where Judson first preached the gospel in the Burmese tongue and buried his little son, Roger Williams. Next he visited the grave of William Carey, the church in Calcutta, and the college in Serampore. Once again Willingham was reminded of the importance of education in the missionary enterprise. In Rome he stood in the pulpit of a small Baptist church to declare the unsearchable riches of Christ with missionary Dexter Whittinghill as interpreter.

A trip that was meant to be a time of relaxation from the daily demands of the Richmond office turned out to be otherwise. Even on shipboard, Willingham could not resist the invitation to preach and lecture and while visiting the various mission stations, the missionaries prevailed upon him to preach, and he was never reluctant to do so. The result was that the man with the world in his heart was never quite the same again—the vision had become an unshakable burden. He never recovered, but Southern Baptists were the richer because he did not. As never before, the corresponding secretary laid bare his heart before churches and before convention after convention. An effective advocate of missions before, afterwards it became his obsession. An editorial in the *Christian Index* observed,

And then Dr. Willingham spoke as one who

had seen with a new vision the workings of sin in men. He felt the inexpressible horror of it all as he had beheld it all in heathen lands. It seemed to us as we listened to him evident that this great soul had entered anew into the sufferings of Christ for sinners, and only the vision of the Christ, the risen and reigning Jesus, could give him hope and cheer and courage in view of the awful things which he had looked upon.[31]

As the work expanded, indebtedness returned. When it appeared at the 1910 meeting of the convention that the necessary funds for advance in the work would not be forthcoming, the *Christian Index* reported that Willingham "seemed crushed. He stood there like a heart-broken hero."[32] The *Index* went on to describe what transpired. "There was a strange feeling that pervaded the audience. C.C. Carroll, Kentucky, came to the platform and made one of those old-fashioned impromptu addresses. He said if we left this Convention with no provision for that debt of $90,000, that it was an acknowledgment that we are whipped." Even though the Proportionment Committee had recommended that no collections be taken at the meetings of the convention, it was evident that the messengers longed to respond immediately to the corresponding secretary's appeal. In the midst of the debate on the report of the Proportionment Committee, J. L. Gross was given the floor to take an offering. Enthusiasm for foreign missions had never been higher. Many were

moved to make sacrificial gifts. By midnight $25,000 had been raised toward retirement of the debt. For sometime, it had been evident that R. J. Willingham had captured the hearts of Southern Baptists—it now appeared that the convention had also caught a glimpse, for the moment at least, of Willingham's vision of a thousand

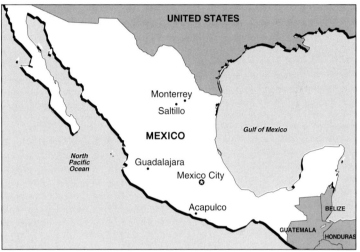

Mexico

Macedonias crying in the night "Come over and help us."

In the Midst of Conflict

It was obvious that Willingham was without a peer when he was presenting the cause of missions to an audience, large or small. He was no less effective in handling the problems that constantly called for his and the board's attention.

Gospel Mission Movement

One of the major problems the board faced was the defection of a number of missionaries who had embraced the Gospel Mission Movement in China. In Memphis, Willingham already had encountered a simi-

Faculty, Madero Institute, Saltillo, Mexico, 1894: front row, left to right: missionaries Lillian McDavid, Mae Bagby (Mrs. A.B.) Rudd, A.B. Rudd and Mexican Baptist leader, Mr. Cardenas; back row: missionaries, from left: Sarah Hale, Lucy Carter Cabiniss, Ida Hayes, and Adie Barton

the mission in Saltillo, Mexico. W. D. Powell became the storm center of a growing controversy among the missionaries over his character and conduct. Early in his missionary service in Mexico, Powell had been able to gain the confidence and friendship of Governor Madero. In fact the governor offered to give property to the Foreign Mission Board for a girls' school in Saltillo. Tupper explained that Southern Baptists could not accept such property from the government because of their principle of church-state separation. Therefore, instead of accepting the offer as a gift, the board purchased the same and established the Madero Institute. This was indeed a remarkable development and an indication of Powell's effectiveness as a missionary. Also, he had been in Mexico less than three years when he led eight churches to form an association in Saltillo (December 1884). Apparently, Powell's younger colleagues and the more recent additions to the missionary force in Saltillo resented his heavy-handed leadership and questioned his close ties with the governor. Charges were brought against Powell that the board was forced to take seriously.

Willingham made two trips to Mexico specifically in an attempt to resolve the conflict but with limited success. After each visit, it appeared that a reconciliation had taken place but in both cases it proved temporary. Finally, the missionaries opposing Powell put their charges in writing. The

lar problem in the person of J. R. Graves, the founder and chief exponent of the Landmark movement, and a member of his church. As with Graves, he expressed the kindest personal appreciation for the missionaries while rejecting the principles and practices of the Gospel Mission advocates. His attitude went a long way in effecting a reconciliation with the remnant that returned to work again under the direction of the Foreign Mission Board.

W. D. Powell

Another conflict that called for much prayer and

W. D. Powell

diplomacy over a period of two or three years, involved the board in the affairs of

board considered them at length in its 8 June 1898 meeting in Richmond. Two days later, according to board policy, Powell was given an opportunity to answer the charges which he did to the satisfaction of those members present. Upon hearing his defense the board decided "that nothing has been shown to the Board which ought to impair confidence in bro. Powell's Christian character, and therefore dismisses further consideration of the charges."[33]

Shortly after this meeting Powell resigned, as did the missionaries who had brought the charges against him. Whereupon, the board decided to close the Madero Institute. Although Powell would later serve the board by assisting in the Judson Centennial Campaign, dissension among the brethren resulted in the loss of missionaries and a golden opportunity to make an impact for Christ through the Madero Institute. The theological institute which Powell had established, did become in time the Instituto Zaragoza which was a forerunner of the Baptist Seminary in Torreon.

The Snuggses of China

Willingham and the board were more successful in resolving the problem relating to the Snuggses of China than they were in the Saltillo situation. Charges were brought against the E. T. Snuggses by the South China Mission. Subsequently, the Snuggses appeared before the China Committee of the board in Richmond on 13 January 1913 and were given an opportunity to answer the charges brought against them. After hours spent in the hearing and in prayerful deliberation, the committee recommended

that the Snuggses not return to the South China Mission.

Naturally unhappy with this decision, the Snuggses carried their cause before sympathetic associations in South Carolina. Subsequently, a delegation from the South Carolina Convention was sent to Richmond to confer with the board about a possible solution to mounting problems. The board relayed the information to the South China Mission with the suggestion that perhaps some adjustment could be made to the satisfaction of all parties concerned. The South China Mission responded that if the board thought it best to reappoint the Snuggses that a new station could be established at Pakhoi, Kwangtung Province.[34] Consequently, Edward Thomas Snuggs and his wife, Josephine, were reappointed in 1914. Edward served twenty-one more years and his wife until her death in 1932.

Person to Person

Willingham identified with the missionaries and defended them before many a thoughtless critic but he was not adverse to offering advice upon occasion. To a new appointee to Japan, he wrote:

When you first get to Japan it would be well to be slow to speak and swift to hear. It is impossible for new missionaries to give wise counsel on problems when the conditions are unknown to them and entirely different from anything they have ever known. To speak too strongly at such times only gets the poor opinion of those already acquainted with the work.[35]

To another missionary, lonely, frustrated, and worn out, he suggested that he obviously needed another missionary colleague with whom he could share the responsibili-

Foreign Mission Board meeting in its "rooms" in Richmond's First Baptist Church, 1898; R.J. Willingham, stands at left. Seated around table, from left: C.H. Ryland, T.P. Matthews, M.A. Jones, C.H. Winston, W.E. Hatcher, J.B. Hutson, John Pollard, H.A. Bagby, Wm. Ellyson, A. Parsons, H.R. Pollard, J.C. Williams, J.M. Mercer, R.H. Pitt and George Cooper.

ty of the work. Angrily, the exhausted man replied: "If you think I have not enough sense to direct the work, send out a man who can do it; but remember that as long as I have charge of it, it will be managed by—-from——, and not by R. J. Willingham from Richmond." Willingham replied: "Dear Brother——: Your last letter shows that you are worn out and that you need a rest. Now, just pull up and get out into the country and let things go for a week." The missionary later commented, "I think that was the biggest thing he could have done. He got at my heart and he kept it."[36]

More serious problems such as the case of a missionary in Japan, who had become addicted to drugs is a case in point. Instead of calling for his resignation or dismissing him outright, the board, upon the recommendation of its medical advisor, called him home for treatment. He was then sent to Kelley Hospital, in Baltimore, for treatment, but he left within a few days because of a death in the family. Throughout the difficult experience, the board kept the missionary on salary and paid his travel and medical expenses.

T. B. Ray, who was associated with Willingham for a number of years, gave an insider's opinion of Willingham's relationship with those most closely related to him on the staff.

The one thing he objected to was the quibbling about non-essential details. We did not always agree, but whenever we did not agree, the man responsible for the department involved in the decision was left to follow the course he thought best. The consideration, above all things, with him was the good of the cause. When he saw that his associates were placing the cause first, it made little difference to him if they differed with him about the methods of procedure.[37]

The Board at Work

The Foreign Mission Board was the hub of the far-flung missionary enterprise of Southern Baptists. As countries were added and colleges, theological seminaries, and hospitals multiplied, the work grew more and more complex. The organization of the board had remained essentially the same as it was in 1845. It was made up of vice presidents, managers, and the staff. During Willingham's administration, the board was reorganized and the staff enlarged.

A Limited Staff

When Willingham assumed his responsibilities, he was met by R. T. Bryan, a missionary on furlough from Shanghai, China, who had been asked to delay his return in order to manage the work of the office until a new corresponding secretary was elected. After a number of years Bryan wrote: "It was my privilege to be in Richmond when Dr. Willingham began work as secretary, and to go with him to his office on his first day. He dropped down on his knees at the table and said, 'Let us begin with prayer.'" This was no dramatic pantomime for the new secretary. From the first day to his last, he and the staff began each day with prayer. Bryan attributed his large influence and his effectiveness as secretary in a large measure to this fact.

The Southern Baptist Convention was on record opposing assistant corresponding secretaries for its boards, without realizing how short-sighted such a policy was. Nevertheless, this was the situation when

Willingham became the corresponding secretary. He wrote a missionary of his frustration. "We are trying to get along without an assistant secretary, but it means hard work for me. Still, I enjoy it. I *love* missions and I have good health. Best of all, I have the privilege of talking to our Father and having His guidance and grace."[38] Willingham had a capacity for hard work which served him well. He reported that up to fifty letters a day were received, some of which required from two hours to half a day to answer. After answering the mail and making entries, he reported, "we must get off tracts and Journals, as requested, and make deposit of funds in the bank. This work takes until two or three o'clock. The books must then be posted and new business taken up."[39]

In the same article in which he gave a glimpse into a day at the office of the Foreign Mission Board, he invited "every brother and sister in our bounds to visit." He was convinced a visit to the "Mission Rooms" would enlighten and inspire any visitor. But when would he have had time to visit with them? He had little spare time from the work and none at all for idle conversation. In fact he had a cardboard sign made upon which was printed MY BUSY DAY. This was a none-too-subtle reminder to the "drop ins" to cut the visit short for he had work to do.

In addition to all his other duties, Willingham was for a time editor of the *Foreign Mission Journal*. Under his leadership, it not only paid its way but became a source of income for the board. Then, in a thoughtless moment the convention voted in 1895 to combine the *Journal* with *Home*

Fields of the Home Mission Board, a decision probably inspired by I. T. Tichenor, who was always jockeying for an advantage in the interest of the Home Mission Board. History now repeated itself. Subscriptions fell off to the extent that within the year, there were fewer subscribers for the combined journal than there had been for the *Foreign Mission Journal* alone. The next year the convention reversed itself.

Although Willingham had no named assistant, he did not labor alone. In the office, he first had the help of R. T. Bryan. After Bryan returned to China, Willingham was fortunate in securing the assistance of R. E. Chambers, who had been appointed a missionary to China but could not go for the lack of funds. Chambers served faithfully and well for eight months. Finally, the convention in its fiftieth anniversary meeting, recognized the impossible load Willingham was attempting to carry and authorized the board to secure the services of an assistant secretary. E. Y. Mullins, pastor of the Lee Street Baptist Church, Baltimore, was chosen associate secretary. He began his duties on 1 September 1895. Although Mullins possessed a fine mind and a missionary

> *The diversity of professions represented on the board was considered an asset, for every issue could be viewed from a number of vantage points...*

heart, he served only six months before accepting the call of the Baptist church in Newton Center, Massachusetts. Mullins was succeeded on 20 August 1896 by J. A. Barton, pastor of the North Edgefield Baptist Church, Nashville, Tennessee.

The Managers of the Board

Much of the work of the Foreign Mission Board was carried on by local managers who lived in Richmond and its environs. These were able and dedicated laymen and ministers who met at least once a month and occasionally two or three times a month. When Willingham came to Richmond, the managers consisted of four professors, two lawyers, one physician, seven pastors, one banker, one broker, one merchant, one editor, and one college treasurer. The diversity of professions represented on the board was considered an asset, for every issue could be viewed from a number of vantage points before a final decision was reached. The managers were divided into committees, with one for each country in which Southern Baptists had missionaries. By 1909, the work demanded more but smaller committees. In addition to a committee for each of the six countries (Argentina, Brazil, Italy, Mexico, China, Japan) in which Southern Baptists had work, there were committees on Africa, Finances, Appointments, Publications, Ways and Means, Woman's Work, and Young People's Work.

P. T. Hale, editor of the *Birmingham Baptist,* gave his impressions of the board after visiting one of its meetings. He was struck with the enormous amount of time and concentrated attention that the members of the board gave freely to the work, "their deep and fraternal interest in the missionaries, and their business-like care to wisely apply every dollar intrusted to them by the churches, as their stewards."[40] He was also impressed with Willingham and his relationship to the managers. "After seeing more of his [Willingham's] work and zeal and plans, I am more than ever convinced that the Lord selected him for this great work. Let us not merely send him money to send forth laborers, but pray for him and for them."[41]

Since its beginning, the Foreign Mission Board had commanded considerable time and the best efforts of a succession of able men. Among these was H. H. Harris, twenty-nine years professor of Greek at Richmond College, and from 1895 to 1897, professor at Southern Seminary. During his tenure on the faculty of the college, he was a member of the Foreign Mission Board for nineteen years, the last nine of which (1886-1895) he served as president of the board. During Harris's term as president, Willingham was called to the secretaryship of the board. Before the Southern Baptist Convention began to limit the terms of the members of the various boards and agencies of the convention, a few families were represented on the Foreign Mission Board for more than a half a century.

William Ellyson was a member of the board and like his father, a Richmond business man. He became a close personal friend of the new corresponding secretary and was with him when he died. He was the son of Henry Keeling Ellyson, who served on the board twenty years and who published at his own expense *The Southern*

Baptist Foreign Mission Journal. Another father and son combination was that of Dr. T. P. Matthews, who was not only a member of the board but who became the first official physician of the board. His son, Dr. W. (Billy) P. Matthews succeeded his father in both positions. L. Howard Jenkins served in many different capacities with the board from corresponding secretary to president of the board. His son, L. Howard Jenkins, Jr., succeeded him. H. W. Gwathmey was elected to the board at the organizational meeting of the Southern Baptist Convention in Augusta in 1845. For almost forty-one years he served as its recording secretary. He was joined on the board by his son, Basil Manly Gwathmey, who served some thirty years, making a total of seventy-nine years in which a Gwathmey father and son served Southern Baptists on the Foreign Mission Board. These father and son combinations gave the board both continuity and stability in the formative and often uncertain years of the board's existence.

Staff Reorganized and Enlarged

By 1906, the work of the Foreign Mission Board had grown to the extent that it had become evident to those familiar with the demands upon the Richmond office that an enlarged staff was an absolute necessity. The board could no longer rely so completely upon its willing and capable managers to carry the increasingly heavy load of the numerous responsibilities of the board. A succession of assistant corresponding secretaries had served with varying degrees of efficiency since 1895. After three years as assistant secretary, A. J. Barton resigned to become corresponding secretary of the

Arkansas Baptist Convention and was succeeded by E. E. Bomar, pastor of the First Baptist Church of Spartanburg, South Carolina, in 1900. Bomar was followed five years later by W. H. Smith, who came to the board on 22 January 1906 from the pastorate of the First Baptist Church of Columbus, Georgia. The staff was enlarged and reorganized that year. Smith was named editorial secretary and served as acting corresponding secretary during Willingham's long absence in 1907. T. Bronson Ray was added to the staff as educational secretary.

In an attempt to relieve the corresponding secretary of the constant necessity of giving a considerable amount of his time to fund-raising, the board also employed S. J. Porter as field secretary, a position reminiscent of the old agency system. Shortly afterwards, upon the recommendation of Willingham, the convention territory was divided into three areas with a field secretary assigned to each. And yet the financial deficit continued to increase because the income failed to match the cost of institutional expansion.

Before the end of Willingham's administration, the growth of the work overseas had grown to include much more than direct evangelism and church planting. There were now six hospitals in China, and theological seminaries in Canton, China (first building provided during Willingham's administration); Ogbomosho, Nigeria; Rome, Italy; Torreon, Mexico; Fukuoka, Japan, and Buenos Aires, Argentina. In addition to the seminaries, colleges were organized in Recife and Rio de Janeiro, Brazil, and in Shanghai and Hwanghsien, China. Publishing houses were also established in China, 1899; Brazil, 1901; Japan, 1904; and Mexico, 1904. It is not surprising that the debit side of the treasurer's report for 1 November 1909 reported $201,500 in time loans and call loans of $10,406.25.[42] The month before, the board had authorized the employment of an office assistant at a salary of $1,100 a year.[43] Apparently, this move was another attempt on the part of the board to free Willingham from the purely secretarial work of the office in order that he might give himself to his weightier responsibilities.

A Multifaceted Ministry

Willingham used all the tools of the trade to promote the cause to which he was giving the last ounce of his energies. First among these was the pulpit. His family complained that he was gone from home much too often. He answered that if he could not preach, he would have to give up the secretaryship and go back to the pastorate. His wife and children recognized his commitment and not only accepted it but became a vital part of his support system.

The Willingham home was indeed a "hall of highest human happiness." His dedicated wife, Corneille, was largely responsible for making it so. The nine children loved their mother and adored their father. Even though it was Mrs. Willingham's responsibility to manage the home, his presence made it sparkle. A strict disciplinarian, Josiah Willingham loved his family and enjoyed being with them. Whether it was a romp with the younger children or an impromptu walk with the older ones, they coveted his attention. Morning prayer time around the table was never neglected, even in the presence of the numerous visitors who were frequently guests at the table. Sunday afternoons often found the whole family gathered around the piano singing the songs of Zion. Father and children also enjoyed playing games together. The children even made a game out of the serious business of raising the annual budget of the Foreign Mission Board. As the denominational year drew to a close, the children vied with one another in announcing the pledges of the various state conventions as the telegrams began to arrive at the front door of the house. It was, indeed, difficult for the corresponding secretary, and for his family, to be absent from the home so much—but it was as necessary as it was painful. How much Willingham cared for his family was evident when he allowed his insurance to lapse in order to use the money previously used for premiums to meet the expenses of college tuition for his children.

...the work overseas had grown to include much more than direct evangelism and church planting. There were... hospitals... seminaries... colleges... publishing houses...

Perhaps Willingham was at his best preaching on missions before a large audience. An editorial in *The Alabama Baptist* commented:

He seems the very incarnation of Foreign Missions, and when he talks one is swept along with mighty enthusiasm. It is impos-sible to hear him and withstand his message. Call it what you will, but he has the power to move men, and make them feel that the most important thing in the world is to give the gospel to the heathen.[44]

At the close of a meeting of the Southern Baptist Convention, a messenger asked T. P. Bell, "What is there in Willingham's speaking that produces such effect?" Bell answered, "He is the incarnation of a great cause, and that cause speaks out through him, without let or hindrance. It is not Willingham, it is Foreign Missions."[45]

Willingham was equally effective on the campus of the seminaries and colleges. W. B. Glass, a missionary for forty-two years in China and the father of missionaries Lois Glass and Eloise Cauthen, recalled the impact he had upon his life when a student at Baylor University.

The most notable occasion that I now recall was in the autumn of 1900, when the Texas Convention met in Waco in the old Baptist Tabernacle which stood on the same lot with our dormitory. It was Sunday afternoon. The hour had been set apart for a great mass meeting on Foreign Missions. The review of the world-field, world-conditions and the appeal for men and women to answer the call of God for laborers by Dr. Willingham was the most powerful I have ever heard. A great audience of 3,000 souls was moved as by a mighty wind.[46]

A few days later, Glass confided to one of his professors, J. S. Tanner, that he had decided to answer the call of God to foreign missions.

The *Foreign Mission Journal* had become under Willingham's leadership an increasingly valuable means of getting the missionary message into Southern Baptist homes.

As time permitted, he wrote articles for the *Journal*. The editorship of the *Journal* was particularly important to him. John Jeter Hurt attributed the effectiveness of Willingham's administration to the varied tools he used, including the *Journal*, but above all to the centrality of the gospel in all that he did.

> And that calls us back to the man and the method that moved the Convention every year. He believed in the Mission Journal, and circulated it wherever he went. He saw the value of charts, and sold them all over the South. He felt the need of study classes, and exhorted the people to foster them. He felt the presence of enormous debts that had to be lifted. He sounded all these notes in proper places, but the one vital note was never neglected—whether in sermon, speech, or private appeal. And that note was the note of my text, namely, The Jesus who died for you and me died for the others also.[47]

Just as his predecessors, Willingham found it necessary to involve himself in fund-raising efforts. A few excerpts from his reports, mainly in letters to his family reveal how much time and energy were involved in trying to keep the foreign mission enterprise afloat. "I got into Houston last night after dark, in time for prayer meeting; made a talk and got some money. Left there before day this morning and now at these folks' door. I talked to the business man at one o'clock." Again he wrote, "To give you an idea of how busy I am: I spoke five times yesterday and got up at 3:00 this morning and came home, and have a world of work before me."[48]

It is not surprising in view of the way in which Willingham drove himself that his health began to fail. When an attack of vertigo forced him to seek treatment and relaxation at a spa, he chafed at the exile from his work but his sense of humor was still intact. He wrote home, "Well, I am here at this monotonous, hum-drum, do-nothing, loafing place. If it does not kill, it ought to cure, for there ought to be some recompense for staying here. If I were well, I would charge at least $100 or $200 to stay here a week."[49]

[Willingham] began to realize that he was not... indestructible and yet he could not refrain from giving himself without reserve to the work.

Big of body, mind, and heart, Robert Josiah Willingham was no longer thirty-nine. After his tour of the mission fields in Asia and Europe, he began to realize that he was not indestructible and yet he could not refrain from giving himself without reserve to the work. Two events took an unusual toll of this man who had given so much of himself for the cause: the death of his little son, Holcomb, of scarlet fever at five years of age; and the recurring debt of the board, which like a bad dream would not go away. Besides, he could not resist the call of the pulpit, even from other denominations. Presbyterians and Lutherans, as well as Northern Baptists, all laid claim to his services. But there came a time when he had to curtail his engagements sharply.

On 22 October 1913, T. B. Ray, who worked closely with Willingham, noticed that the corresponding secretary did not appear well. He sent for Dr. W. P. Matthews, the board's physician, who diagnosed the problem as a stroke. This forced Willingham to absent himself from the office for the first time in years. He recovered sufficiently to perform the wedding ceremony for his youngest daughter, Carrie, but he never fully regained his stamina. He continued to go to the office every day but after three or four hours of prayer and planning with the staff, he was forced to call it a day. J. F. Love recalled those difficult days: "Every morning during those months of trembling and decline he would come to the Mission Rooms, give us his counsel, dispatch some part of the work himself, and

Southern Baptist Convention, 1912, Oklahoma City

before leaving call us together for prayer."[50]

Willingham's illness prompted a major reorganization of the staff. The committee of the board charged with this responsibility worked out the titles of members of the staff and delineated their corresponding duties. The committee was careful to give the rationale for the change.

> *The committee feels certain that it represents not only the wishes of this board, but of Southern Baptists generally when it declares its own conviction that the contin-*

ued presence of our beloved secretary in this work, even though with necessarily lessened responsibility and activity, will be a benediction and a blessing which we could ill afford to lose.[51]

The plan of reorganization called for four secretaries: Willingham was named general secretary; W. H. Smith became the corresponding secretary; T. B. Ray was made foreign secretary, and J. F. Love was named home secretary. This was clearly an interim arrangement.

Before his stroke, Willingham had tendered his resignation to the board in its meeting on 14 March 1913 but the board refused to consider it, knowing full well that the corresponding secretary would continue to serve as long as God gave him breath—and the members of the board were not mistaken. The board was already well into the Judson Jubilee celebration, that held such great promise of relieving its paralyzing indebtedness. Many thought it inconceivable that the goals could be achieved without Willingham.

The Judson Centennial

On 12 June 1912, the Foreign Mission Board formed a Judson Centennial Committee. T. Bronson Ray was asked to direct this campaign because the board desired not only to honor Adoniram Judson, who a hundred years before had sailed to India, but also to raise a substantial amount of cash, enough to retire the indebtedness of the board, which had by January 1912 risen to some $89,000.

The board also made ambitious plans to advance on all fronts. One of the dreams that Willingham and the board entertained was a theological seminary for Europe (1911). This, like other plans for advance, had to wait on funds which were not forthcoming. Even a biography of Lottie Moon, which the North China Mission had requested C. W. Pruitt to write, was approved but not funded. Willingham had repeatedly written in the last years of his life of the difficulty of trying to meet the world's desperate needs without adequate finances. Now it appeared that at last a means for expansion was at hand. The expected income was allocated for every country in which Southern Baptists had work. A definite amount for each object was specifically designated. Hopes and enthusiasm ran high. Within the four years designated for the centennial celebration, $1,064,289.51 was raised. Unfortunately, Willingham did not live to see that day. He had completed his God-appointed task.

A Missions People

Robert Josiah Willingham was stricken on his way to Sunday School at the Second Baptist Church on Sunday 20 December 1914. Feeling ill, he stopped at the Jefferson Hotel. His doctor was called and his family gathered. Close friends prayed upon hearing the news and those who could dropped by for a brief visit. Just when it appeared that he would recover, he breathed his last. Memorial services were held throughout the convention, the first of which was conducted in the Second Baptist Church of Richmond. Upon that occasion, R. H. Pitt, editor of the *Religious Herald* read a resolution that put the life of R. J. Willingham in perspective.

The Foreign Mission Board has had during its sixty-nine years of history three chief secretaries, all three remarkable men and each of the three fitting in a peculiar and striking way into the period of his service, meeting with notable success the conditions of the work during his incumbency.[52]

After summarizing the work of Taylor and Tupper, Pitt shared the conviction of the board when he said:

Dr. Willingham soon became recognized as one of the greatest missionary secretaries in the whole country. He saw the work of the Foreign Mission Board make marvelous advance during the twenty-one years while he was secretary. The contributions to the work grew from $106,332 in 1893 to $587,458 in 1914. The number of missionaries in the foreign fields was 94 when he became secretary. Now there are 300 missionaries. The number of native converts has increased from 3,228 to more than 30,000 at the present time.[53]

In 1893, Southern Baptists had no mission hospitals. In 1914, there were eight staffed by eleven medical missionaries. It was Willingham's conviction that the missionary witness acquired credibility as human needs were met by those motivated by the love of Christ. Hence for him, medical missions was one of the most effective means of Christian witness. Publishing houses were also first established during his administration.

Statistics provide one criterion for evaluating Willingham's contribution but there would have been none without the bedrock convictions that drove him to give the full measure of his life to the cause of missions. A committee comprised of R. H. Pitt, W. H. Smith, J. F. Love, and T. B. Ray published a memorial in honor of Dr. Willingham, in which this tribute is found.

> *Dr. Willingham was, above all things, a foreign missionary. There was ever before him a vivid realization of the need of Christ in all the world. He believed sincerely that men everywhere are hopelessly lost without a saving knowledge of Jesus as Saviour. To the making of Christ known in the remotest regions of the world, Dr. Willingham devoted every atom of strength at his command. His vision of the coming of the Lord Jesus Christ from heaven to reveal to men the saving grace of the Father was even clearer than his vision of the world's need. Hardly ever did he make an address without portraying the divine origin of missions. He became, to a remarkable degree, the embodiment of the missionary impulse.[54]*

The great century of missionary advance for Southern Baptists has been the twentieth century. They were fortunate that at the helm of a remarkable group of men who comprised the Foreign Mission Board stood Robert Josiah Willingham, who in the first decade of the twentieth century enlarged the missionary vision and set the course for Southern Baptists to become truly a "missions people."

ENDNOTES

1. Minutes, FMB, 23 July 1893, 404. The Minutes of the board were all handwritten before Willingham's tenure. The handwritten Minutes were uniformly well done.

2. Ibid., 407.

3. Quoted in Elizabeth Walton Willingham, *Life of Robert Josiah Willingham* (Nashville: The Sunday School Board of the Southern Baptist Convention, 1917), 64.

4. Cited, ibid., 74-75.

5. Cited, ibid., 28.

6. *Encyclopedia of Southern Baptists* (Nashville: Broadman Press, 1958), s.v. "Willingham, Robert Josiah," by E. C. Routh, gives a different set of dates for

Willingham's seminary education. He writes: "On Jan. 1, 1878, Willingham entered Southern Baptist Theological Seminary and was ordained by the First Church, Macon, Ga., June 2, 1878." The records of Southern Seminary have Willingham enrolling in 1877 and graduating in 1879.

7. Willingham, *Willingham,* 43.

8. Ibid., 44.

9. Ibid., 57.

10. Ibid.

11. H. H. Harris, *The Foreign Mission Journal* XXV (September 1893): 34.

12. Ibid.

13. Willingham, *Willingham,* 130.

14. Lottie's "call loan" was $2,625 and that of Bryan was $2,364.11.

15. R. H. Pitt, *Religious Herald* LXIX (April 9, 1896): 2.

16. *Proceedings,* SBC, 1896, 20.

17. Ibid., 21.

18. *Foreign Mission Journal* XXX (June 1898): 486.

19. *Annual,* Southern Baptist Convention, 1901, 57. (Hereafter referred to as *Annual,* SBC.) Thus, Willingham used a term that would recur frequently in the annals of the Foreign Mission Board especially when incorporated into its "Program of Advance" as projected by M. T. Rankin in 1947 and 1948.

20. Ibid., 67.

21. Justo Anderson, *Historia de los Bautistas* (El Paso, Texas: Casa Bautista de Publicaciones, 1990), 3:174.

22. See Santiago Canclini, comp., *Escritos de Pablo Besson,* 2 vols. (Buenos Aires: Junta Bautista de Publicaciones de la Convencion Evangelica Bautista, 1948), 2:223-225. For a biography of Besson, see Santigo Canclini, *Pablo Besson: Un Heraldo de la Libertad Cristiana* (Buenos Aires: Junta de Publicaciones de la Convencion Evangelica Bautista, [1933]).

23. Anderson, *Historia de los Bautistas,* 3:186.

24. James W. Bartley, Jr., "A History of Uruguayan Baptists with Particular Reference to Church Growth" (Ph.D. diss., Southwestern Baptist Theological Seminary, Fort Worth, Texas, 1972), 93.

25. Ibid., 94, 95.

26. Ibid., 96.

27. Anderson, *Historia de los Bautistas,* 3:220. Anderson wrote: "Por muchos años no había pastores uruguayos; habia una dependencia total sobre obreros importados de otros paises. Estos obreros trabajaron bien, pero la obra no se arraigó en el suelo oriental."

28. Minutes, FMB, 9 September 1909, 244-245.

29. Minutes, FMB, 16 December 1909, 266.

30. Willingham, *Willingham,* 169.

31. Cited in Willingham, *Willingham,* 188.

32. Cited, ibid., 194.

33. Minutes, FMB, 11 June 1898, 163-64.

34. The Snuggses' case first came before the board on 13 January 1913 and was not satisfactorily settled until the decision of the board to reappoint them on 8 January 1914.

35. Willingham, *Willingham,* 227.

36. Ibid., 222.

37. Ibid., 210-11.

38. Ibid., 77.

39. Ibid., 79.

40. Cited by ibid., 85.

41. Ibid., 86.

42. Minutes, FMB, 2 November 1909, 264.

43. Minutes, FMB, 19 October 1909, 259.

44. Cited in *Willingham,* 129.

45. George Braxton Taylor, *Virginia Baptist Ministers, Fifth Series, 1902-1914 with Supplement* (Lynchburg, Virginia: J. P. Bell and Company, Inc., 1915), 468.

46. Willingham, *Willingham,* 134.

47. Ibid., 150.

48. Ibid., 98.

49. Ibid., 112.

50. Ibid., 269.

51. Minutes, FMB, 20 March 1914, 15.

52. Willingham, *Willingham,* 274-75.

53. Ibid., 276.

54. Quoted in ibid., 277. The memorial is also recorded in the Minutes of the Foreign Mission Board.

Rising Expectations– Diminishing Returns

*eldom, if ever, have the fortunes of Southern Baptists and their Foreign Mission Board so closely paralleled those of the nation and its people than during the period preceding and following the Great Depression. These were the "boom and bust" years embracing the first World War and the Stock Market crash of 1929 and its aftermath.

In days of unbounded optimism, the Seventy-five Million Cam-

Joblessness plagues the Depression years.

paign was projected over a five-year period (1919-1924) and the Cooperative Program was inaugurated in 1925. The Foreign and Home Mission Boards were to be the major recipients in both of these attempts at a more financially responsible undergirding of the missionary efforts of Southern Baptists. When the projected goal was oversubscribed, the mission boards expanded their work accordingly. But when the expected revenues were not forthcoming, the boards found themselves in financial difficulty. They had overextended themselves. Retrenchment

became the only means of survival. Because the Cooperative Program was only in its infancy, it failed to provide sufficient funds to change the situation.

Southern Baptists faced the grim prospect of going out of the foreign mission business. Creditors relentlessly demanded that the board pay its debts. The board was caught in a cruel dilemma. To meet the demands of the creditors would mean that there would be nothing left by which to carry on the work—to refuse meant the loss of credibility. The board chose the latter course and for a time it suffered the embarrassment of not paying its debts; also it appeared that the board would be forced to suspend its overseas operations. Fortunately, this was not the last chapter in the saga of the Foreign Mission Board or of the convention. Both would learn from the experience and Southern Baptists would be the wiser because of it.

The Convention of 1915

The 1915 meeting of the

In the halcyon days of postwar optimism, Southern Baptists launched and over subscribed the Seventy-five Million Campaign. Both the Foreign and Home Mission Boards expanded their work on the strength of the pledges. When expected funds did not materialize, due to the Great Depression, the denomination found itself heavily in debt. J.F. Love, the corresponding secretary, died and the board floundered. T.B. Ray, his successor, found the situation unmanageable. Missionaries were recalled and others not appointed.

Southern Baptist Convention in Houston, Texas in May could be labeled "the missionary convention." The death of Robert Josiah Willingham a few months earlier raised the cause of missions, particularly foreign missions, to a prominence possibly unequaled in any previous convention. Even though Willingham was dead, he was very much alive in the minds of those who were present.

While B. H. Carroll's picture, who had died in November of the previous year, was given a full page in the 1915 *Annual of the Southern Baptist Convention,* as was generally true with the death of prominent Southern Baptist leaders, the memory of Willingham was given greater prominence. In addition to his likeness, photographs of his boyhood home and of the Concord Church in which he made his profession of faith, are found in its pages. A two-page spread contained a glowing tribute to Willingham's twenty-one years as secretary of the board, a part of which read:

> *In 1893 there was hardly a church in the whole convention that had any adequate conception of its duty to foreign missions, if we are to measure the interest of the church by its contributions. Then Virginia led all the states with a total contribution of $22,803; in 1914 Virginia again led with $80,655. It would be a remarkable story, if we could tell it, how the great Secretary went from church to church and with burning appeals aroused the people to do far greater things. Often with a single supreme effort he increased the contributions of a church many-fold for world-wide missions.[1]*

Not a session of the convention was without some reference to the missionary purpose of the Southern Baptist Convention. On the first day of the con-

vention, J. F. Love, home secretary of the board, presented an abstract of the board's annual report. On the second day, the Efficiency Committee, chaired by E. C. Dargan, gave an optimistic projection of mission giving. "If we increase in gifts during the next decade, as we have in the last, we shall be giving millions for Home and Foreign missions every year. . . ."[2] On the third day, the Judson Centennial Committee reported that $357,000.00 had been raised during the past year, making a total of $959,000.00 since the campaign began. Since the war had interrupted the Judson Centennial Campaign, the board asked the convention to extend it one more year. This request was granted.[3] The evening session of the third day was given to foreign missions. A film was shown, a missionary sermon was delivered by H. L. Winburn of Kentucky, six missionary appointees were introduced, and upon a motion from the floor, Saturday afternoon was set aside for all foreign missionaries in attendance to address the convention.

The Foreign Mission Board report contained a number of sections presented by various members of the board. In its printed form, the report totaled 150 pages, including photographs and maps of every country in which Southern Baptists were at work. The maps of the missions in China also contained inserts to help the reader visualize the location of the missions and their stations in relation to the provinces in which they were located. Also, enlightening bits of information detailed both problems and successes in proclaiming the gospel across national, religious, and linguistic barriers. The report from the Shantung Baptist Association contained encouraging news:

The year 1914 closed with two of its missionaries in Manchuria, ten in western Shantung, and three in Shensi—fifteen in all. We now have eight churches, six having been organized during the year, with a membership of 692. There are nineteen outstations. Three hundred and fifty-nine have been baptized this year.[4]

This report gave Southern Baptists a glimpse of the methods used to introduce the gospel to those who had never heard:

In June, while the wheat harvest prevented country work, the Tengchow workers concentrated their efforts on the city. Every morning they met for prayer and Bible study, and every afternoon they went out carrying banners, put a small organ down on some good residence street and began to sing, men and women together. Soon the doorways and street would be crowded. The women workers scattered themselves in the doorways and talked to the women, and the men preached in the open street. The plan was to eventually preach on every street in the city, but it has not yet been fulfilled. Many portions of Scripture were sold; some of the same people, day after day, followed from street to street, and many and cordial were the invitations given to visit in homes where before no foreigner or Christian had ever been.[5]

A special committee of the board chaired by R. H. Pitt, editor of the *Religious Herald*, reported on "The Present Secretarial Force of the Board." After giving a brief account of why the board now had three

secretaries instead of one, Pitt assured the convention that the work was being carried on efficiently and harmoniously. "It is pleasant to report that our three brethren, Dr. Smith, the Corresponding Secretary; Dr. Love, the Home Secretary; and Dr. Ray, the Foreign Secretary, have worked together without a particle of friction and in most loving cooperation."[6] The arrangement had worked so well, that there was apparently

According to the minutes of the 1915 annual meeting of Woman's Missionary Union in Houston, "The chair recognizes the following visiting missionaries: Minna Roseman, St. Louis; Georgia Barnett, Louisiana; Mary E. Kelley, Illinois; Mary Neutzler, Brenham, Texas; Alice Thomas, Brazil; Florence Jones, China; Ida Hayes, Mexico; Willie Kelley, China; Connie Bostick, China; and Lucile (Mrs. W.H.) Clark, Japan."

no thought of replacing the three secretaries with a chief executive. It must have come as a complete surprise, therefore, when the convention approved a recommendation from the Efficiency Committee to amend the constitution to provide for the election of the corresponding secretaries of the boards by the convention.[7] The Foreign Mission Board had been electing its corresponding secretaries since 1846 and had no reason to assume that the procedure would be changed.

In the evening session of the fourth day of the convention, the Committee on Nominations gave its report which "was adopted without a dissenting vote." In order to remedy a deficiency in the Supplemental Report of the Efficiency Committee, W. H. Wolfe of Texas, offered a resolution

> *that it be the object and intention of the Convention that the Corresponding Secretary of each of the three Boards elected by the Convention be the executive officer, and responsible to the Board and to the Convention for the work of all the departments of the Board of which he is Corresponding Secretary.*[8]

This left no doubt regarding the role of J. F. Love, who had just been elected by the convention as the corresponding secretary of the Foreign Mission Board.

The Reaction
of the Foreign Mission Board

Evidently the Efficiency Committee believed that it had a mandate from the convention to adjust the organization of the boards in the interest of greater efficiency at less cost. The board's reaction to this unexpected development was that of careful compliance.

J. B. Hutson, president of the board, called a meeting of the board for 27 May 1915. All three secretaries were present. The first order of business was to record the actions of the convention. A committee was then appointed to "nominate the other secretaries of the Board and designate their duties and titles. . . ."[9] Nothing was said in

this meeting about the election of Love as the corresponding secretary, even though he was present. Doubtless, the situation was a delicate one that threatened the harmonious relationship of the staff as well as the fellowship among the members of the board. Its annual meeting was scheduled some two weeks later on 16 June.

At this meeting, thirteen of the eighteen state members were present along with all fifteen local members, the president and the secretaries. Shortly after the reading of the minutes from the previous three meetings, the board went into an executive session. After reviewing the situation that led to the organization of the board with three secretaries, William Ellyson turned to the action of the convention in Houston. On behalf of his committee, he recommended "that the Board recognizes Rev. J. F. Love, D.D., as Corresponding Secretary with full and immediate responsibility to the Board and the Convention for all departments of our Foreign Mission work." Then the committee, adhering literally to the wording of the Efficiency Committee's report, recommended that both W. H. Smith and T. B. Ray be assigned essentially the same duties that they had previously discharged, but now "under the general supervision of the Corresponding Secretary." The last recommendation set the annual salary of Love at $3,500.00 and of Smith and Ray at $3,200.00 each.[10]

The next day a committee charged with studying the feasibility of continuing to employ field secretaries in order to promote the work of the Foreign Mission Board among the churches, proposed that three secretaries be appointed for the three geo-

J. Franklin Love

graphical sections into which the convention had been divided. Whereupon, C. J. Thompson was appointed for the Eastern, and C. D. Graves for the Central Section.

James Franklin Love, 1859-1928

James Franklin Love, who had been home secretary less than a year, was elected by the Southern Baptist Convention during its meeting in Houston to succeed R. J. Willingham as corresponding secretary. This was clearly not a decision of the managers of the board but one thrust upon them by what appeared to be a hasty action without prior consultation. The board formally recognized J. F. Love in his new position at its annual meeting in June. If the convention were going to select one of the three secretaries to serve as *the corresponding secretary*, why did the Committee on Nominations nominate J. F. Love for this position? It must have been that the convention leaders, who recommended Love to the nominating committee, thought him the best qualified. He probably was the best known of the three secretaries throughout the convention.

Before becoming home secretary of the Foreign Mission Board, Love had served as state secretary of missions of the Arkansas Baptist Convention and for eight years as the assistant corresponding secretary of the Home Mission Board. Prior to these positions, he had served as a pastor. His pastorates included two churches in his native North Carolina, one in Virginia and an associate pastorate with J. W. M. Williams of the First Baptist Church of Baltimore. Love's experience was to prove an invaluable asset in his new responsibility.

J. F. Love was born near Elizabeth City, North Carolina, on 14 July 1859. His was a devout family. It is not strange, therefore, that early in life James manifested a concern for spiritual matters and was an avid reader.[11] He attended Wake Forest College but never graduated. Later he was awarded a D.D. degree from his alma mater, and one from Baylor University as well. He married Caroline Gregory, although not a Baptist; she was a young woman of culture, superior intelligence, and from an outstanding family. After they were married, Caroline became convinced that she ought to be baptized. She surprised her husband with the request: "I want you to baptize me." He inquired; "Has someone influenced you?" In answering, she held up a book, saying: "This is what did it." It was something he had written, setting forth the Baptist position on baptism.[12]

Somehow, in addition to his other responsibilities, Love found time to write. Numerous articles and books came from his pen. Among the books were *Today's Supreme Challenge to America, The Mission of Our Nation, The Union Movement,* and *The Unique Message and Universal Mission of Christianity.*[13]

In travels, Love exceeded Willingham. For six months he toured the missions in Asia, calling together the missionaries in regional conferences to discuss their work. Later he traveled extensively in South America, Europe, and the British Isles. In 1923 Love was attending a congress of the

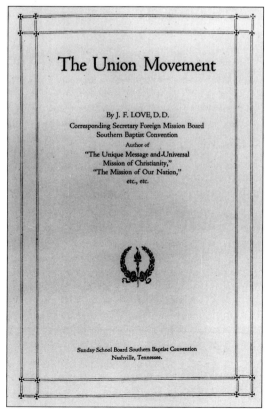

Love's The Union Movement, *1918*

Baptist World Alliance in Stockholm, when he suddenly became deathly ill. He recovered and continued in office until a stroke claimed his life on 3 May 1928.

Defining the Role of the Foreign Mission Board on Church Union

At the same meeting of the board in which J. F. Love was recognized as the corresponding secretary, a committee was appointed to draw up a policy statement of the board's relationship to what was termed "the union effort in mission work."[14] In its annual meeting in 1914 the Southern Baptist Convention had approved the "Pronouncement on Christian Union and Denominational Efficiency."[15] This statement, which set forth the theological and ecclesiological position of Southern Baptists, became the immediate source of reference for the Foreign Mission Board's statement on the subject in 1915.

The board believed that it was necessary to make its own statement on church union due to pressures on its missionaries as well as demands from within the denomination for the board to clarify its position. Ever since the International Missionary Conference at Edinburgh in 1910, ecumenical enthusiasm had mounted throughout the Protestant world. Denominationalism was condemned as an unnecessary foreign import on the mission fields and was declared divisive and sinful. Understandably, Southern Baptists felt themselves under attack for being Baptist. At the same time they claimed to support an organic union among the denominations on the basis of the New Testament alone. Since this latest development in the ecumenical movement threatened to disrupt the missionary thrust of the board and to sow discord within the denomination, Love felt the urgency of the issue and attempted to deal with it forthrightly.

The board issued its policy statement "Toward Union Effort in Mission Work" as a part of its report to the Southern Baptist Convention in 1916. The rationale for the statement was given in its second paragraph.

> *We would, as the Southern Baptist Convention has already done, put ourselves on record as cherishing a very tender Christian regard for all who love the Lord Jesus Christ in sincerity, and as desiring the most cordial Christian relationship with those who, like ourselves, are trying to make him known to a lost world. The dissent which this report affirms is made necessary by a general program of union and cooperation which conflicts at certain points with the policies of this Board, and with well-known principles of the denomination which it represents. We regret the necessity for this dissent. The program which provokes it, threatens to hinder rather than help Christian unity. But the issues having been raised, it becomes us to deal with them candidly.[16]*

The statement then proceeded to cite the 1914 action of the convention on denominational efficiency, of which the position enunciated by the Foreign Mission Board was viewed as an interpretation. In four paragraphs the board set itself against: comity agreements; "interchange of church letters"; unapproved cooperation with other sending agencies; and pressures on the mission field to deviate from its denominational goals. A summary statement continued to affirm a spirit of unity with all who acknowledge Christ as Savior and Lord.

> *Again, we would remind all that Southern Baptists are on record by repeated action of the Convention in recognition of that spiritual union which exists among all believers in Christ, and in favor of their organic union as soon as it can be perfected on New Testament lines. We reaffirm these sentiments. We would have all our people recognize the bonds of brotherhood which unite Christians of every name, cultivate a large spirit of fraternity and strive together with others to secure the closest possible impact of our common Christianity upon the social order for the establishment of righteousness in the earth. We would, however, admonish our people at home and abroad to remain true to New Testament principles of faith and church polity, and by so doing, seek to preserve the unity of the denomination, enlist all of our forces for the holy cause of missions, and thus insure the integrity, support and success of this work. J. F. Love, R. B. Garrett, B. D. Gaw, B. C. Hening, Joshua Levering, Wm. H. Smith, T. B. Ray, Committee.[17]*

It was clear from its policy statement that the board had determined to preserve the integrity of the denomination as a God-given task while not eschewing cooperation in a fraternal spirit with non-Baptist communions as long as such cooperation did not involve compromise of the faith. The realities of the mission enterprise had often brought missionaries of various denominations together in matters of mutual concern. Voluntarily, there was already in place in many mission fields a common comity understanding that this statement did not intend to abrogate. The board did intend, however, for everyone, Baptists and others, to understand that it was in total agreement with the convention's position on the ecumenical movement as defined in 1914.

The corresponding secretary's own position was not different from that of the board or of the convention. This much is clear from his book *The Union Movement.* "Rightly understood," Love wrote,

> it [the statement] should promote sound-
> ness, bigness and brotherliness among
> Southern Baptists. It takes care of our
> denominational identity without repressing
> worthy Christian sentiment. It removes dis-
> putes concerning denominational boundary
> lines so that we can live in neighbor-
> ly relations with other Christ-
> ians.

With obvious conviction, he gave the most favorable interpretation possible to the action:

> Baptists can render
> the greatest help to
> those who carry mis-
> sionary burdens by
> faithfully carrying
> their own. While
> doing this, we need
> not restrain a smile for
> a brother who is also
> under the burden. We
> need neither to throw
> away our convictions in
> order to be courteous, nor
> our courtesy in the effort to be
> frank.[18]

Fannie E.S. Heck

Soon, the attention of Southern Baptists, as that of other denominations, was drawn from the ecumenical movement to the war in Europe. The proposed confer-ence on Faith and Order had to be post-poned. Nor was it possible to convene a conference on Life and Work until some years after the war. With America's entry into the conflict, the nation's attention was diverted from other concerns, and the mis-sionary efforts by all denominations virtual-ly came to a standstill.

Internal Problems

The major, perennial, internal problem of the Foreign Mission Board, until the Seventy-five Million Campaign gave a brief respite, was its growing indebtedness. The convention's attempt to alleviate the prob-lem in 1916 created other problems that proved costly in losses of personnel and counterproductive in both mission awareness and income. The finan-cial embarrassment of the board was not a situation brought about by mismanagement by the officers of the board nor by a greater involve-ment of women in the work. In fact, the Wo-man's Missionary Union became increasingly valuable to the board in both the dissemination of missionary informa-tion and in raising funds for projects of the board. The expanded role of wo-men in Southern Baptist mis-sions was due to a considerable extent to a remarkable woman, Fannie E. S. Heck.

Fannie E. S. Heck and the Woman's Missionary Union

That the role of Woman's Missionary Union had become increasingly important in the missionary education of Southern Baptists in the first two decades of the twen-tieth century was largely due to the vision and leadership of Fannie E. S Heck (1862-1915). The Woman's Missionary Union had become such an indispensable part of the Foreign Mission Board's work during her presidency that upon hearing of her death the board paused to pay her a glowing tribute. In part the tribute read:

> The name of Jesus and the cause of Christian missions have a power over the lives of many thousands, at home and abroad, who had been ignorant, careless or hostile had she not so faithfully exemplified them in her life, and compelled respect and love for them by her intelligent devotion to them. This generation has not been blessed with a better example of the womanhood which the New Testament exalts than was shown it in the life and character of our sister.
>
> J. B. Hutson, President
> W. A. Harris, Recording Secretary[19]

Fannie Heck was president of the Woman's Missionary Union of North Carolina from its beginning in 1886 to her death in 1915. Three times during this period she was elected president of the national Woman's Missionary Union for a total of fourteen years. She brought to her task an enlarged vision of what the women should and could do in the educational and promotional aspects of missions. She led the Woman's Missionary Union to adopt courses of missionary study for women and young people. Heck also began a monthly publication entitled *Our Mission Fields*, which later was re-

Cover, **Royal Service**, October 1914

named *Royal Service*. At the time of her death there were 19,000 paid subscriptions. She was also one of the founders of the Woman's Missionary Training School (Carver School of Missions and Social Work), in Louisville, Kentucky. The Woman's Missionary Union Report to the 1915 meeting of the Southern Baptist Convention reflects the contribution that women were making to the work of the Foreign and Home Mission Boards.

The Woman's Missionary Union Report for 1915 was given for presentation to a Committee on Woman's Work, which was made up of six men and no women. The men were well pleased with what the women had done. They were laudatory, and with good reason:

> The twenty-seven years which have passed since our southern sisters started their splendid service have certainly been sufficient to silence any serious opposition. Their works of faith, their labors of love, and their patience of hope have proven beyond peradventure that their organizations have a real place in our church and denominational life.[20]

Convention wide in 1915, the Woman's Missionary Union counted almost 250,000 members in 13,424 affiliated organizations and total contributions to missions of $315,102.41. By this date, the local Missionary Unions were also sponsoring Girls' Auxiliary and Royal Ambassador organizations in every church possible. The emphasis upon the educational program and social service was a distinct legacy of Fannie S. Heck. The 1915 report reflects this emphasis as well as the concern of the committee that social work not be allowed to preempt the gospel:

> *Organized originally to aid in Foreign*

195

Missions, the work (WMU) was soon extended to Home Missions and then to State Missions. Now, by the Personal Service Work our women are endeavoring to meet the need of social service in our churches, and from the start which has been made in this direction, your Committee feels certain that our sisters will not make social service a substitute for salvation, but will treat it as one of the duties which accompanies salvation as a by-product of the gospel.[21]

In spite of the growing financial support of the Woman's Missionary Union and the successful completion of the Judson Centennial Campaign, which had raised over a million dollars, the indebtedness of the board continued to mount. Instead of giving a financial report in 1916 on the status of the centennial fund, the committee used the opportunity to challenge Southern Baptists, faced with the "horror of thick darkness" that had fallen upon the world, to make the choice between "missions and militarism." "The spirit of militarism would lead us backward. The spirit of missions is crying, 'Forward!' What shall we Southern Baptists do?"[22]

Already the nation was beginning to prepare to enter the war in Europe, the effects of the war upon the economy had delayed the completion of the Judson Centennial a year and now threatened to turn Southern Baptists from their primary task. Recognizing the situation that faced the nation and Southern Baptists, the committee exhorted: "Let us here and now . . . by the strategic character of this hour in human history, beseech one another that we put God's service first, that we give our choicest sons, our loveliest daughters to this

war of Immanuel. . . ."[23] The committee closed its report by quoting the Great Commission.

Commission on Efficiency

A Commission on Efficiency was authorized in 1913 to study the "organization, plans and methods" of the convention

with a view to determining whether or not they are best adapted for eliciting, combining and directing the energies of Southern Baptists and for securing the highest efficiency of our forces. . .and to recommend to the Convention of 1914 such changes and modification, if any, as in their judgment would increase the effectiveness of the Convention. . . .[24]

A strong commission was appointed the next day that, in addition to E. C. Dargan, president of the convention, included J. B. Gambrell, of Texas; John E. White, of Georgia, and author of the resolution that led to the formation of the commission; William Ellyson, a vice president of the convention and member of the Foreign Mission Board; and W. W. Landrum, of Kentucky.

The report of the Commission on Efficiency to the convention in 1914 contained recommendations for tidying up the financial practices of the various boards. It suggested that the boards cooperate with the states before giving field agents of the boards free rein in the states. The commission also recommended that the convention adopt a budget. A major section of the report was concerned with making a definitive pronouncement on the relation of Southern Baptists to various facets of the ecumenical movement. This had a direct bearing on the Foreign Mission Board, which later incorporated its basic principles in its own statement on the Church Union Movement.

When the commission made its report to the convention the following year, it had been enlarged to fourteen members and greatly strengthened with the additions of W. D. Powell, long associated with the Foreign Mission Board; J. M. Frost, corresponding secretary of the Sunday School Board; E. Y. Mullins, president of The Southern Baptist Theological Seminary, and J. F. Love, the successor of Willingham. Apparently the indebtedness of the Foreign Mission Board, a continual frustration for the board and embarrassment to the convention, was the primary catalyst that called the Commission on Efficiency into being. At least one member of the commission was in favor of combining the Home and Foreign Mission boards, if the "sentiment among our people could be secured for the change." After thoroughly studying the matter, the commission concluded that "it will be far better to leave the machinery of administration substantially as it is rather than take decisive and hurtful action looking to radical changes."[25]

The commission did recommend that the members of the Foreign Mission Board, elected by the state conventions to represent their respective conventions on the board, should no longer be referred to as "Vice-Presidents" but as "members" or "managers." The question of combining the publications of the mission boards, the Woman's Missionary Union, and the Laymen's Movement was left to each organization in consultation with the others. It further recommended that a report on the proposal be given the following year. The

commission brought its report to a close with a ringing affirmation of Southern Baptists and an optimistic portrayal of the denomination's prospects.

In compliance with the instructions of the Commission on Efficiency, the Foreign Mission Board appointed a committee to study the proposal to combine the *Foreign Mission Journal, Home Fields,* and *Royal Service.* In the 3 May 1916 meeting of the board, the committee reluctantly agreed to combine the three mission periodicals but expressed the opinion that it did not think it wise to combine only two of them.[26] It probably had already received information that the Woman's Missionary Union was not willing to go along with proposed consolidation.

Mission Publications

Besides, W. H. Smith, editor of the *Foreign Mission Journal,* was probably aware that on the two previous occasions when the mission magazines had been combined the results were counterproductive.

When the convention met in 1916, the messengers rejected the recommendation that the decision regarding the merger of the *Foreign Mission Journal* and *Home Fields* be delayed a year by a wide margin (285 for delay and 590 against). The number of negative votes would probably have been even higher except for the fact that George W. Truett was chairman of the committee presenting the report.[27] Evidently, the convention was determined to cut the costs of operating the Foreign Mission Board and in this way deal seriously with the board's growing deficit. This concern became even more apparent in the "Report on Report of Foreign Mission Board."

The committee commenting on the Report of the Foreign Mission Board recommended four changes affecting the operation of the board: (1) the merger of the *Foreign Mission Journal* with *Home Fields* to be published by the Sunday School Board; (2) the employment of only two secretaries: the corresponding secretary and one other; (3) the dismissal of the field secretaries (financial agents); and (4) budget restraints so that "expenditures of the Board for the ensuing year shall not exceed those of the past year."[28]

The recommendations were approved by the messengers. This was an indication that the convention intended to rid itself of the "embarrassing debt." The action was drastic. It had both its positive and negative aspects. Positively, the convention was involving itself in the financial affairs of the board and it was assuming more responsibility for the foreign mission enterprise itself. Negatively, by merging the mission magazines it was cutting the board off from direct contact with the members of the churches. This action would once again be marked by a sharp decline in subscriptions, missionary information, and eventually, income. It also meant that the board would lose one of its very able and dedicated secretaries, William H. Smith.[29]

William Henry Smith, 1859-1935

The recent action of the convention meant that Smith's position was eliminated. Since the board was now permitted only one other secretary in addition to the corresponding secretary, Smith graciously but reluctantly resigned. Shortly after the convention adjourned, he wrote on 10 June 1916 in order "to relieve you of any embarrassment as far as I am personally concerned." In his letter, he took pains to give the board his thoughts on how to gain support for foreign missions and how to raise the necessary funds: "After these years of careful observation and study, I am profoundly convinced that the most vital need of foreign missions is more direct contact with the churches." He then reminded the board of some of its past achievements in which he had had a part.[30] The disappointment Smith felt at this turn of events is evident. "I have said these things in order that I may say further that it has been the dream of years that I might have a large part in fully working out such plans. This service is not possible for me now." He explained that because his colleague T. B. Ray had such extensive knowledge of the foreign mission fields and because the board now was permitted only one assistant secretary, he would defer to Ray.

It is possible that Smith's "deep regret" was intensified by his changing status with the board. Having succeeded Edward E. Bomar on 22 January 1906 as assistant secretary to Willingham, Smith had left the First Baptist Church of Columbus, Georgia, where he had been pastor for more than twelve years. A year or so later he assumed the responsibilities of the corresponding secretary during Willingham's seven months overseas in addition to his other duties. In 1913 when the board was reorganized, he was named corresponding secretary and upon Willingham's death probably expected to continue in that role when the convention intervened.

After the election of J. F. Love as corresponding secretary, Smith was made one of the two assistant secretaries by the board. Once again the convention, in the interest of economy, made it impossible for him to remain in any capacity with the board which he had served sacrificially and well for more than ten years. He had become a casualty, along with the field secretaries, of

> *…[W.H. Smith wrote], "I am profoundly convinced that the most vital need of foreign missions is a more direct contact with the churches."*

the economic squeeze. The board and the convention were the losers. In a long and fitting tribute the board commended Smith to the churches "as a workman that needeth not to be ashamed, as a comrade in Christ in whom there is no guile."[31]

The resignation of W. H. Smith called for a reorganization of the staff. A committee was appointed to nominate the one additional secretary to which the board was entitled by the recent action of the convention. It brought its report to the 15 June meeting of the board, recommending that T. B. Ray be elected secretary. The committee said: "We recognize in him a man whose services could not be dispensed with without serious loss to the work of the Board."[32] Thus, the board had experienced three organizational changes in as many years. At least the mission boards had not consolidated, as apparently some had wished. An alternative proposal was offered in a resolution in the 1916 meeting of the convention that led to the appointment of a committee of eleven to study the feasibility of establishing an "Executive Board which shall direct all of the work and enterprises fostered and promoted by the Convention."[33] This action would eventually lead to the organization of the Executive Committee.

Financing Foreign Missions

Once the convention realized that the financial plight of the Foreign Mission Board was not the fault of the board but rather due to the failure of Southern Baptists to give commensurate with their abilities, the situation began to change. In the convention year 1916-1917, $186,019.85 was paid on the indebtedness of the board. The income that year was the highest in the board's history to date. Counting $212,829.94 from the Judson Centennial Fund, the total amounted to $961,970.48.

Encouraged by this response to a new financial campaign launched by the board in 1916, J. F. Love challenged the convention in a straightforward appeal to rise to the need of the hour. In the Foreign Mission Board Report, he declared: "The magnitude and uniqueness of the foreign mission task demand for this work a place and a proportionate consideration in Southern Baptist benevolences which it has never received." Also, he left no doubt regarding his position on combining the mission boards:

> The denomination cannot combine the consolidated appeal of foreign missions with that of single departments of the home work and save itself from continued embarrassment in the conduct of this enterprise. Embarrassment and severe restraint upon the activities of the Board and its missionaries are inevitable if this fact is overlooked. Foreign missions can be saved and be given great success by according its appeal the distinctiveness which its uniqueness demands.[34]

The committee to which the report of the board was given for review made several recommendations, the first of which called for the sending of thirty-five or even fifty new missionaries, "if conditions and contributions will at all permit."[35] The committee then recommended a challenging budget of $1,250,000. After discussion of the recommendations by J. F. Love and after prayer, the report was amended to increase the figure to $1,500,000. The vote was preceded by an animated discussion in which messen-

gers from every state convention took part. It was clear that foreign missions was once again a priority item on the agenda of the Southern Baptist Convention. A third recommendation asked that the corresponding secretary arrange his schedule so that he could visit as many mission fields as possible.

With the end of World War I, the possibilities of new missionary ventures seemed limited only by the lack of funds. J. F. Love made the most of it. His appeal in the board's 1919 report to the convention highlighted the unprecedented opportunities open to the convention in its seventy-fifth year.

> Whole nations are engulfed in awful sorrow, and men and women are crying out for the help of the Unseen Hand. . . . Supreme need is matched by unprecedented opportunity. The urgency of the situation cannot be overstated. Our duty is declared in tones as loud and as commanding as human need and divine Providence can utter. If Southern Baptists fail in this the Seventy-fifth year of their history to make a program for Foreign Missions which will take care of that with which they are solemnly charged, they will prove themselves unfaithful stewards and unwise statesmen in the Kingdom of God. . . . It is the men of faith and far vision who achieve results in any field.[36]

The Foreign Mission Board Report also contained an abbreviated account of Love's six-month tour of Japan and China and a delineation of immediate needs in terms of personnel and money. In the course of his travels, the corresponding secretary had held fifty-eight conferences with the missionaries in which he discussed the problems of the missions and the methods of

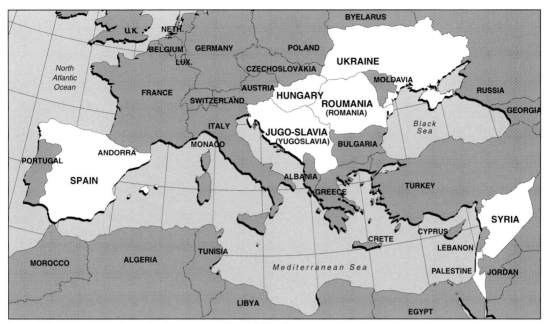

Board enters new countries under the secretaryship of J. Franklin Love.

achieving a more effective witness. He concluded that 153 new missionaries were needed at once for China and Japan at an estimated cost of $1,089,250. Immediate urgent needs for present work called for $2,181,000. It would cost an estimated $105,000 to open the contemplated new work. Another $2,000,000 would be needed during the next five years for the maintenance of old and new work. The figures were mind boggling for a young denomination that numbered no more than three million souls, but the vision of a war-devastated Europe, including Russia, tugged at the heart-strings of the messengers and the response was immediate and overwhelming. No one could have anticipated the unprecedented action of that convention.

The Seventy-five Million Campaign

The committee responsible for making recommendations relative to the Report of the Foreign Mission Board lifted the messengers out of a routine order of business to visualize the desperate needs of a postwar world. W. O. Carver, professor of missions at Southern Seminary, who presented the report, challenged the convention to "effect a more equitable distribution of the money given for denominational beneficences."[37] In addition to the needs of "world evangelism," Carver also emphasized "our obligation to take some part in the religious reconstruction of Europe." The committee also recommended that the Foreign Mission Board assume responsibility for missionaries in Syria, Galilee, and Persia, formerly supported by Illinois Baptists.

The impact of the report and Love's address that followed stirred L. M. Roper, of North Carolina, to offer a resolution which immediately took the form of motion by B.

C. Hening, also of North Carolina, to raise at least $25,000,000 for foreign missions during the next five years. The motion was referred to the Executive Committee. A committee had already been appointed "On Financial Aspect of Our Program," which became by the time it gave its report the "Committee on Financial Aspect of Enlarged Program." Clearly, the committee had caught the spirit of the hour and shared the vision of a world in need that led to its recommendation. "In view of the needs of the world at this hour, in view of the numbers and ability of Southern Baptists, we suggest, (1) that in the organized work of this Convention we undertake to raise not less than $75,000,000 in five years." Apparently the seventy-five million figure was suggested by the seventy-fifth anniversary which the convention would observe in 1920. At the same time, inspired by a similar set of circumstances (postwar optimism and world need), Northern Baptists were attempting to raise $100,000,000 for denominational causes under the rubric of the New World Movement.

Although foreign missions provided the inspiration for the Seventy-five Million Campaign, it became a drive for funds by which all the institutions and boards of the convention would benefit. As such it became the first convention wide effort at a unified financial program and a direct antecedent of the Cooperative Program. It was to be conducted simultaneously in every state convention, according to committee recommendation:

We further recommend that the Executive Committee of the Convention be advised to

plan in cooperation with the state agencies and the organized agencies of the Convention for a simultaneous drive to secure cash and subscriptions to cover the amount named.[38]

After two additional amendments that were designed to implement the campaign, the messengers returned to their respective churches to share the challenge of and to prepare the way for this new and unparalleled venture by Southern Baptists. Later the Foreign Mission Board's allocation of the $75,000,000 was set at $20,000,000. Lee Rutland Scarborough, president of the Southwestern Baptist Theological Seminary, was made general director of the campaign. Under Scarborough's direction and with the help of the Executive Committee and the executive secretaries of the state conventions, quotas were set for each state. The Seventy-five Million Campaign was by far the most carefully organized and best promoted financial campaign in the convention's history. The progress report by the May 1920 convention meeting in Washington, D. C., far exceeded anyone's expectations. Total subscriptions amounted to $92,630,923 with $12,237,827 paid in cash.

The campaign was not just a financial drive. Those who organized and promoted the work called upon the presidents of the Baptist colleges and seminaries to ask the students publicly to dedicate themselves to full time Christian service according to God's will as they understood it. Four thousand young people responded. Expectations were high now that funds would match the volunteers for missionary service. Both the Foreign Mission Board and the Home

Mission Board planned to expand their operations in unprecedented fashion. When the campaign closed, Scarborough announced in 1925, that $58,591,713.69 on the pledges had been paid—$34,039,209.31 less than subscribed. This was a clear indication that the economic picture was something other than it appeared. Other denominations were experiencing similar problems. Even in light of the shortfall, compared with previous missionary offerings, the amount raised was nothing less than phenomenal. During the years of the campaign, state and associational missions received $9,900,785; home missions, $6,622,725; and foreign missions, $11,615,327.[39] The boards, however, had expected much more and had projected their programs on the basis of the pledges. They soon found themselves more heavily in debt than ever before. It was a situation few could have foreseen.

In spite of the relative failure of the Seventy-five Million Campaign, it did something that no other comparable movement had done. It welded a diverse people into a denomination. Southern Baptists had been sometimes dangerously close to disin-

In spite of the relative failure of the Seventy-five Million Campaign,… it welded a diverse people into a denomination.

tegration, due to divisive movements from within and without. Minds and hearts throughout the membership of the denomination were now riveted on missions: state, home, and foreign. Never before had so many young people volunteered for missionary service nor had so many Southern Baptists been involved in sacrificial giving to the cause of Christ. Perhaps the most important result of the campaign was the discovery of a way by which all the causes of the denomination could be adequately financed, for in 1925 the Seventy-five Million Campaign gave birth to the Cooperative Program.

Safeguarding the Integrity of the Baptist Witness

Almost immediately after the armistice, there arose a resurgence of the ecumenical movement that threatened in the minds of some the distinctives of the Baptist faith. As early as 1920, ecumenical leaders from a number of countries met in Geneva to plan conferences to continue the Faith and Order and Life and Work movements. Closer to home, the Interchurch World Movement was launched on 17 December 1918, less than a month after the end of the war, by leaders of several denominational and missionary organizations. It was poorly organized and its purpose as well as its relationship to the denominations poorly defined. By 1920 it had begun to fall apart but not until the Foreign Mission Board was thoroughly alarmed by its perceived threat to its international missionary efforts. In order to preserve the integrity of its witness, the board formulated a statement of faith that all Southern Baptist missionaries were asked to affirm. The committee that commented on the Foreign Mission Board Report was careful to alleviate any fears that the board was attempting to impose a creed upon the missionaries:

> *This is not in any sense offered as a creed, but is intended to represent the general viewpoint of Southern Baptists. It is distinctly understood that neither present nor prospective missionaries are expected to sign this statement, but to recognize it as embodying our general interpretation of New Testament teaching.*[40]

The statement as printed in the 1920 Report of the Foreign Mission Board contained thirteen articles. The distinctive Baptist concepts of the church, baptism, and the Lord's Supper received special attention. While the fundamentals of the faith were clearly presented, as were the Baptist distinctives, fundamentalism was avoided. In addition to the articles to which missionary appointees were expected to subscribe, they were also asked to accept the "pronouncement on Christian union," which had previously been set forth by the board and approved by the convention.[41]

Up to this time no confession of faith had been adopted by the Southern Baptist Convention. The Southern Seminary had asked the members of its faculty to sign an "Abstract of Principles" drawn up by its president, J. P. Boyce, and revised by him in 1887. The Southwestern Seminary adopted the popular New Hampshire Confession of Faith and its successive revisions of 1925 and 1963, but the convention itself owned no confession until 1925. The Statement of Faith published by the Foreign Mission Board was a step in that direction, doubtless

prompted by both the Interchurch World Movement and the World's Fundamental Christian Association (formally organized in 1919). Once the board had set forth its "Statement of Belief," it was ready to turn its attention to what was termed "A Baptist World Program."

A Baptist World Program

In light of the more than $92,000,000 subscribed in the Seventy-five Million Campaign by 1920, the board projected a budget totaling $2,891,203.19 for 1921. This figure included fourteen fields in nine countries. The board proposed to send out 100 new missionaries at an estimated cost of $100,000 and set aside an emergency fund for Europe of $250,000. For fear that the enlarged budget might send the wrong message to the missions, the board voted "that in view of the greatly increased appropriations for the year 1921, the secretaries, Love and Ray, be asked to write letters to the workers on the various fields expressing the hope that these gifts will be a stimulus to our mission institutions and stations to put forth renewed effort toward self-help."[42]

Southern Baptists, a World Missionary Force

Apprehension on the part of some members of the board that the pledges made might not be paid prompted the board to issue a "Call to Southern Baptists." The statement, designed to encourage prompt transmission of funds from the state conventions to the board, appealed to Southern Baptists to do what they had promised and to the states to meet their quotas promptly.[43] In the meantime, year after year, the board, which had expected to receive $4,000,000 a year, began to fall further and further behind in meeting its growing obligations. Nevertheless, the number of countries in which Southern Baptists were working continued to increase.

In 1922, "The Committee on the Foreign Mission Board's Report" announced, with some exaggeration:

> The mission stations of Southern Baptists now nearly encircles the world. We are now at work in eighteen nations, preaching the Gospel of the blessed God to the representatives of an audience of nine hundred millions of people, a territory and audience larger than has ever confronted any other Protestant organization in all time.[44]

A committee, comprised of E. Y. Mullins, chairman; L. R. Scarborough, Texas; J. B. Gambrell, Texas; Z. T. Cody, South Carolina; and William Ellyson, Virginia, was asked by the convention in 1919 to prepare a message of fraternal greetings to the Baptists of the world. The response to the "Fraternal Address," published by the Sunday School Board, and widely distributed by the Foreign Mission Board, was well received. It prepared the way for a consultation between representatives of the Foreign Mission Board, Northern Baptists, Canadian Baptists, and British Baptists (19-23 July 1920) in which the missionary responsibilities for the various countries of Europe were allocated to the denominations involved.

J. F. Love and George W. Truett represented the Foreign Mission Board at the London conference. Back home, they reported that by mutual agreement Southern Baptists were assigned Spain, Jugo-Slavia (Yugoslavia), Hungary, Roumania (Romania), and the Ukraine "with the terri-

tory east thereof." Previously, the board had taken over work sponsored by Illinois Baptists in Palestine, Syria, and Siberia. In addition to these relatively new countries the report of the board in 1921 reminded the convention that "For years Southern Baptists have prosecuted mission work in China—north, central, interior and south China—in Japan, Africa, Mexico, Brazil, Argentina, Uruguay, Chile, and Italy."[45] The following year the number of countries in which the board reported working had grown to eighteen.

Although William Ellyson was a member of the committee charged with preparing the "Fraternal Address," he did not live to see the wide response to the "Address." In its 1920 report to the convention, the board paid tribute to him and eight others who had died in 1919. Among the eight were R. R. Gwathmey, a member of the board for some ten years and the Z. C. Taylors, veteran missionaries to Brazil. Ellyson, a lawyer, had been a member of the board for twenty-eight years, the last three years and nine months of which he served as its president. Before the convention imposed term limits on board members, Ellyson's tenure was exceeded by few. Among these was J. B. Hutson, his immediate predecessor, who served on the board for thirty-five years and as its president for fourteen.

It appears that 1921 set a new record for the number of fields entered in one year by the Foreign Mission Board. The board reported that 1921-1922 was a climatic year in every respect, except in the amount of receipts. In every category by which the board measured progress on its mission fields, there was marked advance over the previous year.[46]

Europe came in for special attention in this report. The board took particular satisfaction in reporting the repeal of the Romanian Ordinance No. 15.831, "under which our Roumanian brethren have suffered disabilities, unjust discrimination, and barbarous cruelty." The board attributed this success to the plans made in the London Conference of 1920 and to the efforts of J. H. Rushbrooke, commissioner for Europe of the Baptist World Alliance.[47] In cooperation with the American Baptist Foreign Mission Society, the board reported that 100,000 copies of the Bible and the New Testament in Russian had been printed and distributed at the cost of only $14,000, or fifteen cents a copy.

Baptist Student Missionary Movement

Shortly after the outbreak of World War I, new interest in missions became evident among Baptist students, probably as a result of the interdenominational Student Volunteer Movement. Three conferences were held during 1914 to explore the possibility of forming an organization that would promote missionary concerns among Baptist students throughout North America. Charles T. Ball, professor of missions at Southwestern Seminary, was granted a leave of absence from the seminary to promote the new movement. His efforts resulted in the movement's first convention in Fort Worth, Texas, during five days in March, 1916. A second convention was held the following year in Louisville, Kentucky, of which, Gaines Dobbins, editor, wrote in *Home and Foreign Fields*, "that they should

have met for five days' study and conference with the subject of missions the one supreme concern is a fact the significance of which can scarcely be overestimated."[48]

The Baptist Student Missionary Movement sparked interest in student work in a number of state conventions and in turn led to the employment of Baptist student secretaries in some states. A student conference was sponsored by the Texas Baptist Convention in 1920 that initiated the Baptist Student Union. Capitalizing on the new interest in missions stimulated by the Baptist Student Missionary Movement, J. F. Love led the Foreign Mission Board to sponsor three sectional meetings for students in the spring of 1920 at Greenville, South Carolina; Louisville; and Fort Worth. From these conferences, Love concluded that "The Lord is again visiting our schools and the hearts of young men and women are turning to the mission fields. . . ."[49]

In order to coordinate the Baptist Student Missionary Movement and the vari-

> *J.F. Love led the... Board to sponsor... meetings for students... and concluded that "The Lord is again visiting our schools and the hearts of young men and women are turning to the mission fields... "*

ous state organizations, the convention responded positively to the reports of the Foreign, Home, Sunday School, and Education boards in 1920. Each report, in what was evidently a concerted and premeditated action, asked the convention to form a committee made up of a representative from each board in cooperation with the Woman's Missionary Union to assume responsibility for the student work within the Southern Baptist Convention. In an agreement with the boards of the convention, the Baptist Student Missionary Movement closed out its work and turned over its financial liabilities to the Foreign, Home, and Sunday School boards. Uncertainty about how to proceed delayed implementing a new student program.

The Report of the Foreign Mission Board in 1921 indicated that the representatives of the boards and Kathleen Mallory, of the Woman's Missionary Union, had already formulated a plan for future student work.[50] It was announced in November. The committee became the Inter-Board Commission, which named Frank H. Leavell the first executive secretary of the new south-wide Baptist Student Union. Memphis was selected for his home office. He, therefore, assumed his new duties 1 January 1922. Apparently, the financial responsibility was to be shared by the Foreign Mission Board, the Home Mission Board, and the Sunday School Board.

The Financial Burden Increases

The only bright spot in the board's otherwise rather dismal financial picture was the sale of a building, at a profit, which had been bought with the Bottoms's fund, and

the purchase of a new piece of property that promised to be adequate for the board's own office building, the purpose for which George W. Bottoms's family of Texarkana, Arkansas, had given $100,000 in 1918. When the gift was first received, the board decided it was best to invest the money until more favorable economic conditions prevailed. Although the newly acquired property could not be occupied immediately, it appeared that the board had done well in these transactions. This was an exception to the board's money management. Its income failed consistently to match expenditures. The board, therefore, was forced to borrow to meet current expenses. Consequently, the call for help became increasingly insistent. It was an ominous sign.

By 1925, the financial plight of the Foreign Mission Board and its consequences were frankly addressed in its report to the convention. After reviewing the impressive gains in baptisms and new churches on the mission fields during the five years of the Seventy-five Million Campaign, the committee bringing the report of the board to the convention in 1925 commented:

> It is not surprising, therefore, that the Foreign Mission Board is in a distressing dilemma. "We must either give more to Foreign Missions; do less Foreign Mission work, or continue to make debt." One thing is sure, we can not continue as we are now going.[51]

The Cooperative Program Offers Hope

The board continued to operate largely on borrowed money. That the financial situation was deteriorating at the same time that its obligations were mounting was due in part to the shortfall from the Seventy-five Million Campaign and in part to the economic straits in which Southern Baptists found themselves. Even though the board had been allocated $11,024,813.79 over the five years 1919-1924, it received only $10,740,496.10 since $554,317.60 was retained by the state conventions to defray the expenses of the campaign. The foreign mission program had been projected by the board upon the basis of $20,000,000 for the same period. The cash receipts of the board in 1924 from the campaign were $1,216,946.28. An additional $240,426.11 was received from other sources. The debt at the end of the year stood at $1,250,792.45. There appeared no way by which the debt could be retired and the work continue. There was a slight glimmer of hope in the new Cooperative Program, from the total receipts of which the Foreign Mission Board was to receive 50 percent in 1926.[52]

Perhaps no one could have foreseen at the time that the immediate future would be so bleak before that hope would become reality. In 1925, the Cooperative Program represented both the fruition and the frustration in the trial and error of previous attempts at convention finance. It was, indeed, the fruition of the original concept of one convention with several benevolences. Gradually the convention had freed itself from the methods of finance inherited from the Triennial Convention and Home Mission Society.[53] The Foreign Mission Board, however, was not to realize the bonanza for missions the new program of finance would provide until the nation had passed through the throes of the Great Depression.

The Crisis of 1927

As receipts continued to decline, the board was forced to borrow $652,921.75 for operating expenses during the convention year ending in April 1927. During the same period, the board made the painful discovery that George N. Sanders, its trusted treasurer, had swindled the Foreign Mission Board out of $103,772.38. The loss was only partially recovered by a bond of $25,000, much too low for one handling such vast sums of money. Sanders had a reputation for honesty and efficiency with the members of the board and the bankers of Richmond. His books had been audited year after year by the A. M. Pullen & Co., Certified Public Accountants. In spite of every precaution against such an eventuality, the treasurer had succeeded in the first such theft in the history of the convention. The board was forced to acknowledge this unconscionable act while at the same time reassuring Southern Baptists of its remedial action.

> The greatest grief of the year was that which was caused by the defalcation of the Board's treasurer. For the first time in the eighty-two years of this Board's history has there been occasion for it to report the loss of a dollar by any official or employee. The defalcation amounted to $103,772.38. We are glad to report that the Board has already realized from the bond and such of the assets as have been disposed of $32,000. The remainder of the assets will probably carry this amount to $57,000, or more. In addition to this sum, friends of the Board are contributing designated gifts to replace more of this defalcation.[54]

After the initial statement regarding this disappointing development, the board took advantage of the opportunity to introduce E. P. Buxton, the newly elected treasurer of the board, to Southern Baptists. He was characterized as a member of "an honored and godly Baptist family" and "an active member in one of our Richmond churches." His qualifications were described as "superb." He was an accountant and teacher of business. C. E. Maddry wrote that he served "through some of the most trying years in the board's history, with fidelity, accuracy, patience and achievement until his well-deserved retirement in 1950."[55]

Retirement in Death

The same report that brought the news of the "defalcation" announced the death of two of the board's veteran missionaries: G. P. Bostick and Solomon L. Ginsburg. In spite of Bostick's defection from the board's service to work under the auspices of the Gospel Mission Movement, he returned to finish his career as a missionary of the Foreign Mission Board. On 21 June 1926 he died in China after thirty-seven years of sacrificial service. Solomon L. Ginsburg, a native of Poland and well known to Southern Baptists through his autobiography, *A Wandering Jew in Brazil,* died in Sao Paulo, Brazil, on 31 March 1927 after a courageous missionary career of thirty-five years.

Less than two weeks before the Southern Baptist Convention convened on 16 May 1928 in Chattanooga, James Franklin Love died. For some time his health had not been good. The burden of the board's worsening financial situation,

his incessant travels on behalf of the missionary effort of Southern Baptists, and, at last, the defalcation of the board's treasurer, all had taken their toll. Relief from his responsibilities came on 3 May after fourteen years and two days at the helm of the Foreign Mission Board. That he had served faithfully and well was evident in the expansion of the work in spite of financial setbacks.

A statistical summary of the period reveals growth in every area of the work. From 298 missionaries and nine fields, the missionary force had almost doubled to number 489 in fifteen fields. The income had more than doubled—from $679,699 to $1,455,801.60. There were 382 churches, 819 out-stations (preaching points), and 5,190 baptisms reported in 1915. In 1928, the missions reported 1,275 churches and 2,861 out stations with a total of 12,542 baptisms.[56]

The death of J. F. Love left the convention with a lingering sadness that is reflected in the tributes paid him so shortly after his death. The Committee on the Foreign Mission Board Report, in commenting upon Love's last days, said: "He was crushed by burdens that we should never have permitted to rest upon him. Truly, his name is to be inscribed on the roll of martyrs of whom the world was not worthy."[57] In its report to the convention, the Foreign Mission Board summarized Love's accomplishments:

> Through his prolific pen and public addresses he sounded in the ears of Southern Baptists a clarion call to worldwide evangelization. By his wise counsel in conference on the fields in the Orient, South America, Europe and the Near East, he brought reassurance and renewed devotion to the mis-

sionaries. His unwavering faithfulness to gospel truths increased loyalty to them wherever he went. His zeal for the spread of the gospel was so unflagging that he pressed on without stint of time and physical strength until he lay exhausted and prone in death. We are bereft over the loss of our loved brother and mighty leader. Indeed, "there is a prince and a great man fallen this day in Israel."[58]

It was difficult for Love's contemporaries to appreciate some of his longer-lasting contributions to the work of the Foreign Mission Board and to the denomination. They were too close to these developments. First, it was Love who insisted upon the denominational pattern in the foreign missionary work of Southern Baptists instead of the plan that was strongly advocated by the International Missionary Council and other organizational expressions of the ecumenical m o v e m e n t . Two, the Statement of Belief, published by the board, reinforced Baptist distinctives and may be seen as the initial step that led to the adoption of the Faith and Message by the convention in 1925. Third, it was Love's appeal to the convention in 1919 for more adequate financing of the convention's foreign mission program that appears to have been the catalyst that sparked the Seventy-five Million Campaign. Fourth, Love's innovative use of planned conferences on the mission fields made for a more

T.B. Ray

realistic use of resources and a more intimate knowledge of the needs and problems of the missions.[59] Fifth, the comity agreement on Europe worked out in cooperation with Northern, British, and Canadian Baptists was a significant and lasting achievement.

While Love lacked the charisma of a Willingham, he made his own unique contribution in strengthening and enlarging the work. The fact that he lacked some of the qualities of his predecessor caused him to develop his own administrative style that in the end may have accomplished more in strengthening the denomination than any one may have realized at the time.

T. Bronson Ray, 1868-1934

Upon the death of the corresponding secretary, the responsibility of his work became that of his associate, T. B. Ray. Ray, a Kentuckian, received his formal education from Georgetown College and The Southern Baptist Theological Seminary, where he earned the Th.M. degree. He was born on 14 August 1868 in Garrard County, the son of William Ray, a devout deacon who was also a country physician, and an equally devout mother, Nancy Jane (Rainey) Ray. His was a home in which stories of missionary exploits were commonly told around the fireside on winter evenings.

His early interest in missions was cultivated by his involvement in the Student Volunteer Movement during his college and seminary days. During the eight years he served as pastor of the Immanuel Baptist Church in Nashville, he was a member of the Tennessee Baptist Board of Missions and the City Mission Board. During these years, he was also president of the Tennessee

Baptist Young People's Union and was responsible for publishing its quarterly. By 1901, he determined the best way to promote missionary education among Southern Baptists was through mission study courses. The idea caught on.

Willingham was quick to see the possibilities of this new approach to mission education. He asked the Foreign Mission Board, therefore, to create the position of educational secretary with T. B. Ray in mind. Ray accepted the call of the board in November 1906 and within six months had organized eighty-four mission study courses. A year later the number had increased to 517. For these courses he edited or wrote a number of books, including *The Highway of Mission Thought, Southern Baptist Foreign Missions, Only a Missionary, Brazilian Sketches,* and *Southern Baptists in the Great Adventure.* For a short time Ray also edited the *Foreign Mission Journal.*

Ray's most lasting contribution to foreign missions may have been the precedent-setting mission study courses that the Woman's Missionary Union has so effectively used through the years, but his most spectacular achievement was the successful leadership he gave to the Judson Memorial Campaign. Upon the reorganization of the board's staff in 1914, Ray became and remained foreign secretary until 1916. When the board was reorganized at the intervention of the convention, he became simply the one additional secretary permitted by the convention mandate. In 1927, he was named associate secretary, and upon the death of J. F. Love the board gave T. B. Ray the title of foreign secretary with the duties of the executive secretary while the board began its search for Love's successor.[60]

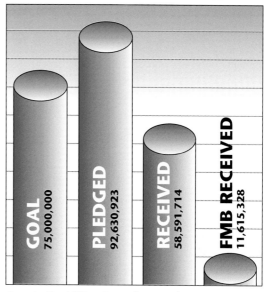

Seventy-Five Million Campaign record

GOAL 75,000,000
PLEDGED 92,630,923
RECEIVED 58,591,714
FMB RECEIVED 11,615,328

A committee was appointed to make a "recommendation for secretaries of the Board" in its meeting on 14-15 June 1928. After deliberation, the committee reported that it was not yet prepared to nominate an executive secretary and asked for more time. This decision was quite unexpected since it appeared a forgone conclusion that Ray would have been nominated. Ray's name was brought up again during the full meeting of the board the following October. After a long discussion, the board referred the matter back to the committee which reported later in the same meeting that it was nominating Solon B. Cousins, a member of the board and pastor of the Second Baptist Church of Richmond. He was elected unanimously, but in November he notified the board that he could not accept the position.

Frustrated, the committee turned to George W. Truett but he declined. Next, J. B. Weatherspoon was invited to become the corresponding secretary but when he failed to accept the call, J. W. McGlothlin was asked to serve but he also declined. Cousins was then asked to reconsider, but he held firm to his earlier decision. The committee also went back a second time to both Truett and McGlothlin but without success. Finally, after reviewing the committee's efforts in its full annual meeting, the board elected T. B. Ray its executive secretary on 2 October 1929. This was a year after he was first nominated for the position and only twenty-seven days before the Stock Market Crash.

The Great Depression

Although the Stock Market Crash on 29 October 1929 caught the nation and most of its economists by surprise, that should not have been the case. The postwar optimism that swept the nation in the 1920's had blinded not only those who speculated heavily in stocks to the bitter realities of unemployment, but also average citizens, including Southern Baptists. In partaking of the national mood of boundless optimism, the convention and its Foreign and Home Mission boards overextended themselves. True, much of the expansion was due to the rising expectations based on the $92,630,923 pledged in the Seventy-five Million Campaign and the attempt to appoint as many new missionaries as possible. Confident that Southern Baptists would rise to the challenge, the board continued to borrow to meet its obligations. Then reality set in.

The nation experienced a financial disaster unequaled in its history during the three years following the collapse of the

Depression takes toll for people everywhere.

Stock Market. Nearly one-fourth of the nation's banks closed. Factories and corporations went out of business at an unprecedented pace and coal mines shut down in Appalachia and in southern Illinois. Because corn was worthless, farmers used it for fuel instead of coal. Thousands of farmers went bankrupt and their farms were sold at public auction to pay off their mortgages. Six to seven million people were out of work, many having lost everything they owned. Shanty towns, called Hoovervilles, sprang up on vacant lots in the large industrial cities. The homeless wandered the streets by day and slept wherever they could at night, even in subways.

The more rural South did not escape the ravages of the depression—nor did Southern Baptists. How one Baptist family survived when the coal mines shut down in Southern Illinois is poignantly described by Robert Hastings in *A Nickel's Worth of Skim Milk.*[61] It would have been surprising if receipts of the Home and Foreign Mission boards had not reflected the inability of Southern Baptists to contribute at previous levels. To complicate matters further, the attention of Southern Baptists, like that of the nation at large, was turned inward. Most were preoccupied with the problems of day to day survival.

Diminishing Returns

In 1929, the income of the board was the lowest in ten years. From 1926 to 1929 eighty-two missionaries resigned and only twelve were appointed.[62] Retrenchment became the order of the day. As the financial condition of the board continued to worsen, missionaries were compelled to delay furloughs due and those on furlough were not able to return unless a year's salary and return travel expenses were "especially provided."[63] In 1930 the budget of the Foreign Mission Board was $1,390,000. By 1932, the cash receipts for the budget totaled only $691,302.00. At this point the convention stepped in and demanded that the budget for 1933 total no more than eighty-eight percent of the previous year's receipts, except for emergency funds. This left a budget of $605,575.76, of which $65,000 was already earmarked for interest due on the board's debt. Fortunately, this dismal situation was the lowest point of the board's fortunes in the twentieth century.

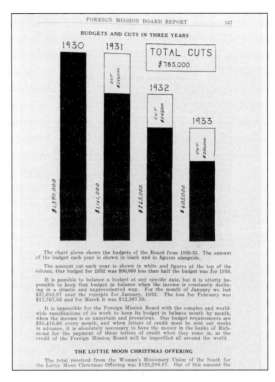

Foreign Mission Board budget, 1930-1933

The result upon the Southern Baptist missionary enterprise was almost fatal. Its human cost was incalculable and T. B. Ray became one of the casualties.

Not realizing that there was no "quick fix" to the board's predicament, it attempted to improve the situation by a change in personnel. Less than five months after T. B. Ray had been chosen executive secretary, the board elected W. Eugene Sallee on 13 March 1930 as home secretary. The twenty-seven year veteran missionary from Interior China served little more than a year before a sudden heart attack carried him away on 15 June 1931. As the financial condition of the board continued to deteriorate, some of its members apparently thought that the situation would not improve until a new executive secretary was elected. Therefore, Ray was asked once again to serve as foreign secretary while a committee was chosen to nominate a new executive secretary.

Charles E. Maddry, a widely recognized executive and Southern Baptist denominational leader, was elected executive secretary of the Foreign Mission Board. He took office on 1 January 1933. Until the October meeting of the board, T. B. Ray continued to serve as foreign secretary. In spite of Ray's earnest request that he be allowed to have some continuing responsibility with the board, he was abruptly terminated, doubtless a victim of "the change of the guard." He was sixty-five at the time. Besides, he had continued the board's educational work, which involved the publication and sale of books at a deficit in spite of the board's financial straits. To soften the blow, "On request of Dr. Maddry, Dr. Ray was given the title of Emeritus Secretary without change of his status as voted this afternoon."[64]

T. Bronson Ray in Perspective

Although retired by the board at the usual retirement age, Ray undoubtedly felt rejected by his brethren. He had been elected executive secretary apparently as a last resort. Then his status was changed less than two years after he had begun to serve in his new role. True, the board's financial condition had not improved—but worsened. Missionary enthusiasm and appointments were at a low ebb. Ray became a victim of the depression and of the loss of confidence of his peers. In less than three months he was dead. He died on 15 January 1934 after twenty-seven years of unselfish

and dedicated service. He had lived and labored through the period of rising expectations to face the results of diminishing returns. "In Memoriam," Solon B. Cousins, speaking for the board, said:

> *Doctor Ray's name will always be associated with the distinctive advances made by our Board during the past twenty-five years. His first service was the creation of a literature adapted to the needs of our people in the study of Foreign Missions. Through the Educational Department, of which he was the first Secretary, he not only wrote and edited suitable books, but also promoted the organization of Mission Study Classes. We owe him a very great debt for vividly bringing the needs of our fields into our churches.*

> *And to his enthusiastic leadership must be credited the success of the Judson Centennial. That movement lifted our Southern Baptists to a high level of missionary interest.*

> *But whether one thinks of the books he wrote, or the campaigns he directed, or the plans he inaugurated; whether one recalls his work as Educational Secretary, Foreign Secretary, Associate Secretary or Executive Secretary, one fact stands out transcendently above all that he did, and that was his devotion to Foreign Missions. To that cause he dedicated his life and in its service he died content. It was in keeping with the ruling purpose of his life that his last service should have been the completion of a book telling the history of Southern Baptist Foreign Missions.*[65]

That book to which Cousins referred was *Southern Baptists in the Great Adventure.* It was edited by the distinguished professor of missions of The Southern Baptist Theological Seminary, William Owen Carver, after Ray's death.

ENDNOTES

1. *Annual,* SBC, 1915, 125.

2. Ibid., 24.

3. Ibid., 37-40.

4. Ibid., 196, 197.

5. Ibid., 197.

6. Ibid., 122, 123.

7. Ibid., 43. Article V of the constitution was amended to read:

Each of these Boards, as elected by the Convention, shall consist of one member from each state cooperating with the Convention, and of a President, Recording Secretary, Auditor, and fifteen other members residing at or near the locality of the Board. No salaried official or employe [sic] of any Board may be a member thereof; but the Convention shall elect for each Board annually a Corresponding Secretary, who may also be named by the Board as its Treasurer if deemed desirable. In case of vacancy occurring between the meetings of the Convention, the Boards are authorized to fill such vacancy. Each Board may elect other Secretaries, a Treasurer, and such other paid officers and employes [sic] as may be necessary for the efficient conduct of its business, and may make such compensation to its Secretaries and other paid officials as it may deem right.

8. Ibid., 65.

9. Minutes, FMB, 17 May 1915, 102.

10. Minutes, FMB, 16 June 1915, 106.

11. George Braxton Taylor, *Virginia Baptist Ministers, Sixth Series, 1914-1934* (Lynchburg, Virginia, J. P. Bell Company, Inc., 1935), 272.

12. Ibid., 273.

13. E.C. Routh, "Love, James Franklin" in *Encyclopedia of Southern Baptists,* vol. 2 (Nashville, TN: Broadman Press, 1958), 809.

14. Minutes, FMB, 13 June 1915, 118.

15. *Annual,* SBC, 1914, 73-78.

16. *Annual,* SBC, 1916, 120.

17. Ibid., 122.

18. J. F. Love, *The Union Movement* (Nashville, TN: Sunday School Board of the Southern Baptist Convention, 1918), 15.

19. Minutes, FMB, 14 April 1915, 125, 126.

20. *Annual,* SBC, 1915, 30.

21. Ibid., 30.

22. Ibid., 34.

23. Ibid., 34.

24. *Annual,* SBC, 1913, 70.

25. *Annual,* SBC, 1915, 23.

26. Minutes, FMB, 3 May 1916, 167.

27. *Annual,* SBC, 1916, 60.

28. Ibid., 61, 62.

29. See B. J. W. Graham, ed., *Baptist Biography,* vol. III (Atlanta: Index Printing Company, Publishers, 1923), 395-401, for more information on Smith's life and work.

30. There are inexpensive plans by which this contact is possible. They were used in 1912 when we raised $580,400. They were used more extensively, though not fully, in 1914, when the Board laid on me the duty of planning the campaign. The Judson Centennial was then in its second year and its claims were being pressed with vigor. Notwithstanding, we received $587,500, the largest amount raised for current support in the history of the work, making a reduction in the debt possible. From Minutes, FMB, 14 June 1916, 172.

31. Minutes, FMB, 13 July 1916, 184.

32. Minutes, FMB, 15 June 1916, 179.

33. Annual, SBC, 1916, 18.

34. Annual, SBC, 1918, 180.

35. Ibid., 62.

36. Annual, SBC, 1919, 198.

37. Ibid., 104.

38. Ibid., 74.

39. For a good summary of the Seventy-five Million Campaign see Frank E. Burkhalter, "Seventy-five Million Campaign" in *Encyclopedia of Southern Baptists,* vol. 2 (Nashville, TN: Broadman Press, 1958).

40. Annual, SBC, 1920, 43.

41. Ibid., 197-99.

42. Minutes, FMB, 6 October 1920, 49.

43. Ibid., 52, 53.

44. Annual, SBC, 1922, 37.

45. Annual, SBC, 1921, 198. The countries listed in this "Report" number only sixteen, while the board reported it was at work in eighteen countries in 1922. Apparently, Switzerland and Czechoslovakia were added to the list. Everett Gill, veteran missionary in Italy, moved to Lausanne, Switzerland to become the representative of Southern Baptists in Europe and the board was involved in the financial support of an orphanage in Czechoslovakia.

46. Annual, SBC, 1922, 180. Below is the statistical table given in the 1922 FMB Report on page 181. The first set of statistics is for the years 1920-21, the second set for 1921-22.

Churches	610	622
Baptisms	6,998	7,891
Membership	59,438	64,251
S. S. Scholars	41,727	53,691
Kindergarten pupils	787	904
Elementary pupils	18,506	22,394
Academy pupils	1,809	2,025
College students	1,007	1,100
Theological students	284	370
Native contributions	$295,694	$465,235

47. Ibid. The board could not refrain from "preaching a bit" when it stated: "Let it be again entered upon

the age of authentic history that Baptists are the consistent and effective champions of religious liberty, just and impartial liberty."

48. Cited in Barnes, Southern Baptist Convention, 193.

49. Ibid., 196.

50. Annual, SBC, 1921, 205.

51. Annual, SBC, 1925, 99. The committee commenting on the Foreign Mission Board Report expressed its frustration in a succinct paragraph:

And singularly enough, this situation faces us at a time when responsiveness to our Foreign Missionaries was never so gratifying. For example, during the five years of the campaign period there were 59,248 baptisms; 706 new churches established; 58,663 new members; an increase of 930 Sunday schools, with 49,400 new pupils.

52. Ibid., 34.

53. Baker, Southern Baptist Convention and its People, 404. Baker explained the significance of the Cooperative Program for the life of the convention when he wrote on page 404:

The significance of the adoption of the Cooperative Program in 1925 resides in its correction of the ambivalence in the financial methods carried over from the society plan in 1845 and its exploiting of the genius of the convention-type program. The Cooperative Program brought the goal of the original constitution of 1845 closer to realization; i.e., the formation of a body to carry on all types of benevolent work desired by its constituency.

54. Annual, SBC, 1927, 161.

55. C. E. Maddry, unpublished history of the Foreign Mission Board, 53.

56. Annual, SBC, 1928, 240-42.

57. Ibid., 51.

58. Ibid., 142.

59. In 1918-1919, Love visited the missions in China and Japan, holding fifty-eight conferences with the missionaries. He closed his visit with a ten day Inter-Mission Conference in Shanghai. The following year, he and Z. T. Cody made a trip to Europe and the Near East to survey the countries for the board. Later in the same year, he led the Southern Baptist delegation which participated in a Baptist conference in London, July 19-23. In 1922, Love made an extensive tour of all the missions in South America, conducting conferences in the process. The following year found him back in Europe where he attended a Congress of the Baptist World Alliance meeting in Stockholm, Sweden. Thus, for five consecutive years, J. F. Love was out of the United States on business for the Foreign Mission Board for months at a time.

60. See E. C. Routh, "Ray, T. Bronson" in Encyclopedia of Southern Baptists, vol. 2 and Taylor, Virginia Baptist Ministers, Sixth Series, 459-63, for additional information on T. B. Ray.

61. See Robert J. Hastings, A Nickel's Worth of Skim Milk (Carbondale: Southern Illinois University, 1972) for a graphically written story of one devout Southern Baptist family and its struggle to survive during the years of the Great Depression.

62. Baker James Cauthen, Advance: A History of Southern Baptist Foreign Missions (Nashville, TN: Broadman Press, 1970), 37.

63. Minutes, FMB, 11 December 1930, 269.

64. Minutes, FMB, 11 October 1933, 41.

65. Annual, SBC, 1934, 159-60.

PART IV

Renewal and Advance

1933-1976

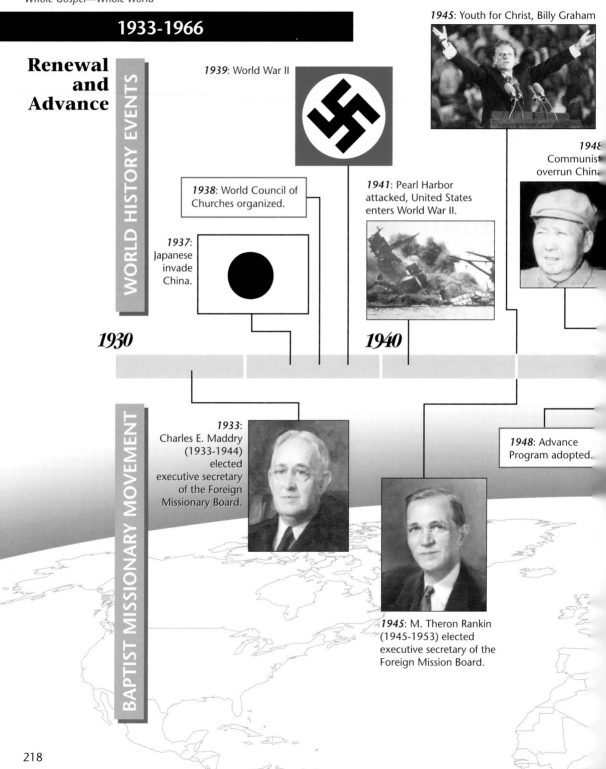

1933-1966

Renewal and Advance

WORLD HISTORY EVENTS

1939: World War II

1945: Youth for Christ, Billy Graham

1948 Communist overrun China

1938: World Council of Churches organized.

1941: Pearl Harbor attacked, United States enters World War II.

1937: Japanese invade China.

1930

1940

BAPTIST MISSIONARY MOVEMENT

1933: Charles E. Maddry (1933-1944) elected executive secretary of the Foreign Missionary Board.

1948: Advance Program adopted.

1945: M. Theron Rankin (1945-1953) elected executive secretary of the Foreign Mission Board.

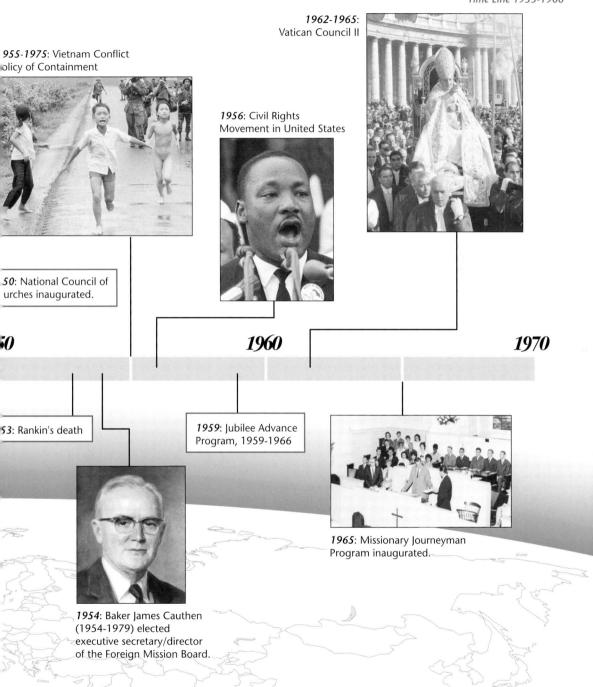

1962-1965:
Vatican Council II

955-1975: Vietnam Conflict
olicy of Containment

1956: Civil Rights
Movement in United States

50: National Council of
urches inaugurated.

50

1960

1970

53: Rankin's death

1959: Jubilee Advance
Program, 1959-1966

1965: Missionary Journeyman
Program inaugurated.

1954: Baker James Cauthen
(1954-1979) elected
executive secretary/director
of the Foreign Mission Board.

A New Spirit

2037 Monument Ave.

Charles E. Maddry brought to the board a wealth of experience in denominational service. He found the board in a state of disarray. The banks to which the board was indebted were demanding payment in full. Maddry's handling of the situation satisfied the bankers and reassured the board. By April 1943, the indebtedness was completely retired. Upon Maddry's retirement, Solon B. Cousins said: "He imparted to us his own faith, courage, vision, and hope. Our unpayable debt to Dr. Maddry is the new spirit he gave us."

hen Charles E. Maddry retired as executive secretary of the Foreign Mission Board, many tributes delineated the achievements of the board under his leadership. None was more revealing than the statement prepared by the board-appointed committee. After summarizing his contributions to the work of the board, Solon B. Cousins and the members of this committee said, "He imparted to us his own faith, courage, vision, and hope. Our unpayable debt to Dr. Maddry is the new spirit he gave us."[1]

Charles E. Maddry

To a considerable extent, this chapter examines the impact of Maddry's "faith, courage, vision, and hope" upon the Foreign Mission Board and its work during his twelve-year tenure.

One indicator of the remarkable turnaround of the board's fortunes during this period is seen in the reversal of its financial situation. In October 1932, the Foreign Mission Board owed the banks $1,110,000 in addition to debts incurred by the various missions exceeding $200,000. Besides, the convention had mandated that the budget for 1933 be adjusted to total no more than 88 percent of the board's actual receipts in 1932.

The total operating budget for 1933, the first year of Maddry's administration, was little more than $600,000. As Maddry often said, "It was an impossible situation." Yet, in less than eleven years the entire indebtedness had been paid. The next year when Maddry retired, the board counted a balance of more than a million dollars in the banks, and the work had not suffered in the process. To the contrary, it had experienced significant growth in every category, with the exception of the

221

limitations imposed upon the missions in Europe and the Orient by the conflicts of World War II.

Charles E. Maddry, 1876-1962

Maddry was fifty-six years of age when he took on the greatest challenge of his ministry. He brought to the board a background of varied experience. Charles was born in the hills of North Carolina on a poor and rocky farm, a few miles from Chapel Hill. His education was at best a now and then affair, both spasmodic and uninspiring, until his eighteenth year. At that juncture of his life, there came a new teacher to the nearby country school different from any he had ever had before. The teacher was enthusiastic about both learning and teaching. He challenged and inspired his students and in the process opened up a new world of literature and knowledge to those who had never dreamed that such a gold mine existed in books. One day J. P. Canaday, the teacher, asked Charlie what he intended to do with his life. The awkward youth, now twenty, replied that he supposed he would farm just as his ancestors had for a hundred and fifty years before him. It was then that Canaday challenged Maddry to consider entering the University

On 2 May 1906 [Charles E. Maddry and Emma Parker]… began marriage and a ministry that would have a global impact…

of North Carolina, only three miles distant. Although, all his life, Charles had heard the bells of the university toll, he had never thought that the school existed for such as he. That conversation changed the course of his life. Later he wrote:

> He had lighted a flame in me that has never gone out. Henceforth life held new meaning, for from that hour a new purpose dominated my life. He was the first ever to tell me that there was something in my life worth striving for and that God is always ready to help those who try to help themselves.[2]

The road ahead was not easy. Since his formal education had been so meager, he entered a preparatory school in Chapel Hill to catch up. Now twenty years old, he found himself attending classes with boys and girls twelve or fourteen years of age, but he persisted in his new-found purpose. Two years later, he entered college still with a deficiency in Latin, which he made up by going back to the high school three times a week during his first year in the university. The hard work of cutting and splitting firewood for the school to pay his tuition and the three mile walk to and from Chapel Hill to his home seemed a small price to pay for the privilege of beginning his university studies.

On the threshold of this new step of faith, his home church, the Mount Moriah Baptist Church, "liberated" him to exercise his gifts of preaching. Upon hearing that Charlie Maddry had been licensed to preach the gospel, the nearby black congregation, whose members his grandfather had befriended when they were a part of the Mount Moriah church, asked him to preach his first sermon in their church. It was an affirming experience for which he was always grateful. From time to time since his conversion and baptism at eleven years of age, he had felt the inner urge to become a minister of the gospel but his sense of unworthiness and innate timidity kept him from sharing his "call" with anyone. When his call became so evident to others, he could no longer suppress the longing of his heart. Hence, the beginnings of his university studies and his ministerial career coincided.

Before finishing the university with his bachelor of philosophy degree, he had become the county superintendent of the public schools of Orange County and pastor of four "quarter-time" churches. Most of the work of the county superintendent was done on Saturdays, his sermon preparation—on Sundays. Upon receiving his degree, he decided that it was time to prepare more fully for the ministry. Once again, and virtually without the necessary financial resources, he took another step of faith: he entered The Southern Baptist Theological Seminary in October 1904.

After a year and a half of demanding but stimulating seminary studies, Maddry decided that it was time to leave the seminary and the teachers he admired for North Carolina. The urge to return to his native state was prompted in part by Emma Parker whom he had planned to marry as soon as he was settled in a pastorate. February 1906 found him in Greensboro, North Carolina, beginning his ministry by dividing time between a small mission church and a new mission in West Greensboro. On 2 May 1906, he and Emma were married in the First Baptist Church of Hillsboro. Thus began a marriage and a ministry that would

have a global impact, although no one may have suspected it at the time.

After the Forest Avenue Church of Greensboro, which he had nurtured from its infancy, became able to walk on its own, he became pastor of First Church, Statesville. The Statesville pastorate was followed by almost five years as pastor of the Tabernacle Baptist Church, of Raleigh, known for its evangelistic outreach. During his Raleigh years, Maddry found himself deeply involved in a fund raising campaign to erect a new building for the Wake Forest Baptist Church, which for lack of an adequate building, was worshiping in the university chapel. When Walter N. Johnson, the pastor, became ill, Maddry was left with the sole responsibility for the successful completion of the campaign. After hundreds of letters and numerous personal appearances, the money was raised and a beautiful church building erected on the campus.

After a four and half year interlude in which Maddry was pastor of the University Baptist Church of Austin, Texas, he was elected secretary of the North Carolina Baptist Convention. His Texas sojourn served to prepare him further for the challenge and task yet unknown. In Texas he became well known for his evangelistic spirit and his ability to raise money for worthy causes. The church in Austin was small but the congregation realized that it needed to build a more adequate and attractive edifice for the future. Baptists in Texas and beyond were made aware of the strategic importance and potential of a Baptist church located two blocks from the University of Texas. With help from the Texas Baptist Convention, the Home Mission Board, and wealthy individuals, sufficient funds were forthcoming to construct an attractive building. Maddry and his family were prepared to spend the remainder of their lives in Texas when a call came to return to their beloved North Carolina. It proved irresistible.

The next twelve years as secretary of the North Carolina Baptist Convention enhanced Maddry's administrative skills and widened his influence, giving him status as a denominational statesmen that few could match. When the Southern Baptist Convention decided to organize a new department of Missionary Promotion under the direction of the con-

George Sadler, left, with J.W. Storer, SBC president (1954, 1955) and L. Howard Jenkins, right

vention's Executive Committee, a search committee, made up of a representative from each of the state conventions, unanimously chose Charles E. Maddry its executive secretary. The purpose of the new department was to promote systematic giving to the Cooperative Program for desperately needed mission support. After eleven and a half years with the North Carolina Convention, Charles and Emma felt it was time to accept a new challenge. For six months, he gave his new responsibility his best and in the process became even more widely known as a man with the world in his heart. It also became evident to several of his friends that he was uniquely gifted and prepared to take the helm of the

Foreign Mission Board.

Maddry Accepts the Challenge

Maddry was in Knoxville, Tennessee preparing to address the Knox County Association when he received a telephone call from the Foreign Mission Board. When he was finally able to return the call, he was informed that the board at its meeting on 12 October 1932 had unanimously elected him its executive secretary. The news took him by surprise for no one from the board had so much as hinted that he was being considered for the position. In a typical understatement he wrote later: "If I possessed any qualification for the position of leadership in the cause of foreign missions of Southern Baptists, it was my enthusiasm and my passion for world missions."[3] While Maddry was undoubtedly surprised that the board would even consider him since he had less than six months before accepted his new position, he must have had some intuition that he would eventually be chosen for the task. So convinced was he that the call of the board was the call of God, within a few days he notified the board of his acceptance of the invitation, resigned from his secretaryship of the Department of Missionary Promotion and moved to Richmond in order to begin his new assignment on 1

January 1933.

A man of less faith or more caution would have turned the board down or imposed some face-saving provisions, in case the board utterly collapsed, for the board was widely perceived as a "basket case."

In an attempt to prepare for a renewed search for leadership of the board, L. Howard Jenkins, its president for more than thirty years, led in its reorganization in 1930. Upon this occasion, T. B. Ray who had first been asked to serve as interim corresponding secretary upon the death of J. F. Love and later corresponding secretary, was made foreign secretary, but still no pastor or denominational leader was found willing to accept the challenge until Charles E. Maddry.

When Maddry was elected executive secretary, Ray was unanimously elected assistant executive secretary. In 1933, Maddry, Ray, the treasurer, his assistant, two stenographers, an "educational secretary" and an office boy comprised the entire Richmond staff. But this situation under the leadership of the new executive secretary was destined to change, as was every aspect of the board during his twelve year tenure.

The Financial Crisis

It was immediately evident that the financial crunch had not only brought the appointment of missionaries to a halt but had caused the board to dismiss several of those on furlough and to place others on leave without salary. In the previous July, twenty-eight missionaries on furlough were told to seek employment in the states until the board could see its way clear to sending them back with some assurance that it could support them. Ten others were told that it was improbable that the board could send them back and seven were detained in the states indefinitely.[4]

The distressing condition of the board became a painful reality to the new secretary at his first board meeting in January 1933. T. B. Ray read the report of the Administration Committee. "We are sorry," Ray said, "that further study of the Board's financial condition on January 1st, makes it more apparent than it was last July that the Board cannot return now any of these detained missionaries to their fields." The report also carried an explanation of its action.

The Board acted as it did in the fear of God in an honest effort to carry out the instructions of the Southern Baptist Convention. Other plans were prayerfully considered, but the one adopted, retaining at home these missionaries, was decided upon as being the one which would present the least embarrassment, disappointment and injury to all the issues and persons involved.[5]

It soon became evident to the new executive secretary that a number of factors had contributed to the financial crisis of the board in addition to the Great Depression. Before these could be addressed, the board was forced to face the issue of indebtedness. The four Richmond banks that held the notes on the loans to the board asked for a meeting with L. Howard Jenkins, president of the board. Maddry and others accompanied Jenkins to the meeting. They were promptly informed that not only must the board pay the $67,000.00 interest on the loans but $150,000.00 on the principal as well. Maddry forthrightly responded that for the board to accede to the bankers' demands would "completely paralyze the

Board as a going concern and bring disaster to all the foreign mission work of the Southern Baptist Convention."[6] Further, he cajoled and warned Burnett, president of the First and Merchants Bank that,

> the Foreign Mission Board had been doing business with these banks for more than ninety years and that they had never lost a cent in principal or interest from our Board. I told them that Southern Baptists were going to continue doing foreign mission work and that if they persisted in their plans, they would put the Foreign Mission Board out of business completely. . . . I told them that our people would pay them every cent they owed them, providing they would allow us to carry on as a going concern. I further reminded them that their notes would be paid, every cent with interest, provided they allowed us to function as agreed upon at the October meeting of the Board. I stated that if they insisted on their demands as announced, their notes were not worth the paper they were written on and that they were planning to "kill the goose that laid the golden egg." Mr. Burnett said, with a smile, that that sounded like common sense to him. He asked for further discussion from his committee and they unanimously agreed to allow us to go on as planned at the October meeting of the Board.[7]

Although the plight of the Foreign Mission Board was not the only financial crisis facing Southern Baptists, it was the most critical. The accumulated indebtedness of all the convention's agencies and institutions in 1933 totaled approximately $6,500,000.00. Clearly, the situation called for concerted action by the entire convention. Before a convention-wide plan materialized, Wade H. Bryant, pastor of the Barton Heights Baptist Church of Richmond, organized a club made up of members of his church who pledged to give twenty-five cents a week on the debt of the Foreign Mission Board. Blanche White, secretary of the Woman's Missionary Union of Virginia, endorsed the plan and promoted it throughout the state. When the Executive Committee met in Nashville on 12 April, it adopted a plan proposed by Frank Tripp which greatly resembled the Bryant plan. This action marked the beginning of the Hundred Thousand Club.

The Hundred Thousand Club plan was designed to enroll one hundred thousand Southern Baptists who would pledge to give one dollar a month over and above their regular tithes and offerings toward the indebtedness of all the agencies of the convention. The plan called for a leader in each church, association, and state. Frank Tripp was asked to be the general leader for the convention. The expenses of promoting the plan were to be paid by the Sunday School Board so that every dollar given could be applied to the principal of the debts. Not only did this effort appear promising, it actually proved effective. Every convention agency became "debt free in '43."[8] The Foreign Mission Board was the first of the agencies to reach this goal and Charles Maddry was largely responsible for this achievement.

The Italian Role

During the early years of the Seventy-five Million Campaign, the Foreign Mission Board had purchased two pieces of valuable property in Rome that had never been used for the projected objects. One consisted of thirty-five acres on a hill overlooking the city. The Fascist government first expropri-

Italian National Baptist Convention, June 1938; European representative, Everett Gill, Sr., left, and Missionary W. Dewey Moore, sit with Maddry

Italy

finally paid the board considerably less than the property's fair value. A valuable piece of property in downtown Rome (Piazza Barberini), which the board had never been able to develop because it was located in a "zone of monuments of antiquity," was in danger of confiscation as well. Just in time, arrangements were made, and with the required consent of Italian Baptists, the property was sold to an international company for $312,500.00. This enabled the board to apply $292,000.00 on its debt. A few months later, Mussolini confiscated the property but not until the transaction was completed and the board had its money in hand. Thus as Maddry wrote: "The Mission Board's credit was saved," and "For once the 'Sawdust Caesar' had been outwitted."[9]

Reluctantly, Italian Baptists played a role in helping to save the credit of the Foreign Mission Board. Maddry was informed by the board's lawyer in Rome

ated twenty acres of the Baptist property and later the remainder. After long and drawn out negotiations the government

227

Urbana Baptist Church, Rome

Mission Board at its February meeting in 1933.[10] The final draft was translated into Italian and presented to the pastors in Rome on 22, 23, and 24 July 1934 during Maddry's European tour. The plan called for a board of directors under which all Baptist work in Italy would be conducted. The Foreign Mission Board also proposed "to turn over to Italian Baptists the church buildings now used strictly for worship and as homes for pastors; it being agreed that no property given by the Foreign Mission Board shall be sold or mortgaged without consent and approval of the Foreign Mission Board."[11] The last provision was finally approved by the Italians only after Maddry warned that the board would "withdraw from Italy unless the plan submitted was adopted."[12] The next day, Maddry wrote in his diary: "When faced with the stern alternative, they [Italian pastors] voted on roll call unanimously to accept legal responsibility & come under their own Board."[13]

that the Italian Baptists insisted that the proceeds from the sale of the Piazza Barberini should go toward enlarging the Baptist work in Italy since the property was originally purchased for that purpose. At the time, after more than sixty years of Southern Baptist missionary efforts in Italy, there was no national organization and the work was heavily dependant upon the board's financial support. Maddry chose the opportunity to impress upon the Italians the importance of forming a National Italian Baptist Union and the adoption of a plan that moved toward a "self-governing, self-supporting, and self-perpetuating" denomination.

The first draft of a proposal drawn up by Maddry was approved by the Foreign

A Brief Respite

After the tension-filled meeting with the Italian Baptists, the Maddrys welcomed a Sunday in Florence, Italy, with their brethren of the city. After Florence, they visited the fabled city of Venice. Their next stop was Oberammergau and its Passion Play. While here they were guests in the home of the man who played Christ. After the performance was over, Maddry recorded his thoughts: "It is so much greater & more Scriptural than I thought. It is beyond description & must be seen to be appreciated. It is the greatest day of my life. I wish everybody in the world could see it—Marvelous."[14]

Missionaries at the Budapest seminary, 1938: missionaries Roy and Lillie Mae Starmer, left, and John Allen and Pauline Willingham Moore, right, with the Everett Gills, center

From Oberammergau to Berlin, the Maddrys joined hundreds of Baptists from around the world who were attending the fifth Congress of the Baptist World Alliance. It was more than a trip of a few kilometers, it was a leap across the centuries. From the first century Palestine of the Passion Play, they found themselves plunged into the rising tensions of a twentieth century Germany in transition. President Hindeburg died just as the congress was preparing to convene. Hitler had already taken over the reins of the Weimar Republic. Several months before, Maddry had been asked to address the congress on "The Implication and Outreach of the Great Commission." Due to time constraints, he was asked to confine his remarks to twenty minutes instead of the twenty-five originally alloted.

Nevertheless, this opportunity to speak to his fellow Baptists gave the new executive secretary exposure to the Baptist world fellowship that enhanced his leadership among Southern Baptists.

Eastern Europe and the Near East

After ten days in Berlin, Maddry and his party toured the Baptist work in Yugoslavia, Romania, and Hungary. Often he was greeted by large and enthusiastic congregations. But he soon discovered more problems existed than he had ever suspected. At Arad, Romania, he was asked to mediate a dispute between warring factions who were doing irreparable damage to the Baptist fellowship, to say nothing of the Baptists' reputation in a Catholic country. Utterly defeated in his efforts in bringing about a reconciliation, he described the situation in his diary.

It is the bitterest factional fight I ever got mixed up in, I think. It is a contest between would-be leaders. All the morning

Baptist church members, in the 1930s, work on their building, Transylvania Province, Romania.

they poured out the[ir] spleens upon each other. We got no where! The favorite method of fighting among these ambitious leaders is by lying & slander.[15]

Leaving the unhappy experience of the Arad quarrels behind, Maddry and his party traveled by train all night in a second class coach, arriving at Bucharest at seven the next morning—"sleepy and tired." Interviews with government officials, in an attempt to gain legal recognition for Baptists in order to carry on the work unhindered, proved fruitless. Discouraged, Maddry wrote in his diary. "Petty persecutions, inspired by the Greek [Orthodox] primate, harassed us at every turn. I will be glad to leave Roumania!"[16]

From Bucharest to Jerusalem, he found no country in which the board had missions without serious problems—some so serious in Lebanon, Syria, and Israel, that he wondered whether or not to recommend that the work be continued. During the entire trip, he was frequently sick and constantly called upon to preach or counsel missionaries, whose competence he seriously questioned. Despite the problems, his diary reflects the joy of fellowship with kindred brethren and the delight at visiting the fabled cities of Europe and the Near East, with the exception of Jerusalem and its holy places. Of these, he wrote:

Went to the Church of the Holy Sepulcher, so called. I feel nothing but disgust for the commercialism of the whole thing. I think it impossible that this garish & loud bedecked [spot] could have been the place of the saviour's suffering, death & resurrection. Every traditional site or anything connected with the Saviour—its all so disappointing.[17]

This first trip overseas for the Maddrys had taken nine days less than four months. They left on 14 June and returned to Richmond on 5 October. Upon their return, he found a mountain of correspondence and other responsibilities awaiting attention. That the new executive secretary had used his opportunity to acquaint himself thoroughly with the work in Europe became evident in the numerous recommendations on Italy, Yugoslavia, Romania, Hungary, Spain, and the Near East approved in the November meeting of the board.[18] The recommendations covered the whole range of Southern Baptist missionary efforts in the countries mentioned. Doubtless the number and complexity of problems of the work in Europe and the Near East impressed upon Maddry the necessity of regional secretaries. By the next year the first of these was elected by the board. In the meantime, the board turned its attention to projects first proposed in its October meeting in 1933.

The Woman's Missionary Union Acts

One of the last announcements of T. B. Ray before his retirement from the board carried the disappointing news that the board could not send missionaries on furlough back to their fields. This state of affairs was unacceptable to the Woman's Missionary Union which proposed to use surplus funds from the Lottie Moon Christmas Offering of 1933 to underwrite the salaries for the remainder of 1934 and pay the "outgoing expenses" of eight new missionaries to be sent out after the meeting of the Southern Baptist Convention.[19] Maddry immediately saw the advantages of this proposal. For one thing, in addition to supplying obvious missionary personnel needs in China, Africa, and Japan, it would send a signal to Southern Baptists that in spite of financial problems the board was still in the mission business. It was a positive move that helped to reverse the policy of retrenchment of "seven lean years," as Maddry referred to the period.[20] With it the spirit of defeatism was slowly replaced by cautious optimism.

... the Lottie Moon Christmas Offering had boosted the fortunes of the board and helped it to continue to function...

The board also adopted five other recommendations of the Woman's Missionary Union involving appropriation of funds for various objects. Some of these proposals included designated items for which funds had been set aside. The board accepted all six "propositions" as presented by Maddry on behalf of the Administrative Committee.[21] Encouraged by the support of the Woman's Missionary Union, the Appointment Committee reported that it had asked eleven young people to attend the April meeting of the board for examination "looking toward their appointment for service with this Board."[22] To an extent not true before, the Lottie Moon Christmas Offering had boosted the fortunes of the board and helped it to continue to function in one of the most difficult periods in its history.

A Charter for Change

As early as the October board meeting in 1933, a Maddry agenda was adopted by the board. It could appropriately be called "a charter for change." It was at this meeting that Ray resigned the position of Assistant Executive Secretary "In order that Dr. Maddry may have the utmost freedom in carrying out the will and policies of the Board, . . ."[23] Taking Ray's letter at face value, the board "relieved [him] of all duties in connection with the Board" and declared the office of Assistant Executive Secretary "abolished effective at once."[24] The board did soften the effect of its actions by voting to continue Ray's salary to the end of the year and after that date to continue to pay him $200.00 a month through the following September. In the evening session upon the recommendation of Maddry, Ray was awarded the title of Emeritus Secretary. The board also proceeded to establish a new position designated, "Office Secretary." Miss Jessie R. Ford was elected to this office. From the actions of the board at this meeting, it was clear that Maddry had the enthusiastic support of the board in establishing the new direction he envisioned for the board.

The Death of T. B. Ray

On 15 January 1934, T. Bronson Ray suddenly died. His death, in a sense, marked the close of one of the most difficult periods in the board's history. In spite of his apparent inability to lead the board out of its financial wilderness and in spite of his own sense of failure, he had continued to maintain an office in the Foreign Mission Board building and to interest himself in the board's ongoing affairs, not an altogether happy arrangement as far as the new executive secretary was concerned. Nevertheless, Ray was genuinely appreciated by the members of the board, who upon the occasion of his death said so.

While citing the many solid accomplishments of T. B. Ray, the committee, charged with the responsibility of preparing the memorial, encapsulated the spirit of the man in the following words:

Editor Routh, center, talks with 1948 missionary appointee, Horace Buddin, and staff member Genevieve Greer.

> *On the walls of the room where he worked might fitly have been written these words: 'This one thing I do—to help Southern Baptists to see their privilege, to feel their obligation, to seize their opportunity, and to do their duty in sending the Gospel of Christ to the ends of the earth.'*[25]

Ray lived just long enough after Maddry's arrival to acquaint the new secretary with the organization of the board and its day to day operation but not so long as to hinder Maddry from providing the board with his own solutions to its long-standing problems.

The Commission

One of the priorities of Maddry's administration was reestablishing the board's own missionary periodical. The *Foreign Mission Journal*, under pressure from the Southern Baptist Convention, had been combined with the *Home Field* in 1916 and published by the Sunday School Board under the title *Home and Foreign Fields.*

Unfortunately, the combined periodical, like previous mergers, failed to prosper. Before the merger, the *Foreign Mission Journal* counted around 30,000 subscribers. When *Home and Foreign Fields* ceased publication twenty years later it had a circulation of 12,184 or about one fourth the total of both mission magazines before the merger. At a time when the Foreign Mission Board most needed the active support of Southern Baptists, it found itself without any continuing direct contact with its constituency. The board took the first step toward remedying the situation by adopting the report of the Committee on Education and Promotion.[26]

In addition to proposing a vigorous new publication policy, the committee recommended the establishment of a Department of Education and Promotion and the employment of a secretary to direct the work. The year, 1934 came and went without a new secretary. Maddry informed the convention in his 1934 report that "we balanced the budget by not electing a Secretary of Education and Promotion and a Field Secretary succeeding Dr. W. D. Powell who retired on February the first."[27] Since the board lacked the personnel and the permission of the convention to launch a new publication immediately, Maddry engineered contracts with seventeen state Baptist papers to carry news stories of the board's activities. In addition, *Home and Foreign Fields, The Baptist Student, Royal Service,* and the *Sunday School Builder* were among the publications tapped to publicize the work of the Foreign Mission Board.

By 1936, the Department of Education and Promotion was completely reorganized and the board's archives were established.[28] Among the duties of the educational secretary that the committee delineated were "preservation and development of the library of the Board with the expansion of its usefulness" and "conservation of all historical records and general data of the Board, . . ."[29] Inabelle G. Coleman was named publicity secretary with the responsibility for all publicity and a number of other duties as an assistant to the educational secretary. Her expertise proved a valuable asset when the board renewed publication of *The Commission.* The following year the Sunday School Board asked to be relieved of the responsibility of publishing *Home and Foreign Fields,* explaining that it had lost money every year of its publication. This was the open door Maddry had long awaited. After consulting J. B. Lawrence, executive secretary of the Home Mission Board, the Foreign Mission Board determined to launch its own missionary magazine, *The Commission.*

The Commission had first been published as a monthly newsletter supplement of the *Southern Baptist Missionary Journal.* Both publications ceased in 1853 when the Home and Foreign Mission Boards decided to publish jointly the *Home and Foreign Journal.* It was Maddry's decision to pick up the old name for the new publication. Four issues were projected for the first year but the response was so encouraging that the board decided on six issues.[30] Maddry edited *The Commission* during its first five years with the help of Miss Coleman who later resigned to become a missionary to China. E. C. Routh followed Maddry as editor in 1943 and two years later, in the board's centennial year, the circulation numbered 65,000, and by 1956 it had reached 119,000.[31] Thus after a hiatus of twenty years the board once again had direct access to the homes and churches of Southern Baptists. Maddry was convinced that the magazine had made a unique contribution to the renewed vigor of the board's work. "I sincerely believe," he wrote, "that *The Commission* has played a major role in the rehabilitation of the work of the Foreign Mission Board at home and abroad."[32] A succession of able editors made such a feat possible but a number of assistants and associates, including Marjorie Moore Armstrong and Ione Gray, dedicated their considerable talents to its continued success.

A Pension Plan

High on the Maddry agenda was a pension plan for retiring missionaries. Shortly after assuming office, Maddry found himself forced to leave Richmond on fund-raising trips on behalf of missionaries whom the board could not return to the field for lack of funds. Some whose meager salaries had not allowed for any investments or even savings, were destitute. In his report to the convention in 1934, after pointing out that missionaries in active service during the "seven lean" years had decreased from 544 to 378, he reported: "One year ago, we made a careful survey and found over fifty missionaries in active service who were already sixty-five and beyond. Many were in the seventies, and four were beyond eighty."[33]

The situation called for action. The deaths of T. B. Ray and both W. D. Powell and his wife in 1934 (for eighteen years missionaries to Mexico) were added reminders that time was running out. Maddry presented the initial plan for pensions and annuities to the Foreign Mission Board at its meeting on 23 November 1933.[34] In agreement with the Relief and Annuity Board, the plan was to take effect in January, 1934. A summary of its provisions was given in the board's report to the convention in its meeting in 1934.

> *The Pension Plan in brief, provides that five dollars per month shall be paid to the Relief and Annuity Board and this Board guarantees to pay each missionary the sum of $500.00 per year if totally disabled while in the service of the Board, or upon retirement at sixty-five years of age, provided the missionary elects to retire at that time. Continued service after that time must be by the vote of the Mission and the approval of the Foreign Board.*[35]

The plan called for an investment of sixty dollars a year out of an annual base salary of $800.00. After twenty years of service this meant that a couple retiring at sixty-five would have an annual income from the Annuity Board of $1,000.00. Maddry told the convention that the new pension plan had been received "enthusias-

tically by the missionaries."[36]

Two years later, the board found it necessary to amend the original retirement provisions. Upon reaching the age of sixty-five, the board declared, all missionaries would be given the title of "Emeritus Missionaries" but in some cases by mutual agreement a missionary could continue to serve year by year until seventy. All retired missionaries were encouraged to remove themselves from their respective fields of service, except in some rare cases when both the board and the mission involved asked a missionary to remain.[37]

In some respects 1936 could be considered a banner year. The total income of the board from all sources was $1,040,574.57. Of this amount, $859,794.74 was received from the churches. The debt of the board, which stood at $1,110,000.00 in 1933, had been reduced to $367,500.00. In addition, the interest paid on the remaining indebtedness through negotiations with the board's creditors had been reduced in three phases from 6 to 4 percent.[38]

One of the happy results of improved finances was that the board could increasingly turn its attention to the expansion of the work and the appointment of new missionaries. Since 1 January 1933, the board had appointed 90 new missionaries and reappointed 28, making a total of 415 in active service. As of 1 April 1937, fifty-six missionaries had retired under the new "pension plan."[39]

Organizational Changes

Maddry had not been in his new position three months, before he realized how woefully inadequate was the Richmond staff of eight for the task committed to it by the Foreign Mission Board. He referred to the situation as an "impossible" one and "determined to do something about it." He wrote: "I realized early in my service with the Board that the work was worldwide in its ramifications and that one man alone could never meet the responsibilities and direct the operations of five hundred missionaries widely separated in sixteen different countries on three continents."[40] After his four months in Europe and the Near East in 1934, he became more convinced of the need of administrative assistance in the form of "District Secretaries."

W.C. Taylor family

Regional Secretaries

Since more than half of all Southern Baptist missionaries were serving in China and Japan, Maddry decided by 1935 to appoint the first one of the "district secretaries" for the "Orient." He already had a missionary in mind for this new position when J. B. Weatherspoon, missionary-minded professor of homiletics at Southern Seminary, suggested that he wait until he had an opportunity to meet a man by the name of M. T. Rankin, a twenty year veteran missionary to China and president of the Graves Theological Seminary. On his trip to China and Japan, accompanied by his wife and the Weatherspoons, Maddry met and was thoroughly captivated by Rankin—so much so that he did not wait until his return to the states but cablegrammed his recommendation to the board that Rankin be elected "Regional Secretary for the Orient." Later, Maddry wrote in his autobiography of this decision: "This was the greatest thing I ever did for foreign missions."[41]

Other secretaries were soon elected by the board for Latin America and Nigeria. W. C. Taylor, for nineteen years a missionary professor in the North Brazil Seminary, in Recife, was the board's choice for both the Spanish-speaking and Portuguese-speaking countries of South and Central America, Mexico, and the Caribbean. Upon the retirement in 1939 of Everett Gill, Sr., who had been designated Superintendent for Europe and the Near East, George W. Sadler, who had served as principal of the Baptist college and seminary in Ogbomosho, Nigeria from 1921 to 1931, was elected secretary for Africa, Europe, and the Near East.

In the 1936 Report of the Foreign Mission Board to the Southern Baptist Convention, Maddry explained the rationale behind the new organizational initiative:

> There was a crying need in all the missions in the Orient for a complete reorganization and unification of the work. The same need existed for closer supervision and more intimate contacts with the work in all lands. To meet this compelling need the Board created the office of Secretary for the Orient, for Latin-America and for Nigeria, West

235

Africa, these positions to be filled by devoted and experienced missionaries serving in these lands.[42]

He went on to explain that the new regional secretaries were considered missionaries at large and on the same salary basis as all other missionaries. "They will spend three years on the field and one year in the homeland."[43]

At first, the new plan was well received at home and on the mission fields. By 1939, however, questions had arisen regarding the purpose and function of the regional secretaries from the South Brazil Mission. The full board at its annual meeting in October 1939 took time to consider the objections raised and to formulate a careful reply. While rejecting most of the criticisms of the South Brazil Mission, the board did order stricken from the Missionary Manual the phrase: "These men will be the eyes, ears, and voice of the Foreign Mission Board on the several fields where they serve, ..." as "contrary to the spirit and purpose of the Board."[44] In addition to a six point statement, the board explained: "District secretaries have been appointed to function as the representatives of the Board in general and of the Executive Secretary in particular. In a sense they are extensions of the Executive Secretary to the field."[45]

As to the charge that such secretaries would interfere with the functions of the missions, the board declared: "They, therefore, do not conflict with the 'spheres and functions' of the Missions anymore than does the Executive Secretary of the Foreign Mission Board."[46] This disclaimer might have been of small comfort to the missionaries if they had been familiar with Maddry's dealings with the Italian Mission.

The board went on to make it a matter of record that the memorial of the South Brazil Mission "constitutes the only expression of disapproval of this policy which the Board has received."[47] There was no turning back the clock. The Foreign Mission Board under Maddry's direction had taken a step into the future in establishing a pattern of missionary operation that would be followed with some variation into the present era.

Apparently no one was quite sure what to call the new secretaries. "District Secretaries," "District Superintendents," and "Regional Secretaries" were titles used at one time or another. Eventually, "Regional Secretaries" became the most common and durable of the various terms used.

The Richmond Staff

As soon as the board could begin to see a way out of its financial morass, it was a forgone conclusion that the staff would be enlarged and reorganized. The first significant addition to the staff was R. S. Jones, missionary to Brazil, who was home on furlough in 1934. He was employed by the board on 1 November of that year as "field representative at large." In a short time he had visited all the states of the convention and conducted numerous schools of missions. Two years later Jones is referred to as "Field Secretary" and still later as "Home Secretary" in charge of deputation work and schools of missions. In 1940 he was made "Field Secretary" for the area west of the Mississippi River with headquarters in Dallas, Texas. Three years later he resigned from the board to accept a position with the Relief and Annuity Board.

The career of R. S. Jones was characteristic of the fluid state of the staff during this period. With high hopes, Maddry reported to the convention in 1936 that the board had elected Claud B. Bowen to the newly created position of "Educational Secretary." Apparently what Maddry and the board had in mind was a personnel secretary, for in addition to Bowen's other duties it was his responsibility "to seek out and find for us suitable men and women for the different kinds of work that are to be done in the lands where we are at work."[48] Bowen promptly reorganized the Department of Education and Promotion. Mary M. Hunter became assistant educational secretary and Inabelle G. Coleman, publicity secretary.

Bowen generated an elaborate report in which the work of the department was divided into three divisions: "Educational, Promotional, and Candidate Work." It appeared that reorganization of the staff was well on the way when Maddry reminded the board at its semi-annual meeting in April 1937 of the need for more staff due to the "growth and enlargement of the work in all departments." He called attention to the need for "at least five workers" in the "growing educational and publicity department." Then he suggested the creation of a "Home Department with the provision for adequate help in this department."[49] However, six months later the "office of Educational Secretary" was abolished "due to the financial condition of the Board."[50] Obviously, Maddry's plans were derailed by unforeseen circumstances.

Perhaps as early as the April meeting of the board in 1937, Maddry was laying the ground work for a personnel secretary who would give his entire time to missionary

Maddry visits Pastor Li, P'ingtu.

candidates. Higher educational standards for appointment for missionary service had already been implemented. By 1937 all candidates seeking appointment were required to make the trip to Richmond in order to undergo a medical examination under the direction of "Dr. James Asa Shield, a noted psychiatrist." Six years later, with the establishment of a Department of Missionary Personnel under the direction of J. W. (Bill) Marshall, its first secretary, the process was further refined. As in all living things,

Nigeria Baptist Mission, 1938

change was becoming and would remain a characteristic of the Foreign Mission Board.

The Traveling Secretary

Every executive secretary of the Foreign Mission Board since James B. Taylor had visited one or more mission fields of the board. The value of such tours was apparent. But none made greater use of the opportunity to travel that the improved means of transportation made possible than did Maddry. In 1934, he was in Europe and the Near East. The next year, he and Mrs. Maddry, accompanied by the Weatherspoons, spent five months in China and Japan. In 1936, the board authorized a trip to South America. This time L. R. Scarborough, president of Southwestern Baptist Theological Seminary, and his wife, along with the W. C. Taylors, missionaries to Brazil, were his traveling companions. A trip to Africa planned for 1937 had to be postponed to the following year. Finally, after spending

ten days with the Italian Mission, Maddry and his party of five arrived in Lagos, Nigeria, on 30 June 1938. After an extensive tour of the missions in Africa, Maddry had completed his goal of visiting every country in which Southern Baptists maintained a missionary presence, and yet "his traveling days" had not come to an end.

Maddry had only been home a few weeks from his African tour when he boarded a ship again—this time for India. The occasion for this trip was a World Missionary Conference, projected for 13-30 December 1938 in Madras, India by the International Missionary Council. Thanksgiving Day found the executive secretary in Paris, where he took advantage of the opportunity to confer with Everett Gill, Sr., the Foreign Mission Board's representative in Europe, and J. H. Rushbrooke, president of the Baptist World Alliance. W. O. Lewis, American secretary of the Alliance, joined the group. The next morning Maddry left his congenial brethren for

Marseilles. After a voyage by ship and a day and night by train, he arrived in Madras. In the process, the sights and sounds of India's teeming millions, especially the plight of its outcasts amidst its sacred cows left their indelible impressions engraved upon his memory. But the conference for which he had come proved disappointing.

The conference itself was well organized. All delegates at Tambaram were assigned to groups which were given certain items from the planned agenda for discussion. Each group prepared a report of its sessions for the plenary meeting at the close of the conference. There was no place on the program for the discussion of issues not appearing on the printed agenda. Maddry attempted to raise the issue of the persecution of Baptists in Romania instigated by the Orthodox Church, but was rebuffed in his group. He determined to raise the issue at the plenary session, but he did so only with the same result. In relating the experience in his autobiography, Maddry wrote:

On the last night of the Conference our report of "findings" came up for adoption. There were beautiful speeches lauding the committee for such a statesmanlike report, and Dr. Mott asked if there was anyone else who desired to speak on the matter. I had sent up a note beforehand asking the right to be heard for ten minutes. The request was granted, and I went to the platform and stated my case. It gave me the chance to get before the whole Conference the fact that while we were there passing platitudes about church union and the beautiful example of almost universal co-operation, there were members of the Conference from Rumania persecuting their fellow Christians called Baptists and filling Rumanian jails with Baptist preachers. Our protest was rejected, as we expected, but delegates from

all over the world, while not voting with us, came offering congratulations for the stand we had taken.[51]

Apparently, Maddry's protest made little impression upon his fellow delegates, for in her account of the conference Ruth Rouse reported that when the delegates of the older and younger churches met together in the plenary session "that complete unanimity had been reached."[52]

During the three weeks from Bombay to New York, Maddry attempted to "redeem the time," much of which he felt had been wasted, by devoting seven hours a day to writing his popular missionary history of

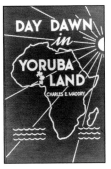

Maddry's **Day Dawn in Yoruba Land**, *1939*

Southern Baptist missionary efforts in Nigeria, published the following year under the title *Day Dawn in Yoruba Land*.

Although the trustees of the board grew a little restless over Maddry's long absences from Richmond, he realized for himself and the work, the trips were absolutely essential. In the absence of any comprehensive history of the board's work, his visits to the mission fields helped to give him, through oral accounts and written documents, a sense of the history of the work. Since he had not served as a missionary himself, the contacts with the missionaries and nationals put faces on problems he had only previously encountered through correspondence and hearsay. Putting his newly acquired knowledge and experience together, he was able to lead the board to formulate policies that led to a more effective use of missionaries and resources around the world. In fact, the executive secretary was on one of his fact-finding trips in Hawaii preparing to preach three times on Sunday, 7 December 1941, when the bombs fell on Pearl Harbor.

Interrupted by War

In spite of disturbing reports of a rising tide of persecution against Baptists in Romania, Italy, and Yugoslavia in 1937-1938, the missionary efforts of Southern Baptists appeared to be making steady, although uneven, progress. Before the Japanese launched their attack against China in 1937, fervent nationalism in both Europe and Asia constituted an ill omen, indeed, for the peace of the world. As early as 1932, the Japanese warlords had launched an invasion of Manchuria, the success of which served as a prelude to the more ambitious aggression against China in July 1937. At the same time, the Third Reich had begun to enlarge the German nation at the expense of its neighbors. With the attack against the Pacific Fleet in Honolulu, America found itself drawn into the enveloping global conflict. Four years earlier, the Foreign Mission Board was forced to take emergency measures to protect the lives of its missionaries while not forsaking its mandate.

Redefining Missionary Strategy in Asia

With the onset of a full scale war in China, the board was faced with the immediate problem of the evacuation of 178 missionaries and 84 children. Most of those in the interior had already taken refuge in the

port cities. The Foreign Mission Board, meeting on 9 September 1937, gave immediate furloughs to those whose furloughs were due to begin in June the following year and to retire immediately four who were already eligible for retirement. Three medical missionaries due furloughs in 1939 were asked to come immediately to the states in hopes of returning as soon as hostilities ceased, possibly within a few months. The board further directed that all missionaries who had not left the interior should be brought out at once. Nine days later the board was called together in Nashville to hear a report from the Administrative Committee of the Executive Committee on financing the anticipated evacuation of the China missionaries and their families.

On 16 September, after hearing a report by the executive secretary of the Foreign Mission Board, the Administrative Committee voted to issue a statement to the Southern Baptist people regarding the crisis in China and the need for funds to evacuate the missionaries. Maddry estimated the total expenditure at $100,000. Therefore, the Administrative Committee gave the board permission to borrow that amount.

Relief Efforts

The deteriorating situation in China called for a gigantic relief effort. Thirty million Chinese were reported displaced. A cholera epidemic was raging in Shanghai and Hong Kong. Dr. Robert Beddoe, of the Stout Memorial Hospital in the Wuchow Province, requested a thousand dollars for the treatment of cholera patients. The board also voted to send a thousand dollars requested by J. W. Decker, of the American

Foreign Missions night, Southern Baptist Convention, San Antonio, 1942

(Northern) Baptist Foreign Mission Society, for relief in Shanghai. By October 1938, the enormity of the devastation in China caused the board to "give its wholehearted endorsement and cooperation to the Church Committee of China Relief" due to the "fact that through this channel we may more effectively minister to the sufferers in China."[53]

It was clear that the war in China had opened up a new day of opportunity for Christians, including Southern Baptists, to demonstrate that Christianity involved more than words. This was the beginning of a new dimension in the missionary witness of Southern Baptists. The board stated as much in its first policy statement regarding the mission of the board and the conduct of its missionaries when confronted with the conflict. "We are servants of a Master for whom seeming disaster is the door to larger opportunity. The proclamation of the Gospel must go on. It is the word of God to suffering, distraught humanity."[54]

Principles of Conduct

While committing itself and its missions to the maintenance of hospitals, schools and churches whenever possible, the board recognized in many cases missionaries were forced to leave, as the state department had advised. On the other hand, the Chinese Baptist leaders expressed a desire for the continued fellowship and support of the missionaries. Therefore, whether a missionary chose to leave or stay was a decision left with each missionary. All missionaries were admonished by the board to maintain a stance of strict neutrality, to take no unnecessary risks, and "to regard their personal safety and that of their Chinese associates as of more importance than the protection of property."[55]

While attempting to maintain an attitude of strict neutrality, the board held Japan accountable for the great loss of its property in China. Maddry estimated the loss at one million dollars or more. The attempt to enlist the services of the state department in pressing its claims with Japanese authorities came to nothing with America's entry into the war.

After Pearl Harbor, the board's concern for the safety of its missionaries reached a new level. Displaced persons, both missionaries and nationals, comprised the most pressing needs with which the board was faced. On 22 December 1941, the board created a "War Emergency Council" to advise the executive secretary. Doubtless Theron Rankin would have been added to the council along with the other regional secretaries, but he was in Hong Kong where he was taken prisoner on Christmas day.

The Southern Baptist Convention

H.W. Schweinsberg signs deed for Colombia seminary property near Cali, bought in 1948 from E.A. deLima, at right, and wife; Missionaries John N. Thomas, left, and J. Ulman Moss, right, watch with Cali notary, Ricardo Nieto.

responded to the emergency by appointing (1940) the "Baptist World Emergency Committee." The War Emergency Council of the board and the Emergency Committee of the convention held a strategy meeting in Atlanta in January 1942. At this meeting, the council recommended a goal of $300,000.00 be raised for relief efforts everywhere the Foreign Mission Board carried on its work. By May 1942, the committee reported to the convention, meeting in San Antonio, that $321,403.14 had been received by the board and that the total emergency fund would likely exceed $400,000.00.[56] In addition to the amount already earmarked for relief, the Emergency Committee reported that Southern Baptists gave $200,000 to the impoverished British Baptist Missionary Society.[57]

By 1944, the relief efforts of the Foreign Mission Board had exceeded all projections. The Board reported to the convention that as of 1 March, 1944, $1,340,820.14 had been received for relief and $1,207,700.14

expended, leaving a balance of $133,120.00. China was the greatest beneficiary of this effort, receiving $657,858.86. Another $100,000.00 was set aside for postwar needs in China and a like amount for Europe. The leadership of the convention from the very beginning of the Sino-Japanese War had tried to get Southern Baptists to look beyond the war to a new day of opportunity. Maddry declared that the best way to prepare for this reconstruction era was to pay off the board's indebtedness. On 14 April 1943, the board was informed that all debts of the board had been paid. It was an elated executive secretary who reported:

We are happy indeed to record the fact that the Foreign Mission Board is out of debt for the first time in more than a generation. So far as we know the Board does not owe a cent to any person or object in the world. We are profoundly grateful for the co-operation of the Board and all of the friends of foreign missions throughout the world who have helped us to lift the burden of debt from our foreign mission enterprise.[58]

New Fields and New Opportunities

Immediately after the Japanese militarists launched an invasion of China, virtually all missionary women and mothers with children were evacuated. Several other missionaries, including a few couples remained in strategic locations in an attempt to carry on the work as long as possible. Missionaries were also withdrawn from

South America: Colombia and Paraguay

to the Philippines to continue their language study, were interned there. M. T. Rankin and five other missionaries of the board were imprisoned in Stanley Prison when Hong Kong fell to the Japanese. It was clear that overt missionary work in Asia would soon, if it had not already, cease.

For years, China and Japan had received the major attention and resources, both in funds and personnel, of the Foreign Mission Board. When Asia no longer provided a viable opportunity for missionary service, Hawaii, Colombia, and Paraguay beckoned for the attention of the board. Displaced missionaries from Asia were "ready-made" for the work in Hawaii, which soon found missionary refugees from the war ministering to other refugees.

After much prayer and considerable thought, Colombia was entered in 1941. The H. W. Schweinsbergs, who had previously served in Ecuador, became the first Southern Baptist missionaries to Colombia. The response to the gospel in this nominally Roman Catholic country was remarkable. Everett Gill told the board in April 1943 of his visit, little more than a year after the Schweinsbergs had begun the work in the living room of their home. "A year later I was privileged to help dedicate two beautiful church buildings, the combined atten-

Japan, with the exception of the Maxfield Garrotts. After the United States became directly involved in the global conflict, 105 missionaries of the board were interned in China, Japan, and Manila. Fifteen missionaries formerly serving in China and Japan transferred to the Hawaii mission which had been organized in December 1940. Fourteen missionaries still were serving, under severe limitations, in Free China (a section in South China), while ten missionaries, eight of whom had earlier transferred from China

dance at Sunday School totalling 476!"[59] The Schwiensbergs were joined by a number of capable and dedicated young appointees who still had to complete at least a year of language study before they could be of much help in the work.[60]

About the same time Southern Baptists decided to enter Colombia, Paraguay (one of the three River Plate republics, along with Argentina and Uruguay) became the object of missionary concern by the Argentine Baptist Convention. Plans were made, in cooperation with the Foreign Mission Board, to begin medical and evangelistic work in Asunción, the capital. While only two missionaries were listed in Paraguay by 1945, a thriving Baptist church in Asunción was beginning to make an impact upon the country through a number of mission congregations and the work of its pastor in a leper colony.[61]

Expansion of the work was not a priority as far as Maddry was concerned. He explained his position to the board on 14 April 1943.

In view of the fact that within recent months the Board has committed itself to the establishment of new work in Hawaii, Colombia, Paraguay, to the entrance into Russia when peace comes, if possible, and to the extension of our already existing mission in Free China, we recommend that for the present, no further expansion in new lands be undertaken.[62]

Maddry was also concerned that a too rapid expansion would involve the board once again in heavy indebtedness. As he put it: "This Board must set its face like flint against the possibility of another paralyzing debt."[63] But the way had been prepared for a major advance in the postwar world.

Board buys property for headquarters building, 2037 Monument Avenue, in 1943.

The Board's New Home

In the October meeting of the Foreign Mission board, 1943, the board voted to buy property at 2037 Monument Avenue for its headquarters building and to dissolve the Exchange Realty Corporation. From the beginning of its operations the board had been located in multi-purpose buildings. Finally in this, its sixth location, the board would own and operate property exclusively dedicated to its use alone. This development was made possible by the George W. Bottoms Memorial Fund.

More than ten years before, Mr. and Mrs. George W. Bottoms of Arkadelphia, Arkansas had given the Foreign Mission Board $100,000 to use as it saw fit. Later, the board, which was housed in rented quarters at the time, asked and received permission to use the fund for the purchase of adequate facilities for the board's headquarters in Richmond. The board then purchased a building on Sixth and Marshall streets. Since the board was not in the real estate business nor equipped to manage rental property, the Exchange Realty

Corporation was formed to administer the Bottoms' fund and manage certain properties previously acquired by the board. With the purchase of the Monument Avenue property, the Exchange Realty Corporation turned all its assets over to the board and ceased to exist.[64]

Maddry Retires

In the same meeting in which the board voted to purchase its first Monument Avenue property, Maddry, who had served as executive secretary since 1933, announced his retirement, effective the first of January 1945. Although, he did not say as much, with the purchase of the new property, Maddry must have felt that his last major objective had been achieved. What he did say was that he would, at the time, be nearly sixty-nine years of age and was convinced that the board needed a younger executive secretary. He was also frank to say that he longed for "a few days of quiet and peace as one comes close to the age of seventy years."[65]

Maddry was a sensitive man upon whom the responsibilities of his office must have always lain quite heavily. Maddry's sensitivity to the missionaries and openness to the work of the Spirit was never more evident than in his visit to China when he attended a mission meeting in the Shantung province held at Chefoo. This was the area in which a great revival broke out in 1932 with remarkable results. During this meeting, Maddry informed the missionaries that reports had come to the States that the North China Mission had gone to extremes in revival and he was asked by the board to investigate the reports. C. L. Culpepper, a

missionary in China, at the time, wrote, "There was a death-like hush which fell over the group. Then W. B. Glass, esteemed professor of our North China seminary, stood and said very gravely, 'Dr. Maddry, I will tell you what I have seen. I know that God has worked in our mission in these past five years.'"[66] Then Glass told of the growth of the seminary from a student body of four to around 150 and how the attendance and membership of the churches had doubled, many of which had become self-supporting. Then others took up the story and told of what they had seen and heard. Then Culpepper said, "I tried to tell him what I'd

1946 Japan missionary appointee, Frances Talley, meets Maddry.

seen. I hid nothing. I told him that the devil had sought to dominate all China, but we had seen him overcome by the power of the spirit." By the end of the afternoon, Maddry was in tears. "Brethren and sisters," he said, " I am going back home and tell my Board that God has been walking in the midst of the North China Mission and we had better go slow in criticizing them!"[67]

Maddry's many arduous trips abroad and the "terrible war," which he was convinced would go on for many more years, at least in Asia, added to his inescapable burden. Too, although physically a big man, he was not a well man. Shortly after his death on 17 September 1962, L. Howard Jenkins gave an intimate glimpse into Maddry's personality.

> It is very difficult to draw a true picture of him, because he was a man of many moods. One day he would be filled with joyous enthusiasm, planning for the future in a big way and perhaps the next day he would be in the depths of despondency, but even then he inspired confidence. There was something there that made you feel everything would come out all right. . . .
>
> His emotions were easily moved, especially for those in distress and for little children. On the other hand, he had a very stern sense of right and wrong and could be very stern in his attitude.[68]

Frequently incapacitated for months at a time, and away from the office during extended mission trips, he was dependent upon the board's staff to carry on in his absence. His usually sound judgment had led the board to assemble a staff of capable and dedicated men and women who could carry on in his absence.

The Staff

In addition to the regional secretaries, notable among these were Inabelle Coleman, Nan Weeks, Marjorie Moore Armstrong, and E. C. Routh, who were all responsible at one time or another for editing *The Commission*. Maddry's personal secretaries, Jessie Ford and Gene Newton, received high praise from him for their efficient service, especially in his absence. When the office of the educational secretary was eliminated, it was Mary Hunter more than anyone else who continued to function in this capacity.

Local Board Members

Without the support and counsel of a committed group of local members, the accomplishments of the board during Maddry's tenure would have been impossible. Among these, three laymen of unusual wisdom and dedication whose terms expired in 1945, stand out. They were: L. Howard Jenkins, president of the board; B. M. Gwathmey, auditor; and Hill Montague, attorney. Two Richmond pastors, who were members of the board from time to time and who also shared in the leadership of the board during the Maddry years, were Solon B. Cousins, pastor, the Second Baptist Church, and Theodore F. Adams, pastor, the First Baptist Church.

The Missionaries

Maddry was the first to admit that the outstanding achievements during the twelve years of his administration were not the accomplishments of one man. Honesty would compel the admission that they were not even that of the staff and elected members of the board but the result of all the components of the missionary enterprise, including the missionaries on the fields. Without these sacrificial and dedicated servants of God, many of whom lost all their earthly possessions, were uprooted, and were imprisoned, the work could not have

C.E. Maddry

continued. But continue, it did. By 1945, there were 502 missionaries in active service of the board.

A Tribute

This chapter ends as it began with a reference to the glowing tribute to the retiring secretary; the committee, asked to prepare an appropriate tribute to Maddry for the board, remembered the situation in 1933: "We were apologetic, on the defensive, and suggestible to the counsels of despair. He imparted to us the contagion of his own faith, courage, vision, and hope. Our unpayable debt to Dr. Maddry is the new spirit he gave us."[69] The board's tribute to Maddry placed the executive secretary in the historical lineage of his predecessors with words of lasting significance.

Our missionary enterprise is the unifying center of Southern Baptists. Its appeal furnished momentum and lifting power for every other cause we support and the Secretary of this Board has from the beginning in 1845 been the symbol and the incarnation of that work. Dr. Maddry satisfied that demand and fulfilled that expectation.

In a sense, in spite of the world at war, the board had been reborn and now faced the future with new-found hope.

ENDNOTES

1. Charles E. Maddry, Charles E. Maddry, An Autobiography (Nashville, Tenn.: Broadman Press, 1955), 138.
2. Ibid., 18.
3. Ibid., 72.
4. Minutes, FMB, 14 July 1932, 323.
5. Minutes, FMB, 12 January 1933, 4.
6. Maddry, *Charles E. Maddry*, 73.
7. Ibid.
8. Merrill D. Moore, "Hundred Thousand Club," in *Encyclopedia of Southern Baptists*, vol. 1. (Nashville, Tenn.: Broadman Press, 1958), 659, 660.
9. Maddry, *Charles E. Maddry*, 87.
10. Minutes, FMB, 9 February 1933, 7-10.
11. Maddry, *Charles E. Maddry*, 83.
12. Ibid., 83.
13. Charles E. Maddry, Diary, 25 July 1934, unnumbered page.
14. Ibid., 1 August 1934, unnumbered page.
15. Ibid., 20 August 1934, unnumbered page.
16. Ibid., 31 August 1934, unnumbered page.
17. Ibid., 12 September 1934, unnumbered page.
18. Minutes, FMB, 10 November 1934, 101, 102.
19. Minutes, FMB, 8 March 1934, 63.
20. *Annual*, SBC, 1934, 156. In the Report of the Foreign Mission Board to the Southern Baptist Convention meeting in Fort Worth, Texas, Maddry described the "seven lean years" (1926-1933) in the following paragraphs:

Truly they have been seven years of terrible struggle and sacrifice, and the number of missionaries in active service has decreased during this period from 544 to 378. All phases of native work, such as evangelism, colportage, primary and middle schools, colleges, seminaries and hospitals, have been discontinued or greatly curtailed. The Seminaries have been closed entirely in Italy, Spain, and Japan. Three hospitals have been closed in China and scores of primary and intermediate schools have been discontinued.

The greatest loss sustained in our foreign mission work during these seven lean years has been in missionary personnel,—not alone in numbers, but in morale and spirit, as well as in health and physical vigor.

We would remind you that your missionaries, as a group, are old or middle-aged men and women. Very few young people have been sent out in seven years, and the ranks are terribly and cruelly thinned and the wavering line is breaking everywhere. One year ago, we made a careful survey and found over fifty missionaries in active service who were already sixty-five and beyond. Many were in the seventies, and four were beyond eighty. These seven lean years have taken a fearful toll of the missionary personnel of this Board.

We believe the worst is over, and we devoutly hope the terrible lean years are past. For the first quarter of 1933 we received for our current budget $241,398.16, while for the first quarter of 1934, we received $313,472.32, a gain in three months of $72,074.16.

21. Ibid.

22. Ibid., 64, 65.

23. T. B. Ray, "Letter addressed to the Foreign Mission Board," Minutes, FMB, 11 October 1933, 37, 38. Following is the entire text of that letter.

To the Foreign Mission Board,

Dear Brethren:

Please let me make a brief and brotherly statement. In making this statement I wish in the outset to say that I believe the coming of our beloved Brother Maddry to the Executive Secretaryship of the Foreign Mission Board, was of the Lord, and I rejoice with all my heart in that happy event. The remarkable response of the denomination to his leadership and the rapidity and comprehensiveness with which he has grasped the problems and details of the work, both at home and abroad, reassures us more and more every day.

In order that Dr. Maddry may have the utmost freedom in carrying out the will and policies of the Board, I suggest that I be relieved of all executive functions and be assigned only such duties as Dr. Maddry and the Administrative Committee may commit specifically to me.

There is a great abundance of matters in connection with which I can render a most worthwhile service. In this service I would find great happiness because it would afford me further opportunity to serve the Board which I love better than my own life.

Cordially and gratefully,

T. B. Ray.

24. Ibid., 38.

25. Minutes, FMB, 8 February 1934, 61.

26. Ibid., 34, 35.

27. *Annual*, SBC, 1934, 156.

28. Minutes, FMB, 12 March 1936, 191, read: That the Virginia Baptist Historical Society be allowed to receive and file the records and correspondence files of the Board now stored in the basement of our headquarters building, with the understanding that they will be stored in their fire-proof quarters in orderly

fashion and that we express our appreciation of this cooperation on the part of the Virginia Baptist Historical Society through the interest of Dr. Ryland. It is to be hoped that very soon some means will be devised for the proper cataloging and filing of these records that they may be available for missionary research.

29. Minutes, FMB, 21 April 1936, 195.

30. Maddry, *Charles E. Maddry*, 76.

31. Marjorie Moore Armstrong, "Missionary Magazines, Baptist" in *Encyclopedia of Southern Baptists*, vol. 2, 864-66.

32. Maddry, *Charles E. Maddry*, 77.

33. *Annual*, SBC, 1934, 156.

34. Minutes, FMB, 23 November 1933, 43 ff.

35. *Annual*, SBC, 1934, 158.

36. Ibid.

37. Minutes, FMB, 21 November 1936, 237. The retirement provisions, according to the Minutes of the board for the dates indicated were as follows:

1. The Foreign Mission Board of the Southern Baptist Convention, in cooperation with the Relief and Annuity Board of the Southern Baptist Convention, has adopted a Pension Plan providing a pension of $500.00 per year for each missionary upon his or her retirement, based upon twenty years of completed service, or in case of total and permanent disability while in the service of the Foreign Mission Board.

2. All missionaries shall be automatically retired from active service and become "Emeritus Missionaries" of the Foreign Mission Board on reaching the age of sixty-five, or at the end of the year in which that age is reached; provided, however, that the Board may, by mutual agreement, continue the employment of missionaries so retired from year to year, in the discretion of the Board until the missionary so retired attains the age of seventy years.

3. In the case of husband and wife, the age of the husband shall determine the time of retirement.

4. The Foreign Mission Board strongly urges all such "Emeritus Missionaries" to remove from the field upon their retirement; but, in special cases, the Board may allow "Emeritus Missionaries" to remain on the field. The request of any such retired missionaries to do so must be made directly to the Board and must have the approval of the Mission and medical committee of the Mission, and upon the agreement with such missionaries:

a. Cannot claim a vote in the Mission or Station where they remain.

b. Shall not undertake any directive or administrative activity in the work of the churches, the Station or the Mission.

c. Shall not occupy a residence required for an active missionary.

38. Minutes, FMB, 7 April 1937, 267.

39. Ibid., 268.

40. Maddry, *Charles E. Maddry, 77.*

41. Ibid., 78.

42. *Annual,* SBC, 1936, 150.

43. Ibid.

44. Minutes, FMB, 11 October 1939, 114.

45. Ibid., 115.

46. Ibid.

47. Ibid.

48. *Annual,* SBC, 1936, 150.

49. Minutes, FMB, 7 April 1937, 269.

50. Minutes, FMB, 13 October 1937, 7.

51. Maddry, *Charles E. Maddry,* 125.

52. Ruth Rouse and Charles Stephen Neill, ed., *A History of the Ecumenical Movement, 1517-1848* (London: SPCK, 1954), 372.

53. Minutes, FMB, 12 October 1938, 70.

54. Minutes, FMB, 13 October 1937, 5.

55. Ibid., 5.

56. *Annual,* SBC, 1942, 108.

57. Ibid.

58. Minutes, FMB, 14 April 1943, 65.

59. Minutes, FMB, 14 April 1943, 121.

60. Ibid. Everett Gill, Jr. reported that

Our missionary staff is located as follows: *Barranquilla:* The H. W. Schweinsbergs and Miss Helen Meredith; *Cartagena:* The Tom Neelys; *Bogota:* The A. R. Daileys. The Jack Combs have arrived in Barranquilla for the study of the language and will be permanently stationed later. Miss Darline Elliott went to Barranquilla this fall to promote our primary school work.

Our purpose is to locate not less than two couples and possibly a teacher in each major city, building a church and a primary school. Surrounding the chapel in Rebolo, a poorer section of Barranquilla, there are 11,000 children with no schools - Catholic, State, or Protestant! When we visited the governor of the province and asked for his advice about establishing a school, he was enthusiastic. Latin America still struggles with illiteracy, inherited from three centuries of Spanish-Catholic domination. But her greatest need is still the Teacher of Galilee.

61. *Annual,* SBC, 1945, 186.

62. Minutes, FMB, 14 April 1943, 65.

63. Ibid.

64. Minutes, FMB, 13 October 1943, 125. The officers of the Exchange Realty Corporation were: L. Howard Jenkins, president; Bill Montague, vice president; and E. P. Buxton, secretary and treasurer.

65. Ibid., 111.

66. C. L. Culpepper, *The Shantung Revival* (Dallas: Crescendo Book Publications, 1971), 77.

67. Ibid., 78.

68. Minutes, FMB, 9-10 October 1962, 131.

69. Maddry, *Charles E. Maddry,* 138.

An End and a Beginning

Bill Wallace

The year 1945 was pivotal in the history of the world and in that of the Foreign Mission Board as well. It marked the end of World War II and the dawn of the nuclear age. The world would never be quite the same again. For the board, it was a time to reflect upon its first century and to plan for a period of unparalleled expansion. Financial solvency had been restored and with it the era of forced retrenchment was now an unhappy memory. At last, it appeared that the Southern Baptist Convention was beginning to match its missionary vision with a new sense of world responsibility. As Southern Baptists prepared to enter their second century, the world began to grapple with the problems of the postwar era.

For Southern Baptists, there was hardly time to think about the past—there was too much to be done. Asia and Europe were awash in the residue of problems left behind by the most devastating war in the history of humankind. In addition, Southern Baptists faced their own set of challenges. Missionaries had been withdrawn and displaced. Numerous mission stations had been closed and mission property confiscated or destroyed. Among the multiplied thousands who lost their lives in the deadly conflict were Baptists—some of them irreplaceable leaders. And the problems of reconciliation were compounded by Communist aggression in both Europe and China.

By 1946, M. Theron Rankin, whose service in China had endeared him to the Chinese people, was peculiarly equipped to lead Southern Baptists in a realistic appraisal of the most pressing needs of that part of the world. With the help of George W. Sadler, secretary for Europe, Africa, and the Near East, Everett Gill, Jr., secretary

M. Theron Rankin

The "war to end all wars" didn't. Therefore, World War II engulfed much of the globe. Missionaries were compelled to leave Europe, China, and Japan for the States or relocate. As a result a number of new mission stations were established overseas. The end of the war brought a brief respite from warfare and missionaries returned to their fields, but Communism in China brought a new wave of destruction and missionaries were forced to leave again. In spite of the loss of China, M.T. Rankin led the board to launch advance.

for Latin America, and Baker James Cauthen, secretary for the Orient, a survey of conditions in the postwar world that Southern Baptists should and could address was begun. This survey was the beginning of the board's preparation for postwar expansion under the direction of a man "who carried the world in his heart."

Milledge Theron Rankin, 1894-1953

M. Theron Rankin was the first foreign missionary to become an executive secretary of the Foreign Mission Board. Appointed to China in 1921, he served first as an itinerant evangelist before becoming professor of New Testament and Greek at the Graves Theological Seminary, in Canton. Contrary to his personal wishes, he was elected president of the seminary when the Chinese president felt compelled to resign, due to the inroads of Communist ideology into the student body. Ten years later, Rankin was elected regional secretary for the Orient, in which position he continued until he became executive secretary of the Foreign Mission Board, in 1945.

The Rankin Family

In retrospect, Theron Rankin appears to have been God's man uniquely prepared for his new responsibilities as executive secretary. The fourth of seven children of Milledge Whitfield and Emma Croxton Rankin, of Newberry, South Carolina, he was born on 28 July 1894. Since his father was pastor of the local Baptist church, it is not surprising that he was converted before reaching his teen-age years. His decision to enter the ministry came during the years he spent at Wake Forest College (now

Rankin reports to the board for the Committee on the Orient, October 1948; Jenkins, presiding; Mary Elizabeth Fuqua, recording secretary, right.

University). His call to missions dates from his student years at Southern Seminary. But the seed that was to germinate and flourish was planted much earlier by intelligent and godly parents. Reflecting upon his boyhood, Rankin later wrote: "We had confidence in our parents because they believed in God. Through their faith they gave to their children, all seven of us, a heritage which no amount of material possessions could provide."[1]

Since the Rankin family was large, Theron learned to share, something for which he was always grateful. He explained that his life was enriched for "the seven of us together received a heritage sevenfold larger than any one of us could have received by himself."[2] The wholesome family life as one among seven children provided a first step in his preparation as a missionary who early in life learned to value the role of the individual in community. For one thing, he learned by experience that life does not consist in, nor is happiness dependent upon, the abundance of things one possesses.

Education

After a year at Furman University, he suspended his college education to earn enough money to continue. After two years as a bookkeeper in the office of a lumber mill in Durham, North Carolina, he resumed his college education, this time at Wake Forest. In the meantime through the influence of John Jeter Hurt, pastor of the First Baptist Church of Durham, his life had taken a new direction. He determined to return to college in order to prepare himself for the ministry. Three years later he graduated from Wake Forest and entered Southern Seminary, in Louisville, in the fall of 1918.

At Southern, the missionary spirit permeated the campus. Once a month, classes were suspended and, as J. B. Weatherspoon wrote, "the whole student body was converted into a 'society for missionary inquiry.'"[3] On one of these missionary days in Rankin's second year, Eugene Sallee, a missionary to China, spoke and Theron dedicated his life to missionary service. Much to his joy, he learned that Valeria Greene, a student in the Woman's Missionary Union Training School, had also made a similar decision. Valeria, the daughter of missionaries to China, was already the object of Theron's affection. Now she became even more so.

China and Marriage

China beckoned and Valeria was appointed a missionary to China in 1920. Theron followed a year later after graduating from the seminary with the Th.M. degree in 1921. Marriage had to wait until each received fresh confirmation that it was,

indeed, the will of God for them to serve together as husband and wife. The desired confirmation was not long in coming, and they were married in the spring of 1922. Valeria continued to teach in the Bible Training School for Women (*Pooi In*) while Theron gave himself to language study.

Rankin soon became aware that missionaries are human and all too often are prone to insist upon their own way—their own projects and the superiority of their own ideas at the expense of the group. He became convinced that the only way strong individuality could be merged into the community of faith and service was by constantly pursuing "godliness . . . brotherly affection . . . and love."[4] These virtues became characteristic of Rankin's missionary career. In the process, he gained the confidence and esteem of his fellow missionaries and the Chinese alike.

The Indigenous Principle

During his years in China, Rankin was dedicated to promoting the indigenous principle among the Cantonese Baptists. For sixty years the mission had operated the seminary. Although the board of trustees was made up of both missionaries and nationals, the seminary's policies, budget, and personnel had to be approved by the Foreign Mission Board, in Richmond. To the Chinese, especially in the rising tide of nationalism, this procedure identified the seminary as a foreign institution. Understandably, they were less than enthusiastic partners in the enterprise so essential to the work. The Executive Committee of the mission, of which Rankin was a member, decided that it was time for a change.

The committee proposed that the mission cease operating the Graves Theological Seminary at the close of the school year in 1933, with the understanding that if the Leung Kwang Association wished to continue such a school, the mission would assist with staff and finances as requested by the association.

The proposal was a risky one but Rankin felt it worth the effort because "it was a step forward in giving the Baptist work an indigenous character."[5] It worked. After the fall term in 1934, Rankin could write: "The session thus far has been the most encouraging one since I have been connected with the school. The Chinese leaders have taken hold with a determination and spirit of consecration which leads me to believe that the Seminary is now planted on a foundation which will not give way. . . ."[6]

As regional secretary for the Orient in 1935, Rankin became even more convinced that the role of the missionary was primarily that of a seed sower and counselor as the Chinese increasingly took the initiative in shaping an indigenous Chinese Baptist denominational life. He wrote:

> *Furthermore, this emerging Baptist consciousness makes it necessary that in our missionary work we be able to die unto ourselves as an American denomination. We cannot expect the institutions and churches which we promote in the Orient to be extensions of the Southern Baptist denomination in America. In the institutions of training we cannot expect to train Chinese to be good Southern Baptists, but we must expect them to be good Chinese Baptists who will be able under the direct guidance of the Holy Spirit to possess their own souls.[7]*

... there are certain responsibilities and duties in the work of missions which the Foreign Mission Board must assume directly...

Regional Secretary for the Orient

Many missionaries, as well as Weatherspoon, thought that Rankin was the ideal choice for the newly created position of regional secretary. But some missionaries viewed the new organizational structure with apprehension and even suspicion. Missionaries were not the only critics of the new plan for many in the states did not understand the situation that prompted Maddry to propose this change in the structure. Some, as the South Brazil Mission was to express later, considered the move unbaptistic because it appeared to establish a hierarchy. Rankin, who was on furlough at the time, was asked by Maddry to write an article explaining the new structure to Southern Baptists. Excerpts from this article reveal how Rankin conceived his role as a regional secretary.

> *It will be the responsibility of this Secretary to act as the Foreign Mission Board's representative on the field. The relationship of the board to the missionaries on the field is in no sense that of an employer to employees. Neither can the relationship of the Secretary for the Orient to the missionaries be that of one who is set over them to exercise authority. The fact is fully recognized, however, by all who are concerned in our missionary work that there are certain responsibilities and duties in the work of the missions which the Foreign Mission Board must assume directly. . . .*

This secretary will seek to become also a connecting link between the Board and the individual work of his fellow-missionaries. In order to do this he will endeavor to spend a part of his time with individual missionaries in the work they are doing, trying to share with them their problems and needs, and to see their tasks as they see them. He will hope to be used as a medium for the exchange of ideas and methods of work as he goes from place to place. He will work also to keep the Board in intimate touch with these individual conditions.[8]

Rankin also indicated that he understood his primary role as that of a missionary alongside his missionary colleagues.

The task which will underlie all other responsibilities is that of being a missionary with his fellow-missionaries in Japan and China. If he cannot fulfill these other duties, and at the same time continue to be a missionary serving with missionaries, he will have failed in the greatest essential.[9]

Through the Storm

In the spring of 1937 Chinese Baptists celebrated the centennial of Baptist work in China and Rankin was encouraged. Wherever missionaries of the board had been at work, he witnessed the growing strength of the Chinese churches, conventions, and institutions. That the Chinese leadership was marked by faith, intelligence, and courage was evident, yet there were still many unreached people groups among the huge population. In spite of a century of progress, Rankin was convinced that the nationals needed the help of missionaries— missionaries who would give themselves primarily to evangelism and church planting. "We need missionaries who will give themselves again to the old method of country itinerating,"[10] he wrote in 1937. In that year, the Japanese invaded China and it appeared as if everything Baptists and others had worked for through a century of Christian witness was swept away "by the destroying hand of war."[11]

In the midst of the devastation Rankin was tempted to despair. But as the calibre of his faith and witness were being sorely tested, he wrote: "Still history teaches us and faith assures us that God's kingdom will go on, that his work, though crushed down, will rise up again with new life and vigor. Storms have come in the past, perhaps as severe as this one. . . ." Then he closed the paragraph with a prayer. "I pray God to give us faith to endure with patience the trials of this storm so that we shall be able to rise up and go forward in his service when it has passed."[12]

"I pray God," [Rankin wrote], "to give us faith to endure with patience the trials of this storm... to rise up and go forward in his service when it has passed."

Before the storm would pass Rankin and his fellow missionaries were to endure much more than they anticipated in 1937. During a Japanese bombing raid, Rankin found himself in a huge culvert, used as a bomb shelter, surrounded by hundreds of Chinese when a little boy thrust his hand into the missionary's hand and looking up into Rankin's face, asked: "Are you afraid?" Although Rankin was afraid, the reassurance of the knowledge of whose he was and whom he served brought renewed faith and he could answer: "No, I am not afraid."[13]

When the United States entered the war, American missionaries who remained in China were rounded up and imprisoned. Hong Kong fell to the Japanese on Christmas Day 1941, and Rankin, along with 300 other Americans, was marched to Stanley Prison. Prison life was grim. The prisoners were put in bare rooms without cots or chairs. Food was scarce and had to be prepared by the prisoners themselves. Rankin was a member of the council of twelve whose responsibility it was to administer the prison. His job assignment included oversight of the kitchen where he spent much of his time baking bread when there was flour. One night he came upon a missionary pilfering food meant for the children. That was too much for the mild-mannered missionary. "Before he knew it," he related to Edna Frances Dawkins, "he had grabbed the man and found himself ready to give him a blow to the face. He even threatened to kill him if he ever caught him stealing the children's food again."[14]

Finally in July 1942, Rankin and thirty-nine other Baptist missionaries were exchanged for Japanese war prisoners held by the United States. At last Rankin was free, minus thirty pounds of his normal weight. Two years later he was elected executive secretary of the Foreign Mission Board.

Executive Secretary

After Maddry requested that the board permit him to retire not later than 31 December 1944, L. Howard Jenkins, president of the board, appointed a committee to recommend Maddry's successor. The committee of ten, chaired by M. W. Egerton, brought its recommendation to a called meeting of the board on 6 June 1944. The committee's recommendation that M. T. Rankin be elected executive secretary was "unanimously and prayerfully adopted."[15]

Celebrating the Centennial

Rankin's first year as executive secretary of the Foreign Mission Board marked the centennial of both the board and the Southern Baptist Convention. The centennial year came and went with little notice. This was not the intention of the Committee on the Centennial Session, which had been instructed by the convention in 1944 to make plans for a Centennial Convention in Atlanta the following year including a pilgrimage to Augusta. Because of the war, with no end in sight, the government issued an order on 5 January 1945 "banning all conventions of an attendance of more than fifty after 1 February 1945."[16] Therefore, the celebration had to be postponed to the following year. In the meantime the end of the war in the Pacific came on 14 August 1945. The government ban was lifted and altered plans for the centennial celebration were implemented at the Miami convention, which convened on 15 May 1946.

The centennial session was held on Wednesday evening in the Bandshell Amphitheater in Bayfront Park. It consisted of a music program, two addresses and a historical film entitled *The Romance of a Century*. Louie D. Newton spoke on "The Work We Sought to Do and Did Begin," and W. R. White gave the keynote address on the convention theme "Carry on with 'Widening Reach and Height-ened Power.'" The music, addresses, and film served to remind the audience of the importance of missions in the organization and continued life of the Southern Baptist Convention. This emphasis was further enhanced by the reprinting of *The Proceedings of the Southern Baptist Convention* (1845) and "The Address to the Public" in the *Annual of the Southern Baptist Convention*, 1946. The entire script by J. E. Dillard, upon which the film *The Romance of a Century* was based, was also published. The script gave special prominence to the formation of the Woman's Missionary Union.

"... it is unthinkable that we shall continue to give only an average of seventy cents per person per year to help all the world outside our own territory,..."

Thursday evening, the second night of the convention meeting, featured, as customary, the Foreign Mission Board. M. T. Rankin presided and presented the missionaries of the board who were present. Charles E. Maddry, who was scheduled to speak on "'Widening Reach and Heightened Power' in Foreign Missions," was prevented from attending due to illness. In his place, George W. Sadler, Baker James Cauthen, the newly elected secretary for the Orient, and

M. T. Rankin each spoke. A prayer of dedication for the more than fifty missionary appointees present was led by C. Roy Angell, well known pastor from Miami.

In this first year of its second century, the convention took two actions which symbolized its rededication to the missionary vision that had marked its deliberations a century before in Augusta. First the messengers approved Recommendation No. 4 of the Executive Committee that provided for a special financial campaign, to begin in July and not to extend beyond September, in order to raise a minimum of three and a half million dollars in cash for world relief and rehabilitation to be administered by the Foreign Mission Board.[17] In a second action, on Thursday evening, a cash offering of more than $10,000 was received for this purpose. While celebrating the past, the convention was clearly thinking of the future and its own global mission.

In giving the Foreign Mission Board's report, Rankin emphasized that two facts stood out against "a background of confusion and destruction." They were: first, "the achievements of world missions are indestructible"; and second, "Southern Baptists must do far more to help save the world than we have been doing." He went on to explain that Southern Baptist missionaries were at that time back in every area of China in which the board had operated before the war. Then he put the needs of a postwar world in perspective and on the hearts of Southern Baptists when he illustrated what he meant:

In the light of the world's urgent need, the Foreign Mission Board's present program can be seen in its tragic smallness. . . . In view of such need, it is unthinkable that we shall continue to send only 550 missionaries to tell the world about Christ; it is unthinkable that we shall continue to give only an average of seventy cents per person per year to help all the world outside our own territory.[18]

Included in the board's report to the convention was an "Historical Sketch" of the Foreign Mission Board by E. C. Routh, editor of *The Commission.* Although brief, it was an accurate outline of the major developments in the history of the board through 1944. In addition to this account of the board's history, Marjorie Moore and Rachel Colvin edited a booklet under the title . . . *that they may have LIFE,* commemorating the board's centennial. Although it may appear that both the convention and the board lacked a sense of history from the paucity of materials produced for the centennial, such was not the case. At first the war circumscribed the events and then the end of the war brought the realities of the present to the forefront that crowded out any temptation to linger longer in the past.

The Limits of Ecumenicity

One of the first tasks Rankin faced upon assuming his new office was to help the board and Southern Baptists define the limits of ecumenicity. It was not merely an academic exercise of the new executive secretary but a vitally important issue, affecting the viability of the denomination. This was not the first time Rankin had faced the ecumenical question but now his attitude would help shape the attitude of the board and its relationship with other mission boards and denominations.

The board's missionaries on the field often worked closely with missionaries of other denominations without formal comity agreements. A spirit of camaraderie with missionaries of other communions had marked Southern Baptist foreign missionary efforts from the beginning. It became even more evident when missionaries of various boards were interned in the same camps by the Japanese. This working relationship was possible because of the commonality of a shared evangelical faith that recognized the unity of those who had committed their lives to Christ. This functional ecumenicity was both voluntary and personal. But for Southern Baptists, ecumenism had its limits.

Although the board had participated in the International Missionary Council and its missions had been participants in various national councils of churches, it was not prepared to embrace principles that would lead to the dissolution of, or the abandonment of, its work as a denominational mission board

A spirit of camaraderie with missionaries of other communions had marked Southern Baptist foreign missionary efforts from the beginning.

responsible for its own policies and programs.

The International Missionary Council

That the board still considered the International Missionary Council in 1943 a viable forum for the exchange of information and a vehicle of interdenominational cooperation is reflected in its relationship to the council. Maddry was sent as a delegate of the Foreign Mission Board to Madras in 1938. In January of 1943, the board made a donation to the council of $500, $200 of which were designated "for the expenses of J. Merle Davis to South America and $300 for the current fund of the Council."[19]

The Foreign Missions Conference of North America

For a number of years, the Foreign Mission Board had been an active member of the Foreign Missions Conference of North America but when the proposal was made that the conference become a member of the North American Council of Churches, doubts were raised about the ultimate goal of the merger. The board declared: "If the Foreign Missions Conference should lose its identity by becoming a part of the North American Council of Churches of Christ, it would mean that our Board would be forced out of a wholesome and helpful fellowship."[20]

Maddry was instructed by the board to make the position of the board clear to the "officials" of the Foreign Missions Conference of North America, indicating that "this Board has no desire to leave" the conference but "if this body of proved usefulness should depart from its ancient posi-tion, it would separate itself from our Board."[21] The issue of ecumenicity for Southern Baptists was even more acute in Japan.

The Church of Christ in Japan

By 1940, all Protestant denominations under pressure of the government formed a united church known as *Nihon Kirisito Kyodan* (Church of Christ in Japan). At first each denomination formed a block that gave the new organization the appearance of a federation of churches. But by November 1942, at the demand of the government, the blocks were discontinued. Supposedly the *Kyodan* had become a monolithic church. The government now had an organization through which it could indoctrinate its membership and control the pulpits. "The Director of the *Kyodan* obeyed all government directives."[22]

The *Kyodan* survived the war and a number of ecumenically-minded Christian leaders of various mission boards sought to reshape the American Protestant missionary presence in Japan to conform to the concept of a United Church of Christ in Japan. In February 1943 the Japan Sub-Committee of the East Asia Postwar Planning Committee met in New York City. Although the Foreign Mission Board chose not to participate, it was asked to respond to the proposal that the various mission boards form a central board that would henceforth carry on mission work in cooperation with the recently created "United Church in Japan."

The Foreign Mission Board's response was forthright and unequivocal. The board replied:

We, therefore, recommend that the

Executive Secretary be instructed to say to the Sub-Committee on Japan of the East Asia Postwar Planning Committee that we can under no circumstances enter into an arrangement for organic church union and control of missionary activity such as this proposal involves. It is our opinion that such a plan violates the essentials of religious liberty and Christian unity.[23]

It is clear from the board's response to these proposals of tighter organizational schemes for cooperative efforts in foreign missions that there were limits beyond which the board was not prepared to go. The problem that had first arisen during Maddry's tenure now became one that Rankin was compelled to address.

The National Christian Council of China

The problems presented to the board by the incorporation of the Foreign Missions Conference of North America with the National Council of the Churches of Christ in the United States of America had been faced before by Rankin in China. The Continuation Committee of the Edinburgh World Missionary Conference sponsored several meetings in various parts of China that resulted in the formation of a Chinese Continuation Committee which led, in turn, to the organization of the National Christian Council in 1922. The hundred member council, the majority of whom were Chinese, was comprised of representatives of various denominational and nondenominational evangelical groups at work in China. Since membership in the council was purely voluntary for the promotion of mutual support and understanding devoid of any attempt to seek doctrinal conformity, Rankin saw no reason why Baptists should

not participate. Rankin also saw some positive benefits of Baptist participation in such an organization.[24]

During his furlough, Rankin determined to make a thorough study of the National Christian Council. W. O. Carver, the widely influential professor of missions at Southern Seminary, encouraged him to make the council the subject of his doctoral dissertation, which he did. In his critical evaluation of the council, Rankin found no problem for Baptists in its original charter and aims but considerable difficulty with its trends. He concluded that the only way the council could be saved from becoming captive to those who would use it to promote the National Church of Christ in China was for Baptists and others, who held to Christian unity but not to organic union, was to remain within the council and seek to hold it true to its original purpose and structure, for, "by the nature of its aims and objectives as an organization, the Council represents the only attempt being made in the Christian work in China toward a sound approach to the problems of Christian unity and fellowship."[25]

In spite of his positive evaluation of the council's structure and stated goals, Rankin was rather apprehensive regarding its future. "Various individual members of the Council and of the staff are unreservedly committed to organic unity and the development of a National Church of China, as is evidenced by their connection with the Church of Christ in China and by numerous utterances."[26] Then, he explained why he felt such a relationship presented a problem to Baptists.

We believe that it is the Council's relation

Rankin with missionaries who spoke to the Southern Baptist Convention, Oklahoma City, 1949, left to right: Ernest Lee Hollaway, Japan; Grayson Tennison, Brazil; William C. Gaventa, Nigeria; and Virginia Wingo, Italy

to this concept of the National Church which constitutes its most serious danger, because we believe, in turn, that the concept of the National Church is a most serious danger to the development of true, spiritual, Christian life in China.[27]

Rankin's experience in China had confirmed the value, and set the limits, of Baptist participation in ecumenical ventures. This time the issue was raised again by the decision of the Foreign Missions Conference of North America to become a part of the National Council of Churches. The board had been a member of the conference from 1893 to 1919 when mounting anti-ecumenical sentiment among Southern Baptists led it to withdraw. In 1938, however, it renewed its membership in the conference and actively participated in its affairs until March 1950.

Out of consideration for Southern Baptists and other denominations whose representatives had expressed misgivings about the proposed merger, the Foreign Missions Conference of North America voted in 1949, not to become the foreign missions division of the National Council.

The remainder of the year saw strenuous efforts on the part of the leadership to accommodate both Southern Baptists and the perceived needs of the National Council, but without success. Searcy Garrison, speaking for the representatives of the Foreign Mission Board attending the fifty-sixth meeting of the Foreign Missions Conference, reported that:

the efforts of a year demonstrate that this [accommodation] cannot be effectively done. If the Foreign Missions Conference is to function effectively for its members who will have membership also in the National Council, it must maintain an organic relationship with the National Council of Churches which will not be in accord with the vote taken in January, 1949, and which will not be acceptable to our Board.[28]

Since plans were made to call a special

Foreign Mission Board exhibit, Oklahoma City convention, 1949

meeting of the Foreign Missions Conference in order to reconsider its relation with the National Council, the committee recommended that the Foreign Mission Board of the Southern Baptist Convention "withdraw its membership in the Foreign Missions Conference and thus leave the conference

261

free to make such changes in its structure and functions as a majority of its members may deem suitable to their needs."[29]

After the foregoing resolution was adopted, the board also voted to withdraw from the Committee on Cooperation, which was the Latin American division of the Foreign Missions Conference.[30] Thus, the ties that had provided an ecumenical outreach for the board and had proved mutually beneficial, were reluctantly broken on the basis of principle. The board could hardly have done otherwise even if it had chosen to do so after the 1949 convention meeting in Oklahoma City. The climate of the convention as indicated by both the report of

Rankin gives charge to new missionaries, J.C. and Betty Abel for Nigeria, left, and John N. and Evelyn Thomas for Colombia, January 1951.

the Committee to Study By-law 17, which was tabled, and that of the Committee to Study Common Problems with Northern Baptists, which was adopted (along with its recommendations), were decidedly anti-ecumenical.[31]

From this point onward, the board would seek informal ways of relating to ecumenical organizations. Edna Frances Dawkins remembered that Rankin continued to cooperate with the Foreign Missions Conference of North America on an unofficial basis even after it had become a division of the National Council.[32] Gene Newton, his secretary, remarked: "He would have liked very much to have had closer cooperation with the National Council of Churches but was held back by tradition."[33]

Missionary Personnel Department

The need for a department that would give itself to the recruiting and processing of missionary candidates had been apparent for some time. The situation became acute with the dissolution of the Department of Education and Promotion, which had been assigned the responsibility of working with missionary candidates. It was fortunate that two years before the end of the war, the board established a Missionary Personnel Department and elected J. W. (Bill) Marshall its first secretary. Marshall, a native of Oklahoma, had been secretary of the Baptist Student Union of Texas for five years before assuming this new position. Upon his election, *The Commission* commented: "We welcome Mr. Marshall to this strategic position. He is to fill a big gap in the present organization of the Foreign Mission Board, the only major one in America which has not had for years a personnel secretary."[34]

After almost a century of operations, the board finally had a department and a secretary devoted to missionary personnel. This does not mean that prior to 1943, nothing was done regarding the selection and preparation of missionary candidates for appointment. Up to this time the work of a personnel secretary had been a shared responsibility. Through the years the executive secretary of the board had carried the major part of the load in recruiting, interviewing, and approving the appointees. According to Gene Newton, who was Maddry's secretary beginning in 1941, it was he who first required candidates for missionary appointment to arrive in Richmond several days early to undergo psychiatric examination at Tucker's Sanitarium. In those

Missions professors Cornell Goerner, Southern Baptist Theological Seminary, right, and Cal Guy, Southwestern Baptist Theological Seminary, confer with Everett Gill, Jr., center, Edna Frances Dawkins, left, and Ellen Libis during 1950 personnel meeting.

days she remembered that Maddry was the personnel department.[35] In spite of the inefficiency of the process, a remarkable number of highly qualified and able missionaries were appointed and the requirements for missionary service were steadily strengthened.

With the coming of Bill Marshall to the board, the whole process of missionary selection became more refined and the requirements for appointment more widely publicized. The first report of the new secretary to the Southern Baptist Convention was made in 1944. In order to emphasize the need for high educational, physical, psychological, and spiritual standards, Marshall pointed out that after World War I one foreign mission board had sent to Asia 103 missionaries of whom forty-three resigned or were recalled within ten years.[36] Marshall, then, proceeded to outline the qualifications for missionaries—qualifications derived from a century of the board's experience. Apparently for the first time, the board was asking that candidates, in

most cases, have "at least one year of successful experience in work similar to that to which the missionary will be assigned. . . ."[37] Every missionary, Marshall insisted, regardless of his assignment must consider himself an evangelist, "a successor to the Apostle Paul."[38]

The year 1947 brought with it optimistic expectations. The devastating war was at an end and in Asia the Communist occupation was confined to Manchuria and North China. Rankin informed the board on 9 January 1947 that he hoped to see 100 missionaries appointed before the end of the year which would bring the total of active missionaries under appointment to 625. By April, fifty-six had been appointed and in May, Bill Marshall resigned to accept the presidency of Wayland Baptist College. At the same meeting of the board, Edna Frances Dawkins was elected assistant secretary in the Department of Missionary Personnel. Although Edna Frances was planning to serve as a missionary to China, Rankin persuaded her to stay in Richmond.

Upon presenting her to the board he explained: "We hope to find a replacement for Dr. J. W. Marshall by the end of the year."[39] Perhaps even at that time he had Sam Maddox in mind.

Maddox was the son of missionaries to Brazil, where he was born. After graduating from Southern Seminary, he served five years in the Army chaplaincy. He and his wife volunteered for missionary service and were appointed but delayed going due to the illness of a son who was injured at birth. After the child's death, Maddox wrote the board, indicating that he and his wife were now free to leave for the mission field. But before he had mailed the letter, he received a telephone call from Rankin, asking him to become the next personnel secretary.[40] As Maddox later told Louis R. Cobbs, "I read him the letter and he said, 'Well I am glad you did because that confirms that we feel we have done the right thing.'" Maddox commented that the board was looking for someone with a missionary commitment who knew the demands of the mission field and had gone through the appointment process. Maddox then related a revealing incident in his move to Richmond. "I remember after I had been there one month that the treasurer came to me and said, 'Sam, what's your salary supposed to be?' I said, 'I just don't know. You'll have to go and ask.' So, he kind of smiled a little bit." Maddox added, "I felt I was where God wanted me to be."[41] This conviction was obviously far more important to the new personnel secretary than the amount of the salary.

Following a pattern Bill Marshall had set, Maddox was soon visiting the seminar-ies twice a year and as many colleges and universities as time would allow. Even though Rankin never saw the 100 missionar-ies appointed in 1947 he had led the board to expect, he reported to the convention in 1951 that in the previous year 111 had been appointed, the first time the board had exceeded a hundred appointments in a given year.[42] The four years 1948-1952 that Maddox was with the board were extremely demanding. He soon found himself away from home two-thirds of the time. There were only two to carry the increasing work load: Edna Frances Dawkins and Ellen Libis, but only Edna Frances shared in the task of interviewing missionary volunteers.

In spite of the growing number of mis-sionary volunteers with whom the small staff was compelled to deal, procedures were initiated whereby every candidate would receive personal attention. Maddox had *The Commission* sent to every person who con-tacted the board about the possibility of missionary service. It also became the estab-lished policy of the personnel department to correspond with every candidate at least once a year. As the appointment process drew to a close, every effort was made to see that no one who arrived in Richmond was turned down by the board, as had some-times happened in the past.[43] Maddox told Louis Cobbs that the most difficult part of the job was to say no. He recalled that Rankin came to his office one day and asked to see a letter Maddox had written to a rejected candidate in whom he was interest-ed. After reading the letter, Rankin said: "Sam, I will never check on you again."[44]

Maddox resigned from the board in December 1952 to accept the call to become pastor of the First Baptist Church of Dothan, Alabama. In part, his departure from the board was prompted by Rankin's proposal to send out only forty missionaries in 1953, due to the financial crunch the board was facing. In announcing Maddox's resignation and expressing his appreciation for his services, Rankin said: "We give him our full moral support in his decision."[45]

Elmer West, pastor of the Glen Allen Baptist Church in Richmond and graduate of Colgate-Rochester Divinity School, had been a member of the Foreign Mission Board two years when he was tapped by Rankin to succeed Sam Maddox. During his two years on the board West served on the Personnel Committee and, therefore, was familiar with its work. His first assignment was to interview students at Southern Seminary a week in mid-February during which Rankin lectured every day on Ephesians. Like his predecessor, Elmer had accepted his new position without discussing salary. West became a very close personal friend to Rankin. He visited frequently in his home. It was he who took Rankin to Johns Hopkins Hospital for additional tests during his last illness.

After Rankin's death, West continued to serve as personnel secretary for ten more

The lack of emphasis on salaries reflect Rankin's own frugality and sense of stewardship.

years.[46] Upon leaving the board in 1963, he returned to the pastorate before going into denominational work. He was called back to the board to serve once again in the Department of Ministries and Deputation in 1980, retiring after another stint of six years, making a total of seventeen years on the staff of the Foreign Mission Board.

The lack of emphasis on salaries reflects Rankin's own frugality and sense of stewardship. West recalled that he finally learned that his annual salary would be $7,500. The area secretaries received a thousand dollars more and Rankin's salary was and remained $10,000 (with no housing allowance), in spite of the fact that the trustees of the board decided to give him a thousand-dollar raise. Rankin answered "If you will give these men (he named a number of staff members) a thousand-dollar raise, you can give me one." Of course, as West recalled, they didn't accept Rankin's suggestion. As a result, Rankin didn't receive a raise either.[47]

In fact, the spirit of dedication marked by sacrifice and frugality apparently marked the entire staff during these years. Gene Newton, who served as Maddry's secretary and until 1948 as the secretary to Rankin, turned down a raise offered her by Maddry because it would have made her salary larger than that of a single missionary. When she retired from the board to marry Thomas Eugene West, Rankin expressed the appreciation of the board for her spirit and service in a tribute that was signed by eighteen members of the board. He spoke of the length, breadth, height, and "the depth of it [appreciation] as revealed in the quality of her personality as felt by those who know her as co-worker and friend."[48]

Department of Missionary Education and Promotion

Rankin announced in his report to the convention in Miami the intention of the board to add a Department of Missionary Education and Promotion as soon as a "directing secretary" for the department could be found. A year later, Frank K. Means was elected secretary on 18 May 1947. The quiet-spoken Means, at thirty-six years of age, brought to the department a solid background in education and knowledge of missions. A native of Missouri, and a graduate of Oklahoma Baptist University and Southwestern Seminary, with both his Th.M. and Th.D. degrees, he had been teaching missions in the seminary since 1939.

In his first report to the convention, Means reflected upon the many facets of his department's responsibility, emphasizing the different functions of promotion of missions among, and the missionary education of, Southern Baptists. These two functions require, he declared, their "own distinctive methods and techniques." Then he revealed something of his thinking when he wrote:

> There are many new areas into which the Foreign Mission Board has either not entered, or has entered very hesitantly. As soon as possible it hopes to secure a specialist in audio-visual aids who will have the general supervision of that part of the program. The whole field of films, slides, film strips, recordings, and radio is one into which the Board has not entered to any considerable degree.[49]

With the arrival of Means, the department and its organization became the subject of careful study. At the time, the

Rankin, right, with J.D. Hughey, 1946

departmental staff included Nan F. Weeks, book editor; Marjorie E. Moore, periodical and non-periodical materials; Mary M. Hunter, literature and exhibits, and Rachel Dickson, church schools of missions. By 1949, the department had been assigned a number of additional responsibilities including: Foreign Mission Week at Ridgecrest, representation at state conventions, and missionary-support correspondence. The staff also had been enlarged to include the new editor-in-chief of *The Commission*, Josef Nordenhaug; Fon H. Scofield, Jr., director of visual education, and Genevieve Greer, editorial assistant.

The Commission

On 15 May 1948, E. C. Routh retired as editor-in-chief of *The Commission*. He had seen the press run of the missionary journal increase from 48,000 to 101,000 during the five years he served as its editor. Upon his retirement, Rankin wrote: "I place Dr.

John Allen Moore prepares to teach missions at Rüschlikon, 1948-1955. Earlier he worked in Eastern Europe and later had assignments as field representative and founding director of European Baptist Press Service.

Routh among the truly great men whom it has been my privilege to know. He has made solid the foundations of *The Commission* and has gone a long way in building the superstructure upon these foundations."[50]

In September, Josef Nordenhaug, a native of Norway and a 1932 graduate of Southern Seminary with the Th.M. and Ph.D. degrees, succeeded E. C. Routh as editor-in-chief. Prior to joining the staff of the board, Nordenhaug had served churches in Kentucky and Virginia. He was assisted in his new responsibility by Marjorie Moore Armstrong, who served as managing editor of *The Commission*.

Audio Visual Aids

The audio visual aids division was the most recent addition to the Department of Education and Promotion. Fon H. Scofield, secretary of visual education and radio for the Baptist State Convention of North

Carolina and instructor in religious education at Wake Forest College (now university) became director of visual education on 1 August 1948. After receiving his M.A. degree from Wake Forest, Scofield pursued graduate studies at Andover-Newton Seminary and Duke University. From a rather modest beginning with the production of filmstrips and slides, with and without sound tracks, the department began the production of two films, authorized by the board: the first featured the work in Colombia, and the second commemorated a century of Southern Baptist missionary efforts in Nigeria.

Assessing the Needs of a Postwar World

Rankin was convinced that before specific recommendations that would give direction to a program of advance could be

By 1947 the George B. Taylor Home, in Rome, enables Italian Baptists and missionaries to minister to families and orphaned children in postwar Europe.

made, a careful survey of conditions where the war had taken its greatest toll must be undertaken. This position represented a consensus of the board. Therefore, an accu-

George W. Sadler meets Hungarian Baptist leaders in Budapest in 1948; to his left, M. Baranyay, treasurer, Hungarian Baptist Union; to his right, Ime Somogyi, president, Mrs. Somogyi and Maude Cobb Bretz; immediately behind Sadler: Barnabas Somogyi, left, and Earl Bretz.

months of 1946 visiting every country in which Southern Baptists had worked before the war. Amidst the destitution and poverty, he found glimpses of hope. One Southern Baptist missionary, Mrs. N. J. Bergtson, had remained in Spain until her health broke. Property seized by the Roman Catholic Church in Barcelona

rate assessment of the most pressing spiritual and social needs of a postwar world became a priority. Fortunately, the board was so organized and communications were such that within two years a plan for advance in foreign missions was ready to be shared with the churches of the convention.

As early as 1946, Rankin could report to the convention that extensive projects in relief and rehabilitation had been launched and made possible by the cash offering of $3,914,085 raised the previous year by Southern Baptists. In addition to meeting the humanitarian needs of "tens of thousands of the destitute in China, Japan, and Europe," church buildings had been restored, schools and hospitals rebuilt and missionary housing provided. This humanitarian effort was not a part of the advance program but indispensable to all else the board hoped to do.[51]

Europe

George W. Sadler spent the first three

and Albacete had been returned to the Baptists. The J. D. Hugheys, who had been appointed by the board to Russia but could

Main building, International Baptist Theological Seminary, Rüschlikon, Switzerland, 1948-1995

not enter due to the closing of the "Iron Curtain," had agreed to serve in Spain. Although Baptists in Italy were poverty stricken, they were spiritually alive. An Italian pastor, Manfredi Ronchi, reported that 292 were baptized during the past year. In Yugoslavia, the John Allen Moores and their theological students, who were forced to leave Belgrade because of the bombing,

Rankin, center, confers with John Allen Moore, left, and J.D. Franks at Nordenhaug inauguration, May 1950.

reactivated the school in Zagreb on 1 March 1946. In Romania, the Baptists had at last received legal recognition as a registered "cult" by the Ministry of Cults.

Hungary was devastated by the war. In 1945 when the war in Europe was drawing to a close, the board received the news that the seminary, orphanage, and two church buildings in Budapest had been bombed.[52] The seminary ceased to function, denominational publications were suspended, and churches were closed. The Baptists of Hungary, therefore, became the major recipients in Europe of the board's relief and rehabilitation fund. With the end of the war, the beleaguered Baptists expressed gratitude for help received and reported progress in the work since the war.

Churches with or without pastors resumed their work, reorganized themselves without any outside help. The value of the great Baptist doctrine about the independent churches was fully proved in the last two years in Hungary. We have eighteen students in our Seminary this year. Seven of them will graduate in next June [1946].

There are already several applicants for next year, and I am sure that by next fall we shall have more than twenty students.[53]

Since 1920 the Foreign Mission Board had been discussing with European Baptists the possibility of establishing an international seminary somewhere in Europe. England and Germany had well established Baptist seminaries but southern Europe had only Bible schools with none on the level of a graduate seminary. Italy, Spain, Romania, the Netherlands, Yugoslavia, and Hungary would particularly benefit from such an institution. Too, it would provide a conference center for the Baptists of Europe. Two world wars had ravaged and divided Europe. Although European Baptists were but a handful compared with the state churches of Europe, Baptist leaders in Europe and the United States were increasingly convinced that Baptists could and ought to establish such an institution that would also foster unity across ethnic and national barriers.

In consultation with European Baptists, it was agreed that the seminary should be located in neutral Switzerland. Accordingly, J. D. Franks was authorized by the board on 6 April 1948 to purchase a choice piece of property in the suburbs of the city of Zürich.[54] Two years later on 5 May 1950, Josef Nordenhaug was elected president of the new seminary. At long last, it appeared that a dream of more than thirty years was about to become a reality in the Canton of Zürich, where the Anabaptist movement first arose during the sixteenth century.

Africa

The war had left Africa relatively untouched, at least as far as Southern Baptist

First Baptist Church, Abeokuta: J. Tanamole Aroyinde interprets for Rankin during Nigerian Baptist Centennial, May 1950.

Mission efforts in Nigeria were concerned. In 1950, Nigerian Baptists celebrated the first century of the Baptist witness in that country. Of course, Baptists of the Richmond African Baptist Missionary Society, which was organized in the home of William Crane, a Baptist deacon, had been at work in Liberia since 1821.

Early in the Nigerian experience, the evangelistic efforts developed around schools and clinics. The work with lepers was particularly fruitful. Illiteracy abounded, therefore schools became centers of evangelism and the training of teachers. On the eve of the first century in spite of losing so many missionaries to the diseases of the continent, Sadler's report to the Southern Baptist Convention was encouraging. At the time there were "119 missionaries under appointment, four teacher-training institutions, four medical centers with doctors, three medical centers with nurses in charge, five secondary schools, 350 day (grammar) schools, one seminary, one Bible school. Baptisms reported during the last convention year totaled 2,044."[55]

Asia

China, Southern Baptists' oldest mission field, had suffered the greatest losses,

At annual Foreign Mission Board meeting, 1948, Everett Gill, left, presents Brazilian Baptists' $2,500 relief check to Sadler.

as far as property and personnel were concerned, of any country in which the Foreign Mission Board was at work. The military aggression of the Japanese war machine was largely responsible for the widespread devastation. Missionary efforts in Japan were brought to a standstill as a result of the war. After Hiroshima and Nagasaki (1945), it was questionable if American missionaries would ever gain acceptance in that country again. In both China and Japan the human suffering and sorrow were beyond computation and to former missionaries, overwhelming.

By July 1946, Rankin was back in China to join Cauthen, the secretary for the Orient. Together they traveled eight thousand miles in an attempt to discover the most pressing needs for relief and rehabilitation and to determine where the board could best use its resources in reoccupying the abandoned missions. Scarcely had he arrived in China when Rankin sent back to Richmond his clarion call to action:

> We must help China! We must share the want and need of these Christian Chinese! China today is a scene of ceaseless confusion. . . . The current of life is sweeping this mass of people along at a mad rate. The tensions of trying to keep from drowning are terrific. Here in this seething city (Shanghai) the drowning thousands disap-

pear from sight underneath the crowds who survive. Stores are filled with food, clothes, and the other necessities of life. Those who have money can survive, but those who have not perish without the notice of the crowds. It is our job to hunt down through this mass of survivors and help the thousands who are perishing.[56]

From describing the dismal condition of the Chinese people, Rankin turned to report on the University of Shanghai, which had risen like the mythical Phoenix bird from the ashes of the war to renewed life. In the early stages of the Japanese invasion, the minutes of the board recorded: "The assassination of President Liu of Shanghai University on April 7th sent a shock of horror around the world and pierced the Baptist heart through with grief. It is for us a major loss to our Baptist Cause in China and a very real loss to the denomination throughout the world."[57] The son of a widowed serving woman, Liu was led to Christ by a missionary. During his ten-year tenure, the Baptist university had risen to a place of prominence and Christian influence. After the death of the forty-two-year-old Liu, the university struggled to conduct classes in other sites off campus before it was officially disbanded in 1942. At the close of the war, the faculty and students returned to the campus and on their own, with only a minimum of help from the mission boards, began to rebuild, refurnish, and reorganize the university. "Today," Rankin informed the board, "we hear reports from the newly elected president of one thousand students who have been back on the campus for some months."[58]

The "newly elected president" was Henry Lin, a Baptist business man and high-ly placed government official who told the Board of Managers, "I believe that God has called me to take this job. I am ready to do it."[59] Rankin emphasized that though the Chinese were ready to rebuild not only the university and the other schools and churches destroyed by the war, they must have the financial help provided by Southern Baptists, for they could not accomplish the enormous task alone. This fact was further underlined by the knowledge that the Chinese members of the board of the university had declined to become a part of the Federated Christian University of East China with three other Christian universities that would have given them "access to larger resources in funds and personnel."[60]

In concluding their survey, Rankin and Cauthen made a number of recommendations. First, they asked that a minimum force of 110 missionaries be maintained in China at a cost of $2,500 a year per missionary instead of the prewar figure of $1,000 each. This adjustment would force the board to use an estimated $200,000 from funds otherwise designated for reserve. Second, they emphasized that in spite of the cost the rehabilitation of property (repair and rebuilding of schools, churches, and missionary housing) must be undertaken immediately. Third, Rankin and Cauthen wrote the board: "The most urgent need for relief funds is in connection with Christian workers. Churches and schools cannot possibly pay salaries on a level with the cost of living. We must provide relief funds to supplement salaries. We should be prepared to make such provision over a period for at least a year, and possibly longer."[61]

Japan in some respects was in worse shape

than China. Not only had the atomic bombs leveled huge sections of Hiroshima and Nagasaki, but other cities, especially Tokyo, had suffered extensive destruction from saturation bombing with enormous loss of life. Of the twenty-one Baptist church buildings, eleven were destroyed, but no pastors died as a result of the air attacks. Perhaps one of the greatest casualties of the war was Christianity itself. The Protestant denominations had been forced into the "United Christian Church of Japan" *(Kyodan)* on the 2,600th anniversary of the founding of the Japanese empire. Originally conceived as a federation of churches with each denomination maintaining its own block, in reality it was little more than a propaganda instrument in close alignment with Shintoism. "Some Christian leaders went so far as to report their election to the Grand Shrine at Ise, the shrine of the Sun Goddess."[62] It also raised money for purchase of six war planes.[63]

By the close of the war, it was questionable whether Baptists could survive as an identifiable denomination in Japan. Since no missionary was allowed in Japan, the board was dependent upon Baptist chaplains serving with the armed forces for news of Japanese Baptists. Chaplain Henry E. Austin, USN, on returning to the States reported that Baptists wanted to return to their own denominational structure "because they feel that the Union Church has fulfilled its purpose in keeping Christianity alive during the war."[64] According to Austin, the Japanese said that "the present Union is no longer working and has made no effort to help the ones who most need help."[65] The Japanese with

Baptist Church, Omuta, Japan; in front, left to right: Pastor Masaji Shirabe, Missionary Maxfield Garrot, Rankin, emeritus pastor Kamori Shimose and his wife; immediately behind Rankin: the Shimoses' daughter, Kiyoko Shimose Shirabe

whom he talked also reported that "the Anglicans, the Presbyterians, and others have already withdrawn from the United Church."[66]

Edwin Burke Dozier was the first Southern Baptist missionary to receive permission to return to Japan. At first it appeared that neither he nor any Baptist would be permitted to enter Japan with the first contingent of American missionaries. The Japan Committee of the North American Missions Conference, consisting of six missionaries, included no Baptist. Lois Whaley wrote that "it seemed there was a definite effort to prevent the return of anyone who might suggest denominational autonomy."[67] Government approval was contingent upon recommendation by the Japan Committee. Finally after six months, Dozier was approved as the Southern Baptist representative. On 30 October 1946, he arrived in Japan, five and a half years after his forced departure.

Dozier was the ideal representative of

Southern Baptists to Japan, the land of his birth. Born in Nagasaki, the son of missionaries, he loved Japan and the Japanese people with a divine passion. This became evident everywhere he went. Upon his first meeting with an old friend, Sadamoto Kawano, he wrote to his wife, Mary Ellen, "After the dinner Ka-wano-San came to greet me, but when I gripped his hand he stood there, sobbing with his whole form shaken with deep emotion. I wept too. Words don't always ex-press the feelings in the recesses of one's being."[68]

Edwin Dozier personified the reconciliation he sought to effect between Japanese and Southern Baptists. He informed his Japanese brethren that Southern Baptists had returned to Japan at the call of God for the primary task of evangelism. As far as the role of Japanese Baptists in this new initiative was concerned, he said: "Our desire is to cooperate with all who hold like faith with us and to serve together as brethren with no overlordship of one group over another."[69]

After traveling extensively throughout the island kingdom and conferring with numerous individuals, he was gratified to see the fruits of his efforts. On 3 April 1947, representatives of sixteen Baptist churches met at Seinan Gakuin (college—now university) in Fukuoka on the island of Kyushu in order to consider the future of Baptists in

Much of the traditional faith of the Japanese people was shattered.

Japan. In their first action, Japanese Baptists voted unanimously to write a letter of apology to the Southern Baptist Convention asking forgiveness, and expressing their "unbounded gratitude for renewed fellowship."[70] The letter also informed Southern Baptists of a very important development:

> *It was unanimously voted on April 3, 1947, by those churches and institutions formerly of the Southwestern Baptist Association to form the Japan Baptist Convention based upon the historic Baptist principles and thereby start anew a Baptist program of evangelism in Japan.*[71]

This action meant that those churches associated with the Foreign Mission Board were separating themselves from the *Kyodan,* as, at least, one Baptist church (Kokura) and fifteen other groups had already done. This also meant that because the churches associated with the American Baptist Foreign Mission Society remained within the United Church, that the new Japan Baptist Convention now considered all Japan its field.[72]

A few weeks after the historic conference at Seinan Gakuin, Baker James Cauthen arrived from Shanghai to join Dozier in making plans for a new missionary thrust in Japan. Together they visited all the churches and schools in Kyushu, preaching in every conceivable place that could accommodate a crowd. The heart-hunger of the people was evident. No longer did the emperor claim to be deity. Much of the traditional faith of the Japanese people was shattered. They heard the preachers gladly. It appeared that a harvest was at hand. With a sense of urgency, Dozier asked the board to send seventy-seven missionaries as soon as possible. Of these, he suggested, twenty-three couples should give themselves to evangelism. The other thirty-one should include teachers, publication workers, agriculturists, and specialists in domestic science, in medicine (doctors and nurses), and in religious education.[73]

The Foreign Mission Board responded as best it could. A number of single veteran missionaries, accompanied by other new missionaries began to arrive as early as July 1947. The United States government limited civilian families from entering Japan unless accompanied by a ton of food for each adult. Pete and Bee Gillespie, from Kentucky, were the first to qualify under this provision. By the last of October, the Maxfield Garrotts had returned and Edwin Dozier, who had been in Japan without his family for more than a year, left for a short furlough. The major accomplishment of Edwin Dozier during that year was a new foundation, which he laid, for the future of the Baptist witness in Japan.

While statistics are important, who can measure the influence of one life completely dedicated to God?

Hawaii

As a result of the war in Asia, the board had relocated in Hawaii some of the displaced missionaries from China and Japan. Charles A. Leonard, missionary to Man-

churia, and Edwin Dozier made a survey of this new mission field. To their surprise they discovered that 37 percent of the people on the islands were Japanese. Many of the Japanese knew no English. English, however, became the main medium of communication for the remaining population with its racial mix of 15 percent Hawaiian, 13 percent Filipino, 7 percent Chinese, and the remaining 28 percent a mixture of several different ethnic groups.

At first the missionaries worked largely with the Wahiawa Baptist Church on the island of Oahu. From there, they branched out among Japanese and Chinese on other islands. All the missionaries cooperated in organizing the Baptist Bible Institute of Hawaii, where several of them comprised the faculty.

After the bombing of Pearl Harbor, Dozier was pressed into service with the Army Signal Corps as a translator. He steadfastly refused to take a commission but continued to work with the Signal Intelligence for the duration of the war. On one occasion he broke a Japanese code. At the same time he had access to the internment camps where he served as chaplain. The Dozier home became the home away from home for many a young American serviceman, at least two of whom, Fred Horton and Chester Young, became missionaries; Horton to Japan and Young to Hawaii. Numerous young people of Japanese parents also came under the influence of the Doziers. Among these were those who became preachers of the gospel or missionaries in Hawaii and Japan, such as, Toshio Hirano, Sue Saito (Nishikawa), and Tom Masaki.[74]

Thus, the Hawaiian interlude became

for Southern Baptists an opportunity for missions unlimited which might never have been if it had not been for the war. By 1947, it was evident from the report of Hannah Plowden that the Hawaiian Mission was well established with eight churches and a total membership of 1031. A full

1948 South Brazil Baptist Mission meeting, Everett Gill, Jr., left, talks with Missionary Jack Cowsert.

complement of Baptist denominational life, including a Baptist Student Union near the University of Hawaii, a Bible institute, a book store, and an active Woman's Missionary Union enhanced the Baptist witness and assured its future.[75]

Latin America

As doors closed in Europe and Asia, the opportunity for expanding the work in Latin America became a reality. The response to the gospel in Colombia, Southern Baptists' newest beachhead in South America, was greater than anyone

had thought possible. This unprecedented growth of new churches and missions did not escape the notice and the opposition of the Roman Catholic Church. The Catholic opposition in Latin America was not limited to mob violence or harassment, legal and otherwise, but a campaign was launched to influence the State Department of the United States to prohibit Protestant missionaries from serving in Latin American countries. Citing various published statements calling for the curtailment of the Protestant missionary enterprise in Latin America, the Southern Baptist Convention adopted a resolution, sponsored by the Foreign Mission Board, at its 1944 meeting in Atlanta, Georgia, highly critical of the Catholic campaign.

Southern Baptists declared that it was not their purpose to defend the Baptist missionary presence in Latin America on religious grounds but upon the basis of the principle of religious liberty and equitable treatment.

The only vital issue here involved is the fundamental ideal of complete religious freedom, first exemplified in human history by the establishment of Rhode Island through the heroic efforts of the persecuted Baptist, Roger Williams. This ideal was later incorporated in the First Amendment of the Constitution of the United States, separating church and state. For this freedom we are asking our Catholic, Jewish, Protestant, and non-religious men to fight and die today.... In spite of this attack on Protestant work, we herewith reassert our historic position to defend the full religious rights of our Catholic neighbors in the United States where they nominally constitute about fifteen per cent of the total population, and to defend the religious rights of all minorities everywhere. On the other hand, we likewise insist that those same God-given rights be granted where we constitute a minority, as in Latin America.[76]

Although Catholic opposition to Protestant missionary efforts in Latin America did not cease, there was a marked improvement in the granting of passports. In spite of the outspoken criticism on the part of the Catholic press, by 1945 there was a notable increase in the missionary force in Latin America. Everett Gill, Jr., secretary for Latin America, reported in the October meeting of the board that

A study of Latin America missionary personnel reveals 82 couples and 66 single workers, or a total of 230 serving in 43 different centers in seven republics. Although some fifty have been appointed for Latin America during the war years, there has been a net gain of only 23 or an average of one new worker per year to each of the six missions. Most of this increase has been absorbed by the rehabilitation of the Mexican and the opening of the Colombian Missions.[77]

While statistics are important, who can measure the influence of one life completely dedicated to Christ? Such was the life of Agnes Graham, missionary to Chile who was a student at the University of Texas and a member of the University Baptist Church when Charles E. Maddry was the pastor there. It was the first Sunday in October 1916, when Agnes, deeply moved by her pastor's sermon, responded to the call to missionary service, saying: "I will go to the ends of the earth as He shall lead." After receiving her degree, Agnes prepared for a

missionary career at the Woman's Missionary Union Training School, from which she graduated in 1920. Shortly afterwards, she moved to Temuco, Chile, where W. D. T. MacDonald, a Baptist preacher from Scotland, had initiated the work. Here, Agnes and three other single missionary women founded the Colegio Bautista that under Agnes' guidance became a junior college.[78] After twenty-seven years in Temuco, Agnes suddenly died. There was no building in the city large enough to hold the crowd attending her funeral. An estimated two thousand followed the casket on foot to the cemetery. "Such was the impact of the life of one missionary," Maddry wrote, "in one city and one country in South America."[79]

Venezuela

Although no missionary was assigned to Venezuela until 1949, the board was financially involved in the country as early as 1945. Before this date the literature of the Baptist Spanish Publishing House was being used by a number of Evangelical groups that prepared the way for direct missionary efforts by Southern Baptists. According to E. Silva Ovalles, a pioneer Venezuelan Baptist pastor, there were evangelical missionaries in Venezuela as early as 1885.[80] Some of these were Baptists or, at least, held to certain Baptist principles and practices. In 1900, the Presbyterians had established a church in Caracas. Twenty-five years later, Mid-Missions, a Baptist missionary society associated with the General Association of Regular Baptists, had entered the southern section of the country. In 1945, the Foreign Mission Board asked Harry Schweinsberg, missionary to Colombia, to make a survey of Venezuela and its needs with the intention of establishing a Southern Baptist missionary presence there. He found conditions favorable and even though Roman Catholic influence was pervasive, Venezuela in the tradition of its liberator, Simon Bolivar, guaranteed religious freedom.

A year later, Everett Gill, Jr. visited Venezuela, and found the situation very encouraging. He reported to the board in December 1946 that Julio Moros, a Baptist pastor, had made an excellent beginning in Caracas, the largest city and capital of the country.

> *Brother Moros, whom we are at present supporting, has already gathered together a splendid group of people, many of them from outstanding families. He has already an average of 100 in his Sunday School after nine months of work. This is nothing short of a miracle in Catholic countries. But under the new regime, Venezuela has become liberal, and a great open door has swung wide.*[81]

Twelve churches from Colombia and three from Venezuela participated in the organization of the Colombo-Venezolana Baptist Convention in February 1950. Evidently the Advance Program upon which Rankin and the staff of the Foreign Mission Board had been working since 1945 was already producing results.

The Call for Advance

In preparation for his call for advance, Rankin gave a summary of the missionary force of Southern Baptists and its distribution through 1947. He pointed out that a total of 625 missionaries were under appointment, including seventy-six who

"... the God in whom we believe, the faith which we proclaim, and the need of the world all call for ADVANCE."

were appointed in 1947. Further, it was evident that the war had led to an increase of the missionary force in Latin America. There were 237 missionaries serving in seven republics of Latin America, 233 assigned to China, 104 to Africa, 24 to Hawaii, 20 to Japan, 15 to Europe, and 12 to the Near East.[82]

Further, Rankin explained that the entire foreign mission enterprise was administered by a staff of thirty-seven persons organized into seven departments: the executive; the Orient; Africa, Europe, and the Near East; Latin America; finance; personnel; and education.

After giving a breakdown of the financial receipts of the board for 1947 of $4,734,288, he announced that the board had in preparation a program of "extensive advance in 1948 and the years immediately following."

> *Six million Southern Baptists cannot continue to answer the world call with 600 missionaries and an average per capita gift of seventy cents a year. The God in whom we believe, the faith which we proclaim, and the need of the world all call for ADVANCE.*[83]

The Advance Program

From the very beginning of his tenure as

executive secretary, Rankin determined to lead the board in a program of missionary advance. The program he presented to the convention three years later was far more ambitious than his initial proposals of 1945. Given Rankin's leadership style, it doubtless represented the collective thinking of the administrative secretaries. During the first three days of January, 1948, they met together in a hotel to work out the details of the Advance Program to be presented to the convention based upon two years of extensive surveys of the pressing needs of the mission fields. It was first presented to a full meeting of the board in April 1948 and to the Southern Baptist Convention the succeeding month.

The Advance Program was presented to those attending the Memphis meeting of the convention on 20 May and referred to the Executive Committee by the convention. Jesse Fletcher summarized it as follows:

The objectives of the Advance Program were: (1) to strengthen the 119 centers in 19 countries where Southern Baptist missionaries serve, and national Baptists in 6 other countries, (2) to open additional centers in strategic areas, (3) to support centers and projects undertaken directly by native Baptist conventions, and (4) to increase our resources in personnel and finances until we have a missionary staff of 1,750, an annual operating budget of $7,000,000, and an annual capital needs budget of $3,000,000 or a total budget of $10,000,000.[84]

The next year, the Executive Committee recommended that 50 percent of the Cooperative Program fund of $4,000,000 be allocated to the Foreign Mission Board and $2,500,000 be set aside for capital needs of the agencies of the convention. The committee also recommended:

That all additional Cooperative Program funds above the six and one-half million dollars and the Convention Operating Budget be given to the Foreign Mission Board for the year of 1950, with the understanding that this is not to be regarded as a precedent for subsequent allocations but rather as a special effort in behalf of the Advance Program of Foreign Missions.[85]

This recommended budget gave Southern Baptists added incentive to give to the Cooperative Program. Foreign missions had moved into the forefront of the convention's concerns and served, as Rankin had expected, to strengthen the entire denomination. "But it will do more than that," he suggested. "It will enlarge the compassion of our souls for a lost world, and will increase our capacities to give to this lost world God's message of salvation without which both we and the world will perish."[86]

In the first year of this new plan for financing the Advance Program, $675,044 was received by the board from the "over and above funds" of the Cooperative Program. And this allocation did not end in 1950 but continued throughout the years of the Advance Program.

Formidable Adversaries

In the same year in which the Advance Program was launched, the board received the ominous news of two powerful and aggressive adversaries that threatened to disrupt the work in both Europe and Asia. The adversaries were Communism and Catholicism. Of the two, Communism proved the most destructive in China, and Catholicism, the most disruptive in Spain.

Catholicism

Since the Reformation of the sixteenth century, the Roman Catholic Church had suffered from a siege mentality. In some parts of the world where it was not the established church of a given country, it had displayed a more tolerant attitude toward other religions, but elsewhere it often used the power of the state to stifle or suppress Baptists and others. Spanish Catholicism, due to its long struggle with the Moors, developed the most fierce variant of this form of Christianity. This was the legacy of the conquistadors throughout Latin America.

Back in Spain, the Franco regime appeared completely subservient to the Roman Church. George W. Sadler reported to the April 1948 board meeting: "One of the most unhappy consequences of the state-church relationship is the discrimination against and persecution of Baptists and other evangelicals."[87] Then he quoted from a letter that J. D. Hughey, Jr., had written on 11 March 1948 to the American Consul General in Barcelona. Two paragraphs from this letter describe the situation as it appeared to him.

There is an intense propaganda campaign being carried on against non-Catholics from the pulpits of the Catholic churches, in pastoral letters of bishops, in the press, and in leaflets which are being distributed in the various cities of Spain. The chief purpose of this propaganda has doubtless been to impress the Government with the undesirability of granting new liberties to non-Catholics or even of continuing the present liberties. I enclose a copy of the leaflet distributed in Albacete in December and also a copy of the parochial leaflet of Gerona published February 29.

Not limiting themselves to words, the fanatical Catholics have raided churches in Granollers, Barcelona, Madrid, Valencia, Albacete, Figueras, and other cities. On January 4 an attempt was made to burn down the Baptist chapel in Albacete. In some places (as in Madrid) the local authorities seem to be disposed to grant protection, whereas in other places the Government seems to be working hand in glove with the propagandists and the "raiders." In Valencia, for example, following a raid on December 8 by a band of young men, the Baptist chapel was closed on the order of the Governor and has not yet been permitted to reopen. The church building is American property. In Denia and Alicante, where we have been trying for months to get permission to build chapels on property owned by my organization (American), it is impossible to get a permit to build or to hold services.[88]

Although in Spain the persecution of Baptists and other Evangelicals never reached the level it did in Colombia during a ten year period of violence, it was serious enough to disrupt the work. In spite of unmarked and locked churches, however, Sadler could report that in a visit to Spain in 1947, he had witnessed the ordination of five pastors, a number of professions of faith, several baptisms and hundreds worshiping together in Madrid, Barcelona, and Valencia.[89]

With the election of John XXIII to the papacy in 1958, and the "Declaration on Religious Liberty" of Vatican Council II in 1965, there has been a marked decrease of overt acts of suppression against Protestants. Unfortunately, Communism's level of violence against forms of Christianity that it could not subvert was far higher and longer lasting than outbursts of Catholic fanaticism.

Communism

The returning missionaries hardly had time to resume their work, interrupted by the war, when the resurging Communist armies swooped down out of Manchuria into North China. Met by the Nationalist Chinese armies of Chiang Kai-Shek, they were only temporarily checked. Like a floodtide, retained at one spot only to break through at others, the Communists soon controlled the entire country.

By January 1948, missionaries were beginning to face the painful fact of the necessity of a partial evacuation of Kaifeng and Chengchow. Mothers with small children moved to Shanghai. The American consul had advised the missions to evacuate all women with children from stations north of the Yangtsze and East of Xian, except those located in cities from which they could be easily moved in case of an emergency. The urgency of following the advice of the consul was punctuated by the murder of five missionaries in January. Three Lutheran missionaries were shot by "so-called bandits" as they travelled on a bus. Two women missionaries of different missionary societies were killed in their homes by Communists in separate incidents.

After receiving this report, the board's Far East Committee asked the members of the board to endorse the following paragraph written by Cauthen, which they did.

With economic insecurity, civil war abounding and the multiplied problems of a war-ravished country trying to feel its way into new life, we are in the midst of a work where we are sustained only by a consciousness that this is God's work. We realistically face the fact that we must project a program of missions under just these conditions or not project any work at all. God chose His servants to come to this land knowing that these were the conditions we will have to face. He who said "Behold, I send you forth as lambs in the midst of wolves," will give us strength, wisdom, guidance and the assurance of His presence adequate to meet whatever is to come.[90]

By making this paragraph their own, the trustees were acknowledging that there were no risk-free opportunities of missionary service. Therefore, only those who were willing to take the risk need apply. One who took that risk and survived the war, only to die at the hands of the Communists, was Bill Wallace.

The Risk Takers
William L. Wallace, M.D. (1908-1951)

Among the 191 Southern Baptists risk takers in China in 1948 when the warnings of the "Red Menace" were first issued by the American Consul, was a single missionary doctor from Knoxville, Tennessee. To close friends and family, he was William; to the Chinese, he became known as *Waa I Saang;* and to most people, he was simply Bill.

At seventeen years of age, while working on a car in the family garage, Bill gave an irrevocable "yes" to the call of God to medical missions. The son of a physician and a member of the Broadway Baptist Church, Bill as a youth had been active in the Royal Ambassador chapter of the church. Quiet and unassuming, he surprised almost everyone when he made his decision public. Long years of preparation followed, first at the University of Tennessee, in Knoxville, followed by medical school in Memphis and residency in surgery at Knoxville's General

Hospital. Turning his back upon a golden opportunity of partnership with an outstanding surgeon, Bill wrote the Foreign Mission Board of his intention to serve as a missionary.

At the time Maddry received the letter from Bill Wallace, he had in his files several from Robert E. Beddoe, missionary doctor and administrator of the Stout Memorial Hospital, in Wuchow, China. Beddoe's failing eyesight had forced him to return to the States for an operation, but the desperate needs of the hospital, which he had built, called him and his wife, Louella, back to China in 1934. From that time on, Beddoe bombarded the board with his pleas for a surgeon. When the news reached the board that a gifted young doctor was now ready to join him, he was elated. Maddry was convinced that Bill was the answer to prayer. On 15 July 1935, Bill Wallace was appointed to China, "ten years to the month from the time he had made his garage commitment and recorded it on the back leaf of his New Testament."[91]

Beddoe, who was an accomplished musician, was distressed to discover that his new colleague was a monotone, devoid of a musical ear so necessary for one who would

At seventeen years of age, while working on a car in the family garage, Bill [Wallace] gave an irrevocable "yes" to the call of God...

speak Chinese. But Bill's skill as a surgeon soon replaced Beddoe's disappointment with delight. He wrote the board, that "Dr. Wallace has already demonstrated that the Board made no mistake in selecting him for this place. He has a keen eye, a steady hand, and a good knowledge of surgical techniques."[92] The veteran missionary was even more pleased to discover that the young doctor was a man of selfless spirit and a compassionate heart. Beddoe predicted that when Wallace's reputation got around, patients would come even from as far away as Canton.[93] He did not expect that to happen so soon but the Japanese invasion stepped up the time table.

Before the end of his first term, Bill's presence had elevated the Stout Memorial Hospital and the cause of Christ to unprecedented prominence throughout South China. Many of those who had formerly resented the hospital's presence and despised the "foreign devils" associated with it had a radical change of heart. For one thing, when the bombs began to fall on Wuchow, the missionaries stayed. When the hospital took a direct hit Wallace, who was in surgery at the time, finished the operation. Between his endless rounds of surgery, Bill witnessed to the love of Christ in word and deed. To the Chinese who had heard sermons before, as Jesse Fletcher wrote, "in Bill Wallace they began to see one, and that made the difference."[94]

When the Japanese occupation of Wuchow appeared imminent, Bill loaded equipment and staff on barges that were pushed up the West River past Nanning to Puseh, a small town where they continued their ministry of healing until the approaching Japanese forced them to move again. The indescribable hardships took their toll. Disease and death did not spare the hospital on the move. Lucy Wright, missionary nurse, joined the staff at Nanning after a year-long adventure in trying to join them. A Chinese nurse filled her in on their experiences. "It was while at Fok Luk that I saw Dr. Wallace refuse his rice allowance and give it to a nurse who was desperately ill with fever." She recounted the time she saw him eating rice that no one else would eat. Then, she said:

> I don't want to offend you, Miss Wright, but we Chinese are not used to seeing Americans or Europeans do things like this. We know the missionaries love us, but there was always a difference. They lived their way and we lived ours, but Dr. Wallace didn't know about the difference. He was one of us; he accepted our portion—all of it.[95]

The love and esteem that the Chinese had for the missionary doctor became visibly evident when Bill lay near death where so many had received renewed health. As the news spread that their beloved doctor was seriously ill, crowds kept a silent vigil night and day just below his window until the word was given that the crisis had passed and the object of their prayers would recover. Few would have dreamed that an even greater crisis awaited the forty-one-year-old surgeon immediately ahead.

As the Communists drew closer to Canton, the South China missionaries were forced to decide whether to go or to stay. Cauthen, secretary for the Orient, had suggested there were three options: leave, stay, or transfer to another country. Whatever the decision, he promised the board's full support. In Wuchow station, there were at the time eight missionaries. Of these, five decided to leave and three to stay. Finally when the Wuchow missionaries asked Jessie Green to leave, she realized her evangelistic work was over. She left. Only Bill Wallace, and a missionary nurse, Everley Hayes, remained and finally, there was Everley—alone. Bill had been murdered.[96]

" ... Dr. Wallace... was one of us: he accepted our portion— all of it."

Him, whose witness the Communists could not discredit, they attempted to destroy. After his arrest as "Truman's spy," on the evidence of a planted pistol found in his bedroom, he was imprisoned on 19 December 1950 and after fifty-three days of humiliation, endless interrogation, and, near the end, torture, Bill was found dead on 10 February 1951. Apparently he had been beaten to death. Upon hearing of Bill's death, M. Theron Rankin wrote:

> The irrefutable quality of Dr. Wallace's love made it imperative that the Communists get rid of him. His life refuted everything the Communists said. They have tried to get rid of the witness of Bill's life. But that is precisely where they will fail. Bill Wallace's witness of God's love in Christ has been made immortal.[97]

Bill was always a man of few words. Once at the prison, he told those who accompanied him, "Go on back and take care of the hospital. I am ready to give my life if necessary." Among his close missionary friends were the Roman Catholic priests of the Maryknoll Fathers, one of whom sent the following tribute to the *New York Times:*

From the orderly science of his medical books he stepped into the reality of one of China's most backward sections, where ignorance and necromancy had always surrounded illness and death. He was the heart of the Stout Memorial Hospital, interesting himself in every patient; going untiringly from operating room to bedside in a never-ending round of charity. With great patience he trained a staff of Chinese doctors and nurses to supplement and extend the great work he was doing.

The Maryknoll Fathers of the Wuchow Diocese mourn the loss of Doctor Wallace whose friendship they esteemed. He healed our malaria, our skin ulcers, and the other illnesses that missioners manage to pick up. He will be mourned by thousands of Chinese, at whose bedside he sat and in whose eyes the name of "Wa I Shaang" will always bring a light of gratitude, though governments may come and go.[98]

Mission Accomplished

On the way back to Richmond from the Southern Baptist Convention in Houston held 6-10 May 1953, Theron Rankin confided in his wife: "I believe it [the Advance] has caught on. I am satisfied. For the first time I feel that I can lay down my work with complete satisfaction about the Advance program."[99] Less than two months later, he laid down his work on 27 June.

In a physical examination in preparation for making a missionary trip to South America with Everett Gill, Jr., a blood test revealed that Rankin had leukemia in an advanced stage. He asked Elmer West to drive him to Johns Hopkins Hospital for a second opinion. The doctors there con-

firmed the earlier diagnosis. Rankin canceled his trip. He still participated in the June board meeting and gave the charge to the new missionary appointees and continued work as long as his strength permitted. He died with the conviction that his dream of Advance was now a shared vision that had only begun to bear fruit. In his last major address to the board in April 1953, he challenged Southern Baptists to dare to follow God through the open door of opportunity.

These are some of the ways [efforts in the postwar world] by which I believe God has brought world Christianity to the door of a new era of advance in the coming of his kingdom among men. Do we dare follow him on through the door? To go with him in the dynamic of his love as he responds to the expectancy of a world hungry for life that is worth living? To see all people of the world as he sees them? To accept with him the responsibility for all men of the world which he accepted in Christ Jesus? To share in his purpose to create of all men new men in Christ?

Do we dare?

Unless we are able to expand our present boundaries of thinking and action concerning God's kingdom, we had better not dare. The world of men in which God is moving today is expecting and demanding far more than can be produced by the token services which organized Christianity has become accustomed to render in the name of our God, who is giving all of himself in Christ for the world.

These forces of advance have been stirring among Southern Baptists. Already they have carried us farther than many of us dared to hope when the Foreign Mission Board announced its program of advance in 1948. But it is becoming evident that we have advanced only to the door, where we are seeing the world in a new way. We are becoming conscious of new dimensions.[100]

During Rankin's administration, Southern Baptists had begun to respond to the challenge of the whole world. A total of 640 missionaries had been appointed during his administration. At the time of Rankin's death, there were 913 under appointment. The board's income in 1944 was $2,885,148.75 in addition to $323,315.47 for world relief. By 1953 it had increased to $9,327,700.13 and $68,022.05 for world relief. The statistic that gave him the most satisfaction was the increase in the per capita giving to foreign missions in twenty years. It had risen from 21 cents in 1932 and 1942, to $1.01 in 1952. At the time of Rankin's death, the board was at work in thirty-three countries, twenty of which had been entered during his tenure.

> *[Rankin] died with the conviction that his dream of Advance was now a shared vision that had only begun to bear fruit.*

In his last major report to the Foreign Mission Board, Rankin reminded the board that Southern Baptists, along with other Christians, only stood at the door of a new period of Advance.

It is my opinion that world Christianity is standing today at the open door of this period of advance. We have not yet entered. What we have done thus far has brought us only to the open door, through which we can catch sight of the dawn of a new day of opportunity and achievement; provided we have eyes with which to discern what is happening in the world.

Through this door, we see a world in commotion. To the ordinary observer, looking through ordinary eyes, it is a world of confusion and human tragedy; a world in which established orders are going to pieces and civilization itself is threatened with collapse. But to him who sees through the eyes of God, it is a world in which God himself is moving to accomplish his purposes of achieving righteousness among men.[101]

In the face of the consuming spread of international Communism, M. Theron Rankin, man of faith and vision, had indeed led Southern Baptists to the open door to Advance. His successor, Baker James Cauthen, true to the Rankin vision, would lead his fellow Baptists through that door into ever widening fields "white unto harvest."

ENDNOTES

1. J. B. Weatherspoon, M. Theron Rankin, Apostle of Advance (Nashville, Tenn.: Broadman Press, 1958), 7.
2. Ibid.
3. Ibid., 12.
4. Ibid., 21.
5. Ibid., 56.
6. Ibid., 58.
7. Cited in ibid., 77.
8. Cited in ibid., 73.
9. Ibid.
10. Ibid., 78.
11. Ibid., 80.
12. Ibid.
13. Ibid., 81. Although Weatherspoon gives a slightly different version of this story, I recall hearing Rankin tell it in a chapel service at Southern Seminary when I was a student there shortly after he was repatriated.
14. Edna Frances Dawkins, Interview by the author, 19 June 1992, Richmond, Virginia. This was Rankin's own account of the episode, as remembered by Edna Frances Dawkins, who while serving on the staff in Richmond became a close personal friend of the Rankins. For years she ate her evening meals with the Rankin family.
15. Minutes, FMB, 6 June 1944, 189.

16. *Annual,* SBC, 1946, 31.

17. Ibid., 48.

18. Ibid., 225.

19. Minutes, FMB, 14 January 1943, 45.

20. Ibid., 69.

21. Ibid.

22. Kenneth Scott Latourette, *The Twentieth Century Outside Europe* (New York: Harper & Row, 1962), 433.

23. Minutes, FMB, 14 April 1943, 69.

24. See Weatherspoon, *M. Theron Rankin, Apostle of Advance,* 35-38.

25. M. Theron Rankin, "A Critical Examination of the National Christian Council of China" (Ph.D. diss., The Southern Baptist Theological Seminary, 1936), 84.

26. Ibid., 94.

27. Ibid., 95.

28. Minutes, FMB, 14 March 1950, 102.

29. Ibid., 103.

30. Ibid.

31. *Annual,* SBC, 1949, 52, 53. The fourth recommendation of the Committee to Discuss Common Problems with Northern Baptists read:

Be it further resolved that, no compact or agreement be formed with any organization, convention, or religious body that would place Southern Baptists in a compromising position, or appear to be a step toward organic union with religious bodies that do not believe in or practice the aforesaid New Testament Baptist principles as set out in this report.

Although it is not stated in so many words, the terms "any organization" or "religious body" referred to the National Council of Churches of Christ. To the best of my memory, for I was present at the time, L. E. Barton and T. C. Gardner presented the reports of their committees and there was no hesitancy in naming the National Council in the heated discussions that followed.

32. Dawkins, Interview. In studying theology with Rankin, Edna Frances remembered that he often said: "'I am more liberal than you,' then he would explain why he could not join in certain ecumenical ventures."

33. Mrs. Gene Newton West, Interview by Elmer West, 17 June 1992, Ashville, North Carolina.

34. *The Commission,* July-August 1943, 2.

35. Gene Newton West, Interview. Gene Newton, a daughter of missionaries to China, became a secretary in the board's office in 1935 and "quite suddenly" found herself Maddry's secretary. Her title was secretary to the executive secretary. She remained after Maddry's resignation to serve as Rankin's secretary until her marriage to Thomas Eugene West in 1948.

36. *Annual,* SBC, 1944, 202.

37. Ibid., 205.

38. Ibid., 204. In summary these qualifications were: 1. good health; 2. between ages 24 and 32; 3. pleasing personal appearance; 4. college and theological degrees; 5. for medical missionaries, an M.D. from a class A medical school with one year of seminary education and two years of internship; 6. emotional balance; 7. a harmonious marital relationship; both husband and wife with a sense of call, and no overwhelming domestic debts.

39. Minutes, FMB, 14 October 1947, 185.

40. Dr. Sam Maddox, Interview by Louis Cobbs, 10 March 1989.

41. Ibid.

42. *Annual,* SBC, 1950, 98.

43. Maddox, Interview.

44. Ibid.

45. Minutes, FMB, 11 December 1952, 221.

46. Elmer West, Interview by the author, 25 June 1992. Elmer West and Edna Frances Dawkins gave me more insights into the life of M. T. Rankin than any other oral sources.

47. Ibid.

48. Gene Newton West, Interview.

49. *Annual,* SBC, 1948, 87.

50. Quoted in the *Annual,* SBC, 1949, 143.

51. *Annual,* SBC, 1946, 73.

52. Minutes, FMB, 21 June 1945, 283.

53. Quoted in *Annual,* SBC, 1946, 89.

54. Minutes, FMB, 9 September 1948, 78.

55. *Annual,* SBC, 1950, 99.

56. Minutes, FMB, 11 October 1946, 95.

57. Minutes, FMB, 11 May 1938, 43.

58. Minutes, FMB, 11 October 1946, 95.

59. Ibid.

60. Ibid.

61. Ibid., 96.

62. Edwin Dozier cited in Lois Whaley, *Edwin Dozier of Japan: Man of the Way* (Birmingham, Ala.: Woman's Missionary Union, 1983), 203.

63. Minutes, FMB, 14 November 1947, 191.

64. Quoted in Whaley, *Edwin Dozier of Japan,* 187.

65. Ibid.

66. Ibid.

67. Ibid., 185.

68. Quoted in ibid., 200.

69. Cited in ibid., 201.

70. Ibid., 208.

71. Quoted in ibid.

72. There can be little doubt that Edwin Dozier was largely responsible for this development. Letters from Dozier to the Foreign Mission Board, excerpts of which were published in the *Annual,* SBC, 1947, pp. 83, 84, indicated that this was the case. He reported that he

told the conference in Fukuoka:

Our primary aim in coming to Japan is to preach Christ, and not the furtherance of a denomination. Nevertheless we at the present know of no better plan than to use our denominational lines which do not prevent us from doing our job because of fears that we might have to compromise certain basic beliefs which we believe essential.

Dozier then delineated in six points why Southern Baptists did not join the Federal Council of Churches and by implication could not be a part of the <u>Kyodan</u>.

Dozier's account of the conference in Japan was followed by an explanation of the board's policy on cooperation with other denominations:

The foregoing statement by Mr. Dozier does not imply any lack of willingness on the part of the Foreign Mission Board to co-operate with other evangelical denominations. Never has there been a time when our missionaries have felt more readiness to work in hearty co-operation with other denominational groups, while adhering to their own earnest convictions.

73. *Annual,* SBC, 1946, 84.

74. Chester Young informed me that Sue Saito Nishikawa was the first native to return to Hawaii to work after studies on the mainland. Converted in the Wagudi Baptist Chapel, that became the Wahiawa Baptist Church (the oldest Baptist church in Hawaii), she graduated from Baylor and Southwestern Seminary. She returned to serve as the educational director of the Olivet Baptist Church in Honolulu. She has also been a most effective leader in the Woman's Missionary Union of Hawaii.

75. *Annual,* SBC, 1947, 109-15.

76. *Annual,* SBC, 1944, 32.

77. Minutes, FMB, 9 October 1945, 13.

78. The word *colegio* in Spanish is not the exact equivalent of the English word college. It simply means school which may go as high as junior college level in the United States.

79. Charles E. Maddry, *Christ's Expendables* (Nashville, Tenn.: Broadman Press, 1949), 100-105.

80. E. Silva Ovalles, "Impacto de los Bautistas en la Obra Evangelica en Venezuela," Lecture delivered at the Undecima Conferencia Teologica "Efraim Silva Ovalles," Seminario Teologico Bautista de Venezuela, Los Teques, Venezuela, 1-5 February 1993, 1, 2.

81. Minutes, FMB, 11 December 1946, 116.

82. *Annual,* SBC, 1948, 86.

83. Ibid.

84. Baker J. Cauthen and others, *Advance: A History of Southern Baptist Foreign Missions* (Nashville: Broadman Press, 1970), 52-53.

85. *Annual,* SBC, 1949, 35.

86. *The Advance Program Must Succeed* (Richmond: Department of Missionary Education and Promotion, Foreign Mission Board, SBC, 1949).

87. Minutes, FMB, 6 April 1948, 15.

88. J. D. Hughey, Jr., to the American Consul General in Barcelona, 11 March 1948. Cited in ibid., 15-16.

89. Ibid., 16.

90. Minutes, FMB, 12 February 1948, 225.

91. Jesse C. Fletcher, *Bill Wallace of China* (Nashville: Broadman Press, 1963), 12.

92. Robert E. Beddoe, China, to Charles E. Maddry, Richmond, Fall, 1936. Cited in ibid., 29.

93. Fletcher, *Bill Wallace of China,* 29.

94. Ibid.

95. Ibid., 96, 97.

96. Minutes, FMB, 8 March 1959, 209. This tribute to Bill Wallace was written by Rankin and first appeared in the minutes but later was sent to the denominational press and picked up by the secular press as well.

97. M. Theron Rankin's tribute to Dr. Wallace, cited in Ione Gray, "Greater Love Hath No Man," *The Baptist Messenger,* 22 March 1951, 5.

98. From a letter sent to the New York Times by a priest of the Catholic Maryknoll Mission, cited in Ione Gray, "Greater Love," 5. The entire text of the letter is found in the Minutes, FMB, 8 March 1951, 207, 208, signed by the (Rev.) Thomas Brack, M.M.

99. Cited in Baker James Cauthen and Frank K. Means, *Advance to Bold Mission Thrust, 1845-1980* (Richmond: Foreign Mission Board, 1981), 57.

100. M. Theron Rankin, "Do Southern Baptists Dare Follow God?" *The Commission,* July 1953, 8-9.

101. Minutes, FMB, 14 April 1953, 10.

A Shared Vision

The September 1953 edition of *The Commission* was dedicated to the memory of M. Theron Rankin. In addition to articles by Ione Gray and J. B. Weatherspoon, there was one by George William Greene, a brother-in-law. Although Greene is listed as the author, the article was essentially Rankin's. Conscious that the deadline was drawing near for his monthly page in the missionary journal, Rankin shared with his brother-in-law his ideas for the article. The result was "Out Beyond."

In the article Rankin had planned to challenge Southern Baptists to venture "out beyond" the usual and the ordinary that frequently keep Baptists from transcending the barriers to an effective witness for Christ in our day and in our world, for "God is calling—calling us as he has his people throughout the ages, calling us 'Out Beyond.'"[1] In this essay, his last verbal legacy, Rankin used history and science to challenge his fellow Baptists to

George W. Sadler, left, with F. Townley Lord, London pastor and BWA president, 1950-1955

catch his vision of advance.

Shocked as they were by the news of the death of their esteemed executive secretary, the members of the board recognized the awesome responsibility with which they were faced. Not quite ready to select Rankin's successor in July, the trustees unanimously chose George W. Sadler, secretary for Africa, Europe and the Near East, as the interim executive secretary and postponed until October, the election of Rankin's successor. In reporting the decision of the board, an editorial in the *Religious Herald* commended Sadler: "Through long years of devoted ministry his gracious spirit and natural gifts have enriched the meaning of missions in the home churches as well as in foreign lands. The administration of the board is in good and capable hands for the months ahead."[2]

Before the meeting of the Foreign Mission Board in October, an editorial in *The Commission* observed that in the called meeting

Baker James Cauthen

Baker James Cauthen was elected to succeed M. Theron Rankin as executive secretary. Both had served as missionaries in China and Cauthen had worked closely with Rankin as secretary for the Orient. Rankin's dream of advance became Cauthen's mandate. He declared: "Our destiny lies in advance. It is only as we march together as a mighty army in a program of worldwide witness for Christ that we can preserve and enrich the spirit of evangelism which means so much to us."

of the board on 9 July the trustees spent much of their time on their knees seeking the Lord's will in the matter. After stating that the demands of the office required a person of great versatility, Frank Means in another editorial delineated the qualities the trustees sought in the next executive secretary.

> *He must be an able administrator, coura-geous denominational leader, prophetic interpreter of influences at work in our world and powerful preacher and speaker. Not only must he possess the ability to dream dreams and see visions, but his con-tagious enthusiasm and selfless devotion must inspire the people in the churches to make the dreams and visions crystallize into solid missionary achievements.[3]*

Baker James Cauthen Elected Executive Secretary

By the October meeting of the board, the trustees had pretty well determined Rankin's successor. As many as three were seriously considered for the position—Means, Sadler, and Cauthen. On Wednesday morning 14 October, L. Howard Jenkins, president of the board, called the trustees into an executive session for the purpose of electing an executive secretary. By secret ballot Baker James Cauthen was elected.[4]

Cauthen's election was not without opposition. Ruben Alley, editor of the *Religious Herald* and Ralph McDaniel, an influential history professor of the University of Richmond, were adamant in opposing Cauthen's election. Their choice was the well known and highly regarded George W. Sadler, who was just a few years away from retirement. Because both Alley

Baker James Cauthen

and McDaniel were so vocal in opposing Cauthen, there was no attempt at making his election unanimous.

Only forty-three at the time, Cauthen was so eminently qualified for the position that Cal Guy, professor of missions at Southwestern Seminary, aptly said, "Baptists would have been shocked at any other choice."[5] Aside from Rankin, himself, Cauthen was the best known among the board's administrative staff, and for most Southern Baptists his name had taken on heroic dimensions. In light of the aura sur-rounding his name, it is surprising that his election was not unanimous, as had been the case with Maddry and Rankin.

The board asked two of its trustees, J. W. Storer, pastor of the First Baptist Church, Tulsa, Oklahoma, and John H. Buchanan, pastor of the Southside Baptist Church, Birmingham, Alabama, to inform Cauthen of his election. After learning of the decision of the board, Cauthen asked Storer and Buchanan if he should meet with the Administrative Committee, but was told to prepare to meet with the full board in the afternoon. At this meeting his remarks revealed the struggle that he and his wife experienced over the prospects of just such a development.

> In praying we sought to know whether we should request the Board not to consider our names at all, but throughout the entire experience there came repeatedly convictions in our hearts that we should leave the matter in the hands of God.

> After earnest prayer throughout the whole Southern Baptist Convention and on mission fields around the world and after careful deliberation on the part of those of you who make up this Board, there has come a sense of direction toward the action taken today. Inasmuch as we have sought to leave our own hearts completely in the hands of God for His direction, we can feel nothing else except a solemn call of duty at this time.

After referring to the spirit of unity that marked the staff of the board, Cauthen named those with whom he would be working.

> It is much encouragement to think of working with honored men of God such as Dr. Sadler, Dr. Gill, Dr. Means, Mr. West, Mr. Deane, Mr. Scofield, and others who make up the staff of this Board. The comradeship which we all enjoy and the team spirit which prevails must always remain an outstanding feature of the life of this Board.[6]

Because of his responsibilities as secre-tary for the Orient, he asked that Sadler continue serving as interim executive secretary until the end of the year.

Baker James Cauthen's Formative Years, 1909-1939

Although already well known for his exploits in China, many were asking what manner of man was this forty-three year old successor to the fallen Rankin? This question could never be answered without some understanding of the forces that had helped to mold the personality of the board's new executive secretary.

Baker James' birth was problematical, not that he was born—that was not the problem but his size was. The attending physician called his father aside and said: "He weighs only three and a half pounds, Mr. Cauthen. He may not make it." Maude Baker Cauthen, the baby's mother, over-heard the doctor's comment to which she replied, "He'll make it," and for emphasis, she repeated, "He'll make it."[7] On that twentieth day of December 1909 Baker's mother may have been the only one who believed her words. Maude Baker Cauthen was an intelligent woman with an iron will and a deep faith. She was convinced that this second son, though tiny as he was, was a gift from God and she gave him back to God. She was determined to help the little fellow, who would carry her maiden name as his first name, make the most of his God-given life.

A few months after Baker's birth, the Cauthens moved from Huntsville, Texas, to Lufkin, a small mill town on the Southern Pacific Railroad in East Texas. They prompt-ly united with the First Baptist Church and almost as soon were involved in an on-going battle between the churches and the saloons. It appeared to be an unequal match, for the seventeen saloons greatly outnumbered the churches, and it would have been—except for the women, particularly Maude Cauthen. She and they were determined to make the town a fit place in which to rear their children, and they won. Lufkin voted liquor out in 1912 and the Cauthens stayed.

Lufkin became a place of sacred memory to "Bake." It was here that he was converted, baptized, and called to preach. It seems that significant milestones came earlier to Cauthen than to his less gifted peers. At sixteen, he graduated from high school and became pastor of his first church. Shortly thereafter he enrolled in Stephen F. Austin College (now university), located in Nacogdoches—only seventy-five miles distant. He preferred Baylor University, for by this time he was convinced that he would preach and hoped for the best possible preparation for his life's work, but funds were insufficient. At Stephen F. Austin he could stay home and commute, which he did.

Ordained to the gospel ministry at seventeen, he soon found life rather demanding. Being a full-time student at college and a part-time pastor left little time for anything else. At first there was only one church, then there were two. The revivals that summer demonstrated that he also possessed the gifts of an evangelist. He could have easily become a full-time evangelist and might have done so except for his determination to prepare himself thoroughly for his life's work. In spite of his preaching

responsibilities, he did not neglect his studies. In fact, at times he found himself preoccupied with doubts that had arisen in pursuing his education. It was during this period of intellectual struggle that A. W. Birdwell, president of the college and a devout Christian, helped the young preacher realize that he did not have to have final answers to all of life's ultimate questions immediately. Cauthen's preaching also helped him weather the storm of doubt that assailed him.

In the spring of 1929, Cauthen received his Bachelor of Arts degree from Stephen F. Austin with a major in English. He had decided to enter Baylor and work toward a master's degree. Upon this occasion Birdwell wrote J. B. Tidwell, a Bible professor at Baylor:

> *Get ready for this young man. He has unlimited potential. He's already a better preacher than most men in Texas, and he just turned nineteen. Don't let his size or his youthful looks fool you. Judge him by the set of his jaw, the fire in his eyes, the persuasiveness of his tongue, and the sharpness of his mind.*[8]

At Baylor, Cauthen found A. K. Armstrong, professor of English and an authority on Robert Browning, an inspiring teacher. It was under his tutelage that he wrote his master's thesis entitled "The Mind of Robert Browning." At the same time, he continued his dual role as both student and pastor. Although he was not averse to socializing, he was very selective in the friendships he cultivated. One of these, Eloise Glass, was the daughter of missionaries in China and a member of the Volunteer Band. Baker found her company and that of her sister Lois most enjoyable.

Baker received his M.A. degree in 1930 from Baylor and in the fall entered Southwestern Seminary. A year or so later Eloise also entered Southwestern and their friendship was renewed. While at Southwestern, Cauthen continued his preaching ministry in the vicinity of Lufkin. He felt fortunate that his churches provided the financial assistance he needed to stay in the seminary, while some of his friends could not do so for lack of funds. Five months before receiving his Th.M. degree, he was called to the pastorate of the Polytechnic Baptist Church, adjacent to Texas Wesleyan College and one of the largest churches in Fort Worth. After Eloise received her degree, they were married on 20 May 1934. Two years later, Cauthen received his Th.D. from the seminary.

Cauthen's doctoral dissertation was devoted to a comparative study of thirteen of the world's living religions, including Christianity. Since there was a vacancy in the missions department, his dissertation and his superior ability made him a prime candidate for the vacant chair. Therefore, L. R. Scarborough, the president of the seminary, asked the twenty-six year old doctoral graduate to become professor of missions. He accepted the invitation without giving up his pastorate.

The next three years would have floored a lesser man. He was both pastor and professor. During this time the Cauthens' two children, Carolyn and Ralph, were born. As he taught missions and preached missions, foreign missions became his own inescapable calling—a development for which Eloise had been hoping and praying

for some time. Baker told the Foreign Mission Board:

> During the past year we became so unmistakably impressed that God was urging us to go to China that we came to believe that we would be untrue to the call of God if we did not offer ourselves for that service. For many months we made it a matter of prayer, and the conviction grew with such intensity that we felt assured it was the voice of God. We, accordingly, have taken this step and rejoice in God's leadership.[9]

Missionary to China, 1939-1953

To become a missionary to China in 1939 was to some people a peculiar form of madness and to others a waste of life. So it was with dismay that Armstrong heard that his favorite and his most brilliant former student, was wasting his life in China.[10] But for Baker and Eloise, it was a divine imperative.

The First Term

Language study in Peking was a frustrating and humbling experience. Mrs. Cauthen found it more amusing than her husband when an official on a train asked to see his passport. (The Cauthens had only been in China three months.) Upon seeing a picture of the two children, who were not with them at the time, the official asked Cauthen if he had two children, to which the missionary replied that he had two wives, much to the amusement of his wife and the Chinese conductor.[11] Cauthen's greatest frustration came from his inability to preach to the multitudes swirling around him. His few opportunities to preach through an interpreter had resulted in a gratifying response. But before the end of his first year of language study, Baker was preaching in Chinese, and looking forward to his first assignment in Hwanghsien, Shantung Province.

The North China mission was still basking in the afterglow of the Shantung Revival and the Cauthens were blessed. Although language study was his primary assignment, Baker was free to do the work of an evangelist as best he could—and nothing could keep him from trying. As the Japanese drew nearer and the hostility toward missionaries increased, so did the conversions. The turbulent times compelled people to think of the certainty of death and the meaning of life. The gospel offered a word of hope in a hopeless society, and Cauthen made the most of it. But then the word came from the American consul to evacuate all women and children. What should they do? Finally all other missionary wives and children left except Eloise and the children, and one other woman.

All too soon it appeared that the Cauthens' missionary career was about to end even before it had hardly begun. To Baker and Eloise, to leave China was unthinkable. Somehow, they determined to stay as long as God provided a way. Maddry wrote that if they were determined to stay in China, they might consider moving to Kweilin, which was located in a section northwest of Canton known as Free China, still under the control of the Nationalists.

They promptly left Hwanghsien for Shanghai, where they attempted to secure a transient visa through Hong Kong, which would be necessary if they flew by night over the Japanese lines into Kweilin. None was forthcoming. As a result, Baker was

forced to take his family to the Philippines until he could make arrangements for them to join him in Kweilin. Back in Hong Kong, after another month, he succeeded in getting the required visa for Eloise and the children the day before he left for Kweilin via Indochina. In company with Hugo Culpepper, Robert Beddoe, and a Chinese physician by the name of Abraham Hsu, Cauthen boarded a steamer for the Kwangchow Peninsula on the northern border of Indochina (Vietnam). From here, dressed as coolies, and using a variety of conveyances, including sedan chairs, cable boats, and a dilapidated bus, they arrived at last in Kweilin minus Robert Beddoe, whom they left with his load of medical supplies at the hospital in Wuchow. Eloise and the children arrived a few nights later at Kukong after a night flight over the Japanese lines from Hong Kong. At last on 31 July, the Cauthens were together again in Kweilin after leaving Shanghai the previous April.

They soon learned that although Kweilin was in Free China, it was not free of Japanese bombs. A siren on top of a nearby hill and a paper lantern on the water tower warned the people of approaching planes. Such alarms gave most of the population time to reach one of the caves in the vicinity. It fell to Mrs. Cauthen's lot while her husband was out on his evangelistic tours to prepare the "get-away kit" for a dash to the caves. In spite of the unsettled times, night by night thousands continued to hear the gospel as the missionaries witnessed to their faith in the refugee-clogged city. An additional opportunity came to Baker to minister to the Flying Tigers at the American air base in Kweilin. In the midst of their stress-filled lives, the Cauthens rejoiced that they were so privileged to serve—she as a teacher in a refugee Bible institute and he as both evangelist and unofficial chaplain to American servicemen.

The Kweilin years were not without their personal anxieties and trials. Little Ralph contracted polio and Carolyn had a bout with paratyphoid fever, but both recovered. Eloise, chilled from a sudden downpour sickened and almost died. One lung had collapsed and Dr. Beddoe, who had been called to her bedside, feared that the other would surely follow. In his desperation Baker asked his fellow missionaries, including Buford Bausom, and several Chinese brethren to join him in prayer for his wife's life. After an anointing with oil and prayer, they waited. The next day Eloise began to show signs of recovery. At the last minute she was evacuated on a stretcher by an air force plane along with Baker and the children. Once again they found themselves forced to leave the China they loved due to the advancing Japanese army. This time they were beginning their much needed furlough after five incredibly difficult but happy years.

Secretary for the Orient

Upon the recommendation of M. Theron Rankin, executive secretary of the Foreign Mission Board, Baker James Cauthen was selected by the board as secretary for the Orient. Although he had been a missionary only one term, his faithfulness to the task and effectiveness as an evangelist had endeared him to his fellow missionaries and the Chinese alike. On 10 October 1945, Rankin informed Cauthen by telegram:

"The Foreign Mission Board unanimously and heartily elected you."[12] Rankin's letter that followed raised in Cauthen's mind a question mark about accepting this new responsibility. Rankin informed Cauthen

Cauthen spars with son, Ralph, at home in Shanghai.

that he would be expected to move to Richmond and make trips to China and Japan, as necessary. Cauthen responded that he had assumed that his office and home would be in Shanghai, as Rankin's had been. He argued further that to live in Richmond would impair his usefulness to the Orient. "When I think of accepting a position which would take me out of the mission field and at the same time would—in my opinion—make me less useful to the Orient than I could be were I actually on the field, I am persuaded that such a step would be at variance with my own convictions."[13] In other words, he was telling Rankin that he could not accept the position if it meant living in Richmond. Eventually Cauthen won out.

In the summer of 1946, Rankin and Cauthen hitched a ride on a military plane to Shanghai. Just two days after taking off in the states they touched down in China. The two missionaries so different in personality attributes viewed the needs of the Orient with one mind and heart. When Cauthen made his first report to the board on 9 April 1946, he echoed the convictions of Rankin.

> *This war has taught us in the Orient that our best investments in a mission program are not in buildings and equipment, but are investments in human life. War can sweep away our investments in property in a matter of a few hours, but war with all of its horrors when it comes upon the Christian community is unable to stamp out among those people the light which they have come to know in Christ.*[14]

The indigenous principle so dear to the heart of Rankin was affirmed by Cauthen in a subsequent paragraph. "The objective of mission[s] always is to plant the gospel of Jesus Christ in an area, foster its development to maturity, and then see that work become self-supporting and independent."[15]

After Rankin returned to the States, Cauthen remained to move into Rankin's former office and reestablish his home—this time in Shanghai. Next, he visited Japan to survey the needs of that country with Edwin Dozier. After the surveys, his first priority was to return all missionaries possible to their stations in China and Japan. This was not possible where the Communists were already entrenched or posed an immediate threat. As the Communists began to envelop the country in 1948, Cauthen redeployed the missionaries serving in China to Formosa (Taiwan), Japan, and countries of Southeast Asia never before entered by Southern Baptists. Some missionaries attempted to stay in spite of the increasingly oppressive measures of the Communist regime. It soon proved impossible to carry

on the work. By the end of 1951, all missionaries had left mainland China. The last to leave was Pearl Johnson.

It was fortunate that Lucy Smith, a missionary assigned to Cauthen's Shanghai office, finally persuaded the secretary to set up an office in Hong Kong in case Shanghai

Lucy Smith

fell to the Communists. Reluctantly, Cauthen agreed. He clung to the hope of remaining in Shanghai to the last minute but learned while on a mission trip to Baguio and Bangkok, where he was assisting the Ed Galloways in getting started in a new assignment, that Shanghai had fallen. At the time, forty missionaries remained in China, twenty-nine in Shanghai and eleven in other cities. Cauthen was never able to return to Shanghai but continued to live in Hong Kong and Japan until September 1952. Before returning to the States, he was able to obtain permission for the missionaries Buford Nichols, Sox Sears, and Charles Cowherd, to remain in Indonesia. They had arrived there with only tourist visas on Christmas day 1951 without any assurance that they would be allowed to stay.

In view of the fact that China was closed to all missionary presence and the dispersion of Chinese in Southeast Asia had made feasible the relocation of former missionaries to China in a number of new fields

Cauthens at home in Richmond, 1953

for Southern Baptists, including the Philippines, Singapore, Malaya, Thailand, Indonesia, and Taiwan, a Richmond office for the secretary for the Orient now made sense to Cauthen. The family, therefore, moved to Richmond in time for the children to enter school in the fall of 1952.

The Changing of the Guard

Personnel changes at the board were a constantly recurring reality. Some directly affected the orientation and effectiveness of the board's work more than others. So it was with the twenty-six year administration of Baker James Cauthen. It could hardly have been otherwise, even though there were so many similarities between Cauthen and Rankin, there was a marked difference in leadership style.

Cauthen's appreciation for M. Theron Rankin and identification with his predecessor's "dream," as reflected in the Advance Program, were transparent. Yet there was a difference that lay in their very different personalities and educational backgrounds. Less than a month after Rankin's death, Cauthen referred to Rankin in his report to the board.

I cannot refrain from adding a paragraph of my own deep personal love for Dr. Rankin. I met him first eighteen years ago when he was in this country just before setting up his office in Shanghai. As was true of so many others who came to know him, my heart was bound to him by the qualities of Christ which I saw exhibited. As a missionary in China I looked upon him with admiration and confidence. When the load he had carried as secretary for the Orient came to rest on me, I found in him at all times a comradeship and understanding, the value of which I could not overestimate.[16]

Then Cauthen went on to express his own commitment to the Advance Program and its goals.

The passing of this great leader calls us all to a rededication to advance in the task of world missions. We must not think of leveling off at some place between where we are today and the goal of 1750 missionaries he set before us. We thank God for one whose ministry has blessed us so signally, and we dedicate ourselves anew to the task lying before us.[17]

It is not strange that Cauthen should feel the way he did about the Advance Program because he had a hand in designing it. Besides, he shared with Rankin complete dedication to advancing the cause of Christ around the world. The Advance Program was, indeed, a shared vision. If it began as Rankin's "dream," as Jesse Fletcher suggested, it became Cauthen's obsession. But before he could reshape the program, a myriad of responsibilities awaited his attention, the first of which was the election of new regional secretaries for the Orient and Latin America.

The New Regional Secretaries

Although Winston Crawley was only

thirty-four when elected secretary for the Orient, he was clearly the choice of the new executive secretary, who was only ten years his senior. Doubtless his educational background appealed to Cauthen for it so nearly paralleled his own. After graduating from Baylor with a bachelor of arts degree, Crawley received his master of arts from Vanderbilt University. Subsequently, he earned both his master and doctor of theology degrees from The Southern Baptist Theological Seminary, where he also served as a teaching fellow in the missions department. An additional factor in Crawley's selection may have been Mrs. Crawley, the former Margaret Lawrence of Lufkin, Texas. Cauthen was a long-time friend of the Lawrence family.

Means meets with Latin America field representatives in 1960; left to right: H. Victor Davis, Charles W. Bryan, William M. Dyal, Jr., and James D. Crane.

Appointed missionaries to China in 1947, the Crawleys were in language study in Peking (Beijing) when the advancing Communist army forced the transfer of the language students to the Philippines. In Baguio, Crawley led in establishing the first Chinese Baptist church organized in the city and a theological seminary, where he also taught. On 7 April 1954 he was elected secretary for the Orient upon recommendation of the Committee on the Orient.

After a year in his new position, Crawley had so proven himself to the satisfaction of the Orient Committee that the members presented a resolution to the board that read: "This year of service has confirmed and deepened our conviction that Dr. Crawley is God's man for the task."[18] Crawley served the board in this capacity until 1968, when he became director of the overseas division.

Everett Gill, Jr., secretary for Latin America died on Sunday morning 25 April 1954. Gill was elected secretary in 1941 and had seen the missionary force in Latin America increase from 169 in five countries to 395 in fifteen. He was characterized by Frank K. Means as possessing "a genial, attractive, compelling personality."[19] In its tribute to "God's man," the board recalled his saving sense of humor and "his sincere interest in every missionary."[20] Two major developments in Latin American missionary strategy were attributed to him: first, he insisted that all appointees attend a language school for one full year before moving to the field and second, he advocated entering a new country in force rather than with a trickle of missionaries over a longer period of time.[21] His death came unexpectedly although he had suffered from ill health for some months.

Gill's sudden death created a vacancy that Cauthen had not anticipated. Prior to assuming his new responsibilities as executive secretary, Cauthen had considered asking Frank Means to become his special assistant "because of his sharp grasp of financial matters," but decided that the responsibility was not one he could "put off on somebody else," but something he was going to have to do himself.[22] Now Means came to mind again as a possible successor to Gill. His eight years in the classroom at Southwestern and seven years as secretary for Missionary Education and Promotion had prepared him well for such a role. Besides he could be of great assistance to Cauthen in the administration of the board. After a trip to South America and the opportunity to com-

Smith, right, with board treasurer, Everett L. Deane, prepares to greet messengers to 1954 Southern Baptist Convention, St. Louis.

pare notes with the missionaries, the decision was made. Frank K. Means was elected secretary of Latin America in October 1954.

The choice of Means proved a fortunate one. His sense of humor reminded missionaries of his predecessor. Fon Scofield remembered an incident on Means's first trip to South America shortly after he had become secretary. He and Scofield were traveling at night by train in Argentina when suddenly the train lurched and Means found himself on the floor. "Looking up, Means said dryly, but with a trace of a smile: 'The next time I change jobs, I'm going to

read the small print in the contract.'" Upon Means's retirement, Scofield said: "Frank Means has never turned to another contract."[23] He served as regional secretary until Latin America was divided first into two and then three areas for administrative purposes. At the time of his retirement, twenty-three years later, Means was area secretary for Eastern South America.

For more than a year the department of missionary education and promotion was without a secretary. In the interim, Frank Means continued to edit *The Commission* and to give some counsel to Rogers Smith, associate secretary, and Fon Scofield, both of whom carried the work load of the department. For the sake of efficiency, the department was reorganized into three divisions: publications, promotion, and audio-visual.[24] In the October 1955 board meeting, Eugene Hill, a twenty year veteran missionary, who had transferred to Malaysia when the Communists forced the missionaries out of China, was elected to succeed Means as secretary of the department the following January.[25] He also became the acting editor of *The Commission.* Of course, Hill, as Means had been, was ably assisted by Ione Gray, the associate editor.

Hill found the prospects of his new task intimidating. He told the board in January:

I do not need to remind you that after twenty years as a journeyman missionary in distant lands, it is not easy to 'shift gears,' change base of operations, and orientate myself in the Occident again. But since I am convinced that this call came from God through this Board, I am determined by God's grace and help to exert maximum effort to lay hold of that for which my Lord has laid hold of me.[26]

George W. Sadler was two years away from retirement when H. Cornell Goerner was asked to become the secretary of Africa, Europe ,and the Near East. Goerner did not move to Richmond until August 1957. This timing gave him an opportunity to travel extensively in the part of the world with which he would relate as secretary before assuming responsibility for the work in 1958. This gradual transition was a wise move, for Sadler was highly regarded by the interna-

Hill, with staff members, Roberta Hampton, left, and Elizabeth Minshew, checks 1959 mission study map.

tional community in Europe and Africa and greatly loved by the missionaries. The Yorubas of Nigeria held a special place in his heart and they loved dearly the "two way big man" (big physically and spiritually, as the Christians of Sanyati Reserve called him).[27]

For more than eighteen years Sadler had served as secretary for Africa, Europe and the Near East. He first went to Africa as a single missionary in 1914 but his first term was interrupted by America's entry into the first World War. For a time he served as a chaplain. After the war, he married Annie Laurie Maynard and promptly attempted to return

to Nigeria but was delayed due to the lack of transportation. More than a year later, with their three-month-old daughter in tow, the Sadlers were back in Nigeria. Thirteen years later they left Nigeria because of the health problems of their son George William. After seven years, during which Sadler was pastor of the Second Baptist Church, Liberty, Missouri, the family moved to Richmond, once again in the service of the Foreign Mission Board.

The return to Virginia in 1939 was in a sense a homecoming for Sadler. A native of Virginia, he had received both his bachelor and master of arts degrees from Richmond College (now university) before departing for Southern Seminary. In fact, in 1928 while on furlough, he earned another master's degree from Columbia University and received an honorary doctor of divinity degree from the University of Richmond. As a man of education and culture, he commanded the respect of Europeans with whom he came into contact. Upon the occasion of his official retirement, he was appointed the board's "special representative to Europe." Among the reasons for continuing to serve, although seventy years of age, he cited the power of the gospel:

We keep going because the gospel is God's power unto salvation to every one that believeth. We heard one believer say it on the slopes of Mt. Lebanon: "I was a robber and I planned to become a murderer. God arrested me. Jesus saved me and now I am his disciple."[28]

Although, according to his daughter Henrietta Ellwanger, one of Sadler's favorite sayings was that the "missionary should work himself out of a job," Sadler had no intention of quitting.[29] It seemed fitting that he should spend his last years of active missionary service with the seminary in Rüschlikon which he had so carefully shepherded through its first eight.

H. Cornell Goerner, like Sadler, went to Southern Seminary with no intention of becoming a missionary. He was convinced that he was called to teach theology. During the course of his studies he began to consider the possibility of serving in Eastern Europe, even Russia. But his friend and mentor, William Owen Carver, convinced him he could do more good by teaching missions than by serving as a missionary. But once he had seen Africa, even the teaching of missions could not substitute for what he began to perceive as God's call. It came during his second trip to Africa in 1955. "Yes, Lord," he said, "Whatever you want me to do to be a part of bringing Christ to this new Africa, I will do."[30] Later, Goerner attended an appointment service in Richmond in which some of his former students were involved. At this time the board asked if he would consider succeeding Sadler. Because of his new commitment to Africa, he unhesitantly said yes. He was elected secretary for Africa, Europe, and the Near East at the April 1957 board meeting. After a three month tour of the mission stations in Africa, he succeeded Sadler on 1 January 1958.[31]

Even before Goerner took office, Sadler had promoted the expansion of Southern Baptist missionary efforts into East Africa. Ghana was entered in 1947, Southern Rhodesia (Zimbabwe) in 1950, and East Africa in 1956. The initial survey into East Africa was made in 1954 by I. N. Patterson

and William L. Jester. Two years later Sadler made a personal survey and discovered needs that could be met by Southern Baptists in Tanganyika and Kenya. In Nigeria the mission strategy had involved in addition to direct evangelism, a heavy emphasis upon education and medical work, particularly among the lepers. Sadler envisioned a similar approach in East Africa. By the time of his retirement as secretary, eight missionaries were at work in four stations—two in Tanganyika and two in Kenya—and a tubercular hospital was projected for Mbeya. By 1958, there were 329 Southern Baptist missionaries in eleven countries in Africa.

During Goerner's nineteen year tenure with the board, Southern Baptists entered

Goerner, right, participates in dedication of Karibongi Baptist Church, Nairobi, Kenya, May 1966; from left; Missionary Davis Saunders, pastors Daniel Mathuku Njuku and John Kariuki.

seventeen new countries in Africa. As was the case in Latin America, by 1963 the work was divided into two areas: Africa, and Europe and the Near East. At the time, 555 missionaries were working under the auspices of the board. By 1973, the number of missionaries had grown to 632 and Africa, itself, was divided into two areas: West

Africa; and Eastern and Southern Africa. Goerner's love for Africa motivated him to become the area secretary for Africa, rather than Europe, when the first division was effected; and to choose West Africa, which included the Francophone (French-speaking) countries, when the second division took place. He continued to serve in this capacity until the end of December 1976.

The board did not succeed in finding a full-time editor for The Commission *until July 1959 when Floyd North joined the Richmond staff as assistant secretary of promotion in the Department of Missionary Education and Promotion.* North, a native of Oklahoma, came to the board from the First Baptist Church of Kirkwood, Missouri, which he had served as pastor for six years. He brought to his new position a rich background in student work, academics, and the pastorate. He received his bachelor of arts degree from Oklahoma Baptist University and his master of theology at Southwestern. He did additional study at the University of Chicago, Vanderbilt, and Peabody.

While the search was in progress for a new editor, Rogers Smith became the administrative associate of the executive secretary. Therefore, North became, in turn, the acting director of the division of promotion. Within four years of Cauthen's election, the administrative staff of the board almost completely changed. Elmer West, secretary of the department of missionary personnel was the one notable exception.

The Priority of Advance

With Rankin's mantle resting upon his shoulders, Cauthen was constantly preoccupied with innovative ways in which he could enhance the concept of Advance and promote it among Southern Baptists. It was not only a vision he shared with his fallen comrade, but it appears to have been the primary motivation underlying every organizational change he made or program he inaugurated. Consistently from board meeting to board meeting and from convention to convention, there were two emphases always present in his reports and sermons: the necessity of more missionaries and the money to support them. This note was sounded the first time he addressed the Southern Baptist Convention in his new role as executive secretary. The theme of his message was "Forward in Mission." It could well have been titled "The Divine Destiny of Southern Baptists." After enumerating in his first three points the various ways in which God had blessed Southern Baptists, he came to the heart of the sermon:

(4) He [God] has preserved a unity throughout our Convention from the Atlantic to the Pacific; so that Southern Baptists walk together in brotherhood.

(5) Most of all, God has preserved in our ranks the preaching of the gospel in clarity, simplicity, power, and compassion.

Therefore, we can conclude that God has raised up Southern Baptists and has bestowed upon them unusual blessings because he expects from them unusual service.

Our destiny lies in advance. It is only as we march together as a mighty army in a program of worldwide witness for Christ that we can preserve and enrich the spirit of evangelism which means so much to us.[32]

Cauthen concluded his address by emphasizing that the two basic requirements for advance were the "choicest young people" completely committed to Christ "for world service" and money in sufficient quantity to "undergird the task for world missions."[33]

In attempting to enlist the support of the constituency of the convention for the cause of Advance, Cauthen first led the board to designate the year 1956-1957 "World Missions Year"; second, to adopt a five year program called "Jubilee Advance"; and third, to affirm "Bold Mission Thrust." Although distinct, these three programs can be considered three phases of the program of Advance.

Bold Mission Thrust, 1976-2000

World Missions Year, 1956-1957

Following Cauthen's address to the convention in 1954, a resolution was adopted by the convention calling for the appointment of a committee of seven to bring to the convention the following year recommendations regarding ways in which the churches of the convention could be *"aroused to action* in increasing their support of all our Convention agencies and particularly world evangelization." The following year (1955), the Committee on World Evangelization brought its report with eight recommendations after which the convention voted to designate the period from October 1956 to the end of the year 1957 as

World Missions Year. The impression that this was no spur of the moment action is further strengthened by the thirteen recommendations for its implementation adopted at the same time. From the resolution in 1954 to the recommendations of 1955, it is not difficult to discern the hand of Baker James Cauthen.[34]

While Southern Baptists were attempting to focus their attention upon the spiritual needs of a world in perpetual crises, three events of 1956 demonstrated how pressing were those needs and how desperate the people. The people of Hungary tried

During 1956 Executive Committee meeting, Nashville, Cauthen, right, talks with fellow executives: Courts Redford, Home Mission Board, left, and James L. Sullivan, Sunday School Board.

Windows of First Baptist Church, Bogota, Columbia, damaged during 1952 religious persecution

in vain to throw off the Communist yoke only to be mercilessly crushed by Russian tanks and artillery. This display of naked brutality shocked the western world. The Suez affair led to the defeat of Egypt by Israel and the end of British hegemony in the region. While the world's attention was focused first on Hungary and then on the Near East, the Roman Catholic Church, with the willing collusion of Franco of Spain and Rojas Pinilla of Colombia attempted to suppress all forms of Protestantism in those countries. Baptist missionary efforts continued in both countries due to the courageous persistence of Baptists and other Evangelicals and the refusal of the Foreign Mission Board to permit totalitarian forces to shape its missions agenda.[35]

In the World Missions Year, Southern Baptists began a new missionary thrust in Africa and by doing so met stiff resistance from Islam and from Roman Catholic competition. Although Sadler reported 75,000 students in Baptist schools in Nigeria and 6,000 baptisms in 1956, in the light of a continent of 112,000,000 people, he realized how little had been accomplished. As a result, he prefaced his request for forty-seven additional missionaries with a quotation from a veteran missionary who said: "It is like reaching the edge of the Promised Land and working ourselves to death on the fringe while others go in to take possession."[36]

Jubilee Advance, 1959-1964

The World Missions Year became the launching pad for the Jubilee Advance. The minutes of the board reveal that Cauthen was turning over in his mind the best way to keep the idea of Advance alive. The first dates suggested for the Jubilee Advance were 1957-1963, but the decision was made to project a five-year program with a differing emphasis each year, the last year of which would coincide with the sesquicentennial of the Triennial Convention in 1964. This convention was the first national organization of Baptists in the United States. It was called into existence specifically to provide support for Ann and Adoniram Judson. Although in the early years, there was an attempt to convert it into a general denominational body, it remained primarily a foreign mission society. Southern Baptists,

Foreign Mission Board Administrative Committee, 1954; facing camera, from left; John Williams, R. Paul Caudill, Theodore F. Adams, W. Rush Loving, and board treasurer, Everett L. Deane

therefore, saw in its 150th anniversary an opportunity to celebrate the common missionary heritage of Baptists in the United States, their historic identity, and their essential unity with other Baptists. It also became for Cauthen and the Foreign Mission Board an opportunity to breathe new life in the program of Advance.

At the February 1956 board meeting, Cauthen proposed a special emphasis for each of the five years preceding the sesquicentennial, culminating in a grand celebration in 1964. He suggested the emphases of the five years be allocated as follows: 1959, world-wide evangelism; 1960, expansion of Sunday School work; 1961, stewardship and enlistment; 1962, church extension and leadership training; 1963, world missions; and 1964, celebration of the 150th anniversary of the Triennial Convention.[37] He also correctly predicted that the Advance goal of 1,750 missionaries under appointment would be met by 1963. Not content with this achievement, Cauthen asked the board to raise the goal to 2,000 missionaries. By such tactics, Cauthen not only led Southern Baptists in an unprecedented expansion, but also shared his enlarged vision of Advance with a denomination that had just begun to realize its potential for world evangelism.

When the Jubilee Advance came to a close with the Southern Baptist Convention meeting in Atlantic City in May 1964, Cauthen declared: "The Baptist Jubilee Advance came into life and made possible progress in every phase of our service for the Lord." He recalled that in 1948 when the Foreign Mission Board inaugurated the Advance Program, the board had under appointment 625 missionaries in nineteen countries compared with 1,832 in 1964, serving in fifty-five countries.[38] This signal achievement was for Cauthen neither a time to engage in triumphalism nor a time to be complacent, but a challenge to greater achievements ahead.

On Thursday evening after C. C. Owen had presented the final report of the Jubilee Advance Committee, Cauthen brought an impassioned address. After reminding the messengers of the heritage of freedom and missions of which all Baptists were the heirs, in the earnestness of his fervent soul Cauthen challenged the convention to send forth around the world "no fewer than 5,000 missionaries."[39] In rhetorical fashion, he rebuked those who would say "it is enough." Then he proceeded to issue a new challenge. "Come, shall we not—at the earliest possible moment—please, for the glory of Jesus around this world in every land that God gives us entry, send no fewer than 5000 missionaries. And do it at the earliest day!"[40]

To this suggestion the audience broke out in spontaneous applause. Cauthen followed this challenge with yet another without which his vision of 5,000 missionaries could never become a reality—a call for unity. The rift that would divide the convention into two warring factions was barely discernable by 1964.[41] The executive secretary, ever sensitive to any threat to Southern Baptist foreign mission efforts, sounded the alarm.

The world may not understand us. The world may see us in convention assembled as we differ as brethren one from the other. For Baptists always differ. You couldn't be Baptists without having varieties of points of view, which we do well to honor one the other as sincere men and women of God.

But let us demonstrate to a world that may not understand—there can be diversity of opinion but great wonderful united brotherhood that binds the convention together like an army that cannot be dissolved. I call upon you in the name of the Great Commission from the Atlantic to the Pacific, and the Canadian border to the Mexican border, in churches large and small—bind your hearts together.[42]

Cauthen referred to this appeal as "a new dimension in the realm of brotherhood, that we should bind our hearts together as a people and love one another."[43] The furloughing and newly appointed missionaries closed the service by marching down the aisles, bearing the flags of many nations, to the tune of the recessional hymn "Forward through the Ages."

Two days later, Southern Baptists joined members from six other Baptist denominations in celebrating the 150th anniversary of the founding of the Triennial Convention in 1814.[44] Once again, missions became the focal point that brought the diverse Baptist communions together in a symbolic demonstration of their common heritage in the United States—a fitting climax to the Jubilee Advance.

The third phase of advance known as "Bold Mission Thrust" did not take shape until the final report of the Missions Challenge Committee in 1976. Bold Mission Thrust was the fruition of the painful but productive work of the Committee of Fifteen, appointed to study the agencies of the Southern Baptist Convention in 1970. However, the year following the Atlantic City convention, Cauthen began to refer to the "New Advance" but the term lacked definition and

soon fell into disuse. Besides, the necessity of reorganizing and expanding the staff of the board took precedence over other matters. New programs were also developed which demanded additional personnel as did an unprecedented outpouring of missionary candidates.

Reorganizing the Administrative Staff

Organization is a necessity in any institution. This was nonetheless true of the Foreign Mission Board. In the early years of the board's existence, much of the work was done by the regents (trustees) of the board,

At Glorieta Baptist Conference Center in New Mexico, 1957, left to right; Cornell Goerner, Rogers M. Smith, George W. Sadler, Baker James Cauthen, Frank K. Means, Eugene L. Hill, and Winston Crawley

who gave generously of themselves and of their time to augment the work of the corresponding secretaries. When Maddry arrived in Richmond, he was dismayed to discover that such a small staff was expected to carry such an enormous work load. Consequently with his administration, the board began its gradual expansion that led to the election of three area secretaries: for the "Orient"; "Latin America"; and, "Africa, Europe and

Cauthen and area secretaries, from left; Winston Crawley, Orient; J.D. Hughey, Europe and Middle East; Frank K. Means, Latin America, and Cornell Goerner, Africa

the Near (Middle) East." Thus, the executive secretary's administrative responsibilities were shared with those closer to the action than the Richmond-based staff.

The Area Secretaries (Directors)

As the work grew and the missionary force increased around the world, it became increasingly difficult for the three regional secretaries to meet the needs of their areas. Therefore, each of the regions was subdivided into areas that called for additional personnel to staff the newly created positions. For example, when Europe and the Middle East were separated from Africa, J. D. Hughey, a Ph.D. graduate of Southern Seminary and missionary to Spain, was elected secretary for Europe and the Middle East; Cornell Goerner became secretary for Africa. A few years later Africa was divided into two areas—West Africa; and Eastern and Southern Africa. Upon this occasion, Goerner chose to remain the secretary for West Africa. In similar fashion, Latin America and Asia were divided.

In addition to dividing one area into two or more, the board also employed field representatives. These representatives were chosen from unusually capable and highly respected missionaries in their areas for the purpose of aiding the area secretaries in administrative responsibilities. Latin America illustrates the process. Like Africa, it was divided first into Middle America and the Caribbean and separated from South America. South America was subsequently divided into Eastern South America and Western South America. Soon after the Latin American area was divided, Hoke Smith, a Th.D. graduate of Southwestern Seminary and a professor of New Testament in the Baptist Seminary, Cali, Colombia, became a field representative for Spanish South America. By January 1970 there were 345 missionaries in the eight countries Smith served. This forty-three year old missionary's ministry was brought to a halt by his sudden death on 25 March 1970. Upon the occasion of his death, Frank Means, secretary for South America, wrote: ". . . the Board has sustained an irreparable loss. God had given him remarkable gifts, and these were all dedicated to his glory."[45]

For eight years, Hoke Smith had served as a field representative. After his death, his responsibilities were divided between Bryan Brasington and Don Kammerdiener.[46] Evidently the system of field representatives had proved its worth, greatly facilitating the effectiveness of the area secretaries, who were stationed in Richmond.

The Richmond Staff

At first the area secretaries lived in the areas that they served. Rankin, however,

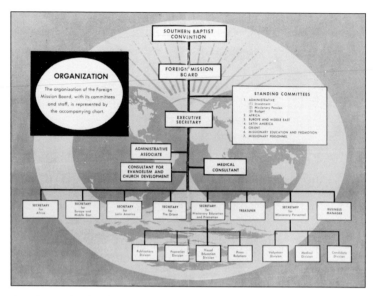

Board organizational structure, 1964

insisted that they move to Richmond and commute to the mission fields as needed for consultation. By 1964, the administrative staff in Richmond consisted of four area secretaries, the secretaries for missionary education and

Ground breaking for new headquarters building at 3806 Monument Avenue, Richmond, April 1957

promotion and for missionary personnel, the treasurer, and the business manager. The executive secretary was assisted by an administrative associate, the consultant for evangelism and church development, and the medical consultant.

As the Richmond staff was enlarged to meet the demands of an ever increasing work load, it became evident that reorganization for purposes of coordination, efficiency, and accountability was imperative. Therefore, the administrative staff was reorganized (1968-1970) into three divisions: Overseas, Mission Support, and Management Services. The Management Services Division was recommended by a consulting firm, the A. M. Pullen Company.

Each division was distinctive and functional. The Overseas Division included the area secretaries and later, the department of missionary orientation. Winston Crawley, secretary for Southeast Asia, became the director of the division. The Mission Support Division initially included the "functional units" (departments) of missionary education and promotion, missionary personnel, public relations, and missionary orientation. Jesse Fletcher, who had served since 1963 as secretary of the department of missionary personnel, became the director of this division. Under his direction the configuration of the division was changed in October 1972 to include: (1) public and press relations; (2) department of missionary personnel; (3) department of missionary education; (4) department of promotion and furlough ministries. The third division, Management Services Division, initially included the departments of the treasurer

Building at Sixth and Franklin, Richmond

Buildings at 2037-2039 Monument Avenue, Richmond

Old First Baptist Church

FMB headquarters building, 3806 Monument Avenue, Richmond

In its 150-year history the Foreign Mission Board has had offices in eight different Richmond locations. Twenty months after it was organized, the board moved into its first home, the basement of the building of First Baptist Church. Twenty-five years and four moves later, the board secured space in downtown Richmond, at Sixth and Franklin; that was 1935. The property at 2037 (later 2037-2039) Monument Avenue was purchased in 1943 and used as is headquarters until 1959, when the present building at 3806 Monument Avenue was occupied.

and business manager and "a unit for the work of the non–administrative staff." Later, an employment office was added. Rogers M. Smith, served as the acting director of this division until Sidney C. Reber, associate missionary serving in Singapore since 1962, became its first director in 1969.

Parallel to the divisions, other staff personnel working closely with the division directors but not within their divisions were known as "consultants." Since the days of Maddry, a medical consultant had become very closely related to the board, especially in relation to the appointment process. Dr. Franklin T. Fowler, a medical missionary to Paraguay and Mexico from 1947, joined the staff as medical consultant in 1961. By 1972, five other consultants had been added to the staff: Joseph B. Underwood, consultant for evangelism and church development; Claude Rhea, consultant in church music; Eugene Grubbs, consultant for Laymen Overseas and Relief Ministries; Richard Styles, public relations consultant; and, Truman Smith, consultant for missionary family life. Most of the consultants were more closely related to the work of the Overseas Division than to other divisions.

During the decade in which the reorganization of the Richmond staff was in progress, there was a realignment of countries with the convention's mission boards. The Branch Committee of the Southern Baptist Convention (1959) recommended the transfer of Hawaii from the Foreign Mission Board to the Home Mission Board and the transfer of Panama and Cuba from the Home Mission Board to the Foreign Mission Board. The realignment of these countries with the two boards was not finalized until the 1970s.[47] Also, Pakistan, Bangladesh (1971) and India were added to the area of Europe and the Middle East.

New Tracks in Missionary Service

Until the 1960s, the Foreign Mission Board had given little thought to short term missionary service. Although there had

Fletcher, right, convenes Missionary Personnel staff, 1965, from left: Louis R. Cobbs, Edna Frances Dawkins, Truman Smith, R. Keith Parks and William W. Marshall.

been preaching missions on the part of state-side pastors and evangelists, no formal programs designed to supplement the work of the career missionary had been devised. With the coming of Jesse Fletcher as associate secretary of the missionary personnel department, this was destined to change.

The twenty-nine-year-old Fletcher had just been refused appointment for missionary service (because of his wife's diabetes) when he was asked to join the administrative staff of the board. At the time, he held the John Town's Chair as professor of the Bible at the University of Texas. A native of San Antonio, Texas, Fletcher was a graduate of Texas Agriculture and Mechanics College (now university) and Southwestern Seminary with both the B.D. and Th.D. degrees. He did further study at the Chaplains' school at Fort Slocum, New York and the University of Richmond. When Elmer West resigned in 1963, Fletcher succeeded him as secretary of the missionary personnel department.

The Missionary Associate Track

Shortly after becoming an associate secretary of the missionary personnel department, Fletcher became involved in developing the board's first new non-career track of missionary service, the missionary associate program. The program was designed for those over the age of thirty-five who felt led "to bear witness overseas" but who could not be appointed as career missionaries, due to age or educational background. The associate was to be "employed" rather than appointed for one term of three to five years, with the possibility of one additional term in exceptional cases. This category of missionary service was expected to utilize persons of specific skills or experience "to fill certain needs" as requested by the missions that would not require the use of another language.[48]

The new Missionary Associate Program was adopted by the board upon the recommendation of Elmer West in its October meeting in 1961. The first missionary associate, Miss Audrey Dyer, a graduate nurse from Minnesota, was employed in December 1961 to serve in the Ire Baptist Welfare Center, Nigeria.[49] In a matter of months there were twelve missionary associates employed by the board and thereafter the number increased rapidly.

The Missionary Journeyman Track

During his years on the staff, Fletcher had become highly regarded by Cauthen. In fact, he was to Cauthen what Elmer West had been to Rankin. When Fletcher was asked to become secretary of the missionary personnel department, he accepted with the understanding that Cauthen would permit him to launch a two year missionary service program for college graduates. Fletcher recalled the conversation. "I said, 'Dr. Cauthen, I'll do it if you will let me have this short term program for young college graduates.'" Cauthen agreed and the Missionary Journeyman Program was born.[50]

At the same board meeting in which the journeyman program was presented, Louis R. Cobbs was invited to join the staff. Fletcher recalled that in the summer of 1964 he and the personnel team of Truman Smith, William Marshall, Samuel DeBord, and Louis Cobbs designed the program. An orientation program of eight weeks was conducted at Westhampton College for the forty-six journeymen who were set apart for mission service at Richmond's First Baptist Church on 10 August 1965. Fletcher was elated. He paid special tribute to Cobbs' role in the process.

There is no way for me to describe adequately my appreciation for the dedication, ingenious organizational abilities, and contagious zeal that Mr. Cobbs has brought to his task. We would want to share any such plaudits with Dr. W. F. Howard, . . . who was granted leave this summer to direct the first Journeyman Training Program.[51]

By April 1967, the continuation of the Journeyman Program was assured as reports from the field reflected not only the career missionaries' acceptance of but also their appreciation for the help of these dedicated and gifted young people. Subsequently, many journeymen from this first contingent were to return later to serve as career missionaries. This has continued to be the case through the years.

The two new missionary tracks accounted for 42 percent of the missionaries sent out by the board in 1969. The department of missionary personnel gave the following breakdown of figures:

> *During the year a record 261 new missionaries reinforced and expanded the efforts of Baptists in 71 foreign fields. This group included 139 career missionaries, 49 missionary associates, 62 missionary journeymen, 1 special project nurse, and 10 reappointments. (Four more of these had a record of prior service overseas in one of the auxiliary program[s].)*[52]

Extended Orientation

In 1954, the department of missionary personnel under the leadership of Elmer West began a period of orientation for new missionaries. It lasted no more than a week and at times included furloughing missionaries as well as new appointees. Prior to the fall of 1967, these sessions were generally held in Richmond. "Beginning in September 1967," Fletcher announced, "all missionaries will complete sixteen weeks of specialized orientation prior to departure for their fields of service."[53] The new orientation program included an introduction to linguistics, customs, culture, history, and the environment of the various countries involved and practical matters such as personal health, mechanics, and bookkeeping.

The first year of the extended orientation was held at Ridgecrest. David Lockard, missionary to Rhodesia (Zimbabwe), was invited to become an associate secretary in the department of missionary personnel to direct the new program. The following year, the program was shortened to fourteen weeks and moved to Callaway Gardens, at a considerable savings to the board but not without incurring the displeasure of the Sunday School Board. Fletcher said: "Bo Callaway made me a deal that cut our cost in half. And Sullivan wrote me and said, 'Why are you doing this? This belongs at Ridgecrest.' And I said, 'I'm doing it because it has to do with mission dollars.' And Cauthen backed me, but it was a sticky wicket."[54] For other reasons, this move proved beneficial for the newly appointed missionaries. In 1969 Fletcher reported, "Living in cottages has given the families needed privacy and comfort. The location has also been better for travel arrangements and weather conditions."[55]

In 1970, missionary orientation was transferred from the mission support division to the overseas division. In setting up the orientation program, Winston Crawley, director of the overseas division had been a member of the orientation council in order to ensure that the program was field related. In speaking about the recommendation of the Committee on Missionary Personnel regarding the transfer, Fletcher observed,

> *After nearly 3½ years in this new program, the reasons for maintaining the orientation in the Mission Support Division from experi-*

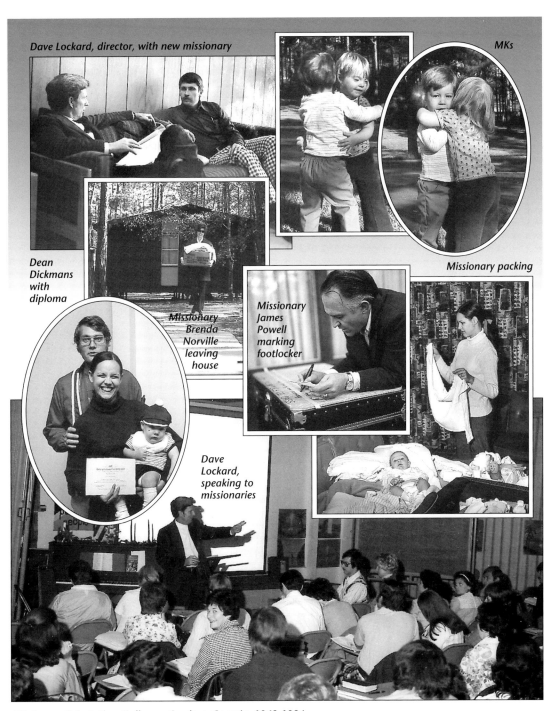

Dave Lockard, director, with new missionary

MKs

Dean Dickmans with diploma

Missionary packing

Missionary Brenda Norville leaving house

Missionary James Powell marking footlocker

Dave Lockard, speaking to missionaries

Missionary Orientation, Callaway Gardens, Georgia, 1968-1984

ence and transition are no longer critical, and the need to identify further Missionary Orientation with field needs and area administration are as critical as ever.[56]

The recommendation was approved by the board. Fletcher and Cobbs remained members of the orientation council of which Crawley was chairman. Eventually, the orientation program would undergo other changes but basically its course had been set and the needs which called it into being were met.

The Committee of Fifteen

The administration of Baker James Cauthen faced its first major crisis in relation to the report of the Committee of Fifteen. Cauthen had

Cauthen presents plaque of appreciation to Porter Routh, SBC Executive Committee executive, May 1979.

been at the helm of the board for twenty years when the committee brought its report to the convention in 1974. He was nearing his sixty-fifth birthday and thought by some to be ready for retirement. The phenomenal growth of the board's missionary enterprise had not been without its problems. The full and part-time headquarters staff had grown to number about 10 percent of the missionaries on the field. As the complexity of the missionary task called for new approaches and new programs, decisions were made that did not please everyone. What was true of the Foreign Mission Board was true to a lesser degree of the other agencies of the convention as well. It appeared to many leaders of the convention that it was time for a close scrutiny and careful evaluation of

all agencies of the convention.

In February 1970, the Executive Committee of the convention established a Committee of Ten to review assignments of the agencies recommended by the "Branch Committee" of 1958-1959. The review was also to include the Executive Committee itself. The Committee of Ten was charged with reporting as soon as possible its findings regarding possible modification of these assignments.[57] E. W. Price, Jr., a North Carolina pastor, was named chairman, and five laymen were added to the committee, making it the Committee of Fifteen.[58]

The work of the Committee of Fifteen soon involved the administrative staff of the Foreign Mission Board in a flurry of meetings and lively correspondence. A workgroup (subcommittee) of the Committee, chaired by Noble Hurley, a layman from Dallas, Texas, met with twelve members of the board's staff and eight elected board members on 28 March 1973 in order to discuss matters of concern. The purpose of this particular meeting was to give the Foreign Mission Board an opportunity to respond to questions that had been raised about certain aspects of its operations.[59]

One of the issues raised regarded mission strategy. Fortunately, the Foreign Mission Board was continually involved in a critical evaluation of its strategy in various areas of the world. In 1968, the board had asked six missionaries to make a study of the "factors affecting the growth and development of Baptist churches in Latin America." The committee brought its report to the board in October 1972. During the study the six missionaries spent thirty-two man-months of on-the-field research, processed 1,198 questionnaires and interviewed 1,222 persons. Copies of the report were provided to members of the Committee of Fifteen.[60] It gave them information that they did not know existed but did not address all their concerns. It did, however, demonstrate the fact that the board could be self-critical and did not lack the initiative to take remedial action when necessary.

After two public hearings and input from numerous individuals, the Executive Committee brought the first recommendations of the Committee of Fifteen to the convention meeting in Philadelphia in June 1972. These recommendations did not relate directly to the Foreign Mission Board. The ten recommendations relative to the Foreign Mission Board were released to the Baptist Press on 4 January 1974. Six days later the article brought an irate reaction from the board in the form of a letter from Jesse Fletcher addressed to "Dr. W. C. Fields, Assistant to the Executive Secretary and Director of Public Relations." Porter Routh, executive secretary and Albert McClellan, associate executive secretary were also included in the salutation. Fletcher wrote on 10 January 1974:

I am writing concerning the approach and terminology used in the BP release of January 4, 1974, entitled "Structure Committee Asks Mission Strategy Revamp."

My concerns can be stated thusly: (1) The story uses terms that imply conclusions not

warranted or asserted by the report of the Committee of Fifteen. (2) The story establishes priority concerns by selection not so designated in the study. (3) The facts do not support the conclusions of the report in many cases, but Baptist Press has reported them without question or effort to determine their accuracy.[61]

In the remainder of the letter, it is evident that Fletcher took exception to both the substance of the article as well as the tone. Fletcher was reacting to the preliminary report as well as to the article. In this he reflected the negative attitude of Cauthen and the administrative staff.[62] Fletcher later wrote in his biography of Cauthen:

When Cauthen and fellow staff members began to read over the recommendations of the committee of Fifteen, they collectively felt misrepresented in the implications of the critique and alarmed at its possible repercussions among the supporting constituency and its potential for the future. . . .

It was obvious to his staff that Cauthen was distressed over the report and frustrated that the subcommittee should recommend that the Convention's Executive Committee assume tasks that he felt had been traditionally entrusted to the agency itself and its elected board.[63]

Upon receiving the report the Administrative Committee of the board met in early February to consider the recommendations of the Committee of Fifteen. Then the full board met in a called meeting on February 12. The recommendation that gave Cauthen and the board the most difficulty was Recommendation 20, which called for an independent committee to review mission strategy, and to propose new strategies. "We think that the development calls for a major review of existent strategy and a bold new development of guidelines for new strategies. These should be developed by a knowledgeable and broad based sympathetic committee as soon as possible."[64]

The board did not object to the study but to the establishment of a committee independent of the board to do the work of the board. The board passed a strongly worded "Resolution" that asked in place of Recommendation 20

> *that the Convention request the Foreign Mission Board to make a major study of foreign mission strategy for the years ahead and in this study secure the widest possible consultation with significant segments of Baptist life, so as to set before the Convention a new challenge of missionary outreach for the final quarter of the 20th Century commensurate with the evident blessings of God upon Southern Baptists and the overwhelming needs throughout the world for the gospel of Christ.*[65]

The rationale for the resolution was given in ten points that provided the agenda for the board's case against Recommendation 20 of the Committee of Fifteen. On 18 February the Executive Committee convened in Nashville with the heads of the agencies to consider the recommendations of the committee. Cauthen and Douglas Hudgins, president of the board, challenged the committee's report point by point.[66] It was clear that Cauthen had come to Nashville to do battle over what he perceived to be an unwarranted attempt on the part of the Executive Committee to usurp the authority of the Foreign Mission Board and said so—pointing out the primary functions of the Executive Committee and the limitations of its authority under the convention's by-laws. Fletcher, who was pre-

sent, reported that after Hudgins had articulated the board's position effectively that Cauthen spoke, which some considered an "overkill." He continued, "There were some strong replies. One Executive Committee member suggested that Cauthen had impugned the motives of the Committee of Fifteen. Cauthen didn't reply but took several other verbal shots to the jaw before the discussion was finished."[67]

Although there is little doubt that Cauthen overreacted, his staunch defense of the board's prerogatives led to Recommendation 20's being changed to call for a "total Convention mission strategy" which would be developed by a committee composed of representatives of the mission boards, the Executive Committee, the Woman's Missionary Union, and the Brotherhood.[68] This committee formulated a substitute "Recommendation No. 20" which called for a committee of twenty-one persons to be appointed by the president of the convention. The new panel was assigned four tasks, the third of which was the most significant. "Involve all appropriate agencies in developing a challenge to Southern Baptists to help meet world needs in the final quarter of this century."[69] This

> *"… Involve all appropriate agencies in developing a challenge to Southern Baptists to meet world needs in the final quarter of this century."*

committee became known as the Missions Challenge Committee which brought its report to the Southern Baptist Convention meeting at Norfolk in 1976.

Warren Hultgren, chairman of the committee, moved that the convention adopt the fifteen recommendations of the committee. They were approved by the messengers. All the recommendations sought to involve every entity of Southern Baptist life in every dimension of missions. Recommendations 1 and 7 were the most significant. Recommendation 1 stated the

primary missions challenge that every person in the world shall have the opportunity to hear the gospel of Christ in the next 25 years, and that in the presentation of this message, the biblical faith be magnified so that all men, women, and children can understand the claim Jesus Christ has on their lives.[70]

Recommendation 7 suggested an expansion of the missionary effort by the use of volunteers such as had already begun. It asked that

the two mission boards be requested to develop as many ways as possible for long and short term involvement of persons in direct mission work in the modern setting, and that in cooperation with other appropriate agencies the boards enlist and guide lay persons with practical and spiritual gifts and callings in all possible phases of mission work, especially such areas as publications, radio and television, medical work, education, etc.[71]

This new missionary thrust made all the pain and agony in the initial battles over "turf" between the agencies worth the effort. The result was "The Bold Mission Thrust." The Committee of Fifteen had called for "bold new plans." Recommendation 13 of the Missions Challenge Committee called for a reaffirmation of the plan "for the years of bold mission, 1977-79. . . ." Others had referred to a "bold mission thrust" and in Kansas City the convention made it official. It still remains for Southern Baptists to make it a reality.

The Ultimate Witness: Meeting Human Need

While the Committee of Fifteen was wrestling with the concept of new mission strategies, the Foreign Mission Board was grappling with how best to bring a gospel witness to the multitudes faced with overwhelming human needs—needs that would not wait. Since World War II both manmade and natural catastrophes have broken out first on one continent and then another.

Coupled with the compounded tragedies of man's inhumanity to man are natural calamities that have left in their wake enormous loss of life and property. In the midst of such developments, missionaries of the board discovered that their attempts to meet the desperate needs of suffering humanity brought an unprecedented response to the gospel. In some cases it was as if the gospel had become credible for the first time because many unbelievers saw in the caregivers an incarnation of the difference Christ makes.

Coordinator for Disaster Relief

For some time the board had been involved in emergency relief efforts. After World War II, the board cooperated with other international relief organizations in an attempt to meet the overwhelming problems of postwar China. In other emergencies the board began to use volunteers to augment the missionary force. To coordinate the use of lay volunteers in various functions, W. Eugene Grubbs was elected consultant for Laymen Overseas and Relief Ministries in 1970. Soon, he was referred to as the coordinator for disaster relief for he found himself increasingly involved in mammoth relief efforts due to a series of natural disasters. In the process, Grubbs enlisted the cooperation of hundreds of laypersons in what became, in effect, a new missionary strategy.

> *"... missionaries have been involved in helping the hungry and the sick, and at the same time offering a message of love, hope and life in Christ."*

Winston Crawley, director of the Overseas Division, pointed out in his report to the March 1975 meeting of the board that the *"medical and benevolent ministries"* were combined for the foreign mission study theme for 1975. Then he proceeded to give the biblical basis for these two programs, which had been assigned to the Foreign Mission Board by the convention. He emphasized "From the very beginning of Southern Baptist mission work, missionaries have been involved in helping the hungry and the sick, and at the same time offering a message of love, hope and life in Christ."[72]

Crawley also reminded the members of the board that the conviction that fueled the medical and benevolent ministries was intrinsic to the nature of the Christian faith. The missionaries in Bangladesh (a new country laid waste by incessant warfare with Pakistan since its independence in 1971) expressed this conviction well. "Please emphasize to our Southern Baptist supporters," they told Crawley, "the importance of our response to the evangelistic opportunities which come to us."[73] They meant that as Christians they could not ignore the appalling, physical suffering that surrounded them, but with the relief efforts, above all else they intended to proclaim Christ to the masses of hurting people. In response, Cauthen announced in the March board meeting that the board after careful study was appropriating $225,194.01 for relief in Bangladesh "where the missionaries are serving."[74]

Tapping the Volunteer Reservoir

The new missionary strategy in the process of being forged in the 1970's included another element, not generally present before—the use of laymen in relief efforts. This became particularly evident in the aftermath of the Hurricane Fifi which swept through Honduras in September 1974, and the devastating earthquake that struck Guatemala on 4 February 1976. While damage and loss of life were much less in Honduras than in Guatemala, the board's response to these natural disasters was similar. In both countries there were missionaries already involved in the work. When disaster struck, the board was alerted and relief funds began to flow. Grubbs, Charles

Bryan, area director, and the missionaries on the field began to assess the damage and organize themselves to meet the emergencies. Because of the proximity of both countries to the United States, a vast reservoir of skilled volunteers was tapped by the board. Medical teams and construction crews were on the ground in relatively brief time. They were either accompanied or followed by evangelistic teams with tents in which services could soon be conducted. Laymen from twelve states participated in the relief and habilitation effort in Honduras. The

Board medical consultant, Franklin Fowler, right, and earthquake relief volunteers set up temporary medical clinic in Bethel Baptist Church, Guatemala City, February 1976.

missionaries reported a year after the hurricane that Honduran Baptists had witnessed the largest number of baptisms in their history. The board was also told that "Baptists are known in Honduras as never before and a spirit of optimism is evident everywhere. A new day has dawned for the Baptist work in Honduras."[75]

In a sense Honduras was a prelude to subsequent Southern Baptist relief efforts of far greater dimensions, the first of which was the February 1976 earthquake in Guatemala. Clark Scanlon, field representative for Middle America, was living in Guatemala City at the time. He wrote a graphic detailed description of the earthquake and the board's response titled *Hope in the Ruins: Love's Response*. It illustrated how the new missionary strategy took shape in the midst of the disaster that snuffed out 23,000 lives and left over a million people homeless.

The tangible results of the cooperative efforts of the missionaries, laymen, and preachers from the United States, Panama, and Mexico were sixteen churches and 350 houses rebuilt and seven hundred and forty converted and baptized by November 1976. Scanlon wrote: "That was the largest number (baptized) in the thirty-year history of the convention. It represented one baptism for every seven Baptists in the country."[76]

The intangible results of the cooperative effort were such that the board's response to the earthquake can never be fully known. But it is evident that without any one of the elements— the herculean efforts of the missionaries and those of almost four hundred laymen, a few women and ministers from twenty state conventions—it wouldn't have come together. Colonel William P. Singleton illustrates the spirit of laymen who somehow found time to give themselves to meet human need in the name of Christ. Singleton carried on his ministry of healing at San Martín, San Andrés, and Chimaltenango under a canopy of colored plastic sheets. Asked how he was able to get off from his heavy round of duties at the Travis Air Force Base hospital in California, the surgeon replied: "By the grace of God. My regular schedule is from daylight to dark with so many schedules to integrate into the day. Yet, I got permission with just two weeks' notice! A miracle."[77] Without the generous support from the Foreign Mission Board of over a half a million dollars, it couldn't have happened. That, too, was due to the grace of God.

The experiences of the missionaries in a series of disasters such as afflicted Nicaragua, Honduras, and Guatemala led to the board's forming medical disaster teams. In October 1979, Harold Hurst, associate to the medical consultant, described the standby units for the board:

> There are four teams of 12-15 men and women who are committed to activation and stand ready to serve under conditions often comparable only to war. Thanks to you, we keep a prepackaged medical clinic that can be airlifted with team members to a scene of a disaster. This clinic is equipped to provide basic medical attention to approximately 5,000 per day and food for the team for 4-5 days. But we move on, knowing that Southern Baptists will respond and additional support will be forthcoming by the time the self-containment is exhausted. This proved to be true, and additional medical supplies and food for distribution were arriving in only two days.[78]

The Cauthens speak to Inez Tiggle who also retired in 1979.

When Hurricane David struck a crippling blow in the Dominican Republic on 4 September 1979, the team and tons of relief supplies had arrived in Bani, the hardest hit city, in three days. Hurst described the effort in the city of 75,000 to 80,000 people, 90 percent of which was destroyed.

> In spite of curfews, no gas, flooded rivers, and washed-out roads, our missionaries did a fabulous job keeping the supply line of food and medicine open, working almost around the clock in an effort that will long be remembered in [the] Dominican Republic. Baptists are a caring people.[79]

Cauthen Retires

At the October meeting of the board, twenty-six years since his election as executive secretary of the Foreign Mission Board Baker James Cauthen announced his intention to retire.

> My 70th birthday comes on December 20, 1979. It is evident, therefore, that my service must come to an end with the Foreign Mission Board at the close of that year.

> It seems the part of wisdom that we make provision at this meeting of the board for the election of a new executive director.

At the meeting of our Administrative Committee last evening I read to them the following statement: "In view of the fact that the executive director will reach in December 1979 the maximum age for service with the Foreign Mission Board as defined by our retirement policy, it seems the part of wisdom to set up at this meeting procedures for electing a new executive director to take responsibility by January 1, 1980."

Cauthen then made explicit suggestions regarding the appointment of a search committee to seek his successor which were adopted by the board.[80]

The board accepted the suggestions and referred the matter to the Administrative Committee, which after discussion and prayer voted to ask the president of the board, in consultation with the two vice presidents, to name the members of the Search Committee and bring a report before the end of the October meeting, if possible. After a time of prayer and worship with the Cauthens, the Administrative Committee presented to the board on 11 October the names of the members of the Search Committee. M. Hunter Riggins, an able layman and former president of the board, was appointed chairman. Four women and two pastors, both of whom were former missionaries, helped to give the committee balance and a depth of experience not always present in such committees.[81] Thus preparation was made for an orderly transition of the leadership of the board.

Cauthen, who had always been slender but healthy, had undergone major surgery in 1976, suffered a heart attack in 1977 and a siege of shingles in 1978. But he refused to stay down. With sheer willpower and characteristic intensity, he continued to lay upon the consciences of young men and women the call of God to Foreign Missions. He recognized that the world had not stood still since his announced retirement, so neither would he. Some wondered why he had not retired at sixty-five. Jesse Fletcher, who knew Cauthen as few people did, believes it was the conflict over the report of the Committee of Fifteen that compelled him to stay on to see the work of the Missions Challenge Committee through to a successful completion. Although his age had caught up with him, the "Bold Mission Thrust" was launched and he could rest assured that his strenuous efforts to keep the Southern Baptist missionary Advance alive had not been in vain.

In Retrospect

By any measure, Cauthen's twenty-six year tenure as executive secretary[82] constituted a remarkable era of missionary advance. Growth from 908 missionaries in thirty-three countries in 1953 to 2,981 in ninety-four countries in 1979 was a phenomenal expansion unparalleled in the twentieth century. There was also a remarkable increase in volunteer involvement, almost non-existent in 1953 to 3,793 in 1979. Total receipts of the board had risen from $16,255,774.24 in 1954 to $70,194,238 in 1979.

It is virtually impossible to state in a few paragraphs the changes in the organization of the board that took place during the Cauthen years. The three areas in which the world was divided for administrative purposes became seven. This development in turn made necessary the organization of the staff into divisions with the additional employment of consultants. The move of the headquarters building and its subsequent enlargement became a necessary corollary to the enlarged staff. The development of an efficient disaster response team headed by board personnel but staffed largely by volunteers made possible one of the most effective evangelistic witnesses in the board's history.

Board chairman Patterson presents plaques of appreciation to the Cauthens during December 1979 meeting.

Tributes showered upon Cauthen at his retirement could easily fill a chapter in this book. Albert McClellan summarized Cauthen's contributions in twelve points now recorded in the Minutes of the Foreign Mission Board.[83] He closed by saying:

> Dr. Cauthen, the first time I heard you speak was at Southwestern Seminary after you returned from Richmond where you had been appointed to go to China as a missionary. That was in April, 1939. The last time I heard you was in Richmond on October 10. I closed my eyes and the forty years fell away. You were the same man with the same enthusiasm, the same conviction, the same purpose, the same fire and the same spirit. If I had not known the difference, I would have thought that it was still the young man speaking. May it always be so.[84]

Those who knew Cauthen well, recognized that he was a strong-willed and tough-minded man with a tender heart. Often after a brusque response to a suggestion or recommendation, he would rethink the issues raised and alter his position. Such was his initial response to the recommendation of an independent advisory committee to work with the Foreign Mission Board in formulating mission strategy. Although rebuffed, the Committee of Fifteen got what it wanted in the Challenge Committee which Cauthen himself was so instrumental in developing. Cauthen prayed it through. Although he was not particularly concerned with developing an overall mission strategy for the board, he came up with an acceptable solution to virtually all parties involved. Through such efforts Southern Baptists became more aware of a world without Christ and of their responsibility for making him known than ever before.

No greater tribute could have been paid Cauthen than that of Keith Parks, his successor, when he declared in his first report to the convention of his intention to walk in Cauthen's footsteps, accepting Cauthen's legacy as his own.

An event of notable significance in 1979 was the retirement of Baker James Cauthen as executive director. His effective 26-year leadership and dynamic proclaiming of foreign missions have challenged and inspired Southern Baptists. His contribution is beyond human definition because it originated from other than a human source. His prayerful, Bible-saturated, single-minded devotion to Christ and his world mission have been used of God to lead this denomination to a remarkable world involvement. Although his physical presence at the Foreign Mission Board will be missed, his influence will continue to be felt. The basic philosophy and primary purpose that Baker James Cauthen declared with such force will remain the operating principles of this agency. The pattern he followed in adapting to changing circumstances will be expanding in light of present realities.[85]

At the last board meeting that Cauthen addressed as executive director, he recognized William O'Brien, secretary for Denominational Coordination and presented him with his fifteen year service pin. Cauthen commended Bill "for his many invaluable contributions" to the work of the board. He then called Inez Tuggle to the front of the auditorium and expressed his deep appreciation for her twenty-seven years of faithful service to the board and to him as his personal secretary. In her brief response, Miss Tuggle said: "And what a great privilege it has been for me to have worked twenty-seven years for the most Christ-like person I have ever known, and for the influence he has had upon my life."[86]

John W. Patterson presented to both of the Cauthens plaques of appreciation individually on behalf of the board. It was fitting that Eloise Cauthen should be so honored. She had always remained in the background, content to share anonymously in her husband's ministry. Although seen but seldom heard, one can never understand Baker James Cauthen or his achievements apart from Eloise Glass Cauthen. Her deep and abiding faith in God and commitment to her husband and his work comprised the indispensable support so necessary for his ministry.

ENDNOTES

1. George William Greene, "Out Beyond," *The Commission*, September, 1953, 31.

2. *Religious Herald*, 16 July 1953, 10.

3. *The Commission*, October 1953, 18.

4. Minutes, FMB, 1953, 91.

5. Jesse C. Fletcher, *Baker James Cauthen, A Man for All Nations* (Nashville: Broadman Press, 1977), 227.

6. Minutes, FMB, 14 October 1953, unnumbered page.

7. Fletcher, *Baker James Cauthen*, 14.

8. Cited in ibid., 40.

9. Quoted in Frank K. Means, "Meet the New Secretary," *The Commission*, January 1954, 3.

10. Jesse Fletcher, "Memorial Service in Memory of Baker James Cauthen," Southwestern Baptist Theological Seminary, 17 April 1985, Audio Tape.

11. Eloise (Mrs. Baker James) Cauthen, Interview by Ken Lawson, Mill Valley, California, 28 February 1983. This story was repeated in a taped interview of Mrs. Cauthen by the author, Richmond, Virginia, June 1991.

12. Fletcher, *Baker James Cauthen*, 171.

13. Cited in ibid., 172.

14. Minutes, FMB, 9 April 1946, 64.

15. Ibid.

16. Minutes, FMB, 9 July 1952, 62.

17. Ibid.

18. Minutes, FMB, 16 April 1955, 53.

19. *Annual*, SBC, 1955, 127.

20. Minutes, FMB, 12 October 1954, 226.

21. *The Commission*, June 1954, 17.

22. Fletcher, *Baker James Cauthen*, 230.

23. Jennifer Hall, "Means Contract Lasted 30 Years," *Foreign Mission News,* 22 November 1977, 28.

24. Minutes, FMB, 11, 12 October 1955, 107.

25. Ibid.

26. Minutes, FMB, 12 January 1956, 161.

27. Ralph T. Bowlin, "His Big Heart Circles Central Africa," *The Commission,* January 1958, 6.

28. George W. Sadler, "We Keep Going," *The Commission,* January 1958, 30.

29. Henrietta Ellwanger, "My Father—As I See Him," *The Commission,* January 1958, 3.

30. Quoted in Ruth Fowler, "A Bond of Love," *The Commission,* December 1976, 20.

31. Fowler, "A Bond of Love," *The Commission,* 1976, 20.

32. The address of Dr. B. J. Cauthen to the Southern Baptist Convention meeting in St. Louis, Missouri, 2-5 June 1954. Cited in Baker J. Cauthen and Frank K. Means, *Advance to Bold Mission Thrust* (Richmond: Foreign Mission Board, Southern Baptist Convention, 1981), 62.

33. Ibid., 62, 63.

34. Baker James Cauthen, "Aroused to Action," *The Commission,* June 1956, 4, 5.

35. The "period of violence" in Colombia against Evangelicals reached a climax in 1956. According to the Committee on Cooperation in Latin America of the National Council of Churches, Evangelicals in Colombia have suffered the following reverses since 1948: 46 church buildings destroyed by fire or dynamite, 75 believers killed because of their religious faith, and more than 200 schools closed by the government. During the month of April 1956 thirty Evangelical churches were reported to have been closed and seven pastors imprisoned. Churches closed included five Mennonite, four Four-Square, ten Evangelical Alliance, seven Inter-American, two Lutheran, and two Baptist in the Amazonas Department. (Minutes, FMB, 14 June 1956, 4.)

36. Minutes, FMB, 9 November 1956, 34.

37. Minutes, FMB, 9 February 1956, 173.

38. *Annual,* SBC, 1964, 121, reported 1,803 missionaries in fifty-three countries. In his address, "By My Spirit," Cauthen updated the statistics (p. 5 of the manuscript copy of the address, Audio-Visual Department, Office of Communications, Foreign Mission Board, 1964.)

39. *The Commission,* June 1964, 29.

40. "By My Spirit," Address by Baker J. Cauthen to the Southern Baptist Convention in Atlantic City, 1964. Typescript, 5, Department of Audiovisuals, Office of Communications, Foreign Mission Board, 1964.

41. Numerous books on the controversy that has divided the Southern Baptist Convention into two, almost equally divided, factions have appeared in the last five years. The most recent is Grady C. Cothen, *What Happened to the Southern Baptist Convention?* (Macon, Ga.: Smyth and Helwys Publishing, 1993). See page 68 ff for a discussion of the early issues.

42. "By My Spirit," 8.

43. Ibid.

44. The Triennial Convention became the most frequent designation of the General Missionary Convention of the Baptist Denomination in the United States for Foreign Missions.

45. Minutes, FMB, 13-15 April 1970, 89.

46. Minutes, FMB, 11 March 1971, 138.

47. Cuba did not become the responsibility of the Foreign Mission Board until much later due to the political situation in that country.

48. *The Commission,* November 1961, 29.

49. *The Commission,* January 1962, 27.

50. Dr. Jesse Conrad Fletcher, Interview by author, 21 April 1993, Fort Worth, Texas.

51. Minutes, FMB, 18 August 1965, 34.

52. Minutes, FMB, April 1970, 86.

53. Minutes, FMB, 10 April 1967, 138.

54. Fletcher, Interview, 11.

55. Minutes, FMB, 8 October 1969, 88.

56. Minutes, FMB, 13 October 1970, 186.

57. Albert McClellan, *The Executive Committee of the Southern Baptist Convention, 1917-1984* (Nashville: Broadman Press, 1985), 240.

58. The Committee members were: E. W. Price, Jr. (NC), chairman; Richard L. T. Beale, III (VA); Doyle E. Carlton, Jr. (FL); Owen Cooper (MS); Noble Hurley (TX); J. Lamar Jackson (AL); Norvell G. Jones (MO); John G. McCall (MS); James L. Monroe (FL); H. Franklin Paschall (TN); Guy Rutland, III (GA); Stewart B. Simms (SC); J. Robert Smith (GA); Rheubin L. South (AR); and T. Cooper Walton (MS). Committee of Fifteen Records, AR. 627-2.

59. Minutes of Foreign Mission Board Workgroup of the Committee of Fifteen, Richmond, Virginia, 23 March 1973.

60. Minutes, FMB, 9-11 October 1972, 128-33. The Report of the Latin America Depth Study Committee was brought to a close with the following statement:

The Latin American Depth Study Committee, created in 1968 by Board action, has now completed its work. At the outset, neither the Board nor the Committee realized what a tremendous job had been assigned to them. What began as a pleasant task soon became an overwhelming assignment requiring painstaking, diligent, mind-stretching, compassionate, dedicated, sacrificial service.

The Committee members chosen were:

A. Clark Scanlon, Middle America, chairman

James P. Kirk, Brazil, secretary

William W. Graves, Caribbean, treasurer

Donald R. Kammerdiener, South Field, Spanish South America

Alan P. Neely, Colombia

Vance O. Vernon, Brazil (p. 133)

61. Jesse C. Fletcher, to W. C. Fields, Porter Routh, Albert McClellan and Executive Committee, SBC, January 10, 1974, 1.

62. Fletcher, Interview.

63. Fletcher, *Baker James Cauthen*, 265.

64. *The Report of the Study Committee of Fifteen to the Executive Committee of the Southern Baptist Convention* (Nashville: The Executive Committee of the Southern Baptist Convention, 1974), 107.

65. Resolution Adopted by the Foreign Mission Board, SBC, 12 February, 1974, 1.

66. In the records of the Executive Committee that are located in the Library and Archives of the Historical Commission is a document entitled "Comments Regarding Areas of Concern as Reported by the 'Committee of 15.'" The section dealing with the Foreign Mission Board contains the board's corrections of the perceived errors of the Committee of Fifteen and clarifications regarding the board's position.

67. Fletcher, *Baker James Cauthen*, 268.

68. Recommendation 20, as amended read:

We ask Dr. E. W. Price, Jr., Chairman of the Committee of Fifteen, Owen Cooper and Stewart B. Simms, representing the Executive Committee, Dr. Baker James Cauthen, executive secretary of the Foreign Mission Board, Dr. Douglas Hudgins, chairman of the Foreign Mission Board, Dr. Arthur Rutledge, executive director of the Home Mission Board, Dr. Jack Lowndes, president of the Home Mission Board, Dr. Glendon McCullough, executive director of the Brotherhood Commission, and Miss Alma Hunt, executive secretary of Woman's Missionary Union, to work out the language of a proposal, to be presented to the pre-convention meeting of the Executive Committee in Dallas, which will challenge Southern Baptists in the final quarter of this century in bold mission advance, encompassing the concerns of the recommendation on Mission Strategy Study and yet recognizing the polity of Southern Baptist Convention relationships.

(The Report of The Study Committee of Fifteen to the Executive Committee of the Southern Baptist Convention, 107.)

69. Minutes, FMB, 14 May 1974, 244.

70. *Annual,* SBC, 1976, 54.

71. Ibid.

72. Minutes, FMB, 11 March 1975, 33.

73. Ibid.

74. Ibid., 22.

75. Minutes, FMB, 8 April 1975, 87.

76. Clark Scanlon, *Hope in the Ruins: Love's Response to Disaster* (Nashville: Broadman Press, 1978), 97.

77. Quoted in ibid., 111.

78. Minutes, FMB, 9-11 October 1979, unnumbered page.

79. Ibid., unnumbered page.

80. Minutes, FMB, 9-11 October 1978, 172.

81. Members of the search committee were as follows: M. Hunter Riggins, Chairman, Travis S. Berry, Charles T. Carter, Mrs. J. E. Collette, John W. Goodwin, Mrs. L. G. Hicks, Jr., Joe Neil McKeever, Mrs. Ray Mullendore, Trevis Otey, John W. Patterson, Mrs. James A. Ponder, James F. Sawyer, Lonnie H. Shull, Jr., Raymond L. Spence, Jr., and Joe E. Trull. Ibid.

82. The term Executive Director replaced Executive Secretary in 1976.

83. Minutes, FMB, 11 December 1979, 109.

84. Ibid.

85. *Annual,* SBC, 1980, 85.

86. Minutes, FMB, 11 December 1979, 109.

PART V

Bold
Mission
Thrust
1976-1992

1967-1992

**Bold
Mission
Thrust**

WORLD HISTORY EVENTS

1967: Continuing
Arab conflict with Israel

1973: Supreme Court
decision: Roe vs. Wade

1975:
Rise of th
New
Religous
and
Political
Right

76

1976: Bicent
of nation's bi

1960

1970

BAPTIST MISSIONARY MOVEMENT

**BOLD
MISSION
THRUST**
Stage 1
(1979-1982)

1976: Bold
Mission Thrust

1980: Keith Parks
(1980-1992), executi
director/president

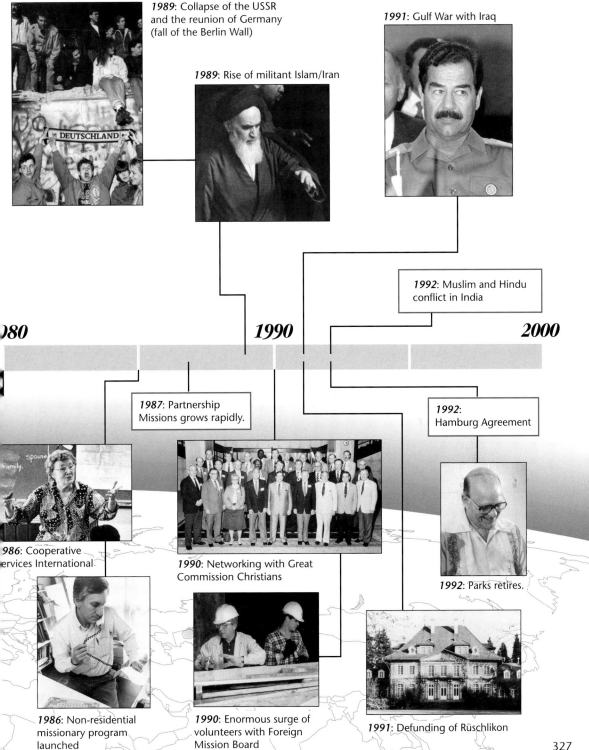

1989: Collapse of the USSR and the reunion of Germany (fall of the Berlin Wall)

1989: Rise of militant Islam/Iran

1991: Gulf War with Iraq

1992: Muslim and Hindu conflict in India

)80

1990

2000

1987: Partnership Missions grows rapidly.

1992: Hamburg Agreement

986: Cooperative ervices International

1990: Networking with Great Commission Christians

1992: Parks retires.

1986: Non-residential missionary program launched

1990: Enormous surge of volunteers with Foreign Mission Board

1991: Defunding of Rüschlikon

327

Into *All* the World

R. Keith Parks

Just as Cauthen made the Advance Program his own, the new president Keith Parks, made the Bold Mission Thrust his marching orders. Parks's emphasis upon evangelism that results in churches became the cornerstone of his mission philosophy which he set forth in seven principles. His creative touch left no part of the board's work untouched. He established the Global Strategy Group as a mission "think tank" to look at the missionary task from the perspective of the needs of the whole world.

The night the Berlin wall came down symbolized an end and a beginning—the end of a divided Berlin and the beginning of a reunited Germany. As the Trabants (little East German-built cars) poured into the Kurfürstendamm (West Berlin's wide boulevard) on the night of 9 November 1989, the sights and sounds of a joyous celebration filled the streets as East and West Berliners heard the news that Checkpoint Charlie had just gone out of business. When additional openings appeared in the wall, jubilant thousands joined in the joyful process of dismantling the de-

Historic November weekend in 1989 heralds the reunited Berlin.

spised barrier that had divided the city for twenty-eight years. Engaging in understandable euphoric exaggeration, the next morning the Berliner Zeitung declared in bold headlines: THE WALL IS GONE—BERLIN IS BERLIN AGAIN.

But more than a wall came down that November night. The Cold War, which began to thaw under the reformist leadership of the Soviet premier, Mikhail Gorbachev, all but melted away when Egon Krenz, the new East German leader, belatedly caught up with the reform movement and ordered the borders opened to free access. His dramatic act caught everyone, even the Soviets and the Germans, by surprise. It was an attempt to salvage the rapidly deteriorating East German society from total collapse.

The destruction of the wall was followed by a series of surprising developments in Europe's Communist nations. The attempted coup in the Soviet Union saw people stop with their own bodies tanks that could easily have crushed them; it also saw the rise to power of another reformer, Boris Yeltsin, the mayor of Moscow.

Scott Sullivan stated the obvious when he wrote in *Newsweek:* "The opening of the Berlin wall last Thursday ended an era. The world has entered a period of unexampled promise and danger."[1]

The repercussions of the collapse of the Soviet Union were world-wide. Although China brutally crushed the rising democracy movement at Tiananmen Square, it has remained far more open than was previously the case. The fragmentation of the former USSR was accompanied by the breakup of nations that had been held together by puppet governments in artificial alliances backed by the armed might of the Soviet Union. In the resulting struggles for nationhood, long suppressed religious and ethnic differences have surfaced to tear apart the fabric of society and lay bare both the irrepressible longings and the pervasive depravity of the human heart. By the same token, the events of the 1980s have highlighted in global dimensions the desperate needs, physical and spiritual, of mankind. Perhaps, the hopeless plight of a lost humanity, outside of Christ, has never been more apparent than during the first years of the last decade of the twentieth century. For such a time as this, Bold Mission Thrust was designed.

> *... the events of the 1980s have highlighted in global dimensions the desperate needs, physical and spiritual, of mankind.*

Just as the Advance Program had been the guiding star of Cauthen's administration, Bold Mission Thrust became the inspiration for the global vision of Keith Parks. The parallel does not end here, for as Cauthen helped to design and set in motion the Advance Program, Parks was a part of the administrative team of the Foreign Mission Board that enabled it to develop the new program, "Bold New Thrusts in Foreign Missions, 1976-2000," which was presented to the meeting of the Southern Baptist Convention at Norfolk in 1976.

Parks Succeeds Cauthen

In the March 1979 board meeting, John W. Patterson, newly elected president of the Foreign Mission Board, called for a progress report from the Search Committee responsible for nominating the board's new executive director. M. Hunter Riggins, chairman, then presented to the board a *Profile* that the committee had drawn up as a guide in its task. Altogether, there were eighteen characteristics listed that the Search Committee considered essential. Five of these give insight into the nature of the qualities of leadership the committee had in mind. Under the category of *"Personal Data"* were: "1. Characterized by the highest of Christian integrity," and "7. Theologically in the mainstream of Southern Baptist life with an appreciation of the rationale behind differing doctrinal opinions." A second category, *"Church and Denominational Data,"* delineated four qualities, the first of which read: "Southern Baptist loyalty and knowledge of our distinctive doctrine, polity, and ways of cooperation." The third category *"Qualities and Abilities"* made seven points relative to

R. Keith Parks

Fort Worth Airport]," Fletcher informed the chairman. "I recommend Keith, but I've committed myself to Hardin-Simmons. I think I need to stay here."[3] On 7 August 1979, the committee was ready with its report. Riggins prefaced his motion to recommend Parks by stating, "The conclusion of the Committee was firm, their decision was unanimous, and it was by secret ballot. It was their feeling that God had brought them together in naming Dr. R. Keith Parks." He then proceeded to move that "Dr. R. Keith Parks be elected Executive Director of the Foreign Mission Board, effective January 1, 1980; and that he become Executive Director-Elect, as of September 3, 1979."[4] Subsequently on 1 January 1980 R. Keith Parks became executive director of the Foreign Mission Board. The following May his title was changed from executive director to president.

Preparation for a World-wide Ministry

No chief executive officer of the Foreign Mission Board before Parks had brought to his task the variety of administrative experiences with the board that were his. From sparsely populated West Texas, Parks took the deep convictions of his faith to the teeming millions (115,000,000 in 1969) on the islands of Indonesia. After fourteen years of missionary service in a number of different assignments, he joined the administrative staff in Richmond upon becoming secretary of Southeast Asia in 1968. Seven years later he succeeded Jesse Fletcher as the director of the Mission Support Division, and after four years in this position, he assumed the responsibilities of executive director of the board on 1 January 1980.

the nominee's ability, two of which stand out. "1. An able administrator who can embrace change, work well with others, and has strong abilities in financial management," and "5. Enthusiastic motivator who is capable of generating loyalty, dedication, and responsiveness from the staff, missionaries and the Board members."[2]

Six months later, the Search Committee was ready with its report. For almost a year the members of the committee had been engaged in the selection process. Eventually, only four persons were asked to meet with the committee for personal interviews. Of the final four, Jesse Fletcher, who had only a short time before accepted the presidency of Hardin-Simmons University, called Hunter Riggins to inform him of his decision to withdraw his name from consideration. "I'm not coming [for the interview at the Dallas-

The preparation of Keith Parks for his world wide ministry began long before he became a missionary. On 23 October 1927, he was born on the high plains of the Texas Panhandle in the town of Memphis, sixty-nine miles southeast of Amarillo. His family, which included two older sisters and a younger brother, attended the First Baptist Church in Memphis. It was here that God touched his heart and the nine year old boy was converted and baptized. Next year his family moved to a farm near Gravelly, Arkansas. Gravelly had only one church and that was a quarter-time Methodist congregation served by a college student. Keith attended a consolidated school twelve miles distant by riding in the back of a truck that served as a school bus. During these years, his parents were largely responsible for his Christian nurture, particularly his godly mother who was known as a "prayer warrior."

Before he entered the eleventh grade, Keith's family moved to Danville, Arkansas. In Danville, the pastor of the Baptist church was a young man by the name of Bill Kirsch. During the year or so under his influence, Keith's interest and participation in the church began to quicken. His father, a cattleman, moved his family to Denton, Texas, where the land held great promise for raising cattle. Keith's senior year found him in the Denton high school and a member of the First Baptist Church. Martha Jean Anderson, who was youth director of the church and part time Baptist Student Union secretary at North Texas State Teachers' College (now University of North Texas) caused Keith to think seriously for the first time about the will of God for his life. One day she probed his conscience by asking: "You know that the Lord has called you to special work, don't you?"

After high school, Keith entered North Texas in Denton. The college years were marked by expanding horizons and by spiritual and intellectual growth. At North Texas, he majored in speech and with David Cotton, a teammate, won the national collegiate debating championship for the university in 1948. That year he graduated with his B.A. degree. The Baptist Student Union became the means by which Keith was brought into a deeper relationship with God. Later, Bill O'Brien, his close personal friend and missionary colleague, described it.

One particular experience stands out. In meditation and prayer Keith describes the impression that God was asking him if he would be willing to do whatever God was asking. His initial response was, "Tell me what it is." Only after much soul-searching he realized that the only answer he could give to God's question was "Yes." Only with his willingness to do whatever God was asking would God reveal what it was that Keith should do. It was soon evident that some form of vocational Christian ministry was the framework of the calling.[5]

Keith was president of the Texas Baptist Student Union in 1947-1948. He was one of four students selected for summer missions on the San Andrés Island in the Caribbean. During that summer he began to think for the first time about the possibility of overseas missionary service, but a definite call did not come until his third year in the seminary. Parks recalled that Jack MacGorman, professor of New Testament at Southwestern, was speaking when he became convinced that it was God's will for him to serve as a missionary somewhere overseas.[6]

After graduation from North Texas, Parks entered Southwestern Baptist Theological Seminary from which he received the bachelor of divinity degree in 1951 and his doctorate in theology in 1955, with a major in systematic theology and minors in Old and New Testaments. The subject of his doctoral dissertation was "A Biblical Evaluation of the Doctrine of Justification in Recent American Baptist Theology: With Special Reference to A. H. Strong, E. Y. Mullins, and W. T. Conner." Both his program of study and his dissertation indicated Parks's strong biblical orientation. His dissertation also revealed that he did not hesitate to examine critically the positions of three highly regarded Baptist theologians on the doctrine of justification in the light of his own understanding of the Bible on the subject.[7] In addition, his studies gave him a solid theological basis for his subsequent life work. Before his Th.D. degree was awarded, Parks served as pastor of a Baptist church at Red Springs, Texas, and for a year was an instructor in Bible at Hardin-Simmons University.

After receiving his B.D., he married Helen Jean Bond whom he had met three or four years earlier at a Texas State Baptist Student Union convention during his tenure as president. While at the seminary, Helen Jean's roommate expressed an interest in Keith but it was Helen Jean who captured his heart. She was the daughter of a professor of English at Hardin-Simmons University. Before receiving her Master of Religious

Four years into his presidency, in 1984, Parks visits friends in Indonesia, including members of Keybayoran Baptist Church in Jakarta.

Education degree from the seminary, she had served as a Baptist Student Union worker in Missouri and Texas, and as youth and music director of the First Baptist Church, Henrietta, Texas. Helen Jean had committed her life to missionary service overseas during her seminary years. The only question that remained was, "Where?" When Keith told her that Indonesia was among the most densely populated countries on earth, that settled it. They decided that they would offer themselves for missionary service in Indonesia.

Blazing New Trails in Indonesia, 1954-1968

Keith and Helen Jean Parks were appointed missionaries to Indonesia in April 1954. Their first assignment was to teach in the Semarang Baptist Seminary on the island of Java. Keith's concern for the multitudes around him to whom he could never hope to present Christ personally compelled him to experiment with new and untried mission strategies.

New Methods of Evangelism

The seminary, which had more students than it could possibly place with churches, provided the means and the Indonesians the laboratory for the innovative experiments. The Indonesians from a variety of ethnic backgrounds reflect the various layers of religion brought to the islands by successive conquests through the centuries. The majority belong to Islam with a sprinkling of the population holding to Buddhism and Hinduism. Christianity was the last of the major religions to infiltrate the island kingdom.[8] Ebbie C. Smith observed that the Muslim faith had provided a thin veneer for the underlying animism of the Javanese in the area where Parks and his students began their new methods of evangelism.[9]

The method was referred to as "Dropping."

On the weekends the students were "dropped" in various locations where there were no churches. All they were to have in their hands was a Bible. They were to experiment in ways that persons could be brought to Christ and churches started with no money and no vast resource of materials. Many different approaches were tried. In some locations invitations to see a movie

about Christ were handed out. For three nights there would be a movie shown, followed by preaching. In other places newspaper ads would appear, followed by students asking if people would like to join a Bible study. Still a third approach was utilized right around the seminary area where people were visited, won to Christ, but no Bible study or church was begun. In this experiment students would return saying people wanted a Bible study. Students began to negotiate with a man who had a vacant building that was then utilized for Bible study to meet the demands of the people asking for it.[10]

After Parks inaugurated the new mission strategy, Smith, who was appointed to Indonesia in April 1960, became responsible for directing the program. He also recalled that Parks was a very effective missionary and the recognized leader among his fellow missionaries.[11] Parks arrived in Indonesia only three years after the first missionaries had transferred there from China. By this time the mission reflected the traditional pattern of mission work as it had been followed in China. He was convinced that the work was too institutionalized and that there would never be enough money to sustain it and to evangelize the masses at the same time. In addition to the innovative approach to starting new churches, the mission under his prodding began to launch out in other directions.

Theological Education by Extension

Ebbie Smith spent his first furlough at Fuller Seminary in order to study with Donald McGavran, the missiologist and church growth specialist, in hopes that he would discover some principles of church growth that could be applied to Indonesia.

He returned to the field convinced of the advantages of theological education by extension over traditional methods. By this time Parks was the director for Southeast Asia but was still very much involved in Indonesia. Upon Ebbie's return to the field, the mission initiated a survey of the churches, pastors, and Baptist leaders regarding every aspect of the mission's work. Bryant Hicks, missionary to the Philippines and Cal Guy, professor of missions at Southwestern were asked to serve as consultants. When the mission met for its annual meeting in 1970 at Tretes, it became a time of soul-searching and spiritual renewal. Parks remembered the meeting as "one of the most moving, spiritual experiences that I've ever had—that I think many of us have ever had."[12]

Tretes became a celebrated event for reasons other than its spiritual blessings. The mission made the radical decision to close the seminary and to conduct theological education through extension centers scattered throughout the country. This, the missionaries reasoned, would make theological education available to laymen and pastors involved in the work in places where growth was taking place. It also avoided the possibility of losing "would be pastors" to the city. The missionaries also determined to give themselves to evangelism and to follow a simpler life-style. Twenty-three years later, Parks summarized the decisions made upon that occasion:

We determined we were going to recommit ourselves to personal evangelism, and a simpler missionary lifestyle. We had bought a lot of colonial-type houses, they were cheap and very reasonable, but it ended up that we

were sort of viewed as the spiritual colonialists, and we said, "We're going to get rid of some of those big houses and live in a simpler lifestyle. We're going to push out where the response is and we're going to start training people." And we decided the only way we could do that was to put a moratorium on the campus theological training, and scatter our faculty, and start training out where the need was, and then as we had a base develop, and a need reemerge to reactivate the central campus. This was never heard by a lot of folks. . . .[13]

The memorandums which Parks sent Cauthen and Crawley never reached them. Therefore, when the reaction occured both in Indonesia and the United States, Parks had some explaining to do. The reports were out that they had "destroyed the seminary, gotten rid of all the missionary houses and were going native." Parks flew directly to Nashville, where Crawley, Cauthen, and others from the board were meeting with the Executive Committee. He explained at length what had transpired in Indonesia. According to Parks, Cauthen's response was not encouraging.

Dr. Cauthen was never enthusiastic about what we had done. He just couldn't bring himself to feel we had done the right thing. He didn't overrule us when I kept telling him we hadn't done away with the seminary—we had dispersed it—but we were coming back. He almost overruled me, but he didn't.[14]

The mission did restore the seminary, but it decided to keep the extension centers as well. Parks attributes the great growth that followed in Indonesia to Theological Education by Extension. "We thought 150 was a large seminary, and it wasn't long until we had 500 in training."[15] There were also some unforeseen benefits from theological education by extension. When the Indonesian government in 1988 refused to renew visas for expatriates, the mission lost a number of missionaries. Subsequently no missionaries could be admitted unless they were engaged in educational work. The extension centers, therefore, provided vocational justification for the missionaries' presence in Indonesia. The program of theological education by extension was also adopted, with gratifying results, by other Southern Baptist missions in Southeast Asia and elsewhere.

For Keith Parks, the fourteen years of missionary experience in Indonesia provided him with the opportunity to test certain missiological principles that subsequently characterized his career as an administrator with the Foreign Mission Board. It was here that he began to develop his conviction that missions should involve primarily evangelism—the kind that results in churches that function within the cultural context of a given society. Since the Southern Baptist work in Indonesia was only three years old, Parks and his colleagues could reshape the missionary effort to conform to a more indigenous approach, almost from the beginning. Parks saw two problems with the older institutionalized pattern.

> *I think we make two mistakes. I think we tend to want to duplicate stateside institutions, and start them relative to what we've been used to here, which means they're foreign for one thing, it also means they are so expensive that we place them years out of reach of the local constituents. So I think on the one hand, we need to keep more simple those initial institutions. The function needs to be done, but it doesn't need to be so elaborately institutionalized.[16]*

While the board sought, certainly since the administration of Theron Rankin, to emphasize the indigenous approach in missionary work, the institutional pattern persisted. It appears that, under Parks's leadership, the board attempted for the first time to apply missiological principles designed to promote indigeny wherever its missionaries were at work. Increasingly the motivational force that made the goal of self-sustaining churches and conventions imperative was the global vision of Keith Parks. He could not see how the board could carry on missions as usual and still have the personnel and finances necessary for sharing the gospel with the unreached peoples of the earth.

Secretary for Southeast Asia, 1968-1975

Parks became secretary for Southeast Asia in June 1968. The concern for a biblically based strategy that had marked his years in Indonesia continued to characterize the thrust of his administration. The missions in his area were all established after the missionaries had been forced out of China. A number of strategy studies were launched in the countries in the area when Parks brought to the board in February 1975 a report titled "Mission Strategy: Southeast Asia Update." It was clear from Parks's report that Vietnam presented the greatest challenge to his own convictions regarding missionary strategy. "In the light of overwhelming human need," he reported, "it was obvious that the Mission had to give itself to a careful evaluation of how we would function in trying to meet that need."[17] As a result of the study, he and the missionaries decided "that the greatest thing we Baptists could do in Vietnam in the face of all the agony and suffering and death and hunger was to concentrate on the development of strong Baptist churches."[18]

Parks illustrated his point by sharing the contents of two letters from missionaries, one in Indonesia and the other in Vietnam. Each letter brought the news of what God was doing when the gospel was preached by missionaries who concentrated on evangelizing and on the forming of churches. This did not mean, he took the pains to explain, that the real human needs of a "warman-

O'Brien, second from right, meets with Communications Committee, April 1987.

gled" people were not being met. To the contrary, with relief and disaster funds from Southern Baptists, the churches in Vietnam had organized a mobile clinic, distributed food and clothing, set up a halfway house for homeless children, and "Christian Love" centers to teach marketable skills. "But the major *programs* of relief and rehabilitation would be determined by the resources and strength of the local Vietnamese Baptists rather than the Foreign Mission Board. . . ."[19] It was clear from this report that conducting missions for Parks was comprehensive, without losing sight of the priority of evangelism.

Director of the Mission Support Division, 1975-1979

In August 1975, Parks succeeded Jesse Fletcher as director of the mission support division. Upon the retirement of Eugene Hill, secretary of the department of missionary education, and the resignation of Samuel DeBord, secretary of the department of promotion and furlough ministries, Parks asked the board for time to study the organization of the division before filling any of the vacant positions.[20] In April 1976, the board approved the reorganization of the missions support division "to include: a *Department of Furlough Ministries, Department of Communications,* and a *Department of Denominational Coordination. . . ."*[21]

The reorganization of the division called for an additional secretary to direct the work of the department of denominational coordination. Parks's choice for this post was William R. (Bill) O'Brien, a Texan, and a graduate of Hardin-Simmons University and Southwestern Seminary with his bachelor and master of church music degrees. O'Brien had served for twelve years as a missionary in Indonesia, teaching music in the seminary and creating radio-television programming for Indonesian Baptists. He was valued by his fellow missionaries quite as much for his innovative ideas as for his musical talents. William W. (Bill) Marshall, a Kentuckian, and a graduate of Georgetown College and Southern Seminary with M.Div. and D. Min. degrees, was asked to serve as secretary of the department of furlough ministries. Previously he had worked in the missionary personnel department and as field secretary in the Middle East. With the election of Tom Hill as secretary of communications, the reorganization of the division of mission support was completed.

Tom and Connie Hill were first appointed to Venezuela but remained in Costa Rica for a number of years to direct the seminary. From 1964, Hill served as an editor with the Spanish Baptist Publishing House in El Paso. When the publishing house was reorganized

Cauthen presents Bible to Parks at January 1980 installation service.

in 1970, he became its administrator. In presenting Hill to the board, Parks said: "His team spirit has been demonstrated through his years as a missionary and in this relationship in El Paso in a very effective way. His leadership in a publication institution remarkably equips him for this specific task that would be his in this organization."[22] With the addition of Tom Hill, Parks had filled out his "team roster." In a further comment regarding the Hills, Parks's sense of humor comes through.

> *I am not sure what complications we will be creating for those involved here in the immediate future or for historians when we seek to replace a Dr. Hill with a Dr. Hill, but I am prepared to run that risk and take great pleasure in introducing to you Dr. and Mrs. Tom Hill at this time.*[23]

The selection of Tom Hill for secretary of the department of communications indicated how Parks wedded principle to function in attempting to find just the right person for a particular responsibility.

> *Early in the process, along with a job description, it was determined that the following five qualifications would assist in an objective way as we sought to seek the Lord's leadership toward a person: A deep commitment to missions, administrative ability, a team spirit, an adequate concept of communications, and an awareness of the Southern Baptist Convention organization. We have reviewed to some degree approximately 50 men and women in seeking a person whom we felt led to recommend.*[24]

The idealism of Keith Parks, and his effectiveness as a missionary and as an administrator could not have failed to impress the members of the search committee, several of whom had worked closely with him for eleven years. Perhaps no one on the board was taken by surprise when the search committee brought its unanimous recommendation that Parks be elected executive director of the Foreign Mission Board.

R. Keith Parks, President, 1980-1992

Monument Heights Baptist Church welcomed the gathering of the Foreign Mission Board, members and staff, the Parks family, and numerous friends for the installation service of R. Keith Parks as executive director of the board at 7:00 P.M. on 7 January 1980. The installation message was delivered by Baker James Cauthen.

In his response, Parks expressed his appreciation for the Baptist heritage, and challenged his audience to grasp the opportunities of the present for the sake of the future. "The richness of our history must be matched by visions and aspirations for the future. And where the past and the future touch, there is the enlightening flashpoint of the ever changing present."[25] Parks predicted that the decade of the 1980s would be "Southern Baptists' greatest decade in global missions." Not unmindful of the cross currents within the convention and of the rising international tensions fed by religious bigotry and intolerance, he expressed his faith in his fellow Southern Baptists. "I am equally convinced that Southern Baptists, if they understand what is at stake and are aware of the opportunities, will allow the Christ who redeems us to spiritually empower us to be his people in this remarkably opportune moment in history."

In the body of his address Parks drove home six points that in a variety of ways would emerge in board policy and programs during his administration. They are mentioned here in the order given with a brief excerpt from each point. I. *Praying* - "If a significant minority of Southern Baptists would give themselves to consistent, earnest, faithful praying, our other needs would be met. It is my pledge to you tonight that I as an individual will open my life to a greater intercessory prayer than ever before." II. *Committing* - "Since we are people whose mission is global missions, every one of us must be committed to whatever segment of the task God calls us." III. *Thinking* - "We as a people called Baptists must give our best thought processes to a strategy for a witness to an entire world." IV. *Giving* - "There are adequate resources to appropriately fund Bold Mission Thrust. Yet, to do so, a remarkable escalation of the

Cooperative Program, the Lottie Moon Offering and other sources of mission dollars must occur quickly." V. *Telling* - "But ultimately and finally, the story of Southern Baptist missions must be told by pastors, WMU leaders, Brotherhood leaders, Sunday School teachers, deacons, lay people, stu-

Parks presents certificates to new missionaries at April 1987 board meeting in Lexington, Kentucky.

dents, youth, by all of us." VI. *Doing* - "The heart of foreign missions is still the telling of the Jesus story and as people accept him as Saviour and Lord, indigenous churches emerge."

Parks brought his message to a conclusion with a ringing affirmation and an earnest appeal. The *affirmation:* "I am convinced that we have been called into the Kingdom for such an hour as this. I believe that the richness of our heritage will enable our future to be richer still." *The appeal:* "It is my prayer that our hearts will be opened wide enough and our spirits adventuresome enough and our wills bold enough that we will not hinder what God is trying to do through us in his world in our generation." He concluded by citing Ephesians 3:11,12 and Paul's benediction in Ephesians 3:20,21.[26]

The term recurring repeatedly throughout Parks's first official address to the board as executive director was "global missions." It was used five times and alluded to many more. It is more inclusive than other terms that he was to use frequently throughout his tenure such as "global evangelism" and the phrase borrowed from Bold Mission Thrust "to present the gospel to everyone in the world by A.D. 2000." Therefore, virtually every action Parks attempted to lead the board to take was in the interest of his concept of global missions. This concept of the whole world was implicit in the title of his column that appeared regularly in *The Commission* titled "World in View" and his program for global missions by the same title published in 1987.

Parks's conviction that God had brought Southern Baptists to the threshold of the last decade of the twentieth century for such a time as this was underlined by the international scene. Resurging religions and the rekindling of ancient racial animosities that had erupted in every part of the world made even more imperative humanity's desperate need of a savior. There was no escaping the turmoil in Iran and India, Israel and Lebanon, South Africa and Cambodia,

Afghanistan and Iraq, inescapable reminders of the hopelessness of the human situation without the transforming power of the gospel of Jesus Christ.

Implementing the Bold Mission Thrust

Capturing the momentum of the vision that had so caught the imagination of Southern Baptists four years earlier, Parks committed himself to its principles and goals with just a hint that its implementation would demand some changes in the board itself. It was in the context of paying tribute to the legacy of Baker James Cauthen in his first report to the convention in 1980 that Parks hinted at changes to come:

> *The basic philosophy and primary purpose that Baker James Cauthen declared with such force will remain the operating principles of this agency. The pattern he followed in adapting to changing circumstances will be expanding in light of present realities.[27]*

From Bold Mission Thrust to the Seven Principles

Two recommendations of the Missions Challenge Committee became so basic to Parks's understanding of the Foreign Mission Board's task as to constitute a mandate for change. They were one and three of the committee's fifteen recommendations. The first recommendation declared the convention's "primary missions challenge that every person in the world shall have the opportunity to hear the gospel of Christ in the next 25 years. . . ." The third recommendation called upon the two Southern Baptist mission boards to:

> *undertake seriously the creative addition of new patterns for work that will help accomplish the objective . . . and that in the development of these patterns, full emphasis be*

placed upon the Bible in the communication of missions, upon research as a fundamental necessity for missions, upon cooperation as a way of magnifying the missions witness of the church, and upon doctrinal integrity as a way of preserving the faith.[28]

These two recommendations were so in tune with Parks's own thinking that he could have written them himself. For some time he had given serious thought to mission strategy from which a critical analysis of "missions as usual" led to a formulation of seven principles of missionary operation. These principles were present in an incipient form from the beginning of his administration as executive director. He was concerned not only for a more effective missionary strategy but also for doctrinal integrity—an integrity that kept faith with the Baptist heritage. The seven principles which he repeatedly set forth before the board, trustees, and staff, included aspects of both of these concerns.

In April 1992, Parks presented to the board for the last time what he termed "Controlling Principles in Southern Baptist Foreign Missions." They are:

1. A biblical basis of all that we do.

2. Our primary purpose is evangelism that results in churches.

3. The incarnational approach which emphasizes the career missionary.

4. The priesthood of the believers, meaning every Baptist is a witness and through volunteer opportunities can be involved personally in missions.

5. The indigenous principle which means that churches which are established are "home grown" or "natural" in their environment.

6. A comprehensive approach, indicating

that we do not focus on one single issue or use one single method but try to express the total scope of ministry to which Southern Baptists are committed.

7. The responsibility of communicating what is happening on the mission field back to Southern Baptists.

All of these strands are interwoven to form one mission fabric. We cannot tear one out without weakening the total.[29]

While these principles constituted the guidelines within which Parks attempted to shape his administration, they led him to make a number of far-reaching changes in the board's operation. These changes were so basic and influential that Louis Cobbs sees Parks's administration as effecting "a paradigm shift" from previous board policy.[30]

The Office of Intercessory Prayer

In his first address to the Foreign Mission Board, Parks insisted on the priority of intercessory prayer. It was the first of his six major points in which he pledged, "We will be praying daily as staff at the Foreign Mission Board building. We plan a prayer room where someone will be interceding throughout the day for world concerns." Then he indicated what he had in mind when he said: "We are committed to sharing prayer needs and prayer answers with Southern Baptists."[31]

Prayer had undergirded the work of the board from its very beginning. Willingham made it a practice, even after his stroke, to meet with the staff every morning for prayer. Cauthen was known as a man of deep personal devotional life. He often reminded the staff and the trustees of the importance of intercessory prayer, but it remained for Parks to lift prayer to a priority function of the staff by setting up the office and assigning to a member of the staff the responsibility for enlisting the prayer support not only of the board but also of the Southern Baptist people. He chose Catherine Walker to direct the prayer ministry of the board.

Parks introduced the veteran missionary from Indonesia at the March board meeting as "special assistant to the president for intercessory prayer." Catherine, a graduate of Wheaton College and the Woman's Missionary Union Training School (now merged with Southern Seminary), was appointed a missionary to China in 1946. Forced out of China by the Communists, she transferred in 1952 along with other missionaries to Indonesia, where she taught, after language school, in the Baptist seminary at Semarang for twenty-six years. She had just retired and settled down in Florida when Parks asked her to join the staff in Richmond as his special assistant for intercessory prayer. For four years she served on the staff of the board until her second retirement in May 1985.

Minette Drumwright, who had served for three years as an assistant to William O'Brien, the executive vice president of the board, succeeded Walker. Mrs. Drumwright, a graduate of Baylor University, was the wife of Huber L. Drumwright, Jr., until his death

Drumright talks with Midwestern Seminary professor, Larry Baker, during 1984 seminary dialogue.

in 1981. While she lived in Texas, Minette was actively involved in a number of organizations, including the Texas Baptist Woman's Missionary Union, of which she was a former vice president, and the Home Mission Board's Women in Evangelism Council. Shortly after Minette assumed responsibility for the office of intercessory prayer, the staff was reorganized. Among the changes that ensued, her office became the "Office of International Prayer Strategy." This change in title reflected a change in emphasis. As Minette put it: "As we began to focus on the unreached world, we decided that the prayer emphasis should include, not replace, but include, focus on the unreached world."[32] As the director of the International Prayer Strategy Office, she was given the responsibility for directing the "development and implementation of intercessory prayer programs designed to motivate Southern Baptists to deeper involvement with overseas missions through intercessory prayer."[33]

Under Drumwright's leadership the intercessory prayer program both changed and expanded. Catherine Walker had edited a monthly newsletter under the caption *Called to Prayer, Called to Pray*, which was changed to *Global PrayerGram*. By 1993 this newsletter had a monthly circulation of some 30,000 and every other month was sent to the missionaries. The prayer office

"Global PrayerGram"

also set up a toll free telephone number, called the "Prayer Line," which anyone could call for a recording of a mission prayer request. This prayer request was changed twice weekly. About 11,000 calls were received monthly in 1992. When a particular event calling for special prayer occurred, Minette explained, the office could declare a "prayer alert" and change the request immediately on the prayer line. In addition, by fax and mail the prayer alert could be in the hands of those on the mailing list in two days. The prayer office was also responsible for the daily staff prayer, which varied from day to day, chapel on Wednesdays, and the spiritual retreat once each year. It is clear that during the twelve years of the Parks administration, prayer not only became a priority, it had become a mission strategy, "not just one of the strategies," Drumwright said, "but the foremost strategy."[34]

Financing Bold Mission Thrust

Parks was not only a man of prayer, he was an astute financier. It did not take him long to realize that the Foreign Mission Board could never achieve the goals of Bold Mission Thrust if the board's receipts from the Cooperative Program continued to decline. In his second meeting with the board as executive director, the board voted that John W. Patterson, president, and the executive director write "J. Howard Coble, chairman of the Program and Budget Sub-Committee, SBC, expressing our great concerns. . . ."[35] Patterson also was asked to write letters to Brooks Wester, chairman of the Executive Committee, and to every member of the board.

The Patterson-Parks letter pointed out that for a decade, the Foreign Mission Board's allocation had continued to decline from a high of 50 percent to less than 46.8 percent. The letter continued to question the division of funds in light of the board's task. "One of the strangest things for a 'bold mission' proposal is that the more the convention receives in challenge funds, the smaller the proportion that will be provided for reaching the 95% of the world's lost people who are outside our national borders." After pointing out that the world's economic condition had lowered by 13 percent the buying power of the board during these same ten years, they said: "Until this entire trend is reversed, we are deceiving ourselves and our Southern Baptist constituency if we continue to talk in terms of Bold Mission Thrust as the guiding principle in our convention financing."[36]

Apparently the lobbying efforts of Parks and Patterson were effective for at the October 1982 board meeting, Carl Johnson, treasurer, reported that the board's allocation of the Cooperative Program receipts for the year ending in September was $44,294,435, a 47.45 percent of the total compared to 46.40 percent the previous year.

Parks's continued concern with the financial support of the board was evident when he proposed a development office in his first reorganization of the board two months later.

Reorganizing the Board

From the time of his election as executive director, Parks had continued to give considerable thought to the reorganization of the board. After seven months of consultation with numerous individuals, he was ready with his report to the trustees. He declared "The original intent [of the reorganization] was to provide creativity, new ideas, and new approaches. By putting knowledgeable, gifted, spiritually sensitive people in new roles, this may be accomplished even faster [than with new personnel outside the present staff]."[37] The new organization was to be operative by May 1.

The most obvious change in the new organization was the new nomenclature, although other changes were far more significant. The corporate model provided the framework of the new board structure. The executive director became the president and the former president of the board became the chairman of the board. This reorganization marked the fourth title change of the chief executive officer of the board since 1845. Until 1933, it remained, with the exception of a short period during Willingham's last illness, "corresponding secretary." From 1933 to 1976, it was "executive secretary" with the exception of the last

Executive Management Group members, from right: Winston Crawley, Keith Parks and Bill O'Brien, talk with missions professor, Alan Neely, during Evangelism and Church Growth Conference, 1981.

two and a half years of Cauthen's administration, when it became "executive director."

The new staff structure reflected the shift in administrative personnel and the creation of the Office of Development under the Office of the Executive. The newly elected vice presidents constituted the Executive Management Group. The titles and corresponding personnel were presented to the trustees in the following format.

Foreign Mission Board
Executive Management Group

Office of the Executive
President........................R. Keith Parks
Executive Vice-president ..William R. O'Brien
Administrative Assistant .Homer E. Beaver
Office of Planning
    Vice-president ....Winston Crawley
Office of Development
    Director ....

Office of Overseas Operation
Vice-president ....Charles W. Bryan

Office of Human Resources
Vice-president ....William W. Marshall

Office of Communications
Vice-president ....*Johnni Johnson Scofield*
Office of Management Services
Vice-president ....*Sidney C. Reber*[38]

After approving the new structure for the board, the trustees voted to establish a committee to update its "By-Laws . . . to coincide with the organizational structure as adopted."[39] At the same meeting, the board heard a report of the Committee to Study the Development and Financial Feasibility of a Missionary Orientation Center which had

Charles W. Bryan, right, talks with Jack Gray, Southwestern Seminary, during Evangelism and Church Growth Conference, 1981.

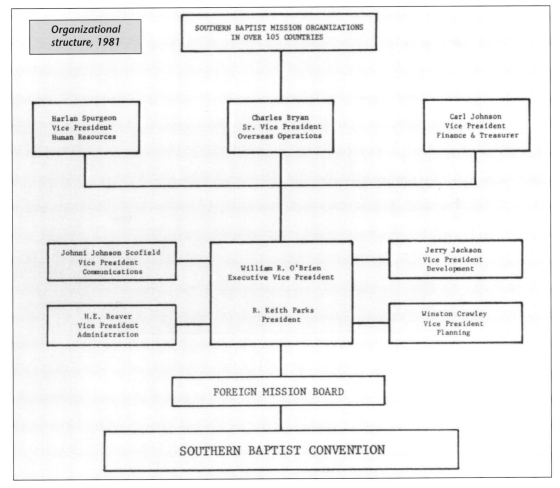

Organizational structure, 1981

SOUTHERN BAPTIST MISSION ORGANIZATIONS IN OVER 105 COUNTRIES

Harlan Spurgeon
Vice President
Human Resources

Charles Bryan
Sr. Vice President
Overseas Operations

Carl Johnson
Vice President
Finance & Treasurer

Johnni Johnson Scofield
Vice President
Communications

William R. O'Brien
Executive Vice President

Jerry Jackson
Vice President
Development

H.E. Beaver
Vice President
Administration

R. Keith Parks
President

Winston Crawley
Vice President
Planning

FOREIGN MISSION BOARD

SOUTHERN BAPTIST CONVENTION

MLC groundbreaking

Housing area

→ East Village
← 12-13
→ 14-17

Sam James on MLC grounds

Dining room

MKs with computers

Missionaries studying class notes

Missionary Learning Center, Rockville, Virginia

been appointed in 1977. This report launched that which became known as the Missionary Learning Center.

The Missionary Learning Center

The Baker James Cauthen and the Eloise Glass Cauthen Missionary Learning Center was dedicated on 10 October 1984. At that time, it had been under construction for two years and in use since April. The board determined to construct the center without using any Cooperative Program or Lottie Moon Offering funds. Ray Spence, chairman of the Development Council reported in the October 1982 board meeting that more than $12,000,000 "had been raised and that 100 percent of the 'old' board members have made pledges to the Missionary Learning Center." The twenty buildings of the center were constructed upon 238 acres near Rockville, Virginia, given by J. Harwood and Louise Cochrane.[40]

For fourteen years missionary orientation had been conducted at the Calloway Gardens in Georgia. While missionary orientation was still conducted at Calloway Gardens, Samuel H. James, former missionary to South Vietnam, was appointed director in 1980. He began a review of the entire operation in order to determine the purpose of missionary orientation. Next he developed program concepts and an undergirding philosophy in preparation for moving to the new location. Architects were then briefed on the unique needs of the new complex. James was succeeded by Timothy T. Brendle in 1985 when he became area director for East Asia. Brendle had been a missionary in Haiti and had served as manager of career orientation before assuming the position. Norman

Burnes became director in 1987. By 1992, the Missionary Learning Center provided eight weeks of a variety of programs for missionary orientation and service. The only time the center, according to Burnes, is not in use is a three week period during the Christmas season. Burnes, a former missionary to Israel and for seven years on the staff of the Office of Mission Personnel, explained that the curriculum of the seven week orientation program, scheduled six times a year for career and associate missionaries, included four areas of study: (1) the biblical and missiolog-

Volunteer Mary Saunders, left, welcomes Keith and Helen Jean Parks to an emergency feeding station in Ethiopia, April 1986.

ical basis of missions; (2) cross-cultural information; (3) relationship with the Foreign Mission Board; (4) self-understanding and personal development.[41] Other orientation programs were organized around the same subjects but were treated within a shorter time frame.

Humanitarian Relief Efforts

By March 1982, the relief efforts of Southern Baptists around the world had grown so rapidly that Parks found it neces-

sary to provide a ratio-
nale for the board's
continued involve-
ment in the growing
phenomenon that
threatened to upset
the balance of the
board's work as a mis-
sionary agency. In his
mind, relief efforts
poorly handled could
militate against his
own axiom that mis-
sions is primarily
evangelism that results in churches. Basing
his remarks upon the philosophy adopted by
the board on 29 June 1978, he justified the
board's continued involvement in humanitarian relief efforts in the name of Christ as
a part of the convention's mandate to the
Foreign Mission Board and an ethical imperative. He told the trustees: "Biblically, philo-
sophically and practically this ministry is a
valid part of our work. It is done in conjunc-
tion with evangelism that results in churches.
This and all other ministries are to strengthen
the witness and growth of churches."[42]

Parks emphasized that the nature of the
Foreign Mission Board and Baptist distinctives determined the limitations that dictated
the use of funds designated for relief.
Southern Baptists expected the funds to be
used, he suggested, for the purpose given,
therefore, the board could not use other agencies to do its relief work since some often used
as much as 25 percent of contributions
received for overhead expenses. They also frequently worked through or used government
agencies to do their work. Too, since the
board was not a relief agency but a missionary

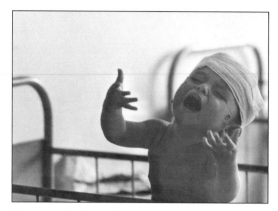

18-month-old victim of 1985 volcanic eruption in Colombia

arm of the denomina-
tion, the relief ef-
forts could be car-
ried on by missionar-
ies, every one of
whom was an evange-
list, and through local
indigenous churches.
These funds also
could be used in long
range relief efforts in
agriculture, well dig-
ging, irrigation pro-
jects, feeding pro-
grams, and in providing medical services
where needed.[43] He concluded his policy
statement with a promise:

*I pledge to you that careful appropriate mea-
sures are being taken with deliberate haste to
accelerate the use of these funds appropriately, but we will not rush into improper or
shoddy arrangements. This ministry will be
done in the name of Jesus. It will augment
evangelism and church growth. It will be an
appropriate part of the total Southern Baptist
foreign mission effort.[44]*

When the pathetic pictures of bloated
and starving children in Ethiopia began to
hit the television screens in the United States,
suddenly the country woke up to the tragic
dimensions that war and famine had
wrought in Africa. The Foreign Mission
Board first entered Ethiopia in 1967 and the
missionaries began work in the Menz-Gishe
of the country's central Shoa region. Ten
years later all Southern Baptist missionaries
were withdrawn due to the political turmoil.
But missionary efforts were resumed in Addis
Ababa, the capitol of the country, in March
1978.

When the famine enveloped the land in

1984, the little band of six missionaries longed to help, particularly in the area and among the people with whom they once worked. Miraculously, they believe, within twenty-four hours, the Marxist government granted the missionaries the requested permission. John Cheyne declared: "I've never gone anywhere I felt so strongly that the power of prayer had paved the way for us."[45] The board granted the necessary funds to rent a bulldozer to open sixty-five miles of road and other vehicles to get the grain to the starving people. Within five months, the five relief centers cut the death rate among children from ten a week to almost zero while in the north, the death rate was fifty a day. For this effort the board appropriated $2,000,000. The long range plans involved agriculture, relief, education, and discipleship training, all in the name of Christ.

Unfortunately Ethiopia was not the only country in Africa devastated by the same deadly mixture of armed conflict and famine. It was fortunate, however, that in Mali and a number of other countries, Baptists had a number of strong churches through which relief efforts could be funneled directly to the people in greatest need.

A year after the famine descended upon Ethiopia and Mali, the snow-shrouded Mount Ruiz erupted in Colombia. The Nevada del Ruiz Volcano had been spewing ash for several days but the authorities assured the towns and villages on its slopes that it had not been active since the 1840s and that there was no cause for concern. They were wrong. While 30,000 residents of Armero, the largest city on the slopes of the mountain, slept, the volcano erupted sending an avalanche of water, ash, and mud cascading down its sides, burying everything in its path. Soon most of Armero was under thirty feet of mud and twenty thousand people were dead, and another four thousand

Missionary Associate Joan Caperton, RN, explains purpose and value of artificial limb to two men at the Baptist Center of Hope.

died in other towns in the path of the gigantic mudslide.

When the nation awoke to the tragedy of the night of 13 November 1985, every emergency relief organization of the country was mobilized to attempt to alleviate the suffering of the living. James Giles, president of the seminary and disaster relief coordinator for the Colombia Baptist Mission, and his wife, Mary Nell, left immediately for what had been Armero. They were joined by Ellis Leagans from Ibagué, seventy miles away. Fifteen Colombian Baptists, among them doctors and nurses, formed the Baptist relief team that soon included other missionaries and members of the Richmond staff.

Many of the mangled survivors were taken to the government hospital in Ibagué where the Baptists began their ministry of loving concern as they shared their faith and hope with the suffering. Tent cities were set up near the destroyed towns in which Colombian Baptists and

The benefits of Partnership Missions have been significant.

missionaries began to minister. With relief funds made available by the Foreign Mission Board, medicine and medical supplies to meet critical shortages, portable generators, food, and blankets, were purchased. Baptists opened up a new "Center of Hope" near the hospital in order to offer therapy and to teach skills needed for the rehabilitation of the victims of the Armero tragedy.

The missionaries and their Colombian brethren worked until they were exhausted. Their witness of selfless service began to bear fruit even within the first weeks of the relief effort. Worship services were held in the refugee camps and families were reunited through the joint efforts of the missionaries and Colombian television stations, which had begun to carry pictures of homeless children at the suggestion of Mary Nell Giles. Also, at the request of local authorities,

Baptists established a rehabilitation center in the Federico Lleras Hospital in Ibagué to equip amputees with artificial arms and legs. A supply of prostheses had been in storage in the country for more than two years. Thanks to Baptists, many amputees were soon walking on a leg or reaching out with an arm made possible by those who sought to minister to the physical and spiritual needs of suffering humanity in the name of Christ.[46]

Volunteers and Partnership Missions

One of the goals of Bold Mission Thrust was 10,000 volunteers a year working overseas with the missionaries by A.D. 2000. The growth of Partnership Missions (state conventions working with the mission in a given country) promised to make this goal a reality. The concept of lay volunteers working overseas under the direction of the missionaries and in partnership with national Christians was not a new idea in the 1980's. In fact, the number of volunteers in various categories had reached a total of 6,213 by 1984. Simultaneously, in the same period, twenty-four three-year partnership arrangements between fifteen state conventions were in effect. Some states were in partnership with more than one country at the same time.

A partnership arrangement in 1985 coupled Kentucky with Kenya. William Marshall, executive secretary-treasurer of Kentucky Baptists and a former missionary, in sharing the plans for "Good News Kenya" scheduled for 1987, said: "It is my desire that Kentucky will become the most mission-minded state in the Southern Baptist Convention."[47] The plans for the evangelistic campaign scheduled for 1987 called for 150 teams. Each team was to be assigned to a church in Kenya matching the skills of the volunteers of a given team with the needs of a particular church. Tract and Bible distribution accompanied personal witnessing with evangelistic services conducted wherever possible. This was the usual pattern, although specialized medical, sports, or work teams have become more common since 1985.

The benefits of Partnership Missions have been significant. For one thing they have changed the lives of the volunteers, raising the level of awareness of missionary work around the world. Even though the number of baptisms have never matched the number of professions of faith in volunteer evangelistic efforts, there is no doubt that many have come to know and to follow Christ as his true disciples. While the missionaries have recognized the problem of being overwhelmed by volunteers ill prepared to understand the people or their culture, they still see value in the volunteer effort, if directed by a sufficient number of career missionaries.

A World to Reach

Keith Parks challenged Southern Baptists in *World in View* to catch step with the Foreign Mission Board's new vision of a world to reach for Christ:

> *If I—if we—are serious about reaching all the world for Christ, should we not open our hearts to allow the Spirit of God to move in us and through us for the sake of seemingly unreachable cities? Why shouldn't we be willing to give prayerful attention to how the gospel can be preached in places that, humanly speaking, seem totally impossible? Is it right for us to assume the Lord God will be prevented from entering where people have said Christianity cannot go? Has God yet said not to be concerned about hard places on our world maps?[48]*

In a sense, Parks's enlarged vision of the foreign mission task was evident in statements that he made in 1980. In the first year of his presidency, after delineating his expectations of the future of missions, he wrote in *The Commission:* "Our options are simple: 1) We can ignore the onrushing tide and be engulfed. 2) We can resist it and be shattered. 3) We can initiate some change and adapt to others and be blessed and a blessing."[49]

The third option was the only viable one for the new president. By 1985, it was evident that far reaching changes in the board's approach to its task were underway. The first was the opportunity to reestablish a witness in China and the second was an enlarged concept of partnership missions—a partnership with other Baptist missionary sending bodies. Other changes yet to follow involved the concept of the nonresident missionary and networking with other "Great Commission Christians." "The Green Alert" was in response to the collapse of the Soviet Union and the new situation that prevailed in eastern Europe after 1989.

Behind the changes mentioned above were a number of discernible factors, the first of which was the Bold Mission Thrust with its goal of proclaiming the gospel to everyone on Earth by A.D. 2000. The second factor was the changing international situation with its new opportunities and its built-in limitations. A third was the contribution to the global strategy planning of David Barrett, editor of the *World Christian Encyclopedia*, who had come to the board as a missiologist specialist on a three-year con-

1989 Baptist delegation to North Vietnam helps with rehabilitation project; left to right: Fred Kaufman, Marvin Raley, MD, Lewis Myers and Keith Parks.

tract in 1983. According to William R. O'Brien, Barrett, an evangelical Anglican, is, "a genius in his field and an outstanding missiological researcher."[50] Of course none of the foregoing would have had any appreciable effect upon the board without the openness and willingness to take risks that characterized both Parks and O'Brien, the new executive vice president of the board. O'Brien explained that Parks was not given to making premature decisions but after consultation, thought, and much prayer he would come to a decision, not always in accord with the advice given—in any case it was always his own decision.[51]

Cooperative Services International

In the June-July 1985 issue of *The Commission,* there was an announcement of the board's action in April when the Office of Cooperative Services International was established specifically to meet a need in China. It had been more than thirty years since all missionaries had been forced out of

the country. Since the death of Chairman Mao, there had been a gradual liberalization of many aspects of Chinese life. One of those was religion. China's Three Self Patriotic Movement, the officially recognized Protestant organization in China, formed the Amity Foundation for promoting "health, education, and social service projects" throughout the country. Charles Bryan, senior vice president for overseas operations, emphasized that missionaries were still not welcome in China and that the board would not be initiating anything but responding to needs as they were identified by the Chinese. Bryan also suggested that the Office of Cooperative Services International would possibly become the agency through which missionaries might be sent to heretofore inaccessible countries.[52]

Partnership Missions Enlarged

The concept of partnership in global mission strategy began to take on other dimensions under Parks's leadership. Increasingly, it became apparent to Parks, with the information provided by Barrett that Southern Baptists were never going to reach the goals of Bold Mission Thrust alone. Barrett pointed out that even if they did achieve the goal of establishing work in 125 countries by the year 2000, this would only constitute half the countries in the world and that in the other half were 10,000 people groups and 300,050 cities with a population of over 100,000 residents in which the gospel was not publicly proclaimed. The fact that one and a third billion people had no chance even to hear the gospel was not lost on Parks and the staff of the board. It occurred to him that one step in addressing that situation was to strengthen partnership relationships with other Baptist groups that also sent out missionaries, or that hoped to do so and with which the board was already working.

In June 1985, the Global Consultation on World Evangelization was held at Ridgecrest, North Carolina with forty-two Baptist participants from twenty-one nations. The agenda was open-ended in order to encourage full participation by all present. The Foreign Mission Board only sent five representatives to the consultation in order not to dominate the meeting and to encourage full and frank discussion on the basis of equal partners. The general consensus was that such a meeting was long overdue. The sharing of ideas was both stimulating and promising.

Networking with "Great Commission" Christians

Two years after the Baptist consultation at Ridgecrest, Parks took the initiative to explore the possibility of a similar consultation with thirty-six of the largest mission sending bodies in the United States. "In order that no one misunderstand the nature of the proposed meeting," he said in issuing the invitation, "if you are interested in trying to reach the world and would like to come together to talk and pray about it with some others who have the same agenda, let's get together." He went on to make it doubly sure that no one mistook the purpose of the proposed meeting when he emphasized: "I am not interested in talking about deep theological differences or missiological approaches. I am certainly not

interested in an organization." Twenty mission boards responded by sending representatives to the conference held at the Dallas-Fort Worth Airport "on fairly short notice."[53]

The results of that meeting have been little known but far reaching. First, Parks said that the first night they came together for a spontaneous prayer meeting. It was such a moving experience that all agreed that each year the weekend of Pentecost, they would challenge their constituents to pray specifically for a "particular unreached people group." Second, with the work of David Barrett, the board had developed the largest missionary database anywhere in the world, which Parks offered to share with mission boards that would agree to use it for missionary purposes and not for publicity. Over a hundred groups have signed the covenant and with a modem have been able to access the database. Third, Parks said: "We found many ways that we could work together more effectively." To illustrate what he meant, he gave the example of the Jesus film produced by Campus Crusade, that the board has used extensively. He remarked that Bill Bright told him that frequently after Campus Crusade showed the film, requests came in for him to send someone to start a church. In speaking to Parks, he said, "That's not what we are there for."[54] Parks replied, "That IS what we are there for." Parks also said that a similar relationship is being established with Christian radio networks.

This whole range of interrelated activity has come to be called "networking with Great Commission Christians." Such activities avoid the problems of more formal ecumenical ties while advancing the cause of

Christ around the world. The same kind of networking has been extended to the program of the nonresidential missionary.

The Nonresidential Missionary

A team of staff members at the board were wrestling with the problem of how best proclaim the gospel to one fourth of the

Global Consultation session, Parks, left

world's population who had never had a chance to hear. They came up with the concept of the nonresidential missionary. The team faced the reality of unfriendly governments that either refused to allow missionaries to reside within their borders or put such restrictions upon them that it made overt missionary activity impossible. If the thousands of people groups living within the borders of these countries were going to be reached for Christ, the group reasoned that it would have to be by missionaries living outside the country who would specialize in learning the language of a particular unreached people and quietly work among the group as the missionary was able to gain access to the area from time to time through a tourist visa or in some other legal manner.

The task appeared formidable. The non-residential missionary would have to become

fluent in the language, knowledgable of the customs, and determine the best avenue of approach to one identifiable people group in a given country. One of the major assignments was to see that the Bible, if not already in a usable language of the specific group, was translated into the group's most widely used language. High priority was given to determining the best means of delivering the message of salvation. The ultimate purpose of all that preceded was to form a church with the newly won converts that in turn could become a self-sustaining witness, utilizing all the opportunities available to nationals of a given country. The vision was certainly a challenging one, but was it feasible? That question could only be answered in the attempt to implement the concept. The concept was first articulated in 1986. Its implementation would take time.[55]

Organizing for Global Strategy

The nonresidential missionary concept was the fruit of a group within the staff in consultation with David Barrett. This group had taken the time to look at the world as it was and pray and plan for a world that could be. For Parks, this was abundant evidence of the value of the investment of time for research and to think through missionary strategy. To make the nonresidential missionary program an integral part of the Foreign Mission Board's global strategy, Parks determined to reorganize the board again.

In speaking to the recommendation of the Transition Committee at the February 1987 meeting of the board, he reminded the board once again of the seven principles that he first presented in 1984. Then he gave the rationale for another reorganization of the board, emphasizing the importance of global strategy.

> *The center of all of this potential change can be summarized in two words: "global strategy." This becomes the hub of these recommendations. All of the other elements in the recommendations are related to that hub like spokes in a wheel. . . .*
>
> *This global strategy revolves around the central expression of the very nature and purpose of God, the continuing theme of the Bible, the expression of The Great Commission and the more modern statement which we call Bold Mission Thrust. Taking all of this seriously, we now commit ourselves to developing a deliberate global strategy to enable Southern Baptists to have our appropriate part in presenting the gospel of Jesus Christ to everyone in the world by the year 2000.*[56]

Following his analogy of spokes in the wheel, Parks labeled each spoke to a particular segment of Baptist life to which the board relates, from the trustees to Southern Baptists as a whole. Commenting on the last spoke, he said, "The degree of difference in foreign missions will ultimately be decided by what happens among Southern Baptists."[57]

The major changes in the organization of the staff were designed to give the area directors more administrative authority and the vice presidents more time to pray and think through mission strategy, not just for their regions but for the entire world. Each vice president was to become a member of the Global Strategy Group, which would replace the Executive Management Group. The area directors were to live in their areas where they could relate more directly to their respective areas. The Office of Cooperative Services International, under which the nonresidential program would be administered, was elevated to parallel the regions, and Lewis I.

Myers, Jr., was named vice president. The standing committees among the trustees were also changed to reflect the changes in the staff.

The proposed reorganization of the staff and the trustees approved by the board at this meeting embraced the following changes:

President -
R. Keith Parks

Executive Vice President -
William R. O'Brien

Vice President of Finance and Treasurer-
Carl W. Johnson

Assistant Recording Secretary -
Nellie P. Walters

Director of Research and Planning -
A. Clark Scanlon

Vice President for Mission Management and Personnel -
Harlan E. Spurgeon

Vice President for Asia and the Pacific -
William R. Wakefield

Vice President for Africa -
Davis L. Saunders

Vice President for the Americas -
Donald R. Kammerdiener

Vice President for Europe, Middle East and North Africa -
Isam E. Ballenger

Vice President for Cooperative Services International -
Lewis I. Myers, Jr.

Associate Vice President for Mission Management -
Thurman E. Bryant

Associate Vice President for Mission Personnel -
Timothy T. Brendle

Standing committees of the board shall [sic] be: Strategy Committee, Administra-tive Committee, Mission Management and Personnel Committee, Communications and Public Relations Committee, Trustee Orientation Committee and the following regional committees: Africa Committee, Asia and the Pacific Committee, The Americas Committee, Europe, Middle East and North

Africa Committee and Cooperative Services International Committee.

The committee structure division will be as follows:
a. The total membership of the board will be divided between the Mission Management & Personnel Committee and the Administrative Committee with no duplication. The membership of the Strategy Committee and the Communications and Public Relations Committee be established by dividing the membership of the Administrative Committee.
Mission Management & Personnel 42
Administrative 41
Strategy 21
Communications and Public Relations .20

b. The Trustee Orientation Committee will be made up of 10 members.

c. Each board member will be assigned to one of the five regional committees. For the testimonies of the missionaries, the members of Cooperative Services International Committee will be divided among the other four regional committees. These committees may meet in subgroups when large numbers of candidates are to be heard.

d. New members preferably will be assigned to Mission Management and Personnel Committee their first or second year on the board.

e. All chairmen of the regional committees will be assigned to the Strategy Com-mittee.[58]

Captivated by his vision of global missions, Parks proposed changing the name of the Foreign Mission Board to the International Board of the Southern Baptist Convention but ran into stiff opposition from all quarters. Traditional use and emotional attachment to the present name were too great. He compromised by asking the board to approve the proposed name over-seas and retain the present name of the board for stateside use. "And then we gave to each mission the right of choice," he said. "They could either register under Foreign Mission Board or the International Board." "And I," he continued, "along with our vice presidents, have two sets of cards—one as president of the International Board and another as president of the Foreign Mission Board."[59]

The newly formed Global Strategy Group took its task seriously. One of its proposals met with widespread negative reaction from among the missionaries and with some misunderstanding. Each mission was asked to take a careful look at its institutions to see whether any should be turned over to national conventions or unions. Parks had long held that the board's primary task was evangelism and the "planting of churches." He conceded that institutions would need to be provided upon occasion but only supported by the missions until national denominational bodies could assume their support. By this proposed survey, it was hoped that a pool of missionaries no longer needed on the older fields could be released for evangelism among unreached people groups.

At the same time the staff proposed the mission surveys, it recommended that at least 70 percent of the missionaries should be spending at least half of their time in "missioning kinds of outreach, new churches and evangelism."[60] Many missionaries who were appointed for something other than evangelism and church planting felt that their work was being denigrated by the administration that had appointed and sent them out for their specialized tasks. Others were upset by the attempt, as they interpreted it, to tell them how to use their time and the desire to move them into the nonresidential pool from a work and a country to which they felt called. In reminiscing about the uproar, Parks said: "I don't know whether you could communicate that [the new 70/30 proposal] without negative reaction or not."[61]

Fine Tuning the New Organization

It seems that during the Parks years the board was in a perpetual reorganization mode. Although appearances are sometimes deceiving, in this case they pretty well reflect the situation. Organizational adjustments became necessary from time to time for a number of reasons. Personnel changes were inevitable and with some of these came certain alterations in the organization of the board. This was particularly true when the O'Briens decided that the invitation extended to Dellanna to become the executive director of the national Woman's Missionary Union should be a matter of serious consideration. After much prayer, the decision was made to accept the invitation and the O'Briens moved to Birmingham, Alabama. At this juncture, Parks decided that the functions of the office of executive vice president should be divided. Bill O'Brien was asked to serve as executive director of public affairs and to continue as director of the global desk while other functions of his office remained the responsibility of the executive vice president. For a year and a half, O'Brien continued as a member of the Global Strategy Group, commuting between Birmingham and Richmond. Don Kammerdiener, who had been appointed a mission-

Global Strategy Group, 1980, prays; from left: Carl Johnson, treasurer; Parks, and vice presidents Don Kammerdiener, Lewis I. Myers, and Davis Saunders.

ary to Colombia in 1962, became executive vice president of the board, responsible for its day-to-day operations, on 1 January 1990.

Two other programs were put in place by 1990. The older "tentmaker" category, which involved no expense other than that of the office in Richmond, was revitalized. The Mission Service Corps was merged with the Journeyman program, to create the new International Service Corps that still provided the Journeyman option for college graduates. A significant change required all candidates to receive the same orientation.[62] The International Service Corps was administered by the Office of Mission Personnel.

The new programs were in place just in time for what promised to be the Foreign Mission Board's greatest opportunity for a new missionary thrust in Europe.

The Green Alert Task Force

The remarkable developments in Europe that led to the breakup of the Soviet Union provided the catalyst that motivated the board to appoint a Green Alert Task Force for the former Soviet Union and its satellites in eastern Europe. Isam Ballenger, vice presi-

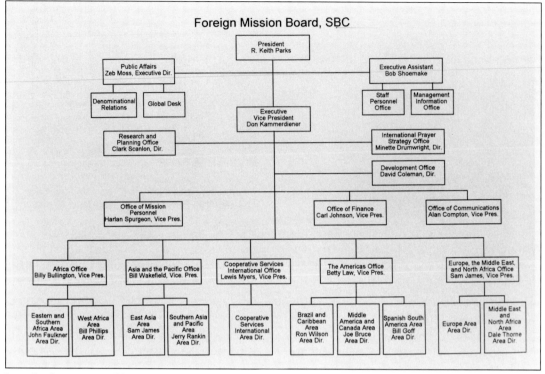

Organization structure, 1992

dent for Europe, Middle East, and North Africa, was named chairman. The other members were: Lewis Myers, vice president, Cooperative Services International (CSI); Keith Parker, area director, Europe; Paul Thibodeaux, associate to the area director, Europe—field deputy for the Task Force; Brian Grim, representative of CSI; Jim Smith, coordinator for Eastern Europe Partnership Missions and representative to the Baltic states; George Lozuk, missionary, USSR.

The purpose of the task force, according to the minutes of the December board meeting, was to establish a

rapid decision-making process to involve all possible Christian resources to meet the unprecedented needs and opportunities in all

lands which have comprised the Soviet Union and to maximize human efforts commensurate with God's activity in our time, specifically 1. to strengthen local Baptists in their effort to evangelize, 2. to provide Christian witness to the unreached/unevangelized peoples and help facilitate appropriate structures for their worship and training, and 3. to provide opportunities for mission involvement in lands which have comprised the Soviet Union.[63]

Two reports were given. The first which concerned mission opportunities in Soviet Central Asia was given by Mike W. Stroope. He gave a breakdown of anticipated needs in terms of missionary personnel, kinds of services, and estimated budget. The total called for 50 career missionaries and 157 International Service Corp missionaries.

The second report containing recommendations for the former USSR was presented by Paul Thibodeaux. He called for an estimated 89 career missionaries, 189 International Service Corp missionaries and 1,289 to 1,469 volunteers. The recommendations of the "Green Alert Initiative" called for a budget of $12,326,785.

It was evident that the members of the task force were convinced that the collapse of Communism in Europe and the dissolution of the USSR presented Southern Baptists with an unprecedented missionary opportunity in Europe and Central Asia. The urgency of acting while the "window of opportunity" remained open was poignantly illustrated by Thibodeaux. Although a considerable amount of time had been given by trustees and staff to the preparation of the Report of the Green Alert Task Force, further discussion was precluded by a reconsidering of the Rüschlikon defunding issue. However, the board did not see to the next item on the agenda until it voted to designate "New Year's Eve, 1991, as a day of prayer, ushering in a year of prayer" for the "nations of the former Soviet Union and that all monies above the 1991 Lottie Moon Christmas Offering be earmarked for the work of the Green Alert Task Force."[64]

The Rüschlikon Issue

During the October 1991 meeting of the Foreign Mission Board, the trustees learned that E. Glenn Hinson, a professor of church history on a sabbatical leave from The Southern Baptist Theological Seminary, was a guest professor at the Baptist Seminary in Rüschlikon. The reaction to this news precipitated a motion to withhold the annual

Donald R. Kammerdiener, left, talks with board chairman, John Jackson, during January 1993 meeting.

appropriation of $365,000 which constituted almost 40 percent of the seminary's annual budget. The motion passed thirty-five to twenty-eight. This precipitous action by the trustees provoked such consternation in European Baptist circles and throughout the Southern Baptist Convention that the board felt compelled to reconsider the Rüschlikon issue in its December meeting. In the meantime, one of the trustees sent a long letter to every member of the board containing a number of quotations from some of Hinson's published works with an admonition not to reverse the board's October decision. In December, the trustees reaffirmed their previous action by a roll call vote of fifty-four to twenty-seven.

When Karl-Heinz Walter, general secretary of the European Baptist Federation, was given an opportunity to speak for the European delegation, "he expressed grief over the judgment which this decision implies about the seminary in Rüschlikon and about the many leaders in Europe who are graduates from that seminary."[65] He also indicated that the action of the trustees had created a more serious problem in that "he did not see the way for a new building up of trust and confidence of future relationships with the European Baptist Union, even though he indicated it was needed for the good of the kingdom on that continent."[66]

In response to Walter, Bill Hancock, chairman of the Foreign Mission Board, defended the action of the trustees while expressing some misgivings about the timing.

> *I believe that the trustees who voted to do what they did this morning have done what they thought was right. It is my feeling they have done what they have done at the wrong time. I have continued to ask when does right end, and where does grace begin, and how long do we give grace.*[67]

Long Standing Problems

For many of the trustees, Rüschlikon had been a festering problem for years. Presidents had come and gone in rapid succession. Until the founding of the Institute of Missions and Evangelism under the leadership of John David Hopper and Earl Martin, neither evangelism nor missions had received much attention in the curriculum. Hardly had John David Hopper, the new president, had time to unpack, when he and Isam Ballenger, vice president for Europe, Africa, and the Middle East, met with the trustees of the board in July 1988 at Glorieta. During this meeting Hopper and Ballenger entered into dialogue with the trustees regarding the perceived problems of the seminary. Upon this occasion Hopper told the trustees, "I want to hear your criticisms of the seminary. I want to correct what has to be corrected."[68] Later in his address, Hopper indicated that

the major problems at Rüschlikon were two—financial and theological —and that it would "take three or four years to get things sorted out."[69]

After the Glorieta meeting of the board, a number of trustees made a trip to Switzerland to assess the situation for themselves. Following the trip, the property was deeded to the European Baptist Federation in October by a vote of fifty-nine to eight. The agreements reached in 1978 and 1983 to continue the annual subsidy through 1992 and for fifteen years thereafter on a gradually reduced level remained intact.

The trustees understood Hopper to say at Glorieta that he intended to move the seminary toward a more conservative theological position. Although he did not actually say so, what he did say could be so interpreted. With this understanding, in April 1991, the Regional Committee voted to recommend to the board a continuation of the subsidy for Rüschlikon "for three additional years at levels not to exceed in 1993 a reduction of 5% of the 1992 base of $365,000. . . ."[70] But in the October meeting of the Regional Committee, Ron Wilson called for reconsideration of the Rüschlikon issue on the basis "that some members of the committee wanted to change their vote."[71] A motion to reconsider was ruled out of order by Steve Hardy, chairman of the committee, as were other attempts to change the April recommendation on Rüschlikon. The following day, however, the committee met in a called meeting to reconsider the Rüschlikon recommendation in light of learning that Hinson had been invited to teach for four months at the seminary. The Finance Committee had already deleted the subsidy from the 1992 budget for the same reason. The majority of the trustees apparently felt that Hopper had betrayed their confidence for Hinson was perceived among them as a liberal. This led to the defunding of the seminary by the board in spite of the agreements of 1978 and 1983.

As Walter had predicted, Baptists in Europe considered the defunding of Rüschlikon a violation of a moral commitment on the part of the Foreign Mission Board. Perhaps that which hurt even more deeply was that Southern Baptists whom they had grown to appreciate and depend upon as reliable partners in the missionary enterprise could apparently no longer be trusted. They were "shocked" by the withdrawal of much needed funds for the seminary and offended by the way in which it was done—unilaterally and without consultation just three months before the next fiscal year. The rupture in relationships between Europeans and Southern Baptists threatened to become permanent.

The Hancock Letter to Southern Baptists

The negative reaction to the defunding of Rüschlikon was no less widespread in the Southern Baptist Convention. In its attempt at damage control, the board asked its chairman, Bill Hancock, to write an open letter to Southern Baptists giving relevant facts influencing the board's decision. After a brief historical sketch of the seminary and an analysis of the cost of educating each student at Rüschlikon in comparison with state-side seminaries, Hancock summarized the situation:

When there have been sporadic financial

Bill Hancock, Foreign Mission Board chairman, 1990-1992, and Parks listen to a report, during April 1992 meeting.

crises at Rüschlikon for 19 years resulting in more severe problems after each crisis; when the cost of operation is evaluated; when student enrollment and cost per student is appraised; when urgent repairs are pending; the question is valid and must be answered, "Is it financially feasible for Southern Baptists to continue supporting an institution with these circumstances anywhere in the world?"[72]

In addition to the familiar charges of liberalism, Hancock wrote: "It is held by many that Rüschlikon does not adequately represent conservative theology."[73] To the charges of theological deviation from biblical teachings on the part of the Rüschlikon faculty, he accused Hopper of violating "trust" and board policy by the establishment of the Friends of Rüschlikon Foundation in 1989 and related actions.

Hancock concluded his letter with a reference to a conference of selected trustees with Hopper, Walter, and Wiard Popkes, chairman of the Rüschlikon board of trustees, before the full meeting of the Foreign Mission Board in December. Apparently, there had been some hopes of resolving the differences and restoring the allocation for Rüschlikon. He wrote that he had made three proposals that were not accepted, which were: "an acknowledgement by the president and trustees of Rüschlikon of their insensitivity to conservative concerns regarding professors and theological positions;" names of professors asked to teach at the seminary "in advance of the fact and not after the fact," and "a full accounting of funds received by Rüschlikon from American sources and how the money is being used."[74] On Friday morning, 6 December, Popkes said the proposals were unacceptable. "Had the European leaders responded to the proposals presented to them December 5 without total rejection," Hancock wrote, "the action concerning Rüschlikon might have been different."[75]

Although the Hancock account of the board's decision to defund the international seminary was a faithful reflection of the majority opinion, it did little to assuage the feelings of those who felt wronged by the action. It did put into a broader context the Rüschlikon situation and raised serious questions about the seminary's continued operation in Switzerland. The Rüschlikon episode from October through December led to a number of developments.

Missionary Reaction in Europe

The reaction on the part of long-time missionaries in Europe was not long in coming. Before the end of January, both Isam Ballenger and Keith Parker had resigned. The *Richmond Times-Dispatch* broke the story on 8 January 1992.

Two key administrators on the Southern Baptist Foreign Mission Board are leaving the Richmond-based missionary agency,

saying fundamentalist trustees have destroyed missionary work in Europe and, as a result, their careers.

Dr. Isam Ballenger, vice president for Europe, Middle East and North Africa, and Dr. G. Keith Parker, area director for European operations, announced yesterday they will take early retirement May 31 and July 1, respectively. Dr. Ballenger is 56 and Dr. Parker, 55.[76]

At the time of their resignations, Ballenger had served twenty-eight years and Parker, twenty-three years. A few weeks later, John David Hopper, who had come under increasing criticism for his fund-raising activities, announced that he and his wife, Jo Ann, (veterans of twenty-seven years) would also resign from the board effective 1 June 1992. A number of other resignations by missionaries serving in Europe followed. At a time when Southern Baptists stood on the threshold of a new day of opportunity and challenge in Europe, their missionary presence was diminished and with it the confidence and good will they had built up in partnership with European Baptists since 1948. Even Romanian Baptists, the only European Baptist group reported to have favored the trustee action of defunding the European seminary, refused to accept $20,000, a part of the Rüschlikon funds reallocated for Eastern Europe. "Because of the misunderstanding raised around this subject and reported by the Baptist Press concerning our stand, we cannot accept this money," wrote the president and general secretary of the union.[77] Parker probably expressed the conviction of most of the missionaries and European Baptists when he wrote: "All our missionaries and staff are deeply committed to the Word of God and to theological integrity, as are all European colleagues. They serve in Christ's name and through their lives and ministries to influence and persuade others. They do not control by money and power. . . ."[78]

From the "trenches" in Spain, came a newsletter that doubtless reflected the sentiment of more than one Southern Baptist missionary in Europe. Bob Worley wrote on 20 November 1992 from Las Palmas de Gran Canaria:

> *All the resignations and controversy this year have been unsettling, but we have simply put our hands in the hand of the One who called us in the beginning, and we trust in him. We do not intend for any person or any circumstance to rob us of the joy of serving Jesus Christ and proclaiming his gospel to those who need it so desperately.*[79]

As the board's work with the European Baptist Federation and its member unions reached an impasse, it was evident that something must be done to reestablish a working relationship. Hence, the Hamburg Agreement.

The Hamburg Agreement

Although, as an emergency measure, Winston Crawley was asked to serve as interim vice president for Europe, Middle East, and Africa, relations between the Foreign Mission Board and the European Baptist Federation had reached an impasse. As Samuel H. James recalled, "At that time, almost all of the European countries had broken relationship with us. They were not requesting any more personnel—they had frozen personnel requests."[80] The Foreign Mission Board recognized that some attempt at reconciliation must be made. In the spring, a delegation from the board attempted to reestablish contact with the European Baptist Federation without success. They were told that when a new vice president was elected then they would consider some kind of meeting.

The Hamburg Consultation

James, who was area director for East Asia, was elected vice president for Europe, Middle East, and Africa at the June 1992 board meeting. He immediately contacted the European Baptist Federation. In the choice of James, Baptists in Europe recognized that the board intended to take its responsibility in Europe seriously. Consequently, the Federation invited the board to send a delegation to meet with its representatives in September. As a result six representatives of the Foreign Mission Board met with seven of their counterparts from the European Baptist Federation in a hotel in Hamburg, Germany on 11, 12 September 1992.

The first session was frustrating. The atmosphere was cool and tense. Virtually every proposal set forth by the Americans was rejected, particularly by the Germans. It was clear that the Europeans were convinced the board had broken its promise to fund Rüschlikon according to prior agreement and in so doing had wronged the seminary and European Baptists. That evening the trustees, once to themselves began to rethink the whole process and to express some misgivings regarding the way in which it was done.

The next morning, after a brief devotional period, Wiard Popkes provoked a sharp response from John Jackson. The conference appeared to be over when LeRoy Smith, chairman of the Regional Committee on Europe, the Middle East, and Africa, expressed his regrets about the way the defunding was done and his sorrow at the anguish it had caused Karl-Heinz Walter and others. "Tears came to his eyes," James recalled. "It was a very emotional moment and I get emotional just thinking about it," he said.[81] Walter stretched his hand across the table and with a handshake, fellowship began to be restored.

Jackson explained that even though the trustees did what they felt was right, they were sorry for the problems their action had caused the European Baptists and for the breach in relationships. He further expressed the feelings of the Southern Baptist delegation that the way in which the defunding was done was not all it should have been. Although, as James reported to the trustees in the October meeting, "never once did the trustees apologize for defunding Rüschlikon," but what they did say led to fruitful dialogue and the Hamburg Agreement.[82] In the report on the Hamburg Consultation, the trustees at the meeting of the board in October were informed that "As the discussions proceeded both parties increasingly recognized the extent of the damage caused by the decision, but they experienced by the grace of God forgiveness in Christ and reconciliation."[83]

The Dorfweil Statement

The Hamburg Agreement which was later ratified by both the European Baptist Federation and the Foreign Mission Board contained ten points setting forth principles by which the board and the federation would work together in reaching Europe for Christ.

At the end [of the Consultation] Karl-Heinz Walter said: 'If we had had this kind of

agreement years ago, we might not have had the Rüschlikon fiasco. This is the first time, to my knowledge, we have ever put in writing a working relationship with any foreign mission board of any kind. We ought to do it with everyone who works with us.'[84]

There is little doubt, as LeRoy Smith said in presenting the Hamburg Agreement to the board, that this was an historic achievement. Basic to all else in the agreement was the first point that contained the five principles drawn up on 28 January 1992 and known as the Dorfweil Statement which were:

1.1   Mutual respect in which the partners deal with each other with candor but with Christian courtesy. (Eph. 4:1-3)

1.2   Spiritual freedom in which the partners, working within a common commitment, recognize and welcome differences of outlook and diversity of practice. (Rom. 15:7; Mark 9:38-41)

1.3   Moral integrity in which the partners honor and maintain solemnly-made agreements. (2 Cor. 1:12-17)

1.4   Genuine consultation in which the partners confer together and aim for mutual consent. (2 Cor. 8:8-9)

1.5   Reciprocal sharing in which the partners learn, work and grow together, each giving and receiving. (Rom. 1:11-12)

All in the Consultation agreed freely, unreservedly and unequivocally that these principles should form the basis of future partnership between the FMB and European Baptists.[85]

In presenting his report, LeRoy Smith, indicated that he was bringing before the board what may well have been "the most important agreement in the history of modern missions." He explained that the reconciliation which made possible the Hamburg

Agreement was due to "only one reason and that is that God wanted the hurts of His body healed and He did it."[86] It appeared to those present that God had wrought out of a less than commendable episode in Foreign Mission Board history a remarkable development. The Hamburg Agreement was ratified by the board on 12 October 1992.

From October to March: Estrangement

In August, 1991, Parks presented to the trustees his vision of the Foreign Mission Board's task throughout the board's sesqui-centennial year 1995 after such time he suggested change of presidential leadership could be smoothly accomplished. At the close of his address, he received a standing ovation. Two months later the climate had begun to change. With the vote to defund the seminary in Rüschlikon in October and Parks's opposition to the action, the tension between him and the trustees mounted.

The first of a series of actions that found Parks and the trustees on opposite sides was a proposal of the Chairman's Council. The council proposed setting up a Search Committee immediately to seek out a new president. After electing a new president the council planned to send the president-elect on a tour of the world which would be followed by a twelve month mission tour by Keith and Helen Jean Parks. This proposal did not set well with Parks. He said: "I thought it was the worst kind of arrangement you can imagine."[87] Later, he said,

I told the group: You totally misunderstood my report in August. I'm not trying to find a way to stay until '95. What I'm trying to do is mobilize the mission impetus of Southern Baptists to capitalize on opportunities that missiologists tell us historically that you have three to five years to capitalize on critical

opportunities. And the clock started ticking in January of '90, so that's what I was trying to say.[88]

In the same meeting in October, Parks found himself in opposition to the action of the trustees when they voted to cut off the board's subsidy to Rüschlikon Seminary. The second vote on Rüschlikon in December acerbated the growing tension between Parks and the trustees. He recalled that at the February board meeting, "I started to go ahead and offer my retirement, but I wanted to make one last appeal to say, 'either give me the mandate and affirmation and let's move on, or tell me you are not going to do that. But I need to know, you need to know.'"[89]

Instead of the mandate, the board voted to hold a retreat in March. The retreat was led by Henry Blackaby of the Home Mission Board. It was, evidently, as the trustees had hoped, a truly spiritual mountaintop experience. It was during this retreat that in spite of expressions of support by individual trustees, Parks decided to retire before 1995. In his own words, he said:

As he [Blackaby] was in some directed prayer time he was talking about death to self and raising the question what were we holding onto that we ought to surrender to the Lord. It became clear to me, in that moment, that the one thing I was holding onto was my role as president of this organization. And it also became clear that the trustees were not going to affirm my leadership.[90]

Since no minutes were taken at the retreat, the record can only reflect the opinion of those who were there. Four trustees in personal conversation agreed with Parks that the retreat was a spiritual mountaintop experience. They also indicated that there were many personal affirmations of Parks during the retreat.[91] But apparently the "mandate" which Parks had sought was not forthcoming. Hence he felt it was the will of God that he retire as president He offered his resignation at the April board meeting.

Parks's announcement that he would retire in 1992 rather than 1995, as previously announced, indicated a recognition that his estrangement with the trustees had reached the point of no return.[92] Parks's decision to retire came at

Parks addresses the board, May 1989.

some conservatives had begun to question Parks's leadership. Upon that occasion, Draper declared: "I want first of all to express how deeply I appreciate and believe in Keith Parks. Keith would tell you that one of the first letters he received after taking this position was one from me expressing confidence and prayers."[94] Then, he addressed Keith directly, indicating his agreement with Keith's emphasis on the priority of missions. "What

the end of a decade of increasingly strained relationships between himself and conservative trustees that began to surface as early as 1982. After the 1982 convention meeting in New Orleans, he wrote: "When we analyzed it carefully, it was apparent that Bold Mission Thrust was not this convention's agenda." Again, he said, "I came away from this convention with a feeling there had been an unconscious shifting of our focus. We did not part with a sense of rededication to our primary task but, rather, polarized around a variety of issues that are not our first priority."[93]

James T. Draper, elected president of the Southern Baptist Convention in June 1982, made his first appearance as president at the October meeting of the Foreign Mission Board. While he affirmed Parks, his dedication and his vision, he also indicated that

you said this morning was brilliantly spoken and is absolutely essential. Our mission work has to be evangelistic, church starting, Bible centered. How can we disagree with that? Nobody can disagree with that, and that has to be. We must not be so overcome in one area or the other that that kind of emphasis does not take the precedence."[95]

In 1984, the board met in Biloxi, Mississippi. In this meeting Parks chose to address the board on the distinguishing marks of Southern Baptists. He pointed out that while Southern Baptists share six major beliefs with other Baptists, their distinguishing characteristic is the nature of their commitment to missions.[96] Then he issued a warning: "Southern Baptists, your destiny— your potential for making a remarkable contribution in my world—is missions. Don't be sidetracked!"[97]

It is clear from a careful reading of the minutes of the board that Parks was increasingly concerned with what has been called the conservative resurgence in the Southern Baptist Convention. This was not because he was not a theological conservative but because he felt the controversy was moving the convention away from its original missionary vision and its distinctive reason for being. Since Parks tried to maintain an apolitical stance, it was a surprise to many when he issued a press release on 22 April 1985 opposing the election of Charles Stanley to a second term as president of the convention. His stated reason for doing so was that Stanley's participation in the denomination was minimal. He and his church were viewed in the vanguard of the movement to dismantle the denomination by accusing the missionaries and institutions of "liberalism." Parks closed his three page document with a plea. "May we not deliberately and unconsciously destroy the most effective mission force in the world today."[98] From this time on, according to O'Brien, Keith Parks was a marked man.[99]

At the October 1988 meeting of the board, Parks felt compelled to address the controversy again after the dialogue on Rüschlikon. He began by emphasizing, as he had repeatedly, that "Missions epitomized the Southern Baptist Convention the day it was born." Then he proceeded to delineate ten points that created an unprecedented challenge for foreign missions. The heart of his message was his concern with the rising crescendo of "misconceptions, suspicion, and distrust that is rampant in our convention."[100] Parks called upon the trustees to repudiate the perception that the trustees of the board were not committed to the priori-

ty of missions among Southern Baptists by declaring their agreement with six statements, the first of which was to "affirm the missionaries and the staff as being theologically sound and evangelistically committed." And the second asked them to "make a wholehearted, unreserved commitment to the continued implementation of the established principles of our mission work."[101]

In response to Parks's request, C. Mark Corts, chairman of the board, appointed a committee to compose a reply to be presented to the trustees in the December meeting

Mark Corts speaks during April 1988 board meeting, Greensboro, North Carolina.

of the board. The resolution composed by the committee, chaired by John Thomas, affirmed the substance of Parks's seven principles in six statements, the first of which began with the reassuring words: "BE IT RESOLVED that the trustees of the Foreign Mission Board 1. Whole-heartedly affirm Dr. Keith Parks, the Foreign Mission Board staff, and our adopted strategy of 'evangelism that produces churches'. . . ."[102] The committee's resolution was approved by the board, and Parks was encouraged. Two years later, however, he felt compelled to address the same

Southern Baptist Convention, New Orleans, 1990

were a true barometer of interest in foreign missions on the part of the messengers, then before his eyes Parks saw the verification of his allegation that the controversy was hurting the cause of missions.

Parks Retires

The resignations of Isam Ballenger and Keith Parker called for a public explanation. Parks felt that it could best be done within the context of a press conference at the headquarters building. After all, Ballenger, a vice president of the board and twenty-eight years in its service, and Parker, area director and a veteran of twenty-three years, deserved to be heard. Besides, Parks's well known position that an unstifled press was best for a free people and the cause of Christ demanded it. Southern Baptists deserved to know why two irreplaceable missionaries felt compelled to resign. All of these factors entered into Parks's decision to call the news conference that in turn prompted William L. Hancock, chairman, to call a special session of the board on Monday 10 February 1992.

It was apparent from the questions of some members of the board that many felt that Parks had erred in giving Ballenger and Parker a platform, as they viewed it, at the board's headquarters. The entire board,

issues again within the context of his own personal pilgrimage.

It was in New Orleans, just before the meeting of the Southern Baptist Convention that Parks felt it necessary to deal with "the something against me" attitude. The point that Parks was attempting to make was that the controversy was hurting the Southern Baptist foreign mission effort around the world. Regardless of the reason Parks felt it necessary to address the board this way, it is difficult to escape the impression that he had assumed an adversarial position in dealing with the trustees.

On Wednesday evening, Parks brought a stirring message on "The Right Time" to the messengers who had taken the time to attend. Of the 37,224 voting in the convention's presidential election on Tuesday morning, less than 3,000 were present on Wednesday night for the Foreign Mission Board report.[103] If attendance at this service

however, went on record affirming the seven principles that Parks had formulated and stated repeatedly were basic to everything the board was doing. After expressing his appreciation for the board's affirmation of the principles and himself, he said: "I continue to get other messages that are contradictory. So, I feel I must share some deep feelings although I have fought against doing so."[104] Then he proceeded to delineate the charges brought against the missionaries and the staff. The Rüschlikon issue and the way in which the board handled it caused him to charge that the trustees had forsaken the indigenous principle. Then he clarified what he had observed: "It appears to me that a shift has occurred when this Board is expecting theological conformity from those who receive Southern Baptist money. I am as concerned about correct biblical belief as anyone is, but to use money to produce it is not the biblical nor Baptist way."[105]

At the close of his report to the board on 8 April, Parks announced his retirement.

Rev. Bill Hancock

Chairman

Foreign Mission Board

Dear Mr. Chairman:

For many months my tenure as president has been a focal point of disruption of our foreign mission effort. The urgent need for decisive leadership has never been greater. Such leadership requires mutual trust and confidence between the trustees and the president. I regret that was not achievable.

In light of this, I have felt a leadership of the Lord to announce my retirement. The effective date is October 30, 1992.

Sincerely,

R. Keith Parks[106]

The Fallout

Among Southern Baptists, the "fallout" of the Parks decision was widespread. First, it was only after the meeting of the convention in New Orleans that the moderates felt so disfranchised that they formed the Cooperative Baptist Fellowship to pursue what they perceived as an abandoned denominational agenda. Second, many missionaries did not understand why Parks stepped down in 1992 when they thought he had committed himself not to retire until 1995. His answer in the form of an open letter frankly stated the reasons. Parks delineated in ten points how he believed the board had changed under the influence of the conservative trustees.[107] Third, in his last annual report to the convention in Indianapolis, he summarized the toll that the controversy had taken on the foreign mission work of the convention. He also cited the shift in emphasis at the annual meetings from missions to politics. Attendance at Indianapolis served to illustrate his point. Of the 17,978 messengers registered, only 4,400 were present for the missionary program. Of those present, an estimated two hundred walked out during Parks's address. Most of those who remained interrupted him time and again by spontaneous applause. But even some of his strongest supporters felt his message was unnecessarily negative. Fourth, during the last months and weeks of his service with the board, Keith and Helen Jean found themselves the recipients of numerous expressions of appreciation from the trustees, missionaries, and friends. Fifth, Parks specifically asked that his retirement be a low key affair and it was. This was in keeping with his own "incarnational" witness. Alan

Thompson, chairman of the Retirement Committee presented pins commemorating thirty-eight years of service with the Foreign Mission Board along with c e r t i f i c a t e s a n d a "R e s o l u t i o n of Appreciation" adopted by the trustees. The resolution listed eleven achievements of the board during Parks's administration.

RESOLUTION OF APPRECIATION

WHEREAS, R. Keith Parks retires as president of the Foreign Mission Board October 30, 1992, completing nearly 13 years of extraordinary service in that position; and

WHEREAS, The following emphases and achievements occurred under his leadership:

*1.	Firmly established "evangelism that results in churches" as the primary goal of the Southern Baptist Convention's foreign mission effort.*

*2.	Recognized prayer as the key to effective foreign mission involvement by setting a personal example and by creating and staffing a prayer office.*

*3.	Introduced to Southern Baptist foreign missions and enhanced within evangelical circles the concept of using non-traditional missionaries to evangelize countries, peoples, segments and cities which cannot be reached through traditional methods. Consequently, helped bring about the use of terms such as "World A" and "NRMs" [nonresidential missionaries] in the missions language and in efforts of every evangelical sending agency and parachurch agency. Encouraged the development of databases that support the thrust of evangelization.*

*4.	Led the staff to move towards a global perspective in planning, strategy and implementing mission efforts, thereby starting to replace the more segmented, turf-conscious and competitive area perspectives of the past.*

*5.	Developed a combined research and planning office and gave attention to database decision-making grounded in and shaped by biblical and spiritual mandates.*

*6.	Championed and maintained a strategic balance between the biblical mandates of discipling believers and evangelizing those who have never heard the gospel.*

*7.	Supported a holistic approach to missions which resulted in an appropriate mix of ministry to both spiritual needs and human needs—of evangelism and social involvement.*

*8.	Made significant advances in placing support and leadership for institutions and evangelism in the hands of national Baptists.*

*9.	Made it possible for individual missionaries to achieve greater success in learning languages and culture.*

*10.	Undergirded and enhanced the approach of selecting career and associate missionaries based on needs identified by the field while also making it possible for more volunteers to serve overseas than served during all the previous years of SBC mission work.*

*11.	Set a personal and corporate lifestyle example of frugality and sacrifice. Funds spent on administrative matters in the United States were kept to a minimum throughout his tenure, which set apart the FMB in this category from other missionary-sending agencies; and*

WHEREAS, He and his wife, Helen Jean, through their personal friendship, exemplary Christian witness, and intense dedication to the cause of world missions, have been of invaluable encouragement to our Foreign Mission Board missionaries, staff, and trustees,

BE IT RESOLVED, That the trustees of the Foreign Mission Board express our gratitude to God and our deep appreciation for the world missions leadership of R. Keith Parks, president of the Foreign Mission Board of the Southern Baptist Convention, January 1, 1980, to October 30, 1992; and

BE IT FURTHER RESOLVED, That the trustees of the Foreign Mission Board express our prayerful desires for God's continued blessings upon Keith and Helen Jean Parks in the years to come.[107]

Unknown to many of the trustees as well as most Southern Baptists were the financial changes brought about largely through Parks's leadership in the years he served as president. Carl Johnson, vice president and treasurer, delineated these accomplishments as follows: (1) Endowment increased from $14 million to $72 million; (2) Contingency reserve from $12,870,000 to $25,000,000; (3) Missionary pensions greatly increased by board's increased contribution; (4) Maximum life insurance coverage per missionary from $20,000 to $100,000; (5) Personal property insurance from $0 to $15,000. Johnson said:

It is probably in the area of missionary support that he will have made his greatest impact in the area of finance at the Foreign Mission Board. . . . Dr. Parks had the courage a lot of others would not have had: to support the staff decision to put the Foreign Mission Board $10 million into debt to make the necessary changes in the missionary pension plan. Not many presidents in their second year in office would have had the courage to do that, particularly at a time when the Foreign Mission Board's budget was a lot smaller than it is now. That debt was finally retired in 1989.[108]

While all missionaries of the board cannot help but be grateful for Parks's leadership in providing more adequate mission support, the Parks legacy was far greater than dollars and cents.

The Parks Legacy

At the time of his retirement, as Parks had indicated at Indianapolis, only two of the major goals of Bold Mission Thrust had been met: that of 10,000 volunteers annually and 125 countries entered by the year 2000. While reaching the goal of 5,000 missionaries may not be impossible, it will take considerable more effort. In 1992, the missionary force stood at 3,918 missionaries with eight years to go. Although the gospel was being preached by Southern Baptist missionaries or volunteers in 126 countries and among twenty-nine additional people groups in other countries, the goal of proclaiming the redemptive message of God's love in Christ was far short of everyone in the world in 1992, but it was still much closer to realization because of Keith Parks and his vision of proclaiming the whole gospel to the whole world.

Perhaps, Parks's greatest legacy was himself. As long as there are Southern Baptists on the earth, his example of integrity and his understanding of the Baptist heritage will continue to challenge them to a reassessment of who they were in the last decade of the twentieth century and what they can be by God's grace in the twenty-first.

ENDNOTES

1. Sullivan, "What do We do Next?" Newsweek, November 20, 1989, 41.

2. Minutes, FMB, 9 March 1979, 104, 105.

3. Dr. Jesse Fletcher, interview by author, 21 April 1993, Fort Worth, Texas, tape recording.

4. Minutes, FMB, 7 August 1979, 249.

5. William R. O'Brien, "Evangelism That Results in Churches," unpublished paper, 1992, 2.

6. R. Keith Parks, telephone interview by author, 15 July 1993.

7. Robert Keith Parks, "A Biblical Evaluation of the Doctrine of Justification in Recent American Baptist Theology" (Th.D. thesis, Southwestern Baptist

Theological Seminary, 1954), 187-90.

8. See Ebbie C. Smith, God's Miracles: Indonesian Church Growth (South Pasadena, Calif.: William Carey Library, 1970), 1-122.

9. Ebbie C. Smith, interview by author, 21 June 1993, Fort Worth, Texas, tape recording.

10. O'Brien, "Evangelism That Results in Churches," 4.

11. Ebbie C. Smith, interview.

12. Dr. R. Keith Parks, interview by author, 19 June 1992, Richmond, Virginia, tape recording.

13. Ibid., 9.

14. Ibid.

15. Ibid.

16. Ibid., 12.

17. Minutes, FMB, 11 February 1975, 21.

18. Ibid.

19. Ibid., 21.

20. The October 1975 board meeting marked the fortieth anniversary of the appointment of Dr. and Mrs. Eugene L. Hill. The Hills were appointed on 16 October 1935 to China along with Lois Glass, the sister of Eloise Cauthen. The twenty-six new missionaries who were appointed at this time constituted the largest group of new appointees sent out by Southern Baptists since the beginning of the Great Depression.

21. Minutes, FMB, 12 April 1976, 172.

22. Minutes, FMB, 12 October 1976, 86.

23. Ibid.

24. Ibid.

25. Minutes, FMB, 7 January 1980, 146. I have taken the liberty of correcting the typos without adding [sic] since to do so would detract from the force of the address. Another inadvertent error is that the response by Parks was titled "Installation Message."

26. Ibid., 146-50. The entire address did not take more than twenty minutes. It was not intended to demonstrate the learning of the speaker or his oratorical skill. It was from Parks's heart to the hearts of Southern Baptists. The call to think in terms of "global missions" resounded throughout the message.

27. Annual, SBC, 1980, 85.

28. Annual, SBC, 1976, 54.

29. Minutes, FMB, 6-8 April 1992, 9.

30. Louis Cobb, telephone interview by author, 21 July 1993.

31. Minutes, FMB, 7 January 1980, 141.

32. Minette Drumwright, interview by author, 8 June 1993, Richmond, Virginia.

33. News and Information Services, Southern Baptist Foreign Mission Board, Richmond, Virginia, 22 February 1991.

34. Minette Drumwright, interview.

35. Minutes, FMB, 11 February 1980, 20.

36. Ibid.

37. Minutes, FMB, 8 April 1980, 42.

38. Minutes, FMB, 11 April 1980, 42.

39. Minutes, FMB, 8 April 1980, 42, 43.

40. Generous friends of the Foreign Mission Board numbering 1,200 or more made possible not only the twenty major buildings of the center and its furnishings but also an endowment for its programs of learning. Numbered among the donors were Cecil B. and Deen Day and Bill Clinton (now president of the United States).

41. Norman Burnes, Director, Missionary Learning Center, interview by the author, 11 June 1993, Rockville, Virginia.

42. Minutes, FMB, 8, 9 March 1982, 3.

43. Ibid., 4, 5.

44. Ibid., 5.

45. Robert O'Brien, "Ethiopia, the 24-hour Miracle," in *The Commission*, February-March 1985, 70.

46. Art Toalston, "After Armero," The Commission, January 1986, 12-19.

47. Cited in *The Commission*, January 1986, 63.

48. R. Keith Parks, World In View (Birmingham: New Hope, 1987), 50.

49. "The Future of Missions: Change," R. Keith Parks, *The Commission*, October 1980, 2.

50. William R. O'Brien, telephone interview by the author, 21 July 1993.

51. Ibid.

52. "Board creates office to respond to China," *The Commission*, June-July 1985, 9.

53. R. Keith Parks, interview by the author, 19 June 1992, Richmond, Virginia. Hereafter referred to as Keith Parks, interview. The meeting was held 17-20 September 1987. See report on the back of *The Commission*, October-November 1987.

54. Ibid.

55. See V. David Garrison, The Nonresidential Missionary: A new strategy and the people it serves (Monrovia, Calif.: MARC, 1990), for more information on the nonresidential missionary concept.

56. Minutes, FMB, 9-11 October 1987, 4.

57. Ibid., 5.

58. From Minutes, FMB, 9-11 February 1987, 7-8.

59. Keith Parks, interview.

60. Ibid.

61. Ibid.

62. In 1993, the Tentmaker Program was discontinued. The Journeyman Program was to be restored to its separate status with a longer period of training. The change was scheduled to be implemented in

January 1994.

63. Minutes, FMB, 9-11 December 1991, 4.

64. Ibid., 5.

65. Minutes, FMB, 10 December 1991, 15.

66. Ibid.

67. Ibid.

68. Transcription of a tape of John David Hopper's presentation on Rüschlikon and its problems to the trustees of the Foreign Mission Board, July 1988.

69. Ibid.

70. Minutes, Regional Committee Meeting: Europe, the Middle East and North Africa, 7 October 1991.

71. Ibid.

72. Bill Hancock, "Open Letter to Southern Baptists," 3 January 1992, 5. The letter was sent to 40,000 addresses at an estimated cost of $10,000.

73. Ibid., 6.

74. Ibid., 9.

75. Ibid., 10.

76. Ed Briggs, "Baptist Mission Leaders to Retire," *Richmond (Va.) Times-Dispatch*, 8 January 1992, B1.

77. Quoted in the Baptist Standard, 18 March 1992, 3.

78. Robert Dilday, "Two top FMB staffers quit, disagree with trustee acts," Baptists Today, 23 January 1992, 1. I have copies in my files of the complete statements which Ballenger and Parker released to the press on 7 January 1992.

79. Prayer letter from Bob and Jerry Worley, missionaries to Spain, 20 November 1992.

80. Samuel H. James, interview by author, 24 August 1993, Richmond, Virginia.

81. Ibid.

82. Ibid.

83. Minutes, FMB, 14 October 1992, no page #.

84. Samuel James, interview.

85. Minutes, FMB, 14 October 1992, no page #.

86. Ibid.

87. Keith Parks, interview, 20.

88. Ibid.

89. Ibid.

90. Ibid.

91. Bill Hall, Leon Hyatt, Jack Bledsoe, and Pat Bullock expressed to me their opinion that there was no attempt at the retreat to force Parks to retire, but there were several personal affirmations expressing a desire that he remain as President through 1995. Personal conversations on 7 and 8 December 1993.

92. Keith Parks, interview, 20. An indication of Parks's alienation from the trustees was indicated by the following statement:

And my perception at that moment, and it hasn't changed, was I could stay for awhile. I couldn't lead, I couldn't be productive, but I could probably stretch this thing out a few months. But the longer I stayed, the longer it will delay this board taking positive, aggressive action around the world, particularly in Eastern Europe.

93. Minutes FMB, 13 July 1982, 3. Keith Parks, "Reflections: Southern Baptist Convention at New Orleans," in *Intercom*.

94. Minutes, FMB, 13 October 1982, 49.

95. Ibid.

96. Minutes, FMB, 9-11 April 1984, 7.

97. Ibid.

98. Bob Stanley, "Parks Won't Back Stanley; Sees Threat to Missions," FMB, 22 April 1985, 3.

99. William R. O'Brien, telephone interview by the author, 21 July 1993.

100. Minutes, FMB, 10-12 October 1988, 10.

101. Ibid., 12.

102. Minutes, FMB, 12-14 December 1988, 27.

103. Grady C. Cothen, *What Happened to the Southern Baptist Convention?: A Memoir of the Controversy* (Macon, Ga.: Smyth & Helwys Publishing, 1993), 75.

104. Minutes, FMB, 10-12 February 1992, 6.

105. Ibid., 7.

106. Minutes, FMB, 6-8 April 1992, 13.

107. The ten points given in the letter are as follows:

—The most important, most incredible one is that a very large percentage of Bible-believing, theologically-conservative Southern Baptists no longer have appropriate representation on boards of trustees. Their money is still solicited but not their representatives nor any contribution of convictions or viewpoints. Southern Baptists desperately need both groups for spiritual balance.

—Decisions are increasingly shaped by ultra-conservative theological interpretations rather than tested and adopted mission principles.

—An atmosphere of trust and respect for differences of viewpoints has been replaced by suspicion, distrust, criticism and intimidation.

—Freedom to disagree has been replaced by expectation of conformity. When issues or problems cannot be discussed honestly, they cannot be dealt with productively or solved.

—Declining career appointments and increasing emphasis on volunteers are bringing an imbalance overseas.

—Some of the trustees without the time, expertise, knowledge or experience to make administrative decisions are increasingly doing staff work instead of fulfilling the role of trustees which is to shape general board policies based on mission principles, acquired understanding and staff input.

—Increasing pressure on the professional news staff to report only "positive" news threatens to destroy the credibility of the press.

—A new development in staff selection is to ask for expressions of loyalty toward trustees and/or the "conservative resurgence."

—An increasing emphasis for missionary appointment is on the four background statements in the Peace Committee report instead of just the Baptist Faith and Message statement.

—The atmosphere created by the convention controversy causes many fine candidates either to believe they cannot be appointed or to decline appointment because they are not comfortable with the present Foreign Mission Board direction.
R. Keith Parks, Richmond, to Missionary Colleagues, 23 October 1992, copy in hand of the author.

108. Minutes, FMB, 12 October 1992, unnumbered page.

PART VI

Epilogue

On the Threshold

The coming of Jerry Rankin to the presidency of the Foreign Mission Board holds the promise of a new day for the board and Southern Baptists. His experience, dedication, and conciliatory stance place him in a position to lead all Southern Baptists into the twenty-first century in unity and renewed hope.

*I*n spite of the retirement of Keith Parks and the resignation of some forty-five missionaries in Europe and a few members of the Richmond staff, the work continued unabated in much of the world. Although the Foreign Mission Board under the leadership of Don Kammerdiener, interim president, found it necessary to reduce the size of the board's staff, due to a shortfall in expected receipts, by the end of 1992 some notable gains were recorded. The number of baptisms, for example, increased from 233,334 in 1991 to 251,901 in 1992. While the number of missionaries under appointment declined by thirteen from an all time high of 3,906 in 1991, new appointments had pushed the figure to 3,978 by June 1993. There were 32,797 Baptist churches on the mission fields in 1992 compared to 27,932 in 1991, an increase of 4,865. By the end of 1992, Southern Baptist missionaries were living and witnessing in 129

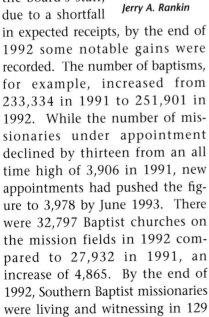

Jerry A. Rankin

countries, exclusive of some thirty other countries in which nonresidential missionaries were at work. During 1993 there were 430 new missionary appointments and by the end of the year, 2,934 were at some stage in the appointment process.

The news that the Foreign Mission Board had elected Jerry Rankin president upon the unanimous recommendation of the Search Committee was met with widespread approval and thanksgiving. Some called it a miracle. Rankin was convinced that it was the Lord's doing. The board's staff breathed a collective sigh of relief and thanked God that a missionary of Rankin's ability and dedication had been chosen.[1]

Jerry A. Rankin Elected President

The election of Jerry Rankin to the presidency of the Foreign Mission Board on 14 June 1993 was the most surprising development in recent board history. This particular episode began on 8 April 1992 when William L. Hancock, chairman of the board, named Joel Gregory, then pastor of the First Baptist Church of Dallas, Texas, chair of a fifteen-member Search Committee to recommend Parks's successor. It was a foregone conclusion that a person identified as a conservative would be the committee's choice. After considering various candidates over an eight month period, the committee decided to recommend Jerry Rankin, a veteran missionary and area director for Southeast Asia. At the last minute, it appeared that the committee's recommendation would be derailed by rumors that the nominee was a charismatic. In response, Gregory declared that Rankin had been grilled extensively on this very issue and was completely exonerated. In fact, Rankin later reported that the committee had interviewed him four times at length. On 14 June 1993, Rankin was elected president of the board by a vote of 59 to 14. Paul Pressler, who had opposed Rankin's election, made a motion, "in the interest of harmony," to make the vote unanimous.

Rankin, a Product of Southern Baptists

In an interview conducted by Van Payne, director of the Office of Communications' Audiovisual Department, Foreign Mission Board, Payne asked Rankin the question, "How do you weigh what the Southern Baptist denomination has meant in your life and development?" He answered, "I am obviously a product of Southern Baptists."[2] Rankin's testimony, given many times since his election, supports this statement.

Jerry was born in Tupelo, Mississippi, on 16 March 1942, but when he was three his family moved to a farm in the suburbs of Clinton, Mississippi. His father believed in the values of farm life for children. As a result, Jerry grew up knowing that milk came from cows and bacon from hogs for he milked the cows and fed the pigs along with the many other chores that demand a farm boy's attention. In the process he learned some of the lessons his father was attempting to teach him through a strong work ethic. Jerry recalls that there was never any question about whether the family would attend church—that was understood. They never missed a service at the First Baptist Church of Clinton, if possible. That was true of Sunday School, Training Union, and Royal Ambassadors, as well, where, he remembers, he first learned about missions and missionaries. But it was under the influence of a Billy Graham crusade in Jackson that at ten years of age Jerry was converted.

Missionaries who visited the church and those who went out from the church to serve in Nigeria and elsewhere began to turn his mind toward the masses without Christ, the thoughts of which kept him awake at night. He was twelve years of age when he decided that he must do something personally about the lost multitudes—he determined to become a missionary.

Jerry found much support in his decision from his home and from his pastor. His pastor, Russel McIntyre, came to Clinton just before Jerry was converted, and it was he who baptized him and asked him to preach his first sermon when he was sixteen. Another member of the church who had a great influence on his life was Billy Ray Smith, a high school basketball coach, who came to Clinton during Jerry's third year in high school. By this time Jerry had begun to report sporting events at the high school for the Jackson *Daily News-Clarion Ledger.* As a sports writer he was closely associated with the devout coach. Jerry continued this extra-curricular activity throughout his college career.

Rankin said that there was never any question about where he would attend college. Although he lived just a short distance from the school, he moved into the dormitory in order to participate more fully in campus life. It was a good decision for he became involved in the student government and active in the Baptist Student Union, of which he became president. During his college years two summers were spent in mission work. The first summer, between his sophomore and junior years, he worked in Vermont and New York; the next summer in the Philippines. En route to the Philippines he was able to visit with missionaries in Japan, Thailand, India, Nigeria, and the Middle East. The missionary experiences of the two summers served to confirm him in the conviction of God's leading in his life. He graduated with a Bachelor of Arts degree from Mississippi College in 1965.

Jerry entered Southwestern Seminary in the fall of 1965. He recalled that the years at Southwestern enlarged his vision and strengthened his sense of God's call. While certain professors were particularly influential in his life, he said, "I think all of our professors, by and large, had an emphasis on spiritual formations in the lives of their students."[3] During his four years at Southwestern, Rankin was involved in a variety of ministries. For three years, he was

youth director and associate pastor of the Sagamore Hill Baptist Church followed by a two year pastorate at the Sadler Baptist Church. During his time at Sadler he also served a year as part-time Baptist Student Union director and as Bible instructor at Grayson County College, Denison, Texas. Rankin received an M.Div. degree in 1969. Later, Mississippi College awarded him a Doctor of Divinity degree.

Before Jerry finished Southwestern, the first of the Rankins' two children, Lori, was born in 1968, and Russell two years later. Mrs. Rankin is the former Bobbye Simons of

WMU executive director, Dellanna O'Brien, right, welcomes Jerry and Bobbye Rankin to WMU annual meeting, Houston, June 1993.

Mobile, Alabama. She graduated from Mississippi College in 1966 with a Bachelor of Science degree; she also attended Southwestern.

Career Missionaries

The Rankins were career missionaries with twenty-three years of varied missionary experience. Appointed in 1970 to Indonesia, they did their language study at Bandung on the island of Java. During their first ten years, Jerry served as a general evangelist with some special short term assignments in India and Bangladesh. For almost five years, he was the associate to the director of South and Southeast Asia and for a year was the administrator for the Southern Baptist missionary effort in India. In 1987, Rankin was named area director for Southern Asia and the Pacific. Since then the Rankins lived in Bangkok, Thailand.

Missionaries depend on the prayer calendar in Royal Service.

During his tenure as area director, Rankin established his base in Thailand in order to have greater access to the 440 missionaries in the seventeen countries comprising the area. His position necessitated frequent trips to Richmond, where he participated in the work of the Global Strategy Group. This aspect of his experience commended him to at least one trustee, who said,

> Rankin's role as an "outside-insider" gave the committee the feeling he knows the FMB's internal affairs but still has an objective view. As area director he operated in two worlds: he was a staff member and sat on the Global Strategy Group, the board's key planning body, but lived and worked overseas except for occasional periods at the FMB's home office.[4]

Although, according to Gregory, Rankin was reported to be a friend of the fundamentalist-conservative political cause, he appears not to have been a "party man." Although, admittedly conservative, he possesses an independent mind with an appre-

ciation of the uniqueness of the Baptist heritage.[5] His first actions as president of the Foreign Mission Board appear to confirm this judgment.

Rankin Acts Decisively

Almost immediately after his election, Rankin made his way to the meeting of the Woman's Missionary Union. His action was as significant as anything he might have said. By it he was saying, "We appreciate you and we need you." He has repeatedly said how much he owes to the Royal Ambassador program, which was initiated by the Woman's Missionary Union. Also, as a missionary he was conscious of the prayers of thousands who read his name on the prayer calendar of *Royal Service.*

In his first meeting with the trustees, Rankin gave an indication of how he hoped to lead the missionary efforts of Southern Baptists. Among other things, he emphasized working together in unity which could only happen when trustees understood the differences between the role of the trustee and that of the missionary staff. He reminded the trustees that missionaries and staff members bring to their role "in most cases, a deep, lifelong commitment and call to missions, extensive experience which shapes our conviction, and a professional level of competency. . . ." Then he frankly said, "I would expect those assets to be recognized and respected."[6]

Later on in his address, Rankin cautioned the trustees against bringing to the board meetings their personal quarrels. "The open forums of this board are not the appropriate venue for voicing and reflecting our unresolved personal differences."[7] He went on to emphasize that the missionary enterprise of Southern Baptists needs the perspective of everyone and that "it is not necessary to compromise personal convictions nor to resolve differences in order to work together in unity and trust."[8]

These statements indicate that Rankin was well aware of the problems that moved Parks to seek early retirement. They also indicate that while he intended to remain open to suggestions from anyone, he planned to exert strong leadership in determining the direction in which the board would move. It was clear that his undergirding conviction was that he owed his new position not to any person or group, but to God alone—the same God who called him to missionary service and endowed him with the gifts of the Holy Spirit.

Rankin's Vision

The heart of Rankin's vision for the Foreign Mission Board is what he perceives to be its God-given task. He told Payne, "We must not lose sight of the fact that our task is to bring lost people to a redemptive experience of knowing Jesus Christ as Lord."[9] This task involves missions and evangelism. Rankin makes a distinction between the two: "Missions is cross-cultural witness of sharing Jesus Christ with the lost. I would emphasize the cross-cultural aspect, as I feel this is the only thing that distinguishes missions from evangelism—leading the lost to know Jesus Christ as Savior."[10] The conviction that God's hand is uniquely upon Southern Baptists in fulfilling his plan for world redemption runs deep in Rankin's soul.

While Rankin is convinced of Southern Baptists' role in achieving God's purpose in the world, he recognizes this conviction must be a shared one for he rightly understands the voluntary nature of the denomination.

> There is a real distinction [between Southern Baptists and other denominations] because of our emphasis on the priesthood of the believer and the autonomy of the local church. . . . Our denomination is just churches cooperating together.[11]

Because of the voluntary nature of the denomination, Rankin recognizes the absolute necessity of restoring the trust factor within the denomination and in the operation of the Foreign Mission Board. This, he believes, is his greatest challenge. All else depends upon it. He explained his position to Van Payne:

> Many people have said to me that they feel the greatest need for the Foreign Mission Board at this time is spiritual leadership that can bring healing, reconciliation, encouragement, unity. Yes, but lead us in a sensitive following of what God is doing in the world. That is worth every price, every effort, whatever the cost, whatever the sacrifice.[12]

What of the Future?

The future of the Foreign Mission Board depends upon the health of the denomination. The healing of the divisions within the convention does not depend upon everyone becoming a moderate-conservative or a fundamentalist-conservative anymore than it depends upon every member becoming a dispensationalist or a supralapsarian Calvinist. But it does depend upon recognizing that unity is found alone in the Lord Jesus Christ and that the denomination exists only for carrying out the Great Commission of our Lord, to whom all authority in heaven and on earth has been given (Matthew 28:18-20).

Missions was the most important contributing factor in the birth of the denomination and foreign missions became its primary focus. In fact, for years the convention was little more than a foreign mission society and only after 1882 became a convention with a functioning Home Mission Board, as provided by its constitution.[13] With the advent of the Cooperative Program and the Executive Committee, Southern Baptists became a denomination. Before this could happen, the convention survived a number of frontal assaults and other more subtle threats to its existence. For those who long to see the Foreign Mission Board proclaim the whole gospel to the whole world, there is hope that Southern Baptists can learn from their past for the sake of those who still wait in darkness for the life-transforming power of that gospel.

The Landmark Movement

J. R. Graves launched a vicious attack against the boards of the convention, especially the Foreign Mission Board in 1859 on the basis that a local church or local associations of churches alone had the biblical authority to appoint and send out missionaries. He and his followers almost succeeded in destroying the struggling foreign mission effort of Southern Baptists but failed when the convention rallied to the support of the board. Significantly, the board also agreed to send out any missionary that a cooperating church or association would appoint, if the church or association would provide the full support and expenses incurred. Thus, the convention was saved from the immediate crisis presented by the Landmark movement.

The Foreign Mission Board was adversely affected by the Gospel Mission movement, which developed in China under the leadership of T. P. Crawford. Under the influence of Graves and the Landmarkers, he stressed both the indigenous nature of churches overseas and their autonomy. Eventually his movement led to the formation of an association in the Shantung Province in North China that withdrew from the North China Mission. It survived but a few years after the death of Crawford. After the turn of the century its few remaining missionaries returned to the board's service. This became possible because of Willingham's willingness to reach out in personal friendship to the dedicated remnant.

Before the Landmark movement had run its course, Southern Seminary lost its president. W. H. Whitsitt, professor of church history and president of the seminary, dared to question, on the basis of his research, the Landmarkers' view of Baptist history. The opposition against him became so great that he finally offered his resignation in 1898. E. Y. Mullins, who was apparently acceptable to the Landmark faction, succeeded Whitsitt to become one of the seminary's greatest presidents. It was he who led Southern Baptists safely through the shoals of the fundamentalist controversy of the 1920s.

The Fundamentalist Movement

The Landmark teachings continued to disrupt the fellowship of Southern Baptists in a number of states with the result that small schismatic groups began to withdraw from the convention, but these schisms were hardly comparable to the disruption caused by the fundamentalists in the Northern Baptist Convention (now American Baptists) as well as other denominations. Fundamentalism in the South left the Southern Baptist Convention almost unscathed except for J. Frank Norris and his Premillennial Baptist Missionary Fellowship which became the World Baptist Fellowship in 1950.

Doubtless there were many reasons why fundamentalism never gained a sizable following among Southern Baptists. For one thing, Norris so wantonly violated so many Baptist ecclesiological principles that his church was excluded, in succession, from the association, the Baptist General Convention of Texas, and the Southern Baptist Convention. Second, under the pressure of vocal fundamentalists within the convention, the Southern Baptist Convention adopted "The Baptist Faith and Message" (its first confession of faith) in 1925. Its preamble disavowed its creedal implications in such terms that it could accommodate the wide diversity of Baptists within the convention. Third, there were no vocal or widely influential "modernists" among Southern Baptists. Fourth, at the time, the cooperative effort in missions,

...the cooperative effort in missions, education, publications and finances was building a momentum and molding a denomination.

education, publications, and finances was building a momentum and molding a denomination. Fifth, there was an adherence by informed Southern Baptists to the essentials of the Baptist heritage, including the fundamentals of the faith that went beyond theory to the application of what was conceived to be the teachings of the New Testament on the church. For these reasons fundamentalism of the 1920s had little effect upon the convention, although a few churches did leave the denomination.

Whether the denomination can recover the momentum of Bold Mission Thrust lost due to the controversy that has increasingly preoccupied the convention since 1979, depends upon the ability of Southern Baptists to surmount it as they did other controversies during the convention's first century and a half. The denomination proved flexible enough in the Landmark, Gospel Mission, and fundamentalist controversies to accommodate the dissidents without betraying its heritage and its missionary vision. The healing of the present divisions within the denomination, as it stands on the threshold of the twenty-first century, awaits the recovery of the distinctive nature of the Baptist heritage and the priority of the convention's missionary vision. The future of the Foreign Mission Board and the viability of the denomination depend upon it.

Is It Worth the Effort?

Is it worth the effort to make possible the continued witness of Southern Baptist missionaries around the world? The answer to that question depends upon whether one is convinced that the missionary witness overseas on the part of Southern Baptists is absolutely essential to the salvation of lost multitudes who otherwise would never know the Christ who saves. To ask the question in another way: is it worth the effort to support a hospital in Bangalore, India, missionaries in the Philippines, or a development team in Ethiopia? The following examples, which could be multiplied thousands of times, give us glimpses into what Southern Baptists are attempting to do overseas.

Bangalore, India

Bangalore is in the state of Karnataka. At the time the Baptist hospital opened, it was the only Southern Baptist witness legally possible in India. The state of Karnataka was one of the most solidly Hindu of any state in the nation. There were only five

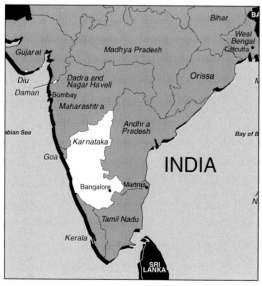

India

Baptist churches in the entire state and Bangalore was a city of one and a half million people when the eighty bed hospital

Bangalore Baptist Hospital in India; a 23-bed addition was completed in 1991.

was dedicated in 1973. Rebekah Naylor, a young missionary surgeon, arrived to assist the other missionaries in the medical and evangelistic ministries in 1974. In those years, she recalled that the medical staff was treating on the average of only ten or twelve patients a day. The missionaries outnumbered the patients.

> *We prayed that this hospital could really be an open door to evangelism and church development. Well, today, it is a different scene. We are a 143 bed hospital in a city of five million. We now average 95 to 100 patients in those beds. I am the only Southern Baptist missionary resident in India, and we now have almost 450 churches in our state of Karnataka in South India. Last year (1992) in our hospital we treated almost 62,000 outpatients, and we admitted more than 6,000 inpatients.[14]*

There is no question about the quality of medical care offered by the hospital or the Christian witness that it bears. This was clearly evident when the hospital accepted an American tourist in India suffering from AIDS. After every other hospital in the city turned the sick man away, the Baptist hospi-

384

tal accepted him. The head of security of the hotel in which the AIDS victim was a guest heard with gratitude Rebekah's explanation: "We are a Christian hospital. It is our policy that we treat anyone, no matter their socio-economic background, no matter their disease status, whatever is their need, we are there to try to meet it."[15] She also said: "I pray with patients always in surgery. There has never been a time that I remember that any patient of any religious back-

Primrose Vasa, left, and Rebekah Naylor talk with a patient after 1983 Sunday morning chapel service.

Rebekah Naylor, M.D.

ground has been unhappy about that prayer before surgery."[16] There are nine chaplains who minister to the spiritual needs of the patients and there are twenty Christian doctors on the staff in addition to Rebekah.

Rebekah Naylor is not only a surgeon (Fellow of the American College of Surgeons) but the administrator of the hospital as well. Her task would be an impossible one without the help of a medical team of doctors (citizens of India) and numerous Southern Baptist volunteers, including doctors, technicians, and nurses. Two volunteers, Joe Ann Shelton and Loeen Bushman, answered Rebekah's call for help in organizing a staff choir of the hospital's medical

personnel. The choir has opened many doors for the gospel that would have remained closed otherwise.

One of the most remarkable developments in the twenty years of the hospital's existence, and much of this time with only one missionary in residence, is the growth of the Baptist work in the region. Where there were only five Baptist churches in the entire state in 1973, by 1993 there were 450 churches. Naylor explained, "The priority for me individually, and for our hospital, is to tell people about Jesus. That is why we are there."[17]

Among the Manobos

Quite a different missionary saga comes from the Philippines. A letter to Keith Parks from Charles H. (Chuck) Morris, at the time stationed in the Philippines, contained an account of the conversion of the "Lost Tribe of Mindanao." It took him three days to walk into the remote mountains where the Manobos lived. There were no roads, only paths, and a crocodile infested river to cross. After reaching the object of his arduous journey, he described what happened:

Mindanao island in the Philippines

Supreme Datu Manlapanag, second from left, and other Manobos, host meal for visitors including Missionary Bob Stanley, left.

Soon after I arrived I met the pakell-lokesen, *the woman leader of the primitive religion of the Manobos. Her beady eyes followed my every movement. Her dress and unique beads identified her as the one experienced in keeping the traditions and laws of the tribe.*

She knew I was there to tell her people about Jesus Christ. I wondered what she was thinking, what she was planning.

It was past midnight and the full moon was reflecting off the frothy Maridajao River. A strange sound jerked me awake. The old woman was squatting on her heels chanting in a tongue I hadn't heard. The noise went on for an hour. . . .

The second night after I had shared the good news of Jesus Christ, the old woman I had heard praying said, "I never thought I would live long enough to see someone come this far to tell us about God. Will you give me permission to pray that tomorrow our people will come down the mountain to hear this message about Jesus Christ?"

About midnight I again heard her praying. Morning light revealed the tribe flowing down the mountain, some having walked two hours. Soon the little hut was packed with 35 adults and three times that many children and young people.

Charles Morris preaches in Manobo village.

For one and one-half hours I told them about Jesus, over and over again the same story. When I invited them to accept Christ the old woman was the first to stand. . . .

At the last service, the translator said to the people, "We have been called the lost tribe of Mindanao. This can't be said any longer. Since brother Morris has brought the gospel to our tribe God has found us."

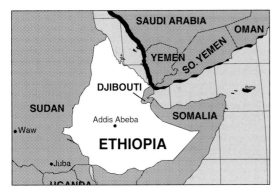

Ethiopia

As I turned to start the long walk back out of the mountains, the old woman crossed her arms, took both my hands in hers and raised her hands toward heaven in an act of benediction and prayer for me. Taking my hands again, she kissed them, and weeping said, "You have become my brother."[18]

Development in Ethiopia

In some respects Ethiopia presents the worst possible scenario as far as the gospel is concerned. During the past twenty years Southern Baptist missionaries have worked under severe handicaps of first a feudal monarchy with a state religion and then a communist dictatorship. Only recently after

1986 Baptist airlift provides supplies for remote feeding stations.

drought, famine, and a civil war, a fragile democracy has attempted to restore the devastated land and provide for an impoverished people. For the first time in two decades the missionaries have been able to carry on their evangelistic and teaching efforts publicly.

The tangible results may seem meager but they are terribly significant. Recently, the Foreign Mission Board received news of two examples of fruit from the "development work."

Women register their babies at the Gundo, Meskel feeding station during 1986 relief effort.

Nearly 40 people completed a spring workshop on MasterLife, a Christian discipleship and Bible study program. More than half are active priests in the Ethiopian Orthodox Church—a common opponent and sometimes persecutor of "Pentays" (a derisive term applied to evangelical Christians).

In the central highlands a tiny band of believers cut off from contact with missionaries for more than a decade after the communist takeover has grown into a 300-member congregation that often attracts 1,000 worshippers. It also has started two other Baptist churches.[19]

The development work consisted of

famine relief in the form of feeding stations and medical clinics in a half dozen remote areas. With the fall of the communist government, water development, reforestation efforts, and veterinary clinics have brought the missionaries in closer contact with the people with promising results in evangelism and discipleship training. A number of small churches are now found in remote areas of the country that promise to produce a harvest as Ethiopian Baptists take the gospel to the people in implementing the development programs under the direction of the missionaries. Jerry Bedsole, a veterinarian and discipleship trainer, wrote the board:

> *Development work allowed Baptists to remain in Ethiopia when communists took over and kicked out all the preachers, including ours. And when the new government came to power they told us up front, "You can preach what you want and where you want as long as you help us develop this country."*[20]

Conclusion

For half of the one hundred and fifty years of Southern Baptist existence, communism has effectively closed the door to the gospel in much of the world. As we stand on the threshold of a new century and a new millennium, Southern Baptists face an unprecedented opportunity. The post communist world is a confused world that has lost its way. At best, tribal and ethnic loyalties have replaced the challenge of the Marxist ideal and at worst, a vacuum has been created in the souls of mankind that waits to be filled and will be by the movement with the vision and the spiritual vitality to seize the golden moment. Can

Southern Baptists, who are suffering from an identity crisis of their own, move into the vacuum with the saving gospel in the power of the Holy Spirit? Does not the answer to this question depend upon our willingness to walk together under the lordship of Jesus Christ who has redeemed us, made us brothers and sisters, and called us to be his disciples?

ENDNOTES

1. Of Jerry Rankin, Don Kammerdiener said, "I think he is a very bright person. . . . He thinks quickly. I think he has deep convictions. . . . I think he will take us in some new directions. . . . As much as we have changed in the last ten years, there is probably more change to come just to stay up with our world. And I am very hopeful that Jerry can bring us into that change." Don Kammerdiener, interview by the author, 9 June 1993, Richmond, Virginia.

2. Jerry A. Rankin, "Getting to know the president," interview by Van Payne, (Fort Worth, Texas, 26 May 1993), *The Commission,* August 1993, 16.

3. Much of the biographical information on Jerry A. Rankin is taken from the author's transcript of the interview of Jerry A. Rankin conducted by Van Payne, 26 May 1993, Fort Worth, Texas.

4. "New FMB president: Jerry A. Rankin," *The Commission,* August 1993, 10.

5. Ed Briggs, "Issue of successor to Parks is fueling fundamentalist rift," *Richmond (Va.) Times-Dispatch,* 12 June 1993, A8.

6. Cited by Ed Briggs, "New president calls end to Baptist mission board war," *Richmond (Va.) Times-Dispatch,* 1 July 1993, B10.

7. Ibid.

8. Ibid.

9. Payne, "Getting to know the president," 21.

10. Ibid., 16.

11. Ibid., 17.

12. Ibid., 20.

13. The election of I. T. Tichenor as corresponding secretary of the Home Mission Board signaled the beginning of a vigorous attempt of the board to claim its birthright as stated in the constitution of the Southern Baptist Convention in 1845.

14. Rebekah Naylor, transcript of missionary message at Gambrell Street Baptist Church, Fort Worth, Texas, 1 November 1992.

15. Ibid.

16. Ibid.

17. Susan Simko, "Missionary Dr. Rebekah Naylor Is Still Declaring Hope in India," *Baptist New Mexican,* 26 December 1992, 1.

18. Charles H. (Chuck) Norris, to Keith Parks, 26 March 1981, quoted in Minutes, FMB, 6 April 1981, 5.

19. Craig Bird, "Ethiopia: years of patience harvest long-term results," Foreign Mission Feature, Foreign Bureau of Baptist Press, 17 August 1993, 1.

20. Ibid., 2.

APPENDIXES

Lottie Moon Christmas Offering 1888-1992

YEAR	TOTAL	YEAR	TOTAL	YEAR	TOTAL
1888-1890	10,295.41	**1930**	200,799.84	**1970**	16,220,104.99
1891	4,984.93	1931	170,724.87	1971	17,833,810.22
1892	5,068.82	1932	143,331.24	1972	19,664,972.53
1893	3,596.48	1933	172,512,.86	1973	22,232,757.09
1894	3,454.73	1934	213,925.81	1974	23,234,093.89
1895	4,501.63	1935	240,455.12	1975	26,169,421.12
1896	3,708.17	1936	292,401.57	1976	28,763,809.71
1897	4,356.42	1937	290,219.74	1977	31,938,553.04
1898	4,493.37	1938	315,000.40	1978	35,919,605.40
1899	5,309.57	1939	330,424.70	1979	40,597,113.02
Decade	49,769.53	**Decade**	2,369,796.15	**Decade**	262,574,241.01
Cumulative	49,769.53	**Cumulative**	4,304,388.34	**Cumulative**	446,320,058.41
1900	6,355.60	**1940**	363,746.30	**1980**	44,700,339.76
1901	6,088.17	1941	449,162.30	1981	50,784,173.38
1902	7,534.27	1942	562,609.30	1982	54,077,464.49
1903	10,957.32	1943	761,269.79	1983	58,025,336.79
1904	11,787.01	1943	949,844.17	1984	64,775,763.83
1905	14,016.49	1945	1,201,962.24	1985	66,862,113.65
1906	17,522.21	1946	1,381,048.76	1986	69,412,195.09
1907	21,272.15	1947	1,503,010.12	1987	69,912,637.50
1908	26,300.15	1948	1,669,683.38	1988	78,787,726.26
1909	27,921.03	1949	1,669,683.38	1989	80,197,870.78
Decade	149,754.40	**Decade**	10,588,019.35	**Decade**	637,535,621.53
Cumulative	199,523.03	**Cumulative**	14,892,407.69	**Cumulative**	1,083,855,679.94
1910	25,283.65	**1950**	2,110,019.07	**1990**	79,358,610.87
1911	28,943.21	1951	2,668,051.30	1991	81,358,723.00
1912	31,875.63	1952	3,280,371.79	1992	80,980,881.11
1913	38,035.63	1953	3,602,554.86	1993	
1914	27,661.48	1954	3,957,821.00	1994	
1915	36,147.97	1955	4,628,691.03	1995	
1916	40,986.35	1956	5,240,745.39	1996	
1917	44,110.83	1957	6,121,585.14	1997	
1918	53,687.39	1958	6,762,448.63	1998	
1919	68,768.82	1959	7,706,847.29	1999	
Decade	395,501.14	**Decade**	46,079,136.50	**Decade**	241,698,214.98
Cumulative	595,025.07	**Cumulative**	60,971,544.19	**Cumulative**	1,325,553,894.92
1920	40,092.77	**1960**	8,238,471.07		
1921	28,615.78	1961	9,315,754.78		
1922	29,583.67	1962	10,323,591.69		
1923	42,677.00	1963	10,949,857.35		
1924	48,677.00	1964	11,870,649.35		
1925	306,376.21	1965	13,194,357.32		
1926	246,152.84	1966	13,760,146.80		
1927	172,457.36	1967	14,664,679.30		
1928	235,274.31	1968	15,159,206.92		
1929	190,130.81	1969	15,297,558.63		
Decade	1,339,567.12	**Decade**	122,774,273.21		
Cumulative	1,934,592.19	**Cumulative**	183,745,817.40		

Cooperative Program Receipts– 1925-1992

Calendar Year	Total Received by Executive Committee, S.B.C.	Percent Increase (Decrease) Over Prior Year	Percentage of Receipts Paid to F.M.B.	Amount Paid to Foreign Mission Board
1925	—	—	—	1,049,518
1926	—	—	—	969,882
1927	—	—	—	905,196
1928	—	—	—	721,859
1929	—	—	—	617,774
1930	—	—	—	542,741
1931	—	—	—	409,470
1932	—	—	—	374,688
1933	—	—	—	292,402
1934	—	—	—	346,017
1935	—	—	—	390,092
1936	—	—	—	421,260
1937	—	—	—	439,550
1938	—	—	—	465,775
1939	—	—	—	504,751
1940	—	—	—	528,910
1941	—	—	—	624,362
1942	—	—	—	719,130
1943	—	—	—	1,030,687
1944	—	—	—	1,358,077
1945	—	—	—	1,776,8084
1946	—	—	—	2,033,873
1947	—	—	—	2,277,000
1948	6,000,837	15.0	35.1	2,107,984
1949	6,330,971	5.5	36.4	2,304,010
1950	7,347,544	16.1	41.0	3,015,294
1951	8,101,421	10.3	42.6	3,451,421
1952	9,076,047	12.0	42.8	3,888,035
1953	9,683,360	6.7	42.3	4,098,520
1954	10,739,497	10.9	44.4	4,772,123
1955	11,648,841	8.5	45.6	5,311,630
1956	13,210,279	13.4	47.0	6,207,709
1957	14,260,301	7.9	49.1	6,995,226
1958	15,598,909	9.4	48.8	7,608,182
1959	17,101,216	9.6	43.7	7,465,912
1960	17,479,428	2.21	45.2	7,909,396
1961	17,715,140	1.35	44.7	7,910,417
1962	18,917,476	6.79	44.7	8,452,410
1963	19,448,028	2.8	46.4	9,019,303
1964	20,891,636	7.42	52.3	10,921,081
1965	22,570,858	8.04	49.3	11,123,505
1966	24,005,046	6.35	49.3	11,829,531
1967	25,169,804	4.85	49.4	12,426,836
1968	25,977,470	3.21	50.1	13,018,000
1969	27,433,440	5.6	50.4	13,836,619
1970	27,925,302	1.79	50.5	14,113,351
1971	29,970,527	7.32	49.6	14,863,351
1972	31,561,729	5.3	48.3	15,252,685

Cooperative Program Receipts (continued)

Calendar Year	Total Received by Executive Committee, S.B.C.	Percent Increase (Decrease) Over Prior Year	Percentage of Receipts Paid to F.M.B.	Amount Paid to Foreign Mission Board
1973	34,701,831	9.95	49.4	17,135,169
1974	38,534,827	11.05	49.5	19,088,150
1975	42,346,099	9,89	48.8	20,667,748
1976	48,049,786	13.47	48.4	23,255,950
1977	53,006,546	10.32	47.3	25,043,318
1978	58,962,826	11.24	47.1	27,775,750
1979	66,228,232	12.32	46.7	30,954,030
1980	73,428,232	10.87	46.9	34,415,900
1981	84,047,692	14.46	46.6	39,168,468
1982	96,730,842	15.09	47.6	46,075,091
1983	103,804,179	7.31	47.8	49,703,612
1984	111,278,558	7.2	50.0	55,639,279
1985	118,668,803	6.64	50.0	59,325,346
1986	126,127,064	6.28	48.6	61,288,796
1987	130,245,412	3.27	48.4	63,061,027
1988	136,830,093	5.06	49.0	68,856,259
1989	138,316,026	1.09	49.8	68,856,259
1990	141,884,080	2.58	49.5	70,228,326
1991	139,357,816	(1.78)	49.5	68,963,377
1992	138,233,623	(.81)	50.0	69,116,808

In Memoriam

The following list includes the names of overseas personnel who died in while on the field in active service with the Foreign Mission Board of the Southern Baptist Convention

Year	Name and Field of Service
1848	Sexton, James, J., M.D., China; Sexton, Anna P. (Mrs. James J.), China
1860	Bond, Alfred L., China Bond, Helena Dameron (Mrs. Alfred L.), China Rohrer, John Q. Adams, Japan Rohrer, Sara Robinson (Mrs. John Q.), Japan
1861	Holmes, J. Landrum, China
1862	Gaillard, Charles W., China
1880	Westrup, John O., Mexico
1884	Pruitt, Ida R. Tiffany (Mrs. C.W.), China
1885	Halcomb, Mattie M. Roberts (Mrs. N.W.), China
1914	Daniel, J. Carey, China
1918	Anderson, John Todd, M.D., China
1919	Taylor, Zachary Clay, Brazil Taylor, Laura Barton (Mrs. Zachary Clay), Brazil
1922	Pierce, L.W., China
1928	Jackson, Ernest A., Brazil Jackson, Janette Beasley (Mrs. Ernest A.), Brazil
1937	Reagan, Lucille, Nigeria
1942	Gray, Rufus Franklin, China
1946	Mein, Elizabeth Fehsenfeld (Mrs. John), Brazil
1951	Hickerson, Julius Raht, Jr., Colombia Wallace, William L, M.D., China
1954	Davis, Martha Mae, Mexico
1955	Carney, Mary Ruth, Brazil Dotson, Hattie Thigpen (Mrs. Clyde J.), Zimbabwe(formerly Rhodesia) Foreman, Blonnye H., Brazil
1957	Oliver, John Samuel, Brazil
1958	Harper, Winfred Ozell (Wimpy), Tanzania
1968	Clark, Eric Herschel, Kenya Smith, Loy Connell, M.D., Nigeria
1969	Edwin Burke Dozier, Japan
1970	Kite, Thelma Elaine Olney (Mrs. Billy O'N.), Zambia Williams, Diane, Philippines Parker, Mary Lorena Stroup (Mrs. Robert R.,Jr.), Zimbabwe Smith, Hoke, Jr., Colombia Brown, Homer A., Nigeria
1971	Potter, Paul Edwin, Dominican Republic Potter, Nancy Ann Roper (Mrs. Paul Edwin), Dominican Republic Mills, Virginia Lee Land (Mrs. J.C.), Liberia Campbell, Eleanore Ayers (Mrs. Charles), Thailand
1972	Compton, Charles Earl, Jr., Brazil Pate, Mavis, Gaza Legg, Mary Leigh Anderson (Mrs. L. Gene), Nigeria Smith, Doris Stull (Mrs. Donald R.), Venezuela
1973	Hopewell, Gladys, Taiwan Wise, Allene Ruth Greenlaw (Mrs. Gene H.), Brazil

Moore, Marian (Mrs. Vernon L.), Malaysia-Singapore

Sanders, Frances Marian, Mexico

1976 Pippin, Martha Ann Smith (Mrs. Ernest C.), Argentina

Bateman, Dallas, Kenya

1977 Clark, G. Harold, Malaysia

1978 Hampton, Wilma Ruth Rodenburg (Mrs. Robert A.), Brazil

1978 Dunaway, Archie G., Jr., Zimbabwe

Harris, Mary Lillian Culpepper (Mrs. Robert L.), Bermuda

1980 Bender, William B., Nigeria

Williams, James A., Yugoslavia

Douglas, Ray, Dominican Republic

Phifer, Dudley A., Zimbabwe

1981 Dunaway, Margaret Lanier (Mrs. Archie G.), Zimbabwe

Clark, Gene B., Japan

1982 Crawford, Linda Lee, Brazil

Jennings, Lois, Brazil

Thomas, Larry S., Tanzania

Burtis, J. Robert, Argentina

1983 Thompson, Roger L., Ecuador

Balyeat, Kent W., Argentina

Herrin, Manget, Grenada

Duncan, Margie J. Rains (Mrs. M.G), Kenya

Hunker, Jeanette Roebuck (Mrs. W. Carl), China, Philippines, Taiwan

Egedy, Betty Chance (Mrs. Charles R.), Nigeria

1984 Verdery, E. Augustus, Switzerland

Yost, Oliver J., Philippines

Fine, Roberta M. Robson (Mrs. Earl M.), Nigeria

1985 Philpott, James Morgan, Mexico

Richard Morris, Taiwan

1986 Senter, Mary Elizabeth Tarlton (Mrs. Jesse George), Liberia

Cowsert, George Bagby, Brazil

1987 Waldron, Troy M., Jr., Ethiopia

1988 Hall, Carl W., Kenya

Billings, Herbert D., Guatemala

Seay, Dudley Alan, Sr., Belize

Seay, Lee Rousey (Mrs. Dudley Alan, Sr), Belize

Noland, Paul Wayne, Brazil

1989 Hull, Wendell R. ("Jack"), Kenya, Tanzania

Fallaw, Billy K., Brazil

Ross, J. Wilson, Baptist Spanish Publishing House

Nottingham, Barry, Burkina Faso

1990 Martin, Nancy C. Palmer (Mrs. R.J.), Liberia

Lovell, Darla, Uganda

Mercer, Dewey Edward, Japan

1991 Fraser, Virginia E., Colombia

Bethea, Lynda Sharp (Mrs. Ralph C.,Jr.), Kenya

Perrin, Margaret Joplin (Mrs. J. Kyle), Japan

1992 Hailey, William Morgan, Sr., Indonesia, Japan, Hong Kong

Tackett, Tonita Noreen, Brazil

Honor Roll of Missionaries
Who Served for Thirty Years or More

This list includes the names of the men and women who served overseas thirty years or longer under the Foreign Mission Board of the Southern Baptist Convention. Time frame: 1845 - 1992. The names are in alphabetical order, by decades, with the number of years served indicated in parenthesis behind each name. An asterick (*) before a name indicates a missionary still in active service as of the end of December 1992.

THIRTY YEARS SERVICE

A Abel, Betty R. (Mrs. John C., Jr.),
   Nigeria (35)
Abel, John C., Jr., Nigeria (35)
Abernathy, Jewell Leonard (Mrs. John A.),
   Philippines, South Korea (32)
Abernathy, John A., China, Philippines,
   South Korea (35)
Adams, Floy White (Mrs. W.W.), China (33)
Adams, W.W., China (34)
Albright, Jean (Mrs. Leroy), Malawi, Zambia,
   Mexico (35)
Albright, Leroy, Malawi, Zambia,
   Mexico (35)
Alderman, Jennie T., China, Taiwan (35)
Alexander, Betty N. (Mrs. Max N.),
   Thailand (31)
Alexander, Cecile P. (Mrs. Mark M., Jr.),
   Argentina (35)
Alexander, Mark M., Jr., Argentina (35)
Alexander, Mary C., China, Hong Kong (35)
Alexander, Max N., Thailand (31)
Allen, Marjorie Hammond (Mrs. James R.),
   Brazil (33)
Allen, James R., Brazil (33)
Anderson, Kitty T. (Mrs. John J.),
   China, Hawaii, Hong Kong (30)
Anderson, Theresa K.,
   China, Philippines (35)
Andrews, Constance (Mrs. William P.),
   Chile (37)
Andrews, William P., Chile (37)
Appleby, Rosalee Mills (Mrs. D.P.),
   Brazil (35)
Applewhite, LaVerne (Mrs. C. Winfield),
   Indonesia (30)
Applewhite, C. Winfield, Indonesia (30)
Austin, Stella A., Nigeria (36)
Ayers, Winnie D. (Mrs. Sanford E.),
   China (33)
Ayers, Sanford E., China (33)
Ayers, Minnie S. (Mrs. Thomas W.),
   China (33)
Ayers, Thomas W., China (33)
B Bagby, Frances A. (Mrs. Taylor C.),
   Brazil (37)
Bagby, Taylor C., Brazil (37)
Bagby, Thelma (Mrs. Albert I.), Brazil (30)
Baker, Dwight L, Israel, India (36)
Baker, Emma E. (Mrs. Dwight L.),
   Israel, India (36)
Baker, Mattie A., Brazil (36)
Barker, Emma J. (Mrs. Herbert W.),
   Taiwan (33)
Barker, Herbert J., Taiwan (33)
Barton, Addie, Mexico (37)
Bausum, Euva M. (Mrs. Robert L.),
   China, Taiwan (33)
Bausum, Robert L., China, Taiwan (37)
Beall, Jeannette E., China (33)
Beddoe, Louella H. (Mrs. Robert E.),
   China (32)
Beddoe, Robert E., China (39)
Bedenbaugh, Betty (Mrs. Charles W.),

Tanzania (31)
Bedenbaugh, Charles W., Tanzania (31)
Bell, B. Wayne (Mrs. Lester C.), Brazil,
    Portugal (32)
Bell, Lester C., Brazil, Portugal (32)
Bender, Novella C. (Mrs. William D.),
    Nigeria (30)
Bennett, Audie (Mrs. E. Preston), Japan (32)
Bennett, E. Preston, Japan (32)
Bennett, Marjorie A. (Mrs. Troy C.)
Bangladesh, Tanzania, Union of South
    Africa (Ciskei), Zambia, Lebanon (33)
Bennett, Troy C., Bangladesh, Tanzania,
    Union of South Africa (Ciskei), Zambia,
    Lebanon (33)
Berry, Edward G., Brazil (32)
Berry, Lois R. (Mrs. Edward G.), Brazil (37)
*Bible, Mattie Lou, Brazil (37)
Bice, Blanche Hamm (Mrs. John L.),
    Brazil (32)
Bice, John L., Brazil (32)
Bitner, Fern W. (Mrs. James H.), Chile (34
Bitner, James H., Chile (34)
Blackman, Gladys Yates (Mrs. Lonnie E.),
    China, Hawaii (36)
Blackman, Lonnie E., China, Hawaii (36)
Blair, Cora H. (Mrs. Martin S.),
    Argentina (34)
Blair, Martin S., Argentina (34)
*Blattner, Doris M., Philippines (30)
Boatwright, Betty Faith (Mrs. C.S.),
    Japan (31)
Boatwright, C.S., Japan (31)
Bond, G. Clayton, Ghana, Togo (32)
Bond, Helen T. (Mrs. G. Clayton), Ghana,
    Togo (32)
Bowdler, George A., Argentina (36)
Bowdler, Ruth N. (Mrs. George A.),
    Argentina (36)
Bowlin, Betty Jean (Mrs. Ralph T.),

Zimbabwe (33)
Bowlin, Ralph T., Zimbabwe (33)
*Bozeman, Marie W. (Mrs. O.K., Jr.), South
    Korea, India (30)
*Bozeman, O.K., Jr., South Korea, India (30)
Bradley, Blanche, China (33)
*Brady, Martha A. (Mrs. Otis W.), Bahamas,
    Guyana, Belize (37)
*Brady, Otis W., Bahamas, Guyana,
    Belize (37)
Branum, Irene T., China, South Korea (36)
Bratcher, Lewis M., Brazil (35)
*Brincefield, Clara M., Chile (30)
Brothers, L. Raymon, Nigeria (33)
*Brown, Bradley D., Liberia (30)
*Brown, Carolyn F. (Mrs. Bradley D.),
    Liberia (30)
Brown, Lorne E., Jordan, Lebanon,
    Tanzania, Zimbabwe, Uganda,
    Kenya (32)
Brown, Virginia (Mrs. Lorne E.), Jordan,
    Lebanon, Tanzania, Zimbabwe, Uganda,
    Kenya (32)
Bryan, Mamie S. (Mrs. R.T.), China (31)
Bryan, Nelson A., China, South Korea (37)
Bryan, Frances Allison (Mrs. Nelson A.),
    China (37)
Bumpus, Claud R., Brazil (35)
Burks, Edgar H., Jr., Nigeria (30)
Burks, Linnie Jane (Mrs. Edgar H.),
    Nigeria (30)
Burt, Daniel H., Jr., Brazil (32)
Burt, Mary E. (Mrs. Daniel H., Jr.), Brazil (32)
C Cader, Burley E., Brazil (36)
Cader, Ulene D. (Mrs. Burley E.), Brazil (36)
Calcote, Gena M. (Mrs. Ralph V.), Japan (35)
Calcote, Ralph V., Japan (35)
Caldwell, Pearl, China (36)
Callaway, Elizabeth (Mrs. Tucker N.),
    Hawaii, Japan, Liberia (34)

Callaway, Tucker N.,
Hawaii, Japan, Liberia (34)
Campbell, Bernadene (Mrs. Charles W.),
Argentina (34)
Campbell, Charles W., Argentina (34)
Campbell, Viola D., Mexico, Spanish Baptist
Publishing House (38)
Cannata, Samuel R.J., Zimbabwe, Ethiopia,
Kenya, Sudan (35)
Cannata, Virginia C. (Mrs. Samuel R.J.),
Zimbabwe, Ethiopia, Kenya, Sudan (38)
Canzoneri, Antonina, Nigeria, Bahamas (37)
Carroll, Betty Alice (Mrs. Daniel M., Jr.),
Argentina, Jamaica (36)
Carroll, Daniel M., Jr., Argentina,
Jamaica (36)
Carson, William H., Nigeria (35)
*Carter, B. Sue (Mrs. J. Dale), Brazil (36)
Carter, Evelyn (Mrs. Pat H.), Mexico (33)
*Carter, J. Dale, Brazil (36)
Carter, Joan, Tanzania, Kenya (32)
Carter, Kate (Mrs. William P.), Chile (37)
Carter, Pat H., Mexico (33)
Carter, William P., Chile (37)
Chambers, Christine C. (Mrs. R.E.),
China (33)
Chambers, Robert E., China (38)
Chappell, Catherine F., Brazil (37)
Chastain, James G., Mexico (32)
Chastain, Lillian W.(Mrs. James G.),
Mexico (32)
Christie, Alonzo B., Brazil (39)
Christie, Anna C. (Mrs. Alonzo B.),
Brazil (39)
Clark, C.F., Jr., Japan (38)
Clark, Charles B., Venezuela (38)
*Clark, Nancy H. (Mrs. Stanley D.),
Argentina (31)
Clark, Pauline W. (Mrs. C.F., Jr.), Japan (38)
Clark, Shirley R. (Mrs. Charles B.),

Venezuela (38)
*Clark, Stanley D., Argentina (31)
Clark, Lucille D. (Mrs. W.H.), Japan (33)
Clark, W.H., Japan (37)
Claxton, Emma O. (Mrs. W. Neville),
Ghana, Nigeria, Dahomey (33)
Claxton, W. Neville, Ghana, Nigeria,
Dahomey (33)
Cobb, Daniel R., Thailand (33)
Cobb, Fannie M. (Mrs. Daniel R.),
Thailand (33)
*Coleman, W. Anita, Japan (31)
Conner, Marie, China, Taiwan (36)
Cooper, Katharine T. (Mrs. W. Lowrey),
Argentina (35)
Cooper, N. June, Japan (35)
Cooper, W. Lowrey, Argentina (35)
*Covington, Robert C., Malaysia, Singapore,
Australia (30)
Cowan, Anna L., Israel, Jordan (36)
Cowsert, George B., Brazil (33)
Cox, Addie E., China, Taiwan (37)
Coy, Betty (Mrs. R. Frank), Chile (33)
Coy, R. Frank, Chile (33)
Cozzens, Katherine, Brazil (33)
*Crabb, Patricia M. (Mrs. Stanley, Jr.), Italy,
Switzerland (34)
*Crabb, Stanley, Jr., Italy, Switzerland (34)
Crabtree, Asa R., Brazil (38)
Crabtree, Mabel H. (Mrs. Asa R.), Brazil (38)
Crabtree, Mildred I., Nigeria (36)
Craighead, Albert B., Italy (37)
Craighead, Rhoda M. (Mrs. Albert B.),
Italy (37)
Crane, Edith (Mrs. James D.), Mexico (36)
Crane, James D., Mexico (36)
Crawford, Frances N., Nigeria, Gaza,
Colombia, Honduras (37)
Crawford, Mary K. China, Hawaii (32)
Cross, Ardis W. (Mrs. Eugene M.), Hawaii,

Philippines (34)

Cross, Eugene M., Hawaii, Philippines (34)

Cummins, Betty N. (Mrs. Harold T.),
Bangladesh, Kenya (32)

Cummins, Harold T., Bangladesh,
Kenya (32)

D Davis, Burton DeWolfe, Brazil (30)

Davis, H. Victor, Brazil (31)

*Davis, Ida A. (Mrs. Robert C.), Hawaii,
Vietnam, Singapore (38)

Davis, J. Edgar, Mexico, Spanish Baptist
Publishing House (38)

Davis, Joyce M. (Mrs. W. Ralph), Nigeria,
Ghana (35)

Davis, Mary G. (Mrs. J. Edgar), Mexico,
Baptist Spanish Publishing House (38)

*Davis, Robert C., Hawaii, Vietnam,
Singapore (38)

Davis, Sara B. (Mrs. Burton deWolfe),
Brazil (30)

Davis, W. Ralph, Nigeria, Ghana (35)

*Dean, Rita D. (Mrs. Pratt J.), Japan (31)

Demarest, Mary C., China, Taiwan (39)

Deter, Arthur B., Brazil (38)

Deter, May S. (Mrs. Arthur B.), Brazil (38)

Dickman, Jean F., Gaza, Yemen (35)

Dickson, Charles W., Brazil (33)

Dickson, Juanita J. (Mrs. Charles W.),
Brazil (33)

*Ditsworth, Mary Alice, Indonesia,
Singapore (37)

Doyle, Gerald W., Ecuador (34)

Doyle, Janelle H. (Mrs. Lonnie A., Jr.),
Brazil (39)

Doyle, Lonnie A., Jr., Brazil (39)

Doyle, Mauriece P. (Mrs. Gerald W.),
Ecuador (34)

Dozier, Edwin B., Hawai, Japan (35)

*Dubberly, Carolyn F. (Mrs. T. Eugene),
Uruguay (32)

*Dubberly, T. Eugene, Uruguay (32)

Dunaway, Archie G., Nigeria, Zimbabwe (31)

Dunaway, Margaret (Mrs. Archie G.),
Nigeria, Zimbabwe (33)

Dunstan, Albert L., Brazil (37)

Durham, Ina M. (Mrs. Jonathan B.), Nigeria,
Burkina Faso (34)

Durham, Jonathan B., Nigeria,
Burkina Faso (34)

Duval, Alice S. (Mrs. Louis M.), Nigeria (32)

Dyer, Anne L., Jordan, Gaza (32)

Dyson, Albert H., Jr., Nigeria,
Sierra Leone (35)

Dyson, Ruth W. (Mrs. Albert H., Jr.), Nigeria,
Sierra Leone (35)

E Elliott, Darlene, Colombia (36)

Emanuel, B. P., Japan, Philippines (38)

*Emanuel, Mary Lou (Mrs. Wayne E.),
Japan (34)

Emanuel, Rebekah Sue (Mrs. B.P.), Japan,
Philippines (38)

*Emanuel, Wayne E., Japan (34)

Emmons, Dorothy E., Tanzania (34)

Enete, Crystal A. (Mrs. William W.),
Brazil (34)

Enete, William W., Brazil (34)

Entzminger, Maggie G. (Mrs. William E.),
Brazil (30)

Entzminger, William E., Brazil (38)

Epperson, Barbara, Nigeria (32)

Ernest, Mary Lee, Hawaii, Malaysia,
Singapore (30)

Eudaly, Marie S. (Mrs. N. Hoyt), Mexico,
Spanish Baptist Publishing House (34)

Eudaly, N. Hoyt, Mexico, Spanish Baptist
Publishing House (34)

Evans, Charles E., Tanzania, Kenya (30)

Evans, Elizabeth (Mrs. Charles E.), Tanzania,
Kenya (30)

Evans, Mary L. (Mrs. Philip S.) China (35)

Evans, Philip S., China (35)

Evenson, Mary V. (Mrs. R. Kenneth), Uruguay, Spanish Baptist Publishing House (35)

Evenson, R. Kenneth, Uruguay, Spanish Baptist Publishing House (35)

F Fairburn, Margaret, Liberia (30)

Faw, Geneva (Mrs. Wiley B.), Nigeria (31)

Faw, Wiley B., Nigeria (31)

Fielder, J. Wilson, China (36)

Fielder, Maudie E. (Mrs. J. Wilson), China (34)

Ford, Ruth L., China, Indonesia (36)

Fort, M. Giles, Jr., Zimbabwe (35)

Fort, Wana Ann (Mrs. M. Giles, Jr.), Zimbabwe (35)

Foster, James A., China, Philippines, Suriname (35)

*Foster, James E., Germany (30)

*Foster, Sylvia (Mrs. James E.), Germany (30)

Foster, Zelma V. (Mrs. James A.), China, Philippines, Suriname (35)

Fowler, Daisey C. (Mrs. F.J.), Argentina (31)

*Fox, Ann R. (Mrs. Hubert A.), Thailand (30)

*Fox, Hubert A., Thailand (30)

Frank, Irma P. (Mrs. Victor L.), China, Hong Kong (32)

Frank, Victor L., China, Hong Kong (32)

Frazier, Ina (Mrs. W. Donaldson), Nigeria (33)

Frazier, W. Donaldson, Nigeria (33)

Fredenburg, Mary Evelyn, Nigeria (39)

Freeland, Estelle, Nigeria, Ivory Coast (35)

Freeman, Zachary P., Argentina (31)

G Galloway, John L., Macao (38)

Galloway, Lillian T. (Mrs. John L.), Macao (38)

*Gammage, Al W., Jr., Philippines (36)

*Gammage, Nettie L. (Mrs. Al W., Jr.), Philippines (36)

Gardner, Hattie Mae, Nigeria (37)

Gardner, Vera, Thailand (30)

Garner, Alex F., Argentina, Paraguay (35)

Garner, Charleta B. (Mrs. Alex F.), Argentina, Paraguay (35)

Giannetta, Amelio A. Brazil, Italy (30)

Giannetta, Lidia (Mrs. Amelio A.), Brazil, Italy (30)

Gilbert, Dorothy (Mrs. James P.), Ecuador (35)

Gilbert, James P., Ecuador (35)

Giles, James E., Colombia, Spanish Baptist Publishing House (36)

Giles, Mary M. (Mrs. James E.), Colombia, Spanish Baptist Publishing House (36)

Gill, Emma W. (Mrs. Everett, Sr.) Italy (31)

Gill, Everett, Sr., Italy (31)

Gillespie, A.L., Japan (31)

Gillespie, Viola R. (Mrs. A.L.), Japan (31)

Ginsburg, Solomon L., Brazil (35)

Givens, Sistie V., Brazil (35)

Gladen, Ruth (Mrs. Van), Mexico (32)

Gladen, Van, Mexico (32)

*Goodwin, J.G., Jr., Korea (37)

*Goodwin, June B. (Mrs. J.G., Jr.), Korea (37)

Gordon, Audrey J. (Mrs. R. Edward), Philippines (30)

Gordon, R. Edward, Philippines (30)

Graham, Finlay M., Israel, Lebanon (39)

Graves, William W., Argentina, Puerto Rico (34)

Grayson, Alda, China, Hawaii (39)

Green. George, Nigeria (38)

Green, Jessie L., China, Malaysia (32)

Green, Lydia W. (Mrs. George), Nigeria (38)

Greene, Lydia, China, Hawaii, Malaysia (34)

*Greenway, Frances, Nigeria, Zimbabwe, Ghana (34)

*Greenwood, Lahoma M. (Mrs. Richard R.),

Guatemala (30)

*Greenwood, Richard R., Guatemala (30)

Greer, Jenell, China, Hawaii, Thailand (39)

*Gregory, Betty G. (Mrs. L. Laverne), Chile,
Costa Rica, Spanish Baptist Publishing
House (35)

*Gregory, L. Laverne, Chile, Costa Rica,
Spanish Baptist Publishing House (35)

Griffin, Alice M. (Mrs. Bennie T.),
Nigeria (39)

Griffin, Bennie T., Nigeria (39)

*Griffin, Clarence O., Indonesia (32)

*Griffin, Ruth P. (Mrs. Clarence O.),
Indonesia (32)

*Griggs, Florence S. (Mrs. John P.),
Zimbabwe (30)

*Griggs, John P., Zimbabwe (30)

Grober, Glendon D., Brazil (31)

Grober, Marjorie S. (Mrs. Glendon D.),
Brazil (31)

Grover, Blanche, China, Hawaii,
Hong Kong (39)

Gullatt, Mary. S. (Mrs. Tom D.), Japan (35)

Gullatt, Tom D., Japan (35)

H Hairston, Martha E., Brazil (37)

Hale, Elizabeth, China, Malaysia (37)

Hamlett, Peter W., China (39)

*Hammett, J. Hunter, Taiwan (34)

Hammett, M. Frances, Nigeria (30)

*Hammett, Patsy P. (Mrs. J. Hunter),
Taiwan (34)

Hampton, Gena (Mrs. James E.), Tanzania,
Kenya (32)

Hampton, James E., Tanzania, Kenya (32)

*Hampton, Roberta, Brazil (39)

Hancock, R. Elaine, Hong Kong (35)

Hardy, Hubert L., Chile (35)

*Hardy, Mavis S. (Mrs. Robert), Japan (39)

Hardy, R. Nell (Mrs. Hubert L.), Chile (35)

Hardy, Robert D., Japan (34)

Harmon, Ethel R., Nigeria (34)

Harper, Elizabeth J. (Mrs. Leland J.),
Paraguay (32)

Harper, Leland J., Paraguay (32)

*Harrell, Ralph W., Tanzania, Kenya (35)

*Harrell, Rosalind K. (Mrs. Ralph W.),
Tanzania, Kenya (35)

Harrington, Edna E. (Mrs. Joseph A.),
Brazil (34)

Harrington, Joseph A., Brazil (34)

Harris, Emogene, Nigeria (31)

Harris, Hendon M., China (34)

Harris, Frances P. (Mrs. Hendon M.),
China (34)

Harrison, Helen Bagby (Mrs. William C.),
Brazil (35)

Harrison, William C., Brazil (34)

Hartwell, Jesse Boardman, China (35)

Hatchell, Jessie E. (Mrs. William F.),
Mexico (30)

Hatchell, William F., Mexico (37)

Hatton, Frances Bumpus
(Mrs. W. Alvin), (35)

Hawkins, Fred. L., Brazil (30)

Hawkins, Mariruth B. (Mrs. Fred L.),
Brazil (30)

Hayes, Arnold E., Brazil (35)

Hayes, Helen F. (Mrs. Arnold E.), Brazil (35)

Hayes, Hermon P., Vietnam, Australia (32)

Hayes, R. Everley, China, Indonesia (36)

Haylock, Arthur R., Honduras (32)

Haylock, Martha H. (Mrs. Arthur R.),
Honduras (32)

Heiss, Donald R., Japan (34)

Heiss, Joyce S. (Mrs. Donald R.), Japan (34)

*Henson, Carol J., Chile (33)

Herring, J. Alexander, China, Taiwan (30)

Herring, Nan T. (Mrs. J. Alexander), China,
Taiwan (30)

Hickman, Jane G., (Mrs. William, Jr.),

Paraguay (39)
Hickman, William, Jr., Paraguay (39)
High, Katharine (Mrs. Thomas O., Sr.),
Nigeria (35)
High, Thomas O., Nigeria (35)
Highfill, Virginia B., Japan (34)
*Hill, D. Leslie, Philippines (30)
*Hill, Janet M. (Mrs. D. Leslie),
Philippines (30)
*Hill, John B., Sr., Nigeria (35)
*Hill, Louise (Mrs. John B.), Nigeria (35)
Hipps, John B., China (38)
Hobbs, Darline A. (Mrs. Jerry), Thailand (34)
Hobbs, Jerry, Thailand (34)
*Holifield, Flora D. (Mrs. Robert A.),
Italy (30)
*Holifield, Robert A., Italy (30)
Hollingsworth Marceille S. (Mrs. Tom C.),
Argentina (31)
Hollingsworth, Tom C., Argentina (31)
Horton, Elvee W. (Mrs. Frederick M.),
Japan (34)
Horton, Frances, Japan (35)
Horton, Frederick M., Japan (34)
Hoshizaki, Asano M. (Mrs. Reiji), Japan (35)
Hoshizaki, Reiji, Japan (35)
Howard, Patsy M. (Mrs. Stanley P.),
Japan (38)
Howard, Stanley P., Japan (38)
Huey, Mary Alice, China, Hawaii (35)
Hull, Dorothy E. (Mrs. W.R.), Kenya (30)
Humphreys, Inez Webb, Venezuela (33)
Humphries, Carol L., Nigeria (34)
Hunker, Jeannette R. (Mrs. W. Carl), China,
Philippines, Taiwan (37)
Hunt, Betty Jane, South Korea (33)
Hurst, Harold E., Honduras (33)
I Ichter, Jerry C. (Mrs. William H.),
Brazil (35)
Ichter, William H., Brazil (35)

J Jackson, Alma M., Brazil (34)
Jackson, Mina G. (Mrs. J.E.), China,
Philippines (38)
Jackson, Shirley, Brazil (32)
Jacob, Robert A., China (33)
Jacob, Floy W., (Mrs. Robert A.) China (34)
Jeffers, Irene, China, Taiwan (36)
Jester, William R., Nigeria (36)
Jester, Daisy Hicks (Mrs. William R.),
Nigeria (36)
Johnson, Sammie G. (Mrs. Leslie L.),
Brazil (38)
Johnson, Leslie L., Brazil (38)
Johnson, R. Elton, Jr., Brazil (37)
Johnson, Elizabeth B. (Mrs. R. Elton, Jr.),
Brazil (37)
Johnson R. Pearle, China, Taiwan, (37)
Johnson, Kate C. (Mrs.William B.), China,
Indonesia (36)
Johnson, William B., China, Indonesia (36)
Johnston James D., Nigeria (32)
Johnston, Juanita, Thailand (36)
Johnston, Marie H. (Mrs. James D.),
Nigeria (32)
Joiner, Elaine (Mrs. Garreth E.), Ecuador (38)
Joiner, Garreth E., Ecuador (38)
*Jolley, Earl E., Argentina (34)
*Jolley, Veta N. (Mrs. Earl E.), Argentina (34)
*Jones, Archie V., Sr., Chile (32)
*Jones, Don C., South Korea (36)
Jones, Florence, China (35)
*Jones, Juanita A. (Mrs. Don C.), South
Korea (36)
Jones, Kathleen C., Indonesia (35)
Jones, Ona K. (Mrs. Samuel L.),
Zimbabwe (32)
Jones, Samuel L., Zimbabwe (32)
Jowers, Alcie P. (Mrs. S. Clyde), China,
Philippines (33)
K Kendrick, Bertie Lee, Hawaii (30)

Kersey, Ruth M., Nigeria (35)
Key, Jerry S., Brazil (34)
Key, Johnnie J. (Mrs. Jerry S.), Brazil (34)
Keyes, Leslie G., Honduras (32)
Keyes, Naomi (Mrs. Leslie G.),
    Honduras (32)
*Kimler, Eugene B., Jr., Venezuela (35)
*Kimler, Eva T. (Mrs. Eugene B., Jr.),
    Venezuela (35)
King, David W., Lebanon (30)
King, Harriette L., China, Malaysia (35)
King, Maxine S. (Mrs. David W.),
    Lebanon (30)
Kirk, James P., Brazil (37)
Kirk, Maxie C. (Mrs. James P.), Brazil (37)
Kirksey, Marilois, Brazil (30)
Knight, Doris L., Nigeria (39)
L Lacey, George H., Mexico (31)
Lacy, Minnie M. (Mrs. George H.),
    Mexico (30)
Lair, Lena V., Nigeria (31)
Lake, John, China (35)
Lambert, Rebekah D., South Korea (35)
Landrum, Minnie L, Brazil (36)
Lane, Dorothea K., Japan (36)
Lanier, Minnie Lou, Brazil (37)
Larson, Edith D. (Mrs. I.V.), China,
    Philippines, Taiwan (39)
Larson I.V., China, Philippines, Taiwan (39)
Laseter, Anne, Chile (34)
Lawton, Ben R., Italy (35)
Lawton, Deaver M., China, Thailand,
    Taiwan (38)
Lawton, Dorothy D. (Mrs. Deaver M.),
    China, Thailand, Taiwan (37)
Lawton, Geraldine (Mrs. Wesley W., Jr.),
    China, Hawaii, Hong Kong, Taiwan and
    Philippines (33)
Lawton, Ida D. (Mrs. W.W., Sr.), China (37)
Lawton, Mary P. (Mrs. Ben R.), Italy (35)

Lawton, Wesley W., Jr., China, Hawaii,
    Hong Kong, Taiwan, Philippines (33)
*Lay, Diana, Ghana (32)
LeSueur, Allie R. (Mrs. David H.),
    Mexico (31)
LeSueur, David H., Mexico (31)
Lea, Ola, China, Taiwan (36)
*Ledbetter, Ethel T. (Mrs. Michael J.),
    Mexico (30)
*Ledbetter, Michael J., Mexico (30)
Lee, Elizabeth M. (Wyatt W.), Mexico (36)
*Lee, Hal B., Jr., France (31)
*Lee, Lou Ann (Mrs. Hal B., Jr., France (31)
Lee, Wyatt W., Mexico (36)
Legg, L. Gene, Nigeria (35)
Lennon, Harriet O. (Mrs. S. Judson),
    Thailand (32)
Lennon, S. Judson, Thailand (32)
Leonard, Charles A., China, Hawaii (38)
Leonard, Evelyn C. (Mrs. Charles A.), China,
    Hawaii (38)
Lewis, Beverley J. (Mrs. Francis L.),
    Indonesia (31)
Lewis, Francis L., Indonesia (31)
*Lindwall, Hubert N., Guatemala (33)
*Lindwall, Sue F., Guatemala (33)
Lingerfelt, James E., Brazil (32)
Lingerfelt, Nelle S. (Mrs. James E.),
    Brazil (32)
Littleton, Ossie P. (Mrs. Homer R.), Nigeria,
    Ghana (33)
Locke, Russell L., Nigeria (36)
Locke, Veda W. (Mrs. Russell L.),
    Nigeria (36)
*Lockhart, Maxine, Nigeria,
    The Gambia (30)
Logan, Dorothy C. (Mrs. William Wayne),
    Nigeria (30)
Logan, William Wayne, Nigeria (30)
Longbottom, Marian C. (Mrs. Samuel F, Jr.),

Hawaii, Vietnam, and Taiwan (35)

Longbottom, Samuel F, Jr., Hawaii, Vietnam, Taiwan (35)

Lovan, Nadine, Ghana (33)

Lovegren, Alta L. (Mrs. L. August), Gaza, Jordan (36)

Lovegren, L. August), Gaza, Jordan (36)

Lowe, Clifford J., China (38)

Lowe, Julia M. (Mrs. Clifford J.), China (38)

*Lozuk, George S.,Venezuela, Commonwealth of Independent States (37)

*Lozuk, Veda Rae (Mrs. George S.), Venezuela, Commonwealth of Independent States (37)

Lunsford, James A., Brazil (36)

Lunsford, Lena J. (Mrs. James A.), Brazil (36)

Luper, J. Daniel, Brazil (37)

Luper, Julia F. (Mrs. J. Daniel), Brazil (37)

*Lusk, Ida B. (Mrs. Richard L.), Hong Kong (32)

*Lusk, Richard L., Hong Kong (32)

Lyon, Alma Ruth M. (Mrs. Roy L.), Mexico, Venezuela (31)

Lyon, Roy L., Mexico, Venezuela (31)

M MacLean, Addie B. (Mrs. Ewart G.), Nigeria (33)

MacLean, Ewart G., Nigeria (33)

Maddox, Effie R. (Mrs. Otis P.), Brazil (39)

Maddox, Otis P., Brazil (39)

Malone, Janis M. (Mrs. William P.), Argentina (32)

Malone, William P., Argentina (32)

Margrett, Anne, Argentina (33)

Marler, L. Parkes, Guam, Greece (30)

Marler, Martha T. (Mrs. L. Parkes), Guam, Greece (30)

Marlowe, Rose, China, Japan (34)

Marrs, Effie K. (Mrs. Frank), Mexico (34)

Marrs, Frank, Mexico (34)

Martin, Earl R., Kenya, Tanzania, Rwanda,

Switzerland (31)

Martin, M. Jane (Mrs. Earl R.), Kenya, Tanzania, Rwanda, Switzerland (31)

*Martin, Pauline, Nigeria (38)

Masaki, Betty Y. (Mrs. Tomoki), Japan (31)

Masaki, Tomoki, Japan (31)

Masters, Helen R., Nigeria (31)

Matthews, Clara L. (Mrs. W. Harold), Philippines (35)

Matthews, W. Harold, Philippines (35)

Mayhall, David N., Nigeria (31)

Mayhall, Ollie W. (Mrs. David N.), Nigeria (31)

McCamey, Georgia (Mrs. Howard D.), Nigeria (31)

McCamey, Howard D., Nigeria (31)

McCormick, Mary R. (Mrs. Hugh P.), Nigeria, Hawaii (35)

McCrea, Jessie R. (Mrs. Tully F.), China (37)

McCrea, Tully F., China (38)

McCullough, Nita, Nigeria (35)

McGavock, Catherine J. (Mrs. J.W.), Chile, Mexico, Baptist Spanish Publishing House (31)

McGavock, J.W., Chile, Mexico, and the Baptist Spanish Publishing House (31)

McGee, Doris T. (Mrs. John S.), Nigeria (33)

McGee, John S., Nigeria (33)

McIlroy, Minnie, Brazil (36)

McKinley, Betty J. (Mrs. James F., Jr.), Bangladesh (33)

McKinley, Hugh T., Zimbabwe (35)

McKinley, James F., Jr., Bangladesh (33)

McKinley, Rebecca (Mrs. Hugh T.), Zimbabwe (35)

McNeely, Gerald A., Spain (32)

McNeely, June H. (Mrs. Gerald A.), Spain (32)

Medling, Mary L. (Mrs. William R.), Japan, Okinawa (33)

Medling, William R., Japan, Okinawa (33)
Mefford, Joseph W., Jr., Spain (32)
Mefford, Lila P. (Mrs. Joseph W., Jr.),
    Spain (32)
Mein, Elizabeth F. (Mrs. John), Brazil (32)
Mein, John, Brazil, Bahamas (38)
Mercer, Dewey E., Japan (36)
Mercer, Margaret Ramona (Mrs. Dewey E.),
    Japan (37)
Meredith, Helen, Colombia (36)
*Meuth, Mary Sue, Indonesia,
    Hong Kong (38)
Mewshaw, Dell S. (Mrs. Robert E.,
    China (31)
Mewshaw, Robert E., China (31)
Middleton, Hubert K. Chile (33)
Middleton, Jean A. (Mrs. Hubert K.),
    Chile (33)
Miles, Fern Harrington, China, Philippines,
    Taiwan (35)
Miles, Virginia, Philippines, Indonesia (36)
*Miller, Charles, Philippines (32)
Miller, Cynthia A., China (30)
Miller, David L., Brazil (31)
Miller, Floryne T., China, Hawaii, Japan (33)
Miller, Glenda G. (Mrs. David L.), Brazil (31)
*Miller, Roberta E. (Mrs. Charles),
    Philippines (32)
Mills, Ernest O., Japan (31)
Misner, Miram L., Indonesia (37)
Mitchell, Anne M. (Mrs. D. Leon),
    Indonesia (32)
Mitchell, D. Leon, Indonesia (32)
Mitchell J. Frank, Chile (36)
Mitchell, Margaret (Mrs. J. Frank), Chile (36)
Moon, Charlotte D., ("Lottie") China (39)
Moon, Hazel F., Nigeria (34)
Moon, J. Loyd, Brazil (37)
Moon, Mary Hazel F. (Mrs. J. Loyd),
    Brazil (37)

Moore, Alice S. (Mrs. W. Dewey), Italy (37)
Moore, Bonnie M., Nigeria (33)
Moore, John Allen, Hungry, Egypt,
    Yugoslavia, Switzerland, Germany,
    Turkey, Austria (39)
*Moore, Marylu, Italy (30)
Moore, Minnie F. (Mrs. J. Walton),
    China (31)
Moore, Pauline W. (Mrs. John Allen),
    Hungary, Egypt, Yugoslavia, Switzerland,
    Germany, Turkey, Austria (39)
Moore, V. Dale, Nigeria (36)
Moore, W. Dewey, Italy (31)
Moorhead, Marion F., Japan (36)
Moorhead, Thelma C. (Mrs. Marion F.),
    Japan (36)
Moorman, Mary Ellen, China (31)
*Morgan, Agnes M. (Mrs. E. Carter), Hawaii,
    Hong Kong (35)
*Morgan, E. Carter, Hawaii, Hong Kong (35)
Morgan, Finis A.R., Brazil (32)
Morgan, Gertrude W. (Mrs. F.A.R.),
    Brazil (32)
Morris, Betty L. (Mrs.Russell R.), Tanzania,
    Jordan Kenya (31)
Morris, Charles H., Malaysia (30)
Morris, Erica H. (Mrs. Charles H.),
    Malaysia (30)
Morris, Russell R., Tanzania, Jordan,
    Kenya (31)
*Moss, Evelyn (Mrs. Zeb V.), Zambia,
    Kenya (34)
Moss, J. Ulman, Venezuela, Colombia,
    Mexico (37)
Moss, Ruth M. (Mrs. J. Ulman), Venezuela,
    Colombia, Mexico (37)
*Moss, Zeb V., Zambia, Kenya (34)
Mosteller, Dorothy B. (Mrs. Paul C., Sr.),
    Thailand (35)
Mosteller, Paul C., Sr., Thailand (35)

Muirhead, Alyne G. (Mrs. Harvey H.), Brazil, Bapist Spanish Publishing House (39)

Muirhead, Harvey H., Brazil, Baptist Spanish Publishing House (39)

Murphey, Martha L. (Mrs. Milton, Israel (30)

Murphey, Milton, Israel (30)

*Muse, James C., Jr., Ecuador (32)

*Muse, Pat S. (Mrs. James C., Jr.), Ecuador (32)

Musgrave, James E., Jr., Brazil (35)

Musgrave, Jane A. (Mrs. James E., Jr.), Brazil (35)

*Myers, Helen G. (Mrs. S. Payton), Nigeria (30)

*Myers, S. Payton, Nigeria (30)

N Neal, Charles L., Mexico (38)

Neal, Hallie G. (Mrs. Charles L.), Mexico (38)

Neel, Bernice, Brazil (35)

Neely, Herbert W., Zimbabwe, Cayman Islands (33)

Neely, Jacqulyn (Mrs. Herbert W.), Zimbabwe, Cayman Islands (33)

Nelson, Edward W., Baptist Spanish Publishing House (32)

Nelson, Enrico A., Brazil (39)

Nelson, Gladys S. (Mrs. Edward W.), Baptist Spanish Publishing House (32)

Nelson, Ida L. (Mrs. Enrico A.), Brazil (39)

Newton, Mary W. (Mrs. William C.), China (36)

Newton, William C., China (39)

Nicholas, Anne Y. (Mrs. R. E.), Gaza (31)

Nicholas, R. E., Gaza (31)

Nichols, Buford L., China, Indonesia (34)

*Nichols, Gilbert A., Paraguay (35)

*Nichols, Mable Deane (Mrs. Gilbert A.), Paraguay (35)

Nichols, Mary Frances (Mrs. Buford L.), China, Indonesia (34)

Nixon, Helen, Colombia (32)

Noland, Betty B. (Mrs. Paul W.), Brazil (30)

North, Henrietta F., China (32)

*Northcutt, Irvin L., Peru, Colombia (31)

*Northcut, Mildred M. (Mrs. Irvin L.), Peru, Colombia (31)

O O'Neal, Boyd A., Brazil (38)

O'Neal, Irma S. (Mrs. Boyd A.), Brazil (38)

*Oates, A. Elizabeth, Brazil (36)

Ogburn, Georgia Mae, Chile (36)

Olive, Howard D., Philippines (31)

Olive, Marjorie D. (Mrs. Howard D.), Philippines (31)

Oliver, A. Ben, Brazil (37)

*Oliver, DeVellyn, Philippines (35)

Oliver, Edith (Mrs. A. Ben), Brazil (37)

Oliver, Edward L., Japan (39)

Oliver, Susan P. (Mrs. Edward L.), Japan (39)

Orr, Donald L., Colombia (33)

Orr, Violet R. (Mrs. Donald L.), Colombia (33)

Orrick, B.W., Uruguay (37)

Orrick, Vera H. (Mrs. B.W.), Uruguay (37)

*Owen, Evelyn, Japan (37)

Owens, Carlos R., Tanzania, Kenya, Namibia (35)

Owens, Myrtice T. (Mrs. Carlos R.), Tanzania, Kenya, Namibia (35)

P Parker, Sarah Gayle (Mrs. Earl), China, South   Korea (36)

Parker, Earl, China, South Korea (36)

Parker, F. Calvin, Japan (38)

Parker, Harriett H. (Mrs. F. Calvin), Japan (38)

Parker, John A., Chile (37)

Parker, Ruby H. (Mrs. John A.), Chile (37)

Patterson, A. Scott, Nigeria (39)

Patterson, Ione Geiger (Mrs. A. Scott), Nigeria (35)

Patterson, Frank W., Mexico, Spanish Baptist Publishing House (33)

Patterson, Pauline G. (Mrs. Frank W.), Mexico, Spanish Baptist Publishing House (33)

*Pearce, Sydney F. (Mrs. W. Boyd), Kenya, Tanzania (30)

*Pearce, W. Boyd, Kenya, Tanzania (30)

Pemble, Margaret (Peggy), Brazil (33)

Pender, S. Auris, China, Hawaii, Malaysia (33)

Penkert, Doris L., Brazil (33)

*Pennell, Elinor H. (Mrs. Wayne A.), Indonesia, Philippines (32)

*Pennell, Wayne A., Philippines (32)

Perryman, Maurine, Jordan (31)

Pettigrew, Ruth, China, Hong Kong (39)

*Phillips, Gene D., Zimbabwe (37)

*Phillips, Jean J. (Mrs. Gene D.), Zimbabwe (37)

Pierce, Ethel M., China (37)

Pierce, L. W., China (31)

Pierson, Coy Lee C. (Mrs. Abel P.), Mexico (30)

Pierson, Abel P., Mexico (30)

Pike, Harrison H., Brazil, Angola (33)

Pike, June H. (Mrs. Harrison H.), Brazil, Angola (33)

*Pinkston, Florence G. (Mrs. Gerald W.) Indonesia, Union of South Africa (Ciskei) (36)

*Pinkston, Gerald W., Indonesia and the Union of South Africa (Ciskei) (36)

Pinnock, Mrs. Samuel G., Nigeria (33)

Pinnock, Samuel G., Nigeria (33)

Plampin, Carolyn G. (Mrs. Richard T.), Brazil (31)

Plampin, Richard T., Brazil (31)

Plowden, Hannah, China, Hawaii (39)

*Plunk, Mell R., Jamaica, Argentina, Colombia (30)

*Poe, Eleanor O (Mrs. Joe T.), Chile, Spanish Baptist Publishing House (36)

*Poe, Joe T., Chile, Baptist Spanish Publishing House (36)

Pool, Elizabeth R. (Mrs. J. Christopher), Nigeria (38)

Pool, J. Christopher, Nigeria (38)

Popp, Violet, Jordan (36)

Posey, J. Earl Jr., Philippines (32)

Posey, Mamie Lou (Mrs. J. Earl, Jr.), Philippines (32)

Powell, Rosa H. (Mrs. J.C.), Nigeria (37)

Powell, J.C., Nigeria (37)

Q Quick, Mary J. (Mrs. Oz J.), China, Philippines, Hong Kong (36)

R Raborn, John C., Hong Kong (32)

Raborn, Nelwyn M. (Mrs. John C.), Hong Kong (32)

Ragland, James K., Lebanon (38)

Ragland, Leola K., Lebanon (38)

Raley, Frances B. (Mrs. Harry L., Sr.), Taiwan (36)

Raley, Harry L., Sr., Taiwan (36)

Randall, Ruth, Brazil (38)

Rankin, Manley W., China, Hawaii, Malaysia (38)

Rankin, Miriam T. (Mrs. Samuel G.), China, Hawaii, Hong Kong (32)

Ray, Bonnie Jean, China, Hawaii (35)

Ray, Daisy P. (Mrs. Jefferson F.), Japan

Ray, Daniel B., South Korea (39)

Ray, Frances D. (Mrs. Daniel B., South Korea (38)

Ray, Janet G. (Mrs. Rex), China, South Korea (34)

Ray, Jefferson F., Japan (37)

Ray, Rex, China, South Korea (34)

*Reece, Gwendolyln D. (Mrs. Z. Don), Nigeria (34)

*Reece, Z. Don, Nigeria (34)

Reid, Alma (Mrs. Orvil W.), Mexico (32)

Reid, Orvil W., Mexico (37)

Renfrow, Harold E., Brazil (31)

Renfrow, Nona M. (Mrs. Harold E.), Brazil (31)

Reno, Alice W., (Mrs. Loren M.), Brazil (30)

Reno, Loren M., Brazil (30)

Richardson, J.W.H., Jr., Nigeria (37)

Richardson, Margaret S. (Mrs. J.W.H.,Jr.), Nigeria (37)

Ricketson, Robert F., China, Philippines (33)

Ricketson, Bettie A. (Mrs. Robert F.), China, Philippines (36)

Riddell, Gerald F., Colombia, Chile (36)

Riddell, Olive, China (34)

Riddell, Virgie T. (Mrs. Gerald F.), Colombia, Chile (36)

Riffey, John L., Brazil (32)

Riffey, Prudence A. (Mrs. John L.), Brazil (32)

Roberts, Frances E., Paraguay, Argentina (36)

Roberts, Hoyt M., Honduras (30)

Roberts, M. Louise (Mrs. Hoyt M.), Honduras (30)

*Roberts, Marie (Mrs. Will J.), Kenya (31)

*Roberts, Will J., Kenya (31)

Robison, Martha B. (Mrs. Oren C., Jr.), Nigeria, Liberia (34)

Robison, Oren C., Jr., Nigeria, Liberia (34)

Rogers, C. Ray, Indonesia, Malaysia, New Zealand, Singapore (30)

Rogers, Joyce C. (Mrs. C. Ray), Indonesia, Malaysia, New Zealand, Singapore (30)

Rogers, Lillie O., Malaysia, Singapore (33)

Roper, C. Anita, Nigeria (38)

Roper, John A., Jr., Gaza, Jordan (35)

Roper, Ruth A. (Mrs. John A., Jr.), Gaza, Jordan (35)

Ross, J. Wilson, Mexico, Spanish Baptist Publishing House (39)

Rummage, Laverne R. (Mrs. Ralph L.), Zimbabwe (31)

Rummage, Ralph L., Zimbabwe (31)

Runyan, Elizabeth B. (Mrs. Farrell E.), Nigeria, Senegal (35)

Runyan, Farrell E., Nigeria, Senegal (35)

S Sallee, Hannah F. China (39)

Sampson, Mary H., China, Philippines, Taiwan (38)

Sanderford, Dora Jean M. (Mrs. Matthew A., Sr.), Uruguay, Spanish Baptist Publishing House (35)

Sanderford, Matthew A., Sr., Uruguay, Spanish Baptist Publishing House (35)

Sanders, Edward O., Indonesia (34)

Sanders, Eva, Nigeria (37)

Sanders, Jaletta J. (Mrs. Edward O.), Indonesia (34)

Sandlin, Annie, China (37)

Saunders, Letha M., Brazil (33)

Saunders, Mary Lucile, China, Philippines (39)

Scaggs, Josephine A., Nigeria (36)

Scarlett, Lenora, China (38)

Schmidt, Darleen W. (Mrs. Sidney P.), Malaysia, Singapore (31)

Schmidt, Sidney W., Malaysia, Singapore (31)

*Schochler, Lowell C., Brazil (31)

*Schochler, Melba G. (Mrs. Lowell C.), Brazil (31)

Schwartz, Evelyn, Hawaii, Indonesia (37)

Schweinsberg, Dorothy B. (Mrs. Henry W.), Colombia, Spain (37)

Schweinsberg, Henry W., Colombia, Spain (37)

Sears, Grace B. (Mrs. William H.), China (35)

Sears, William H., China (31)

Sharpley, Dan N., Brazil (35)

Sharpley, Doris A. (Mrs. Dan N.), Brazil (35)

*Shaw, Carroll W., Zimbabwe, Union of South Africa (34)

*Shaw, Jackie H. (Mrs. Carroll W.),
   Zimbabwe, Union of South Africa (34)
Shelton, Mary S. (Mrs. Ray E.), Uruguay (36)
Shelton, Ray E., Uruguay (36)
Shepard, Jean P. (Mrs. John W., Jr.),
   Japan (35)
Shepard, John W., Jr., Japan (35)
Sherer, Helen M. (Mrs. Robert C.), Japan (31)
Sherer, Robert C., Japan (31)
Sherwood, Eunice A. (Mrs. W.B.), Brazil (31)
Sherwood, W.B., Brazil (34)
Shoemake, Dorothy D. (Mrs. Howard L.),
   Colombia, Ecuador,
   Dominican Republic (34)
Shoemake, Howard L., Colombia, Ecuador,
   Dominican Republic (34)
Short, James M., Jr., Mexico (34
Short, Jaxie, China, Hong Kong (34)
Short, Sara Beth (Mrs. James M., Jr.),
   Mexico (34)
Skinner, Frances L. (Mrs. William),
   Paraguay (37)
Skinner, William, Paraguay (37)
Sledd, Betty Jean S. (Mrs. Max D.),
   Nigeria (31)
Sledd, Max D., Nigeria (31)
Small, Mary B., Zimbabwe, Zambia (35)
Small, Tom G., Zimbabwe, Zambia (35)
*Smith, Carolyn B. (Mrs. William L.),
   Brazil (30)
Smith, Cathryn L, Brazil (37)
Smith, Dixie S. (Mrs. Murray C.),
   Uruguay (30)
Smith, Donald R., Venezuela (34)
Smith, Edna B. (Mrs. J. Leslie), Indonesia,
   Guam, Malaysia (33)
Smith, Elizabeth F. (Mrs. James W.),
   Israel (34)
Smith, J. Leslie, Indonesia, Guam,
   Malaysia (33)

Smith, James W., Israel (34)
*Smith, Lewis R., Hong Kong (34)
Smith, Lucy E., China, Hong Kong,
   Japan (32)
Smith, Murray C., Uruguay (30)
Smith, Shelby A., Ecuador, Trinidad (34)
*Smith, Shirley A. (Mrs. Lewis R.),
   Hong Kong (34)
*Smith, William L., Brazil (30)
Smyth, Frances H., Brazil (38)
Smyth, Jerry P., Brazil (38)
Snell, Oleta E., Chile (32)
*Snow, Laura Frances, Chile (38)
Snuggs, Harold H., China (39)
Snuggs, Grace M. (Mrs. Harold H.),
   China (38)
Sowell, Ermine B. (Mrs. Sidney M.),
   Argentina (38)
Sowell, Sidney M., Argentina (38)
*Spann, Bettye C. (Mrs. J. Frederick),
   Brazil (31)
*Spann, J. Frederick, Brazil (31)
Spann, Jimmie D., Uruguay, Mexico (31)
Spann, Norma S. (Mrs. Jimmie D.), Uruguay,
   Mexico (31)
Spear, Bobby L., Thailand (38)
Spear, N. Jeannie (Mrs. Bobby L.),
   Thailand (38)
Spencer, Alvin E., Jr., Japan, Okinawa (33)
Spencer, Doris S. (Mrs. Alvin E., Jr.), Japan,
   Okinawa (33)
Spessard, Rosemary, Thailand (32)
Spiegel, Betty W. (Mrs. Donald J.), Brazil (32)
Spiegel, Donald J., Brazil (32)
Stainer, Ethne A., Yemen (33)
Stallings, Hattie, China (31)
*Stampley, Mary D., Ghana, Philippines (32)
Stamps, D. F., China, Hawaii (35)
Stamps, Elizabeth B. (Mrs. D.F.), China,
   Hawaii (35)

*Stamps, Glenna M. (Mrs. Stanley), Honduras (30)

*Stamps, Stanley D., Honduras (30)

Stapp, Mary S. (Mrs. Charles F.), Brazil (30)

Starnes, H. Cloyes, Korea (31)

Starnes, Mary Jo (Mrs. H. Cloyes), Korea (31)

Starns, Fanny L., Thailand (34)

*Stennett, Elizabeth G. (Mrs. William W.), El Salvador (30)

*Stennett, William W., El Salvador (30)

Stephens, Irene C. (Mrs. S.E.), China (37)

Stephens, Marjorie L., Nigeria (34)

Stephens, Peyton, China (31)

Stewart, Dorine Hawkins, Brazil (32)

Stewart, Martha G., Nigeria (39)

*Stewart, Maxine A. (Mrs. Robert R.), Thailand (35)

Stewart, Reba C., China (32)

*Stewart, Robert R., Thailand (35)

Stouffer, Paul W., Brazil (32)

Stouffer, Peggy S. (Mrs. Paul W.), Brazil (32)

Stover, Josephine W. (Mrs. T.B.), Brazil (38)

Stover, Thomas B., Brazil (32)

Strother, Green W. China, Malaysia (32)

Strother, Martha Lucille K. (Mrs. Green W.), China, Malaysia (32)

Stuart, Malcolm W., China, Hawaii (36)

*Sturgeon, H. Eldon, Mexico (36)

*Sturgeon, Jo Ann (Mrs. H. Eldon), Mexico (36)

Summers, Mabel, Israel, Jordan, Gaza, Lebanon (36)

Sutton, J. Boyd, Brazil (34)

Sutton, Jo Ann (Mrs. J. Boyd), Brazil (34)

*Swenson, Ann, Mexico (30)

Swenson, Erhardt S., Argentina (34)

Swenson, Anna M.G. (Mrs. Erhardt S.), Argentina (34)

*Swicegood, Audrey P. (Mrs. Glen M.), Brazil (30)

*Swicegood, Glen M., Brazil (30)

T Taylor, Ada L., (Mrs. James J.), Brazil (37)

Taylor, E. Fay, China, Indonesia, Hong Kong (39)

Taylor, George Boardman, Italy (34)

Taylor, James J., Brazil (35)

Taylor, Laura B. (Mrs. Zachary C.), China, Brazil (30)

Taylor, Maye Bell, Brazil (35)

Taylor, Zachary C., Brazil (37)

Teal, Edna E., China (32)

*Templeton, J. Logan, Jr., Hong Kong, Japan (31)

*Templeton, Mildred G. (Mrs. J. Logan, Jr.), Hong Kong, Japan (31)

Tennison, Betty J. (Mrs. Grayson C.), Brazil, Portugal (33)

Tennison, Grayson C., Brazil, Portugal (33)

Terry, Adolph J., Brazil (33)

Tharpe, Edgar J., Hawaii, Hong Kong (31)

Tharpe, Gertrude A. (Mrs. Edgar J.), Hawaii, Hong Kong (31)

*Thomas, Bill Clark, Singapore, Germany, Thailand, France (30)

*Thomas, Ruth A. (Mrs. Bill Clark), Singapore, Germany, Thailand, France (30)

Thompson, Cecil L., Argentina, and Spanish Baptist Publishing House (35)

Thompson, Jean W. (Mrs. Cecil L.), Argentina, and Spanish Bapist Spanish Publishing House (35)

Tilford, Lorene, China, Taiwan (37)

Tinkle, Amanda, Nigeria (34)

Tipton, Mary B. (Mrs. William H.), China (36)

Todd, Pearl, China, Japan (35)

Tolar, Jack E., Nigeria (30)

*Tribble, C. Lamar, Bolivia (30)

*Tribble, Elizabeth Watson (Mrs. C. Lamar),
Bolivia (30)
*Troop, J. Eugene, Brazil (33)
*Troop, Leona M. (Mrs. J. Eugene),
Brazil (33)
Trott, Edward B., Brazil (32)
Trott, Freda Lee P. (Mrs. Edward B.),
Brazil (32)
*Tucker, H. Robert, Venezuela, Colombia,
Canada, Russia (30)
*Tucker, Margaret R. (Mrs. H. Robert),
Venezuela, Colombia, Canada,
Russia (30)
Tumblin, Frances D. (Mrs. John A.),
Brazil (36)
Tumblin, John A., Brazil (37)
*Turnage, Cherry (Mrs. Loren C.), Colombia,
Iran, Scotland, Netherlands (34)
*Turnage, Loren C., Colombia, Iran,
Scotland, Netherlands (34)
V Van Lear, Marie, Nigeria (38)
Vanderburg, Ruth, Indonesia (31)
Vaughn, M. Edith, Brazil (35)
Verner, Marjorie J. (Mrs. W. Eugene),
Ghana (35)
Verner, W. Eugene, Ghana (35)
*Viertel, Joyce C. (Mrs. Weldon E.),
Bahamas, Barbados, Philippines, Baptist
Spanish Publishing House, Lebanon (32)
*Viertel, Weldon E., Bahamas, Barbados,
Philippines, Baptist Spanish Publishing
House, Lebanon (32)
W *Wagner, Lucy E., South Korea (38)
Walden, Ruth, Nigeria (30)
Waldron, Veda M., Argentina (32)
Walker, Catherine B., China, Indonesia (34)
Walker, Mary F. (Mrs. William L.),
Japan (39)
Walker, William L., Japan (39)
Walworth, E. Harvey, Mexico (33)

Walworth, Martha T. (Mrs. E. Harvey),
Mexico (33)
Ware, James H., China, Hawaii (39)
Ware, Mary L. (Mrs. James H.), China,
Hawaii (39)
Watson, Frances S. (Mrs. James O.),
Argentina, Paraguay, Philippines (31)
Watson, Hazel T. (Mrs. Leslie), Japan (35)
Watson, James O., Argentina, Paraguay,
Philippines (31)
Watson, Leslie, Japan (35)
Watson, Lila, China, Taiwan,
Hong Kong (38)
Watson, Annie M. (Mrs. Stephen L.),
Brazil (36)
Watson, Stephen L., Brazil (36)
Watson, Thomas L., Uruguay, Peru (33)
Welmaker, Ben H., Colombia (30)
Welmaker, Janis L. (Mrs. Ben H.),
Colombia (30)
Wester, Blanche C. (Mrs. William S.),
Zimbabwe, Malawi (33)
Wester, William S., Zimbabwe, Malawi (33)
Westmoreland, James, Zimbabwe (33)
Westmoreland, Wynema M. (Mrs. James),
Zimbabwe (33)
Whirley, Carlton F., Nigeria (32)
Whirley, Enid P. (Mrs. Carlton F.),
Nigeria (32)
White, Dan R., Spain (31)
White, Frieda B. (Mrs. Dan R.), Spain (31)
*Whitson, Betty A. (Mrs. David H.),
Tanzania (30)
*Whitson, David H., Tanzania (30)
Whittinghill, Dexter G., Italy (38)
Whittinghill, Suzy T. (Mrs. Dexter G.),
Italy (33)
Whorton, Mary Jane, Nigeria (37)
Wiggs, Bonnie B. (Mrs. Charles W.), South
Korea (32)

Wiggs, Charles W., South Korea (31)

Williams, James T., China (38)

Williams, Laurie S. (Mrs. James T.), China (38)

Williams, Leslie S. (Mrs. William J.), Nigeria (30)

Williams, Thelma, China, Hawaii, Philippines, Taiwan and Hong Kong (34)

Williams, William J., Nigeria (30)

Williamson, Guy S., Mexico (31)

Williamson, Julia H. (Mrs. Guy S.), Mexico (31)

Willis, Miriam, Argentina, Paraguay, Gaza (36)

Wilson, Billie H. (Mrs. Ernest C., Jr.), Brazil (31)

Wilson, Ernest C., Jr., Brazil (31)

*Wilson, George R., Jr., Hong Kong (31)

*Wilson, Sarah G., Argentina (36)

Wingo, Virginia, Italy (33)

*Witt, Mary, Brazil (30)

Wolfard, Rodney B., Brazil (35)

Wolfard, Sue W. (Mrs. Rodney B.), Brazil (35)

*Wood, Jean Powell (Mrs. Norman W.), Zambia, Mauritius (31)

*Wood, Norman W., Zambia, Mauritius (31)

Woodward, Frank T., China, Hawaii (39)

Woodward, Mabel E. (Mrs. Frank T.), China, Hawaii (39)

Wright, Joyce H. (Mrs. Morris J.) Wright, Japan, Spanish Baptist Publishing House (35)

Wright, Morris J., Japan, Spanish Baptist Publishing House (35)

Y Yancey, Mary Ellen, Nigeria (38)

Yocum, Alfred W., China, Korea (39)

Yocum, Daisy D.(Mrs. Alfred W.), China, (33)

Yong, Ch'in S., China (36)

Young, James M., Jr., Gaza, Yemen (32)

Young, June B. (Mrs. James M., Jr.), Gaza, Yemen (32)

FORTY YEARS SERVICE

A Allen, Edith A. (Mrs. William E.), Brazil (40)

Allen, William E., Brazil (40)

Anderson, Minnie Susan, Nigeria (43)

B Barrett, Clifford, China, Taiwan (41)

Bartley, James W., Jr., Uruguay (41)

Bartley, Peggy Jean P. (Mrs. James W.,Jr.), Uruguay (41)

Bedford, A. Benjamin, Argentina (41)

Bedford, La Nell W. (Mrs. A. Benjamin), Argentina (41)

Berry, Olga O. (Mrs. William H.), Brazil (41)

Berry, William H., Brazil (41)

Blair, Dorothy S. (Mrs. W. Judson), Argentina, Spanish Baptist Publishing House (40)

Blair, W. Judson, Argentina, Spanish Baptist Publishing House (40)

Bratcher, Artie P. (Mrs. Lewis M.), Brazil (40)

Britton, Nannie S. (Mrs. Thomas C.), China (45)

Britton, Thomas C., China (45)

Brower, Cornelia, Chile (44)

Bryan, Catharine, China (43)

Buster, W. Ray, Brazil (40)

C *Campbell, Vera L., Japan (43)

Carson, Grace S. (Mrs. William H.), Nigeria (43)

Clement, Lora A., China, Singapore (43)

Congdon, Esther B. (Mrs. Wilfred H.), Nigeria (42)

Congdon, Wilfred H., Nigeria (43)

Connely, Frank H., China, Japan (40)

Connely, Mary S. (Mrs. Frank H.), China, Japan (41)

Cowsert, Grace B. (Mrs. Jack J.), Brazil 40)

Cowsert, Hilda B. (Mrs. George B.),
    Brazil (41)

Cowsert, Jack J., Brazil (40)

Crawford, Martha F. (Mrs. Tarlton P.),
    China (41)

Crawford, Tarleton P., China (42)

Culpepper, Charles L., Sr., China, Hong
    Kong, Taiwan (41)

Culpepper, Charles L., Jr., China,
    Taiwan (41)

Culpepper, Ola L. (Mrs. Charles L., Sr.),
    China, Hong Kong, and Taiwan (41)

Culpepper, Donal J. (Mrs. Charles L., Jr.),
    China, Taiwan (41)

D Deal, Barbara W. (Mrs. Zach J.,Jr.),
    Colombia (40)

Deal, Zach J., Jr., Colombia (40)

Dodson, Flora E., China, Hong Kong (40)

Dozier, Maude B. (Mrs. C. K.), Japan (44)

Dozier, Mary Ellen W. (Mrs. Edwin B.),
    Japan (40)

Dunstan, Sally S. (Mrs. A.L.), Brazil (46)

E Ewen, Bettye Jane, Nigeria (41)

F *Fite, Horace W., Jr., Brazil (43)

*Fite, Salle Ann T. (Mrs. Horace W., Jr.),
    Brazil (43)

Franks, Martha L., China, Taiwan (40)

G Garrott, Dorothy C. (Mrs. William
    Maxfield), Japan (42)

Garrott, William Maxfield, Japan (40)

Ginsburg, Emma M. (Mrs. Solomon L.),
    Brazil (45)

Glass, Jessie P. (Mrs. Wiley B.), China (43)

Glass, Lois C., China, Taiwan, Japan (40)

Glass, Wiley B., China (41)

Goldfinch, Frances M. (Mrs. Sydney L.),
    Uruguay, Paraguay and Costa Rica (42)

Goldfinch, Sydney L., Uruguay, Paraguay,
    Costa Rica (42)

Graham, Julia S. (Mrs. Finlay M.), Israel,
    Jordan, Lebanon (43)

Graves, Alma O., Nigeria, Hawaii, Japan (40)

Graves, Janie S. (Mrs. Rosewell H.),
    China (49)

Greene, Valeria Page (Mrs. G.W.), China (43)

H Hagood, Martha, Japan, Nigeria (40)

Hallock, Edgar F., Jr., Brazil (44)

Hallock, Zelma C. (Mrs. Edgar F.,Jr.),
    Brazil (44)

Hamlett, Lettie S. (Mrs. P.W.), China (43)

Harris, Robert L., Peru, Bermuda (40)

Hart, Joseph L., Argentina, Chile (43)

Hart, Lois E., Argentina (41)

Hart, Tennessee H. (Mrs. Joseph L.),
    Argentina, Chile (43)

Hartwell, Anna B., China (47)

Hatton, Katie J. (Mrs. W. Alvin), Brazil (40)

Hatton, W. Alvin, Brazil (40)

Hawkins, Thomas B., Argentina (41)

Hawkins, Lou Ellen C. (Mrs. Thomas B.),
    Argentina (41)

Hayes, Alice J. (Mrs. Charles A.), China (41)

Hayes, Charles A., China (41)

*Hill, Evelyn P. (Mrs. Ronald C.),
    Thailand (41)

*Hill, Ronald C., Thailand (41)

Hollis, Emma C. (Mrs. James D.), Hong
    Kong, Macao (40)

Hollis, James D., Hong Kong, Macao (40)

*Hoover, Annie, Japan (44)

Hudgins. Frances E., China, Thailand (41)

Hundley, Lillie M., China, Hawaii,
    Lebanon (44)

Hunker, W. Carl, China, Philippines,
    Taiwan (40)

J Jackson, John E., China, Philippines (40)

Johnson, Pearl, China, Taiwan (43)

K Kelly, Willie, China (43)

Kolb, M. Ann (Mrs. Raymond L.), Brazil (43)

Kolb, Raymond L. Brazil (43)
Koon, Victor, China, Hawaii (41)
L Lancaster, Cecile, Hawaii, Japan (40)
Lanneau, Sophie S., China (43)
Lawton, Olive A., China, Taiwan (41)
Lawton, Wesley W., Sr., China (41)
Leavell, Cornelia, China, Hawaii, Hong
   Kong, Macao (40)
Lide, Florence C., China, Nigeria (40)
Lide, Francis P., China, Philippines, Hong
   Kong, Macao (46)
Lide, Bettie S. (Mrs. Francis P.), China,
   Philippines, Hong Kong, Macao (46)
Lide, Jane W., China (43)
Lindsey, Margaret L. (Mrs. Robert L.),
   Israel (43)
Lindsey, Robert L., Israel (43)
Lovegren, Mildred E., China,
   Hong Kong (41)
Lowe, John W., China (42)
Lowe, Margaret S. (Mrs. John W.),
   China (42)
M McConnell, H. Cecil, Chile (45)
McConnell, Elizabeth Buck (Mrs. H. Cecil),
   Chile (45)
McCormick, Hugh P., Nigeria, Hawaii (40)
McDaniel, Charles G., China (41)
McDaniel, Nannie B. (Mrs. Charles G.),
   China (41)
McMillan, Henry H., China, Bahamas (42)
McMillan, Lelia M. (Mrs. Henry H.), China,
   Bahamas (42)
McNealy, Walter B., Brazil (40)
McNealy, Ymogene A. (Mrs. Walter B.),
   Brazil (40)
Mein, David, Brazil (41)
Mein, Lou Demie S. (Mrs. David), Brazil (41)
Moore, R. Cecil, Chile (44)
Moore, Mary M.P. (Mrs. R. Cecil), Chile (44)
Morris, J. Glenn, China, Thailand (41)

Morris, Pauline L. (Mrs. J. Glenn), China,
   Thailand (41)
Morrow, Aurora Lee Koon, China,
   Hawaii (41)
Murray, Katie, China, Taiwan (40)
N Nichols, Sophia, Brazil (43)
O Oliver, Virginia W. (Mrs. John S.),
   Brazil (41)
P Parker, Alice, China (40)
Parker, Lucy Wright (Mrs. Earl), China,
   South Korea (42)
Patterson, Ira N., Nigeria (41)
Patterson, Sara Lou B. (Mrs. Ira N.),
   Nigeria (41)
Perry, May E., Nigeria (40)
Pierce, Nellie M. (Mrs. L.W.), China (45)
Porter, Margaret J. (Mrs. Paul C.), Brazil (40)
Porter, Paul C., Brazil (40)
Pruitt, Anna Seward (Mrs. C.W.), China (48)
Pruitt, C.W., China (47)
Q Quarles, James C., Argentina,
   Uruguay (44)
Quarles, Helen Taylor (Mrs. James C.),
   Argentina, Uruguay (44)
Quarles, Lemuel C. Argentina, Uruguay (40)
Quarles, Jennie S. (Mrs. Lemuel C.),
   Argentina, Uruguay (40)
Quick, Oz J., China, Taiwan (42)
R Rankin, Grace T. E. (Mrs. Manly),
   China, Hawaii, Malaysia, Singapore (42)
Ridenour, Crea, Colombia (45)
*Rohm, Alma H., Nigeria (43)
Ross, Jimmie M. (Mrs. J. Wilson), Mexico,
   Spanish Baptist Publishing House (40)
Ryan, S. Roberta, Chile, Spanish Baptist
   Publishing House (42)
S Sallee, Annie J. (Mrs. W. Eugene),
   China (41)
Saunders, Joel R., China (42)
Saunders, Mabel E. (Mrs. Joel R.), China (41)

Sears, A. Darlyne H. (Mrs. Stockwell B.),
China, Indonesia, Malaysia,
Singapore (42)
Sears, Stockwell B., China, Indonesia,
Malaysia and Singapore (42)
Shumate, Margie, China, Hong Kong,
Thailand (44)
Simmons, E.Z., China (41)
Simmons, Maggie M. (Mrs. E.Z.), China (42)
Smith, Olive Bertha, China, Taiwan (41)
Spence, Marjorie, Chile (40)
Stapp, Charles F., Brazil (42)
Starmer, Lillie M. (Mrs. Roy F.), Rumania,
Italy (40)
Starmer, Roy F., Rumania, Italy (40)
Stephens, Mary T. (Mrs. Peyton), China (48)
Stuart, Edyth B. (Mrs. Malcolm W.), China,
Hawaii (42)
T Tatum, Ezra F., China (45)
Taylor, Grace C. (Mrs. William C.),
Brazil (41)
Taylor, Sara Frances, Argentina (43)
Taylor, William C., Brazil (41)
Terry, Lulie S. (Mrs. A.J.), Brazil (45)
Tipton, William H., China (41)
Truly, Elizabeth, Nigeria (40)
W Walne, Claudia M. (Mrs. Ernest N.),
Japan (42)
Walne, Ernest N., Japan (42)
Ward, Josephine, China, Taiwan (45)
Weeks, Wilma J., China, Hawaii,
Indonesia (41)
Wells, Grace, China, Hawaii, Indonesia (40)
West, Edith O., Brazil (40)
Westbrook, Charles H., China (40)
Whaley, Charles L., Japan (40)
Whaley, Lois L. (Mrs. Charles L.), Japan (40)
Wheat, Ruby, China, Philippines,
South Korea (40)
Whilden, Louisa (Lula), China (45)

White, Kate (Mrs. Maxcy G.), Brazil (44)
White, Maxcy G., Brazil (44)
White, G. Pauline, Brazil (42)
Whitten, Charles W., Argentina, Colombia,
Spain, and Equatorial Guinea (40)
Whitten, Nella D. (Mrs. Charles W.),
Argentina, Colombia, Spain and
Equatorial Guinea (40)
Wilburn, Mary Jo McMurray, Uruguay,
Spanish Baptist Publishing House (43)
Womack, Ruth, Nigeria (40)
*Wyatt, Joyce C. (Mrs. Roy B.), Colombia,
Spain, Chile (40)
*Wyatt, Roy B., Colombia, Spain, Chile (40)
Y Yates, Matthew T., China (41)
Yates, Eliza M. (Mrs. Matthew T.), China
(47)
Young, Neale C., Nigeria (41)

FIFTY YEARS SERVICE
Bagby, Anne L. (Mrs. William Buck), Brazil
(56)
Bagby, William Buck, Brazil (56)
Bryan, Robert T., China (51)
Graves, Roswell H., China (57)

Chronology of Countries Entered 1846–1992

he Southern Baptist Convention was organized in 1845 and established its Foreign Mission Board the same year. Across 150 years, Southern Baptist missionaries have gone to countries and peoples beyond the borders of the United States of America. Country names have changed. In more recent years, it has been increasingly necesssary to think of people groups, political and/or geographic entities as well as countries. In the following chronology of "countries entered," note that:

1. The term "entered" is defined to be the year in which Southern Baptist missionaries first arrived to live and work in a given country or place. The term "withdrawn" is defined to be the year in which missionaries ceased to live and work in a given country or place, meaning, in some cases, redeployment to assignments in other locations.

2. For some countries — e.g., Australia, New Zealand and many places across Europe, the Middle East, and North Africa — the preferred term for missionary is now "fraternal representative."

3. Countries are listed chronologically by date of entry and by the country name in use at the end of 1992 (prior country names and/or other relevant data are indicated in a bracket following the country name). In some cases, as indicated, missionaries have been withdrawn from a given country, sometimes to return at a later date; sometimes not. In other cases, missionaries have been redeployed to assignments in other countries.

4. In recent years a number of missionaries work among peoples or in places that cannot be openly identified due to concern for the safety of the missionaries.

Year	Country or other entity
1846	China [withdrawn 1951]
	Liberia [withdrawn 1871; reentered 1960]
1850	Nigeria
1870	Italy
1880	Mexico
1881	Brazil
1889	Japan
1903	Argentina
1906	El Paso Baptist Spanish Publishing House [though established in Mexico, moved to El Paso, Texas, 1916]
1910	Macao
1911	Uruguay
1917	Chile
1921	Israel [Palestine before the state of Israel, 1948]
1923	Romania [withdrawn 1949; reentered 1991]
1924	Spain
1935	Hungary [withdrawn 1942; reentered 1989]
1938	Yugoslavia [withdrawn 1941; reentered 1955, withdrawn 1957; reentered 1977; work continued in Croatia]
1940	Hawaii [statehood: 1959; last missionary retired 1964]
1941	Colombia
1945	Paraguay

1947	Ghana [Gold Coast: independence, 1957]
1948	Guatemala
	Lebanon
	Philippines, the
	Switzerland
	Taiwan
1949	Costa Rica
	Hong Kong
	Thailand
	Venezuela
1950	Ecuador
	Korea, South
	Peru
	Zimbabwe [Southern Rhodesia: independence, 1980]
	Singapore
	Malaysia
1951	Bahamas
	Indonesia
1952	Jordan
1954	Gaza
	Honduras
1956	Kenya [British East Africa: independence, 1963]
	Tanzania [Tanganyika: independence, 1963]
1957	Bangladesh [East Pakistan: independence, 1971]
1959	Portugal
	Vietnam [withdrawn 1973]
	Malawi [Nyasaland: independence, 1964]
	Zambia [Northern Rhodesia: independence, 1964]
1960	France
	Okinawa [returned to Japan, 1972]
1961	Germany [West and East Germany reunited; the former East Germany entered 1992]

	Guam
1962	Dominican Republic
	Guyana [British Guiana: independence, 1963]
	India
	Trinidad and Tobago
	Uganda
1963	Jamaica [withdrawn 1979]
1964	Luxembourg [withdrawn 1967]
	Togo
	Yemen
	Guadeloupe
1965	Austria
	Libya [withdrawn 1976]
1966	Bermuda
	Ivory Coast
	Turkey [withdrawn 1979; reentered 1990]
1967	Belgium
	Botswana
	Ethiopia
	Morocco
	Angola [withdrawn 1975; reentered 1983]
1968	Iran [withdrawn, 1979]
	Namibia [South West Africa: independence, 1990]
	Antigua*
1969	Senegal
1970	Benin [Dahomey: independence, 1960]
1971	Laos [withdrawn 1975]
	Suriname [Dutch Guyana: independence, 1975]
	Burkina Faso [Upper Volta: independence, 1984]
1972	Barbados
	Greece
1973	Mozambique [withdrawn 1975; reentered 1984]

Niger Republic
1974 Dominica
1975 El Salvador
Grenada
Panama
1976 Nicaragua [withdrawn 1982; reentered 1990]
St. Vincent
* began as outreach from Trinidad; now center for outreach to other Leeward Islands (including Anguilla, Montserrat, and St. Kitts-Nevis)
1977 Belize [British Honduras: independence, 1981]
Bophuthatswana
Cayman Islands
Martinique
Rwanda
South Africa
Sri Lanka
Seychelles [withdrawn 1978]
Tortola [withdrawn 1981]
1978 Haiti
Bolivia
Mauritius
Reunion
United Kingdom [Scotland, England, Wales, Northern Ireland]
1979 Transkei [homeland in the Union of South Africa]
1980 Sudan [withdrawn 1984]
Egypt
1981 Brunei [withdrawn 1985; reentered 1988]
Equatorial Guinea
1982 Gambia, The
Turks and Caicos Islands [withdrawn 1989]

Guinea
Norway
1983 Netherlands Antilles
Swaziland
St. Lucia
Mali
Fiji
Nepal
New Zealand [withdrawn 1991]
1984 Pakistan
Australia
Sierra Leone
1985 Zaire
Finland
1986 St. Martin/St. Maarten
Canada
1987 Lesotho
West Samoa [withdrawn 1990]
Vanuata [withdrawn 1988]
Carribean Baptist Communications Mission
New Caledonia [withdrawn 1993]
Bahrain
1988 Guinea
Netherlands
Ciskei [homeland in the Union of South Africa]
1989 Venda
1990 Kuwait [withdrawn 1990]
Cambodia
Czech Republic
1991 Bulgaria
Poland
Commonwealth of Independent States [Russia, Belarus, Ukraine]
1992 Dubai, United Arab Emirates
Guinea-Bissau

List of Photographic Credits

Photographic Credits

Institutions
Foreign Mission Board, SBC
    Richmond, Virginia
Home Mission Board, SBC
    Atlanta, Georgia
Southern Baptist Historical Library and
Archives
    Nashville, Tennessee
Southwestern Baptist Theological Seminary,
    Fort Worth, Texas
Sunday School Board, SBC
    Nashville, Tennessee
Woman's Missionary Union, SBC, Archives,
    Birmingham, Alabama.
    Used by permission.
Boatwright Memorial Library, University of
    Richmond, Richmond, Virginia
Seminary Library, Union Theological
    Seminary, Richmond, Virginia
The Bettmann Archive
    New York
UPI/Bettmann
    New York
The Valentine Museum
    Richmond, Virginia
Virginia Baptist Historical Society
    Richmond, Virginia
Virginia State Library and Archives
    Richmond, Virginia

Donors
Charles Beckett
Edith M. Jeter
William Winn

Photographers
Marjorie A. Armstrong
Paul Brock
Erich Bridges
Bob Desbien
William Estep
George Green
Bob Harper
Warren Johnson
Sandy King
Stanley Leary
James E. Legg
G.E. Miltz, Jr.
Charles H. Morris
Floyd H. North
Van Payne
Joanna Pinneo
Gerald Riddell
Don Rutledge
Mary Lucile Saunders
Fon H. Scofield, Jr.
V. Lavell Seats
Lawrence R. Snedden
Mark Snowden
Charles E. Warren

Index